The author and contributors

Carol von Pressentin Wright has been writing and revising editions of *Blue Guide New York* since 1980 and has also authored *Blue Guide Museums and Galleries of New York* and *art/shop/eat New York*. She has published on women's health (Yale University Press) and cooking (Simon and Schuster) and contributed to the *Encyclopedia of New York City*. Her work has appeared in *The New York Times*, *Ceramics*, and other periodicals and has been translated into Chinese, Hebrew, and Romanian. She was born on Staten Island and received a graduate degree from Columbia University as a Woodrow Wilson fellow.

Francis Morrone is an art and architecture critic for *The New York Sun*, where his column "Abroad in New York" appears every Thursday. He writes book reviews, film criticism, etc. for various publications. He has written six books, including *An Architectural Guidebook to Brooklyn*. He lectures widely, teaches occasionally, and works on exhibitions.

Kate Hill holds an undergraduate degree in history from Barnard College; she is presently in London, studying for an MA in Asian art at Christie's Institute of Art.

Simon Harding holds a degree in history from Cambridge University and postgraduate degrees in linguistics and botany. He has also completed his doctoral research in marine biology with a specialism in geology.

BLUE GUIDE

NEW YORK

Carol von Pressentin Wright

Somerset Books

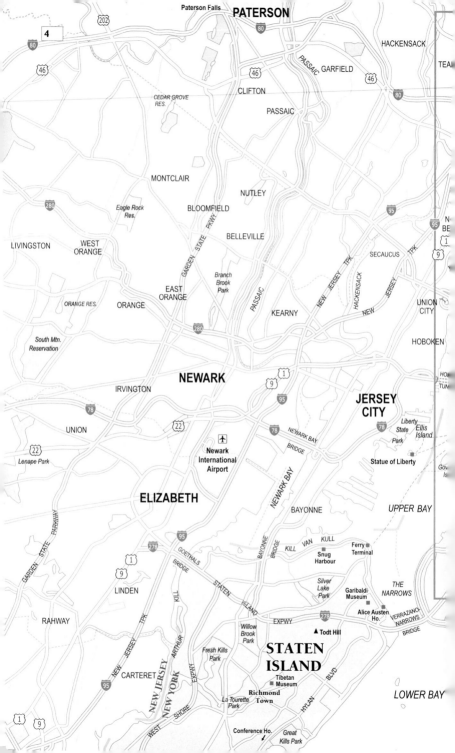

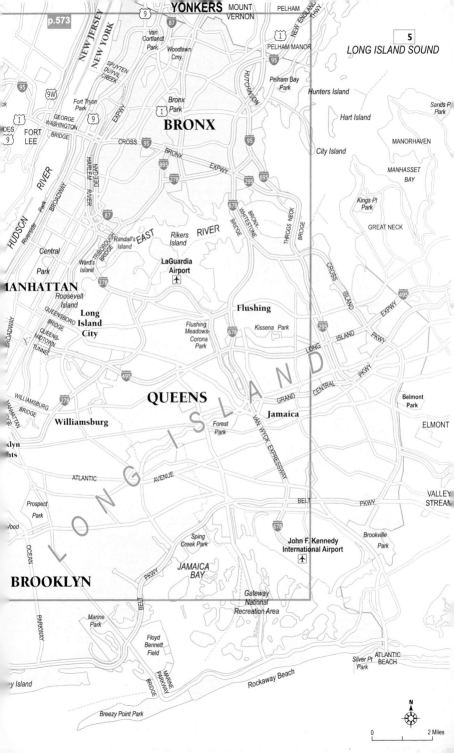

Fourth edition 2008

Published by Blue Guides Limited, a Somerset Books Company
Winchester House, Deane Gate Avenue, Taunton, Somerset TA1 2UH.
www.blueguides.com
"Blue Guide" is a registered trademark.

ISBN 978-1-905131-23-5

A CIP catalogue record of this book is available from the British Library.

Distributed in the United States of America by
WW Norton and Company, Inc.
500 Fifth Avenue, New York, NY 10110.

The author and the publishers have made reasonable efforts to ensure the accuracy of all the
information in *Blue Guide New York*; however, they can accept no responsibility for any loss, injury
or inconvenience sustained by any traveller as a result of information
or advice contained in the guide.

Statement of editorial independence: Blue Guides, their authors and editors, are prohibited from
accepting any payment from any restaurant, hotel, gallery or other establishment for its inclusion in
this guide, or for a more favorable mention than would otherwise have been made.

Every effort has been made to contact the copyright owners of material reproduced in this guide.
We would be pleased to hear from any copyright owners we have been unable to reach.

All other acknowledgements, photo credits and copyright information are given on p. 584,
which forms part of this copyright page.

Your views on this book would be much appreciated. We welcome not only specific
comments, suggestions or corrections, but any more general views you may have: how this
book enhanced your visit, how it could have been more helpful. Blue Guides authors and
editorial and production team work hard to bring you what we hope are the best-researched
and best-presented cultural guide books in the English language. Please write to us by email
(editorial@blueguides.com), via the comments page on our website (www.blueguides.com)
or at the address given above. We will be happy to acknowledge useful contributions in the
next edition, and to offer a free copy of one of our titles.

CONTENTS

THE ARCHITECTURE OF NEW YORK CITY

by Francis Morrone

New York's architecture, from earliest Dutch days to the beginning of the 19th century, wore the unaffected look of a vernacular evolved in accord with the basic needs of rugged colonial life and—before electricity or gaslight—the natural rhythms of the day. But it also evolved in accord with the sense of rightness of the ordinary builder, his matter-of-fact taste and pride in the thing well made, attaining an affectless handsomeness and comeliness that appeals to us no less today than it did to the man or woman of the 17th or 18th centuries.

Our earliest extant buildings are the very few that date from the period of New Netherland, a colony of the Dutch West India Company, and these are outside Manhattan. In Brooklyn, the Pieter Claesen Wyckoff house (5900 Ralph Avenue) has a part going back to 1652, near to the earliest settlement of Brooklyn's interior; additions to the house date to 1740 and 1820. Here we see the classic Dutch farmhouse style, with the distinctive gambrel roof, overhanging eaves, and clapboard walls. What's missing is the surrounding farmland. The oldest part of the John Bowne house (*see p. 499*) dates to 1661 with additions made in 1680, 1696, and c. 1830. Flushing, then a town and now part of the Borough of Queens, was a center of Quaker life in the Dutch period. The Flushing Friends' Meeting House dates to 1694, with an addition in 1716–19, making it the oldest house of worship in continuous use in New York City today (*see p. 498*). Note the date, however: by 1694, the Dutch had long ceased to rule a place now called New York, so named when in 1664 New Netherland passed to James, Duke of York and Albany and brother of King Charles II of England.

The new British colonial administration of 1664 chose to respect all Dutch property rights, with the result that few of the Dutch left. That is why most of what we regard as "Dutch colonial" among New York's very old buildings is actually from the British colonial period, which lasted until 1783. An example is the Wyckoff-Bennett house at 1669 East 22nd St in Sheepshead Bay, Brooklyn, built c. 1766. From the Dyckman house, c. 1785, on Broadway at 204th St in Upper Manhattan (*see p. 460*), we see the persistence of Dutch ways even after America gained its independence. Both the Wyckoff-Bennett and the Dyckman are classic Dutch farmhouses.

The British colonial period (1664–1783)

On Staten Island, on Hylan Boulevard in the Tottenville section, Bentley Manor, built by Christopher Billopp, a captain in the Royal Navy, in c. 1675 represents the earliest appearance of distinctively British, as opposed to Dutch, houses in the present bounds of New York City. A simple, handsome house, with rhythmically patterned multi-pane windows, it is built of local fieldstone, unlike the clapboarded Dutch dwellings, and is a colonial variation on the Christopher Wren house type from the

time of Charles II. (It is also known as "Conference House," as the site of ill-fated negotiations among American and British representatives in 1776; *see p. 511*)

A city house of the Wren type is Fraunces Tavern (54 Pearl St). This is a speculative reconstruction from 1904–07 of the 1719 town house of Étienne De Lancey, a Huguenot whose family was the richest in 18th-century New York (but which chose the wrong side in the Revolution). In later years the house was made an inn and a tavern by Samuel Fraunces, and it is there that General Washington bade formal farewell to his officers in 1783. The house then served a variety of uses, was remodeled, decayed, suffered fire damage, and, while never having technically been pulled down, bore, by 1900, not the faintest resemblance to its 18th-century appearance. At that time, the Sons of the Revolution engaged one of their number, the Staten Island architect William Mersereau, to rebuild the house to what it may—or may not—have looked like. It is, in any event, a good approximation of c. 1720 taste.

In the 1760s, on Broadway between Fulton and Vesey Sts, St. Paul's Chapel rose to serve Trinity Parish's "uptown" congregants. By the time it was built, James Gibbs, architect of London's St. Martin-in-the-Fields, had replaced Wren as the principal form-giver to British architecture. That is to say, he designed buildings and produced "pattern books" that suggested to local vernacular builders how they might build—or provided them with detailed plans for buildings. Thus we say that St. Paul's is a Georgian church in the Gibbs mode. The exterior walls are of local schist. Inside, the pastel color scheme, the original Waterford chandeliers, and the large Palladian window all testify to the non-sacramental Anglicanism that the later Gothic Revival rebelled against. This could as easily be the setting of a cotillion as of a worship service. In 1789, after George Washington took the oath of office as America's first president, he and his party attended a service at St. Paul's; needless to say, the *Te Deum* in those days was recited not sung—the architecture would suggest as much. (At the 1865 memorial service for President Lincoln at the Gothic Trinity Church on Broadway at Wall Street, the *Te Deum* was sung.)

The so-called Morris-Jumel Mansion is a country house on 160th St at Edgecombe Avenue in Harlem. In 1765, when the original house was built, the countryside around here possessed all the sylvan majesty we still experience north of the city in the lower Hudson River valley. The estate's grounds stretched all the way from the Harlem to the Hudson rivers. An Englishman, Roger Morris, built the house; like the De Lanceys, he and his family fled New York at the end of the Revolution. Later, Stephen Jumel, a wealthy importer, purchased the property. His wife was the notorious former courtesan Eliza Jumel (*see p. 447*). The porch of this lovely clapboarded house takes the same basic form as St. Paul's Chapel: four full free-standing columns supporting a broad triangular pediment. A feature of the house is its abundance of intricate balustrades, an emblem of high class. Today the mansion is a "historic house museum" and well worth visiting.

The Federal style

A fascinating glimpse of changing tastes may be had at 7 State St in Lower Manhattan, where a man named James Watson built his house in 1793. Though the British had

ceded New York to the Americans ten years before, most New Yorkers were of British extraction, and to British taste did they cling. The Gibbs-Georgian style of the house was of a type that had remained virtually unchanged in New York for 30 or more years. By 1806, when the house was roughly doubled in size, the new taste had made its way across the Atlantic from Britain to America. Though we chose to call it "Federal," acknowledging it as the dominant style of the new republic, the changes introduced to the Georgian architecture of Gibbs came from the Scots-born brothers Robert and James Adam, architects of Chiswick House, Kenwood House, and other outstanding buildings in England from the late 18th century. The Adams introduced curving forms and delicate notes like slender, attenuated columns. At 7 State St, the later half of the façade curves, like a movement in a waltz, and bears a screen of skinny columns. It's a thrilling house, certainly the best thing of its period remaining in the city (*pictured on p. 51*).

New York is famously a city of row houses (or terrace houses as they are called elsewhere in the English-speaking world), and perhaps the earliest surviving example in the city stands at 18 Bowery, built in 1785–89 as the home of Edward Mooney (*see p. 113*). The red-brick house is in the Gibbs mode. The lintels are "splayed" and paneled, the doorway is flanked by twin marble columns supporting a tight triangular pediment, and the double-hung windows are of six-over-six sash, which would remain standard in New York for many years. The use of marble rather than brown sandstone (i.e. "brownstone") for trim indicates that this was a grand house in its day. Today the Georgian façade bears Chinese characters—for this is in Chinatown—and they somehow seem not the least out of place.

The city's most famous country house of the years of the young republic is Archibald Gracie's waterside cottage located at the present-day East End Ave at 88th St (*see p. 380*). Gracie began building his house in 1799, at a time when the countryside around there lured the city's mighty families the way the Hamptons does today. The sight that most impressed the Frenchman de Tocqueville when he visited New York in the early 1830s before writing his classic *Democracy in America*, was that of the grand country houses lining the East River waterfront of Manhattan north of the built-up part of the city. Gracie Mansion, as we call it, has a very broad porch and a simple, graceful interplay of shuttered six-over-six windows, slender columns, and "chinoiserie" balustrades that make this a splendid example of the Federal country-house style (*pictured on p. 280*). It seems built for relaxation and delight. We see in the inland addition, the Susan B. Wagner Wing of 1966, the persistence of architects' interest—amounting to mastery—of the Georgian vocabulary. Gracie Mansion was from Fiorello La Guardia in the 1940s to Rudolph Giuliani in the 1990s the official residence of the Mayor of New York. Michael Bloomberg chose to remain in his own East 70s town house, perhaps because he was the first mayor for whom a move to Gracie Mansion did not represent a step up in living standards.

Gracie Mansion is probably our oldest extant Federal-style country house. Perhaps the oldest town house in the Federal style is the Stuyvesant-Fish house of 1803–04 at 22 Stuyvesant St, on what was once the estate of the Dutch West India Company manager Peter Stuyvesant. Here we see the characteristics common to all the Federal-style

city houses of New York: Flemish-bond brickwork (alternating headers and stretchers), six-over-six windows, doorway practically flush with the housefront, low stoop, the elegant columns and sidelights, a semi-elliptical fanlight, and dormers. For 30 years the New York house façade changed very little. This was a high-class town house in its day, built by Peter Stuyvesant's great-grandson for his daughter, Elizabeth, and son-in-law, Nicholas Fish.

The Stuyvesant-Fish house was completed while New York's finest public building of the period was under construction. City Hall (*see pp. 83–84*) was built in 1802–11, and—remarkably considering the growth of the city—remains New York's city hall, where the mayor has his office and the City Council convenes. The exterior architecture we credit to a Frenchman, Joseph François Mangin, and is in the Louis XV style, expertly executed by an architect who obviously had had thorough training. Though today it may appear quaint and diminutive, surrounded as it is by towering sky-scrapers, City Hall in 1811 had a majestic presence. It may have been New York's first building meant not merely to be convenient and comely but to excite us with beauty and grandeur—a work of "architecture," so to speak, as opposed to "building." There had, before Mangin, been a French architect in New York, Pierre L'Enfant, whose surviving work includes the altar decorations in St. Paul's Chapel (which is just down Broadway from City Hall). L'Enfant befriended George Washington and won the commission to plan the new capital city on the Potomac River. But Mangin's work really represents the intro-duction into New York of a French influence that would in time overtake the British influence. Inside City Hall, it's all Federal-style Georgian. The interior architect was the son of an Ulster Scot, John McComb Jr. He and Mangin dominated the architectural pro-fession in the newly independent city. McComb also designed the country house of Alexander Hamilton, now the Hamilton Grange National Monument in Harlem. The house was completed in 1802; Hamilton was killed by Vice President Aaron Burr (his political rival) only two years later. McComb's City Hall interior is among the most elegant the Federal period has to show us in New York. The "flying staircase," with its sweeping curves and no visible means of support, rising up through a splendid rotunda, is pure Adamesque exuberance, and one of the loveliest things in New York.

A fine institutional building in the Federal style is the former Roman Catholic Orphan Asylum (32 Prince St; *map p. 581, D4*) of 1825–26, established by the American Sisters of Charity. The doorway of this building, as with so many Federal-style buildings, bears special mention, with its typically elegant, slender columns, sidelights, and arched fanlight. Each style of architecture through the ages seems to do one thing better than any other, and the Federal had mastery of the doorway treat-ment, a simple and lovely arrangement that no one thought superfluous even in so humble a building as an orphanage.

Few buildings until the late 1820s deviated from Federal orthodoxy. And it is not surprising that the style should have had such staying power—or that it would be revived (along with other Georgian styles) in the late 19th and throughout the 20th centuries. In 1899, New York's most important architecture critic, Montgomery Schuyler, would say of the early 19th-century Federal-style houses of Manhattan that

they were "the most respectable and artistic pattern of habitation New York has ever known."

One rather remarkable deviation occurred in 1809–15 when Mangin designed the city's first Roman Catholic cathedral. St. Patrick's Old Cathedral (so-called nowadays to distinguish it from the later, vastly larger St. Patrick's on Fifth Avenue) stands on Mott St right across Prince St from the former Orphan Asylum, with which it was associated. Mangin, daringly for the time, chose a Gothic design, several decades before the mature Gothic Revival set in. Truth be told, Mangin's Gothic was—albeit intriguing—picturesquely awkward, and though the church we see today bears the appearance of a substantial rebuilding that occurred following an 1860s fire, the Mott St façade nevertheless retains its striking strangeness. This is not the Gothic that would later devour the 19th century.

The Greek Revival

When a style finally overtook the Federal it was the Greek Revival, which though it bore superficial similarities to the Federal (they both may be called "Neoclassical"), nonetheless gave expression to a city that by 1830 or so had become a significantly different place from the city of Federal days. Projects undertaken by a great New York mayor and governor, DeWitt Clinton, affected forever the appearance—and the architectural pretensions—of the city. In 1811, Clinton's appointed commissioners issued their plan to guide the city's growth northward up Manhattan island. Where, London-style, the city had grown organically in a tangle of often crooked streets, henceforward the entirety of the island not yet developed (roughly north of Houston St) would take form on a topography rigorously denuded of any of its natural features (hills leveled, forests felled, streams and lakes filled, marshes drained) and platted in a rectilinear "gridiron" of north–south avenues and east–west streets divided into uniform lots of (usually) 25ft by 100ft. Federal houses, typically built in small clusters of three or four, diminutive in size and modest in appearance, related well to the short blocks and bending byways of the old city. The new city suggested grander treatments.

Clinton's other city-changing achievement was the Erie Canal, which opened in 1825. At 363 miles in length it more than tripled the length of the longest canal yet built, and may have been the largest public-works project undertaken since ancient times. Certainly the world was startled to see what America (in fact, what New York) was capable of. By linking New York Harbor via the Hudson River to the Great Lakes, and the rich agricultural lands of the American interior, the canal ensured that New York's port would for more than a century be the nation's most important. Before the canal New York had at most handled nine percent of the nation's exports. By 1860, that number had risen to more than 60 percent. The canal may be said more than anything to have made inevitable New York's rise to commercial preeminence in America. With that preeminence came breathtaking growth, and the historic churn of New York architecture, the constant tearing down and building up of the city, its relentless growth northward, then its doubling back and reaching into the sky as no city had done—or would, for some time, do or dare to do.

The Greek Revival buildings of New York speak to us of Erie Canal days, of a city's lofty aspirations, and of the values of an increasingly self-confident people. Grecian forms had in fact entered New York architecture in the 1790s following publication of James Stuart and Nicholas Revett's seminal *Antiquities of Athens*. The high tower added to St. Paul's Chapel in 1793 adapted its design from the Choragic Monument of Lysicrates, as drawn by Stuart (it is perhaps the oldest example of "Grecian" architecture in New York). Yet it was Roman forms—or at least the arch, the dome, the curving bulge, and the treatment of the orders as ornamental appurtenances without pretense of structural purpose—that prevailed in the Federal style. At 29 East 4th St stands a remarkable town house (now the outstanding Merchant's House Museum; *see p. 158*) that demonstrates how the Federal transitioned to the Grecian (and how marvelously they could be combined). On the outside the house (built in 1831–32) is largely Federal, though the elaborate iron fence bears Grecian motifs and also signals a change in the nature of New York residences toward an increasing separation of public and private realms. Most Federal houses were built in a time when transportation was primitive. There was as yet not such a thing as "suburban" living. People worked very close to where they lived—often, for example in the artisans' quarter that grew up west of Broadway where the World Trade Center would later rise, in the same or adjacent buildings. An extant example is the marvelous Federal-style frame house at 17 Grove St (*see also p. 142*), where a sashmaker named William Hyde lived and, in the adjacent wooden structure, practiced his craft. But the Erie Canal era saw the introduction first of the horse-drawn omnibus—which rode rockily on the block-paved streets of the city—and then of the revolutionary horsecar, or horse-drawn street railway, in which the cars' wheels were fitted onto iron rails. These provided smooth, swift transport, and placed less stress on the horses. Thus New Yorkers clamored to settle the newly gridded uptown streets—in so doing to create ever greater distance between homes and workplaces.

This in turn created or fed a cult of domesticity that is often expressed in our Greek Revival row houses, with their elaborate passages from sidewalk to inside the house. Look for example at the houses at 1–13 Washington Square North (*map p. 581, D3*), a celebrated row erected in 1832–33 shortly after the former paupers' burial ground the houses face had been remodeled into a public square, from which time the area boomed. First there is the iron fence, as at the Merchants' House Museum, with anthemion-crested posts and fretwork such as we see painted on Greek vases. The fence opens to an areaway prior to the first step of the stoop. The stoop itself is a wide thing, with thickly balustraded railings terminating in stout stone blocks. At the top of the stoop a landing leads to full fluted columns—chubby ones, not the attenuated things we see in Federal houses. What's most important is that the Grecian columns are pushed out from the front of the house—not set into it, as in the Federal. Here the columns rise up to a full, heavy entablature that creates a second, sheltered landing past which we finally come to the front door. Four distinct parts make up this passage, which involves opening a gate and standing on a roofed landing before ever going inside. In Federal houses, on the other hand, like the typical examples from the

1820s at 4–10 Grove St, you could often in a single bound (sometimes a single step) make your way from inside the house to the sidewalk. With the Greek Revival this was no longer so.

The term "Greek Revival" conjures images not of row houses but of temple-front structures. What we see on Washington Square North, or more typically in the "Cushman Row" on 20th St between Ninth and Tenth Aves (*map p. 580, B2; see p. 187*), where sandstone pilasters replace marble columns, is an adaptation of the temple front to a building type—the 25-ft-wide urban house—that would at first seem ill-suited to such a treatment. In New York the architect most responsible for the spread of Grecian taste was Minard Lafever. No Greek Revival houses he may have designed in Manhattan remain. But many of the thousands of extant houses in that style were drawn by builders from the several "pattern books" through which Lafever spread the Grecian gospel. When the English-born architect Calvert Vaux, who co-designed Central Park, called Lafever the "Sir Christopher Wren of America," it was because Lafever, like Wren, developed house types that were readily reproducible by humble builders, yet that also helped to form a congenial style for city streets.

Of Lafever's designs outside Manhattan, we have the outstanding examples (at last authoritatively attributed to Lafever by the architectural historian Barnett Shepard) at Snug Harbor on Staten Island (*see p. 508*). Lafever's buildings form a grand ensemble of fully temple-fronted marble structures. Other survivors of the city's Greek temples include the former Custom House of 1833–42, now the Federal Hall National Memorial, on Wall Street (*see p. 69*). This was designed by the outstanding architects of the time, Alexander Jackson Davis (who was Herman Melville's friend) and Ithiel Town.

Across the river, Brooklyn was incorporated as a city in the midst of the Grecian era; consequently, Brooklyn City Hall (now Borough Hall) bears the temple-front style. It was built in 1845–48 though derives from designs of fully a decade earlier. At Snug Harbor, on Wall Street, and in Brooklyn the buildings are imposing (which is the point of the temple front) and austere; note the absence of ornamentation. Especially striking in each example is the broad triangular pediment supported by the free-standing colonnades. The pediments have raked cornices, which in Classical architecture served as frames. The ancient Greeks themselves filled in these frames with elaborate figure sculpture. Yet the Americans left them bare. It's like going into a gallery and seeing empty picture frames adorning the walls. Why is this? Partly it's to do with the romanticism of the times, expressed not only in nature-worship but in worship of Antiquity, which itself was accessed by intellectuals through the cult of ruins. It may be said that we patterned our Grecian buildings less after how the Greeks built, than by how nature decayed the Greek buildings, stripping them of their color and ornamentation, leaving them as somber totems of ancient civilizations. Then again, we see in all the arts and crafts of early America a striving after humbler forms than those to be found in European work—our fabled "republican simplicity," which found a profound outlet in our "Grecian" architecture, not to mention in the Greek dresses our ladies wore to garden parties, the fretted patterns on our ceramic dishes, and countless town names (Athens, Georgia; Syracuse, New York).

The Gothic Revival and Medievalism

The Romantic era gave New York not only its cult-of-ruins Greek architecture but also the passionate Medievalism we imported from Britain. Here again Mr. Lafever led the way. Mangin valiantly if strangely essayed the Gothic in his St. Patrick's Old Cathedral (*see p. 12 above*). But that is really an eccentric work, a stylistic outlier. The real Gothic Revival doesn't start up until the late 1830s. This is the "archaeologically correct" Gothic—sometimes serving deep liturgical strivings—that Augustus Pugin developed in Britain. An Englishman, Richard Upjohn, is generally credited with introducing the style in New York, at Trinity Church (1839–46) on Broadway. However, Lafever designed the Washington Square Reformed Church, on the east side of Washington Square, before Upjohn designed Trinity; and the Lafever building, not the Upjohn, may be said to have inaugurated the mode that with variations persisted well into the 20th century. Alas, Lafever's church is gone, but we can see his approach to Gothic if we go to Brooklyn Heights (*map p. 470*). Holy Trinity Church, on the corner of Clinton and Montague Sts, was built in 1844–47, and his First Unitarian Church (Church of the Saviour), on Pierrepont St at Monroe Place, in 1842–44. Holy Trinity's English Gothic has a lacy exuberance that we also find in the Gothic designs of James Renwick Jr., such as Grace Church in Manhattan, completed in 1846 (*see p. 160*). Both Lafever and Renwick were aesthetes, interested in Gothic as one among several historical styles from which to choose for its appropriateness to a given project. Upjohn, by contrast, belonged to the New York Ecclesiological Society, which sought to import the values of Britain's Cambridge Camden Society, which promoted the Gothic as part of a broad-based reform movement seeking to restore the Catholic liturgy to the Anglican (or, in America, Episcopalian) rite. The Ecclesiologists, whose hero was Pugin, were dedicated churchmen. When Upjohn designed a church—an outstanding example besides Trinity is Grace Episcopal Church (1847–49) on Grace Court at Hicks St in Brooklyn Heights—he wished for every stone, every rib of the ceiling vault, every piece of glass to play its proper and approved role in the liturgical pageant of the Mass. Renwick and Lafever merely acceded to clients' wishes and Lafever, especially, helped spread the Gothic to denominations that found it beautiful but had no historical claim on it or liturgical interest in it—after all, the Unitarians of Brooklyn Heights did not debate transubstantiation!

We call the 1840s and 1850s the period of the "Early Gothic Revival." The Gothic, in many variations drawn from many sources, remained a dominant note thereafter in New York architecture. French and Italian Gothic influences soon joined the English. Renwick's St. Ann's Episcopal Church (1867–69) on Henry at Remsen Sts in Brooklyn Heights is an outstanding example of what was often called—much to the consternation of the man for whom it was named—"Ruskinian Gothic." The English writer John Ruskin, whose magnificent prose transfixed Victorian readers in both Britain and America, had written, in his *Stones of Venice* and other works, of the richly ornamented, polychromatic Gothic of Venice, suggesting that no building in the world merited emulation more than the Doge's Palace of the 14th century. Many architects, each in his own way, employed the style, or at least the tics, of the 14th-century

Venetians so admired by Ruskin, whose Medievalism replaced Pugin's. This was an idealized Medievalism to be sure. The chivalric knight, the pious peasant, and the monastery were storybook antidotes to the increasing harshness of life in the industrialized cities of the 19th century, with their pollution, appalling labor and housing conditions, constant epidemics of deadly diseases, and massive infestations of vermin. Romanticism was in general a looking back or away from these pestilential conditions, in hopes of forgetting or remedying them—and in hopes of reclaiming or retaining noble values (however spurious) that the present age had no use for (piety, for example). Ruskin's Medievalism became a full-on political movement that eventuated in, among other things, the creation of Britain's Labour Party. So all of that is implicit when you look at the 1870s and 1880s buildings with their pointed windows, spiky towers, studied asymmetry, zebra stripes, exotic masonry, and so on.

This strain of Medievalism extended to all types of buildings, not just churches. Two Englishmen, Calvert Vaux and Frederick Clarke Withers, both followers of Ruskin, designed the Third Judicial District Courthouse (also known as Jefferson Market Courthouse, now Jefferson Market Library) of 1874–77 on Sixth Ave at 10th St in Greenwich Village (*see p. 146*). It has polychromatic masonry, a picturesque skyline with high conical towers, stained glass, and relief sculptures of scenes from *A Midsummer Night's Dream*. At the time, it was voted by architects as one of their most admired buildings in America; a generation later, a reaction set in against "Victoriana," and such buildings as this were demolished in waves. The just-a-bit-over-the-top, exuberantly picturesque Gothic romanticism of Jefferson Market Courthouse is—like London's St. Pancras Station—very much the sort of thing we imagine when we think "Victorian architecture." A private house in the same vein is the one on the south side of Gramercy Park, just west of Irving Place (*map p. 581, D2*), remodeled from two ordinary brownstone row houses in 1881–84 by Calvert Vaux and George K. Radford for New York governor Samuel J. Tilden (*see p. 176*). A commercial building in this style, and perhaps the city's finest work in "Venetian Gothic," is the modestly scaled building at 8 Thomas St (1875–76; *map p. 582, C2*), designed by a very talented architect, J. Morgan Slade, who died tragically young.

The prestige of the Gothic may be inferred from its use in three of the city's greatest building endeavors of the 1860s and 1870s: St. Patrick's Cathedral, Central Park, and the Brooklyn Bridge. St. Patrick's, on Fifth Avenue between 50th and 51st Sts, was built between 1858 and 1879, with its fantastic twin towers coming in 1888. Renwick (an Episcopalian) designed this replacement for the old cathedral downtown, and turned to a combination of English and French Gothic forms for the exterior, which is in white marble from Westchester County, just north of the city. His lacy ornamentation, exuberant freestanding gables like those found in France, the soaring towers (which taper more dramatically than any cathedral towers of the Middle Ages), made this perhaps the most extraordinary building that had been erected in New York up to its time. Renwick was forced into many compromises, for he had to squeeze the church into a single lot of the Manhattan grid, and his ingenious adaptations made this one of the most original Gothic buildings of the 19th century. The interior is dazzling as well, patterned

partly after Westminster Abbey and York Minster; alas, it is too brightly and harshly illuminated most of the time. The enamel-painted aisle windows, in a Renaissance classical style by Lorin of Chartres, are perhaps the finest of their kind in the city.

The Brooklyn Bridge was built in 1870–83. The original design was by a German-born engineer—actually, a great polymath—named John Roebling, who pioneered the manufacture of steel wire cable and already had to his credit the longest suspension bridge in the world, the Cincinnati–Covington Bridge across the Ohio River. The new bridge would have a central span half as long again. As the longest suspension bridge ever built, and the greatest work of steel construction ever undertaken—and not least for its haunting beauty—the bridge outclassed even the Erie Canal as a monument of New Yorkers' ingenuity and ambition, and the world's attention was riveted. Note that in the design of the great granite towers of the bridge, at the time the most skyline-dominating structures in New York, Roebling chose the pointed arch of the Gothic.

Central Park grew out of a public parks movement led by the newspaper editor and poet William Cullen Bryant and the influential landscape gardener Andrew Jackson Downing. Their devotees included a journalist named Frederick Law Olmsted, who visited England in 1850 and was deeply impressed by Sir Joseph Paxton's Birkenhead Park in Liverpool. An English devotee of Paxton, the London architect Calvert Vaux, emigrated to America to work in Downing's firm. Eventually, Olmsted, who had been hired to superintend the clearing of the land for the park, and Vaux, who had taken over Downing's firm following the master's tragic death in a steamboat accident, teamed up on the "Greensward Plan," which won the 1858 competition for the park's design. Here we see the English ideal of *rus in urbe* magnificently transplanted to American soil. Closely related to romantic Medievalism, Central Park embodies the notion that the antidote to the harsh city is to get rid of some of it and make it over into a verdant fairyland of compacted landscapes that could not possibly follow one upon the other in nature itself, but which in the hands of artists might serve to brighten the souls of otherwise benighted denizens of the great, monstrous metropolis. The park also follows the romantic landscape painting of the time, the Hudson River School of Thomas Cole, Frederic Church (one of Ruskin's favorite artists), and others, whose pictures often served as models for the intricately composed vistas of Vaux and Olmsted's park, which has itself rightly been characterized as one of the greatest works of art of the 19th century. Note that nearly all of Vaux's park structures—service buildings, bridges, etc.—are in the Gothic style. An exception would be the flamboyantly Moorish Bethesda Terrace (*see p. 289*), that Vaux helped to design but that we credit largely to yet another Englishman, the eccentric genius Jacob Wrey Mould (*see p. 289*), friend of Walt Whitman and former assistant to the British designer Owen Jones.

A later, highly original strand of American Gothic is represented by two Bostonians influenced by Henry Adams, the American patrician pessimist and lover of the Middle Ages. Ralph Adams Cram was responsible for the reworking in Gothic of the originally Romanesque Cathedral of St. John the Divine (1911–41), while he and his brilliant partner Bertram Goodhue designed St. Thomas Church on Fifth Avenue at 53rd St (1905–13), its neo-Gothic reredos one of the world's greatest (*see p. 259*).

Two things need noting before we go on. The first is that this roster of names—Upjohn, Renwick, Vaux—tells us that the age of the professional architect had dawned in New York. Henceforward, all important buildings would be designed directly by architects, not put up by builders based upon pattern books. Second, the Greek Revival, the Gothic Revival, and the contemporaneous Italian *palazzo* style brought us the earliest stone-faced buildings. Such works as the former Custom House on Wall Street, Grace Church and St. Patrick's Cathedral, and the A.T. Stewart dry-goods emporium (built 1845–46 with several later add-ons) on Broadway between Reade and Chambers Sts, which took after the Pall Mall club-house style of Sir Charles Barry, all bore white marble façades. The marble was from local sources, as was the other principal stone that came into use for full façades at this time, the soft sandstone, brown or reddish-brown in color, quarried in New Jersey, New York State, and Connecticut. Trinity Church wears an earthen coat of New Jersey brownstone, which often suited the somber purposes of the Ecclesiologists. The soft stone also suited the speculative developers of the row upon row upon row of houses revetted in it. The red-brick Greek Revival front yielded to the brownstone front when changing fashions in the 1850s dictated richly carved stone ornamentation. The middle class demanded houses with intricately carved console brackets and elaborate window enframements, and such houses could be built rapidly enough to keep pace with the frenetically growing city only if a soft stone could be used—soft making it easier (and cheaper) to quarry, and easier (and cheaper) to carve. Again for ease and cheapness a great deal of the stone was mishandled, with the result that water absorption caused severe scaling of the stone fronts of many New York houses over the years. It is likely that the speculators who built these houses did not foresee that they would be valued and preserved by future generations.

Apartment houses

Multiple-unit dwellings first came to New York in the form of tenant houses, or "tenements," built for the very poor, especially the Irish and German immigrants who flooded the city in the 1840s and 1850s. At first several families of Irish would cram together in a Federal-style house that had been erected for a single family then abandoned in the northward trek of fashion. Then purpose-built multi-family dwellings came in. For several decades, multi-family dwellings were considered suitable only for the very poor. But in the second half of the 19th century, as the final, complete covering of Manhattan island's gridded streets appeared imminent, apartment houses for the middle and upper classes became an economic necessity.

The first apartment house was the Stuyvesant, on East 18th St between Third Ave and Irving Place, designed by Richard Morris Hunt and built in 1869. Unfortunately, it no longer stands, though several noteworthy examples of "first generation" apartment houses still do survive. The famous Dakota was completed in 1884 (72nd St at Central Park West). The Osborne, at 205 West 57th St, was built in 1883–85 (with later additions). Its architect, James E. Ware, also devised the prototype of what we call the "old-law tenement" (*see box on p. 122*). In 1879, Ware's prototype for a

slightly more healthful tenement design was adopted as law by New York City. This coincided with the most extensive build-out of tenements in the city's history, such that by the turn of the century a majority of New Yorkers resided in old-law tenements, of which block after block remain—the Lower East Side and the west Midtown neighborhood called Hell's Kitchen particularly abound in them.

Before such laws, the only decent tenements were those constructed by philanthropists as "model tenements." Men like Brooklyn's superb Alfred Tredway White, who was born into great wealth and devoted his life to the physical reform of his native city, attempted to show that decent housing for the working class could be built and still yield modest profits. White's Tower and Home Buildings and Workingmen's Cottages, built in 1876–79 on Hicks St between Warren and Baltic Sts in Cobble Hill, Brooklyn, and his Riverside Buildings, built in 1890 on Columbia Place at Joralemon St in Brooklyn Heights, are the city's outstanding examples of model tenements. The architects of both developments, William Field & Son, were, like White, a product of Brooklyn's influential community of Unitarian social reformers. (White incidentally also helped found the splendid Brooklyn Botanic Garden, where there stands a monument to him designed by Daniel Chester French.)

Buildings such as the Dakota (*see p. 414*), with their generous interior courtyards, electricity, elevators, high-ceilinged rooms, and so on provided not only more amenity than the tenements but often more than single-family row houses. The Upper West Side of Manhattan did not begin to develop in earnest until the 1880s, when the steam-powered elevated railway made the area swiftly accessible to the business centers downtown. From the time of the Dakota onward, the area took shape as perhaps the first apartment-building neighborhood in America. When the Interborough Rapid Transit subway supplemented the Els in 1904, a wave of speculative apartment house construction ensued, and many of the city's most classic and beautiful examples of the type rose in rapid succession. The Ansonia Hotel (1899–1904) on Broadway at 73rd St was built by the eccentric developer William Earl Dodge Stokes, who is credited with its flamboyant design together with the French architect Paul Émile Duboy, possibly the first major French architect in the city since the days of Mangin. The Ansonia bears the hallmark lavish ornamentation of the Belle Époque, though it is well to note that at 17 stories it would have been by a monstrous margin the tallest building in Paris at the time. Arguably the most beautiful of the Upper West Side buildings is the Apthorp (1906–08), on Broadway at West 78th St. Designed by Clinton & Russell, the full-block building has a magnificent vaulted entryway on Broadway leading to a large interior courtyard. The entry is designed as though it were a triumphal arch, with figure sculpture as fine as any in the world. With most apartment buildings we do not know the names of the sculptors who embellished them with work unvaryingly of the highest refinement. We only know that the anonymous craftsmen of this era were often Italian immigrants, many descended from long lines of carvers—thus establishing the direct link between the Renaissance in Italy and the "American Renaissance" of the late 19th and early 20th centuries.

The Romanesque Revival

We must step back for a moment at this point and round out the story of Victorian architecture in New York before looking at the revolution in taste of the late 19th century. Besides the Gothic, the earlier medieval style of the Romanesque also gained traction. Its earliest instances include Richard Upjohn's Church of the Pilgrims on Henry St at Remsen St in Brooklyn Heights (1844–46; now Our Lady of Lebanon Church), where the Congregationalist parishioners wished a simpler style than the Gothic of the Anglo-Catholic revival, with which they wanted nothing to do. In Manhattan, the Astor Library (now Joseph Papp Public Theater) at 425 Lafayette St was built in three phases (southern wing 1849–53, central section 1856–69, northern wing 1879–81) with each part perfectly mated to what came before, all in the popular German Romanesque style, or *Rundbogenstil* (round-arched style). Italian Catholics, who came to New York in large numbers toward the end of the 19th century, found a cool welcome at best in the Irish churches of the city, so, in forming their own parishes, rejected the dominant Gothic of the Irish in favor of an Italian Romanesque such as we see at the Church of St. Anthony of Padua, designed by Arthur Crooks and built in 1888 on Sullivan St between Prince and Houston Sts in the southern, once heavily Italian, part of Greenwich Village (*map p. 580, C4*). The inspiration for this and so many other Italian churches in New York was the 13th-century San Francesco, in Assisi.

But America made the Romanesque its own when in the 1870s and 1880s the architect Henry Hobson Richardson, who was based in New York in his early career but grew to prominence after moving to Boston, worked his own refinements on French Romanesque models and created the "Richardsonian Romanesque," which dominated American architecture of the 1880s and early 1890s. Only minor early works by Richardson survive in New York City, but his acolytes abounded here, especially in Brooklyn, which experienced rapid growth during the heyday of the Richardsonian style. Two architects merit note. Frank Freeman designed masterpieces of the Richardsonian Romanesque (sometimes borrowing elements directly from Richardson designs, both built and unbuilt). Examples are the mansion of the industrialist Herman Behr, on Pierrepont St at Henry St in Brooklyn Heights (1888–90), and the former Brooklyn Fire Headquarters (1892) at 365 Jay St in downtown Brooklyn. Between 1887 and 1892 C.P.H. Gilbert designed 20 of the 46 houses on the exquisite one-block-long Montgomery Place, between Prospect Park West and Eighth Avenue, in Park Slope, Brooklyn, all in inventive variations of the Richardsonian Romanesque. The house at 46 Montgomery Place, in particular, is a symphony in elegant, golden Roman brick. Hallmarks of this style include walls of rough masonry blocks, often sensuously contrasting with elegant brickwork and delicate terra-cotta adornments. This was the style dominant in American cities during the era of westward expansion depicted in most of Hollywood's Westerns, which evoke similarly to the architecture a combination of raw, urgent power and the civilizing grace notes of refined ornamentation.

The first New York architect to use ornamental terra cotta was George B. Post in his Brooklyn Historical Society of 1878–81 (*see illustration on p. 473*). Because a single mold

could yield literally countless instances of a particular ornamental form, terra cotta answered to its era's penchant for lavish embellishment, which would have been impossible to achieve on such a wide scale if all the ornament had to be carved. Another—and earlier—form of molded ornamentation was cast iron, from which whole building façades were made beginning in the 1840s and 1850s. One of the city's earliest extant examples is the beautiful Haughwout Building in SoHo (*illustrated on p. 101*). That building also had the first steam-powered passenger elevator (1857) in the world. SoHo has America's largest concentration of cast-iron façades (*see p. 104*).

The Beaux-Arts era and Georgian Revival

The Richardsonian style yielded to a new Classicism that marked a definitive end to Victorian experimentation and historical Romanticism. The first American to attend the École des Beaux-Arts in Paris was Richard Morris Hunt, already mentioned as the designer of the city's first apartment house—a building type he was familiar with from the eight years he lived in the Paris of Louis-Philippe. In New York Hunt established a practice where his employees were also pupils, who received training as though in a Beaux-Arts atelier in Paris. George B. Post, for example, apprenticed in Hunt's atelier. Hunt himself helped lead the charge to the new Classicism, and was heavily involved in the World's Columbian Exposition in 1893 in Chicago, where the grand-manner Classicism of the white buildings, arranged harmoniously along broad boulevards and piazzas and lagoons, provided the public with a vision of beautiful cities that was very different from the *rus in urbe* of Central Park. For the next half century or so America's native Jeffersonian anti-urbanism yielded to an urban grandeur that made of New York a classical city to compare with the likes of St. Petersburg, Vienna, Dublin—and even Paris.

Yet it was not Hunt so much as a firm called McKim, Mead & White, formed in the late 1870s, that led the way. White and his partner Charles Follen McKim met when they both worked for Henry Hobson Richardson. Richardson had, like Hunt, been to the École des Beaux-Arts, as had McKim; White, for financial reasons, was unable to attend. Their first New York masterpiece (begun in 1882) was the ultra-refined Italian Renaissance-style Villard Houses, grouped around a courtyard on Madison Avenue between 50th and 51st Sts (*see pp. 235–36*). Joseph M. Wells, a brilliant designer in the firm (he died very young and never became a partner), was in charge of the exteriors. It is almost inconceivable that this scrupulously sober ensemble followed by only five years the drunken gallimaufry of Vaux and Withers's Jefferson Market Courthouse. Change was in the air.

The Villard Houses were faced in brownstone, which was *de rigueur* at the time. The stone is expertly handled and a joy to behold. Nonetheless, Wells had specified Indiana limestone, a light-colored metamorphic rock that young architects had begun to think suited the brilliant skies of New York—a city on Rome's southern latitude that had always been treated as though it were on London's northern latitude. The client, Henry Villard, overruled Wells, and went with the conventional material. Soon, however, McKim, Mead & White would lead the way out of the brownstone era. Stanford White

excelled at the combination of golden Roman brick with light-colored terra cotta to achieve sumptuous effects even on tight budgets, as at Judson Memorial Baptist Church (1888–93, with later additions) on Washington Square South, and the clubhouse of the Century Association (1889–91) at 7 West 43rd St. For his Metropolitan Club (1891–94) White turned to gleaming marble. The Italian Renaissance supplied McKim, Mead & White's models, though the firm adapted them in often strikingly original ways, not least in the manner of applying the models to new building types like the tall apartment house or railroad stations.

We call this the Beaux-Arts era because Parisian values ruled. Many of the architects had not only studied in France, as we have seen, but were intense Francophiles. Yet the British influence was not thrown off so easily. McKim and White were in the vanguard of the rediscovery and reappraisal of America's colonial architecture, and they largely begat the Georgian Revival that has, since the 1890s, not shown any signs of going away. It may in the end be the most enduring contribution of this firm to American architecture. An outstanding New York example of McKim's work in that vein is his house for James J. Goodwin, built 1896–98 at 11–13 West 54th St. An example by White would be the former Colony Club (now American Academy of Dramatic Arts) of 1904–08, at 120 Madison Ave.

For many years McKim, Mead & White was without question New York's most prestigious—and busy—architectural firm. Other leading Beaux-Arts firms included Carrère & Hastings, who designed the New York Public Library (1898–1911) on Fifth Ave at 42nd St; Warren & Wetmore, architects of Grand Central Terminal (1903–13, in association with Reed & Stem) on 42nd St at Park Ave; and York & Sawyer, specialists in awe-inspiring banking interiors such as that of the Central Savings Bank (1926–28) on Broadway at 73rd St. The outstanding architect in this vein was the Philadelphian Horace Trumbauer, whose sometime partner in design, Julian Abele, was the first African-American to attend the École des Beaux-Arts. They gave us the superb mansion of James B. Duke on 78th St at Fifth Ave (*see p. 315*), a limestone beauty of such refined proportion that it claims few rivals among French classical houses—even in France.

We often—and, often, not incorrectly—associate the Beaux-Arts with lavish display, whether in civic buildings (Cass Gilbert's United States Custom House, 1899–1907, on the south side of Bowling Green; *see p. 42*) or rich men's mansions (Carrère & Hastings's house for Henry Clay Frick, 1913–14, later remodeled into the Frick Collection, on 70th St at Fifth Ave; *see p. 299*). The Georgian Revival, on the other hand, shows a quiet, refined sensibility. In 1897 Edith Wharton and her architect friend Ogden Codman Jr. wrote *The Decoration of Houses*. It influenced a decorator named Elsie de Wolfe (later Lady Mendl), whom Stanford White hired to create the interiors for the Colony Club. Not one for mahogany and gilt, she used light-painted walls, chintz fabric, and trellises to create airy, almost whimsical rooms. The new spirit announced by the limestone architecture of the 1890s was becoming ever brighter, lighter, and more carefree, unshackled by opulent display, made for living. The period of 1910 to 1925 may be the most delicious in all the architectural history of New York. It is also the period of female emancipation (and the end of constraining clothing for women), of "free love" and

lifestyle experiments to which the 1960s are a mere footnote, and of the birth of a new popular music in New York—itself the perfect accompaniment to the new architecture.

The age of "gentrification"

When Manhattan island filled up and residences began to be stacked one on top of another, a concomitant phenomenon was the first-ever return of the bourgeoisie to their abandoned downtown homelands, which had in the interim become working-class areas. Not until a British sociologist coined a word—"gentrification"—in 1964 did we have a name for the phenomenon, but this was the golden age of it. In 1909 Frederick J. Sterner, a prominent architect from Denver, completely remodeled an 1840s Greek Revival brick row house at 139 East 19th St, a block south of Gramercy Park (*map p. 581, D2*). He removed the, in his word, pompous stoop; stuccoed over the brick façade and painted it a cream color; installed red roof tiles; gave the new basement entrance art-pottery accents; gutted and remade the interior with wood paneling in a linenfold design; and made the small rear yard into a fantasy of the Tuscan countryside. At around the same time, artists were discovering the joys of living and working in stables (or mews houses), as at MacDougal Alley, off MacDougal St half a block south of 8th St in Greenwich Village. It was in MacDougal Alley that Gertrude Vanderbilt Whitney, whose summer home growing up had been the 70-room villa *The Breakers* in Newport, Rhode Island, kept a tiny house and sculpture studio (*see p. 144*) and founded the Whitney Museum of American Art. The First World War gave further momentum to the new spirit as New York society ladies such as Anne Vanderbilt and Anne Morgan, whose Francophilia led them to volunteer their services in French military hospitals during the war and who as a consequence had witnessed up-close the most horrible carnage, found that after the war the old opulent way of life was no longer what they wanted. They and other ladies, including Elsie de Wolfe, hired Mott B. Schmidt, a young architect of the Georgian Revival whose wife was a decorator in Miss de Wolfe's firm, to design an ensemble of simple but elegant houses in an East Side slum called Sutton Place (*see p. 277*), where the ladies were, for a few years at least, surrounded by tenements and gritty factories. Around the same time, the British Garden City ideal promoted by Ebenezer Howard influenced the design of an exquisite planned community in the old town of Newtown, which had become part of the Borough of Queens. Called Forest Hills Gardens and masterfully laid out by Frederick Law Olmsted Jr. (a more talented designer than his famous father), it and similar developments in New York and elsewhere caused the historian John Lukacs to label this period of the "breeze of beauty" in American life.

The age of the skyscraper

While the domestic ideal became ever more relaxed and intimate, on the commercial side everything was about size in New York. We'd begun putting elevators (first steam-powered, then hydraulic, then electrical) in buildings in the late 1850s. First with iron then with steel framing we eventually created building frameworks that relieved external walls of any load-bearing function, rendering them "curtain walls" draped over

steel frames. And the New York skyline shot up in the air. We had a quick succession of "tallest buildings in the world": the Park Row Building in 1899, the Singer Building (since demolished) in 1908, the Metropolitan Life Insurance Company Tower in 1909, the Woolworth Building in 1913, the Bank of the Manhattan Building in 1929, the Chrysler Building in 1930, and the Empire State Building in 1931. By the First World War, New York had so many really tall buildings that the city was visually unique; perhaps not since medieval Constantinople had any city's appearance so awed the first-time visitor. After the war, the city took on a global prominence—in finance, industry, shipping, and selling—commensurate with its growing scale.

As had earlier happened with tenements, a lack of regulation in the design of tall buildings led to overbuilding of lots. A number of tall buildings in a row cast whole sections of the city into darkness. In 1916 the city adopted the first comprehensive municipal zoning legislation in American history. Among the code's provisions was the requirement that tall buildings step back at prescribed intervals to allow sunlight to penetrate to the streets. From 1916 until 1961, when the code was changed, all of New York's tall buildings bore the stepped silhouette that architects soon came to see not as an aesthetic hindrance but its opposite, as allowing for plays of volumes and indentations that resulted in dramatic forms. A Beaux-Arts firm like Warren & Wetmore expertly applied classical detailing to the stepped-back skyscraper with their brilliant New York Central (later Helmsley) Building of 1927–29, at 230 Park Ave. But by this time the classical skyscraper had begun to yield to modern forms, at first in the guise of Art Deco, though that term (like "gentrification") would not be coined until the 1960s. Ralph Walker, a highly individualistic architect with the firm of McKenzie, Voorhees & Gmelin (later Voorhees, Gmelin & Walker), designed the ex-New York Telephone Company Building (1923–27) on West St at Vesey St (now the Barclay-Vesey Building; *see p. 63*). He applied to the stepped-back skyscraper the fashionable modern ornamentation that originated in France and was promoted by the French government at the 1925 Exposition Internationale des Arts Décoratifs et Industrielles in Paris. The result was a kind of "jazz architecture," what we later would call the Art Deco skyscraper. At One Wall Street Walker went further, experimenting with the limestone "skin" of the building, folding it in wavy patterns that recalled the linenfold paneling Frederick J. Sterner designed for the interior of his house at 139 East 19th St in 1909.

Ely Jacques Kahn designed the Bricken Casino Building (1931) on Broadway at 39th St with a kind of bias-cut pattern to the stepped-back massing, recalling a Vionnet gown. The skyscraper had entered a period of high inventiveness. The most stunning of all was the Chrysler Building (42nd St at Lexington Ave), the tallest in the world in 1930, topped off by a stylized version of a Mycenaean helmet. As unlike anything else in architecture as the top of the Chrysler Building was, so the same could be said of the building's lobby, an eccentric triangular space with a rich palette of red Moroccan marble, Mexican onyx, Siena marble, and elaborate wood marquetry (*see p. 233*). The Empire State Building (Fifth Avenue at 34th St), 202ft higher than the Chrysler, was completed in 1931, altogether in a more sober style but still characteristically Art Deco, again with the signature use of varied marbles in the lobby, and

with a distinctive crown meant at first to be used as a dirigible mooring mast. Throughout the 1930s, John D. Rockefeller Jr. built Rockefeller Center on the Midtown site bounded roughly by 48th and 51st Sts and Fifth and Sixth Avenues. The ensemble originally comprised 13 buildings (later extended) grouped harmoniously around formally designed open spaces, one of them being the dramatic Promenade leading west from Fifth Avenue with the tall RCA Building terminating its vista: it was one of the first instances of terminating a vista with a skyscraper, something that because of the grid it was hard to do in Manhattan.

The later 20th century

After the Second World War, it may be said that New York, however briefly, stood in importance among the world's cities as no city had since ancient Rome—it was the undisputed capital of just about everything. As though to signal that New York had at last become a truly international city, the builders of skyscrapers turned to the so-called International Style. Where Art Deco was modern because it employed modern ornamentation, the new style was modern in that it dispensed with ornamentation altogether, offering up stark metal and glass. Competently handled, the new style yielded its share of winners. Lever House, designed by Gordon Bunshaft of Skidmore, Owings & Merrill, rose at 390 Park Ave in 1950–52, the first glass-walled skyscraper built in the dense masonry core of the city. It seemed to float, a shimmering, light-as-a-feather building that showed how exciting the new style could be. The Seagram Building, cater-corner to Lever House at 375 Park Ave, went up in 1956–59, designed by the German Ludwig Mies van der Rohe. Faced in bronze and tinted glass, and set behind a generous marble plaza, the building evoked the austere glamour of a self-important (though perhaps not self-confident) city. The rapid proliferation of these Modernist buildings, however, drawn from the repertoire of world-weary 1920s intellectuals, were, the philosopher Allan Bloom once said, like Bobby Darin singing "Mack the Knife." The architects knew the words, but not their nihilistic meaning. By the time of the former PanAm Building (200 Park Ave) by Emery Roth & Sons, with exterior styling by the Bauhaus panjandrum Walter Gropius, New Yorkers were proud to hate the new architecture.

Worst of all was how federal government money was put to use ripping down old neighborhoods of tenements and row houses and replacing them with brick or concrete high-rises set within parklike "superblocks"—a supposed solution to mass housing based on 1920s prototypes by the Swiss-French architect called Le Corbusier. Corbusier built nothing in New York, but like Henry Hobson Richardson his acolytes were everywhere either doing his bidding or—as Ruskin felt about his acolytes—getting it all wrong. Whichever the case, the Corbusian virus spread across the world's cities, not least New York, in a pandemic of destruction. New York's "master builder" since the 1930s, Robert Moses (none of whose official titles betrayed that he held such power as Haussmann held over mid-19th-century Paris), built in accord with this vision, creating a city of vast high-rise housing estates and automotive high-speed roadways. The bulldozing and rebuilding went by the name "urban renewal." Its

orthodoxy was challenged in the late 1950s and early 1960s by a brilliant writer named Jane Jacobs, and also by a historic preservation movement that succeeded in passing the 1965 Landmarks Preservation Law, such that by the early 2000s some 25,000 buildings in the five boroughs were legally protected from demolition or inappropriate alteration.

Public interest in architecture reached a high level in the 1980s, a creative and often confused decade in which architects questioned everything they had been doing. Philip Johnson, one of the major figures of the mid-century Modernist revolution, designed a skyscraper that looked like a Chippendale dresser (the Sony Building; *see p. 242*). Architects began using veneers of luscious masonry—cut paper thin, like deli roast beef, because developers weren't willing to pay the cost of whole blocks of the stuff. The result wasn't a return to the look of the old masonry city but a kind of weird, flimsy stage-set version of it. That we remain amply capable of the real thing—solid masonry construction, classical style—is evidenced by the Carhart Mansion (2006) on 95th St just east of Fifth Avenue, designed by Zivkovic Connolly.

New York has always had rather an insular architectural culture. We have one Mies van der Rohe building, a façade by Walter Gropius, nothing by Le Corbusier, and only an interior by Alvar Aalto. In the 1990s all this began to change as New York embraced the chi-chi world of "starchitects," the globe-trotting celebrity architects such as Daniel Libeskind, Rem Koolhaas, Frank Gehry, Santiago Calatrava, Jean Nouvel, Christian de Portzamparc, Norman Foster, Renzo Piano, and Richard Rodgers, all of whom at long last got their coveted chances to design in New York. Portzamparc's LVMH Building on 57th St just west of Madison Avenue is an exciting exercise in wavy glass that seems in part a homage to Ralph Walker and Ely Jacques Kahn. Some other works by starchitects have not worked so well. In Brooklyn, Frank Gehry has designed a city-within-the-city called Atlantic Yards, including a basketball arena and a tower he has named "Miss Brooklyn." The project, hailed by some, has also met with stern opposition. It and many other projects have attempted to cash in on a red-hot Brooklyn real-estate market that was created by young people buying "fixer-upper" brownstones in the 1960s and '70s when social strife and crime had depressed outer-borough property values. The reclamation of the old neighborhoods and the preservation and adaptation of old houses may, when the starchitects' publicity inevitably subsides, turn out be the most enduring architectural news of the turn of the new millennium.

THE GEOLOGY
OF MANHATTAN

by Simon Harding

For anyone interested in geology, Manhattan offers a rare opportunity. Under the cement, steel, and glass lie layers of geological deposits, animal bones and modern rubbish covering millions of years. To a large extent the geology of Manhattan has determined its early and more recent history.

The island of Manhattan is built on three main strata: Manhattan schist, Inwood marble, and Fordham gneiss. The island sits near the famous Cameron Thrust Fault and the Hartland Formation. To add to its geological complexity, the area marks the southernmost boundary of the Laurentide ice sheet that once covered most of North America. The ice retreated 27,000 years ago and the glaciation created not only Long Island (moraine and outwash) but almost all of the features of the NYC region. As the sea encroached, the archipelago of New York City was created—in geological terms a mere 6,000 years ago. Mastodon bones found under Broadway and Dyckman St in Upper Manhattan testify to the period when giant fauna ruled the land. In Inwood Hill Park you can see the potholes carved by violent whirlpools of melting ice and rocks, also from this period, that drilled deep cylindrical holes. The pattern of early human settlement in Manhattan was largely determined by its geology, from massive rock features to the soil that sustained the flora and fauna on which the hunter-gatherers depended.

Manhattan today is one of the best places in the world for geo-archaeological research. Every time the foundations for a new building are dug or a tunnel bored, something of interest emerges. A simple walk through Midtown or Lower Manhattan will show you the current sites. There is approximately $50 billion of proposed construction scheduled for the next 20 years, including a substantial amount of tunneling and mining, including subway tunnels of over 20ft in diameter, and the construction of caverns over 100ft wide for stations associated with the Second Avenue Subway Project. These projects will reveal another chapter in Manhattan's geology.

Even a glance at the Manhattan skyline reveals the power of geological influence. The dips in the geological strata account for the gap you notice between the midtown and downtown skyline. This is because the tall buildings must be based on bedrock and not the glacial till in the geological valleys. In fact, most of the modern landscape of Manhattan and the Bronx only has a thin veneer of soil, developed after the last glaciation. You can see the effects of this last glaciation best along the edge of the Hudson River.

Where to see the rocks

The American Museum of Natural History (*see p. 395*) has a mass of information on local and exotic geology, as well as a renowned and extensive collection. The

museum also organizes local geological tours. The best places to see the rocks *in situ* are Central Park, Inwood Hill Park (*see below*), or just outside Manhattan in the New Jersey palisades along the Hudson River. If you drive over the George Washington Bridge (*map p. 573*), you can see the expanses of bedrock along the highway cuttings (although it is illegal to stop). The geologist John McPhee in fact opens his famous book *Basin and Range* with a scene in which geologists study the George Washington Bridge cut: "Geologists on the whole tend to be inconsistent drivers. When a roadcut presents itself, they tend to lurch and weave. To them, the roadcut is a portal, a fragment of a regional story, a proscenium arch that leads their imaginations into the earth and through the surrounding terrain."

A walk through Central Park will open up a new vista of geological interest. Here you can study the famous glacial grooves and striations on the Umpire Rock (near Heckscher Ballfields), or erratics scattered in the park from the New Jersey palisades sill. Some of these erratics (rocks carried and dumped by glaciers) have been built into the park walls but a few remain, particularly near the ponds. Exposures of Manhattan Schist are scattered throughout the park.

Finally, there is the fascinating Inwood Hill Park (*map p. 573*) in Upper Manhattan (the closest subway stops are the A train's 207th St station and the IRT number 1 train's 207th and 215th St stations). The park consists of two giant ridges as high as 220ft with a valley in between. The park is famous geologically. "There is no better place in the city to see the geology and all its relationships," says Sidney Horenstein, a geologist at the American Museum of Natural History. "You can see expanses of Inwood marble, outcroppings of Manhattan schist, boulders of billion-year-old Fordham gneiss and glacial striation and potholes."

An excellent background to Manhattan geology is *The Foundation Geology of New York City* by Charles Baskerville, who has probably done more mapping in the "Big Apple" than anyone. His article appears in the *Geological Society of America, Reviews in Engineering Geology* series (vol. 5, 1982), "Geology Under Cities." A xerox copy is available for $4 (current at the time of writing) from the New York State Geological Survey. Baskerville has recently also produced several maps (1:24,000) depicting both the geology and engineering geology of Manhattan, the Bronx, and parts of Queens and Brooklyn.

CHRONOLOGY

1524 Giovanni da Verrazano, working for Francis I of France, explores New York Bay and the North American coastline.

1609 Henry Hudson, seeking a water route to the Orient for the Dutch East India Company, explores the harbor.

1613 Adriaen Block and crew winter in Lower Manhattan, building a new ship after their first, the *Tyger*, burns.

1614 Block explores Long Island Sound, and makes the first map of Manhattan.

1624 Thirty Dutch and Walloon families sent by the Dutch West India Company settle in New Netherland, a territory reaching from the Delaware to Connecticut rivers.

1625 First permanent settlement is made in Lower Manhattan and named New Amsterdam.

1626 Governor General Peter Minuit "purchases" Manhattan Island from the Native Americans (*see p. 47*).

1636 Settlers Jacques Bentyn and Adrianse Bennett buy land from Native Americans in Brooklyn.

1638 First ferry line established from Fulton Ferry in Brooklyn to about present-day Dover St in Manhattan.

1639 Jonas Bronck, a Dane, buys part of the Bronx from Native Americans. David de Vries and others settle Staten Island but are driven out by Native Americans.

1642 The religious tolerance of New Amsterdam attracts dissenters from New England.

1643 Native American uprisings in New Amsterdam, New Jersey, and Staten Island; they continue intermittently until 1655.

1645 First permanent settlement in Queens at Vlissingen (Flushing).

1647 Peter Stuyvesant becomes governor.

1653 Peter Stuyvesant builds a fortified wall, river to river, at the present latitude of Wall St, to keep out the British, trading rivals of the Dutch.

1654 First permanent Jewish settlement; Asser Levy and 22 others arrive, fleeing persecution in Brazil.

1661 First permanent settlement on Staten Island.

1664 The British capture New Amsterdam and rename it New York after James, Duke of York, brother of King Charles II.

1673 The Dutch recapture New York and rename it New Orange.

1674 Treaty of Westminster brings Anglo-Dutch War to a close; New York becomes British once again.

1686 The Dongan Charter gives the city a form of municipal government that remains in force until modern times.

1693 Frederick Philipse builds King's Bridge across the Harlem River, joining Manhattan island to the mainland.

1713 First Staten Island ferry.

1732 First theater opens near present Maiden Lane.

1754 King's College, now Columbia University, founded as city's first college.

1763 French and Indian War closes with Treaty of Paris, confirming English control of North America.

1765 British Parliament passes Stamp Act, raising revenues to support British troops in America. Delegates from nine colonies meet in New York and denounce the Act.

1766 Stamp Act repealed in England. St. Paul's Chapel dedicated.

1767 British again increase taxes and restrict colonial self-government. Anti-British sentiment grows.

1776 Declaration of Independence marks beginning of Revolutionary War. British occupy Brooklyn after Battle of Long Island and take control of all of Manhattan by Nov 17.

1783 Treaty of Paris concludes Revolutionary War as Britain recognizes independence of the 13 colonies. British Army leaves New York.

1784 New York City becomes the capital of the state and nation.

1789 US Constitution ratified. George Washington becomes nation's first president.

1790 Federal capital moves to Philadelphia. First census puts city population at 33,000.

1791 Yellow fever epidemic stimulates development of Greenwich Village.

1792 Buttonwood Agreement leads to formation of New York Stock Exchange.

1796 Robert Fitch tests experimental steamboat on Collect Pond.

1797 Albany becomes state capital.

1803 Cornerstone laid for present City Hall.

1806 First New York free school opens.

1807 Robert Fulton demonstrates his steamboat on the Hudson River.

1811 John Randel Jr. heads group of commissioners who plan New York's rectilinear street grid.

1812 City Hall opens. US declares war on Britain; port suffers in trade war and is fortified against possible British attack.

1814 Treaty of Ghent ends War of 1812.

1820 New York becomes nation's largest city, with population of 123,706.

1825 Erie Canal opens, greatly enhancing the importance of New York as a port and making it the gateway to the Midwest.

1827 State legislature ends all slavery in New York State.

1831 New York University founded as University of the City of New York.

1832 New York and Harlem Railroad, a horsecar line, opens along the Bowery and Fourth Ave from Prince St to 14th St.

1834 Village of Brooklyn incorporated as City of Brooklyn.

1835 "Great Fire" destroys 674 buildings near Hanover and Pearl Sts.

1837 Business panic; city losses total some $60 million.

1841 St. John's College, now Fordham University, founded in the Bronx.

1842 Croton Aqueduct brings water to a reservoir on the site of Bryant Park.

1846 Potato famine in Ireland swells immigration.

1847 Madison Square Park laid out.

1848 Political uprisings increase immigration from Germany.

1849 Free Academy, the precursor of City College, opens on Lexington Ave at 23rd St. Astor Place Riot demonstrates incompetence of police force.

1850 Giuseppe Garibaldi arrives in Staten Island during period of exile.

1851 *New York Daily Times*, now the *New York Times*, begins publication.

1853 State legislature authorizes Central Park. World's Fair held in Bryant Park.

1855 Castle Garden becomes immigrant station. First model tenement built at Elizabeth and Mott Sts.

1856 City buys land for Central Park.

1858 Calvert Vaux and Frederick Law Olmsted chosen to design Central Park. Macy's founded.

1859 Cooper Union opens. Otis passenger elevator installed in Fifth Avenue Hotel.

1860 City's population reaches 813,669, including large number of immigrants.

1861 American Civil War begins.

1863 Draft Riots against conscription into the Union Army (those who could pay a $300 fee were exempted) paralyze the city for three days.

1865 Civil War ends. Municipal fire-fighting system replaces volunteer companies.

1867 Prospect Park opens in Brooklyn. First tenement house law attempts to set standards for ventilation, sanitation, and room size.

1868 First elevated railroad opens on Greenwich St from the Battery to Cortland St, a cable system with both moving and stationary engines.

1869 Rutherford Stuyvesant builds city's first known apartment houses on East 18th St.

1870 Work begins on Brooklyn Bridge. Pneumatic subway opens under Broadway from Warren to Murray Sts. Ninth Avenue El reaches 30th St.

1871 Grand Central Depot opens. "Boss" Tweed arrested, closing a period during which city government reached a low point of inefficiency and corruption.

1874 Part of the Bronx annexed to New York City.

1877 Alfred Tredway White opens model tenement houses in Brooklyn.

1879 "Dumbbell" tenement plan by James F. Ware wins competition for model tenement. Plan condemned by tenement reformers but widely adopted.

1880 Sixth Avenue El reaches 155th St. Metropolitan Museum of Art opens. Broadway illuminated by Brush electric arc lamps.

1882 Thomas Edison opens generating plant at 257 Pearl St, making electricity commercially available.

1883 Brooklyn Bridge opens.

1886 Statue of Liberty inaugurated. Elevated railway joins Manhattan and Bronx.

1888 Great Blizzard. First building with steel skeleton erected (Tower Building at 50 Broadway).

1891 Carnegie Hall opens. New York Botanical Garden opens in the Bronx.

1892 Immigration station opens on Ellis Island.

1895 Harlem Ship Canal opens along Harlem River. Rest of Bronx annexed to New York City.

1898 Greater New York created by joining the five boroughs under a single municipal government. Population of 3.4 million makes it the world's second largest city behind London (4 million).

1899 Croton Reservoir in Bryant Park razed.

1900 Subway construction begins. Blacks begin moving to Harlem. Census shows tenements house 70 percent of city's population.

1901 Tenement House Law institutes "New Law" tenements, superseding dumbbell plan.

1903 Williamsburg Bridge opens, making northern Brooklyn accessible to the poor of the Lower East Side.

1904 IRT subway opens from City Hall to West 145th St.

1905 Municipal Staten Island ferry opens.

1908 East River subway tunnel links Manhattan and Brooklyn. First Hudson tunnel links Manhattan and Hoboken. IRT Broadway line reaches Kingsbridge section of the Bronx.

1909 Queensboro and Manhattan Bridges open.

1910 Pennsylvania Station opens.

1913 The present Grand Central Terminal opens. The Armory Show introduces New York to "modern art."

1916 Nation's first zoning resolution, divides city into residential and commercial areas and restricts height and bulk of buildings.

1923 "Setback" law restricts configuration of tall buildings.

1929 Stock market crashes; Great Depression begins.

1931 Empire State Building and George Washington Bridge open. Floyd Bennett Field opens as city's first municipal airport.

1932 Mayor James J. ("Beau James") Walker resigns after Seabury Investigations reveal rampant corruption.

1933 Fiorello La Guardia elected mayor. IND subway opens to Queens.

1934 New York City Housing Authority formed to clear slums and build low-rent housing.

1936 Triborough Bridge opens.

1938 La Guardia's City Charter goes into effect, centralizing municipal power.

1939 North Beach Airport opens; soon renamed for La Guardia. New York World's Fair of 1939–40 opens in Queens.

1940 Queens–Midtown tunnel opens. Brooklyn–Battery Tunnel begun.

1941 US enters World War II. New York becomes major Atlantic port. Brooklyn Navy Yard operates at full capacity.

1945 World War II ends. United Nations charter passed.

1946 UN selects New York as permanent headquarters.

1947 Stuyvesant Town, middle-income housing for returning war veterans and their families, is built along East River Drive.

1948 New York International Airport, known as Idlewild, officially opened; now called John F. Kennedy International Airport.

1950 Brooklyn–Battery Tunnel opens after construction delay caused by war. City population at all-time high: 7,891,957.

1952 Lever House opens, first of the glass-box skyscrapers.

1957 Fair Housing Law outlaws racial discrimination.

1959 Ground broken for Lincoln Center.

1960 Completion of Chase Manhattan Bank marks beginning of construction boom in lower Manhattan.

1961 New zoning law offers incentives for public amenities, plazas, arcades.

1963 Pennsylvania Station demolished.

1964 Race riots in Harlem and Bedford-Stuyvesant. World's Fair of 1964–65 opens in Queens. Verrazano-Narrows Bridge opens, ending relative isolation of Staten Island.

1965 Landmarks Preservation Commission established to save city's architectural heritage. New laws allow increased Asian, Greek, Haitian, Dominican immigration. First power blackout.

1966 Ground broken for World Trade Center (estimated cost of $250 million).

1970 First New York City Marathon is run, with 126 males and 1 female participating. McSorley's Old Ale House is forced by the courts to admit women.

1973 Construction of Twin Towers at World Trade Center completed.

1974 City's financial position worsens, as loss of middle class and departure of businesses erode tax base while costs of social services increase.

1975 Cash-flow problems and inability to sell more municipal bonds bring city to verge of insolvency. South Bronx becomes symbol of urban despair as 13,000 fires break out in 12-square-mile area.

1977 Power blackout, lasting 25hrs, results in widespread looting and vandalism. *A Chorus Line* opens.

1978 Radio City Music Hall saved from demolition. Supreme Court decision preserves Grand Central Terminal. Federal government gives city $1.65 billion in long-term loan guarantees. "Pooper scooper" law requires pet owners to clean up after their dogs.

1980 Census assesses population at 7,086,096, with sharp decline in city's white population, moderate increase in black population, and substantial increase in Hispanic population. Blacks and Hispanics account for 48 percent of city's population.

1981 City re-enters long-term municipal bond market. Construction begins at Battery Park City.

1982 IBM Building opens on Madison Ave. *Cats* opens, ushering in the era of the Broadway blockbuster.

1983 *A Chorus Line* sets Broadway record with 3,389th performance. City enacts "antisliver" law, which limits height of buildings that are less than 45ft wide.

1986 Statue of Liberty celebrates 100th anniversary.

1987 Stock market crashes as Dow Jones average plunges 508 points in one day. World Financial Center opens in Battery Park City.

1989 David Dinkins is elected first black mayor. B. Altman & Company department store closes after 124 years in business.

1990 Ellis Island reopens as a museum.

1991 African Burial Ground discovered near City Hall (*see p. 89*).

1993 World Trade Center is bombed. Six die, more than 1,000 are injured. Staten Island bids to secede from Greater New York.

1994 High-tech industries reach New York with development of "Silicon Alley" around Broadway in the West 20s. Staten Island's secession bid quashed by courts.

1997 Times Square rehabilitation in full swing. Crime rate falls. *Cats* establishes new longevity record (6,138 performances).

2000 City's population tops 8 million, confirming it as nation's largest: 3.6 million whites, 2.2 million Hispanics, 2.1 million blacks, and fewer than 800,000 Asians. *Cats* finally closes after 7,485 performances.

2001 On Sept 11, two commercial airliners hijacked by Islamic terrorists deliberately crash into the Twin Towers of the World Trade Center. More than 2,800 people killed.

2002 Tourism drops and economy shrinks in wake of World Trade Center disaster. Guggenheim Museum scraps plan for Frank Gehry building on downtown waterfront.

2004 Statue of Liberty, closed after Sept 11 attacks, reopens to the public.

2006 World Trade Center rebuilding officially begins.

2008 New Museum of Contemporary Art opens in a new building on the Bowery.

BOROUGH OF MANHATTAN (NEW YORK COUNTY)

To many people New York is synonymous with Manhattan, a slender island 12.5 miles long, 2.5 miles wide, with a total area of 22.6 square miles. It is the third largest borough in population (1.611 million from census data for 2006), and the smallest in size. Manhattan's highest altitude is about 268ft and its lowest, sea level.

Topographically there remain only a few vestiges of Manhattan's appearance before the Dutch came. Southern Manhattan is flat, a coastal plain lying over a fairly shallow stratum of Manhattan schist, the bedrock on which its skyscrapers stand. Again in Midtown, bedrock lies close to the surface, supporting a second great concentration of towering buildings. In its more northerly reaches, however, the island's natural topography is more evident: in Central Park's outcroppings of Manhattan schist laced with granite intrusions and striated by glacial scratches; in Fort Tryon Park and Inwood Hill Park, two schist ridges bisected by the fault valley that underlies Dyckman St, in the ridges of Morningside Heights once used by rock climbers to hone their skills; and in the valley of West 125th St, slashing diagonally across the regular north–south street grid.

Manhattan is encircled by rivers, the Hudson (once called the North River) on the west; the East River, actually a tidal inlet from Long Island Sound on the east; and the Harlem River on the northeast, part of which, the Harlem Ship Canal on the north, is an artificial channel dug at the end of the 19th century to facilitate navigation.

Manhattan is the engine that drives the city's economy, with more corporate headquarters than any other location nationwide. Wall Street is the center of the nation's financial industry; Madison Avenue is synonymous with the advertising industry. The borough's culture industry brings tens of millions of tourists every year to enjoy its offerings.

Downtown Manhattan seems largely to have recovered from the economic devastation that followed the September 11 terrorist attacks, and is enjoying a boom that clogs the streets with construction equipment and shrouds the buildings with scaffolding.

The disparity in wealth that is affecting the entire United States is particularly keenly felt in Manhattan. As working-class people and small businesses are forced out by rising costs, the neighborhoods are threatened with a loss of individuality. In the financial district as elsewhere, office towers and hotels are being converted to condominiums, with such prominent buildings as the former headquarters of J. Pierpont Morgan's bank, the Plaza Hotel, and the Woolworth Building all becoming residential, at least in part.

Manhattan neighborhoods

If Parisians think of themselves living in such-and-such an *arrondissement*, Manhattanites think of themselves as living in a certain neighborhood—Greenwich Village, or the Meatpacking District, or the Upper East Side. As the demographics and economics of the island have changed, Manhattan has attached new names to old

neighborhoods, either to polish a tarnished image (Clinton, formerly Hell's Kitchen) or to establish an identity for a drab, anonymous area (TriBeCa).

The island was settled from south to north, with its oldest neighborhoods in what is today called Lower Manhattan. The first Dutch settlement was near what is presently the Battery, then an area of marsh similar to the Dutch lowlands. The Financial District, a residential area for the Dutch, had already begun to assume some public functions when the British took over in 1664. Battery Park City, west of the World Trade Center site and built on landfill largely excavated when the World Trade Center was first built, includes the World Financial Center and a planned residential community. North of it are the Civic Center, Chinatown, Little Italy, and the Lower East Side, the last three of which saw the influx of large immigrant populations toward the end of the 19th century. The East Village, once simply considered part of the Lower East Side, gained new recognition (or notoriety) as the home of the counterculture during the 1960s. The eastern East Village—Avenues A through D—is called Alphabet City, and is changing rapidly.

On the Lower West Side, north of Battery Park City are Tribeca and SoHo, former industrial areas, now gentrified. Above Houston St are Greenwich Village, once a village outside of "New York" Downtown; and the Meatpacking District, formerly the Gansevoort Market, where bloody butcher aprons have, by and large, given way to designer duds, and "gritty" has evolved into "gritty chic." Chelsea developed the same way a decade earlier, but with the added fillip of high-powered art galleries on its far west side, which moved up from SoHo. The eponymous garment industry has mostly left the Garment District, between 34th and 42nd Sts on the West Side, but the Theater District to its north still thrives, with Times Square at its spiritual center. North of that, on the West Side, are Hell's Kitchen, politely known as Clinton; the Lincoln Center neighborhood; and the Upper West Side.

In the eastern parts of Midtown are Park and Madison Avenues, with their newer glassy or older masonry office towers; and several residential districts to the east: Murray Hill, Kips Bay, and Turtle Bay—named for geographical features that no longer exist.

Central Park divides the East Side from the West Side above 59th St. The Upper East Side includes some of the most expensive residential real estate in the city—particularly along Fifth Avenue as well as in elite neighborhoods like Sutton Place and Beekman Place—as well as Yorkville, once an uptown immigrant neighborhood for Germans, Czechs, and Hungarians. Above 96th St lies East Harlem, formerly an Italian enclave, now known as El Barrio or Spanish Harlem.

On the West Side, Central Park West and Riverside Drive are the finest residential areas. The commercial avenues are Broadway, Amsterdam Avenue, and Columbus Avenue, all of which offer restaurants, bars, and shops geared to an affluent middle class. North of 96th St is Morningside Heights, dominated by Columbia University, the Cathedral of St. John the Divine, and other major educational and religious institutions. To the east and below Morningside Heights lies the Harlem plain, home to the nation's most famous black community. Upper Manhattan consists of the neighborhoods of Washington Heights and Inwood, both residential. The Cloisters in Fort Tryon Park is the major cultural institution in Upper Manhattan.

THE STATUE OF LIBERTY
& ELLIS ISLAND

The Statue of Liberty and Ellis Island are two of New York's most famous and beloved landmarks, places of pilgrimage for Americans and foreigners alike. The statue, a marvel of 19th-century French engineering, has become a symbol of freedom and democracy, while Ellis Island remains a potent symbol of the millions of immigrants who poured into this nation seeking a better life.

Visiting the sites

Map p. 4. Subway: 1 to South Ferry; 4, 5 to Bowling Green; R to Whitehall St. Bus: M1, M6, M15. Open daily at least from 9:30–4, extended hours summer and holidays; closed Dec 25. Access to Liberty Island by ferry only. The round trip takes about 1hr 15mins, with stops at Ellis Island and the statue. In good weather, expect long waits and large crowds. Your ferry ticket will enable you to visit the museum on Ellis Island and the grounds of Liberty Island. If you wish to enter the pedestal of the statue, you will need a Monument Pass, free when you purchase a Reserve Ticket (with a specified time slot). A limited number of Monument Passes are available on a first-come, first-serve basis every day at the ferry dock, but are often in short supply.

If you know when you want to visit the statue, it is wise to get a Reserve Ticket and Monument Pass in advance. Reserve Tickets also shorten waiting time by allowing you priority entry to the security check line. If you do not know precisely when you will visit the Statue, you can buy a Flex Ticket, good for three days. A Flex Ticket will shorten your waiting time in the security line, but does not include a Monument Pass. During the summer and holiday periods, advance tickets can shorten long waits. Call the ferry company at 1 877 LADY TIX or reserve online at www.statuecruises.com.

The Monument Pass allows you to visit the Museum Gallery and the Pedestal Observation Deck, with sweeping panoramic views. You will also be able to see the interior structure of the statue, though you cannot ascend beyond the pedestal. There is no access to the statue itself. Visitors entering the monument are subject to secondary security screening. For further information, T: 212 363 3200 or www.nps.gov/stli.

THE STATUE OF LIBERTY

The Statue of Liberty, the best-remembered work of sculptor Frédéric-Auguste Bartholdi, dedicated in 1886 and properly called *Liberty Enlightening the World*, is surely the most famous piece of sculpture in America, rising in majesty on Liberty Island in direct view of ships entering the Upper Bay. A gift of the people of France, the figure stands on a granite pedestal donated by the American public. Her head is surrounded by a radiant crown, while her feet step forth from broken shackles; in her uplifted right hand is a torch; her left holds a tablet representing the Declaration of

Independence. The statue stands on a pedestal of Stony Creek granite inside the star-shaped walls of Fort Wood. The fort was part of the city's defenses for the War of 1812 against Great Britain, during which the British imposed blockades on European ports, seized American ships, and impressed American sailors into the British navy in an attempt to prevent American shipping interests from supplying Napoleonic France.

HISTORY OF THE STATUE

The inspiration for the Statue of Liberty came primarily from Édouard de Laboulaye (1811–83), a jurist, professor, and authority on US Constitutional history, and Frédéric-Auguste Bartholdi (1834–1904), a sculptor of monumental ambitions. Laboulaye wanted to identify the destiny of France, then ruled by a monarch, with that of a democracy, but he knew anything too close to home would be inflammatory. He proposed a joint Franco-American monument and introduced Bartholdi to the project. The statue's iron skeleton was devised by Alexandre-Gustave Eiffel, whose reputation at the time rested with his iron trusswork railway bridges but would be enhanced by the famous tower that bears his name.

The size of the statue imposed technical difficulties, which Eiffel solved with great ingenuity. He devised an interior framework consisting of a heavy central iron pylon supporting a lightweight system of trusswork that reaches out toward the interior surface of the statue. The hammered copper "skin" of the figure, only $3/32$ of an inch thick, is bound together in sections by steel straps and joined to the trusswork in such a way that it "floats" at the ends of hundreds of flexible attachments, accommodating wind and thermal changes.

Fundraising presented its own challenges. A committee called the French-American Union was formed to raise money, coordinate publicity, and so on. The French sponsors raised about 400,000 francs (an estimated $250,000, though some recent scholars estimate the figure at nearly 600,000 francs, or $450,000) from the general public. The campaign began with a banquet at the Hôtel du Louvre (successful), followed by a concert for which Charles Gounod wrote a cantata (a fundraising failure), a painted diorama of New York harbor for which visitors paid an entrance fee (successful), and the sale of signed and numbered clay models of the statue (also successful). When the head was completed, it was set up on the Champ de Mars and tickets were sold to visitors, who could climb 36 steps and look out through the windows in the crown. In all, there were 100,000 subscribers, including 181 towns, and the majority of masonic lodges in France.

The statue itself was constructed in Paris by the firm of Gaget, Gauthier et Cie, and assembled outside Bartholdi's workshops. On July 4, 1884, the figure was formally presented to the United States. Then it was dismantled and shipped to New York in 214 crates. The crates sat unopened for more than a year as the

American side of the Franco-American committee struggled to raise money to build the pedestal (designed by French-trained architect Richard Morris Hunt). In 1885, the committee was considering returning the statue or letting another city try to raise the money for it when *New York World* publisher Joseph Pulitzer (of Pulitzer Prize fame) promised to print the name of every donor in his paper, even if the gift were only a penny. Within three months the final $102,000 had been raised—from 80,000 donations.

On Oct 28, 1886, President Grover Cleveland dedicated the statue during spectacular ceremonies culminating in fireworks and the unveiling of the face. The statue soon became a tourist attraction, later a promise of hope offered to immigrants, and eventually a powerful symbol for the US itself.

After nearly a century of wear and tear, a restoration campaign refurbished the statue in time for her centennial celebration. The only visible exterior change was the replacement of the former glass torch by a gilded one, as Bartholdi had envisioned. Inside, the wire mesh that long enclosed the spiral staircase was cleared away so that the great volumes of the body and the billowing folds of the robe soared above the circular staircase.

STATUE STATISTICS

Height of statue alone	151 ft
Height of pedestal	89 ft
Height of torch above sea	305 ft
Weight	225 tons
Waist measurement	35 ft
Width of mouth	3 ft
Length of index finger	8 ft
Size of fingernail	13 by 10 inches
Weight of fingernail	about 3½ pounds
Length of nose	4 ft 6 inches
Approximate fabric in gown	4,000 square yards
Length of sandal	25 ft
Approximate women's shoe size (US)	879

The museum

In the lobby, the **Torch Exhibit** displays the original torch as altered by Gutzon Borglum in 1916 after it was damaged in an explosion (*see p. 40 below*). Unfortunately, the remodeled torch leaked badly, hastening the corrosion of the statue's interior. During the 1984–86 restoration, French metal workers fashioned a gold-plated copper flame lit by reflection (the sculptor's original conception) to replace the old flame, illuminated from within. Upstairs, the **Statue of Liberty Exhibit** explores the conception and construction of the statue, its impact on new arrivals, and its exploitation as an image for commerce or propaganda. The exhibit also includes a plaque bearing "The New Colossus," Emma Lazarus's famous sonnet (1883), written as part of the fund-raising for the pedestal. Its lines "Give me your tired, your poor/Your huddled masses yearning to breathe free …" have come to symbolize the statue's promise of hope. Visitors can view the interior of the statue and its marvelous engineering through a glass ceiling.

ELLIS ISLAND NATIONAL MONUMENT

Map p. 4. Open at least from 9:30–4, extended hours summer and holidays; closed Dec 25. T: 212 363 3200; www.nps.gov/elis. For access, ticket and security information, see p. 35 above. Originally a low-lying sandbar, Ellis Island lies about a mile southwest of Battery Park in Upper New York Bay. It is the site of the former United States Immigration Station, through which an estimated 12 million immigrants passed on their way to a new life in America. The island consists of two land masses separated by a ferry slip. The museum stands on the original island, to the right of the slip. To the left of the slip stand derelict hospitals and other buildings left over from the immigration service.

HISTORY OF ELLIS ISLAND

The Native Americans called Ellis Island *Kioshk* (Gull Island); the Dutch bought it from them in 1630, and named it Little Oyster Island. During much of the 18th century, the British called it Gibbet Island, after several pirates who were hanged there in the 1760s. At the time of the Revolution it was owned by Samuel Ellis (d. 1794), who had a farm in New Jersey, sold general merchandise in Manhattan, and leased out part of the island to a fishermen's tavern. After his death, the federal government acquired it (1808) for a then-exorbitant $10,000 to build a fort. Like the other fortifications built at about this time, it was intended to protect the city from a British naval invasion in the War of 1812, but saw no action. From 1835–90 it served as an ammunition dump, threatening nearby New Jersey residents with the possibility of accidental explosions.

In 1890, when the federal government took over the immigration service, Ellis Island was designated as the site of the main receiving station, and an immigrant station opened in 1892. The first immigrant to be admitted was 13-year-old Annie Moore, born in Cork, Ireland, who arrived as a steerage passenger on the SS *Nevada*, with her two younger brothers. The station, primarily constructed of Georgia pine, burned to the ground five years later, fortunately without loss of life, but most of the immigration records from 1855–90 were destroyed. In 1898 construction began on the present station and the immigration service moved to Battery Park. The new fireproof buildings opened on Dec 17, 1900, and that day received 2,251 immigrants. Federal inspectors processed the immigrants, detaining those who would be unable to earn a living and weeding out paupers, criminals, prostitutes, the insane, and those suffering from contagious diseases or professing beliefs such as anarchy or polygamy.

Until 1902, when President Theodore Roosevelt appointed William Williams as Commissioner of Immigration, immigrants were often abused or robbed. After Williams' reforms, problems arose primarily from overcrowding. In 1907, the peak year of immigration, 1,004,756 people entered the US through Ellis Island, approximately twice the number the station was designed to handle.

The heavy influx continued until 1915, when World War I closed transatlantic shipping. Under the National Origins Act (1924) immigrants were processed in their own countries and thereafter Ellis Island became under-used and increasingly expensive to maintain. In 1954 the last detainee, a Norwegian sailor who had jumped ship, was released; the station closed and the island was vacated. The buildings began to deteriorate rapidly, ravaged by weather and damp sea air, and stripped by vandals. Gradually, the government became mindful of the island's historic importance and in 1965, it became part of the Statue of Liberty National Monument. In 1990, the Main Building opened as a museum. The rest of the island awaits restoration and is not open to the public.

The **Main Building** (1897–1900; Boring & Tilton), formerly the Immigrant Receiving Station, is built in French Renaissance style, of red brick laid in Flemish bond, with exuberant granite and limestone trim. At the corners four 100-ft towers rise to spire-topped domes. Three arched entrances on each side ascend above the second story. An early description of the building remarked on its "bloated" detailing, and suggested that these oversized features made the building easier to recognize from ships in the harbor.

The names of more than 600,000 immigrants who entered here are inscribed on the American Immigrant Wall of Honor to the right of the Main Building. Along with the names of myriads of uncelebrated people are the names of some who became famous (or notorious), including Russian-born composer Irving Berlin (who wrote "God Bless America") and the Sicilian-born gangster "Lucky" Luciano.

Inside the Main Entrance is the **Baggage Room**, where immigrants waited before climbing to the second floor to the imposing **Registry Room** (200ft by 100ft by 56ft), which has been left largely empty to heighten its emotional impact. Until 1911 it was divided by iron pipes into a maze (whose appearance in old photos suggested cattle pens), through which immigrants wound their way past the various inspectors. The building was designed to handle 5,000 immigrants a day, but on April 17, 1907, the peak day, 11,747 were processed.

The barrel-vaulted ceiling of Guastavino tile replaced a plaster one, destroyed by the Black Tom explosion (1916; *see box below*) on a nearby New Jersey wharf. Despite the decades of neglect when the building was abandoned, only 17 of the 28,880 tiles needed to be replaced during the restoration of the 1990s.

THE BLACK TOM EXPLOSION

On July 30, 1916, more than a thousand tons of munitions exploded on the Black Tom Wharf in nearby Jersey City, rocking the harbor with the force of an earthquake estimated at 5.0–5.5 on the Richter scale. The explosives had been stored on the wharf en route to the Allies in World War I. Shrapnel from the blast hit the Statue of Liberty, and the shock waves—which knocked down the plaster ceiling of the Registry Room at Ellis Island—were felt as far as Philadelphia. The explosion is attributed to German agents, who sabotaged the munitions so they would not reach Britain and France.

Exhibits of photos and artifacts throughout the building shed light on the process by which immigrants were screened; on view are pieces of baggage, photographs, and treasured personal possessions brought by the immigrants; a dormitory room has been restored to its 1908 appearance; other exhibits detail the station's abandonment, decay, and restoration, and explore the history of immigration.

GOVERNORS ISLAND

Map p. 4. Open during summer, usually Tues–Sat. Park information, T: 212 825 3045; or www.nps.gov/gois. The Governors Island Ferry departs from the Battery Maritime Building adjacent to the Staten Island Ferry in Lower Manhattan. Tickets available through New York Water Taxi; T: 212 749 1969; www.nywatertaxi.com. Same-day sales at the Governors Island ferry slip, Sat only, subject to availability.

Situated in New York Harbor between Lower Manhattan and Brooklyn, Governors Island (172 acres) is a place of great beauty that has been largely insulated from the commercial and political forces that have shaped the rest of the city. It offers breathtaking, wide-angle views of the downtown skyline and the harbor, as well as a collection of historic military buildings, notably two 19th-century forts. New York City and State jointly own the island, except for the 22 acres that constitute Governors Island National Monument, operated by the National Park Service.

The forts were built during the run-up to the War of 1812 (*see p. 30*) to protect the city from invasion by sea. Fort Jay (1798; rebuilt 1803), a star-shaped fortification of sandstone blocks, stands on the site of earlier earthworks. It is named for John Jay, first chief justice of the United States. Quickly outmoded, it was replaced by Castle Williams (1811), a circular red sandstone fort whose three tiers of guns rake the harbor channels. Its designer, Colonel Jonathan Williams of the Army Corps of Engineers, was a grandnephew of Benjamin Franklin and the first superintendent of West Point.

Governors Island got its name from the British, who took over from the Dutch in 1664, and in 1698 set it aside for the "accommodation of His Majesty's governors." The island's long military history began before the Revolutionary War and continued until 1997 when the Coast Guard moved its facility.

LOWER MANHATTAN: LOWER BROADWAY & BATTERY PARK

Map p. 582, C4. Subway: 1 to South Ferry; 4, 5 to Bowling Green; R to Whitehall St. Bus: M1, M6, M15.

New York City owes its historic supremacy among American cities to its closeness to the sea, and nowhere are these ties more obvious than at the southernmost tip of Manhattan, where the East and Hudson Rivers converge and empty into New York Bay.

ALEXANDER HAMILTON CUSTOM HOUSE

The former United States Custom House (1907), at 1 Bowling Green, stands on the probable site of New York's first permanent settlement. Today it houses the US Bankruptcy Court and a branch of the National Museum of the American Indian.

NEW AMSTERDAM'S FIRST FORT

In 1624 the Dutch ship *Nieuw Nederlandt* deposited eight men on what is now Governors Island and continued upstream to settle others at the present site of Albany. These men, sponsored by the Dutch West India Company, and the families who followed them, moved to the southern shore of Manhattan, where they built rude shelters and a fort to protect themselves from Native Americans.

The original fort (1626), Fort Amsterdam, more or less where the Custom House stands today, consisted of a crude blockhouse protected by a cedar palisade. As the town grew, and alternately fell under the jurisdiction of the Dutch, the British, the Dutch again, and the British once more, the fort was strengthened and appropriately renamed. The last such structure, called Fort George after the reigning British monarch, remained until after the Revolution, when it was torn down in 1789 to make way for Government House, intended as the residence for the new nation's president.

In 1892 the US Treasury announced an architectural competition for a custom house—an important building, since customs revenue was essential to the nation's budget in the years before income tax. Architect Cass Gilbert won the competition with a plan intended to symbolize the commercial greatness of the nation and of the city.

A triumph of Beaux-Arts exuberance, the façade is adorned with emblems of commerce and the sea. In the window arches are heads of the eight "races" of mankind. Above the cornice, statues representing 12 great commercial nations of history stare down on Broadway, while the head of Mercury, Roman god of commerce, crowns the

The Custom House rotunda.

capital of each of the 44 Corinthian columns encircling the building. Gilbert commissioned Daniel Chester French, best known for his statue of Abraham Lincoln in the Lincoln Memorial (Washington, D.C.), to design the heroic limestone statues of the four continents. Left to right they are *Asia, America, Europe*, and *Africa*. The groups reflect early 20th-century cultural attitudes: Asia and Africa, meditative and somnolent, sit at the periphery; Europe, robed in a Grecian gown, sits enthroned among the achievements of the past. America, with a sheaf of maize on her lap, looks dynamically forward, while Labor turns the wheel of progress on her right, and on her left a Native American kneels, eyes downcast.

The main entrance leads into a hallway finished in opulent marbles, at either end of which a spiral staircase mounts the entire height of the building. In the center of the main floor is the great **rotunda** (135ft by 85ft by 48ft high). The ceiling, constructed of 140 tons of tile and plaster (no steel), was engineered by Rafael Guastavino. Trained as an architect in Spain, Guastavino arrived through Ellis Island in 1881. His tile-work also appears in the Cathedral of St. John the Divine, Ellis Island's Registry Room, and Grand Central Station. Just below the dome are frescoes (1937) by Reginald Marsh, a painter who specialized in New York City life, mostly low but sometimes high. These panels depict early explorers and an ocean liner entering New York harbor. One famous panel shows the movie star Greta Garbo surrounded by the press. The murals were financed by the Treasury Relief Art Project, which supported artists with government commissions during the Depression.

The National Museum of the American Indian (Heye Center)
Open daily 10–5, Thurs until 8; closed Dec 25; T: 212 514 3700; www.si.edu/nmai.
In 1989 the Custom House became the new Heye Center, a satellite space of the Smithsonian's larger National Museum of the American Indian, in Washington, D.C.

> *George Gustav Heye* (1874–1957)
> The Museum of the American Indian was born from the obsession of George Gustav Heye, who gathered most of its collection. The son of a wealthy German oil baron, Heye took a job in Arizona as an electrical engineer and soon began collecting Native American artifacts. At first he acquired things a few at a time. Later he collected wholesale, criss-crossing the West and financing expeditions to Central and South America. The collection opened to the public in 1922, in a building at Audubon Terrace (Broadway at 155th St) in Washington Heights. The museum's goals today reflect attitudes toward Native American cultures and art that have evolved since Heye died. Heye's own insatiable collecting methods are no longer condoned, and the museum is required by law to return to the tribes sacred objects and human remains.

The museum's astonishing collections range geographically from the Arctic to Tierra del Fuego and chronologically from prehistoric times to the present. Highlights include feathered headdresses and buffalo-hide robes from the Plains Indians; masks and ceremonial wood carvings from the Northwest Coast tribes; feather-work from the Amazon; and Peruvian and Navajo fabrics. A good selection of objects from the permanent collection (800,000 objects and more than 80,000 photographs) is always on view, while changing exhibitions showcase the work of contemporary Native Americans.

LOWER BROADWAY

The small fenced plot of lawn, sycamore trees and a fountain, just north of the main façade of the Custom House, is **Bowling Green Park**, the city's first park. During the Dutch colonial period, this area was an open place at the south end of *de Heere Wegh* ("the Main Street," now Broadway) and was used as a cattle market; hence the name of Marketfield St, a block east. Later the area became a parade ground and still later a bowling green, leased in 1733 for the annual fee of one peppercorn per year. The Bowling Green Fence (1771) was built to keep the park from collecting "all the filth and dirt in the neighborhood" and to protect an equestrian statue of George III, torn down on July 9, 1776 by a crowd of patriots, stirred to action by the public reading of the Declaration of Independence. The original fence survives, although the mob made off with the ornaments which capped the posts. Just beyond the park, a flagpole commemorates the evacuation of the British troops on Nov 25, 1783 (*see box below*).

EVACUATION DAY

New York, a vital port city at the entrance of the Hudson River, was a crucial battleground during the Revolutionary War. In Sept 1776, George Washington and his men retreated from Manhattan and fled south along the Jersey Coast. British troops occupied the city for seven years, and life was harsh. On Nov 25, 1783, Washington made his triumphal return to Manhattan with New York governor George Clinton, who declared a public holiday (Evacuation Day) and repaired to nearby Fraunces Tavern for a celebration. As a parting defiant gesture, the British nailed a Union Jack to the flagpole at Fort George and greased the pole. A sailor named John Van Arsdale used cleats to climb up and replace the flag with the Stars and Stripes. For many years, the city commemorated Evacuation Day with a flag-raising ceremony at Battery Park, in which one of John Van Arsdale's descendants did the honors.

While lower Broadway no longer harbors the offices of the great transatlantic steamship lines, it still maintains fragile ties to its maritime past. **No. 1 Broadway** (1884), once the United States Lines Building (on the west side of Bowling Green), is marked by decorative tridents, shells, and fish on the façade and doorways labeled for first- and cabin-class passengers.

The building at **25 Broadway**, locked and empty at the time of writing, began as the Cunard Building (1921; Benjamin Wistar Morris), the first major building to appear in New York after World War I. The Renaissance Revival façade features arched entrances leading into an arcade along the first floor and columned loggias above. Behind the façade lies one of the city's great interiors, with an ornate domed ceiling, wall paintings of world steamship routes, and frescoes depicting the ships of famous explorers—all of which proclaim the romance of steamship travel in a manner suitable to the company that launched the *Queen Mary* and the *Queen Elizabeth*.

On an island in front of 25 Broadway, Arturo Di Modica's bronze ***Charging Bull*** (1989) symbolizes the city's financial district while providing myriads of tourists with a photo opportunity. Di Modica created the bull secretly and at his own expense, trucking it at night to the front of the New York Stock Exchange, and leaving it there on Dec 15, 1989. The Stock Exchange had it hauled away, but the Department of Parks and Recreation responded to public protest and moved it here. Di Modica has offered the statue for sale, so long as it remains where it is, but as yet there have been no buyers.

Across the street at 26 Broadway is the **former Standard Oil Building** (1922), designed by Carrère & Hastings. The façade curves to follow Broadway, but the tower, best seen from Battery Park, is aligned with the north–south grid of the streets, an architectural concession to the uptown skyline. Decorated with huge Ionic columns at its base and crown, it is the epitome of the Neoclassical skyscraper, New York's

special contribution to urban architecture of the early 20th century. On top a structure resembling an oil lamp conceals a chimney. Reliefs of oil lamps flank the main entrance, and the names of former company executives, including John D. Rockefeller, adorn the marble walls of the vestibule.

THE MUSEUM OF JEWISH HERITAGE: A LIVING MEMORIAL TO THE HOLOCAUST

Map p. 582, B4. 36 Battery Pl (First Pl). Open Sun–Tues and Thur 10–5:45, Wed 10–8, Fri 10–3. Extended Fri hours during Daylight Saving Time, except on the eve of Jewish holidays. Closed Sat, Jewish holidays, and Thanksgiving Day. Free Wed 4–8. T: 646 437 4200; www. mjhnyc.org. Attractive kosher café with harbor views. Free admission to café and memorial garden (no exit to exhibits). For a guided walk in Battery Park City, see p. 59.

Located near the south end of Battery Park City, this museum (opened 1997) explores Jewish life and culture from the late 19th century, through the Holocaust, to the present. The hexagonal form of the building, the work of Roche, Dinkeloo and Associates, suggests a Star of David without the points, and the six tiers of the ziggurat roof are said to symbolize the six million Jews killed in the Holocaust.

The core exhibit beginning on the first floor is dedicated to the traditions of Jewish life, with artifacts and photos detailing ceremonies surrounding birth, marriage, and the seasons of the Jewish year. The second floor, the War Against the Jews, explores the Holocaust, from the rise of Hitler to the liberation of the death camps. Photos and artifacts are supplemented by remarkable video oral histories by survivors. On the third floor, the only floor with natural light, the theme is Jewish Renewal, that is, Jewish history after World War II, including the Eichmann trial, the founding of the state of Israel, the survival of Jewish customs into the present, and the contributions of Jews to American culture. Also on the third floor is the **Garden of Stones**, a memorial garden designed by Andy Goldsworthy. Eighteen boulders are drilled with holes in which dwarf oak trees have been planted. The garden is a metaphor for the tenacity of life, and is dedicated to people who died in the Holocaust and those who survived. It is hoped that as the trees grow, the trunks will fuse to the stones, suggesting nature's power of survival even under the harshest conditions. From the garden are views over the harbor.

BATTERY PARK

Map p. 582, C4. For information (Battery Conservancy), T: 212 344 3491; www.thebattery.org. There is a restaurant at the south end of the park (Battery Gardens; T: 212 809 5508).

The name of Battery Park recalls a row of cannons that defended the original fort and stood near the present sidewalk west of the Custom House. Situated on filled land, the 23-acre park offers spectacular views of the harbor, and a group of monuments recalling New York's maritime and commercial history.

The Netherlands Memorial Monument, depicting the mythical sale of Manhattan to the Dutch, apparently paid for in goods worth $24.

The Eisenhower Mall

Near the intersection of State St, Bowling Green, and Battery Place, just outside the park fence, is the **Battery Park Control House** (1904–05), the original entrance to the Bowling Green station of the city's first subway. Designed by Heins & La Farge, an architectural firm better known for its work on the Cathedral of St. John the Divine, it is a fine example of the influence of the École des Beaux-Arts. The flagpole near the park entrance is the **Netherlands Memorial Monument**, given to the city in 1926 by the Dutch as a token of affection for the city's founders. The flagpole base bears a map (now barely visible) of Manhattan in Dutch times and a representation of the legendary Native American receiving goods worth $24 for the island from Peter Minuit.

Between the flagpole and Castle Clinton stretches the Eisenhower Mall (1970). When the Dutch arrived, New York's shoreline only extended to about the midpoint of the present mall. Towards the end of it stands Fritz Koenig's *Sphere* (originally dedicated 1971), moved here temporarily from the plaza of the World Trade Center, where it was battered and buried by debris from the falling towers on September 11, 2001. Originally conceived by Koenig as a memorial to world peace through trade, the 45,000-lb brass sculpture now memorializes those who perished in the tragedy. Koenig, who at first did not want his work re-installed but later came to New York to oversee the reconstruction, remarked: "It was a sculpture, now it's a monument … It now has a different beauty, one I could never imagine. It has its own life—different from the one I gave to it."

Castle Clinton, Pier A and the Promenade

Open every day 8:30–5; closed Christmas. Exhibits sometimes closed in inclement weather; T: 212 344 7220; www.nps. gov/cacl.

The squat red sandstone walls of Castle Clinton National Monument were raised before the War of 1812 to protect the harbor from a naval invasion. Beyond the main gate, the passageway opens into a circular parade field surrounded by the fort's massive walls. Inside are historical exhibits and the ticket kiosk for the Circle Line ferry to the Statue of Liberty and Ellis Island.

CASTLE CLINTON: TWO CENTURIES OF ADAPTIVE RE-USE

The original fort, the Southwest Battery, was situated on an island connected to the mainland by a 200-ft wooden causeway with a drawbridge. In the early years of the 19th century, British attacks on American ships suggested that war might be imminent. Virtually defenseless at the time, New York began the construction of four forts: Fort Wood on Bedloe's (now Liberty) Island, Fort Gibson on Ellis Island, Castle Williams on Governors Island, and the Southwest Battery here.

Built in 1808–11 from plans by John McComb Jr., one of New York's earliest native architects, the walls facing the harbor were pierced by a row of 28 black 32-pounders which could sweep the harbor shore to shore; those facing the land housed powder magazines and officers' quarters.

The fort was untested during the war, and in 1817 it was renamed Castle Clinton to honor DeWitt Clinton, mayor of the city and later state governor. In 1824, it opened as Castle Garden, an entertainment center where audiences enjoyed balloon ascents, fireworks, scientific demonstrations (Samuel F.B. Morse's "wireless telegraph"), political speeches (Daniel Webster, Henry Clay), and receptions for heroes (the Marquis de Lafayette, Andrew Jackson). In 1845 the fort was roofed over, and Castle Garden became a venue for more serious cultural fare, reaching its apogee on September 11, 1850, when P.T. Barnum staged the American début of Jenny Lind, the "Swedish Nightingale," before a sellout crowd of over 6,000.

After more than a quarter of a century, Castle Garden closed its doors to the theatergoing public and reopened them (1855) to immigrants streaming in from abroad. By this time the island had been joined to Manhattan by landfill, forcing immigration officials to fence off the depot from the swindlers who preyed on bewildered new arrivals. The station welcomed more than eight million people from 1855 until 1890, when the Immigration Service became a function of the federal government. Two years later Ellis Island opened.

In 1896 Castle Garden became the New York Aquarium. In 1941, despite the aquarium's immense popularity, Robert Moses, then Commissioner of Parks and head of the Triborough Bridge Authority, closed it down, determined to raze the fort in revenge for the defeat of a bridge to Brooklyn that he proposed, which would have run through and over Battery Park. Concerned citizens lobbied to preserve the fort, and in 1946 Congress declared it a National Monument.

The American Merchant Mariners' Memorial (1991), inspired by the sinking of the American merchant vessel SS *Muskogee* by the Germans in 1942.

To the right of Castle Clinton is the **Korean War Veterans Memorial** (1991; Mac Adams), *The Universal Soldier*, a 15-ft black granite stele with the silhouette of an infantryman excised from the center.

Dramatically sited in the water south of the long pier, the **American Merchant Mariners' Memorial** (1991; Marisol Escobar) depicts three men on a sinking lifeboat, a fourth in the water. The scene was reconstructed from a photograph taken by a German sailor whose U-boat torpedoed the SS *Muskogee* in 1942, leaving the men to drown. Later, an American seaman, captive on a German supply ship, saw the photograph, which had been published in a magazine. The watery setting heightens the work's impact as the figure of the drowning man emerges and recedes from the river with the ebb and flow of the tide.

Jutting 300ft out into the river is **Pier A** (1884–86), one of the oldest piers remaining in the Hudson. The tower of the **Fireboat Station**, originally a lookout, holds a clock donated (1919) by Daniel Reid, a founder of US Steel, to honor servicemen who died in World War I. Until 1959, the pier served as headquarters for the Harbor Police and thereafter was used by the Fire Department's marine division. At the time of writing there were plans to renovate it as a ferry checkpoint and visitor center.

All along the waterfront are the **Gardens of Remembrance**, beautifully planted with native grasses and flowers, and honoring survivors of September 11, 2001. The decorative railing of the sea wall is the Battery's first public-art initiative, *The River That Runs Both Ways*, a name that describes the Hudson's estuarial nature. Artist Wopo Holup's 37 cast-iron panels (2000), divided by wavy bronze bands representing the river, evoke the history of the Battery: the images above the water-line suggest human history, while those below refer to the ecological story of the river from the glacial era to the present.

Battery Bosque

To the left of Castle Clinton, between the fortress and the park known as Battery Bosque, stands Luis Sanguino's *The Immigrants* (1973, dedicated 1983), a bronze statue paying homage to the eight million immigrants who passed through Castle Clinton's gates during its 35 years as the Immigrant Depot Station.

The centerpiece of the **Battery Bosque**, 3.75 acres of parkland with benches and food kiosks (*open seasonally*), is a granite fountain whose spiral water jets are irresistibly tempting to children on hot days. Further south, the great bronze eagle of the **East Coast War Memorial** (1961; Albino Manca) faces out to sea. Eight marble pylons bear the names of over 4,000 Americans who perished in Atlantic coastal waters during World War II.

The path leads east out of the park past the Marine Flagpole. Just inside the park fence, in a small enclosure of its own, is the little **Oyster Pasty Cannon**, dating back at least to the Revolution.

Peter Minuit Plaza

NB: At the time of writing, portions of Battery Park and Peter Minuit Plaza (the triangle between the ferry terminal, State St, and Whitehall St; map p. 582, C4) were inaccessible because of construction for the subway, but the redesigned plaza will contain its former monuments, as described here.

South of Battery Park are two ferry stations. One is the glassy new Whitehall Terminal (2005) for the **Staten Island Ferry**. The only direct commuting link between Staten Island and Manhattan, it is also one of New York's great sightseeing bargains (*see p. 507*). South of the ferry terminal is the beautifully restored **Battery Maritime Building** (1909), at 11 South St, a fine old relic of the days when many ferries plied the East River.

Rectory of the Shrine of St. Elizabeth Ann Seton, a remnant of old Manhattan, attributed to John McComb Jr., New York's first native-born architect. 17 State St towers behind.

Constructed of sheet steel, it is elaborately decorated with rivets, latticework, rosettes, and marine designs. The terminal is most dramatic when seen from the water, its open-mouthed arches gaping against the severe geometry of the skyscrapers behind it. The Governors Island ferry leaves from here.

Peter Minuit Plaza is named for the Dutch governor, who in 1626 made the most famous real estate deal in the city's history, allegedly "purchasing" Manhattan from Native Americans for 60 guilders, a sum worth $24 according to traditional rates of exchange. The park contains a monument to New York's first Jewish immigrants, a group of Sephardic refugees fleeing persecution in Brazil. Their ship, bound for Holland, was seized by pirates; a few days later the pirates were overtaken by a French frigate whose captain charged the refugees for a voyage to Amsterdam but brought them to New Amsterdam instead. The Jews arrived in Sept 1654, and despite Peter Stuyvesant's opposition they were allowed to remain and engage in commerce. Peter Stuyvesant's town house, built in about 1657, stood near the present intersection of State and Whitehall Sts. It was renamed Whitehall by the first English governor of New York.

OLD MANHATTAN

Herman Melville (1819–91), author of *Moby-Dick*, was born at 6 Pearl St, now the site of **17 State St**, a wedge-shaped tower with a curved wall of mirrored glass. The red-brick **Rectory of the Shrine of St Elizabeth Ann Seton**, originally the James Watson House (7 State St, facing Battery Park), is the only survivor of a time when State St was an upper-crust residential street. Designed in two sections (east wing 1793, west wing 1806), it has been attributed to John McComb Jr. The details of the façade reflect its Georgian and Federal heritage: the marble plaques in the brickwork, the oval windows on the west wall, the splayed lintels above the rectangular windows. Its most distinctive feature, however, is the curved wooden portico that follows the street line, its tapered Ionic columns said to be made from ships' masts. After the Civil War an Irish immigrant, Charlotte Grace O'Brien, inspired the Roman Catholic Church to buy the house and establish the Mission of Our Lady of the Rosary, a haven for immigrant Irish girls. The Mission now operates the building as a shrine to Elizabeth Seton (1774–1821), the first American-born saint, canonized in 1975.

During the Dutch colonial period **Broad St** (*de Heere Gracht*) was a canal for drainage and shipping. The British filled it about 100 years before the Revolution, by which time it was polluted; but the extra width of Broad St remains as evidence of the former canal. Pearl St, on the edge of the East River before landfill pushed out the shoreline, was named for the opalescent shells that dotted its beaches. At Bridge St, the city's first bridge crossed the canal.

The small brick plaza between Water St, South St, and Coenties Slip East is **Vietnam Veterans Plaza**. Dominating it is a greenish glass-brick wall (1985; William Britt Fellows and Peter Wormser), 70ft long and 14ft high, etched with words written home

by American soldiers in Vietnam. Once the park, then called Jeannette Park, was a favorite haunt of idle seamen, a tree-shaded trapezoidal plot created when Coenties Slip was filled in during the late 19th century. Named after the ship *Jeannette*, which took part in the tragic polar expedition of 1879–81, the park originally followed the shape of Coenties Slip. The **East River slips** (Coenties Slip, Old Slip, Peck Slip) were originally docking areas for ships. As the coastline was pushed out by landfill, breakwaters were built and the slips were dredged to provide adequate draft. Eventually they were filled in to create new land, but the old names and street configurations remain.

FRAUNCES TAVERN & MUSEUM

Map p. 582, C4. 54 Pearl St (Broad St). Museum open Mon–Sat 12–5. Closed Sun, New Year's Day, Good Friday, and Christmas Day. Free admission Washington's Birthday, Flag Day, and July 4; T: 212 425 1778; www.frauncestavernmuseum.org.
Fraunces Tavern is the centerpiece of one of the few full blocks of 18th- and early 19th-century buildings to have escaped both the Great Fire of 1835 (*see p. 55 below*) and successive downtown building booms. The present tavern is a reconstruction (1907) of a mansion built (c. 1719) for Stephen (or Étienne) De Lancey. Since no graphic records survived, William Mersereau's reconstruction was based on an analysis of the building's structure and studies of similar buildings, but was nevertheless a groundbreaking endeavor in architectural preservation.

HISTORY OF FRAUNCES TAVERN

In 1762, Samuel Fraunces, a West Indian, possibly of French ancestry, bought the De Lancey house and opened it as the Queen Charlotte Tavern; he renamed the tavern after himself when the Revolution broke out. Fraunces was well known as a cook, renowned especially for his desserts, which may have influenced George Washington in his selection of the tavern for his farewell to his officers when he temporarily retired to private life. Fraunces's abilities later earned him the position of chief steward to Washington during most of his presidency.

In 1785 Fraunces leased the building to the government for office space; later he sold it to a Brooklyn butcher. During the 19th century the building deteriorated along with the rest of the neighborhood, becoming at its nadir a hotel for transients. After being badly burned several times (1832, 1837, 1852), it remained derelict until its purchase in 1904 by the Sons of the Revolution of the State of New York, who restored it. Today the Fraunces Tavern block, protected by landmarking, is dwarfed by the huge office buildings surrounding it.

Above the restaurant is **Fraunces Tavern Museum**. Governor George Clinton and George Washington celebrated the retreat of the British from Manhattan at the tavern on

Nov 25, 1783, and on Dec 4 Washington bade farewell to his troops in the Long Room (second floor) now refurbished as room in a late 18th-century tavern. The museum has many objects related to the colonial period and to Washington himself (including a lock of his hair and a piece of his pew from St. Paul's Chapel). The Clinton Room, furnished as a dining room, is notable for its historic hand-printed wallpaper. Galleries on the third floor offer changing exhibits on early American history and culture.

THE STONE STREET HISTORIC DISTRICT

Occupying the block between Pearl and South William Sts and Coenties Alley is the austere, brown stone **No. 85 Broad St** (1983; Skidmore, Owings & Merrill). The purchase of the air rights from the small-scale Fraunces Tavern Block Historic District buildings across the street paved the way for this 30-story building. Near the corner of Coenties Alley and Pearl St (displayed under the arcade below sidewalk level) are parts of walls from buildings unearthed during the city's first archaeological dig (1979–80). One of the buildings was the Dutch colonial *Stadt Huys* or City Hall, which began as a waterside tavern in about 1641. It was converted to the Town Hall when New Amsterdam was granted its municipal charter in 1653, and served not only as a meeting place, but as a jail, debtors' prison, courthouse, and public warehouse. No. 85 Broad St obliterates the section of **Stone St** between Coenties Alley and Broad St, but brown paving stones in the lobby outline the former path of the old street (*currently not open to the public*). Stone St, probably the city's first paved street, was formerly *Brouwers Straet*, named for its breweries.

Further north, however, the old streets, which approximate the street plan of New Amsterdam, have fared better. This district, first built up with wooden buildings during the 17th and early 18th centuries, burned "to an indistinguishable mass of ruins" during the Great Fire of 1835 (*see box opposite*), according to a contemporary observer. Within a year brick Greek Revival buildings with ground-floor shopfronts and warehouses above were rising from the rubble of this then-vital waterfront neighborhood. Many survive on Stone, South William, and Pearl Sts, some with picturesque early 20th-century alterations in a mishmash of styles. Building details here include original granite lintels and star-shaped tie-rod plates, as well as later whimsical neo-Dutch, neo-Tudor, and neo-Gothic façades. At night Stone St has become the center of a busy social scene, with tables set up in the alley, drawing local business professionals.

Mill Lane is named after a large windmill for grinding grain built by the Dutch in 1626, which once stood approximately at the intersection of Mill Lane and South William St (formerly Mill St). The mill had a meeting room on the second story which in the 1680s was rented to the city's first Jewish congregation, Shearith Israel. (Two millstones can be seen at Shearith Israel's current synagogue on Central Park West; *see p. 415*). In 1729 the congregation, many of whose members were descendants of those refugees from Brazil who had arrived in 1654 (*see p. 52 above*), purchased land south of the mill for 100 pounds sterling plus a loaf of sugar and a pound of tea, and built their first synagogue there (site of 26 South William St).

Delmonico's Restaurant (1891) at 56 Beaver St, a decorative pile of brownstone, terra cotta, and orange iron-spot brick, is the most recent incarnation of one of New York's historic restaurants. The columns flanking the door, which remain from an earlier Delmonico's, were believed to have been excavated at Pompeii. In the 19th century, Delmonico's chef is said to have invented baked Alaska and lobster Newburg. Today the restaurant is a high-end steakhouse.

Hanover Square

Hanover Square (actually a triangle bounded by Pearl St, Stone St, and a street also called Hanover Square) was once a public common in a fine residential district. The most notorious early resident was William Kidd, a sea captain hanged in England in 1701, for piracy. At the end of the 17th century the area became the city's first Printing House Square, home of New York's first newspaper (1725), the *New-York Gazette*, published weekly by William Bradford. **India House**, 1 Hanover Square, is one of the city's finest surviving Italianate brownstones (1851–54), built for the Hanover Bank. At the time of construction this *palazzo* exemplified a new direction in New York commercial building, as modest brick counting-houses were replaced by grander buildings based on European models. The New York Cotton Exchange (1870–86) and the Haitian consulate later occupied the building. In 1914 it became India House, a social center for shipping executives and merchants involved in international commerce. In the center of the square, the **British Memorial Garden** commemorates British victims of 9/11. The landscaping has been designed by Julian and Isabel Bannerman, and the abstract map of the counties of England in the paving stones is by Simon Verity, who also worked on the stone carving at the Cathedral of St. John the Divine.

THE GREAT FIRE OF 1835

Early New York, constructed mostly of wood, suffered many fires. Hanover Square was the center of one of the worst, the Great Fire of 1835. On the night of Dec 17, a gas explosion ignited stockpiles of dry goods and chemicals, and, whipped by winter winds, the blaze raged out of control. Sub-zero temperatures froze the fire hoses, and by noon the fire had incinerated Hanover Square. When the blaze finally burned itself out, it had destroyed over 20 acres and more than 650 buildings, including all the Dutch colonial structures in downtown New York.

New York City Police Museum

100 Old Slip. Open Mon–Sat 10–5; T: 212 480 3100; www.nycpolicemuseum.org.
The "fortified" Italianate Renaissance *palazzo* in the middle of Old Slip (*map p. 583, D4*) is the former **First Precinct Police Station** (1909–11), now containing the New York City Police Museum, with a fine collection of police memorabilia. The ground-floor entrance hall has been restored to resemble a station house around the turn of the 20th

century. Among the exhibits are displays of vintage police uniforms and examples of police vehicles, historic badges, weapons and nightwatch rattles—used as early as the 1650s to alert the public to danger. On the second floor, exhibits of historic and bizarre weapons include a cane with a concealed pistol and an iconic sawed-off double-barreled shotgun fitted into a violin case. On the third floor a long-term exhibit documents the role of the NYPD during the 9/11 crisis, with a video, remarkable photos, and artifacts, including objects altered by the heat and falling rubble of the Trade Center buildings.

THE SOUTH STREET SEAPORT MUSEUM & HISTORIC DISTRICT

Map p. 583, D3. Visitor Center at 12 Fulton St. Exhibits and ships open April–Oct usually 10–6; closed Mon; restricted hours off season; T: 212 748 8600; www.southstseaport.org. The beautiful Federal and Greek Revival commercial buildings around Fulton St and the East River piers in the South Street Seaport Historic District stand as reminders of South St's glory days when it was a center of world trade. The **South Street Seaport Museum**, a museum without walls, offers a collection of restored buildings—counting-houses, saloons, hotels, and warehouses—as well as permanent and changing exhibitions, historic ships, and a program of walking tours and events.

SOUTH STREET: FORMER WORLD TRADE CENTER

Until the years after the Civil War, the city's maritime activity focused on the East River, which lies on Manhattan's lee side and is less affected than the Hudson by ice, flooding, and the prevailing westerlies. During the early 19th century Fulton St became a major thoroughfare leading to the waterfront and the Fulton Ferry (1814) to Brooklyn. A produce market for Brooklyn and Long Island farmers (1822) eventually evolved into the legendary Fulton Fish Market. The opening of the Erie Canal (1825) flooded New York with Midwestern industrial and farm products, and 500 new shipping firms sprang up around South St to handle the new business. By the 1840s, trade to California and to China burgeoned, spearheaded by the firm of A.A. Low on Burling Slip (now John St). But after 1880 when steamships superseded the great sailing vessels and trade moved to the Hudson's deep-water docks, the area fell into decline.

After nearly a century of neglect, preservationists fought to save the old port, chartering the museum (1967) and acquiring historic buildings and ships. By the mid-1970s, financial pressures had pushed the preservationists into an uneasy alliance with the city and a commercial developer, whose work is evident in the shopping malls and other ventures that dot the area. In 1983 much of the present restoration opened, including a rehabilitated Schermerhorn Row.

Schermerhorn Row (1812) is the seaport's architectural centerpiece, on the south side of Fulton St between South and Water Sts. In 1793, Peter Schermerhorn, a ship chandler, bought the land as water lots, filled it in, and constructed 12 Georgian-Federal-style red-brick commercial buildings on speculation. These handsome buildings, with their steeply raked slate roofs and walls of handmade brick, had warehouse space downstairs and accounting offices above. The corner building was later converted into the Fulton Ferry Hotel.

The north side of Fulton St was once the turf of the **Fulton Fish Market**, long the most important wholesale fish distribution point on the eastern seaboard. The market dated back to 1822 when vendors were allowed to set up stalls in a wooden building here. By 1831, the butchers downstairs were complaining that runoff from the upstairs fish-gutting operations was seeping down to their stands. The fish dealers were exiled to a wooden shed on the water, behind

Schermerhorn Row.

which floated "fish cars" with live fish, a satisfactory arrangement until the turn of the 20th century when polluted waters poisoned the fish. Nevertheless, the market survived fires, crime, corruption, and crowding, until 2005, when it moved to the Bronx, exiled by outmoded facilities, development pressures, and transportation bottlenecks.

WATER LOTS & LANDFILL

To raise money, the city sold water lots—land between high and low tides that was under water half the time—to merchants with the provision that they fill and build on them. To do so the owners constructed wooden cribs and filled them with cartloads of refuse—often old bottles, and broken crockery. The fact that the shoreline of Lower Manhattan was pushed riverward by several blocks has in recent years led to some startling archaeological discoveries, for example Adriaen Block's ship under the World Trade Center site (*see p. 62*).

The piers

The Pavilion on Pier 17, to the left, is a mall with shops, restaurants, and a gorgeous view of the Brooklyn waterfront and Brooklyn Bridge. To the right on Pier 16, are two exhibition ships. On the north side is the *Ambrose Lightship*, built in 1908 to mark the entrance to the deepwater Ambrose Channel leading to New York harbor. The lightship was replaced in 1932 by a tower and beacon. The *Peking*, a four-masted ship (1911) from Hamburg, is one of the last sailing vessels built for commercial purposes. The *Wavertree* (1885), a square-rigged iron-hulled ship from England, is not currently open to visitors. The *Pioneer* is used for harbor trips and sail-training programs.

Water and Beekman Streets

The three **Greek Revival warehouses** (1835–36) at 207–11 Water St are among the best remaining in the city, their granite steps, lintels, piers, and cornices still intact. Two of the museum's satellite exhibition spaces are in the row. The **Walter Lord Gallery** at 209 Water St has a spectacular collection of ocean liner models and memorabilia. At 211 Water St, a museum has recreated the l9th-century printing shop of **Bowne & Co. Stationers**, whose working presses turn out business cards and stationery instead of the broadsides and handbills they produced formerly. The Italianate building at 213 Water St (1868), with its ground-floor cast-iron façade, served as a warehouse for a tin company. It now houses the **Melville Gallery** (exhibitions, museum programs).

At the corner of Water and Beekman Sts, turn right and walk toward the river. One of the most charming houses in the historic district is **no. 142 Beekman St** (1885) on the corner of Front St. Built for a member of the Schermerhorn family and first occupied by a fish dealer, the house is decorated with marine motifs: starfish on the tie-rod ends, cockleshells on the cornice, and fish wriggling on the terra-cotta keystones.

A WALK THROUGH BATTERY PARK CITY

Subway: 4 or 5 to Bowling Green; 1 to Rector St. Bus: M1 (weekdays), M6, M9.

This walk, from south to north along the Esplanade in Battery Park City, is one of the most beautiful in New York City, offering views across the Hudson River to the New Jersey waterfront, landscaped gardens, public art, and even creature comforts—seating, cafés, restaurants, and shops. The walk also takes in the Skyscraper Museum and the Winter Garden, centerpiece of the World Financial Center, whose lobby provides the best available view of the World Trade Center construction site. Parks open 6am–1am daily.

Battery Park City, the result of thoughtful urban planning, sits on 92 acres of man-made land in the Hudson River. In the mid-1960s, as commerce fled uptown and the unused Hudson River piers rotted in the water, Governor Nelson Rockefeller conceived of Battery Park City as a way to revitalize the downtown area and the decaying waterfront, providing housing as well as saving millions of dollars by finding a use for the rock and earth excavated from the World Trade Center site. In 1968 the state, which owns all landfill in the river by riparian rights, created the Battery Park City Authority to develop the area.

In 1979 architects Alexander Cooper and Stanton Eckstut created the master plan, which extended the Manhattan street grid into the landfill area and called for a north–south Esplanade joining the commercial central area with the residential neighborhoods proposed for both ends. Design guidelines emphasized the human scale and variety of New York's successful older neighborhoods.

On the ground floor of the Ritz-Carlton Hotel and Condominiums is the **Skyscraper Museum** (*39 Battery Pl near First Pl, open Wed–Sun 12–6; T: 212 968 1961; www.skyscraper.org*). The permanent collection includes such artifacts as annotated photos documenting the construc-

tion of the Empire State Building and part of an I-beam from the 1890s. Changing exhibitions focus on the structure, design, and economic and social consequences of tall buildings. Roger Duffy of Skidmore, Owings and Merrill designed the galleries, whose mirror-polished stainless steel floors and ceilings create the vertiginous sensation of walking suspended in air.

Next to the Jewish Heritage Museum at 20 Battery Pl (*see p. 46 for coverage*) is an Italian restaurant (with good views), Gigino at Wagner Park (*T: 212 528 2228; www.gigino-wagnerpark.com*).

The 3.5 acres of **Robert Wagner Jr. Park** (1996) are named for a lifelong public servant (d. 1993). The gardens were designed by Lynden B. Miller, whose work can also be seen in the Conservatory Gardens in Central Park and Bryant Park. Toward the river two brick pavilions offer a café and viewing platforms. Sculpture includes Tony Cragg's bronze *Resonating Bodies* (1996), near the *allées* at the park entrance: two giant bulbous shapes suggesting a tuba and a lute. According to the sculptor, the undulating lines on the surface represent the forms of energy (light, heat, gravity) to which all bodies are subject. Nearby are Louise Bourgeois's three-foot granite *Eyes* (1995) with protruding pupils, and

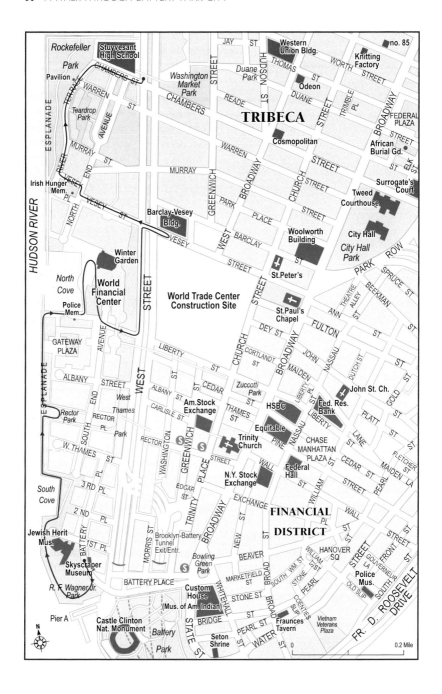

Jim Dine's *Ape & Cat (At the Dance)* (1993).

South Cove presents a meditative landscape with thoughtfully sited rocks, a wooden jetty, and plantings of grasses and flowers. A block uptown opposite West Thames St is Richard Artschwager's *Sitting/Stance* (1988), a sly group of out-sized, outdoor "furniture" in granite, aluminum, and wood.

Rector Park, at Rector St, a residential square surrounded by apartment build-ings, was designed to recall the quiet elegance of Gramercy Park, or other neighborhoods of civilized scale. At the mouth of the park, facing the Esplanade, is *Rector Gate* (1988; R.M. Fischer), a 43-ft skeletal gateway of stainless steel and decorative metal, illuminated at night.

At the intersection of Albany St is Ned Smyth's **The Upper Room** (1987), an ele-vated bluestone plaza surrounded by columns of pinkish concrete with coarse, colorful pebbly aggregate. The columns closest to the river have been interpreted as Egyptian papyrus plants, palm trees, or perhaps chess pieces.

The apartments of **Gateway Plaza** (1982) are dour and reminiscent of post-war Soviet block housing. They were built before the Cooper-Eckstut master plan. A little bit inland, just past the dog-run, is Stuart Crawford's *Police Memorial* (1997), a granite wall inscribed with the names of New York police officers killed in the line of duty. Nearby, a stream of water rises from small fountain, runs through a narrow channel, and falls into a still pool. The falling water represents the officers' lives and untimely deaths.

At the midpoint of the promenade is **North Cove**, which usually has a handful of mega-yachts berthed in its marina. In front of the glassy building is an instal-lation of stone steps, benches, and stools (Scott Burton); on the railing overlooking the cove are quotations from Walt Whitman, among others.

The hub of Battery Park City is the **World Financial Center**, whose five office towers were designed by the firm of Cesar Pelli between 1985 and 1988. The spectacular **Winter Garden**, with its palm trees and great glass windows, is used for exhibitions and arts events. Debris from the fall of the Twin Towers severely dam-aged the 120-ft glass-domed atrium and the marble floor, and crushed the aerial bridge that formerly linked it to the World Trade Center across West St. The atrium itself became an escape route for thousands of workers in the towers who fled west toward the river. In the ensuing months, the sixteen 43-ft *Washingtonia robusta* palm trees, brought from the Sonoran desert, died, unable to survive the cold rain sluicing in through the cracked and misshapen dome.

The building reopened in Sept 2002, after only a year of concentrated and ded-icated reconstruction. The palm trees have been replaced, as have the floor and the marble steps leading up to a new wall, 110ft wide and 60ft tall, of German industrial glass overlooking the World Trade Center site. Visitors flock here, though at the present the view includes only a construction site. On ground level a long-term installation offers photos, models, and a timeline of the construc-tion, fall, and rebuilding of the World Trade Center. Around the atrium are shops, restaurants, and cafés.

A description of the World Trade Center site follows overleaf. If you wish to con-tinue the walk up the Esplanade, see p. 63.

THE WORLD TRADE CENTER SITE

The World Trade Center was a complex of seven buildings centered around a five-acre plaza bounded by Vesey, Liberty, West, and Church Sts. Most famous were the Twin Towers, two boxy 110-story office buildings designed by Minoru Yamasaki, which initially drew criticism for their size and ungainliness, but eventually became familiar icons for the city and even for the nation. All seven of the original buildings, constructed between 1972 and 1987, were destroyed on September 11, 2001, when Islamic terrorists deliberately crashed two fully fueled Boeing 767s into the towers.

The huge pile of debris was cleared away by the spring of 2002, and a replacement for 7 World Trade Center (2006; David Childs of Skidmore, Owings and Merrill) now stands just north of the former plaza at 250 Greenwich St. Construction for Daniel Libeskind's Freedom Tower, 1,776 ft high to symbolize the date of American independence, began in 2006. At a site where there are so many competing interests, it is not surprising that conflict, litigation, financial overruns, and a series of decisions made and then abandoned have dogged the planning and design.

The site, called Ground Zero, will eventually be reconstructed with office towers designed by celebrity architects and arranged more or less according to a master plan by Daniel Libeskind, architect of the Jewish Museum in Berlin. A new transportation hub by Santiago Calatrava will replace the PATH (Port Authority Trans Hudson) station linking New York and New Jersey, destroyed by the buildings' collapse. There will be a memorial, *Reflecting Absence*, by Michael Arad with landscape designer Peter Walker, recreating the footprints of the two towers as pools of water, and a museum elucidating the events surrounding the tragedy. At present, however, the Trade Center site remains a 16-acre, 70-ft-deep hole, from which new construction is only beginning to rise.

THE ORIGINAL WORLD TRADE CENTER EXCAVATIONS

In 1916, subway excavations at Greenwich and Dey Sts (within the World Trade Center site) uncovered the charred timbers of the *Tyger*, the ship on which Dutch explorer Adriaen Block had sailed across the Atlantic in 1612. The *Tyger* burned in the harbor in 1613, and Block and his followers spent the winter in New Amsterdam, building another vessel, the *Onrust* ("Restless"), in which they explored Long Island Sound before returning to Holland. In 1967, during excavations for the World Trade Center, workmen unearthed a bronze breech-loading swivel deck-gun, also probably from the *Tyger*, since Block was sued by the Dutch Admiralty for loss of the ship's cannons. The exhumed relics are now at the Museum of the City of New York (*see p. 376*), while the rest of the *Tyger* still lies buried below the World Trade Center site.

South of the site at 120 Liberty St is the **Tribute WTC Visitor Center**, a storefront museum established by the September 11th Families' Association to tell the story of the tragedy (*open Mon, Wed–Sat 10–6; Tues and Sun 12–6; T: 866 737 1184; www.tributenyc.org. Tours of the WTC site offered by guides connected to the WTC community*). Five galleries recount the story of the Trade Center beginning with its construction, through its existence as an office building where 40,000 workers spent their days and another 150,000 passed through daily, through the events of September 11 and its aftermath. Among the artifacts on view are a chunk of the fuselage of one of the planes, with a window opening virtually intact; the unremarkable contents of the pockets of one of those who died in the tower; and two pistols melted together by the heat of the flames.

Contd. from p. 59.

North of the World Trade Center but not part of it is the former **Barclay-Vesey Building** at 140 West St (Barclay and Vesey Sts), now the Verizon Building. Built in 1926 by the New York Telephone Company as an office tower and telephone switching center, it was the first major building by architect Ralph Walker, as well as New York's first Art Deco skyscraper, and the first building to turn the restrictions of the 1916 Zoning Law (*see p. 68*) to aesthetic advantage. The Barclay-Vesey Building has long been admired for the arcaded sidewalk along Vesey St (formerly a shopping arcade) and for the lavish Art Deco ornament inside and out—plant forms, baby flutists, elephants whose ears spiral into nautilus shells, and bells (symbol of the phone company). (*NB: At the time of writing, the lobby was not open to the public; should it reopen, its ceiling paintings and ornamentation make it well worth a visit.*)

At the foot of Vesey St, the **Irish Hunger Memorial** (2002), on a half-acre cantilevered platform, commemorates the Irish potato famine, which sent hundreds of thousands of immigrants to the New World, beginning in the 1840s. The centerpiece of the memorial is a ruined stone cottage (c. 1838) donated by artist Brian

Tolle's extended family. It was brought from Ireland, reconstructed stone by stone, and surrounded with Irish grasses, heather, wild flowers, and stones bearing the names of Ireland's counties. There is a self-guided tour and audio presentation.

Demetri Porphyrios's picturesque **Pavilion** (1992) at the foot of Warren St offers shelter from the sun or inclement weather. Porphyrios, an architect and theorist, is internationally known for his classically-inspired buildings. Four stout Doric brick columns and 12 thin wooden pillars support a square wooden roof at the Pavilion's center and periphery. Beneath the roof a platform with low stone steps provides seating.

Near the foot of Chambers St, Tom Otterness's **The Real World** (1992), a series of small bronze, often pudgy, cartoonish figures, depicts a comic and yet sinister world in which money and power are motivating forces. Little workers push giant pencils or roll giant pennies; a dog tied to a water-fountain eyes a cat, which eyes a bird, which eyes a worm.

At 345 Chambers St is **Stuyvesant High School**, renowned for its programs in science and math. The school, which has several Nobel laureates among its graduates, is open by competitive exam and free to New York City students.

THE FINANCIAL DISTRICT

Map p. 582, C3. Subway: 2, 3, 4, 5 to Wall St; R to Rector St. Bus: M1 (weekdays, marked South Ferry), M6.

WALL STREET

Wall St is a short street, about a third of a mile long, which runs between Broadway and the East River. Ever since the New York Stock Exchange moved here in 1903, this thoroughfare, sometimes called simply "The Street," has been synonymous with New York's financial industry. Today, however, the neighborhood is in a state of flux, as is obvious to any visitor from the heavy equipment clogging its narrow streets and the construction cranes towering overhead. Many of the elegant early 20th-century commercial buildings, constructed for premier banks and major corporations, are being converted to residential uses. Hotels, restaurants, and shops are arriving. And while major financial corporations are returning from Midtown—where they relocated after the World Trade Center attacks—they are not coming to Wall St, whose buildings are too old, too small, and too technologically obsolete.

Strolling in the Financial District does give a sense of an earlier New York, though some of the buildings whose interiors were formerly open to visitors are no longer accessible, and security is extremely tight, especially around the New York Stock Exchange.

HISTORY OF WALL STREET

Wall St gets its name from a wall, erected in 1653 during Peter Stuyvesant's tenure, which stretched river to river at the northern edge of the settlement, ostensibly to protect the Dutch town from its British neighbors. Fortunately for the townspeople, the wall was never needed for defense. Though the original plan called for a palisade of whole tree trunks sharpened and driven into the ground, the wall was actually constructed of planks instead. These proved overpoweringly attractive to homeowners as sources of firewood or lumber for household repairs, and so in 1699 the British had the wall torn down as useless.

TRINITY CHURCH & CHURCHYARD

Map p. 582, C3. Church open weekdays 7–6, Sat 8–4, Sun 7–4. Churchyard open (weather permitting) weekdays 7–4, until 5 during daylight-saving; Sat and holidays 8–3. T: 212 602 0800; www.trinitywallstreet.org. Tours of the church daily at 2pm. Concerts on Thur at 1pm. Museum open Mon–Fri 9–11:45 & 1–3:45, Sat 10–3:45, Sun 1–3:45.

At the head of Wall St on Broadway stands Trinity Church, once the loftiest building in the neighborhood, now overshadowed by gigantic office buildings. Despite its modesty in size and conception, Trinity Church is probably New York's most famous house of worship, because of its dramatic setting. It is also one of the wealthiest—as befits a parish situated in a district so unabashedly devoted to Mammon.

HISTORY OF TRINITY CHURCH

The wealth of the parish stems from a land grant made in 1705 by Queen Anne, which included the land west of Broadway between Fulton and Christopher Sts—an impressive chunk of lower Manhattan. (The queen also granted the church the rights to all unclaimed shipwrecks and beached whales.) Although the parish no longer owns the entire parcel, it is still one of Manhattan's largest landholders, using the revenue from its holdings to support its programs. The present church is the third on the site. The first (1698) was a stone building facing the river, paid for by all citizens, who were taxed for the construction regardless of religious denomination. That church was burned in 1776 and remained in ruins until long after the Revolution. A second church (completed 1790) was demolished in 1839 after a heavy snowfall damaged the roof. The present church dates from 1846.

The church is 79ft wide and 166ft long; its tower including the spire stands 281ft above the ground: for many years it was the highest point in Lower Manhattan. Richard Upjohn, the architect, was one of the principal exponents of the Gothic Revival movement in the US, and Trinity was one of the first Gothic Revival churches in the nation, as well as the first Gothic Revival church in the city. Its flying buttresses, stained-glass windows, Gothic tracery, and medievally inspired sculpture impressed and pleased 19th-century New Yorkers, though Upjohn's choice of brownstone for the façade drew criticism. Until the construction of Trinity Church, brownstone (*see p. 415*) was generally used as a cheaper substitute for marble, granite, or limestone, but since Trinity parish could well have afforded marble, the choice was probably made for aesthetic reasons. The Romantic movement, making itself felt in architecture as well as the other arts, favored the use of dark building materials, which were considered "picturesque" and "natural"—that is, close to the colors of the landscape.

The church doors are modeled after Lorenzo Ghiberti's famous bronze doors of the baptistery of the cathedral in Florence. They were designed by Richard Morris Hunt and donated by William Waldorf Astor. Karl Bitter, who won the competition for the construction, executed the main west doors, whose panels illustrate biblical scenes as follows: right door (top) *The Four Horsemen of the Apocalypse*; (center) *The Annunciation*; (bottom) *Jacob's Dream*. Left door (top) *The Throne of Heaven*; (center) *The Empty Tomb*; (bottom) *The Expulsion from Eden*. J. Massey Rhind and Charles H. Niehaus designed the doors on the north and south sides.

The Empty Tomb: bronze panel by Karl Bitter from the west door of Trinity Church.

Architect Upjohn controlled all the details of the church. He designed the chancel window, one of the earliest American examples of stained glass—though the glass itself was made in Germany, since no American craftsman at the time possessed the requisite skills. He also decided that no memorials should disfigure the nave (untrue to the Gothic spirit in his opinion), so he planned the Monument Room on the south side of the church. The altar screen behind the main altar was given (later) by John Jacob and William Astor in memory of their father. Made of Caen stone and marble, it was designed by Frederick C. Withers. On the side of the building a small museum documents the history of the church.

Trinity churchyard

The church sits in a beautiful churchyard, its two acres a welcome spot of green in the Financial District. Some of the gravestones are quite old and striking, their incised frizzle-haired angels and grinning death's heads reminding onlookers of inevitable mortality. The oldest stone (north of the church) belongs to Richard Churcher, who died at the age of five in 1681. Other more elaborate monuments mark the burial places of renowned figures: Robert Fulton, whose *Clermont* proved that steamboat travel was economically viable; Alexander Hamilton; William Bradford, the publisher of the *New-York Gazette*; and Captain James Lawrence, whose nautical tombstone brings to mind his famous remark about not giving up the ship. Near the Broadway sidewalk on the north side of the church is the burial place of Charlotte Temple, a

young lady of genteel background who was seduced and abandoned by a British officer and immortalized in a long but popular novel by Sarah Haswell Rowson. *Charlotte, A Tale of Truth* was published in 1791 in London, reprinted in Philadelphia in 1794, and quickly went through 160 editions.

The impressive Cross in the center of the northern portion of the graveyard commemorates Caroline Webster Schermerhorn Astor, queen of New York society in the later decades of the 19th century (*see p. 313*). At the northeast corner of the plot is a large tribute to the Martyrs of the American Revolution, who died while imprisoned by the British in a sugar house (*see box below*).

THE "SUGARHOUSE" MARTYRS

During the 18th century one of the city's prime industries was distilling rum, made of raw sugar or molasses from the West Indies. The rum was exported to Africa in exchange for slaves, a series of transactions known as the "Triangular Trade." The Van Cortlandts' sugar house, a warehouse used for refining and storing sugar, near the northwest corner of the present Trinity Churchyard, was one of several warehouses converted to prisons during the Revolution. Conditions were foul, and the common soldiers, crowded and underfed, suffered from successive outbreaks of smallpox, cholera, and yellow fever; many starved or froze to death.

The American Stock Exchange and Equitable Building

The **American Stock Exchange** (not to be confused with the New York Stock Exchange; *see overleaf*) at 86 Trinity Place (Thames St), is visible to the west of Trinity Churchyard. This handsome Art Deco building (1930; Starrett & Van Vleck) holds the city's second major stock exchange. It was known as the New York Curb Exchange, because before 1929 its brokers stood on the curb at the north end of Broad St and signaled with hand and arm movements to their colleagues in the windows of the New York Stock Exchange.

The **Equitable Building**, at 120 Broadway (Pine and Cedar Sts) has become famous as the building that provoked the first restrictions on skyscraper design in New York. In order to maximize available rental space and hence profits, the architect Ernest R. Graham designed the Equitable Building (1915) to rise 39 stories straight up without setback, filling an entire block and darkening side streets and adjacent buildings. It was the largest office building in the world, its floor area more than 30 times its footprint. The following year the city passed the Zoning Resolution of 1916 (*see box overleaf*), which insured that such blockbuster buildings would not be built again in the city.

Wall Street skyscrapers

One Wall St, the former Irving Trust Company (later the Bank of New York Building) at the corner of Broadway, is one of New York's finest Art Deco skyscrapers, the

masterpiece of Ralph Walker of Voorhees, Gmelin & Walker, completed in 1932. The building, clad entirely in limestone, rises 654ft to a chamfered crown (which formerly had an observation lounge). The exterior detail emphasizes the building's verticality and its setbacks illustrate the provisions of the Zoning Resolution of 1916. The Gothic pointed windows echo the forms of Trinity Church across Broadway. To some observers the building appears to have been chiseled out of a single block of stone; to others its curtain wall suggests folds of undulating drapery.

Walker, who had recently designed the Barclay-Vesey Building (*see p. 63*), outdid himself with the interiors of this building. The Reception Hall, where wealthy and corporate clients awaited their private bankers, is decorated with glass mosaics by Hildreth Meière that shade from a dark burgundy at the bottom to a flaming orange at the top. The irregularly shaped tesserae, manufactured in Berlin, are embedded in a mesh of gold lines that suggest a web, or perhaps the fault lines in minerals.

"WEDDING CAKE" SKYSCRAPERS

The 1916 zoning law accounts for the "wedding cake" silhouettes of so many older New York towers. The amount of setback required was determined by running an imaginary plane up from the center of the street at a predetermined angle and requiring the profile of the building to remain within this boundary. After setbacks had reduced the building size to 25 percent of the site, the tower could rise straight up. (In 1961, amendments allowed buildings to rise straight up without stepping back if they covered no more than 40 percent of the site; the law also established absolute limits on building size and offered incentives for including public amenities.)

No. 14 Wall St, built as the Bankers Trust Building (1912) by Trowbridge & Livingston, is notable for its stepped pyramidal roof, later adopted by the firm as its logo: "A Tower of Strength." Inspired by the campanile of St. Mark's in Venice (a design used earlier by Napoleon Le Brun for his Metropolitan Life Tower), the building was the first of several in the Financial District to display a recognizable form on the skyline. The windowless, seven-story pyramid contained rooms for storage as well as the building's mechanical apparatus, including a smokestack, which vented at the top and sometimes gave the building the appearance of a volcano about to erupt. J.P. Morgan was to have occupied the 31st floor as an apartment, but he never did: the *New York Times* ran a headline in 1912 that said, "No Morgan Bower Atop Bankers Trust: The $250,000 Wonderland Where He Was to Rest Is Really Empty and for Rent."

The New York Stock Exchange

The New York Stock Exchange, the world's largest exchange in terms of dollar value, is one reason why New York is a preeminent city of the capitalist world. (*Since the World*

Trade Center attacks, the building has not been open to visitors, and security in the immediate neighborhood is extremely tight.) Like Federal Hall up the street, the Stock Exchange building is a "temple," dating from the period (1903) when Classicist architecture was *de rigueur* for all important public buildings. George B. Post designed the original building; the 22-story addition (1923) is by Trowbridge & Livingston. The sculpture on the pediment, by John Quincy Adams Ward and Paul W. Bartlett, is *Integrity Protecting the Works of Man*. The works in question (flanking *Integrity*) are the mechanical arts, electricity, surveying, and building on the left; mining and agriculture on the right.

Shortly after the end of the American Revolution, the Congress sitting in Federal Hall issued about $80 million in bonds to pay for the war debt. A central marketplace became necessary for these securities, and after a few years of informal trading outdoors and in coffee houses, a group of 24 brokers got together and drew up the "Buttonwood Agreement" (May 17, 1792). The name of the document commemorated a buttonwood or sycamore tree on the north side of Wall St, between William and Pearl Sts, near which the brokers used to meet. The stock exchange was formally organized in 1817, and moved to the present site in 1865.

FEDERAL HALL NATIONAL MEMORIAL

Map p. 582, C3. 26 Wall St (Nassau St). Open Mon–Fri 9–5, closed federal holidays. Free. Guided tours at 10, noon, and 2; T: 212 826 6888; www.nps.gov/feha.
Federal Hall is one of New York's most important historic sites, although the historical events predate the present building.

In the early 18th century the British City Hall (begun 1699; demolished 1812) stood on this site. There John Peter Zenger, the confrontational publisher of the *New York Weekly Journal*, was tried in 1735 for libeling the royal governor. Zenger's acquittal established a precedent for freedom of the press that would later be reaffirmed in the Bill of Rights. After the Revolution, the Congress met in the former city hall. George Washington took the oath of office in 1789 on the second-floor balcony, wearing what was for the period a simple suit of brown cloth. The hall was renamed Federal Hall in honor of New York's prestigious position as the nation's capital (the federal government was moved to Philadelphia in 1790).

The present building was constructed as a US Custom House (completed 1842), designed by Alexander Jackson Davis with Ithiel Town, who won the architectural competition. The design, which combined a Greek Doric portico and an elaborate domed interior, is said to evoke both the democratic ideals of ancient Greece and the power of the Roman Empire. Federal Hall, closed from 2004–06 for repairs to its foundation, whose cracks were exacerbated by the fall of the buildings at the World Trade Center, has been handsomely restored.

The exterior

This severe and elegantly proportioned building is one of the finest examples of Greek Revival temple architecture in the nation. A wide flight of steps leads to eight 32-ft

fluted Doric columns of Westchester marble that support an architrave and unadorned pediment. There is a second columned portico on the rear of the building facing Pine St, an unusual feature. On the western wall are evenly spaced pilasters.

On the steps is a heroic statue of George Washington (1883) by John Quincy Adams Ward, probably the sculptor's most famous work. He relied for historical accuracy on a full-length marble statue made from life in 1786 by the admired French sculptor Jean-Antoine Houdon. Ward shows the president at the moment of the inauguration, lifting his right hand from the Bible on which he swore his oath. (The Bible is usually on view in the Inaugural Gallery.)

John Quincy Adams Ward (1830–1910)
Ward was one of the nation's most important 19th-century sculptors, classically trained and apprenticed to Henry Kirke Browne in Brooklyn. Ward opened his own studio in New York in 1861 and achieved his first major success with *The Indian Hunter* (1866), now in Central Park (*see p. 288*), which brought him notable commissions for public sculptures such as this one. He has been praised for combining the grace of Classical sculpture with psychological intensity, especially evident in his masterful statue of Henry Ward Beecher (*see p. 468*) in Brooklyn's Cadman Plaza, a work that admirers of American sculpture will want to seek out.

The interior

The vaulted masonry ceiling of the rotunda was one of the few forms of fireproofing available when the building was constructed. A ring of beautifully carved Corinthian columns supports the dome; the details of the capitals can be seen close up from the balcony level. One of the vaults from the sub-treasury is open for display. In the basement is another ring of columns, squat and thickset, supporting the upper floors.

The Visitor Information Center has listings of cultural events and programs downtown. The George Washington Inaugural Exhibit includes models of the original City Hall and Federal Hall, as well as memorabilia relating to the inauguration, and information about New York Harbor and the national parks surrounding it. This permanent exhibit is supplemented by temporary exhibits on such subjects as the Draft Riots during the Civil War and the Bill of Rights. On the ground floor are the old coin vaults (1878) dating from the building's period as a US sub-treasury, which at the end of the 19th century contained as much as 1,700 tons of gold and silver coins.

Wall Street's classic banks

Across the street from Federal Hall at 23 Wall St, the **former Morgan Guaranty Trust Company** (1913; Trowbridge & Livingston) was the bank of J.P. Morgan, who more than any other man epitomized Wall Street power and the stupendous acquisition of

John Quincy Adams Ward: *George Washington* (1883).

wealth. The building is noteworthy for its elegance and restraint. The Wall St façade still bears traces of a tragic explosion caused by a carriage loaded with TNT, which killed 33 passers-by and injured 400 others in 1920. Anarchists were suspected, but the crime remains unsolved.

No. 30 Wall St (William and Nassau Sts) was once the site of a Greek Revival bank (1826; Martin E. Thompson), which later became the US Assay Office. In 1915, the building was torn down and its marble façade eventually incorporated into the American Wing of the Metropolitan Museum of Art (*see p. 345*), where it faces the Garden Court. The present building dates from 1921, when York & Sawyer, also architects of the Federal Reserve Bank, designed this rusticated *palazzo* with its great iron window screens as a new Assay Office.

At 40 Wall St is the **former Bank of Manhattan** (1929; H. Craig Severance & Yasuo Matsui). Planned as the world's tallest building during a period when architects were exercising secrecy and cunning to top their competitors, 40 Wall St lost out to the Chrysler Building. The uptown architects surreptitiously added a stainless steel spire to their structure, previously 2ft shorter than 40 Wall St, thus to become tallest in the world—until the completion of the Empire State Building two years later. The green pyramidal tower and spire make it a familiar part of the downtown skyline. The present owner, Donald Trump, has added his name in large letters to the façade.

At 48 Wall St is the **former Bank of New York** (1927; Benjamin Wistar Morris), distinguished in the downtown skyline by its Georgian-style cupola. Founded by Alexander Hamilton in 1784, it is the oldest commercial bank in the country. Located in the grand old banking hall, the Museum of American Finance (*open Tues–Sat 10–4; T: 212 908 4110; www.financialhistory.org*) offers exhibits on markets, money, banking, and entrepreneurship.

Across the street at 55 Wall St is the venerable **National City Bank Building**, remarkable for having been constructed in two stages. The first section (1842; Isaiah Rogers), a three-story Ionic temple with an imposing domed central hall, belongs to the same period and architectural tradition as Federal Hall. The 16 granite columns, quarried in Quincy, Massachusetts, and hauled up Wall St by 40 teams of oxen, make an impressive façade for the building, which first served as the new Merchants' Exchange, replacing the one destroyed in the Great Fire of 1835. Later used as the custom house, the building was remodeled by the firm of McKim, Mead & White in 1907, when the Custom House at Bowling Green opened. The architects doubled the volume of the building by adding the upper stories, which are surrounded by a tier of Corinthian columns.

Beaver St, which joins Wall St to the right, is named for the rodent whose pelts played such a large part in the city's early economy that it appears on New York's coat of arms.

No. 70 Pine St (1932; Clinton & Russell) is recognizable on the skyline by its Gothic crown and spire. Near the Pine and Cedar St entrances are large models of the building. During the 1920s and '30s, designers made considerable use of sculptural models and it is possible that the architect, having gone to so much trouble to

construct the models, had them installed here. Formerly the Cities Service Building, 70 Pine St has a lavish Art Deco lobby, with brown and beige tones of marble and polished aluminum decoration.

CHASE MANHATTAN PLAZA & THE FEDERAL RESERVE BANK OF NEW YORK

The Chase Manhattan Tower (1960; Skidmore, Owings & Merrill, principal designer Gordon Bunshaft), which occupies the enlarged block bounded by Pine, William, Liberty, and Nassau Sts, is now an ordinary-looking skyscraper, but in 1960 it was considered remarkable. First, its presence here was testimony to the bank's decision in the late 1950s to remain downtown when the financial community seemed on the brink of flight uptown, a decision that stimulated the rapid growth of the area in the late 1960s. Second, with its severe, unembellished forms and surfaces of glass and steel, the building became the first example in lower Manhattan of the International Style.

HISTORY OF THE BANK

The Chase Manhattan Bank was the successor to the Chase Bank (named after Salmon P. Chase, secretary of the Treasury under Abraham Lincoln and originator of the national banking system) and the Manhattan Company, formed by Aaron Burr and others. In 1799 Burr and a group of investors organized the Manhattan Water Company, with the apparent intent to provide the city with an adequate, safe water supply. An unobtrusive clause included in the charter gave the investors the right to form a bank and engage in financial activities. Although the Manhattan Water Company did lay several miles of wooden pipe to carry water, its primary interest quickly became banking—and maybe always had been. Alexander Hamilton claimed that Burr used his banking privileges to enhance his political career, and this vociferous and sustained criticism of the bank was yet another source of hostility between the two men. In 2000, Chase Manhattan and J.P. Morgan & Co. merged to become J.P. Morgan Chase.

The bank's outdoor plaza, a large expanse of pavement inaccessible from Liberty St, was the first in the area, a gratuitous act at the time, since the building predates the Zoning Resolution of 1961, which offered developers additional floor space in exchange for public plazas and other amenities. It is adorned by Isamu Noguchi's sunken Japanese garden, whose black basalt rocks were brought from Japan by the sculptor. Originally the fountain contained fish, but they had to be rescued from the effects of air pollution and from people's irrepressible desire to throw coins into fountains.

In 1972 the owners installed the sculpture *Group of Four Trees* by Jean Dubuffet, a 43-ft, 25-ton fabrication supported by a steel skeleton and constructed of fiberglass,

aluminum, and plastic resin, materials the artist hoped would withstand air pollution; the polyurethane paint used on the surface is essentially the same kind used to paint lines on streets. The sculpture has been called handsome, humane, amusing, and ominous; critics were quick to point out what they felt was the ironic juxtaposition of an institution that epitomizes the moneyed establishment and a work by an artist who called himself anti-bourgeois and claimed to be influenced by children, criminals, and psychotics (Dubuffet coined the term Art Brut).

Federal Reserve Bank of New York

The Federal Reserve Bank of New York, at 33 Liberty St (*for tours—reservations required—T: 212 720 6130*), fills the entire block bounded by Maiden Lane, Liberty, William, and Nassau Sts with its massive institutional stolidity. Philip Sawyer, of York & Sawyer, the principal architect for the building (1924), had studied in Italy, and his design reflects the fortified palaces of the great Renaissance families whose wealth and power made them institutions in their own right. The Palazzo Strozzi in Florence is the bank's principal model, and the superbly-crafted wrought-iron lanterns flanking the doorway on Maiden Lane are almost exact replicas of their Florentine predecessors. They were executed by Samuel Yellin, whose work also adorns the former Cunard Building on lower Broadway.

Beneath the bank are five subterranean levels containing offices and bullion vaults, where gold from foreign countries is stored. International transactions are consummated by simply moving the gold from one vault to another without its ever seeing the light of day. The **American Numismatic Society**, due to open in TriBeCa in Hudson Square (*map p. 582, B1*), has the nation's largest collection of coins, paper money, and medals, as well as currency from all over the world. At the time of writing the new gallery had not yet opened (*T: 212 571 4470; wwwnumismatics.org*), but a long-term exhibition on the history of money is on view here (*weekdays 10–4; free*).

Former Marine Midland Bank and Zuccotti Park

The **former Marine Midland Bank Building** (140 Broadway at Liberty St), now the HSBC Bank Building (Hong Kong and Shanghai Banking Corp), is a smooth, dark tower that soars straight up without setbacks. Designed by Gordon Bunshaft of Skidmore, Owings & Merrill (1967) during an earlier downtown building boom (he also designed the Chase Manhattan Tower; *see previous page*), it is New York's first dark-glass office tower. On the Broadway side stands another creation by Isamu Noguchi: his red steel and aluminum ***Red Cube*** (1968), not really a cube but a three-dimensional parallelogram, poised on one vertex. Like the building, which is trapezoidal rather than rectangular, the *Cube* is both balanced and irregular.

Opposite it, on the other side of Broadway, is **Zucccotti Park** (formerly Liberty Plaza), reopened, redesigned and improved in 2006 (it is named for a civic activist and real estate mogul). Formerly noteworthy for its expanses of pavement, the park has been landscaped, repaved with pink granite, and provided with in-ground lighting, benches, and tables. In the northwest corner of the park, closest to the World

Isamu Noguchi: *Red Cube* (1968).

Trade Center site, is J. Seward Johnson's bronze **Double Check** (replicated from the 1982 original), a businessman reading a memo. New to the park is Mark Di Suvero's heroically scaled *Joie de Vivre*, a towering intersection of red I-beams (1998), formerly installed at the entrance to the Holland Tunnel.

One Liberty Plaza, on the northwest corner of Liberty St and Broadway (1972; Skidmore, Owings & Merrill), later and less successful than the former Marine Midland Bank across the street (*see above*), replaced the much-admired Singer Building (1908; Ernest Flagg), which at 41 stories was the tallest building in the world for 18 months, taller by far than Trinity Church, which had held the record for almost 50 years. The Singer Building, with its bulbous mansard top, was the last of the slender downtown towers, soon to give way to massive bulk of such behemoths as the Equitable Building (also visible from here; *see p. 67 above*).

JOHN STREET METHODIST CHURCH

Map p. 582, C3. Open Mon, Wed, Fri 11–5 (subject to change); T: 212 269 0014, www.john-streetchurch.org.

At 44 John St stands the John Street Methodist Church, which has steadfastly

occupied this property since 1768. It is the oldest Methodist congregation in the country. The present building (1841) is the third on the site and an early example of the Italianate style. The wide-board flooring, entrance stairway, pews, and light brackets along the balcony were preserved from an earlier building of 1817, demolished when John St was widened.

The first congregation, mainly Irish Methodist immigrants who had come to this country in the early 1760s, was led by Philip Embury and Barbara Heck. Mrs. Heck, Embury's cousin, came home one day to find her husband, brother, and friends gambling at cards in the kitchen; she broke up the game (an early illustration shows her tossing the cards into the fire), and entreated her cousin, a former preacher, to re-assume his duties. Embury began preaching at his home in 1766, but when his living room became too crowded, the group rented the upper story of a rigging loft. In 1768 they purchased this property on John St, and Embury drew up plans for the original chapel, a stone building faced with plaster, which he literally helped build.

One of the early sextons of the church was Peter Williams, a black man whose parents were slaves of a family living on Beekman St. Williams converted to Christianity and became sexton of the church. When his owner returned to England after the Revolution, the church trustees, thinking it embarrassing for a well-known Christian to be sold publicly at auction, bought Williams privately for 40 pounds. He repaid his purchase price over a period of years and was formally emancipated in 1785. Williams went into the tobacco business, prospered, and eventually founded the Mother Zion Church, the first black Methodist church in New York. In the basement of the church is the **Wesley Chapel Museum**, with the church's first altar rail, a clock sent by John Wesley, and Embury's Bible and lectern, among other artifacts.

ST. PAUL'S CHAPEL, CITY HALL, & THE CIVIC CENTER

Map p. 582, C3–C2. Subway: 2, 3 to Park Pl; 4, 5 to Fulton St; A to Broadway-Nassau. Bus: M1, M6.

ST. PAUL'S CHAPEL & CHURCHYARD

Map p. 582, C3. Open weekdays 10–6, Sat 8–3, Sun 7–3; T: 212 233 4164, www.saint-paulschapel.org. Mon noon concerts; exhibition on the church's role in the World Trade Center aftermath.

St. Paul's Chapel faces Broadway between Fulton and Vesey Sts. It is Manhattan's only remaining colonial church (1766), built as a subsidiary chapel of Trinity Church for worshipers who lived too far uptown to make it down to Wall St. During the British occupation, while other churches became stables, prisons, and hospitals, St. Paul's Chapel served British officers as their house of worship. Unlike Trinity Church, St. Paul's Chapel survived the fire of 1776, thanks to the efforts of a bucket brigade that carried water from the Hudson. It became the most important Anglican church in the city and was used by George Washington following his inauguration at Federal Hall.

After the World Trade Center disaster, the chapel served both as a place of refuge for workers at Ground Zero and as a temporary memorial for visitors, who attached messages and memorials to the fence in front of the church.

The exterior

Commonly attributed to Thomas McBean, of whom little is known, St. Paul's shows the influence of St. Martin-in-the-Fields, London, though executed in homely native building materials—rough, reddish-gray Manhattan schist and smooth brownstone. When built, the Georgian-style church stood in a field, facing west to the river, but as Broadway became an important thoroughfare, a portico and entrance were added facing east. On the east porch is the tomb and monument of Brigadier General Richard Montgomery, mortally wounded in the Battle of Quebec, Dec 25, 1775. The monument, by sculptor Jean-Jacques Caffieri, pays tribute to the cause of freedom: on the right of the obelisk are a Phrygian cap (given to freed Roman slaves), broken swords, and a club of Hercules with a ribbon inscribed "Libertas Restituta" ("Liberty Restored"). The tower and steeple were added later, in 1794.

At the rear of the church, the burial ground contains gravestones of moderately prominent early New Yorkers (the most famous were buried in Trinity churchyard). Among them are George Frederick Cooke (d. 1812), a famous English actor whose monument was financed by Edmund Kean, an even more famous English actor; and Thomas Addis Emmet (d. 1827), an Irish patriot and lawyer exiled from British territory after serving a prison term for treason.

The interior

The interior is beautiful, painted in pale colors, graced by slender Corinthian columns supporting a barrel-vaulted ceiling. The Palladian window glazed with clear glass on the chancel wall and the 14 Waterford crystal chandeliers (which survived the shock waves of the collapsing Twin Towers) give the space an airy lightness. The chandeliers, organ case, and the elaborately carved pulpit and communion rail all date from before the Revolution. Over the pulpit are three feathers, the emblem of the Prince of Wales. Pierre L'Enfant, best known as city planner of Washington, D.C., may have designed the gilded wooden sunburst behind the altar. The pew where George Washington worshiped, originally canopied, is in the north aisle; in the south aisle is the Governor's Pew, reserved first for royal

St. Paul's Chapel interior, with its lovely, light Palladian window at the east end, and its Waterford crystal chandeliers.

governors, now for the state governor. The other pews have been removed. At the rear of the church is a memorial to the lawyer John Wells (d. 1823), the earliest known marble portrait bust by an American sculptor (1824; John Frazee).

AROUND ST. PAUL'S

The former **American Telephone and Telegraph Building** (1915–22) at 195 Broadway (Fulton and Dey Sts) is perhaps most famous for something it no longer possesses: a gilded statue, *Genius of the Telegraph* (Evelyn Beatrice Longman), nicknamed "Golden

Boy," which became a corporate icon for AT&T. The statue, a male nude, clutching a fistful of lightning bolts and girded by a length of telephone cable, now stands at AT&T headquarters in New Jersey. The building is noteworthy for its eight tiers of Ionic columns resting on a tier of Doric. The parade of columns continues in the monumental lobby, which also has a plaque commemorating the inventor of the telephone, Alexander Graham Bell, and a bronze and marble work by Chester Beach entitled *Service to the Nation*. Its central figure, wearing headphones, his hair frizzled by lightning bolts, poses before a map of the US, its major cities linked by long-distance telephone wires.

Further north at 22 Barclay St, **St. Peter's Roman Catholic Church** (1838; John Haggerty and Thomas Thomas) is Manhattan's oldest Roman Catholic church, standing on the site of its predecessor, the first Catholic church in the city. Since the regulations outlawing Roman Catholicism in Britain applied to the US during the colonial period, it was not until 1785 that the congregation was able to purchase this land from Trinity Parish and lay the cornerstone for the original building. The present granite church has an Ionic portico with six massive columns and a wood-framed pediment. In the central niche a statue of St. Peter holds the keys to the eternal kingdom.

THE WOOLWORTH BUILDING

The Woolworth Building at 233 Broadway (1913; Cass Gilbert; *map p. 582, C3*) was the world's tallest when completed, and though it was eclipsed in 1930 by the Chrysler Building, it remains one of the city's most luxuriantly detailed skyscrapers.

F.W. Woolworth enjoyed a classic 19th-century American rags-to-riches career, starting out as a farm boy and beginning his life's work clerking in a general store. During this apprenticeship Woolworth became convinced that customers would patronize a store where they could see and even finger the merchandise and buy without having to haggle over prices with intimidating clerks. After a few false starts he proved himself right in a grand way, opening his first successful five-and-ten-cent store in 1879 and expanding it eventually into a chain. By 1913 he was able to pay $13,500,000 in cash for this building.

The care and attention that Woolworth devoted to the smallest details (he personally picked out the bathroom fixtures and the mail chutes), the extravagant expenditures for beautiful materials and fine craftsmanship, and the grandiose conception of the whole make the building a monument to its owner's career and a visual delight in a less opulent age.

When the Woolworth Building officially opened, the Rev. S. Parkes Cadman, a Brooklyn minister and radio preacher known for the intensity of his sentiments, noted that the building inspired "feelings too deep even for tears" and dubbed it "The Cathedral of Commerce," a nickname that stuck.

The exterior

Predating the 1916 zoning restrictions (*see p. 68*), the building covers its entire site. It rises about 300ft straight up from the street, its verticality emphasized by the

The tip of the Woolworth Building pierces the clouds in 1928, when it was still the tallest sky-scraper in the city.

light-colored piers which ascend in an unbroken line straight to the top of the main section. The tower then soars another 400ft, ending in a delicate crown surrounded by four smaller towers (total height 792ft). At street level, around the elaborate door-way arch, are carved figures of young men and women at work—earning the money, according to some early observers, to shop at Woolworth's. Masks above the second floor represent four centers of civilization—Europe, Africa, Asia, and America—a motif Cass Gilbert used earlier on the Custom House at Bowling Green (*see p. 43*).

The interior

(The interior is well worth seeing, though with the tightened security downtown, the lobby has recently been closed to visitors.) The walls are covered with golden-toned marble quarried on the Aegean island of Skyros; the vaulted mosaic ceilings in blue, green, and gold have bird and flower patterns intended to recall the Byzantine mosaics of Ravenna. The only relief in all this magnificence (neither Gilbert nor Woolworth was known for a sense of humor) comes from a set of sculpted figures beneath the arches leading to the lateral hallways near Broadway, which depict Woolworth and some of his builders: Woolworth clutches a big nickel; Cass Gilbert peers through his pince-nez at a large model of the building; Lewis E. Pierson, president of the Irving Bank, first tenant of the building, gazes at a stock ticker tape.

CITY HALL PARK

Map p. 582, C3–C2. Subway R, W to City Hall; 2, 3 to Park Pl; 6 to Brooklyn Bridge-City Hall. Bus M1, M6, M15.

City Hall Park, 8.8 acres bounded by Broadway, Park Row, and Chambers St, is one of the oldest public gathering places in the city. The park contains monuments of its historic past, as well the beautiful and elegant City Hall. (The pedestrian walkways of the Brooklyn Bridge are accessible from the eastern edge of the park.)

HISTORY OF CITY HALL PARK

The Dutch used the area as a commons—shared land for pasturing livestock and holding public ceremonies—and for a windmill (1691). By the early 18th century, this land stood at the outskirts of the city and seems to have been relegated to use for people on the fringes of society. Between 1736 and 1760 a poor house and a debtors' prison known as the New Gaol were constructed, as well as a barracks and a powder house for the city's defenses. Just to the north the city's blacks were permitted to bury their dead (*see p. 89 below*).

As hostilities escalated before the Revolution, the presence of the barracks brought local patriots and British soldiers into conflict. At 6pm on July 9, 1776, the Declaration of Independence was read to George Washington's troops, assembled there with a large crowd. After the reading, the crowd grew raucous and headed downtown to the Bowling Green to pull down the statue of George III.

The park has hosted both celebrations and protests. It is the destination of the traditional ticker-tape parade through the Canyon of Heroes (the section of Broadway beginning at Bowling Green and ending here). There have been demonstrations and rallies against police violence (1849, 1998), the high price of flour (1837), and same-sex marriage (2004); as well as others in favor of labor unions (1836, 1850), and immigrant rights (2006). In 2000, the park reopened after a $14-million restoration of its plantings and monuments. The excavations uncovered coins, pot shards, long clay pipes, several intact skeletons, and areas with jumbled bones from burials elsewhere.

Park Row

Park Row, an early center of theatrical activity, later became the center of the city's newspaper industry, close to City Hall (political news) and to the slums of the Lower East Side (sensational human interest stories). In its prime, "Newspaper Row," as the street was known, ran from Ann St (where James Gordon Bennett's marble New York Herald Building was built on the site of P.T. Barnum's American Museum in 1866) to Chatham Square, and was divided by the approaches to the Brooklyn Bridge into a northern section for the foreign-language press, and a southern section which

belonged to the great New York dailies. In one grand row facing City Hall Park stood buildings housing four of the city's greatest papers: Joseph Pulitzer's *New York World*, Charles Anderson Dana's *New York Sun*, the *New York Tribune*, founded by Horace Greeley, and the *New York Times*, revitalized by Adolph Ochs. When Joseph Pulitzer died in 1911, New York had 14 daily newspapers, 12 of them published on Park Row.

The elaborate brick **Potter Building** (1886) at 38 Park Row is an important early office building from the period before the skyscraper, and an early example of architectural terra cotta for fireproofing. (Its developer, Orlando B. Potter, owned a previous building on this site which burned in 1882, and he understandably wanted its replacement to avoid the same fate.) Its flamboyant mix of Queen Anne, Neo-Grec, Renaissance Revival, and Classical motifs distinguished it from its more subdued contemporaries.

At 41 Park Row between Beekman and Spruce Sts is the **former New York Times Building** (1857; later enlarged). The first home of the *Times* was both imposing (its height of more than 80ft gave it a grand panoramic view) and elegant, with plate-glass windows on the ground level, frescoed walls, and marble floors. This luxury started a trend in newspaper buildings, which until then had humbly reflected the status of the industry. It was also fireproof, surviving the 1882 blaze that destroyed its neighbor.

The area around Nassau and Spruce Sts and Park Row was known as **Printing House Square** when the statue of Benjamin Franklin (c. 1872; Ernst Plassmann), publisher of the *Pennsylvania Gazette*, was erected. Today the ramps to the Brooklyn Bridge fill much of the former open space.

Monuments in City Hall Park

In the center of the park stands a reconstructed **fountain** (1871) by Jacob Wrey Mould (*see p. 289*), which in 1920 had been shipped off to Crotona Park in the Bronx, where it was vandalized. The perimeter fence replicates an 1820s original taken down in 1865 to make space for a large post office, which itself was torn down in 1939. Contrasting paving stones mark the perimeters of long-gone buildings, including the windmill and the British barracks, and the aforementioned post office.

A bronze statue of **Nathan Hale** (1890; Frederick W. MacMonnies) faces City Hall. The Revolutionary spy is best remembered for the words "I regret that I have but one life to give for my country," allegedly uttered just before he was hanged by the British. The portrayal represents MacMonnies' romantic conception of Hale as a handsome youth (he was 21) in an impassioned attitude of defiance. One of Hale's contemporaries, however, described him as having "shoulders of moderate breadth, his limbs straight and very plump."

On the west lawn stands a **monument to the "Liberty Poles,"** erected in the years before the Revolution by the Sons of Liberty, a group of tradesmen, workers, and army veterans, who harassed the British government and propagandized against taxation policies. The poles, ancient symbols of resistance to tyranny, deliberately provoked the British garrison. Five successive poles stood on private property in sight of the barracks; the most impressive was one erected in 1770, an 80-ft pine ship's mast sunk in a 12-ft hole and girded with iron hoops, as is the present pole.

North of City Hall on the east side of the park, a bronze **statue of Horace Greeley** (1890; John Quincy Adams Ward) shows the famous newspaperman relaxing in a bronze upholstered chair with bronze fringes, a newspaper draped over his right knee. Greeley founded the *New York Tribune* and guided it to eminence. Famous also for his advice to an unknown fortune-seeker, "Go West, young man," Greeley is known to have been careless about his dress and personal appearance, a quality Ward has captured.

THE SUBWAY BENEATH THE PARK

Sealed behind concrete doors under City Hall Park is the city's first subway station (1904), out of service since Dec 31, 1945, by which time subway cars became too long to navigate the tight loop of track. Designed by Heins & La Farge, whose work includes the Cathedral of St. John the Divine as well as the first phase of the New York subway system, the elegant appointments—chandeliers, leaded skylights, a vaulted Guastavino ceiling, and decorative tile work—are legacies of the City Beautiful Movement. The New York Transit Museum sponsors occasional tours of the station (*T: 718 694 1867; www.mta.info/mta/museum/programs.htm*).

CITY HALL

Map p. 582, C2. City Hall may be visited only by a guided tour (organized by the Art Commission of the City of New York), which also visits the Tweed Courthouse; T: 311 or, outside New York City, 212 639 9675 or book online at www.nyc.gov/html/artcom. One non-reservation tour meets weekly (Wed at noon, first come, first serve) at the Heritage Tourism Center, located at the southern end of City Hall Park on the east side of Broadway at Barclay St. At the time of writing, the portraits in the Governor's Room were being restored, a few at a time. City Hall (1811), one of the New York's architectural treasures, houses a noteworthy collection of portraits of city mayors and 19th-century celebrities, including 13 paintings by John Trumbull, best known for his depiction of people and scenes associated with the Revolutionary War. The most important works in the collection hang in the Governor's Room on the second floor, though portraits and busts are located throughout the public areas of the building. The present City Hall is the third building to house the municipal government, after the *Stadt Huys* on Pearl St and the 18th-century City Hall on Wall St that later became Federal Hall (*see p. 69*).

The building

Novelist Henry James, with his usual keen eye, hailed City Hall for its "perfect taste and finish … reduced yet ample scale, … harmony of parts … and modest classic grace." Less articulate observers have called it the best City Hall in America.

Constructed during the opening decades of the 19th century (1803–11), when the nation was searching for an architectural style that would reflect its youthful republican ideals, the building is an outstanding example of the Federal style. Though similar in its Classicism to the government buildings then on the drawing boards or under construction in Washington, D.C., City Hall is unusual in its adoption of French classic details, notably the garlanded swags and flat pilasters on the façade, which make it less austere than most of its contemporaries. One of the architects, Joseph François Mangin, was a French immigrant; the other, John McComb Jr., was a native New Yorker, brought up in the tradition of master builders. The two won a prize of $350 for the design of the building.

CITY HALL

The cost of the original marble on the façade distressed the city fathers, who wanted a cheaper brownstone finish; McComb lobbied for marble at least for the front and sides, leaving only the rear façade a dull brown (Alabama limestone replaced both brownstone and the original marble in 1956). A copper figure of *Justice* stands on top of the cupola, replacing a similar wooden figure by John Dixey, an Irish immigrant sculptor.

In the interior, the lobby walls are covered with the original white Massachusetts marble. Beyond the lobby is the **rotunda**, with a beautiful circular staircase and a dome with a clear glass oculus, supported by ten Corinthian columns. The design for this space is probably McComb's. On the second floor, the **Governor's Room** first served as an office for the governor when he visited the city and as a reception room; now it also serves as a museum celebrating New York's civic history.

The collection

In 1790, while New York was enjoying its brief fling as capital city of the nation, the

Common Council, the city's chief legislative body, commissioned John Trumbull to paint a portrait of George Washington and another of George Clinton, the state's first governor. In 1805 the Council expanded the program to include all the governors and mayors who had served since the Revolution. Seven years later, with the country embroiled in the War of 1812, the Council decided to honor several heroes of that struggle by adding their likenesses to the roster. This tradition of officially sponsored portraits of governors and mayors continued through the mayoralty of Fiorello La Guardia (1934–45), with subsequent portraits donated as gifts. Thus the series constitutes a gallery of celebrities—New York politicians, war heroes, and foreigners who caught the public eye. Because the artists commissioned to paint them were notable figures in the contemporary art world, the collection also chronicles changing styles of portraiture during the 19th century. Especially noteworthy are works by the first generation of post-Revolutionary artists—John Wesley Jarvis, Thomas Sully, Samuel F.B. Morse, John Vanderlyn, George Catlin, and Rembrandt Peale.

The two portraits by John Trumbull, on the end walls of the central room, show the artist at the height of his powers. Trumbull, who served as Washington's aide-de-camp, depicts his subject as commander-in-chief of the Continental Army on Evacuation Day (*see p. 45*), against a background showing the Bowling Green and the Upper Bay. Trumbull's portrait of George Clinton, brigadier general in Washington's army, seven-term governor of the state, and opponent of the US Constitution, depicts him against a background of the Hudson highlands and burning American ships, a reference to his unsuccessful defense of Fort Montgomery during the Revolution.

Samuel F.B. Morse, who later became known as the inventor of the telegraph, had ambitions as a history painter, but failing to receive major commissions painted portraits to make a living. His portrait of the Marquis de Lafayette, considered one of the most important works in the collection, was painted in 1824 while Lafayette was on a triumphal tour of the country.

Among the portraits of heroes of the War of 1812 are several by English-born John Wesley Jarvis. Thomas Sully contributed the portrait of Commodore Stephen Decatur, accorded a hero's welcome for his naval victories when he visited the city in 1812; and one of the engineer General Jonathan Williams, after whom Castle Williams on Governors Island is named. Samuel L. Waldo painted John McComb Jr., architect of City Hall.

John Vanderlyn was advised by Aaron Burr to study in Paris, to absorb the style of the French Neoclassical and Romantic painters. Vanderlyn's portraits in the collection include President James Monroe, General Andrew Jackson, and Mayor Philip Hone (known less for his administrative skills than for his diary, which detailed city events in the 1830s and 1840s). He is shown as an old man with busts of Washington and Franklin in the background.

George Catlin later achieved renown as a painter of the American West, documenting the way of life of the Great Plains Indians. First trained as a lawyer, he became an artist in the early 1820s and was completely self-taught. His portrait of DeWitt Clinton is typical of his early work.

THE TWEED COURTHOUSE

The Art Commission tours of City Hall also include the former New York County Courthouse (1872, John Kellum; rear addition 1880, Leopold Eidlitz; *map p. 582, C2*), now housing the Department of Education. The building is better known as the "Tweed" Courthouse because William M. "Boss" Tweed and his "Ring" embezzled impressive sums of money from the city during its construction. In 1858 the city Board of Supervisors agreed to a preliminary expenditure of $250,000 for a new criminal courthouse, the cornerstone of which was laid in Dec 1861. By the time the building was finished ten years later, the cost had risen to somewhere between $12 million and $13 million—the exact figures were concealed during the ensuing scandal—of which an estimated $8.5 million ended up in the pockets of Tweed and his cronies. They hired contractors who padded their accounts and then kicked back to the politicians most of the difference between what the work actually cost and what the city paid for it. Thus a plasterer named Andrew J. Garvey appeared in the records as receiving $45,966.89 for a single day's work, a sum which earned him the title "Prince of Plasterers."

Tweed rose from humble beginnings to wealth, power, and fame through the machinery of Tammany Hall (*see p. 171*), the most powerful organization in Democratic Party politics. He never held a high city office himself, but was a kingmaker who profited from friends in high places. Although he and his "Ring" fleeced the city in other ways, it was the disclosure of the cost overruns of this courthouse that precipitated Tweed's exposure, downfall, and ultimate imprisonment. His fall was swift and spectacular; he was tried in a courtroom in this building, and he died in prison, poor and friendless, in 1876.

The main section facing Chambers St was the work of Kellum, who designed an imposing Italianate *palazzo*. Kellum died in 1871, and Eidlitz, who had entirely different ideas as to what the courthouse should look like, took over. He added the neo-medieval wing to the south, instead of an entrance matching the Chambers St approach, and developed many of the interior spaces, including the polychrome brickwork in the famous rotunda.

THE CIVIC CENTER

Map pp. 582, C2–583, D2. Subway: 4, 5, 6 to Brooklyn Bridge-City Hall; J, M, Z to Chambers St. Bus: M1, M6.

Beyond City Hall lies the Civic Center, with a collection of government buildings dating from the late 19th century to the present. The location was chosen almost by default, the boggy ground making the neighborhood unsuitable for high-rise commercial construction, and the nearby slums during the early years of the 20th century making it unattractive for anything else.

The Municipal Building

The Municipal Building (1907–14; McKim, Mead & White) at 1 Centre St, northeast

of City Hall Park, has been applauded as a great civic skyscraper. Like other early skyscrapers, it is divided horizontally into an elaborate base (impressive to the pedestrian), a simple central tower, and a monumental top designed to occupy a conspicuous place in the skyline. The central arch in the ground-level colonnade formerly straddled Chambers St, forming a monumental gateway to the slums of the Lower East Side, but now acts as a grand entrance to Police Plaza. Above the colonnade are shields with the insignia of Amsterdam, Great Britain, New York City, and New York State. The winged figures flanking the arch represent *Guidance* (left) and *Executive Power* (right). The panels over the smaller arches are (left) *Civic Duty*, which shows the city conferring the law upon its citizens and (right) *Civic Pride*, depicting the citizens returning the fruits of their labors to the city. Above, relief medallions depict *Progress* (left) and *Prudence* (right). Adolph A. Weinman's 25-ft statue on top of the building, *Civic Fame* (1913–14), holds a laurel branch and a crown with five turrets symbolizing the five boroughs. Made of copper hammered over a steel frame (like the Statue of Liberty), the gilded statue stands 582ft above the street.

Inside, to the north of the entrance arch, is CityStore (*open Mon–Fri 9–4:30; closed federal holidays*), the official municipal store, with books, gifts, and memorabilia including used horseshoes from NYPD mounted police. The central arch has an imposing coffered ceiling; bronze ornamental work decorates the lobby. On the south side of the building an arcade with a vaulted ceiling finished with Guastavino tile makes the subway entrance one of the most imposing in the city. Among the city offices is the Marriage Chapel, where couples getting married "at City Hall" take their vows.

Police Plaza

Beyond the central arch Police Plaza is bounded by the remnants of a former warehouse district on the east, by the Brooklyn Bridge approaches on the south, and by existing municipal buildings and irregular streets in other directions. The site recommended itself to planners only because the city could conveniently purchase its many small land parcels at a reasonable price.

On the south side of the plaza is the **Rhinelander Sugar House Prison Window Monument**. The Rhinelander Sugar Warehouse, built (1763) on the corner of Rose (formerly the name of the southern extension of Madison St) and Duane Sts, became a prison for American soldiers when the British occupied New York during the Revolutionary War, as did other sugar houses (*see p. 67*). The sugar house was razed in 1892, but a window was incorporated in the Rhinelander Building (1895), which stood here until it was demolished (1968) for Police Plaza.

The sculpture in the center of the three-acre brick plaza is Bernard (Tony) Rosenthal's *Five in One* (1971–74), its five interlocking oxidizing steel disks said to symbolize the five city boroughs. **Police Headquarters** (1973; Gruzen & Partners) is a 15-story building of brick and reinforced concrete, its ground level containing an auditorium, meeting rooms, and holding and interrogation rooms for prisoners.

Surrogate's Court

At 31 Chambers St (Centre St) is the Surrogate's Court (*lobby open Mon–Fri 9–5*), also known as the Hall of Records (1899–1907; John R. Thomas and Horgan & Slattery). Like the Woolworth Building, with which it is roughly contemporary, the Surrogate's Court was built as a monument, and the impulse of civic pride that inspired the design is expressed in the elegance and costliness of both the façade and the interior. The former is lavishly ornamented with sculpture appropriate to the building's first function as a guardian of historical records. Flanking the Chambers St entrance are two sculptural groups by Philip Martiny: *New York in Revolutionary Times*, represented by a proud female figure wearing a helmet, and (right) *New York in Its Infancy*, a woman wearing a feathered headdress. The frieze above the portico bears eight figures representing prominent early New Yorkers, including Peter Stuyvesant (third from left), and DeWitt Clinton (third from right). The cornice figures facing Reade and Centre Sts represent the arts, professions, and industries.

Inside, the walls of the foyer are faced with yellow-toned Siena marble. Above the doorways at each end of the rooms are sculptural groups by Albert Weinert: *The Consolidation of Greater New York* (east door) and *Recording the Purchase of Manhattan Island* (west door). On the ceiling a mosaic by William de Leftwich Dodge, a Paris-trained muralist, is organized into panels depicting Greek and Egyptian deities. The Greek divinities in the corners are *Themis* (Justice), *Erinys* (Vengeance), *Penthos* (Sorrow), and *Ponos* (Toil). On the end walls are mosaics, also by Dodge, with unimaginative but descriptive titles: *Searching the Records* and *Widows and Orphans Pleading Before the Judge of the Surrogate's Court*. Above the central landing of the grand staircase in the lobby is a stucco relief of the seal of New York City (*see box below*).

THE CITY'S SEAL

First adopted in 1686, the seal recalls the city's early history. Upon shield are the sails of a windmill, recalling the days when New York was New Amsterdam; above and below are beavers and flour barrels representing the fur trade and milling industry, both fundamental to the city's early economy. A sailor and Native American support the shield, which rests on a horizontal laurel branch bearing the date 1625, the year the Dutch established New Amsterdam. Above is an American eagle with wings displayed; on a ribbon encircling the lower half of the design are the words "Sigillum Civitatis Novi Eboraci" ("Seal of the City of New York"). *Eboracum* was the Roman name for York in England; James, Duke of York was the first proprietary ruler of New York under the English.

Recycled municipal buildings

The **former Emigrant Industrial Savings Bank Building** (1909–12) at 51 Chambers St (Broadway and Elk St) was founded in 1850 by the trustees of the Irish Emigrant

Society to protect the financial resources of Irish immigrants and to teach the virtues of thrift and industry. The bank succeeded from the outset, gradually widening its dealings to include people of many nationalities. It is currently used by the city government.

On the northeast corner of Broadway and Chambers St (280 Broadway) is the former Sun Building, originally the nation's first department store, the **A.T. Stewart Marble Palace** (1846; Trench & Snook), and now owned by the city. Alexander Turney Stewart did for merchandising at the upper end of the economic scale what F.W. Woolworth did at the lower end. He brought together many different types of merchandise under a single roof, selling clothing in fixed sizes at fixed prices and freeing shoppers from the psychological demands of bargaining. Furthermore, Stewart shrewdly saw the need to turn shopping into entertainment, and to that end built the Marble Palace, which initially drew shoppers in droves. By 1862, however, fashionable society had begun shopping further uptown, so Stewart moved up Broadway to a new palace, the Cast Iron Palace, between 9th and 10th Sts, retaining the Chambers St store as a warehouse. Stewart also built a mansion on Fifth Avenue at 34th St, a $3-million extravagance that set the standard for younger generations of millionaires.

The Marble Palace is an early example of the Italianate style, which replaced the Greek Revival style as the city's dominant architectural fashion. Contemporaries admired the store for its palatial dimensions, beautiful white marble façade, and elegant details (for example the classical masks in the keystones over the second-story windows). When the building opened, the slender Corinthian columns on the ground floor framed display windows so large that Stewart had to order the plate glass from France.

From 1917–50 the *New York Sun* occupied the building, its motto displayed on the four-faced bronze clock on the Chambers St corner: "The Sun, it shines for all."

AFRICAN BURIAL GROUND NATIONAL MONUMENT

Map p. 582, C2. Memorial open Mon–Sun 9–5 except Thanksgiving, Christmas, and New Year's Day. Visitor center open weekdays 9–5, except federal holidays; tours Mon–Fri 10am and 2pm; tours of African-American sites in Lower Manhattan by reservation; T: 212 637 2019.

The African Burial Ground at the intersection of Duane and Elk Sts is one of the 20th century's most significant archaeological finds. In 1991, during excavations for the nearby Federal Building at 290 Broadway, workers came upon what turned out to be the skeletal remains of more than 400 African Americans, as well as hundreds of burial artifacts. Period maps showed the area to be part of the "Negroes Burial Ground," seven-plus acres that reached south through City Hall Park, west to Broadway, and east to Centre St. The larger site is believed to contain the remains of 15–20,000 people, free and enslaved, stacked in layers.

HISTORY OF THE BURIAL GROUND

The Dutch introduced slavery to New Amsterdam in 1626, using slave labor for building Fort Amsterdam, laying roads, and performing domestic work. When the English took over in 1664, the city became an active center of the African slave trade, and by 1711 there was a slave market on Wall St at the East River. In 1697, Trinity Church may have contributed to use of the present site, ordering that "no Negroes be buried within the bounds and limits of the church yard of Trinity Church." The Burial Ground is thought to have been in use until about 1794, when the Chamber of Commerce acquired part of the land to lay out Chambers St. The neighborhood was soon leveled and filled for building construction, and as development continued through the centuries, the memory of the Negroes Burial Ground was lost.

In 1994 the excavated remains were sent to Howard University for forensic study, research that focused on the economic and social conditions affecting the skeletons. About nine percent of the burials were children younger than two, and another 32 percent were prepubertal. Both adults and children showed signs of poor nutrition, and it was determined that the average age of death for both men and women was somewhere in the low- to mid-thirties.

The monument and visitor center

The imagery of the monument, designed by Rodney Léon, a Brooklyn-born architect, recalls traditional African burial practices. Two slabs of granite angle upward to create the hull-like Ancestral Chamber. The chamber opening, between two reflecting pools, leads to a sunken court, whose walls are inscribed with African symbols. In the center

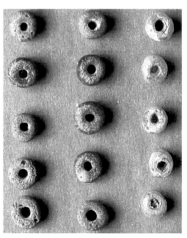

an Africa-centric map of the world is carved into the granite floor. The federal government commissioned several works of art for the Weiss Building, which will become part of the permanent visitors' center. They include Clyde Lynds's *America Song* (1995), a stone, steel, and fiber-optic wall sculpture (on the exterior wall to the right of the entrance); Barbara Chase-Riboud's *Africa Rising* (1998), a bronze female figure that

Yellow and turquoise glass bracelet beads from the grave of a woman aged about 50. Such beads, thought to be of Venetian manufacture, were commonly traded to Africa in the 18th century.

suggests both Umberto Boccioni's Futurist figures and the Winged Victory of Samothrace; and Houston Conwill's floor mosaic, *The New Ring Shout* (1998).

FOLEY SQUARE

North of Centre Street lies Foley Square, named after politician Thomas F. Foley (1852–1925), a kingmaker but never an office-holder. Foley helped Al Smith become governor and kept William Randolph Hearst—who had attacked him in his newspapers—from becoming either governor or a US senator.

In the center of the square stands Lorenzo Pace's *Triumph of the Human Spirit* (2000), a 50-ft black granite sculpture which takes its inspiration from the antelope forms of West African art (specifically that of the Bambara people). The monument honors all Africans brought to America, and the boat-shaped base alludes to the "Middle Passage," the transportation of slaves across the Atlantic.

THE COLLECT POND

Until the beginning of the 19th century much of the present square lay beneath the waters of the Collect Pond (from the Dutch *kolch*, a small body of water). Known for its depth (60ft) and purity, the spring-fed pond drained into the Hudson. Much of the land on western side was marshland called the Lispenard Meadows. In the 18th century tanners settled here because the water supply was essential to their business, but in 1730 Anthony Rutgers, a landowner, petitioned the city for the swamp and pond which he then began to drain, to the distress of the tanners. The city gained title to the pond in 1791. In 1796 John Fitch tested a prototypical steamboat on its waters. Though successful technologically, the boat never achieved the fame of Robert Fulton's *Clermont*, which steamed up the Hudson in 1807. Fitch eventually abandoned his craft in the pond and left town.

Around 1800 the city began filling the pond and draining the Lispenard Meadows. By 1807, cartloads of dirt and garbage were being dumped into the pond, eventually forming a foul-smelling island 12–15ft above the water. In 1809 Canal St was laid out and a sewer built beneath it to drain the springs which formerly fed the pond. By 1811 the pond had disappeared altogether.

The stench, the sinking of land still undermined by springs, and the encroachment of the dry goods trade into nearby streets drove out people who could afford to live elsewhere. By the early 19th century the neighborhood was a slum, inhabited by freed slaves, immigrants, and the undifferentiated poor. By 1840 it had become notorious for crime, its worst section called Five Points at the intersection of Park, Baxter, and Worth Sts. Houses were rotten and overcrowded, with people packed into windowless basements or relegated to "back buildings" hastily erected in dark rear yards by eager landlords.

At 1 Foley Square (southeast corner) is the **Thurgood Marshall United States Courthouse** (1933–36; Cass Gilbert; completed by Cass Gilbert Jr.). Gilbert, who also designed the Supreme Court in Washington, intended this to be a counterpart. It has a gilded top like the Municipal Building (*see p. 87 above*) and a heroic portico (50-ft Corinthian columns) facing Foley Square like the County Courthouse to its north (*see below*). The building houses the US District Court and the Federal Court of Appeals. In 2003 it was renamed to honor Thurgood Marshall, the first African-American Supreme Court Justice, famous for his work on civil rights.

On the northeast corner of Pearl St at Foley Square is the **New York County Courthouse** (1913–27; Guy Lowell), home of the New York State Supreme Court. The grand portico in the Roman Corinthian style is three columns deep and about 100ft wide. The carving in the tympanum above the portico (sculptor Frederick W. Allen) shows *Justice with Courage and Wisdom*. Atop the pediment are statues representing *Law* (center) flanked by *Truth* and *Equity*. The niches of the porch shelter two female figures (by Philip Martiny) removed from the Surrogate's Court on Chambers St in 1961 when the city widened traffic lanes there. The figure with the shield and city coat of arms (left) is *Authority*, while her companion *Justice* (right) rests her foot upon a bundle of records.

Further north at 100 Centre St (between Leonard and White Sts) looms the bulk of the **New York City Criminal Courts Building** (1939; Harvey Wiley Corbett), formerly the Manhattan Detention Center for Men and better known as "The Tombs." The name originated with an earlier prison on the site, built in a gloomy hollow so deep that the massive prison walls hardly rose above the level of Broadway some hundred yards to the west. Officially known as "The Halls of Justice," it was built (1836–38) in the Egyptian Revival style, with trapezoidal windows, lotus columns, and emblems of the sun god. This prison was called "The Tombs" partly because of the funereal associations of the architectural style and partly because of its dismal function and appearance. It served as the city jail until 1893, when a second prison, Romanesque Revival in style but still called "The Tombs," replaced it.

A WALK THROUGH TRIBECA

Subway: N, R to Canal St (Broadway); 6 to Canal St (Lafayette St). Bus: M6.

TriBeCa, an acronym devised in the 1970s by realtors to enhance property values in the Triangle Below Canal St, is a trapezoidal neighborhood known for its intriguing combination of wealth and grit. The grit comes from its days as part of the Lower West Side, when food purveyors once roasted coffee or distributed dairy products and merchants haggled over wool in the 19th-century industrial buildings here. The wealth is more recent, attributable in part to a spillover from SoHo. Today the apartments of celebrities and other well-heeled people occupy the upper floors of former manufacturing lofts and warehouses. At street level are shops with well-designed displays, as well as restaurants where reservations are made weeks in advance, and small amounts of food (albeit exquisitely prepared) command high prices. (There are also more modest establishments.) The TriBeCa Film Festival, founded in 2002 to revitalize the neighborhood after the September 11 attacks, has become a major cultural event (late April–early May). This walk takes in some examples of TriBeCa's 19th-century industrial architecture, as well as its 21st-century flair.

The walk begins at Canal St and Broadway. Lispenard St, a block south of Canal St, is named for Leonard Lispenard: at the end of the 18th century, much of what is now TriBeCa was owned either by Trinity Church (the western part) or by the Lispenard family (the eastern part). The two groups developed their property separately, with separate street grids. The eastern part has many cast-iron buildings, as does SoHo to the north. In the western section, closer to the Hudson, are brick warehouses, many in the Romanesque Revival style. The arrival of the A.T. Stewart Department Store, downtown a few blocks on Chambers St (*see p. 89*), sparked development on Broadway and the side streets, where stores, lofts, and houses were built. Photographer Matthew Brady had a portrait studio near Franklin St at 359 Broadway for six years (1853–59), before he made his mark documenting the Civil War.

Around the time of the Civil War, industrial buildings began to replace the earlier Greek Revival houses and shops. The cast-iron-fronted building (1861) at **55 White St** (Franklin Pl), with its keystone-crowned arches and Corinthian columns (the capitals are now gone), was deemed so handsome by Daniel D. Badger, whose iron foundry supplied the material, that he featured it in his 1865 catalogue. The building housed a saddlery and, later, drapery and textile firms.

The triangular pediment of 46–50 White St identifies the Italianate **Woods Mercantile Buildings** (1865), faced upstairs with Tuckahoe marble (dingy at present) and with cast iron at street level. Across the street at 49 White St is the undulating façade of the **Civic Center Synagogue** (1967; William N. Breger Assocs), built decades before this neighborhood became a Historic District.

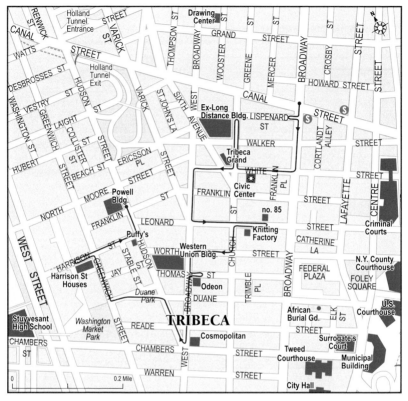

In the block north of Walker St at 32 Sixth Ave is the former **Long Distance Building of the American Telephone & Telegraph Company** (1930–32; Voorhees, Gmelin & Walker), a large Art Deco building with polychrome brickwork and V-shaped piers. Formerly called the "Tower of Speech," the building had direct circuits to several hundred cities; inside as many as 5,000 operators manually connected long-distance calls. The decoration of the lobby lionizes the power of telephony. A tile map on the wall proclaims that "Telephone Wires and Radio Unite to Make Neighbors of Nations." A mosaic on the ceiling depicts the continents as female figures linked by golden telephone wires.

In the triangle further south at 2 Sixth Ave is the **Tribeca Grand Hotel**, an expensive boutique hotel whose advent in 2000 reflected TriBeCa's arrival as a hip neighborhood.

On the northeast corner of West Broadway at **2 White St** stands a small, brick-and-frame two-story Federal house with its original gambrel roof and dormers (1809). It survives from the days before commercial development spread north from Downtown, when this was a well-to-do residential area. Though constructed in the opening years of the 19th

century, the house harks back to an earlier style. The original owner was prominent in city affairs and also owned a plaster factory.

The **Knitting Factory** at 74 Leonard St (Broadway and Church St) was founded on Houston St in 1987 as a venue for experimental music, jazz, poetry, art, and films; over the years it has changed ownership and lost some of its avant-garde sheen. There are three performance spaces within the multi-level club, catering to different levels of musical professionalism (*T: 212 219 3055; www.knittingfactory.com*).

The cast-iron building at **85 Leonard St** (1861) is the only structure in the city that can be positively attributed to James Bogardus, generally considered to be the father of cast-iron architecture in the US. This building is practically a catalogue of decorative possibilities: fluted columns (formerly with leafy capitals), lions' heads, rope moldings, bearded faces, dentiled moldings, faceted keystones, egg-and-dart trim, stylized leaves.

James Bogardus (1800–74)

High-school dropout though he was, Bogardus nevertheless had a vision: he foresaw the possibilities of bolting together sections of cast iron into façades or even whole buildings. His importance arises primarily from his patents for constructing buildings with mass-produced cast-iron sections and as a building contractor. Bogardus was a prolific inventor, patenting devices for engraving postage stamps, spinning cotton, cutting rubber, and pressing glass. Between about 1848–60, he promoted iron buildings because they were fireproof and efficient to build. In 1858 he wrote *Cast Iron Buildings: Their Construction and Advantages*, in which he described the method of supporting the weight of construction on columns rather than with masonry walls; it was a first step in the development of skeleton framing, which eventually made skyscrapers possible.

The **Western Union Building** (1930; Voorhees, Gmelin & Walker) between Thomas and Worth Sts (front entrance at 60 Hudson St) is an imposing Art Deco building by architect Ralph Walker (whose Barclay-Vesey Building stands further downtown; *see p. 63*). Nineteen tons of brick shade the façade from deep red brown at the bottom to bright salmon at the top, not unusual for Art Deco brickwork. When it opened, the building housed telephone, telegraph, and ticker machinery, as well as a messenger service and classrooms where Western Union messenger boys could continue high school. The lobby gloriously exemplifies Art Deco materials and techniques, its interior finished in brown brick, with recessed lighting, leaded glass windows, geometrically patterned brickwork, and marble flooring.

On the southeast corner of Thomas St (named for Thomas Lispenard, a son of Leonard Lispenard; *see p. 93 above*) is **The Odeon**, 145 West Broadway (*open late, breakfast on weekends; T: 212 233 0507*). Converted in 1980 from a vintage cafeteria to a casual American eatery, it

was the first of many stylish restaurants to follow the artists to TriBeCa.

The cast-iron building at **147 West Broadway** (1869), just off the southeast corner of Thomas St, is closer than most in its imitation of stone, down to the incised blocks on the façade and the quoins on the corners. While early cast-iron buildings in the area often simulated stone, later ones exploited the natural properties of cast iron and were more elaborate.

Bouley Bakery/Café & Market at 130 West Broadway (at Duane St) offers three floors of good things to eat in or take out. Its chef, David Bouley, whose haute-cuisine restaurant is across the street, was a TriBeCa pioneer.

The **Cosmopolitan Hotel**, at 95 West Broadway (Chambers St), is said to have opened around 1850 as the Gerard House, when, according to the 1939 *WPA New York City Guide*, its proximity to the piers made it attractive to gold miners back from California, who "staggered into the lobby after a trip around the Horn, dumped their gold-dust, went out to the barber, and came back 'unrecognizably clean.'" Refurbished a decade ago, it is a favorite budget hotel.

Walk back up Hudson St to **Duane Park**, a small triangle with benches and plantings, the first land bought by the city specifically as parkland. The history of the plot can be traced back to 1636 when it belonged to Annetje Jans, a Dutch farmer. The farm was later sold to the English governor and then confiscated by the Duke of York (later James II), who in turn gave it to Trinity Church. The city bought it in 1795 for five dollars. James Duane (1733–97) was the city's first mayor after the

Revolutionary War and later a federal judge. At 179 Duane St, the Duane Park Patisserie (*open Mon–Sat 8–6:30, Sun 9–5; T: 212 274 8447; www.madelines.net*) offers pastries, coffee, and tea.

Around the park are late 19th-century buildings, including no. **173–75 Duane St** (1879; Babb & Cook), one of the area's earliest Romanesque Revival buildings. No. 171 Duane St has a cast-iron front (1859) grafted onto an earlier Federal house. The large brick Romanesque Revival building on the northwest corner of Hudson St, **165 Duane St**, was built for Leopold Schepp, who developed a process for drying coconut that assured his fortune; millions of coconuts were processed and packaged here. According to a contemporary account in the *New York Times*, Schepp had a "temper that would make the North Pole melt," but later in life "he established a foundation to give grants to boys who vowed to abstain from bad habits." The Dutch-style building across the street at **168 Duane St** (1887; Stephen Decatur Hatch) was a factory for packing eggs and making cheese before it was converted to condominiums. The ground-floor spaces of some of these buildings today house antiques shops and galleries of beautifully crafted furniture.

The name of **Washington Market Park** (1983) recalls the city's largest food market, which stood in this neighborhood for almost 150 years. The market building occupied a block bounded by Fulton, Vesey, Washington, and West Sts in what is presently the northwest corner of the World Trade Center site, but its activities as a distribution center for produce, as well as

cheese, butter, eggs, and candy, spread into the surrounding streets along West St as far north as Canal St. The market, a large building divided into stalls, offered everything from codfish cheeks to bear steaks; it was supplanted by the Hunts Point Market in 1967, as plans for the World Trade Center and the rehabilitation of the neighborhood took shape.

Near Greenwich St on Harrison St—named for Harrison's Brewery, which stood near the river in pre-Revolutionary days—is a row of nine 18th-century Federal-style brick town houses, known as the **Harrison Street houses** (1796–1828). Nos. 25, 37, 39, and 41 Harrison St were built by John McComb Jr., New York's first native-born architect (he designed City Hall), who lived in one of them.

At 6 Harrison St is the **former New York Mercantile Exchange** (1886; Thomas R. Jackson), a five-story, gabled brick Queen Anne-style building with a handsome tower facing the Hudson River and rusticated granite pillars at the base. The tall second-story windows opened onto the trading floor, where on a good day at the turn of the 20th century $15,000 worth of eggs changed hands in an hour. The exchange was organized in 1872 as the Butter and Cheese Exchange, for commercial objectives (fostering trade, reforming abuses) and also social ones (promoting good fellowship, providing for the widows and orphans of members). On the ground floor is Chanterelle, an elegant, established, and expensive restaurant (*T: 212 966 6960; www.chanterellenyc.com*). **Puffy's Tavern**, on the southwest corner of Harrison and Hudson Sts (81 Hudson St), dates back to Prohibition, and still has its old-fashioned bar, tile floor, jukebox, and dart board (*open daily 4–4; T: 212 227 3912; www.puffystavern.com*).

The **Powell Building** (1892; Carrère & Hastings; 105 Hudson St at Franklin St) was formerly known as the Pierce Building for its developer, Henry Pierce, head of the firm that made Baker's Chocolate. It is an early work by Carrère & Hastings (later famous for the New York Public Library on Fifth Ave at 42nd St and the Frick Mansion), probably their third project in New York (the first two no longer remain). After Pierce's death, the building was sold to Alexander Powell, a candy manufacturer, who enlarged it top-to-bottom and side-to-side. Nobu, another restaurant that made TriBeCa a culinary destination, occupies the ground floor (*T: 212 219 0500; www.myriadrestaurantgroup.com*).

THE HOLLAND TUNNEL

Two blocks north of Franklin St are the ramps for the Holland Tunnel, the first Hudson River vehicular tunnel, completed in 1927 and named after its chief engineer, Clifford M. Holland. When it opened, the tunnel was heralded as a triumph of engineering, in large part for Holland's solving the ventilation problems of a long vehicular tunnel. It is operated by the Port Authority of New York and New Jersey; its tubes (roughly a mile and a half long) carry more than 34 million cars annually.

SOHO

Map p. 582, C1. Subway: N, R, W to Prince St; 6 to Spring St; D, F, V to Broadway-Lafayette. Bus: M6 to Houston St and Broadway.

SoHo, the area SOuth of HOuston St, is endowed with the city's greatest concentration of cast-iron architecture and one of its denser concentrations of shopping opportunities, with stores ranging from high-end boutiques to sidewalk carts. Some of the side streets, particularly those in the southern end of the district, retain their Belgian block paving, granite sidewalks, and iron loading platforms. Broadway is the busiest street, especially on weekends; West Broadway is less frenzied than Broadway. Greene St offers many examples of cast-iron architecture.

History of SoHo

After the Revolution, SoHo's great farms were subdivided and the area developed as a quiet residential suburb. By 1825 it had become the most densely populated part of New York. By 1840 it had become highly fashionable, and in the 1850s expensive hotels and retail stores of sterling reputation lined Broadway while the side streets began sporting brothels, dance halls, and casinos, some of them elegant. As the carriage trade vanished uptown, industry filled the vacuum. During the decades between 1860 and 1890, most of the cast-iron architecture so admired today was constructed, the buildings serving as factories or warehouses, often with shopfronts on the ground floor. Appealing as they may seem now with their Corinthian columns, Palladian windows, or French Second Empire dormers, many functioned as sweatshops where immigrants from southern and eastern Europe endured 12 or more hours a day of tedious labor. SoHo and Little Italy still sit side by side, and what is left of the Italian population, especially visible in warm weather on the streets west of West Broadway, particularly Sullivan St, is descended from those overworked immigrants.

Although the sweatshops were legislated out of existence, in part by immigration quotas that stanched the flow of cheap, uneducated, and hence acquiescent labor, SoHo remained industrial until the middle of the 20th century. Gradually the cast-iron buildings became outmoded and inconvenient, and SoHo's paper-box companies, tool and die factories, and wool remnant companies moved elsewhere. In 1959 the City Club of New York published an influential report labeling the area, then known as Hell's Hundred Acres (because of its frequent fires) or as The Valley (a lowland between the architectural highs of the Financial District and Midtown), an industrial slum with no architecture of note.

In the early 1960s artists attracted by those same empty commercial buildings began moving in, illegally converting the space to apartments. In the late 1960s SoHo was an artist's Eden. Rents were cheap, space was plentiful, and society was made up mostly of other artists. By 1970 SoHo had become a boomtown for real estate dealers, art dealers

SoHo façades on Broadway.

(some headed downtown from the Upper East Side), and artists who, if not becoming rich, were at least forming a coherent artistic community. Film, video, and "performance" art—the avant-garde media of the 1960s—became staple commodities of SoHo artistic life. Experimental dance and drama flourished. Cooperative galleries opened.

Today the SoHo of artistic legend is a victim of its own success. As the galleries brought in a moneyed clientele, rents soared. Artists, except for the most successful, moved elsewhere—to Brooklyn or the far edges of the Lower East Side. Gradually the galleries, including the highly successful ones, began their own exodus to Chelsea and also to Brooklyn. SoHo's museums have either departed or disappeared. A four-star hotel opened in 1996, the first new hotel in the area for more than 100 years.

BROADWAY FROM WEST HOUSTON TO BROOME STREET

Along Broadway south of Houston St are shops with clothes best worn by the young and adventurous, as well as stylish shoes and other accessories. The Ruskinian brick and stone building at 575 Broadway (corner of Prince St) was built (1882; Thomas Stent) for Rogers Peet, a men's clothier established in 1874 (which lasted until the mid-1980s). A century later, redesigned by Arata Isozaki (1992), it housed the SoHo branch of the

Guggenheim, built during the museum's period of global expansionism. Redesigned again (2001) by Dutch architect Rem Koolhaas, it has become a showplace for Prada.

On the ground level of 560 Broadway, at Prince St, in another masonry building by Thomas Stent (1883), **Dean & DeLuca** is one of the city's fine food stores, famous for its displays. The store first opened in SoHo in 1977, moved to this location in 1988, and now has branches nationwide. Formerly the upper floors of the building constituted a vertical mall of art galleries, but few remain.

Little Singer Building

The former "**Little Singer Building**" (1904; Ernest Flagg), across the street at 561–63 Broadway, was built by the architect of the bigger Singer Building downtown, demolished in 1967 (*see p. 75*). Despite ugly ground-floor modifications, this 12-story steel-framed skyscraper (a building type less than ten years old when it was built) is extremely handsome. Most notable are the terra-cotta panels, delicate curls of dark green wrought iron, large expanses of plate glass, and the great arch beneath the cornice. The L-shaped building wraps around the corner of Prince St, enveloping 565 Broadway next door (1859; John Kellum), whose carved marble Corinthian columns evoke the days when Ball, Black & Co. purveyed jewelry to society.

The **Scholastic Building** (2000), next door at 557 Broadway, is the last work of the celebrated Italian architect Aldo Rossi, who died in 1997 before construction began. It sits between the Little Singer Building and the Rouss Building, echoing the red terra cotta and green-painted cast iron of the former and the classical columns of the latter. A more severely industrial façade faces Mercer St.

At 555 Broadway the façade of the handsomely maintained **Rouss Building** (1889; Alfred Zucker), still proclaims the success of merchant Charles "Broadway" Rouss, who came debt-ridden to New York from Maryland and so flourished that he took the street's name as his own and had it emblazoned on his storefront.

The **bishop's crook lamppost** in front of 515 Broadway dates from around 1900, when it and others of its kind replaced older gaslights introduced in the 1860s. In 1896 this classic lamppost—with its tendrils, scrollwork, and acanthus leaves—designed by Richard Rodgers Bowker, began to appear on city streets.

Bloomingdale's SoHo, 504 Broadway (near Broome St), in an elegantly remodeled building (1860), is more stylish than its heftier uptown sister. It opened in 2004 in place of Canal Jeans, an iconic SoHo store which sold moderately priced vintage clothes, military wear, feather boas, and, of course, jeans. Canal Jeans has moved to Brooklyn.

Haughwout Building

In the once supremely elegant Haughwout Building (1857; John P. Gaynor) at 488–92 Broadway (*map p. 582, C1*), Eder V. Haughwout sold china, glassware, chandeliers, and silver (to the White House and lesser householders) from the ground-floor showroom. Designed in the Italianate *palazzo* style common to many early cast-iron

Detail of the Haughwout Building, one of the most famous cast-iron façades in Manhattan.

buildings and perhaps even modeled on Sansovino's Libreria Marciana in Venice, the Haughwout Building (sometimes inappropriately called the Parthenon of Cast-Iron Architecture) was a pioneering structure. It was one of the first New York buildings whose floor loads were carried by a cast-iron skeleton instead of masonry walls, and the very first to feature a passenger elevator with a safety device, a steam-driven, cable-and-drum contraption invented by Elisha Otis. The economy of casting many forms from the same mold fostered the repetition of detail on cast-iron buildings such as this one, whose basic motif—a round-arch window between slender Corinthian colonnettes flanked by larger Corinthian columns—is repeated 92 times in four tiers on two façades. It is this repetition, the result of a practical and economic principle, that makes for the frequently invoked harmony of the building.

WEST BROADWAY & WOOSTER STREETS

West Broadway (*map p. 582, B1–C1*) used to be the main street of SoHo, the place to be seen gallery hopping on Saturdays. Like its mirror, East Broadway, the street got its name from its intended function, relieving the congested traffic on Broadway, four blocks east. It is also SoHo's widest street and the western frontier of the historic district (only the east side of the street lies within the protected district, so that building fronts on the west side have been altered extensively).

The New York Earth Room and The Drawing Center

At 468 West Broadway, near Houston St, is a brick Romanesque Revival building (c. 1885), with round arches relieved by cast-iron floral swags in the spandrels. Next door, at 472–78 West Broadway, the first-floor pilasters of the one-time brick warehouse have been decorated with floral designs including cast-iron sunflowers.

Upstairs at 141 Wooster St, near Prince St, is the **New York Earth Room** (1977), one of two long-term projects of the Dia Art Foundation in SoHo and an example of "Earth" or "Land" Art by sculptor Walter De Maria. The Room (*open mid-Sept–June Wed–Sun 12–6; closed 3–3:30; ring bell to left of door for entry; T: 212 473 8072; www.earthroom.org*) consists of 280,000 lb of dark damp earth, piled to a uniform depth of 22 inches in a starkly white gallery. Like some other works by De Maria, the installation seeks to explore the relationship between the natural world and the constructs of civilization.

The block between Spring and Prince Sts on West Broadway was once the hotspot of the gallery scene. The legendary Leo Castelli opened his gallery at 420 West Broadway in 1971. Castelli (1907–99), long acknowledged as the dean of the Pop Art movement, made his name representing Jasper Johns, Robert Rauschenberg, Roy Lichtenstein, and Andy Warhol, and later showed Minimalists, Conceptualists, and Neo-Expressionists. Castelli was famous for discovering unknown artists and nurturing them through long careers, as well as for convincing Europeans of the importance of American art.

Walter De Maria's second SoHo installation, *Broken Kilometer*, has been on view at 393 West Broadway (Spring and Broome Sts) since 1979. The work, mathematical

and precise, consists of 500 polished, two-meter brass rods. They are laid on the floor in five parallel rows of 100 rods apiece, with each row 80mm further apart than the previous one (*open mid-Sept–June Wed–Sun 12–6; closed 3–3:30; T: 212 989 5566*).

The Drawing Center at 35 Wooster St (near Grand St) was founded in 1977 to foster appreciation of drawing as a major art form (*open Tues–Fri 10–6; Sat 11–6; T: 212 219 2166; www.drawingcenter.org*). It mounts six or seven highly regarded exhibitions yearly in its main space (a handsome cast-iron building dating from 1886), and also across the street in the Drawing Room at 40 Wooster St. Exhibitions have ranged from Rajasthani miniatures, to visionary architectural drawings, to work by contemporary artists, for example Kara Walker, whose first public exhibition was at the Drawing Center.

Behind most cast-iron fronts are buildings of conventional internal structure with brick bearing walls, wooden beams, and joists supporting wooden floors. But occasional buildings like this one (1866; Samuel Curtiss Jr.), have a system of slender cast-iron columns supporting the floors, an arrangement which permitted a very open interior (and hence a lot of rentable space). Such columns, usually painted white, were often fluted, and embellished with elaborate Corinthian capitals.

GREENE STREET

Greene St is named after Revolutionary War general Nathanael Greene. At its northern end, near Houston St, it offers fine examples of cast-iron architecture (*see box overleaf*), and, more recently, of fine European design, particularly furniture and clothing.

The brick Federal house (c. 1824) at **139 Greene St**, its original dormers and lintels more or less intact, is one of the few buildings remaining from SoHo's early period of residential development. The house has been in an arrested state of renovation for several decades. The elaborate building at **121–23 Greene St** (1883; Henry Fernbach), with its fluted pilasters, Corinthian columns, and ornate cornice, all painted a smooth cream color, is a fine example of this prolific architect's work. The sidewalks are monolithic granite slabs, some with their edges rounded to form curbing.

At the southwest corner of Greene and Prince Sts, nos. **112–14 Greene St** has a famous *trompe l'oeil* mural (1975) by Richard Haas. With wit and precision the mural reproduces on the brick eastern wall of the building (1889; Richard Berger) the cast-iron detail of the northern façade. The cast iron in turn suggests masonry construction— banded corner pilasters resembling masonry blocks, colonnettes standing on pedestals and supporting impost blocks, protruding cornices ending in decorative blocks supported by consoles. Thus the painted mural imitates cast iron imitating masonry.

On the west side of Greene St between Spring and Prince Sts are three cast-iron buildings (nos. 93–95, 97, and 99), all designed in the Neo-Grec style by Henry Fernbach in 1881. On the east side of the street, on the sidewalk near 110 Greene St, is Françoise Schein's steel subway map embedded in the pavement; created in 1986, its proper name is *Subway Map Floating on a New York Sidewalk*.

SOHO'S CAST-IRON ARCHITECTURE

Cast-iron architecture, which was developed during the later decades of the 19th century, served as a major alternative to masonry architecture during a period when cast iron was inexpensive and steel was not yet readily available. SoHo's commercial buildings, with their elegant, prefabricated cast-iron façades, once a source of personal and civic pride, later suffered the ravages of neglect—disfigured by ugly ground-floor modernizations or dimmed by layers of dull paint. In 1973 the SoHo Cast-Iron Historic District was created to protect a 26-block tract—bounded by West Broadway, Houston, Crosby, and Canal Sts—with the largest concentration of cast-iron architecture in the world. Today many of these structures have been handsomely restored.

Early cast-iron architecture, adorned with the familiar quoins, columns, and consoles of the Classical tradition and painted tan, buff, or cream, was designed to imitate marble or limestone. Sometimes cast-iron plates were even grooved to resemble blocks of stone mortared together. Eventually iron-founders, many of whom had previously dealt in stoves, safes, and lawn furniture, began offering catalogues of ornaments from which the client or architect could select, combining the elements in simple or lavish compositions. As long as patterns could be carved and molds made, elaborate ornaments could be cheaply reproduced, allowing businessmen who could not afford stonecutting to enjoy the prestige of fluted Corinthian columns or floral swags, bolted onto their buildings and painted to look like stone. While the earliest cast-iron buildings hark back stylistically to Italy (Sansovino's Libreria Marciana in Venice and the Roman Colosseum were much admired), later examples were based on French renaissance, Second Empire, or Neo-Grec styles.

In one sense cast-iron architecture was standardized: the ornaments were machine-made, mass-produced, and as interchangeable as parts of a Winchester rifle, which allowed the architect great scope and originality, as the general exuberance of these SoHo buildings demonstrates. The elements of a façade were separately cast, the smaller pieces bolted together at the factory, and the whole façade laid out with pieces numbered and tested for fit. It was all then shipped to the construction site where the front was assembled and permanently bolted into place.

Spring and Broome Streets

Spring St (*map p. 582, B1–D1*) takes its name from a spring tapped by Aaron Burr's Manhattan Water Company, whose ostensible purpose was to supply drinking water to the city but which quickly evolved into a banking company instead. A former well at Broadway and Spring St became the grave of one Juliana (or Gulielma) Elmore Sands, whose body minus shoes, hat, and shawl was found floating there on Jan 2,

1800. In a sensational 19th-century murder case, her fiancé was acquitted of the crime (Aaron Burr and Alexander Hamilton defended him).

The building at 72–76 Greene St (1872; J.F. Duckworth), with a monogram cast on the central pilaster between the doorways, was once a warehouse of the Gardner Colby Co. Most of the other buildings on this block between Spring and Broome Sts were designed by Henry Fernbach and John B. Snook in the early 1870s and used by firms dealing in rug clippings, wool rags, and fabric remnants. No. 66 Greene St (1873; John B. Snook) was built as a store for the Lorillard tobacco company.

Further down Greene St at the corner of Broome St (469–75 Broome St) is the Gunther Building (1871–72; Griffith Thomas), a warehouse for furrier William H. Gunther. The elegant corner turning, with its curved panes of glass, is notable. For several decades beginning in the 1960s, the building housed a cooperative art gallery and artists' studios.

The "Queen of Greene Street"

The vista along the block between Grand and Canal Sts, little changed since the 19th century, reveals the city's longest continuous row of cast-iron architecture, built between 1872 and 1896, when SoHo was rapidly becoming industrial. The *pièce de résistance* of the block between Grand and Canal Sts, known familiarly as the "**Queen of Greene St**," is no. 28–30 Greene St (1872; J.F. Duckworth), a grandly ornate Second Empire building crowned with a stupendous mansard roof. The tall broad windows flanked by half-round columns, the keystoned segmental arches, the central two-window bay rising the full height of the building to a broken pediment, and the elaborate dormers with balustrades, modillions, pediments, and finials offer a wealth of architectural ornament.

During the 1850s, when nearby Broadway sparkled with theaters, hotels, and casinos, Greene and Mercer Sts were notorious for their brothels. While the houses on the southern end of the streets near Canal St catered to sailors from the ships docked in the Hudson, the houses further north appealed to a wealthier clientele. An 1859 *Directory to the Seraglios in New York*, written by an anonymous "Free Loveyer," recommends a Miss Clara Gordon at 119 Mercer St, "beautiful, entertaining and supremely seductive," who is patronized by Southern merchants and planters, and a Mrs. Bailey of 76 Greene St, whose comfortable and quiet "resort" is within a few moments' walk of Broadway and the principal hotels.

CANAL STREET

NB: For the section of Canal St in Chinatown, see p. 109.
Canal Street (*map p. 582, C1–A1*), which runs river to river connecting the ramps of the Holland Tunnel to those of the Manhattan Bridge, is a crowded crosstown thoroughfare and a busy street market for everything from electronics and industrial plastics to Chinese vegetables and gold jewelry. Cars and trucks jam the roadway, the

drivers on occasion expressing their impatience by leaning on their horns. Pedestrians jam the sidewalks, their progress impeded by sidewalk vendors, by merchandise spilling from open storefronts, food stalls, and by the sheer volume of foot traffic. The awnings, billboards, advertising placards, and other signs posted on almost every available flat surface make the street visually chaotic. On its western end, Canal St forms the northern border of TriBeCa; in its mid-section it borders SoHo; further east it separates Chinatown to the south from Little Italy (increasingly becoming the escape valve for Chinatown) to the north. The sidewalk crowd and the merchandise and food offerings change accordingly.

Canal St owes both its name and its exceptional width to a canal proposed by the city fathers in 1805 to serve as a storm drain, a household sewer, and a conduit siphoning off the waters of the Collect Pond near present Foley Square (*see p. 91*). By the 1820s both street and canal had been paved over, a mixed blessing: while the covered sewer alleviated the mosquito problem, the stench it created depressed both property values and morale until adequate air traps were installed.

Around Mercer Street

On the northeast corner of Canal and Mercer Sts stands the **former Marble House** (1856–65; Griffith Thomas), 307–11 Canal St, once the home of the Arnold Constable Dry Goods Store and currently being restored. Only the Canal St façade of Marble House actually involved marble; the sides and rear of the building made do with humble brickwork. During the 1850s and 1860s the neighborhood boasted several such fine stores, including Lord & Taylor's, ultimately the victor in its perennial rivalry with Arnold Constable's, then located a block north at Broadway and Grand St.

Mercer St, still paved with its 19th-century Belgian blocks, is named after Hugh Mercer, a surgeon and brigadier general in the Revolutionary War. The building at no. 11 (1870) began as a warehouse for the India Rubber Company. It still retains its vault cover, also known as an illuminated sidewalk or light platform, with glass discs embedded in the iron stoop to permit sunlight to illuminate the storage vault below, a system invented in 1845 by one Thaddeus Hyatt.

The Italianate building housing two banks at 254–60 Canal St (Lafayette St) may have been designed by James Bogardus (*see p. 95*). It dates from 1857; its half-round window arches and Medusa-head keystones at the fourth-floor level suggest his work.

CHINATOWN,
LITTLE ITALY & NOLITA

Map p. 583, D1–D2. Subway: 6 to Canal St; 4, 5 to Brooklyn Bridge; B, D to Grand St. Bus: M15, M103. The Museum of Chinese in America (see p. 115) offers walking tours Sat at 1; reservations required; T: 212 619 4785. The Explore Chinatown kiosk at Canal and Baxter Sts has maps and information; open 10–6, weekends 10–7; www.explorechinatown.com.

While many of Manhattan's other ethnic enclaves are shrinking or gentrifying, Chinatown is expanding eastward beyond its original boundaries into the Lower East Side and northward into Little Italy. The neighborhood surges with energy. Pedestrians jostle one another on the narrow sidewalks; merchandise crowds the display windows; signs in English and Chinese hang from virtually every storefront.

Visitors come for the ambiance, for bargains, and for food, as well as for knockoff designer handbags and perfume. Sunday is the busiest day, when Chinese who have moved out to the suburbs return to the old neighborhood.

A chef and her interpreter buying ingredients in Chinatown in the 1940s.

HISTORY OF CHINATOWN

Chinatown grew only slowly for centuries. Although the China trade brought sailors and merchants from the Far East in the late 18th century, only about 150 Chinese had established residence a hundred years later. It was not until the completion of the Transcontinental Railroad in 1869 that the Chinese population grew significantly. Peasant laborers brought to build the railroad found themselves without work, and the increasing racial hostilities in the West drove many eastward in the late 1870s. Other Chinese arrived from Cuba, where they had been imported by cigar makers and quickly excelled at hand rolling. In 1870 one Wo Kee established a general store in a house on Mott St, the first mercantile establishment in Chinatown; he sold shark fins, opium, tea, medicines, and incense.

National exclusionary laws and minuscule immigration quotas kept Chinatown's population small relative to other immigrant groups for another hundred years; other laws prevented the naturalization of Chinese already in this country and barred wives and families from arriving, so that Chinatown long remained a "bachelor" society. Most of the immigrants during this period arrived from Guandong (Kwangtung or Canton) province in southeast China and settled in "old" Chinatown, maintaining their language (Cantonese) and cultural traditions. Jobs open to these arrivals were those where English was not necessary—rolling cigars or working in hand laundries, restaurants, and the garment industries—all of them low paying and labor intensive.

When the quotas were lifted in 1965, a new surge of immigration began, changing the political structure, geography, and cultural makeup of New York's Chinatown, which became the largest in the country by 1980. Arrivals from Hong Kong, Taiwan, and the Chinese mainland swelled the population and created new Chinatowns in Queens (Flushing), Brooklyn (Sunset Park and Bay Ridge), and elsewhere.

Many of the newer arrivals are rural Fujianese, and many have arrived illegally. The 1993 fiasco of the *Golden Venture*, a ship carrying illegal immigrants which ran aground off Queens, brought to light the scope of the problem and the plight of these often impoverished and ill-educated arrivals. The presence of the new immigrants, whose loyalties are to mainland China and whose language (one of the many dialects of Fujianese) is not understood by earlier settlers, has impacted Chinatown politics, long dominated by speakers of Cantonese, who were loyal for the most part to Taiwan.

Chinatown remains plagued by poverty, overcrowding, and physical deterioration; its housing and business space is largely substandard. It supports an underground economy that includes sweatshop labor (in restaurants and garment factories), counterfeiting (of trademarked luxury items), and the smuggling of illegal immigrants.

CANAL STREET

In its western reaches, Canal St marks the southern boundary of SoHo (*see p. 105*), but east of Broadway, it is definitely Chinese. At the intersection with Centre St, the former Golden Pacific National Bank (1983) is vividly decorated in blue, red, gold, and green, and styled with sweeping tile roofs and galleries. The bank, once the pride of Chinatown, collapsed in 1985, causing panic among depositors.

The pagoda-shaped kiosk of the Explore Chinatown Campaign, located in the triangle of pavement near Baxter St, was set up after the September 11 attacks to help Chinatown recover from the ensuing economic damage.

At 83–85 Mott St (corner Canal St) is an architectural mélange of East and West, housing the **Chinese Merchants' Association** and the headquarters of the On Leong Tong, a bakery and a beauty parlor.

THE TONGS OF CHINATOWN

Chinatown's *tongs*, basically neighborhood and business associations, were formed at the turn of the 20th century as immigrant aid societies. They offered legitimate services—language assistance, credit unions and loans, social outlets—and they settled disputes among individuals and between rival groups of immigrants. The two strongest were Hip Sing and On Leong, who came to control many businesses and also became involved in crime, prostitution, gambling, and drugs. Until the 1970s the *tongs* were unchallenged in Chinatown, but as the demographics changed, they lost power. On Leong was said to control Mott St, and the Hip Sings had Pell St as their turf.

The eastern end of Canal St near the Bowery, the city's second largest jewelry district, glitters with dozens of shops offering gold and diamonds. In the 1930s Jewish immigrants fleeing Nazi Germany opened stores here on the fringes of the Lower East Side, but after World War II, many jewelers moved up to Midtown around West 47th St. Most of the downtown merchants now are Asian. The imposing domed building on the corner of Canal St and the Bowery (58 Bowery), now a branch of HSBC (Hong Kong and Shanghai Banking Corporation), was built in 1924 as the Citizen's Savings Bank.

At 139 Canal St, near the ramps to the Manhattan Bridge, is the ticket booth and loading area for the legendary Fung Wah Bus, a cheap service to Boston's Chinatown. Fung Wah ("magnificent wind") began as a van service in 1997, and developed into an intercity transport company, serving Chinese and also young budget travelers. The company has been cited for federal safety violations and for using drivers who do not speak English, but has been said to provide the allure of living on the edge. The **Mahayana Buddhist Temple**, at 133 Canal St (Manhattan Bridge Plaza), is the largest Buddhist temple in Chinatown, with an imposing golden image of the Buddha.

THE MANHATTAN BRIDGE

The Manhattan Bridge, the third East River crossing, built after the Brooklyn and Williamsburg Bridges, is notable for its ceremonial approach, arch, and colonnade (1912; Carrère & Hastings; Gustav Lindenthal, bridge engineer).

Feelings ran high over the design, for though the Brooklyn Bridge, which opened in 1883, had evoked enthusiasm both as a feat of engineering and as an object of beauty, the Williamsburg Bridge, which followed in 1903, was considered ugly. The disputing parties were engineers, whose interests were primarily technical, and architects, whose goals were aesthetic. Plans for the Manhattan Bridge thus went through numerous modifications as architects and bridge commissioners came and went.

An early plan was scrapped in about 1901 and the bridge redesigned by Henry Hornbostel, an architect whose belief in "artistic" engineering resulted in a proposal which included eye-bars instead of the usual cables to support the roadway. City officials, however, preferred suspension cables, and Carrère & Hastings (designers of the New York Public Library and the Frick Museum) were hired to replace Hornbostel. The bridge, with its 1470-ft span, opened in 1909.

Meanwhile the World's Columbian Exposition in Chicago (1893), awakening public interest in Neoclassical architecture, had given birth to the City Beautiful movement. From these enthusiasms sprang plans for improving the approaches to the bridge. Carrère & Hastings, who had studied at the École des Beaux-Arts in Paris, the cradle of the Neoclassical movement, were well qualified for such an undertaking. The Manhattan approach originally featured an elliptical landscaped plaza, which surrounded the actual roadway.

The approach ends in a monumental arch and colonnade, the arch modeled after the 17th-century Porte St-Denis in Paris, the colonnade after Bernini's colonnade at St. Peter's Square in Rome. The frieze over the arch opening by Charles Cary Rumsey is said to have been inspired by the Panathenaic procession on the Parthenon frieze, suitably Americanized. It depicts a group of four Native Americans on horseback hunting buffalo. The choice of this subject matter may seem peculiar on a classical arch signaling the approach to a modern steel suspension bridge linking two boroughs of a large city, but such frontier themes were popular at the turn of the 20th century.

Flanking the arch opening are two large granite sculptural groups by Carl Augustus Heber: the *Spirit of Commerce* on the north side and the *Spirit of Industries* on the south. Above the arch opening (36ft by 40ft) is a cornice and a low attic story decorated with lions' heads. The interior of the arch is barrel-vaulted and coffered. The arch is set in the middle of a colonnade of Tuscan columns (31ft high) above which are cornices with balustrades which connect the columns to one another and to the arch.

MOTT & MULBERRY STREETS

Mott, Pell and Doyers Streets form the center of "old" Chinatown. Mott St is named after Joseph Mott, a prosperous pre-Revolutionary butcher, who also ran a tavern at what is now 143rd St and Eighth Ave. The **Eastern States Buddhist Temple** at 64 Mott St was the first Chinese Buddhist temple on the eastern seaboard, founded in 1962. The **Chinese Community Center** at 62 Mott St is run by the Chinese Consolidated Benevolent Association, formed in 1883 by established merchants to help newly arrived countrymen survive in business and in America. It provided language assistance, loans, and social contact for the early immigrants, mediated disputes, and served as a link between the Chinese and American communities.

At 32 Mott St stood Chinatown's oldest continuously operating store, **Quong Yuen Shing**, founded around 1899. It went out of business in 2003, victim of the economic downturn after the September 11 attacks, but has reopened under new management as Good Fortune Gifts. Chinatown was particularly hard hit, losing both tourists and customers who worked at the former World Trade Center. Many of the garment factories shut down for weeks, since the trucks could not make deliveries through the debris-clogged streets.

The **Church of the Transfiguration** (1801), at 25 Mott St (Mosco St), built as the Zion Episcopal Church, now serves a Roman Catholic parish, with masses given in Cantonese, Mandarin, and English. The modest rubblestone building belongs to the Georgian tradition with its triangular pediment, simple tower, and unusual pointed-arch windows. The copper-clad spire was added in 1868.

Columbus Park (opened 1897), facing Mulberry St between Bayard and Worth Sts, represents a triumph for early social reformers who spurred passage of the Small Parks Act in 1887. This park, formerly known as Mulberry Bend Park, replaced Mulberry Bend, a violent slum which reformer Jacob Riis called "the worst pigsty of all." Nowadays people use the park to practice tai ch'i, play mahjong, or simply enjoy the passing scene. Along Mulberry St facing the park are funeral homes, florists, and other related businesses, including shops that sell goods for the afterlife—fake money and paper houses, traditionally burned at the funeral to provide for the deceased.

The **Chinatown Ice Cream Factory** at 65 Bayard St (Mott and Elizabeth Sts) sells homemade ice cream that comes in flavors ranging from prosaic vanilla to exotic lichee, red bean, and green tea. (*Open daily 11am–10/11pm; T: 212 608 4170.*)

DOYERS STREET & CHATHAM SQUARE

Crooked, narrow Doyers St (*map p. 583, D2*) was originally a cart lane leading to Anthony Doyer's distillery at the southern end. The bend in Doyers St was once known as "Bloody Angle," recalling a turn-of-the-20th-century *tong* war during which the two powerful families, the Hip Sings and On Leongs, battled one another. On the site of the present Post Office at 6 Doyers St stood the Chatham Club, where Irving Berlin, born Israel Baline, waited tables. Across the street at 5–7 Doyers St is the site

of the original Chinese Opera House, which in 1910 was acquired for a mission run by Tom Noonan, an ex-convict who dispensed charity to the Bowery bums until his death in 1935. Pell and Doyers Sts are lined with beauty and barber shops, so many that Pell St is nicknamed "Haircut St."

The **former Edward Mooney house** at 18 Bowery (Pell St) is the city's oldest row house (c. 1785). Mooney, a meat wholesaler and amateur racehorse breeder, built the house on land forfeited after the Revolution by Tory James De Lancey. The house is Georgian in its proportions and in its details: the door hood, the lintels with splayed keystones, the quarter-round and round-headed windows facing Pell St. The generous number of windows reveals Mooney's wealth, since glass, manufactured in the middle colonies only after about 1740, was an expensive commodity. In the mid-19th century the house became a brothel; more recently it has been an off-track betting parlor, and is now a mortgage lender.

Facing Chatham Square at Division St and the Bowery is Liu Shih's bronze statue of Confucius, presented in 1976 as a gift from the Taiwanese government. It stands in front of **Confucius Plaza** (1976), the only new housing built in Chinatown between the 1960s and early 1980s. Division St marked the division between the farms of James De Lancey and Henry Rutgers in pre-Revolutionary New York.

Chatham Square

Chatham Square (*map p. 583, D2*), bounded by a tangle of intersecting streets (Park Row, St. James Place, Oliver St, East Broadway, Catherine St, Division St, the Bowery, Doyers St, Mott St, and Worth St), used to mark the border between Chinatown and the Lower East Side. Before the Revolution it was named for William Pitt, Earl of Chatham and Prime Minister of Great Britain; because Pitt was supportive of the colonies, the name was not changed after the British departed. The **Kimlau War Memorial** (1962; Poy G. Lee), an arch with a pagoda-style top on one of the traffic islands, is dedicated to Chinese-Americans who died in the US armed services during World War II. On another traffic island east of the arch stands a former bank building, brightly painted and topped with a traditional Chinese curved roof; built in 1977, it is one of the first buildings in Chinatown that was architecturally "Chinese." (*At the time of writing, the building was unoccupied and covered with scaffolding.*)

In the neighborhood to the south and east of Chatham Square remain several landmarks from the period of earlier immigrations. The **Mariners' Temple** (1844–45) at 12 Oliver St (corner of Henry St) was built as the Oliver Street Baptist Church when this neighborhood was just developing. It was bought by the Mariners' Temple in 1863, serving as a social mission for seamen, immigrants, and later, Bowery derelicts. Today its congregation is largely Hispanic. The building, roughly contemporary with the nearby St. James Church, is constructed of stone laid in random courses, plastered over (where visible to the street) and grooved with false joints to give it the smooth appearance characteristic of the Greek Revival style.

Between Oliver and James Sts is the small, forlorn **First Shearith Israel Graveyard** (1683), the earliest surviving burial ground of the city's first Jewish congregation (*see*

p. 54). An earlier cemetery, then outside the city, was consecrated in 1656 on land granted by Peter Stuyvesant, but its location is unknown. The earliest stone in the present graveyard dates from 1683. During the Revolutionary War, General Charles Lee placed several guns in "the Jew Burying Ground" as part of the city's fortifications; 18 Revolutionary soldiers and patriots are buried here, among them Gershom Mendes Seixas, who removed the Torah scrolls to Stratford, Connecticut, during the British occupation. As the congregation moved uptown, it established two other cemeteries, one at West 11th St and another at West 21st St.

At 32 James St between St. James Place and Madison St is the **St. James Roman Catholic Church** (1835–37), a severe brownstone Greek Revival building, the façade ornamented only by rosettes on the door lintels and a carved scroll and anthemion above the central doorway. Originally the church served Irish immigrants. Alfred E. Smith, who rose to fame as a social reformer, four-time governor, and Democratic candidate for President in 1928, was baptized here. He received his entire education at St. James School, across the street.

East Broadway: "Fouzhou Street"

East Broadway, one of the streets surrounding Chatham Square, is sometimes called "Fouzhou Street" because so many Fujianese live nearby (Fouzhou is the capital of the province of Fujian). Here are Fujianese herbal shops, hair cutters, food markets, dating services, and driving schools. Facing East Broadway from Chatham Square is a statue (1997) of Lin Ze Xu (1785–1850), a Fujianese government official known for his integrity and for resistance to the opium trade. On the base of the statue is inscribed in English and Chinese "Say no to drugs." Since New York's Fujianese are sometimes stereotyped as drug dealers, the choice of Lin made an obvious point. Furthermore, the mere presence of the statue suggests the political impact of the new immigrants, sympathetic to mainland China, for whom Lin has become, since the mid-20th century, a figure of anti-imperialism and national unity. The statue counters the older figure of Confucius, a block away, placed there by the Cantonese-speaking, generally pro-Taiwanese earlier immigrants.

LITTLE ITALY

Map pp. 582, C1–583, D1. Subway: B, D to Grand St; 6 to Canal St. Bus: M1, M103.
Mulberry St from about Canal St to Kenmare St is the spine of Little Italy, an ethnic enclave dating from the 1880s that in recent decades has become increasingly Asian. The Italian population has aged or moved away, and today Little Italy has become a tourist draw, attracting visitors to its cafés, "red sauce" restaurants, and ethnic food stores. The neighborhood is at its most lively during two annual festivals: the feast of St. Anthony of Padua, held during the first two weeks of June and centered on Sullivan St in the southern part of Greenwich Village (*map p. 580, C4*); and the feast of San Gennaro held around the week of Sept 19, and occupying several blocks of

Mulberry St. Images of the saints are carried through the streets and at night arcades of lights turn the neighborhood into a carnival.

In the neighborhood

Da Genaro's restaurant at 129 Mulberry St (corner of Hester St), named for the patron saint of Naples (San Gennaro; St Januarius), occupies the site of the original Umberto's Clam House, where in 1972 mobster Joe "Crazy Joey" Gallo was shot down while eating *scungilli* (whelks) on his 43rd birthday. At 149 Mulberry St near Grand St stands the **Stephen van Rensselaer House** (1816), covered with stucco, which dates from the Federal period and still retains its original dormers. For many years it hosted Paolucci's, another of Little Italy's old-style restaurants.

Grand St still retains some Italian food shops and cafés, offering authentic products, including fresh pasta, cheeses, cured meats, and olive oil. The Ferrara Café (founded 1892) at 195 Grand St (between Mulberry and Mott Sts) advertises itself as New York's first espresso bar and oldest *pasticceria*.

The former **Odd Fellows Hall** (1847–48) at 165 Grand St (Centre St) is one of the city's earliest Italianate buildings. This immense brownstone pile was built as the home of a fraternal and mutual aid society; apparently it was not sufficiently large, as two more stories were added in 1881–82. At the corner of Centre and Grand Sts one of the city's few antique bishop's crook lampposts remains.

THE MUSEUM OF CHINESE IN AMERICA

At the time of writing, MOCA was due to open at a new location at 211–15 Centre St (Grand and Hester Sts) in a large space designed by Maya Lin, known for the Vietnam Veterans Memorial in Washington, D.C. Map p. 582, C1. T: 212 619 4785; www.mocanyc.org.

MOCA documents the experience in the Western Hemisphere of Chinese immigrants and their descendants. The museum began (1980) as the Chinatown History Project, founded by Chinese-American historians, artists, and students, who realized that the memories of first-generation immigrants would vanish if not recorded. The collection includes humble artifacts (musical instruments, a slipper for a bound foot, a coal-heated iron like those used by immigrant laundry workers, and small-scale handmade furniture for cramped tenement spaces), as well as photos and archival documents (letters from wives in China to their husbands here, immigration papers). After more than 20 years of collecting—both personal stories and objects—the museum has one of the most important archives of Chinese life in the Americas.

At 240 Centre St is the **former Police Headquarters** (1905–09), set apart from the surrounding tenements and loft buildings by its grand scale and Baroque

flamboyance. Its grandeur was intended to enhance the image of the relatively new and rapidly expanding police force. The main entrance on Centre St is flanked by lions and embellished by a large New York coat of arms and five statues representing the five boroughs. The police moved out in 1973, and in 1987 the building was converted into luxury condominiums. The lobby is as extravagant as the exterior.

The **Storefront for Art and Architecture** at 97 Kenmare St (Mulberry St and Cleveland Pl) is a not-for-profit organization wedged into a small triangular building, designed by architect Steven Holl and artist Vito Acconci (*open Tues–Sat 11–6; T: 212 431 5795; www.storefrontnews.org*). The front panels of the building flip up or down or left or right, creating several possible configurations. Exhibitions here are often imaginative and adventurous.

NOLITA

While Chinatown has expanded into Little Italy, the neighborhood to the north, NoLIta (North of Little Italy; *map pp. 582, C1–581 D4*), has gentrified to become a kind of SoHo East. Its boundaries are roughly Houston and Broome Sts on the north and south, and Lafayette St and the Bowery on the west and east. The southern Italian families who lived here have been replaced by well-to-do urban professionals, whose pocketbooks will support the neighborhood's chic boutiques and restaurants. The tree-lined streets and low-rise architecture make it a pleasant place to stroll.

The Roman Catholic Orphan Asylum and neighborhood

The former Ravenite Social Club at 247 Mulberry St was the hangout of John Gotti (1940–2002), the boss of the Gambino crime family for many years. Gotti, known also as the Teflon Don and the Dapper Don, raised thuggish behavior to celebrity status, and was sometimes seen posing with tourists outside the club. Information collected from FBI wiretaps here was instrumental in sending him to prison. Since the Mafia departed, the building has done time as a shop for chic bags and shoes.

At 32 Prince St, on the southwest corner of Mott St, is the former **Roman Catholic Orphan Asylum** (1825–26), an unusually large Federal-style building with brownstone trim, its handsome doorway (*see p. 11*) framed with slender Corinthian columns and topped with a fanlight (now filled with stained glass). It is now St. Patrick's Convent and Girls' School.

The former **Fourteenth Ward Industrial School of the Children's Aid Society** (1888–89) at 256–58 Mott St, later the Astor Memorial School, and a Gothic Revival reminder of Little Italy's past as an immigrant slum, has been converted to apartments. Industrial schools were established by charitable organizations to fill the gap between the tenement and the public school, taking in street children and teaching them the rudiments of citizenship as well as reading and writing. The architects were Vaux & Radford; Vaux, who collaborated with Frederick Law Olmsted on Central Park, was responsible for the beautiful terra-cotta ornament.

St. Patrick's Old Cathedral

St. Patrick's Old Cathedral at 233 Mott St (Prince St) was originally the cathedral church of the see of New York and is the oldest Roman Catholic building in the city. Designed by Joseph François Mangin (co-architect of City Hall), it was begun in 1809 and finished six years later (the War of 1812 intervened). When the present St. Patrick's Cathedral on Fifth Avenue was completed in 1879, it became a parish church. The original building, an early Gothic-style church, was gutted by fire in 1866, and its present appearance only hints at its former self (*see also p. 12*). The smooth-faced, windowless façade confronting Mott St is dignified in its severity; the rubblestone side walls contain pointed-arch stained-glass windows. A low wall surrounds the churchyard, which includes a gravestone of Pierre Toussaint (1766–1853), born a slave in Haiti and revered for his ministrations to the poor and plague-stricken (best view from the rear of the church facing Mulberry St).

At 295–309 Lafayette St (filling the block between Mulberry, Houston, Lafayette, and Jersey Sts) is the imposing brick Romanesque Revival **Puck Building** (1885–86), which long served the printing industry, first as the home of the humor magazine *Puck*. At the corner of Houston St and above the main entrance on Lafayette St are figures of Puck, top-hatted and cherubic, by Caspar Buberl, an immigrant from Bohemia.

THE LOWER EAST SIDE

Map p. 583, D1–E1. Subway: F to East Broadway-Canal St. Bus: M9, M15. Lower East Side Visitor's Center (261 Broome St, between Orchard and Allen Sts; map p. 583, D1) open daily 10–4; T: 866 224 0206; www.lowereastsideny.com. The Lower East Side Business Improvement District, also at 261 Broome St, offers tours (free) of the Orchard Street Shopping District; meet at Katz's Deli (corner of Ludlow and East Houston Sts), April–Dec Sun at 11am; T: 212 226 9010. The Lower East Side Conservancy gives guided walking tours (fee) to historic sights and synagogues, including some interiors not otherwise open to visitors; T: 212 374 4100; http:nyc-jewishtours.org. In addition to guided visits to its own tenement, the Lower East Side Tenement Museum offers neighborhood tours (fee); meet at the museum's visitor center, 108 Orchard St; T: 212 431 0233; www.tenement.org.
NB: Many shops are closed on Sat, the Jewish Sabbath.

Like the rest of downtown Manhattan, the Lower East Side, long an immigrant neighborhood, is in the midst of rapid change. Chinatown is encroaching from the west and 19th-century tenements are being converted to luxury apartments. Yet the neighborhood retains something of its past—ethnic eateries, synagogues in various states of disrepair or restoration, and a street of bargain shopping. Historic institutions, for example the Educational Alliance and the Henry Street Settlement, continue to serve the neighborhood's newer immigrants.

Blue (2007; Bernard Tschumi), the luxury condo symbolic of what is happening to the Lower East Side.

HISTORY OF THE LOWER EAST SIDE

In the 18th century much of what is now the Lower East Side belonged to the city's wealthy landowners, the Rutgers family (of Dutch origin) and the De Lanceys (of French Huguenot origin). After the Revolution, loyalist James De Lancey saw his estate confiscated, broken up, and sold off as building lots, in part to butchers, grocers, cartmen and other former tenants. Henry Rutgers cut up his riverside land and leased out parcels to shipwrights, sail-makers, and rope-makers.

By 1850 the pressures of immigration were beginning to be felt, and the Lower East Side started to decline economically. Former captains' mansions on East Broadway became shops; single-family row houses were sold off for a quarter of their value of 30 years earlier, or were knocked down and replaced by tenements. The ethnic makeup of the district was also shifting. Between 1846 and 1860, large numbers of Irish immigrants sought relief in the US and many settled here, at least until the next wave of immigration swept them out. Many joined the building and maritime trades and later became municipal workers, policemen, firemen, and eventually politicians and lawyers. At mid-century Germans, both Jews and gentiles, also arrived, a group that included skilled workers and craftsmen, who actively pursued their trades, forming trade unions and working men's associations. They assimilated with relative ease and took their places in society as merchants, jewelers, clothing manufacturers, furriers, professionals, and bankers.

In 1881, however, revolutionaries assassinated Czar Alexander II of Russia, and the ensuing pogroms and political repression led to a wave of Russian and Eastern European Jewish immigration that entirely changed the Lower East Side and still affects the ethnic makeup of New York. Of the almost two million Jews who came to the US from Russia, Poland, and Romania between 1881 and 1914, many settled at least temporarily on the Lower East Side (60,000 between 1880 and 1890). At the century's end it was the most densely populated place on earth.

Most of the Jewish immigrants found work peddling or in the needle trades, whose skills could be learned quickly. They toiled 12–14 hours a day for little money and under miserable conditions. Women and children contributed by sewing, making paper flowers, and shelling nuts at home.

The high-water mark of immigration came in the early years of the 20th century; but while new arrivals were pressing at the barricades of Ellis Island, established residents were beginning to move on. They went out to Brooklyn across the East River bridges; they took the elevated railway uptown or to the Bronx; they rode the subway under the Harlem River or to Brooklyn. The immigration laws of 1924 virtually stopped all new arrivals from Eastern Europe, and as the existing population drained away, the area became less crowded and also less vital.

After national quotas were eased in 1965, new immigrants—many of them East Asian and Latino—replaced those who had left.

THE HEART OF THE NEIGHBORHOOD

Writers of the late 19th century considered **Hester St** (*map p. 583, D1*), site of the neighborhood's busiest pushcart market, the quintessential ghetto street, ringing with the shouts of vendors, the haggling and chattering of women, the cries of children who darted through the crowds playing games and making swift raids on the pushcarts. A sympathetic reporter from the *Times* in 1898 found the street scene touching and attractive. Another reporter for the same journal described it as the filthiest place on the western continent, whose inhabitants were slatternly, lawless (they had failed to empty their garbage cans at a specified hour), and indecent.

During the same period **Allen St**, then darkened and dirtied by the Second Avenue El, became a haven for prostitution. A local minister complained that the women openly solicited from the stoops of tenements adjoining his church. Michael Gold in his autobiographical novel *Jews Without Money* (1930) recalled the time when prostitutes sat out on the sidewalks in chairs sunning themselves, their legs sprawled indolently in the way of anyone who wanted to pass by.

Orchard St, named for the apple orchards on the 18th-century farm of James De Lancey, is the district's main shopping street, especially busy on Sundays. Like Hester St, it once had a pushcart market that stretched a few blocks north and south of Delancey St. For unskilled immigrants with little English, the pushcarts represented one of the few ways to eke out a living. Obstructive and insanitary, the carts were outlawed by the city in the 1930s. Today the street is a jumble of shops—some old, some new, some cluttered with merchandise, some artfully arranged. The street is closed to traffic Sunday during business hours while shoppers, hungry for bargains, finger the leather coats and winter jackets hanging on racks, or haggle with shop-owners over handbags, underwear, and home decorating fabrics.

The Eldridge Street Synagogue

Towering above the neighboring tenements on this cramped street (*map p. 583, D1*) is Congregation Khal Adath Jeshurun with Anshe Lubz ("Community of the People of Israel with the People of Lubz"), better known as the Eldridge Street Synagogue (1886–87; *for tour information, T: 212 219 0888; www.eldridgestreet.org*). Other Lower East Side synagogues had been built by Western European Jews, but this was the first established by Eastern European Ashkenazi Jews, a congregation sufficiently wealthy to hire the prestigious architectural firm of Herter Brothers to design their house of worship. It is built in a mixture of Gothic, Romanesque, and Moorish Revival styles that illustrate the mid-19th-century trend in synagogue architecture. The barrel-vaulted upstairs sanctuary is an outstanding example of synagogue decoration, with great brass chandeliers (gaslit in early days) and Victorian glass shades, a large rose window in the west wall, a towering ark carved in walnut, and elaborately designed pews.

In its early years this was the grandest synagogue on the Lower East Side, drawing so many worshipers on the high Holy Days that police were called in to control the crowds. Ben Shahn, Eddie Cantor, and Jonas Salk belonged to the congregation. But

in the 1930s, as the Jewish population of the Lower East Side shrank and the fortunes of those who remained diminished during the Depression, the building fell on hard times. The main sanctuary was sealed off, and services were held in the basement. The roof began to leak and rapid deterioration followed. The not-for-profit Friends of the Eldridge Street Synagogue, founded in 1986, raised funds for a $16-million dollar restoration, completed in 2007.

The former **Jarmulowsky's Bank** at 54–58 Canal St (Orchard and Allen Sts), founded 1873, was one of several small private Jewish banks established when financial conditions eased enough for local residents to save a few dollars. Unfortunately several of these institutions failed, taking with them savings painfully culled from sweatshops, factories, and small businesses. This bank, founded by Sender Jarmulowsky, an immigrant from Russia, survived until Aug, 1914, when the state banking superintendent closed it with assets of $654,000 and liabilities of $1,703,000. Jarmulowsky's sons, who were by then managing the bank, were indicted for fraud. The depositors eventually recovered some of their losses. Although Jarmulowsky lived uptown in Carnegie Hill, he was president of the nearby Eldridge Street Synagogue.

Lower East Side Tenement Museum

Map p. 583, D1. 97 Orchard St (Visitor center at 108 Orchard St). Open Mon 11–5:30, Tues–Fri 11–6, Sat and Sun 10:45–6. Tour tickets are sold for day-of-purchase tours and also online; reservations recommended on weekends. The visitor center has a free 25-min video on the history of the Lower East Side as well as a shop with a thoughtful selection of books on immigration, local history, etc. T: 212 431 0233; www.tenement.org.

This museum, a former tenement, was founded in 1988 to preserve the heritage of the nation's immigrants, honoring the millions who lived on the Lower East Side and in other immigrant ghettos. Five apartments in this six-story Italianate brownstone (1863) have been restored to their 19th-century appearance; a visit (*guided tour only*) recreates the experiences of the families who lived here.

The city's most famous pickle store, **Guss' Pickles**, is at 85 Orchard St near Broome St. Izzy Guss, a Russian immigrant, opened his first pickle shop in 1910, with earnings from his produce pushcart. The shop still sells quarter sours, half sours, kosher sours, sauerkraut, and olives from large barrels.

TENEMENTS

Tenements, built to exploit all available space and maximize the return for the landlord, were one of the horrors of immigrant life. They can be classified as pre-Old Law (before 1879), Old Law (1879–1901), or New Law (after 1901); in general, the earlier buildings were worse than later ones, since each successive law laid new restrictions on landlords and builders. The Tenement Museum building is a pre-Old Law tenement, built when the law made no requirements of builders.

In 1850 one Silas Wood built a "model" tenement on Cherry St "with the purpose of providing cheap lodging." His tenement, Gotham Court, was five stories tall and had about 144 two-room apartments. Six years after its completion, it housed over a thousand tenants.

In 1867 the city passed an act that promised improvement. Technically, landlords were required to provide fire escapes and to connect toilets with sewers instead of cesspools, but for every requirement the law provided a loophole. The next attempt at amelioration came in 1878 with a contest for a design that fit the standard New York 25ft by 100ft lot, and would afford safety and convenience to the tenant and profit for the landlord. The prize-winner, the "dumbbell" tenement, soon became synonymous for all that was miserable in tenement design: two tenements were constructed side by side with an airshaft, often only a foot or so wide, between them, which gave the buildings their characteristic dumbbell shape, while providing virtually no air or light to the lower rooms on the airshaft. The population of a five-story building based on this plan could and often did reach 100–150 people, since poor families sublet space. The Tenement House Act of 1879 did provide some improvements: there had to be running water either in the house or yard; buildings had to contain one toilet for each two apartments.

In 1901 reformer Lawrence Veiller helped enact a law forbidding further construction of dumbbell tenements. Instead of the narrow airshaft, the law required a light court at least 4¹/₂ ft wide. Toilets were required in each apartment and windows in each room. Unfortunately the 1901 law came too late, since by 1893 some 1,196 dumbbell tenements already blighted the Lower East Side.

THE ESSEX STREET MARKET & ITS NEIGHBORHOOD

Occupying the block of Essex St from Delancey to Rivington Sts (*map p. 583, E1*) is the **Essex Street Market** (*open Mon–Sat 8–7, individual shop hours may vary*). Built in 1940 to house pushcart peddlers whom Mayor Fiorello La Guardia legislated off the streets, the market offers food for all tastes—Latino, Jewish, and upscale urbanite: chicken gizzards, *nopales* (cactus stems), sherry vinegar, fish cheeks, prime cuts of beef, and artisanal cheeses. Schapiro's Wine, founded in 1899 and formerly on Rivington St, has a booth; the company's kosher wine, now made in upstate New York, once advertised itself as "the wine you can almost cut with a knife."

Towering over the rest of the neighborhood at 105 Norfolk St (Delancey St) is a 16-story residential tower (2007), **Blue**, by celebrity architect Bernard Tschumi. The luxury condominiums sold at prices up to nearly $4 million. Clad in rectangular panels of dark and lighter blue, the building evokes for some observers the energy of Mondrian's *Broadway Boogie Woogie*. The tower's irregular form—bulging on one side, cantilevered over a smaller neighboring building, and slanting inward on top—arises from zoning considerations and setback requirements. Blue occupies the former parking lot of Ratner's, a legendary Jewish dairy restaurant, which closed in 2003.

Seward Park High School (Ludlow, Essex, Broome, and Grand Sts), occupies the site of the old Essex Market Court House and Ludlow Street Jail. The jail held prisoners whose offenses came under the jurisdiction of the Sheriff of the County of New York as well as violators of federal laws. Prisoners with enough money could buy fancier accommodations in the jail, a system that naturally led to abuse. William M. Tweed (*see p. 86*), jailed here while serving time for defrauding the city, availed himself of these privileges: he occupied a two-room cell with flower pots on the window sills, and even had a piano to ease the tedium of prison life. Tweed died in the jail in 1878.

At 367 Grand St is **Kossar's Bialys**, a bakery apparently unchanged since it was founded in 1936 (*open Sun–Thur 6am–8pm, Fri 6–2, closed Sat*). The store's specialty, *bialys* (rolls with ground onions patted into the center of the dough), were reputedly invented by the bakers of Bialystok in Poland. Also for sale are *pletzels* (onion flatbreads), *bulkas* (small loaves), and sesame sticks. The **Bialystoker Synagogue** (1826) on Bialystoker Place (also called Willett St), originally the Willett Street Methodist Episcopal Church, is a plain late Federal building with walls of random fieldstone. The Jewish congregation from Bialystok bought the building in 1905.

EAST BROADWAY

The **Educational Alliance** at 197 East Broadway near Jefferson St (*map p. 583, E1*), organized in 1889, was one of the most important early agencies formed to help the massive influx of Eastern European Jews adapt to the alien culture of America. The Alliance was founded by a group of German-Jewish philanthropists, many of them immigrants who had arrived a generation earlier, prospered, and moved out of the

ghetto. These "uptown" Jews saw Americanization as the key to self-reliance and freedom from want. The Alliance held classes for immigrant children to prepare them for the public school system and gave courses in English and civics to adults to ready them for naturalization. It provided facilities for taking showers, an important service in a tenement-ridden slum where bathtubs were rare.

Relations between the "uptown" Jews who founded the Alliance and the "downtown" Jews who used it remained prickly for a long time. The assimilated uptowners found the new immigrants backward, "oriental," and slovenly; people who needed lessons in hygiene as well as English. The "greenhorns," or new immigrants, found the German Jews condescending and insensitive to their natural desire to perpetuate their culture. Today the Alliance carries on its work, although those who use its facilities are Puerto Rican, Asian, and black as well as Jewish.

Opposite Jefferson St is the **Seward Park Branch of the New York Public Library** (1909; Babb, Cook & Welch), 192 East Broadway, founded as an early branch of the public system and built with funds given by Andrew Carnegie. It offered a large collection of books in Yiddish, and in its early years long lines sometimes formed at the door as people waited to get in. Today the collection includes books in English, Chinese, Spanish, Russian, and Hebrew, as well as Yiddish.

Seward Park (opened 1903) is named after William H. Seward (1801–72), governor of the state of New York, US senator, and secretary of state under Abraham Lincoln. In 1898 settlement workers Lillian Wald (*see box opposite*) and Charles Stover founded the Outdoor Recreation League to build playgrounds on city-owned land for children who otherwise played in the streets. Across from Seward Park is the **Forward Building** (1912; 173–75 East Broadway, Jefferson and Rutgers Sts), built for the *Jewish Daily Forward*, the country's most influential Yiddish daily newspaper. The first-floor frieze includes portraits of Karl Marx and Friedrich Engels. In the later years of the 19th century, the Lower East Side was a hotbed of political activity with clubs and organizations—mostly of left-wing persuasions—meeting in the cafés and meeting halls. Some organizations put out their own propaganda; the most successful of these left-wing publications was the *Forward*, but the Yiddish Communist daily, *Freiheit*, and Emma Goldman's anarchist *Mother Earth* were also published on the Lower East Side. The *Jewish Daily Forward* (founded 1897) rose to prominence under Abraham Cahan (1860–1951), an immigrant from Lithuania. Cahan dictated the editorial policy of the paper, which had close ties to the Socialist Party, but reported on the whole spectrum of immigrant Jewish experience. Intimate in tone and straightforward in diction, the *Forward* told of the everyday events of the Lower East Side. Cahan wrote about the the iniquities of bosses who imposed unbearable working conditions; his paper explained baseball to the greenhorn and offered advice on the use of the pocket handkerchief. The paper's most famous feature was the *Bintel Brief* ("Bundle of Letters"), a column in which readers unburdened themselves of personal problems. A mother writes that her adult daughter ridicules the old-country modes of dress, speech, and even cooking. A working father worries because his daughters hang around with street boys, no better than gangsters. In 1974 the paper moved to 49 East

33rd St. In the 1930s the circulation was 275,000; in 2000, published as a weekly, it had a circulation of some 26,000 in English and about 7,000 in Yiddish.

THE HENRY STREET SETTLEMENT

The buildings of the **Henry Street Settlement** (1827, later additions; *map p. 583, E1*) at 263–67 Henry St (near Montgomery St) attract attention architecturally as late-Federal residences, constructed in what was once a semi-rural setting at the edge of town. They were built for prosperous shop-owners, ship's captains from the South Street Seaport area, and others in the maritime trades. Only the central building has survived with original details intact: the wrought-iron stoop railing with open box newel posts; the areaway fence with knobby finials (sometimes said to be acorns symbolizing hospitality, an attribute also attached to the pineapple, which appears as a finial on the newel post of no. 263); the louvered shutters on the first-story windows; and the paneled doorway flanked by slender columns. The settlement's arts' programs take place in the Henry De Jur Playhouse and the Abrons Arts Center, 466 Grand St near Pitt St (*T: 212 598 0400; www.henrystreetarts.org*).

Lillian Wald (1867–1940)

Lillian Wald, who founded the Henry Street Settlement, remains one of New York's great figures, a compassionate, gentle, yet shrewd and worldly woman who devoted herself tirelessly to the poor. Awakened to a sense of vocation by a visit to an immigrant home, she moved to a fifth-floor walk-up at 27 Jefferson St and began her rounds, fighting ignorance, disease, malnutrition, rats, and bigotry. She raised money, largely through the assistance of philanthropist Jacob Schiff, who gave two of the Henry St buildings to the settlement. Coming from a bourgeois German-Jewish family, Wald gradually grew to accept these strange Eastern European immigrants as her own people and became an important liaison between the "uptown" and "downtown" Jews, who often found themselves at odds with one another.

St. Augustine's Episcopal Church (1827–29) at 290 Henry St was originally the All Saints' Free Church, "free" because the pews did not have to be rented. At the back of the balcony in this small Georgian-Gothic church built of Manhattan schist are two "Slave Galleries," where black worshipers were segregated from the rest of the congregation. Although slaves were legally emancipated in 1799 in New York State, many were not actually freed until later. The congregation is now largely African-American.

ON & BELOW EAST HOUSTON ST

Russ & Daughters (*open Mon–Sat 9–7, Sun 8–5:30; T: 212 475 4880; map p. 581, E4*)

at 179 Houston St (Allen and Orchard Sts) was founded by Joel Russ, an immigrant from a *shtetl* in Eastern Europe. He began selling herring from a wagon in 1911 and opened his first store on Orchard St in 1914. His three daughters Ida, Anne, and Hattie became partners the business, allegedly because they were more pleasant to the customers than their father was. The store sells caviar, smoked and salted fish, salads, and dried fruit and nuts.

Katz's Delicatessen, at 205 Houston St (Ludlow St), is an old-style deli with a large dining room (*open daily from 8am until at least 8:45pm; T: 212 254 2246; www.katzdeli.com*). Founded in 1888, it is still famous for its jaw-stretching, mouth-watering pastrami sandwiches, and for its slogan, "Send a salami to your boy in the army," which was coined in World War II.

On the roof of Red Square (1989), an apartment building whose name aptly describes its color and shape, at 250 East Houston St (Aves A and B), a **statue of Lenin** salutes downtown Manhattan with a stiffly upraised arm. Commissioned by the Soviet government but never put on display because the Soviet Union unraveled, the statue was recovered from a dacha outside Moscow and installed here in 1994. A randomly numbered clock covers the water tower.

Congregation Anshe Chesed and Chasam Sopher Synagogue

Congregation Anshe Chesed (1850; Alexander Saeltzer), at 172 Norfolk St, is the oldest surviving structure in the city built as a synagogue, and the original home of New York's third Jewish congregation (after Shearith Israel and B'nai Jeshurun). Designed by the architect of the Astor Library (now the Public Theater), it was once resplendent with Gothic Revival pointed-arch windows and delicate tracery. Its various owners reflect the successive waves of Jewish immigration in the neighborhood: built by a German congregation, Anshe Chesed ("People of Kindness"), it later housed a Hungarian immigrant group, and eventually became Congregation Anshe Slonim ("People of Slonim"), named for a fondly-remembered village in Poland. Anshe Slonim, dwindling in size and resources, abandoned the building in 1974. In the early 1980s it was sealed against vandalism and threatened with demolition. Sculptor Angel Orensanz bought the building (1986) and restored it; today as the Angel Orensanz Foundation and Center for the Arts, it is used for performances and exhibits.

Chasam Sopher Synagogue (1853), at 8 Clinton St (near East Houston St; *map p. 581, F4*), is the second oldest surviving synagogue in the city, built for a German-Jewish congregation which moved uptown in 1886. A group from Poland purchased the property and renamed it Chasam Sopher ("Seal of the Scribe") to honor Moshe Sofer (or Schreiber, in the Germanized form), a scholar and rabbi, born in Frankfurt in 1762. This red-brick building is constructed in the round-arch Romanesque Revival style, although its appearance has been altered by the loss of the original parapets topping off the towers.

Rivington Street

Rivington St (*map pp. 581, F4–583, D1*) is named after James Rivington (1724–1803),

publisher of *Rivington's New York Gazetteer*, a Tory newspaper which attacked the American revolutionary movement. Rivington's sentiments and abrasive personality earned him the hostility of American patriots, who destroyed his presses, and stole his type fonts, a serious theft since no American foundries produced type of the same high quality as Rivington's imported English fonts. Undaunted he returned to England and got new equipment, came back to New York, and started another loyalist newspaper. In 1781, he had a change of heart, and became a spy for General Washington.

Streit's Matzoh Company, 150 Rivington St (at Suffolk St), was founded in 1916 (*open Mon–Thur 9–4:30; T: 212 475 7000; www.streitsmatzos.com*). It is the sole remaining bakery in Manhattan producing matzoh, an unleavened bread used especially during Passover, turning out some 2.5 million pounds during the holiday. The building is currently for sale; Streit's long tenure on Rivington St, it seems, may soon be over.

The **Hotel on Rivington**, at 107 Rivington St (Ludlow and Essex Sts), arrived in 2005, a glassy, high-style high rise in a brick low-rise neighborhood. On the ground floor is THOR (an anagram of the hotel's name), a restaurant, with a café open to the street in good weather (*T: 212 796 8040; www.hotelonrivington.com*).

GREENWICH VILLAGE

Map pp. 580–81. Subway 1 to Christopher St-Sheridan Square; A, B, C, D, F, V to West 4th St; N, R, or W to 8th St-NYU. Bus M1, M3, M5, M6, M20.

Greenwich Village is—or was—America's bohemia, its Left Bank, a cradle of creativity and individuality and artistic fulfillment. Novelists have pounded out their masterworks here; the little theater movement began here; Abstract Expressionists developed a new form of painting in Village studios; "Beat" poets, anarchists, advocates of birth control and free love have vocalized their ideas in the Village's living rooms, cafés, and coffee houses. Today the Village is no longer the center of New York's artistic life. The bars and coffee houses where Dylan Thomas, Eugene O'Neill, Jack Kerouac, and their friends drank, spouted poetry, or observed the human condition are largely gone, though some have become sites of pilgrimage. Nevertheless the Village's irregular streets and small-scale architectural survivals still make much of the neighborhood rewarding to explore.

HISTORY OF GREENWICH VILLAGE

When Washington Square was still marshland traversed by Minetta Brook, a Native American settlement stood in present-day Greenwich Village. The Dutch divided the land into farms. Under the British the area became known as Greenwich (Green Village), a name that first appears in city records in 1713. A few large landholders dominated the landscape: Trinity Church in the West Village; Sir Peter Warren, who purchased 300 acres in 1744; and such established families as the De Lanceys, Lispenards, and Van Cortlandts. By the 1790s, however, the estates were being broken up as the city spread northward, in part fleeing epidemics of yellow fever and other diseases, and in 1799 the streets were mapped.

Between 1825 and 1850 the population of the Village quadrupled. Since its inhabitants were predominantly native born, the area became known as the "American Ward," a title that lost its accuracy toward the end of the century. By 1870 the Village had become a backwater, fashionable commerce passing it by, leaving a vacuum filled by immigrants. First came the Irish and a black population who settled south of Washington Square; they were displaced by Italians in the 1890s and a second, poorer, wave of Irish who settled around Sheridan Square. Federal, Greek Revival, and Italianate row houses gave way to tenements, while shops and hotels were converted to warehouses or manufacturing lofts suitable for exploiting immigrant labor.

Around the turn of the 20th century, the Village entered its halcyon period. Because of its relative isolation, its historic charm, and the indifference of a foreign

population who had their own concerns, the Village attracted a radical, avant-garde element of American society. Here were cheap rents and freedom from the late-Victorian sexual and material values that dominated middle-class American culture. Soon the place swarmed with radical social and artistic activity: Max Eastman founded *The Masses* (1910), a paper whose publication was suppressed in 1917 because it opposed the war; the *Seven Arts* (founded 1916), whose columns integrated political and artistic ideas, met a similar fate. Clubs like the "A" Club and the Liberal Club became forums for woman suffrage, birth control, anarchy, and free love.

Among the theater groups flourishing in the opening decades of the 20th century were the Provincetown Players, whose productions displayed the talents of such playwrights and performers as Eugene O'Neill, Edna St. Vincent Millay, and Bette Davis. The Theater Guild, which started as the Washington Square Players, moved uptown in 1919 and became an innovative force in American theater. Resident Village writers included Sherwood Anderson, Theodore Dreiser, John Dos Passos, and Van Wyck Brooks as well as poets E.E. Cummings, Hart Crane, and Marianne Moore.

The isolation of the Village came to an end when Seventh Avenue South was rammed through it in the 1920s, and in the 1930s a second subway line linked the Village to the rest of the city. Real estate developers began tearing down the old row houses and replacing them with apartments, a process that accelerated after World War II. Still, for about a decade after the war, the Village remained central to the city's counterculture. In its bars—the Minetta Tavern and especially the San Remo Café (MacDougal St at Bleecker St)—the original members of the Beat generation hung out. (Jack Kerouac, Allen Ginsberg, and Gregory Corso lived elsewhere because the Village was already too expensive: only William Burroughs, whose parents sent him a monthly allowance, lived in the Village, on Bedford St.) Others who drank at the San Remo during its heyday were James Agee, Merce Cunningham, John Cage, William Styron, and W.H. Auden.

Avant-garde painters also congregated in the Village. The Cedar Street Tavern (which used to be at 24 University Place, but was originally on Cedar St) was their favored watering-hole, a working-class bar where Willem de Kooning, Jackson Pollock, and Franz Kline caroused. During the folk revival of the 1960s, such artists as Simon and Garfunkel, Joan Baez, and the most famous of all, Bob Dylan, followed an older generation of folk musicians (Woodie Guthrie and Pete Seeger) to the Village.

Because of its long-standing tolerance, the Village had a large homosexual community for many years and has been a base for feminist and gay activists, but it also attracts middle-class and professional people who, perhaps because of the traditional Village sense of community, have frequently and visibly exercised themselves in political and social causes.

SHERIDAN SQUARE & BLEECKER STREET

Christopher Park (Christopher St at Seventh Ave South; *map p. 580, C3*) is often mistaken for Sheridan Square, since it contains a statue (1936; Joseph Pollia) of General Philip Sheridan (1831–88). Sheridan, a successful Union general during the Civil War and a ruthless exterminator of Native Americans thereafter, is remembered for the (oft misquoted) remark, "the only good Indians I saw were dead." The park also contains George Segal's *Gay Liberation* (1992), two same-sex couples, all four cast in bronze and painted stark white, a work appropriately sited, since Christopher Street was long the center of the Village's gay community. Sheridan Square (bounded by Washington Place, Barrow St, and West 4th St) has a pleasant small garden, but is otherwise undistinguished, though its name is well known. The classic *WPA New York City Guide* (1939) called it "the Times Square of Greenwich Village."

THE STONEWALL RIOTS

The riots at the Stonewall Inn, 53 Christopher St, were a turning point in the struggle for gay civil rights. In the early morning hours of June 28, 1969, police raided the bar, an easy target as it operated without a liquor license and apparently had connections to organized crime. Gay patrons usually met police intrusions passively, submitting to arrest without protest because they feared publicity. This night, however, a hostile crowd gathered on Christopher St; customers and passers-by threw paving stones and bottles at the police and attempted to firebomb the bar when the outnumbered police barricaded themselves inside. The rioting, which continued for several days, presaged a new militancy among gays. Gay Pride parades, held toward the end of June in many cities worldwide, commemorate the uprising.

The Northern Dispensary and Gay Street

The **Northern Dispensary**, bounded by Waverly Place, Grove St, and Christopher St, is a triangular building on a triangular plot, the only public building from the Federal period still standing. Built in 1831 by a local mason and carpenter, this austere little brick building offered free medical care to the poor (Edgar Allan Poe was treated for a cold in 1837) and continued to do so for more than 150 years. The vagaries of Greenwich Village geography make it possible for the building to have two different sides facing a single street and one side facing two streets, since Waverly Place forks at its southeast corner and Christopher St joins Grove St along its northern façade.

Crooked, block-long **Gay St**, between Waverly Place and Christopher St, is still graced by several small, dormered Federal houses. In the 19th century, Scottish weavers lived here, and off and on until about 1920 the area was a residential enclave for the Village's black population. During Prohibition it harbored the Pirate's Den, a

speakeasy where the waiters reputedly refused to give change. Novelist Ruth McKenney, who lived at no. 14, made Waverly Place famous in her play *My Sister Eileen*, later adapted as the musical comedy *Wonderful Town*, which recounted her adventures in the bohemia of the 1930s.

St. Joseph's Church

St. Joseph's Church at 371 Sixth Ave (Waverly Pl and Washington Pl) is the city's second oldest Roman Catholic Church building (after "old" St. Patrick's; *see p. 117*) and one of its earliest (1833) Greek Revival churches. The architect was John Doran, about whom little is known. The main façade belongs to the then-emerging Greek Revival tradition, with its smooth surface, two large Doric columns, low pediment, and frieze. The corner quoins and the rubblestone masonry on the side walls hark back to the Federal period; the arched windows on the front date from 1885, during a restoration after a fire. John McCloskey (1810–85), an early rector, became America's first cardinal. The interior preserves many of the original architectural features, but suffers from the addition of stained-glass windows.

WASHINGTON SQUARE

Washington Square (*map pp. 580, C4–581, D4*), once marshland though which Minetta Brook wandered on its way to the Hudson River, is often considered the heart of Greenwich Village. The area's first inhabitants, after the Native Americans, were some black slaves freed by the Dutch beginning in 1644 and granted land for farming. Toward the end of the 18th century the land became a potter's field and a hanging ground. In 1826 the field was converted to a parade ground and in 1827 the park was laid out, attracting the well-to-do, whose houses rose along its perimeter. In 1835 the park was the site of the first public demonstration of the telegraph by New York University professor Samuel F.B. Morse. In 1837 New York University constructed its first building on the east side of the park, a handsome Gothic Revival building.

In the early 1950s Robert Moses, then Parks' Commissioner and always a highway advocate, decided to push a highway over, under, or through the park to ease downtown traffic on Fifth Avenue, a project that Villagers defeated after a decade-long struggle. In the 1960s folk singers performed regularly by the fountain. Today the park swarms with activity during good weather: parents and children, students, chess players, street performers—and the occasional drug dealer.

Washington Arch and its sculpture

Washington Arch (dedicated 1895), designed by Stanford White, modeled on the Arc de Triomphe in Paris, dominates the northern entrance to Washington Square Park. The present marble arch replaced a temporary wood and plaster arch erected (1889) to commemorate the centennial of George Washington's inauguration. Henry James, returning to New York after a long sojourn in Europe, had a low opinion of the arch, calling it "the

lamentable little Arch of Triumph which bestrides these beginnings of Washington Square—lamentable because of its poor and lonely and unaffiliated state ... this melancholy monument." Fifth Avenue ran through the arch until 1964, when the park was redesigned and closed to traffic at the urging of Village residents.

The frieze is carved with a design of 13 large stars, 42 small stars, and the initial "W" repeated at intervals between emblems of War and Peace; in the spandrels are figures of Victory. Sculpted against the north side of the eastern pier is *Washington in War* (1916; Hermon A. MacNeil), the commander-in-chief flanked by *Fame* (right) and *Valor*. On the west pier is *Washington in Peace* (1918; A. Stirling Calder), showing the statesman with *Justice* and *Wisdom*, holding a book inscribed "exitus acta probat" ("the end justifies the deed"). The sculptor was the father of Alexander Calder.

Washington Square North

Throughout the 19th century attractive row houses faced the square on three sides, but now only Washington Square North, from Fifth Avenue to University Place, suggests the former gentility of this neighborhood. William Dean Howells, editor and critic, took note of the economic gulf between the "international shabbiness which has invaded the southern border" and the "old-fashioned American respectability which keeps the north side of the Square in vast mansions of red brick." Henry James, though he did not live in the neighborhood very long, expressed fondness for Washington Square, which, he said, had "a kind of established repose which is not of frequent occurrence in other quarters of the long, shrill city; it has a riper, richer, more honorable look."

The western portion of the street was developed (late 1820s–50s) by individual owners, and the houses reflect various styles—Federal, Greek Revival, and Italianate. Nos. 21–23 are Greek Revival mansions (1835–36) with columned doorways, long parlor windows, and fine ironwork, considered in its day especially suited to park settings. The parlor window balcony at no. 21, with anthemion and Greek key motifs combined on a wheel, is especially handsome.

The earliest house on the square (no. 20) is one of the city's few remaining Federal mansions, constructed 1828–29 as a country residence and converted into apartments in 1880 by Henry Hardenbergh, architect of the Plaza Hotel. The keystone and blocks in the arched doorway and the panels in the lintels are decorated with a vermiform design.

The original buildings from 18 Washington Square North to Fifth Avenue have been demolished, including Henry James's grandmother's Greek Revival house (no. 18), which provided the setting for his 1880 novel *Washington Square*. In 1951 the entire site was sold for an apartment house, dismaying the locals, who waged a losing battle against what they considered the wanton development.

The houses extending from Fifth Avenue east to University Place, nos. 1–13 Washington Square North, are known simply as **The Row**. Built in 1831–33, they

Greek Revival row houses on Washington Square North.

form one of the city's first examples of controlled urban design (*see also p. 13*). The fronts are red brick; the basement stories and trim are marble, as are the porches and massive balustrades. Along the street runs an iron fence with anthemia, lyres, and Greek key motifs. Yet even this fine row has not escaped alteration. The house at no. 3 is a Victorian replacement. Today the buildings are used by New York University. Among the Row's famous residents have been Edith Wharton, Edward Hopper, William Dean Howells, John Dos Passos (who wrote *Manhattan Transfer* at no. 3), and architect Richard Morris Hunt (who lived at no. 2 from 1887–95).

A half block north on the east side of the avenue is **Washington Mews** (Fifth Ave and University Pl), a private alley. The buildings on its north side were stables built in the 19th century, while those on the south were built in the 1930s on land formerly part of the back gardens of the houses facing Washington Square.

NEW YORK UNIVERSITY

New York University (*map p. 581, D4*) was founded in 1831 by a group of business and professional men including Albert Gallatin, secretary of the Treasury under Thomas Jefferson. The university, nonsectarian and "modern" in its curriculum, offered practical as well as classical courses to a middle-class student body, providing an alternative to Episcopalian and conservative Columbia College. Today it is a highly regarded university, enrolling more than 50,000 students in its undergraduate colleges and graduate schools. Among its early faculty members was Samuel F.B. Morse, painter, sculptor, and inventor of the telegraph and Morse code.

For years the school has been Greenwich Village's largest landowner, which has prompted confrontations with residents over expansion plans. During the early 1960s architects Philip Johnson and Richard Foster produced a master plan to unify the campus which, though originally more ambitious, resulted only in three bulky buildings faced with bright red sandstone—the Tisch Building, the Meyer Physics Building, and Bobst Library. More recently NYU has expanded into surrounding neighborhoods. South of the square the University demolished a house on West 3rd St, where Edgar Allan Poe lived in 1844–45 while writing "The Raven," and "The Cask of Amontillado." The campus has also extended northward toward Union Square.

The university once had an uptown campus on University Heights in the Bronx, designed by Stanford White, but sold it during a period of fiscal crisis (for both the city and the university) in 1973. Successful fundraising has resulted in the building boom as well as the transformation of NYU from a regional university to a nationally recognized research facility.

The Silver Center

The Silver Center for Arts and Science, at the corner of Washington Square East and Washington Place, replaces a Gothic Revival structure torn down in 1894, whose tower rooms were rented to students, including Winslow Homer, Walt Whitman, and inventor Samuel Colt. Today it houses the university's fine arts museum, the Grey Art

Gallery (*entrance at 33 Washington Pl; open Tues, Thur, Fri 11–6; Wed 11–8; Sat 11–5; closed Sun, Mon, major holidays; T: 212 998 6780; www.nyu.edu/greyart*). The gallery mounts imaginative and often adventurous exhibitions—both from its own collection and from other sources—that have drawn praise for their high quality; many emphasize the historical, cultural, and social contexts of the art they display. The permanent collection is strong in American paintings from 1940 onward, including work by Romare Bearden, Elaine de Kooning, Helen Frankenthaler, Arshile Gorky, Adolph Gottlieb, Kenneth Noland, and Ad Reinhardt. Picasso's monumental public sculpture *Bust of Sylvette* (*see p. 140*), belongs to the collection. Other strengths include European prints, and contemporary Asian art.

The **Brown Building** at 29 Washington Pl (Greene St), which now houses NYU science laboratories, is named for Frederick Brown, a realtor and art patron, who bought it and gave it to NYU. It is infamous as the site of a disastrous industrial fire (*see box*).

THE TRIANGLE SHIRTWAIST COMPANY FIRE

Built in 1900 as a ten-story manufacturing loft, the building cost $400,000 to construct. The owners declined to have a sprinkler system installed for another $5,000 because they considered the building fireproof. On March 25, 1911, fire broke out at about 4:30pm in the upper stories where the shirtwaist company employed some 500 workers, mainly Jewish and Italian immigrant girls. Most of the stairwell doors had been locked to prevent employees from leaving their posts or stealing; the few available stairways were narrow and winding; the fire escape, unable to bear the weight of the fleeing workers, tore free from the wall; and the fire department ladders reached up only six stories. Before the fire was brought under control, perhaps 20mins later, 146 workers had died, most jumping for their lives and perishing on the pavement ten floors below. The owners were acquitted of manslaughter and received some $65,000 more in insurance than they paid out in claims (a profit of $6,445 per victim). The fire, however, eventually brought about improved safety regulations for the workplace and still remains a landmark event in the history of labor reforms.

Washington Square South

NYU buildings, including the massive red sandstone Bobst Library (1973; Philip Johnson and Richard Foster), dominate Washington Square South. The newest addition is the Kimmel Center for University Life (2001; Roche, Dinkeloo and Associates), which contains student lounges, offices, dining rooms, and the Skirball Center Theater, the largest performing arts space south of 42nd St.

Judson Memorial Church

At 55 Washington Square South (Thompson St) stands the Judson Memorial Church

(*map. 581, D4*), affiliated with the Baptist Church and United Church of Christ. It was named by its founder Edward Judson after his father Adoniram Judson (1788–1850), first Baptist missionary to Burma and compiler of an English-Burmese dictionary. The younger Judson focused his missionary zeal close to home, building the church with its back door on the edge of an immigrant neighborhood but facing the bluebloods of Washington Square North across the park, thus setting the congregation on the path of social and political activism it still follows. The adjoining campanile and Judson Hall were intended as fundraisers for the ministry of the church. In recent years the church has sold off real estate to support its programs and revitalize its historic building.

With the help of contributions from eminent Baptists, including John D. Rockefeller, the church hired architect Stanford White to design the complex and chose leading artists to decorate the church. This is in fact one of only four churches designed by White (1892), and is considered a masterpiece. The building and adjoining square bell-tower, built of amber Roman brick with terra-cotta moldings and panels of colored marble, are generally Romanesque Revival in style, influenced by Stanford White's Italian travels, though White included Byzantine and Renaissance elements as well. The two-story hooded doorway between the church proper and the adjacent campanile (now belonging to NYU) is one of the building's finer features.

The style of the Meeting Room inside (*open during services and events*) is simple, reflecting the emphasis of Baptist worship on preaching and baptism. The 17 **stained-glass windows**, by John La Farge, the largest collection in the country, are remarkable both for their design and their technique. La Farge pioneered opalescent glass, said to be America's only original contribution to the Art Nouveau movement, and his technique was later widely imitated by Louis Comfort Tiffany and others. The opalescent glass here imitates marble and stone, and the images in the tall round-arched windows suggest—though in two dimensions instead of three—the niche sculptures of Italian Renaissance masters. Judson had hoped to commemorate Baptist missionaries in these figures, but the windows cost more than $1,000 apiece and the realities of fundraising curtailed Judson's plan. Some of the faces of the saints and patriarchs depicted are said to depict donors. At the south end is a marble baptistery with a decorative panel designed by Augustus Saint-Gaudens, the cost of which ($5,000) was donated by Joseph Blachley Hoyt, who made a fortune selling belts and shoes.

MACDOUGAL STREET, MINETTA LANE & BLEECKER STREET

The Café Wha? at 115 MacDougal St (West 3rd St; *map p. 580, C4*) dates back to the 1960s when Bob Dylan, Janis Joplin, and Jimi Hendrix played here. The **Provincetown Playhouse** at 133 MacDougal St (West 4th and West 3rd Sts) was founded by struggling actors and writers as a Cape Cod summer theater (1915).

St. Anthony, detail of a window by John La Farge (c. 1892). The window memorializes the Rev. John B. Walton (1810–70) and his wife Rebecca (1810–81), a Baptist missionary team.

Eugene O'Neill joined the group and one of his plays, *Bound East for Cardiff*, achieved such success that the Provincetown Players opened a New York season in 1916 using the parlor floor of a house at 139 MacDougal St. In 1917 they remodeled the present building—then a stable and bottling works—into a small theater. Among the plays first produced were *The Emperor Jones* and *The Hairy Ape* by O'Neill, whose work changed the shape of American drama. The company went under after the stock market crash of 1929; after many years of hosting independently produced plays, the theater was taken over by the theater department of NYU in 1998.

The building at no. **137 MacDougal St** once housed the Liberal Club, with Polly Holliday's restaurant downstairs, a famous eating and meeting place for artists and intellectuals in the first decades of the 20th century. Polly's lover, anarchist Hippolyte Havel, served as cook and waiter, and gave the place its own cachet by shouting "bourgeois pigs!" and other insults at the patrons, who nonetheless remained loyal. Another watering place, whose site is now a small garden at the southwest corner of West 4th St and Sixth Avenue, was the Golden Swan, known by its intimates as the Hell Hole, whose clientele included thugs as well as bohemians, and which later provided the setting and some characters for O'Neill's *The Iceman Cometh*.

Minetta Lane commemorates Minetta Brook, which flowed from former hills near Fifth Avenue and 21st St to the Hudson River near Charlton St. Some sources say the name comes from a Native American name, *Manetta* ("devil water"); others say the Dutch called it *Mintje Kill* ("little stream"). Minetta St, which intersects Minetta Lane a half-block west, follows the course of the brook. The walls of the **Minetta Tavern** at Minetta Lane and 113 MacDougal St, which opened in 1937, are covered with pictures of illustrious clients. Perhaps the tavern's most unusual patron was the legendary Joe Gould, whose exploits and eccentricities were chronicled by *New Yorker* writer Joseph Mitchell. A Harvard graduate, Gould lived in the Village by his wits and on the charity of friends for three decades, gathering material for his magnum opus, "An Oral History of Our Time." The work, consisting of innumerable conversations, was reputed to have reached 11 million words when Gould died in a mental institution in 1957. It was never found.

MacDougal-Sullivan Gardens Historic District

The MacDougal-Sullivan Gardens Historic District is a group of 24 houses (1844–50) south of Bleecker St (MacDougal St and Sullivan St) sharing a common back garden. In the mid-19th century this land belonged to Nicholas Low, a banker, land speculator, and legislator, who subdivided the property and built the houses as an investment. Although a large immigrant population altered the social makeup of the neighborhood in the late 19th century, the Low family resisted the temptation to tear down the houses and replace them with more profitable tenements. Then in 1920 William Sloane Coffin, scion of the W. & J. Sloane furniture company, hit upon the idea of modernizing the old row houses to provide moderate-cost housing for professionals. He bought the block and converted the buildings to apartments, selling off the houses facing Bleecker and Houston Sts to finance the project. Although the façades

have been significantly altered, the district remains interesting as an example of early urban renewal and for creating a common garden from small individual plots.

Bleecker Street

Bleecker St (*map pp. 580, C4–581, D4*) is named after Anthony Bleecker, an early 19th-century man of letters, who owned the land ceded to the city for the street. In this part of the Village it was the main street of the immigrant Italian neighborhood, and became the boulevard of bohemia in the 1950s. The San Remo at the corner of Bleecker and MacDougal Sts was a favorite bar with the Beat generation. Le Figaro (186 Bleecker St), a coffee house, also remains from those days, though the clientele has changed. The legendary Bleecker St Cinema at no. 144, where viewers saw such then-avant-garde films as Kenneth Anger's *Scorpio Rising* and Jonas Mekas's *The Brig*, fell victim to real estate pressures and closed in 1990. Of the street's famous entertainment venues, only the Bitter End (147 Bleecker St) remains.

The building at **160 Bleecker St** (Thompson St), now called the Atrium, was originally Mills House No. 1 (1896; Ernest Flagg), a philanthropic low-income housing project, and later also the home of the Village Gate, a venue for music, comedy, and theater. During its glory days the great jazzmen of the 1960s and '70s displayed their talents here, and the revue *Jacques Brel is Alive and Well and Living in Paris* delighted audiences for four years. The club closed in 1994. Flagg designed the Singer Building (*see p. 75*) and homes for the wealthy, including the Scribner family, but he was also interested in high-density housing for the less affluent. This building, palatial in scale but cut up into tiny single rooms, was intended for men who could not afford boarding-house rates. It was named for Darius Ogden Mills, who financed it expecting only a modest five percent profit. With some justification *Scribner's* magazine described Mills House as "A Palace at Twenty Cents a Night." Its 1,500 rooms faced either the streets or the open, grassy interior courts, and the hotel had modern bathrooms, lounges, restaurants, and smoking rooms. Eventually it deteriorated into the Greenwich Hotel, with a down-and-out clientele.

La Guardia Place

On the east side of La Guardia Place (Bleecker and West 3rd Sts; *map p. 581, D4*) is Neil Estern's **statue of Fiorello La Guardia** (1994), who was born in the nieghborhood at 177 Sullivan St in a building that collapsed in 1987. The statue depicts the short, stocky mayor (*see box overleaf*) open-mouthed in mid-sentence, gesticulating with his hands, and striding forward. As the sculptor said, "He was always railing against something, some injustice or corruption."

The New York chapter of the American Institute of Architects, along with several other architectural institutions, is located in the **Center for Architecture** at 536 La Guardia Place. The galleries offer rotating exhibitions (*open Mon–Fri 9–8, Sat 11–5; closed Sun; T: 212 683 0023; www.aiany.org/centerforarchitecture*).

Installed in the courtyard of the apartment complex called Silver Towers (south of Bleecker St between Mercer St and La Guardia Pl) is a monumental sculpture

modeled from a smaller work (1934) by Pablo Picasso, entitled **Bust of Sylvette**. The original, representing the profile of a girl with a ponytail, was only 2ft high, painted on a piece of bent metal. The concrete enlargement (1967) by Norwegian sculptor Carl Nesjar is 36ft tall and weighs 60 tons.

Fiorello La Guardia (1882–1947)

Mayor from 1934–45, Fiorello H. La Guardia was renowned for his fighting spirit and ferocious temper, his boundless energy and ambition, and his facility in seven languages. Born in 1882 to a Jewish mother (from Trieste) and an agnostic Italian father, raised as an Episcopalian, married first to a Catholic and then a Lutheran, La Guardia was a living example of the city's ethnic diversity. He was a liberal, a reformer, and an irate opponent of graft.

A shrewd politician himself, he nonetheless professed contempt for politicians calling them "tin horn gamblers," but was usually able to turn his political independence to his own advantage. When he campaigned in Little Italy he carried a copy of *Il Progresso* and spoke Italian; on the Lower East Side he spoke Yiddish and carried *The Daily Forward* (*see p. 124*). Elected during the Depression as a reformer, La Guardia gained the confidence of President Roosevelt and was able to secure federal aid for many local projects—public clinics, housing developments, parks and playgrounds, sewers, bridges, and La Guardia Airport—at the same time providing jobs for thousands of the unemployed. He was the only reform mayor to be re-elected, proving his dominance over Tammany Hall, the entrenched Democratic party machine (*see p. 171*). He considered his greatest achievement to be the increased honesty and efficiency in municipal government he brought about in New York through his own actions and throughout the country by force of example.

La Guardia has been called the most colorful mayor since Peter Stuyvesant. His flamboyant personality and unbounded energy were the stuff of legend. During a newspaper strike, he read the comics over the radio. On occasion he conducted symphony orchestras (his father was a musician). He followed firefighters into burning buildings and went on raids with the police. He died of pancreatic cancer at the age of 64 and is buried in Woodlawn Cemetery in the Bronx.

THE WEST VILLAGE

Block-long, gingko-lined **St Luke's Place** (Leroy St between Hudson St and Seventh Ave South; *map p. 580, C4*), named for the nearby chapel, has a row of Italianate houses whose aura of settled repose characterizes much of the West Village. Built in the early 1850s for prosperous merchants, many of whose livelihoods were tied to the Hudson River, the houses still have the red-brick façades typical of the earlier Greek

Revival style. However, they incorporate such fashionable Italianate details as brown-stone trim, door hoods supported by carved consoles, bold cornices, tall stoops with rather elaborate cast-iron railings, high rusticated basements, and deeply recessed doorways with double doors. Marianne Moore, Paul Cadmus, and psychedelic guru Timothy Leary have all lived here, but the block's most famous resident was James J. ("Jimmy") Walker, the popular, high-living mayor of New York from 1926 until his resignation under a cloud of fiscal scandal in 1932. His home was at no. 6.

The playground across the street is **James J. Walker Park**, originally St. John's Burying Ground of Trinity Parish (which owned the West Village up to Christopher St under a 1705 land grant from Queen Anne). During excavations for the park, workers uncovered a stone marked "Leroy," which rumor identified as the grave marker of Louis Charles, son of Louis XVI and Marie Antoinette (*le roy* means "the king" in old French). Although the dauphin may have been smuggled out of prison after his parents' death, he surely did not die in Greenwich Village. Leroy St is named, more prosaically, after Jacob Leroy, alderman, successful merchant—and commoner.

Bedford Street

Bedford St (*map p. 580, C4*) was mapped before 1799 and named after its precursor in London. James Vandenburgh, master mason of Trinity Church, lived at no. 68 in 1821, another reminder of Trinity's influence in the West Village. At **75½ Bedford St** is a house only 9½ ft wide, distinguished both as the narrowest house in the Village and as a residence of Edna St. Vincent Millay. Built in 1873, it was wedged into a former carriage alley; the brick facing came later. Edna St. Vincent Millay (1892–1950), poet, playwright, and actress, arrived in Greenwich Village in 1917, illuminating bohemian society with her beauty and intoxicating personality. Millay is probably one of very few people named after a hospital: her middle name honors the Greenwich Village hospital (St. Vincent's), where the staff had saved the life of a family member. In 1923 when she won the Pulitzer Prize, she lived briefly in this house.

The **Isaacs-Hendricks House**, at 77 Bedford St (Commerce St), the oldest house in the Village, was built in 1799 as a farmhouse by Joshua Isaacs, but has been altered and retains little of its original appearance. Around the sharp bend in the street are two remarkable houses, nos. **39 and 41 Commerce St** (1831 and 1832), facing one another across a central courtyard. Although local legend says a sea captain built them for two feuding daughters, records attribute them to a local milk seller. The mansard roofs were added in the 1870s.

Chumley's restaurant at 86 Bedford St (Grove and Barrow Sts) is a hangover from Prohibition days. It opened in 1927 disguised as a garage, and operated as a speakeasy, catering to Edna St. Vincent Millay, John Steinbeck, Willa Cather, and others whose thirst was not quenched by the Volstead Act. A "secret" entrance through the alley door facing Pamela Court allowed patrons to enter unobtrusively and exit the same way if the police raided. In commemoration of those clandestine times, the restaurant does not advertise its presence with a sign, although the liquor license is visible through the barred window. (*At the time of writing the restaurant was closed. Its future is uncertain.*)

Grove Street

The clapboard house at **17 Grove St** was built in 1822 by William Hyde, a window-sash maker. Although the house has been considerably altered—a Greek Revival doorway added in the 1830s or 1840s, a third story with a gingerbread cornice in 1870, and an obtrusive fire escape later—it is still the best preserved of the Village's few wood-frame houses. Behind it at **100 Bedford St** stands Hyde's workshop (1833). Designer and amateur architect Clifford Daily, whose greatest project stands next door, "renovated" it in the 1920s using moldings and other trim salvaged from demolished 19th-century houses.

The bizarre house known as "**Twin Peaks**," at 102 Bedford St (Grove St), was built in 1830 as an ordinary frame house and redesigned (1926) by Clifford Daily as a stuccoed, gabled, and half-timbered extravagance. Daily, who believed that Village artists needed inspirational surroundings to court the muse, persuaded financier Otto Kahn to undertake renovation of the house, which would be turned over to artists, writers, and actors who could then live free from financial pressures. The resulting house, said to be a replica of a house in Nuremberg, contains bricks from the old Madison Square Garden, a Second Avenue tenement, and an Upper West Side apartment. The opening ceremonies were held in 1926. Princess Amelia Troubetzkoy sat on one peak making a burnt offering of acorns (to the god Pan) while actress Mabel Normand sat atop the other peak christening the building with the customary bottle of champagne.

Grove Court, entered between 10 and 12 Grove St (Bedford and Hudson Sts), one of the Village's hidden architectural enclaves, is group of shuttered brick houses built (1853–54) as dwellings for workmen. Remarkable nowadays for its serenity, the court has a boisterous past, earning at different times in its history the names "Mixed Ale Alley" and "Pig's Alley." Nos. 4–10 Grove St, a group of Federal houses (1834), retain many original features: hand-wrought ironwork including boot-scrapers in the stoop fences, small dormers, and paneled doorways.

St. Luke in the Fields

At 487 Hudson St (near Grove St) is the Church of St. Luke in the Fields (1822; *map p. 580, B4*), designed as part of an unusual complex, attributed to Clement Clarke Moore (*church open Mon–Fri 10–2 & 5:45–7, Sun 7:30–3. Garden open Mon–Sat 7–8, Sun 7–7; main gate at 487 Hudson St; hours may change seasonally*). The church began as an independent Episcopal institution on land donated by Trinity Church, but in the late 19th century, as immigrants overwhelmed the neighborhood, the genteel congregation fled uptown to Convent Avenue at West 141st St, and in 1891 Trinity Church bought St. Luke's, making it a chapel of Trinity Parish, which it remained until 1976. Built of brick rather than the more customary rubblestone, St. Luke has a low, bulky, square tower unadorned with a steeple, reflecting the austerity of the Federal style. Badly damaged by fire in 1981, it was reconstructed and expanded (1981–85) by Hardy Holzman Pfeiffer Assocs.

In its early years, the church was flanked by 14 town houses, built by James N. Wells (who also built houses on nearby Grove St) as part of a complex designed along

with the church. Six remain (nos. 473–77 and 487–91 Hudson St, all built in 1825), as does the handsome vicarage in the churchyard.

The ten-story dark brick building at 641 Washington St (filling the block bounded by Washington, Greenwich, Christopher, and Barrow Sts) was originally the **US Appraiser's Stores** (1899), a warehouse for goods passing through customs. Later it served as a federal archives building and a post office; it has been renamed "The Archives" and converted to condominiums. Imposing in scale, it typifies the Romanesque Revival style at its best, with strong brick arches at ground level, rounded corner turnings, and successive bays of arched windows.

Lucille Lortel Theatre

The Lucille Lortel Theatre (121 Christopher St; *map p. 580, B4*), is named after its former owner, "the Queen of Off-Broadway," whose 70-year career was marked by a daring commitment to new plays and young talent. Lortel (1900–99), born Lucille Wadler, gave up acting in 1939 in deference to her wealthy husband. She had a barn moved to their Connecticut estate, intending to raise horses, but restrictions on feed during World War II scuttled that plan; instead Lortel founded the White Barn Theater in 1947, far from the commercial pressures of Broadway. She began producing plays by fledgling and unfamiliar playwrights, challenging actors and directors to move in new directions. In 1955 her husband, tired of her spending so much time in Connecticut, bought this theater, then called the Theatre de Lys, as an anniversary gift. She opened it with a revival of the *Threepenny Opera*, starring Lotte Lenya, that ran for seven years. Over her long career, Lortel mounted more than 500 productions, including work by Edward Albee, Ugo Betti, Eugene Ionesco, Athol Fugard, Sean O'Casey, Terrence McNally, and Langston Hughes, many of the plays exploring themes of injustice or discrimination.

THE FAR WEST VILLAGE

The house at **121 Charles St** (Greenwich St; *map p. 580, B4*) is oddly rural, with wide clapboards, double-hung windows, and unexpected angles and proportions. Tucked away on a small triangular plot amidst larger commercial buildings, the house, which may date from the 18th century, has been moved twice. It was brought to its present location in 1968 from York Avenue and 71st St, where it was a back house with no street frontage. When the building was threatened with demolition, the owner purchased this small piece of land and had the house trucked here.

At 567 Hudson St on the corner of West 11th St is the famous **White Horse Tavern** (founded 1880), once a watering hole for Norman Mailer, Jack Kerouac, and other writers. Dylan Thomas's prodigious drinking bouts, however, have made it a destination for that poet's admirers. On Nov 3, 1953, Thomas announced that he'd had "eighteen straight whiskies. I think that's the record," probably an apocryphal remark, but one which became an urban legend anyhow. The next day Thomas fell into a coma, and on Nov 9 died in St. Vincent's Hospital.

Bank and Bethune Streets

Bank St (*map p. 580, B4–B3*) was once an important financial center. In 1798 the Bank of New York, on Wall St, established a branch bank on a nameless Greenwich Village lane to be used for emergencies (the downtown branch was threatened with quarantine for yellow fever); during the smallpox epidemic of 1822 other banks came for similar reasons. Today, attractive homes line the block and cobblestones line the street.

Westbeth at 55 Bethune St (the block bounded by Bank and Bethune, Washington and West Sts) is an artists' community with living and working space for visual and performing artists, occupying the bulky industrial building formerly used by the **Bell Telephone Laboratories** (1900; Cyrus L.W. Eidlitz). Among the technological advances engineered here were the transistor and the transatlantic telephone, but its greatest artistic contribution in the old days was the production on its sound stage of parts of *The Jazz Singer*, the first commercially successful "talkie." In 1965, after the phone company moved out, the building was renovated by Richard Meier and converted to studios and artists' housing with federally subsidized rents. At one time or another Robert de Niro, Merce Cunningham, and Diane Arbus lived and/or worked within its walls.

Abingdon Square

Abingdon Square (*map p. 580, B3*) is named after Charlotte Warren, who married the Earl of Abingdon. Although many British place names were changed in 1794, after due consideration by the City Council Abingdon Square was allowed to remain Abingdon Square because the earl and his wife had been sympathetic to the American Revolution. Charlotte's father, Admiral Sir Peter Warren, was one of Greenwich Village's great 18th-century landholders. A true adventurer, Warren went to sea as a 12-year-old, rose to his own command at age 24, made a fortune as a privateer, and married Susannah De Lancey. He eventually owned some 300 acres and built a mansion on the block now bounded by Charles, Perry, Bleecker, and Washington Sts. He returned to England before the Revolution, became a member of Parliament, and acquitted himself brilliantly in society. He died in 1752 at the age of 49, and is buried in Westminster Abbey.

Abingdon Square contains the Greenwich Village War Memorial (1921; Philip Martiny), a bronze figure of an American soldier carrying a flag.

WEST 8TH–WEST 14TH STREETS

In 1931 Gertrude Vanderbilt Whitney (*see pp. 317–18*) founded the Whitney Museum of American Art in the building at 8 West 8th St (*map p. 580, C3*) that now houses the **New York Studio School**. She had already remodeled a stable at 19 MacDougal Alley as her own sculpture studio, and in 1908 had given significant financial support to The Eight, a group of artists whose work offended the genteel taste of the era. Her Whitney Studio was a place where artists could gather, exchange ideas, and show their work.

THE FORMER MABEL DODGE HOUSE

At 23 Fifth Ave, on the northeast corner of West 9th St, stood the house—well known in Village lore—where Mabel Dodge held her famous "evenings." In 1912 Mrs. Dodge and her wealthy husband rented the second floor of the house, which she had fitted out in white, including a white bearskin rug in front of a white marble fireplace. Inviting anarchists, poets, artists, sculptors, and journalists, she organized her evenings around a theme—psychoanalysis, birth control, or the labor movement. Featured speakers included A.A. Brill, "Big Bill" Haywood (leader of the "Wobblies" or Industrial Workers of the World), and anarchist Emma Goldman. The evenings, covered by the press, sometimes degenerated into quarrels, but were nonetheless considered symbolic of the Village's artistic and intellectual eminence. In 1919 Mrs. Dodge moved to Taos, New Mexico, where she instituted another salon, had an affair with D.H. Lawrence, and married a Pueblo Indian named Antonio Luhan.

The Center for Jewish Life and Church of the Ascension

The former Lockwood de Forest residence (1887), at 7 East 10th St near Fifth Avenue (*map p. 581, D3*), now NYU's **Center for Jewish Life**, has unusual East Indian decorative details, including an ornate bay window and carved door frame, both of teakwood. A celebrated designer, de Forest worked in India where he developed an interest in traditional Indian woodcarving. He also designed the teakwood trim for the Carnegie Mansion family library, and with his brother gave a room from an Indian Jain temple to the Metropolitan Museum of Art (*see p. 361*).

On Fifth Avenue at West 10th St stands the **Church of the Ascension** (1840–41), a fine brownstone Gothic Revival church by Richard Upjohn, the architect who later designed Trinity Church. In 1844 President John Tyler was married here to Julia Gardiner, whom a contemporary diarist described as "one of those large fleshly Miss Gardiners of Gardiners Island." In 1885–88, the church was "modernized" by Stanford White, an early project by the firm of McKim, Mead & White. McKim designed the pulpit; John La Farge painted the altar mural, which is considered one of his best works; Louis Saint-Gaudens (brother of the better-known Augustus) designed the marble reredos. Next to the church at 7 West 10th St is the Rectory (1839–41), a Gothic Revival row house, daringly innovative for its day, with asymmetrical massing, drip moldings, a steep roof and large chimney, pointed dormers, and a rough brownstone façade.

West 10th Street

A number of houses on this pleasant street have interesting architectural and social connections. Etiquette expert Emily Post (1873–1960) once lived at no. 12 (1846), built by her architect father, Bruce Price. Emma Lazarus wrote "The New Colossus"

("Give me your tired, your poor…"; *see p. 38*) while living at no. 18. The row of houses at nos. 20–38 (1856–58) is known either as Renwick Terrace, since it is attributed to James Renwick, or as the English Terrace since it was influenced by rows or "terraces" of town houses in London. Stylistically these Anglo-Italianate or "English basement" houses depart from the usual Italianate brownstone in having low stoops (three or four steps instead of ten or twelve) and round-arched single windows and doorways on the ground floor. Like other mid-19th-century brownstones, Renwick Terrace was planned as part of a unified streetscape, with cornices, rooflines, and window levels aligned to create an impressive architectural vista. Dada artist Marcel Duchamp, a chess aficionado, moved to no. 28 in 1959, across the street from the Marshall Chess Club, which is still at no. 23.

No. 58 West 10th St (c. 1836) was remodeled by Stanford White. Behind it stood a back house (now joined to the main building) where the Tile Club once met. This nationally important society of artists claimed such members as Augustus Saint-Gaudens, Daniel Chester French, and John Singer Sargent. Across the street stood Richard Morris Hunt's Studio Building at 51 West 10th St. Clients included Winslow Homer, John La Farge, Albert Bierstadt, Frederick MacMonnies, Saint-Gaudens, and French.

Jefferson Market Library and Garden

The former Jefferson Market Courthouse at 425 Sixth Ave (*map p. 580, C3*) dates to 1877, designed by Central Park architect Calvert Vaux and Frederick Clarke Withers. It is now a branch of the New York Public Library system. Turreted, towered, gabled, carved, and further embellished with stained glass and ironwork, the building exemplifies Victorian Gothic architecture at its most flamboyant. Voted the nation's fifth most beautiful building in 1855, it stood empty from 1945 until 1967, when (after a struggle by preservationist Villagers) Giorgio Cavaglieri remodeled it for its present use. The Library has a special collection of books about the history of the city and especially Greenwich Village.

The courthouse stands on the site of the Jefferson Market, one of the city's primary 19th-century produce markets. The old market (founded 1833) had a tall wooden fire-tower with a bell to alert volunteer firefighters, the precursor of the present main tower originally used for the same purpose. Assembly rooms above the market sheds doubled as courtrooms, so that when the present building was constructed, it became part of a complex that included a brick jail and a reconstructed market building. Harry K. Thaw, who murdered architect Stanford White (*see p. 181*), was tried here, and found "insane." Mae West was tried here on obscenity charges, paying a $500 fine, and spending one day in jail and nine more in the workhouse on Welfare (now Roosevelt) Island.

A superb example of Victoriana: the Jefferson Market Library. In the mid-19th century it was considered one of the most beautiful buildings in America.

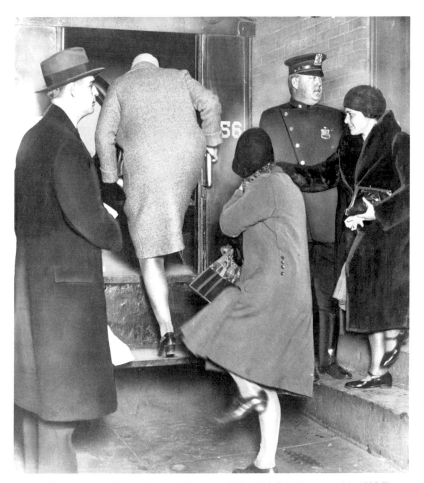

Women from the Birth Control Research Bureau on West 15th St being arrested in 1929. The patrol wagon was to take them to Jefferson Market Courthouse in Greenwich Village.

In 1927 the jail was demolished and replaced by the infamous Women's House of Detention (1931), a massive Art Deco building, long a village landmark or eyesore depending on the beholder's point of view. The women's prison, originally intended for the temporary detention of women awaiting trial, was more successful architecturally than socially, and as conditions within it deteriorated, its grim bulk bore unpleasant associations for Villagers, especially since the inmates could often be heard shouting out of the windows. In 1973–74 it was demolished. Its site has been converted to the **Jefferson Market Garden** (entrance on Greenwich Ave; *open afternoons*

except Mon, weather permitting, April–Oct), a third of an acre graced with borders of annuals and perennials, magnolias, yellowwoods and holly bushes, and a pond for koi and shubunkin goldfish.

Patchin Place, Milligan Place, and the Second Jewish Cemetery

Patchin Place at West 10th St (Sixth and Greenwich Aves), is a secluded mews with ten brick houses built in 1848 by one Aaron D. Patchin. Theodore Dreiser lived here in 1895 while still an obscure journalist, and E.E. Cummings, the occupant of no. 4, enjoyed its serenity for some 40 years.

Milligan Place, on Sixth Avenue between West 10th and West 11th Sts, another enclave of 19th-century houses clustered around a tiny triangular courtyard, is named after Samuel Milligan, who purchased farmland here in 1799 and, according to legend, hired Aaron Patchin, later his son-in-law, to survey it. The houses (c. 1852) are said to have accommodated Basque waiters from the former elegant Brevoort Hotel on nearby Fifth Avenue and French feather workers who dealt in ostrich and egret plumes for millinery.

About a quarter of a block along the south side of West 11th St (near Sixth Avenue) is the small triangular remnant of the Second Cemetery of the Spanish and Portuguese Synagogue, also known as the Second Shearith Israel Synagogue, once a larger, rectangular plot. This graveyard opened in 1805 when the synagogue's first burial ground at Chatham Square (*see p. 113*) was full. It was used until West 11th St was cut through in 1830, obliterating most of it, though the congregation petitioned the city to retain the part of the cemetery that did not lie in the way of the street. Still buried here is Ephraim Hart, a founder of the New York Stock Exchange. (Most of the bodies were removed to West 21st St near Sixth Avenue, where the congregation established its third graveyard, used until 1852 when a new law prohibited burials within the city limits.) The present Shearith Israel cemetery is on Long Island.

First Presbyterian Church and Salmagundi Club

The **First Presbyterian Church** (1846, Joseph C. Wells; south transept, 1893, McKim, Mead & White; chancel 1919) on Fifth Avenue at West 12th St (*map p. 581, D3*) replaced an earlier one on Wall St after the street was rebuilt as a commercial neighborhood following the Great Fire of 1835. The present church was built at a time when Gothic Revival architecture reigned supreme in New York, at least in church buildings, and Joseph C. Wells, an immigrant from Britain, created here a fine example of that style, based on English models. The crenellated central tower, for example, is based on that of Magdalen College, Oxford, and the Church of St. Saviour in Bath. George Templeton Strong, the 19th-century diarist and a congregant of Episcopalian Trinity Church, found this building "a travesty of a Gothic church." As it rose, Strong found that it grew "uglier and uglier, and when its tower is finished it will resemble a corpulent Chinese gander with its neck rigid, stout, and tall."

Across the street at 47 Fifth Ave (near 12th St) is the **Salmagundi Club** (1852–53), the only survivor of the great mansions that once ennobled lower Fifth Avenue. The

building belongs to the Italianate tradition, with its boldly rusticated basement, high stoop and grand balustrade, ornate door hood supported on foliate consoles, and lavish cast-iron work on the parlor window balconies. Built for Irad Hawley, president of the Pennsylvania Coal Company, the mansion is now owned by the Salmagundi Club, the nation's oldest artists' club, founded in 1871 as a sketching club. Among its members were John La Farge, Louis Comfort Tiffany, and Stanford White. The name "Salmagundi" (whose origins cannot reliably be traced back beyond the French *salmigondis*—a salad of minced veal, anchovies, onions, lemon juice, and oil) was adopted by Washington Irving and his collaborators as the title of a periodical whose pages satirized New York life. The club offers art classes and has a gallery (*open during exhibitions daily 1–5; T: 212 255 7740; www.salmagundi.org*).

Forbes Galleries

Map p. 581, D3. Open Tues–Sat 10–4; closed Sun, Mon, legal holidays. Reserved Thur for group tours. Free. T: 212 206 5548; www.forbesgalleries.com.
The Forbes Galleries (1985), at 60 Fifth Ave (West 12th St), showcase the collections of *Forbes* magazine, which largely reflect the interests of former publisher, Malcolm S. Forbes (1919–90), known for his extroverted and lavish lifestyle and his passionate enthusiasms. On display are toy boats, toy soldiers, antique games including historic Monopoly boards, and a gallery of trophies—the usual cups and urns along with some rather odd testimonials to moments of triumph. During his days as a publishing magnate, Malcolm Forbes amassed a much larger collection, which included nine Fabergé imperial eggs and important historical papers—among them documents handwritten by Abraham Lincoln, Robert E. Lee, Albert Einstein, and others. Since Forbes's death, parts of the collection have been auctioned off, including the eggs, which were sold to a Russian billionaire in 2004 for a sum estimated at $100 million.

THE NEW SCHOOL

The New School, originally the New School for Social Research, occupies several blocks between Fifth and Sixth Avenues, from West 10th St north to West 14th St, though the campus extends to other parts of the city. The school, actually a university with eight divisions, was founded in 1919 to offer college-level courses for all "intelligent men and women," and remains one of the city's innovative educational institutions.

History of the New School

In the 1920s the New School broke ground by introducing psychoanalysis to the American public, and was the first college to offer courses on black culture (taught by W.E.B. DuBois). Teachers who lectured in the school's six rented brownstones in Chelsea included Lewis Mumford, Franz Boas, and Bertrand Russell. During the following decades it became a "university in exile" for intellectuals fleeing Nazi Germany and Fascist Italy, and after World War II the school welcomed returning

veterans and other working adults whose lives had been disrupted by the war. During the 1950s, Hannah Arendt, W.H. Auden, and Robert Frost offered lectures. In recent decades, the Mannes College of Music and the Parsons School of Design have become part of the New School, which has also added a school of management and urban policy, a drama school, a program in jazz and contemporary music.

The Alvin Johnson Building and art collection

In 1930 the New School commissioned Joseph Urban to design its first permanent home, now the Alvin Johnson Building at 66 West 12th St (*map p. 580, C3*). Known for his sometimes extravagant stage sets and theater designs, Urban tried to make this Modernist building unobtrusive on a street where most of its surroundings are small in scale. After trying various color schemes, he chose rows of black and white brick alternating with bands of windows set in black frames. The upper stories are recessed to de-emphasize the building's bulk. Inside (*though student ID is required for admission*) is a landmarked egg-shaped auditorium, beautifully and accurately restored in 1995 (including the ceiling, painted in nine tones of gray) by the firm of Ohlhausen DuBois. Works from the New School's collection are on rotating display in the hallways, classrooms, and lobbies of the buildings. Most of the collection is contemporary, much of it from the last decade; works reflect the school's diversity and commitment to freedom of expression, and its historic involvement with avant-garde art. Recent commissions include works by Kara Walker, Sol LeWitt, and Martin Puryear. The most famous works are the city's only murals by José Clemente Orozco (1931), a series often referred to as *A Call for Revolution and Universal Brotherhood*, paintings which explore themes of exploitation, revolution, the brotherhood of man, and the dignity of labor. Thomas Hart Benton's *America Today* murals were commissioned by the New School, but are now on view in Midtown (*see p. 270*).

THE EAST VILLAGE

Map p. 581. Subway: 6 to Spring St; N, R, or W to Prince St. Bus: M103 to Prince St; M6 to Prince St at Broadway (walk six blocks east).

In recent years, the population of the East Village, bounded by East Houston St, East 14th St, the Bowery and Third Avenue, and Avenue D, has included Bowery bums, immigrant working-class families, middle-class sometimes middle-aged "hippies," artists and writers, young professionals, and a surging population of students. Because of historical circumstance—sudden and rapid development as a fine residential area in the early 19th century, followed by an equally rapid decline when commerce invaded Broadway and immigrants crowded into the Tompkins Square neighborhood—the district preserves architectural traces of its evolution in strange juxtaposition.

HISTORY OF THE EAST VILLAGE

Until the 1960s the East Village did not exist as a distinct neighborhood. Its eastern blocks were part of the sprawling Lower East Side, populated by Slavs, Eastern European Jews, Germans, and, later, Latinos. Its western sector, around Astor Place, was a decaying remnant of a formerly aristocratic neighborhood.

In the 1950s a few "beatniks" moved in—Jack Kerouac and Allan Ginsberg among them—and during the next decade artists, writers, musicians, and other exponents of the burgeoning counterculture were drawn here by low rents. By the mid-1960s the area had become known as the East Village. The blocks around St. Mark's Place pulsed with intellectual energy: there were cafés, bookstores, theaters, coffee houses, and "head shops," where drug paraphernalia was sold. By the mid-1970s the counterculture had faded, and in the 1980s the neighborhood was beset by drug abuse and crime and also by tensions between cultural groups, of which the 1988 Tompkins Square Park riots (*see p. 167*) were one expression.

Since the 1990s, as the city has recovered economically, the East Village has gentrified apace: coffee bars abound; condos, some elegantly designed, soar above the remaining tenements; and in at least one large, deluxe grocery store, mothers pushing strollers forage for cactus pears where addicts formerly gathered to buy crack.

THE BOWERY

Bowery (*map pp. 583, D1–581 E4*), one of Manhattan's oldest streets, runs about one mile, from Chatham Square to Cooper Square, and for long was associated with

loneliness, poverty, and alcoholism. Originally an Indian trail, the Bowery got its name from the Dutch word for farm (*bouwerie*), when the area was farmland on the northern fringes of the city. During the 18th century the Bowery was part of the Boston Post Road, and in the early 19th century the street traversed a fine residential area, though the neighboring streets further downtown (Chrystie, Elizabeth, and Forsyth Sts) had already attracted slaughterhouses and factories for lard, soap fats, and candles. In the mid-19th century, the Bowery glittered with the lights of theaters; it witnessed the first blackface minstrel show in the city, the first stage version of *Uncle Tom's Cabin*, and toward the end of the century hosted several Yiddish theaters.

After about 1870, as the slums encroached on both sides, the Bowery began a long slide into poverty, with the arrival of beer halls, distilleries, and cheap lodgings. The worst were flophouses, where the lodger slept on the floor, his space chalked out for him by the proprietor. During the Depression the Bowery's cheap hotels, doorways, and all-night restaurants offered the army of the unemployed a place to spend the night, or wait until times got better. In the 1940s and '50s there were still several bars per block, and until 1968 the Salvation Army operated a mission, doling out free food, coffee, and counseling.

Today the flophouses are gone and much of the street has come to life. Between Grand St and Delancey Sts the Bowery houses a discount and wholesale lighting district that arose to supply the nearby theaters with gas fixtures for the stage and front of house. Further south, between Delancey and East Houston Sts, is the wholesale kitchen supply district, which arrived here in the 1930s.

"In the Bowery, midnight in a cheap underground lodging cellar. Only 5 cents a spot." A 19th-century artist's impression of a flophouse.

The New Museum of Contemporary Art

Map p. 581, E4. 235 Bowery. Open Wed noon–6, Thur and Fri noon–10, Sat and Sun noon–6; free Thurs 7–10; café open same hours; T: 212 219 1222; www.newmuseum.org.

The New Museum of Contemporary Art is the only museum in Manhattan devoted exclusively to the work of living artists. It was the first institution in the city to exhibit such now prominent artists as Jenny Holzer and David Hammons; it also gave major solo shows to John Baldessari, Leon Golub, Hans Haacke, Ana Mendieta, and Martin Puryear, long before their reputations were established.

The museum was founded in 1977 by Marcia Tucker, a former curator of painting and sculpture at the Whitney Museum of American Art. Tucker's ideas about showing living artists outside the mainstream and her misgivings about established museum management led her to start a museum that would focus on the newest art, displaying only works created in the past decade. Originally the New Museum planned to buy works and sell them ten years later so that the collection would continuously renew itself, but this plan was not carried out and the museum does have a permanent collection, though the emphasis is on changing exhibitions and on presenting art in its political and social contexts.

In its 30 years of existence the museum has moved from a cramped space on Hudson St to a few rooms in the New School, to Broadway in SoHo and, in Dec 2007, to its arresting new space on the Bowery. The architects, Kazuo Sejima and Ryue Nishizawa, based in Tokyo and not well-known in this country, have designed a building that resembles a seven-story, off-kilter stack of boxes, clad in shimmering aluminum mesh—a startling modern presence on this formerly dingy stretch of the street. Inside are open floors of column-free exhibition space, with windows and skylights that offer unexpected views.

Two cemeteries

Within a block of one another are two small cemeteries. The larger is the **New York City Marble Cemetery** (1831), at 52–74 East 2nd St, whose handsome monuments and gravestones are visible through the fence (*open by appointment, donation requested; T: 212 228 6401; www.nycmc.org*). President James Monroe was interred here but was later removed; still remaining are early mayor Marinus Willett, several Roosevelts, and Preserved Fish, member of a fine New York family, and seemingly the victim of his parents' fondness for punning. The cemetery name includes the word "city" to distinguish it from its nearby predecessor, the New York Marble Cemetery. The **New York Marble Cemetery** (*usually open on fourth Sun of month, March–Nov 11–3, as well as several other weekends throughout the year; see www.marblecemetery.org*) on the west side of the street, half way up the block of Second Avenue between East 2nd and East 3rd Sts, was the city's first nonsectarian graveyard, built as a commercial venture after burials were outlawed south of Canal St. The vaults are underground, but the names of the families who bought them are inscribed in plaques on the wall.

Interior stairwell of the New Museum of Contemporary Art.

At 319 Bowery (East 2nd St) the **Amato Opera Theatre** is a local cultural institution (*T: 212 228 8200*) run by Anthony and Sally Amato, who founded it in 1948. In its minuscule house (107 seats facing a 20-ft stage), the Amato gives talented singers the chance to sing full-length roles and offers the public low-price tickets. The late lamented rock club CBGB stood across the street at 319 Bowery.

The Bayard-Condict Building

Slightly outside the boundaries of the East Village stands one of the city's little-known architectural treasures, the only New York building by Louis H. Sullivan, considered by many to be the creator of the skyscraper. The Bayard-Condict Building (1897–99), at 65–69 Bleecker St, tucked away at the north end of Crosby St (*map p. 581, D4*), reflects Sullivan's dictum that a skyscraper should be a proud and soaring thing. (The best view is from Crosby St near Houston St.) Slender vertical piers over the interior structural columns alternate with even more slender vertical columns between the windows. The sumptuous terra-cotta surface decoration of leafy and geometric forms, seed pods, tendrils, vines, and gargoyle lion-heads, culminates in an ornate cornice beneath which six angels hover with outspread wings.

First called the Bayard Building to honor one of the city's oldest families (though no Bayards were involved in the project), this 13-story office tower was undertaken by the United Loan and Investment Co., which hired Sullivan. Already known for his work in Chicago, Sullivan had attracted attention for his radical theories on sky-scraper design, which stressed function as a determinant of form, the importance of new building materials, and their influence upon design.

His first plan incorporated a freestanding steel skeleton with 14-inch structural columns and exterior brick walls only 12 inches thick. Unfortunately, the con-servative city building code disallowed this design and insisted upon thickening the lower walls and columns. With the loss of floor space and rental income, the United Loan and Investment Co. became unable to afford the building and sold it to Silas and Emmeline Condict. The building was beautifully restored in 2002–03, with 1,300 of the 7,000 terra-cotta pieces cleaned and re-glued; the original storefronts were replaced and the capitals of the ground-floor columns recreated from one that still existed in the basement of the Brooklyn Museum.

Bond Street

At the corner of Bond St and the Bowery (330 Bowery) is the **Bouwerie Lane Theatre** (1874; Henry Engelbert), built as the Bond Street Savings Bank. The architect, working with a modest 25ft by 100ft building lot, managed to suggest the massive grandeur formerly associated with bank architecture, a difficult undertaking since the short side of the lot faces the Bowery, the more important thoroughfare. The Corinthian columns, the cornices at every floor, the quoins and rusticated piers, all masquerade as stone, though they are cast iron.

For a while in the 1830s and 1840s, Bond St was the cynosure of fashion, but the creep of commerce up Broadway put an end to its eminence; its fine homes became

Terra-cotta angels and luxuriant foliage on the Bayard-Condict Building.

boarding houses and offices. By 1870 it was solidly commercial. Now converted to apartments, no. 1–5 Bond St, the **former Robbins & Appleton Building** (1879; Stephen D. Hatch), was built for the proprietors of the American Waltham Watch Co. The ground floor was also headquarters for publisher D. Appleton & Co., whose torches of learning are above the main doorway. The building, with its tall mansard roof, is a dramatic example of the French Empire style. The large expanses of plate glass were made possible by the strength of iron under compression, so that a few widely spaced columns could support a sizable façade.

Bond Street is being recast as a habitat for the wealthy, with luxury condos by famous architects rising on the block between Lafayette St and the Bowery.

Great Jones Street

The land for **Great Jones St** was ceded to the city by Samuel Jones, a prominent lawyer and the city's first comptroller (1796–99), with the stipulation that the street bear his name. New York already had a Jones St; for a while it had two, until Samuel Jones suggested calling his street "Great Jones St." At no. 44 is the firehouse of **Engine Company 33** (1898; Ernest Flagg and W.B. Chambers), a satisfyingly flamboyant, impeccably maintained Beaux-Arts building dominated by a monumental three-story arch. Among its elegant details are a deep cornice with scroll brackets, tall French windows, and ornamental railings. The bold Romanesque Revival **Schermerhorn Building** on the northwest corner of Great Jones and Lafayette Sts (376 Lafayette St) was built (1888) by Henry J. Hardenbergh as a warehouse; Hardenbergh is better known for the Plaza Hotel

and the Dakota Apartments. On the northeast corner of the intersection, at 399 Lafayette St, is the former **De Vinne Press Building** (1885; Babb, Cook & Willard), a stark Romanesque Revival building of dark brick with terra-cotta trim. Massive and simple, it is remarkable for its appearance of weight and strength. Theodore De Vinne (1828–1914) was a successful printer and distinguished scholar of the history of printing.

The Merchant's House Museum

Map p. 581, D4. 29 East 4th St (Lafayette St and the Bowery). Open Thur–Mon 12–5; closed Tues, Wed, major holidays; T: 212 777 1089; www.merchantshouse.com.

This remarkably preserved Greek Revival house remains from the days when the neighborhood was the city's finest. Inside are the furnishings and personal possessions of the Tredwell family, who lived here for almost 100 years. Known also as the Seabury Tredwell House, the three-story brick town house (1832; attrib. Minard Lafever) was built on speculation by a hat merchant dabbling in real estate. The building was then purchased in 1835 for $18,000 by Seabury Tredwell, a prosperous hardware merchant and importer. It stayed in the family until Tredwell's eighth and last child, Gertrude (b. 1840), died there in 1933; it became a museum three years later. Fortunately for posterity, Gertrude threw nothing away.

The outside of the house has a steeply slanted dormer roof and a handsomely detailed doorway typical of the late Federal period. The interiors are Greek Revival in style, with beautiful moldings and plasterwork. There are three floors of period rooms, with furniture ranging from a Federal sofa with hand-carved eagles, and gondola chairs covered with black horsehair, to such Tredwelliana as needlework, gloves and hats, underclothes, and chamber pots. In the ground-floor kitchen the cast-iron stove remains installed in the original cooking hearth.

LAFAYETTE STREET & GRACE CHURCH

In 1804 John Jacob Astor paid $45,000 for the land where Lafayette St now runs (*map p. 581, D4–D3*). While waiting for land values to rise, Astor leased it to a Frenchman who created a pleasure ground called Vauxhall Gardens, with summer pavilions where visitors could buy light refreshments, and a remodeled greenhouse where those so inclined could indulge in heavier drinking. In 1825 Astor reclaimed the gardens, carved out the street, originally named Lafayette Place, and sold lots facing the new street for more than $45,000 apiece, the price of the entire parcel only 20 years earlier. John Jacob Astor never lived on Lafayette St, but his son William B. Astor did—opposite Colonnade Row at 34 Lafayette Place, in a house described by a contemporary as a "plain but substantial-looking brick mansion."

Colonnade Row

On the west side of Lafayette St (nos. 428–34) stand the remains of **Colonnade Row**

(1833; attrib. Alexander Jackson Davis), once highly desirable residences. First named La Grange Terrace after the country home of the Marquis de Lafayette, Colonnade Row originally had nine houses joined by a monumental two-story Corinthian colonnade. The houses (built on speculation and faced with white Westchester marble cut by Sing Sing prisoners) were purchased eagerly by such notables as Franklin Delano, grandfather of Franklin D. Roosevelt. Colonnade Row enjoyed only a brief moment of social splendor, as commerce continued moving up Broadway, depressing residential land values. By the 1860s the Astor mansion had become a restaurant, a neighborhood church had been converted to a boxing ring, and the five southernmost houses of the row opened as the Colonnade Hotel. When Lafayette St was extended south to the City Hall area in the 1880s, the remaining houses on the street became tenements and rooming houses or were torn down to make way for warehouses and factories. In 1901 the Wanamaker warehouse replaced the Colonnade Hotel.

The Public Theater

Directly opposite Colonnade Row is The Public Theater, at 425 Lafayette St between 4th St and Astor Place. (*Map p. 581, D3; T: 212 539 8500; www.publictheater.org.*)

The Public Theater grew out of the New York Shakespeare Festival, founded by Joseph Papp, born Yosl Papirofsky, a larger-than-life figure whose entrepreneurial skills and artistic courage changed the face of the American theater. Papp rose from an impoverished childhood in Brooklyn to bring free Shakespeare to New Yorkers and to become the driving force behind the Public Theater. Through its history the Public has championed new and challenging work; nurtured the careers of emerging black, Asian, and female playwrights; and cast black and Asian actors in classic roles. The theater opened (1967) with the musical *Hair*, which moved to Broadway a year later. Profits from *Hair* and later *A Chorus Line*, which ran for a then-record 6,137 performances, underwrote less mainstream plays, and in this, too, Papp broke new ground. The theater has produced classic plays with stellar casts and it has introduced new work by David Mamet, John Guare, Sam Shepard, Vaclav Havel, David Hare, Suzan-Lori Parks, and others. Plays from The Public have won 40 Tony awards, 141 Obies (Off-Broadway awards), and four Pulitzer prizes.

The grand theater building has a complicated history, built in three separate sections and then remodeled when it was threatened with demolition in the mid-20th century (south wing 1849–53, Alexander Saeltzer; center wing 1856–59, Griffith Thomas; north wing 1879–81, Thomas Stent; remodeled 1966, Giorgio Cavaglieri). The building opened in 1854 as the Astor Library, the only public benefaction of tight-fisted John Jacob Astor, who ostensibly dedicated it to working people, but kept it open only during the daytime when workers couldn't use it. When the Astor Library merged with the Lenox and Tilden collections in 1912 to form the nucleus of the New York Public Library system (*see p. 208*), the Hebrew Immigrant Aid Society took over and used the building from 1921–65 in its work of resettling Eastern European immigrants. In 1966, after HIAS moved out, Joseph Papp convinced the city to buy the building and remodel the interior under the guidance of Giorgio Cavaglieri, who also brilliantly

recycled the Jefferson Market Library in Greenwich Village. Within the building are five performance spaces and Joe's Pub, a cabaret.

Astor Place

On the traffic island on the east side of Astor Place is a 15-ft weathering steel cube (1966) by Bernard (Tony) Rosenthal. Balanced on one apex, the work is entitled *Alamo*, a name derived from a remark by the sculptor's wife that the piece had the strength and feeling of a fortress. The Astor Place subway entrance across the street (Fourth Ave and East 8th St) is a cast-iron reproduction (1985) of an original subway kiosk. The station below (1904; Heins & La Farge) is one of the best subway restorations in the city, with murals by Milton Glaser.

THE ASTOR PLACE RIOT

The building at 13 Astor Place stands on the site of the Astor Place Opera House, now remembered chiefly for the Astor Place riot (May 10, 1849). An already bitter theatrical rivalry between English actor William Macready and his American counterpart Edwin Forrest—fanned by working-class anti-British and anti-aristocratic sentiments—erupted into violence during a performance of *Macbeth*. The audience hurled garbage at Macready while a mob outside assaulted the building with bricks and paving stones. The militia summoned from a nearby armory was eventually ordered to fire into the crowd. Estimates of casualties differ, but the usual count is about 30 dead and 150 wounded.

Grace Church

Grace Church (Protestant Episcopal), which lifts its delicate spire at the corner of Broadway and East 10th St (*map p. 581, D3*), has been praised as New York's finest Gothic Revival church (1843–47; James Renwick Jr.); it was also once its most socially desirable. The white marble façade, quarried by Sing Sing convicts as an economy measure, is known for its delicate stonework and fine proportions. The octagonal spire (1888) replaced a wooden steeple—another economy measure instituted by the building committee; unfortunately the marble spire cost 2/3 the original cost of the whole church.

Inside, the chancel window known either as the "Te Deum" window or the "Church Triumphant" window is by Clayton and Bell (1879), an English firm with an overtly medieval style. The Pre-Raphaelite windows by Henry Holiday (also English) in the north and south aisles represent an attempt to fuse medieval and 19th-century sensibilities. The **rectory** (north of the church), designed by Renwick at the same time as the church, is one of the city's earliest Gothic Revival dwellings, replete with pinnacles, gables, quatrefoil ornamentation, and traceried windows.

Grace Memorial House (1882–83; James Renwick Jr.), at 94–96 Fourth Ave, east of the church, is now used by the Grace Church School. By the late 1870s the parish

served by Grace Church was no longer exclusively wealthy, and the church needed facilities for its poorer members. Levi P. Morton, vice-president of the United States under Benjamin Harrison, donated money in memory of his wife for Grace Memorial House, first a day nursery, then a home for young women of modest means, and still later a rehabilitation center for girls. The building, originally two Greek Revival town houses, was altered to its present appearance by Renwick, who added the façade, the gable, and other features. No. 96 Fourth Avenue was later duplicated by Clergy House at 92 Fourth Ave (1902; Heins & La Farge) to make a symmetrical group of buildings. Later Neighborhood House (1907; Renwick, Aspinwall, & Tucker), at 98 Fourth Ave, was added in the same style.

THE ST. MARK'S HISTORIC DISTRICT & COOPER UNION

The St. Mark's Historic District (*map p. 581, D3–E3*) lies within the boundaries of Peter Stuyvesant's original farm or *bouwerie*, purchased in 1651 from the Dutch West India Company and extending from the East River to Fourth Avenue, from about present-day East 5th to East 17th Sts. (The Stuyvesant mansion's probable foundations were uncovered in 1854 during excavations at 129 East 10th St.)

The governor's great-grandson, Petrus Stuyvesant, developed part of the estate. In the late 1780s his property was mapped into lots along a grid of streets oriented to the points of the compass. Building began around 1800, but the city moved to impose its own scheme for development based on the Commissioners' Plan of 1811, which featured a street grid oriented to the long axis of Manhattan Island. Although the city generally closed existing streets or tore down buildings that did not conform to its plan, the Stuyvesant St neighborhood was allowed to remain, largely in deference to its wealthy families, including the Stuyvesants themselves.

Renwick Triangle and the Stuyvesant-Fish Residence

The houses at 112–28 East 10th St and those directly behind them (23–35 Stuyvesant St) comprise **Renwick Triangle** (1861; attrib. James Renwick Jr.). This group of 16 residences was built on land belonging to Hamilton Fish, who sold it under the condition that no "noxious or offensive establishments"—breweries, slaughter houses, soap or glue factories, tanneries, cattle yards, or blacksmith shops—be built there. Before restrictive zoning laws, such covenants were the sole means of ensuring residential tranquillity. The houses, built with red Philadelphia pressed brick and brownstone trim, have rusticated ground floors, bold cornices, and fully enframed upper-story windows; many have fine cast-iron railings.

At 21 Stuyvesant St near Third Avenue is the **Stuyvesant-Fish Residence** (1803–04; *see also p. 10*), which dates from the earliest period of development of the Stuyvesant property. Built by Petrus Stuyvesant as a wedding present for his daughter Elizabeth and her husband, Nicholas Fish, the house is one of the city's grandest

Federal residences, declaring the Stuyvesant wealth in its unusual height and width (28¼ ft). The east windows indicate that it was built as a freestanding (not a row) house. Hamilton Fish (1808–93), born in this house to Elizabeth and Nicholas Fish, inherited from a childless relative half a million dollars and went on to become governor of New York, US senator, and secretary of state. The house, now owned by Cooper Union, is a residence for the university president.

Cooper Union

The Cooper Union for the Advancement of Science and Art is a private college, which offers free tuition to all its students. Occupying the area bounded by Third Avenue, 7th St, the Bowery, and Astor Place, the **Cooper Union Foundation Building** (1859; Frederick A. Peterson; later remodelings) embodies the innovative genius of its founder both in its physical plant and in the institution it houses.

Peter Cooper (1791–1883)
Cooper, a self-educated genius, designed the first American locomotive, promoted the Atlantic cable with Cyrus W. Field, and helped develop Morse's telegraph. His fortune, however, came largely through an ironworks in Trenton, New Jersey, and a glue factory in Baltimore. Unlike others of his breed, Cooper recognized that his wealth had come from the "cooperation of multitudes," and turned his millions to philanthropy. By establishing the Cooper Union as a free educational institution to give students the equivalent of a college degree while stressing also the practical arts and trades, Cooper provided for others the education he would have wished for himself. Requiring no other credentials than a good moral character, Cooper Union opened its doors to women as well as men, to adults as well as young people.

Built of brownstone in the Italianate style, the building incorporates some of the first wrought-iron beams used anywhere, beams which Cooper developed from train rails and for which he built the necessary rolling machinery in his Trenton plant. Later, Cooper's beams evolved into I-beams, which when translated into steel became the backbone of the modern skyscraper. The upper stories, added in the 1890s, once housed the collection of decorative arts that later became the nucleus of the Cooper-Hewitt Museum. Outside, just south of the main entrance, is a **statue of Peter Cooper** (1897) by Augustus Saint-Gaudens, who had received his early training as a night student at the Cooper Union. The bronze statue sits beneath a marble canopy designed by the sculptor's friend Stanford White.

On the right side of the lobby a staircase leads down to the Great Hall, an auditorium with arcades of supporting granite arches. One of Cooper's aims in founding the Union was to establish a forum where great issues of the day could be freely discussed. Here Henry Ward Beecher, William Cullen Bryant, and William Lloyd

Garrison spoke against slavery. Here Abraham Lincoln made his famous "right makes might" speech in 1860, winning the support of the New York press and hence the presidential nomination. Later the auditorium housed the People's Institute, offering lectures to education-hungry Jews from the Lower East Side.

LITTLE UKRAINE

The city's Ukrainian enclave stretches along Second Avenue from about East 4th to East 14th Sts, with East 6th and 7th Sts at its heart (*map p. 581, E4–E3*). "Little Ukraine" reached a population of about 60,000 after World War II as Ukrainians fled Soviet control, but dwindled thereafter until the collapse of the Soviet Union, when more immigrants arrived. While younger Ukrainians are leaving for the suburbs, the neighborhood still has vital cultural institutions.

The Ukrainian Museum

Map p. 581, E4. 222 East 6th St (Second and Third Aves). Open Wed–Sun 11:30–5; T: 212 228 0110; www.ukrainianmuseum.org.

The handsome four-story new museum building (2005), designed by Ukrainian-American architect George Sawicki, brought to fruition 15 years of planning. When the museum was founded in 1976 in a modest brownstone on Second Avenue, Ukraine was a republic of the Soviet Union, its culture and heritage suppressed by that of the monolithic USSR. The mission of the museum was to bring to public attention Ukraine's existence and to preserve its cultural heritage. The collection at the time focused on Ukrainian folk art, including costumes, embroidered textiles, metalwork, *kilims*, and *pysanky*—the brilliantly decorated Easter eggs whose origin dates back to pre-Christian fertility rituals. The museum also built a photographic archive documenting Ukrainian architecture, people in native dress, and the history of immigration to the United States. These things are still on display in the museum, though with less emphasis.

Since Ukraine regained its independence in 1991, the museum has focused more on its fine arts collection, and in particular on Ukrainian artists of the 20th century. First among them is Alexander Archipenko, the Modernist sculptor, who was the subject of the inaugural exhibition in the new space. Among the works in the permanent collection are luminous watercolors by Oleksa Hryshchenko (Alexis Gritchenko), woodcuts by Jacques Hnizdovsky, and brilliantly-colored flower paintings by Arkadia Olenska-Petryshyn, who studied with William Baziotes and Robert Motherwell. The museum has a significant collection of works by Nikifor, Poland's most noteworthy primitive artist, among whose favorite subjects were the Orthodox churches and wooden buildings of his native Krynica. As the museum builds its permanent collection, changing exhibitions rely on generous loans from Ukrainians here and abroad. A show on Ukrainian Modernists showed work by El Lissitsky, Kazimir Malevich, and Alexander Rodchenko, who are usually thought of as Russian but considered themselves Ukrainian, as well as by artists little known in this country.

On and around East 7th Street

Onion-domed, Byzantine-style **St. George's Ukrainian Catholic Church** (1977) at 30 East 7th St is the largest institution in the community. On the north side of the street, the Surma Book and Record Company, at 11 East 7th St, has been a family business since 1918. It sells traditional Ukrainian Easter eggs (*pysanky*), embroidered blouses, decorative wooden plates, and other crafts.

McSorley's Old Ale House opposite the church, at 15 East 7th St, is one of the most venerable and atmospheric saloons in the city, claiming 1854 as its opening date. It is said that Abraham Lincoln drank here in 1860; in due time he was followed by Babe Ruth, Will Rogers, and Woody Guthrie. The walls are covered with memorabilia and the floor with sawdust. Joseph Mitchell and E.E. Cummings wrote about the place; John Sloan painted scenes of both the bar-room and the back room. Women were not permitted until 1970, when it became illegal to exclude them.

Nearby Ukrainian establishments include the **East Village Meat Market**, at 139 Second Ave; the **Ukrainian National Home**, 140–42 Second Ave, a community center with an inexpensive, home-style Ukrainian restaurant whose specialties include *kielbasa*, stuffed cabbage and *pierogi*; and Veselka at 144 Second Ave, a restaurant which has served handmade *pierogi* and goulash to generations of local Ukrainians (*T: 212 228 9682; www.veselka.com*).

ST. MARK'S PLACE

St. Mark's Place, the blocks of 8th St from Third Avenue to Avenue A, is famous for its bohemian associations. When first developed in the early 19th century, it was a fashionable street, its houses set back from the sidewalks to give the impression of spacious elegance, but during the 1960s St. Mark's Place became the focus of the counterculture. Today the street has a shopping strip with tattoo parlors, goth and vintage clothing stores, and ethnic restaurants. The building (1885) at no. 12 was once the social hall of a German shooting club, its identity marked by the ornamental terra-cotta target and crossed rifles on the upper part of the façade. In the 1920s the Polish National Home (Polski Dom Narodowy), an immigrant support organization, made use of nos. 19–25 St. Mark's Place for a social club with a dance hall and a restaurant. Andy Warhol rented the place and created The Dom, a downstairs dance hall, with the Electric Circus upstairs, a club with a light show and other mixed media special effects.

THE YIDDISH RIALTO

Second Avenue from Houston St to East 14th St, once called the Yiddish Rialto (*map p. 581, E4–E3*), was the home of a vital theatrical tradition beside whose dramas the rest of the theater community paled. The plays, written for an unsophisticated

audience, implausibly coupled tragic events with song-and-dance routines, low comedy, and extravagant tableaux. For Eastern European immigrants who spoke no English, the Yiddish theater was an escape from a brutal reality, virtually the only entertainment available; journalist Hutchins Hapgood noted in 1902 that people whose weekly wage was only $10 willingly spent half their income on the theater. The Yiddish theater thrived until the 1930s, when the Depression and the decline of a Yiddish-speaking audience brought its glory years to a close.

The building that houses the Village East Cinemas, 189 Second Ave (corner of East 12th St), was constructed as the **Yiddish Art Theater** (1926), later becoming the Yiddish Folks Theater, the Phoenix Theater (1953), and a movie theater (1991). The building, seating 1,236, was one of the last Yiddish theaters, designed in a multi-cultural style with Moorish, Byzantine, and Middle Eastern elements, both on the façade and in the interior.

Nearby restaurants include Veniero's Café, 342 East 11th St (at Second Ave), a coffee shop and *pasticceria* founded in 1894 by immigrants from Sorrento in southern Italy, and the De Robertis Pasticceria, 176 First Ave (East 11th and East 10th Sts), whose tiled floors and walls and old-fashioned showcases date back to its founding in 1907.

The famous Second Avenue Delicatessen, founded in 1954, stood at 156 Second Ave (10th St) until it closed in 2005. In front of the former restaurant Lebewohl's "Walk of Yiddish Stars" remains embedded in the sidewalk, Hollywood style, commemorating celebrities of the Yiddish theater. Among them are Boris Tomashefsky, who billed himself as "America's Darling," and Jacob Adler, the best dramatic actor of his generation, who performed Shylock on Broadway in Yiddish while the other actors spoke English. The original owner, Abe Lebewohl, was murdered in 1996, a crime still unsolved. Lebewohl's nephew reopened the deli in 2007 on East 33rd St (*www.2ndavedeli.com; see p. 543*).

The **Ottendorfer Branch of the New York Public Library** (1884) at 135 Second Ave (St. Mark's Place and East 9th St), originally the Freie Bibliothek und Lesehalle, is a bright red-brick building with terra-cotta ornament, donated by newspaper publishers Oswald and Anna Ottendorfer to the local community. It is now part of the city public library system. Next door at 137 Second Ave is the **Stuyvesant Polyclinic Hospital** (1884), founded and endowed by the Ottendorfers as the German Dispensary. Designed in an energetic neo-Italian Renaissance style, the clinic, now part of the Cabrini Medical Center, is architecturally noteworthy for its terra-cotta ornament, which includes portrait busts of physicians and scientists.

The famous **Fillmore East** stood at 105 Second Ave (East 6th and East 7th Sts); such legendary rock stars as Jimi Hendrix, Janis Joplin, The Who, and The Doors performed here before it closed in 1971.

ST. MARK'S-IN-THE-BOWERY CHURCH

On the west side of Second Avenue at 10th St (*map p. 581, E3*), St. Mark's-in-the-Bowery Church (1799; Protestant Episcopal) is the second oldest church in the city

after St. Paul's Chapel (*see p. 77*). Built on the probable site of Peter Stuyvesant's own chapel, St. Mark's, which originally served an affluent, conservative congregation, has long been one of the city's most socially active churches and an important cultural center, supporting poetry, dance, and theater.

The building

The rubblestone walls and simple triangular pediment date from the church's late-Georgian, rural beginnings. Thereafter St. Mark's enjoyed the services of prominent architects. The lovely Greek Revival steeple was added in 1828 (Martin E. Thompson and Ithiel Town) and an Italianate cast-iron portico was built in 1854, keeping the church abreast of architectural fashions. The brick Sunday School building (1861) was designed—or at least supervised—by James Renwick. The rectory (1899) was designed by Ernest Flagg. Flanking the main doorway are two marble lions (one a copy of Donatello's *Marzocco*, the emblem of Florence) and, outside the portico, two granite statues of Native Americans based on drawings by Solon Borglum, brother of the more famous Gutzon Borglum. Commissioned by the church, they were executed by the Piccirilli brothers (*see p. 393*) and symbolize Aspiration and Inspiration. At the west end of the porch is a bust (1939; O. Grymes) of Daniel Tompkins (1774–1825), a governor of New York State known for liberal reforms in education, the criminal code, and human rights. He is buried in the graveyard.

The interior, steeple, and roof were severely damaged in 1978 when a worker's torch ignited the wooden gallery on the second floor. In 1980 a new bell was installed, dedicated to the workers, many of them youthful laborers from the neighborhood, who rebuilt the church. After the fire, the interior was restored, retaining much of the original detailing, including the 19th-century stained-glass windows on the lower level. The upper windows are replacements.

The graveyard and churchyard

The graveyard (on the left-hand side of church; *sometimes locked*) was the scene of a ghoulish kidnapping in 1878 when the body of department store millionaire A.T. Stewart (*see p. 89*) was exhumed and carted off for $20,000 ransom. It was recovered two years later. Resting undisturbed are Commodore Matthew Perry, Daniel Tompkins and members of the prominent Fish, Goelet, Schermerhorn, Stuyvesant, and Livingston families.

The entrance to the churchyard is on the other side of the church. Here stands the old church bell, cracked by the heat of the 1978 fire. Unlike the present electronically operated carillon, it was rung by a rope, and tolled the deaths of John F. Kennedy, Robert F. Kennedy, and the Rev. Dr. Martin Luther King; after Dr. King's assassination it was rung only to celebrate the end of the Vietnam War. Here also are the **remains of Peter Stuyvesant**, entombed in the church wall; nearby (to the right of the porch) is a statue of the governor sculpted in the Netherlands (1911) by Toon Dupuis. A plaque commemorates W.H. Auden, who lived in the neighborhood and was a parishioner of the church.

TOMPKINS SQUARE PARK

The 16-acre Tompkins Square Park (*map p. 581, F3*) is named after onetime governor Daniel Tompkins, whose remains lie at St. Mark's-in-the-Bowery (*see above*).

Originally part of a salt marsh called Stuyvesant Swamp, the park was given to the city by the Stuyvesant family in 1833. Through the years it has witnessed two historic riots and many political demonstrations—sparked by poor economic conditions, oppressive labor relations, the Vietnam War, and gentrification, among other causes. The first riot occurred in 1874 when police, mounted on horseback and wielding clubs, suppressed a gathering of 7,000 unemployed people hoping for work relief during a financial depression. The second, in 1988, was a confrontation between police and local residents angry over enforcement of a curfew that prevented home-less people from staying overnight in the park.

In 1936, Robert Moses had the park designed in its present configuration—many small patches of green interrupted by curving walkways. It is said that he chose this plan as a means of crowd control, to discourage large demonstrations and gatherings.

The park monuments were restored and new playgrounds (and a popular dog-run) opened in 1991.

Park monuments

Visible through a gate leading to the playground on the north side of the park is a marble monument whose eroded features depict a boy and girl looking at a steam-boat. It is a **memorial to the victims of the *General Slocum***, an excursion steamer that burned in the East River on June 15, 1904. The steamship company and even the manufacturer of the life preservers were woefully negligent in failing to provide adequate safety equipment; after the fire broke out the captain failed to ground the burning ship on a nearby island. Some 1,021 people, virtually all of them women and children from this then-predominantly German neighborhood, burned or drowned in the tragedy. Many men, kept from the outing by their jobs, lost their entire families; for the bereaved, the Tompkins Square neighborhood became too full of painful mem-ories, and most departed for other German communities within the city after the disaster. As the Germans moved out, Jews moved in, changing the ethnic character of the area within a few years. The *General Slocum* disaster was the city's largest single loss of life until the September 11 attacks.

Near the 9th St entrance is the **Temperance Fountain** (1888; Henry D. Cogswell). On the canopy is a statue of Hebe (goddess of youth and cup-bearer to the Olympian deities); beneath is a fountain intended to encourage the healthful consumption of water instead of alcohol. Cogswell was a dentist, who made a fortune fixing the teeth of prospectors in the Gold Rush and investing in San Francisco real estate.

Near the southwest entrance to the park is a **statue of Samuel Sullivan Cox**, "the letter carrier's friend," an Ohio congressman who earned this appellation by sponsor-ing legislation that raised wages and gave salaried vacations to postmen. The statue (1891; Louise Lawson) was commissioned by the mailmen of America and first

erected in Cooper Square, where it occasioned criticism that the figure resembled a floor-walker (a department-store employee) beckoning an approaching customer. When Saint-Gaudens's figure of Peter Cooper was installed there (*see p. 162 above*), Congressman Cox was moved here.

Around the square

Along the north side of the park stands a handsome row of houses built in 1846 when the Tompkins Square neighborhood was felt to have an auspicious future. The houses on the south side, built just a year later, were described at the time of completion as "new and desirable tenements," but their ground floors were designed as stores to be rented for $200 a year, an indication of the coming decline of the area. By the 1850s German immigrants had begun to displace the previous residents and the one- and two-family houses were sliced up into rooming houses or razed to make way for profitable tenements. By the 1860s the area was described as dirty, seedy, and dusty; 4th St between Avenues A and B was called "Ragpickers' Row," while 11th St from First Avenue to Avenue B became "Mackerelville."

In the neighborhood

The **Tenth Street Baths** (1892), at 268 East 10th St (First Ave and Avenue A), are the only traditional Russian-Turkish steam baths remaining in Manhattan. Years ago there were many such establishments, modeled after their Old World predecessors, serving people whose homes lacked bathtubs. The children of immigrants subsequently shunned them as too old-fashioned, but today the Tenth Street Baths serve a clientele that includes many Russians, but also New Yorkers young and old.

On the southwest corner of 10th St and Avenue A is **St. Nicholas Carpatho-Russian Orthodox Church** (1883; James Renwick Jr. and W.H. Russell), a congregation founded by immigrants from Carpathian Ruthenia, now in western Ukraine. The Rutherford-Stuyvesant family built the church as a missionary chapel of St. Mark's-in-the-Bowery, who sold it to the present owners in 1925. The interior is distinguished by tiled walls, stained glass, and carved wooden beams.

At 151 Avenue B (9th and 10th Sts) is the **Charlie Parker House** (c. 1849; *map p. 581, F3*), where the great saxophone player lived with his companion, Chan Richardson, from 1950–54. The couple had an apartment on the ground floor; two children were born during their stay. At the time Parker was world-famous, already recognized as a major innovator in jazz, but his life was spinning out of control. He died in 1955, his death hastened by drug use; Chan Parker (she used his name but they were never married) died in 1999 in France. The house itself, modestly remarkable as one of the city's few remaining Gothic Revival town houses, retains its original pointed-arch entranceway and double wooden doors.

UNION SQUARE TO MADISON SQUARE

UNION SQUARE PARK

Map p. 581, D3–D2. Subway L, N, Q, R, W, 4, 5, 6 to 14 St-Union Square. Bus M1, M2, M3, M6, M7, M9. Walking tours Sat at 2pm depart from the Abraham Lincoln statue at the 16th St transverse; T: 212 460 1200.

Union Square Park has emerged as the center of an energetic commercial and residential neighborhood, surrounded by an Off-Broadway theater district and enlivened by the city's largest Greenmarket.

Union Square was first named Union Place (1811) because it stood at the junction of the two main roads out of town: the Bowery Road, which was a section of the Boston Post Road, and the Bloomingdale Road, which was the Albany Post Road (now Fourth Avenue and Broadway respectively). In 1839 when the park opened, Union Square was surrounded by fine homes, as well as restaurants, theaters, and hotels. Toward the century's end, the square became the heart of Ladies' Mile, a promenade of fashionable stores that stretched along Broadway from Eighth to 23rd Sts; by 1900 both commerce and art had moved uptown to Madison Square, leaving Union Square to languish.

The park has long been a gathering place; it was the site of the first Labor Day Parade on Sept 5, 1882. In the years before World War I, the park became a center of political dissidence, for anarchists, socialists, "Wobblies" (members of the Industrial Workers of the World), and communists. A decade later, mass meetings sometimes developed into confrontations with the police: most famous were a gathering protesting the execution of anarchists Nicola Sacco and Bartolomeo Vanzetti (Aug 22, 1927) and a Depression labor demonstration (March 6, 1930) attended by 35,000 workers and sympathizers. Public outcry after police injured 100 demonstrators at this meeting secured the park as a place of assembly, making it the heart of radical political activity.

In the 1970s the park fell on hard times, plagued by drug dealers and considered dangerous. Its recovery is due in part to development at its edges, to the arrival of the popular Greenmarket in 1976, and to the restoration of the park beginning in 1985. Today it is surrounded by thriving businesses and busy restaurants.

Monuments in the park

The equestrian **statue of George Washington** (1856), facing East 14th St at the southern end of the park, is by Henry Kirke Brown, known for his equestrian statues. One of Brown's finer works, it commemorates Washington's entrance to the city on Evacuation Day (*see p. 45*). John Quincy Adams Ward, later known for his portrait busts, was trained by Brown and assisted him with this statue. In the southwest corner is Kantilal B. Patel's bronze (1986) of **Mohandas Gandhi**, the Indian nationalist and advocate of non-violent resistance, an appropriate resident of a park long associated with political

protest. Near the southern edge of the park at East 15th St stands a bronze **statue of the Marquis de Lafayette** (1876; Frédéric-Auguste Bartholdi) presented by France in gratitude for American support during the Franco-Prussian War. Bartholdi, best known for that other monument of Franco-American friendship, the Statue of Liberty, depicts Lafayette offering his sword to the cause of American independence.

Near the center of the park stands the base (36ft diameter; 9½ ft high) of the **Independence Flagstaff** (1926; Anthony De Francisci), whose bronze reliefs contrast the evolution of government under democratic and tyrannical rule. Formerly called the Charles F. Murphy Memorial, after a Tammany Hall boss (*see opposite*), the flag-pole was financed by $80,000 of Tammany money collected on the 150th anniversary of the signing of the Declaration of Independence. The **Union Square Drinking Fountain** nearby (1881; Karl Adolph Donndorf) was donated by philanthropist Daniel Willis James to promote the virtue of Charity, represented allegorically by a mother with her infant and child atop the pedestal. The bronze **statue of Abraham Lincoln** at the north end of the park (1868; Henry Kirke Brown) was originally criticized for the dowdiness of Lincoln's suit. North of the statue is a colonnaded pavilion dating from the 1930s.

South of the park: *Metronome*

A colossal piece of public sculpture, *Metronome* (1999), by Kristin Jones and Andrew Ginzel, covers ten stories of the façade of 1 Union Square South (14th St between Fourth Ave and Broadway). Variously described as "enigmatic," "pretentious," and "the most prominent commission of a public artwork in the city since the Statue of Liberty," the work is said to be a meditation on time—geological, astronomical, historical, and "real." It consists of disparate elements: a wall of rippling brick, a two-ton hunk of concrete fabricated as a boulder; a six-foot hand (enlarged from Henry Kirke Brown's statue of Washington in the park; a five-foot hole that emits steam (referencing the energy of the urban scene); a "pendulum" that emits sound at noon and midnight. To the left of this central composition, a 15-place digital clock simultaneously measures the time passed since midnight (left to right) and the time remaining until the next midnight (right to left)—in hours, minutes, seconds, and tenths of a second, with the middle digit recording hundredths of a second, whirling at illegible speed. To the right a gold colored sphere rotates with the phases of the moon. The artists were chosen through a competition organized by the Public Art Fund.

East and North of the park

The **former Union Square Savings Bank** (1907) at 20 Union Square East (East 15th St), with its handsome Corinthian colonnade, recalls architect Henry Bacon's most famous accomplishment, the Lincoln Memorial in Washington, D.C. Today the Daryl Roth Theater, one of several Off-Broadway houses in the neighborhood, occupies the building. The **Union Square Theatre**, 100 East 17th St (Union Square East and Park Ave South), offers its performances in the Colonial Revival former headquarters of Tammany Hall (1929; *see box opposite*).

TAMMANY HALL

Tammany Hall, later synonymous with the politically corrupt Democratic Party machine, began in New York as the Tammany Society in 1788. Earlier Tammany societies had been instituted in Philadelphia and elsewhere, named for a legendary Native American, Tamanend, of the Lenni Lenape tribe, whose deeds and personality assumed heroic proportions: he was thought, for example, to have created Niagara Falls during an epic battle with an evil spirit. Tamanend became symbolic of the new republic, and was sometimes celebrated as St. Tammany, patron saint of America.

After the Revolution, the Tammany societies became a means for supporting republicanism (and opposing the revival of an aristocratic elite). Unlike the city's more exclusive clubs, the Tammany Society was open to anyone who paid a small membership fee. The ordinary members, "braves," were drawn largely from the ranks of artisans and tradesmen; the leaders were "sachems." They met monthly at their "wigwam," to eat, drink, and talk politics. During celebrations, braves and sachems paraded through the streets wearing Native American garb.

The organization quickly became politicized. William M. "Boss" Tweed owed his start in politics to the society, which recruited him from the ranks of his volunteer firefighters' company, whose logo, a snarling tiger, later became the symbol of Tammany Hall. As immigration swelled the population of the city, Tammany Hall expanded its power base by attending to the needs of the new arrivals, finding work for them, enabling them to gain citizenship, and eventually controlling their votes, a strategy that kept Tammany in power for generations. The sachems of Tammany Hall were also the powerful politicians who ran the Democratic Party organization. Tweed and others like him rewarded loyalty with lucrative contracts.

After Tweed's fall in 1871, John Kelly headed Tammany Hall, converting it from a rabble of competing interests to a disciplined political apparatus. Kelly, the first of ten Irish bosses, introduced a hierarchical system that involved every unit of electoral politics, from the city precincts up to the highest levels of state government. Ethnic groups within Tammany's embrace included the Irish first and foremost, but also Jews and Germans.

The organization peaked in 1928, when its candidates filled the offices of governor (the respected Al Smith) and mayor (the high-living James J. Walker). The next year Tammany opened its fine new building on Union Square. Only three years later Tammany Hall had lost its stranglehold on city politics. In 1931 Walker was forced from office. In 1932 Franklin D. Roosevelt, a Democrat but an opponent of Tammany, was elected president. Roosevelt took control of federal patronage and also promoted the candidacy of Fiorello La Guardia, running on a Republican-Fusion ticket. In 1943, unable to meet the mortgage payments, the Tammany Hall sachems sold the building to the Ladies' Garment Workers Union.

The **Union Square Greenmarket** (*open Mon, Wed, Fri, Sat 8–6*), in the parking lot to the north of the park, brings city dwellers farm-fresh produce, potted plants, baked goods, and flowers from "the country," i.e. anywhere outside the five boroughs. Its arrival in 1976 helped spur the redevelopment of the park and neighborhood. There is a busy outdoor café, Luna Park, here during warm weather (*T: 212 475 8464*).

WEST & NORTH OF UNION SQUARE

The Center for Jewish History

Map p. 580, C2. 15 West 16th St (Fifth and Sixth Aves). Free gallery spaces open Sun 11–5, Mon–Thur 9:30–5, Fri 9–3; closed Wed and Sat. The Yeshiva University Museum galleries have an entrance fee and are open Sun 11–5, Tues–Thurs 11–5; closed Mon, Fri, and Sat. All exhibition spaces closed Jewish holidays, and major national holidays. T: 212 294 8301, www.cjh.org.

The Center for Jewish History (opened 2000) is an umbrella organization that brings together the American Jewish Historical Society, the American Sephardi Federation, the Leo Baeck Institute, Yeshiva University Museum, and YIVO Institute for Jewish Research. Each institution emphasizes a different aspect of Jewish experience: the Yeshiva University Museum (founded 1973) looks at Jewish intellectual and cultural achievements over 3,000 years of history; the Leo Baeck Institute (founded 1955) documents the history of German-speaking Jews; the American Jewish Historical Society (founded 1892) illuminates American Jewish life from 1500 to the present; the American Sephardi Federation (founded 1984) focuses on Jews whose families originated in Syria, Turkey, Morocco, Yemen, and Egypt. YIVO Institute for Jewish Research (founded 1925 in Vilna) is the only pre-Holocaust scholarly institution that successfully transferred its holdings to the Western Hemisphere.

The collections, shown in changing exhibitions, include 100 million archival documents, half a million books, and more than a thousand family trees. The tens of thousands of artifacts include Emma Lazarus's handwritten sonnet "The New Colossus"; a letter of Thomas Jefferson denouncing anti-Semitism; Sandy Koufax's first baseball uniform (signed); and Yiddish sheet music commemorating the sinking of the *Titanic*.

Ladies' Mile

The section of Broadway running north from the park was once the home stretch of Ladies' Mile, a shopping district in the late 19th century for well-to-do women. Palatial department stores and fine office buildings occupied the prominent intersections along Broadway. Several remain, though their ground floors have been altered and their functions have in many cases changed. (Another strip of the Mile runs along Sixth Avenue between West 18th and West 23rd Sts.)

The **former Arnold Constable Dry Goods Store**, 881–87 Broadway (East 18th to East 19th Sts), (1869, with later additions), was designed by Griffith Thomas, architect of Marble House, the original Arnold Constable store on Canal St (*see p. 106*). Thomas faced the Broadway wing with marble—the only suitable material according to Aaron

Arnold. The store grew and expanded along 19th St, becoming one of the city's finest emporia, and Thomas eventually duplicated the Broadway façade in cast iron along Fifth Avenue, wrapping the imposing mansard roof around the entire building.

The **former W. & J. Sloane Store** (1882), across the street at 880–88 Broadway (East 18th to East 19th Sts), is a six-story brick building with cast-iron decoration, wide windows, and classical detailing. The Sloane brothers immigrated from Kilmarnock in Scotland, a town known for carpet-weaving, and began selling carpets, oriental rugs, lace curtains, and upholstery fabrics. Eventually expanding into furniture, the Sloanes decorated mansions for the city's wealthiest families, and eventually intermarried with Vanderbilts and Whitneys. The store followed the carriage trade uptown in 1912. Both the Sloane and the Constable buildings are now occupied (fittingly) by ABC Carpets and Home, a high-end home furnishings store risen from humble beginnings (1897) on the pushcarts of the Lower East Side.

The **former Gorham Manufacturing Co. Building**, at 889 Broadway (East 19th St), brick with a chamfered corner turning that once rose to a tower, was built (1883) as an investment by the Goelet family, who began as hardware merchants and ascended to the upper echelons of New York society. It was an early multi-use building, with showrooms for Gorham silver and ecclesiastical metalwork downstairs, and apartments above. Another family investment, the one-time **Goelet Building** at 900 Broadway (East 20th St), is conspicuous for its fine brickwork and sweeping arches. Built (1887) by McKim, Mead & White, it stands on the site of the Goelet mansion, whose large garden was populated by peacocks and other exotic birds with clipped wings.

The **former Lord & Taylor store**, 901 Broadway (East 20th St), built in 1869, is best seen from the east side of Broadway. It is the fourth and grandest Lord & Taylor emporium, a cast-iron French Second Empire confection by James H. Giles, an architect known for his work in this style. The two-story arched entranceway on Broadway and the fine corner turning with its tall display windows and marble columns are gone, but the imposing corner tower and its high mansard roof remain.

Theodore Roosevelt Birthplace National Historic Site

Map p. 581, D2. 28 East 20th St (Broadway and Park Ave South). Open Tues–Sat 9–5, except Christmas Day, New Year's Day and Thanksgiving; Guided tours given on the hour, 10–4. Admission charge for adults; children under 16 and senior citizens free; T: 212 260 1616; www.nps.gov/thrb.

Theodore Roosevelt, the 26th president of the United States, was born in a house at this address on East 20th St and lived there until he was 14. The present house is a reconstruction (1923; Theodate Pope Riddle), built as a memorial to the president after his death in 1919.

At the time of Roosevelt's birth (1858), this four-story brownstone was an upper-middle-class home in a comfortable residential neighborhood. Theodore's parents moved uptown in 1872, but the house remained in the family until 1896, when it was sold. In 1916, the house was demolished and replaced by a commercial building.

After Roosevelt's death, the Women's Roosevelt Memorial Association rebuilt the home (fortunately it was the mirror image of the neighboring house, which had belonged to Roosevelt's uncle) and redecorated the interior as it had been.

The house contains five rooms of period furniture, about 40 percent of it from the immediate family, with another 20 percent contributed by Roosevelt cousins and more distant relatives. The museum also has an excellent collection of Roosevelt memorabilia, including a set of obelisks from a trip the family made to Egypt, Roosevelt's christening gown, and his diaries.

STUYVESANT SQUARE & ENVIRONS

Map p. 581, E2–E3. Subway L to 1st or 3rd Ave. Bus M15, M101, M102, M103.

Stuyvesant Square, a four-acre park bisected by Second Avenue, was once part of Peter Stuyvesant's farm. In 1836 Peter Gerard Stuyvesant, the governor's great-great-grandson, sold the acreage to the city for $5, with the understanding that the city would fence and landscape it as a park, thus enhancing the value of his own surrounding land. The city procrastinated, and only after years of litigation (Stuyvesant was a lawyer) did the city erect the fence, plant trees, and construct fountains. By the 1850s, the area was attracting sedate religious institutions and well-to-do residents, who built Greek Revival and Italianate houses, some of which still remain.

The bronze statue of peg-legged Peter Stuyvesant (1941) in the western section is by Gertrude Vanderbilt Whitney, founder of the Whitney Museum (Stuyvesant lost his right leg fighting the Spanish in the Caribbean before he became governor of the colony of New Netherlands). In the northeast corner of the square is Ivan Meštrović's statue (1963) of composer Antonín Dvořák, brought here in 1997 from Avery Fisher Hall in Lincoln Center. Between 1892–95 Dvořák was the director of the National Conservatory of Music of America, nearby on 17th St.

West of Stuyvesant Square

Along East 16th and 17th Sts, between Stuyvesant Square and Third Avenue, are several fine late Greek Revival and Italianate row houses built in the 19th century. The earliest Greek Revival houses (1842–43) are at 214–16 East 18th St; one of the latest is at 245 East 17th St (1883), the only remaining residence in the city built by Richard Morris Hunt.

Protestant Episcopal **St. George's Church** on Rutherford Place (East 16th and East 17th Sts facing Stuyvesant Square) is a formidable Romanesque Revival brownstone (1856; Otto Blesch and Leopold Eidlitz), probably best remembered as J. Pierpont Morgan's church because as an elder he ruled it with an iron hand. Morgan (*see p. 202*) also donated the land on which the present parish house stands. The first church (1847) burned in 1865 but was rebuilt according to the original plans, although at the time of the reconstruction the rector insisted on an evangelically simple interior without the customary altar and reredos. The original church had two tall spires, but

they were weakened by the fire and removed (1888). African-American baritone Harry T. Burleigh, the grandson of slaves, sang in the choir for many years. He introduced Dvořák to Negro spirituals, and his arrangement of "Swing Low, Sweet Chariot" is said to have inspired the theme of the largo of Dvořák's *New World Symphony*. At 4 Rutherford Place is St. George's Chapel (1911), an elaborate Byzantine-Romanesque companion to the more somber church next door.

Stuyvesant Town

Stuyvesant Town, bounded by First Avenue and Avenue C (14th–20th Sts; *map p. 581, E2–F2*) is an immense and institutional-looking housing project built shortly after World War II (1947) by the Metropolitan Life Insurance Company, primarily as affordable housing for returning servicemen. In 1947 the waiting list numbered some 110,000, and through the years "Stuy Town" has been home to firefighters, teachers, nurses, and other middle-income tenants. In 2006 both Stuyvesant Town and its northern neighbor, the somewhat more upscale Peter Cooper Village, were sold to an international real estate firm for the record-breaking price of $5.4 billion.

The present Rutherford Place Apartments at 303–05 Second Ave (East 17th–East 18th Sts) began as the **New York Lying-In Hospital** (1899), a philanthropically-supported maternity hospital that provided care for immigrant women of the Lower East Side. J.Pierpont Morgan contributed $13 million to this Classical Revival building, designed by Robert H. Robertson, an architect known for heavyset Romanesque Revival churches. Decoration on the ornate façade includes portrait heads of children, and bas-relief babies in swaddling clothes derived from those by Andrea della Robbia on the foundling hospital in Florence.

GRAMERCY PARK

Map p. 581, D2. Subway 6 to 23rd St.

Gramercy Park is New York's only private residential square. It is surrounded by a lovely old iron fence, Greek Revival houses, 19th-century clubs, and, most recently, an expensive new apartment hotel.

The name "Gramercy" harks back to the Dutch colonial period when the area was called *Krom Moerasje* (crooked little swamp; or *Crommessie*, crooked little knife) after a marshy brook that wandered from Madison Square to the East River near 18th St. Samuel Bulkley Ruggles, a lawyer and small-scale urban planner, bought a 20-acre farm in 1831, drained the marshland, and laid out a park to increase the value of his land. Around the park he designated 66 building lots and sold them with the stipulation that only lot owners could have access to the park. His wishes are still in force: except for a brief period during the Draft Riots of 1863, when troops camped inside the eight-foot iron fence, the park trustees have resisted all intrusions, including a proposed cable car line (1890) and an extension of Lexington Avenue (1912). Only residents facing the square who pay a yearly maintenance fee are granted keys.

Gramercy Park West and the Sage House apartments

Along Gramercy Park West are fine Greek Revival town houses. Dr. Valentine Mott (d. 1865), a prominent surgeon and a founder of Bellevue Hospital, lived at no. 1. The buildings at nos. 3–4 Gramercy Park West (c. 1840; attrib. Alexander Jackson Davis) are distinguished by their original cast-iron verandas with profuse Greek Revival ornamentation—anthemia, meanders, and floral motifs. This lacy ironwork, more familiar in southern cities such as Charleston and New Orleans, was considered a rustic touch especially appropriate to houses facing parks or enjoying deep front yards. A pair of Mayor's Lamps stands at no. 4, once the home of James Harper, mayor of the city (1844–45) and a founder of Harper & Bros publishers.

The Sage House apartments, just north of the park at 4 Lexington Ave and East 22nd St (next door to the apartment hotel), occupy the former **Russell Sage Foundation** (c. 1914), a lavishly handsome Renaissance Revival palace in the Florentine style, whose frieze proclaims the foundation's purpose: "For the Improvement of Social and Living Conditions." Sage—financier, railroad builder, and stock market entrepreneur—left a fortune of some $60 million when he died in 1906. His widow used $15 million of her inheritance to establish the foundation. Among its philanthropic acts was the construction of Forest Hills Gardens in Queens, an attempt at model housing. Grosvenor Atterbury was the architect for both Forest Hills Gardens and this building.

Gramercy Park South

The brownstone **National Arts Club** at 15 Gramercy Park South near Irving Place (*T: 212 475 3424; www.nationalartsclub.org*) was built (1845) during the Gothic Revival period of the 1840s as two houses. It was remodeled (1884, Vaux and Radford) for Samuel J. Tilden during the heyday of a more flamboyant Victorian Gothic style. Tilden, scourge of the Tweed Ring (*see p. 86*), governor of New York State, and the Democratic presidential candidate who lost by one electoral vote in 1876, was wary of assassination attempts, so he had rolling steel doors installed behind the lower windows and an escape tunnel built to 19th St. Tilden spent much of his money on his collection of rare books, which along with the Astor and Lenox endowments formed the core of the New York Public Library collection. Architecturally the building's attractions include polychrome decoration, asymmetric bays, heavy lancet windows, and a set of medallions portraying Goethe, Dante, Franklin, Shakespeare, and Milton. The National Arts Club bought the property in 1906. The Club sponsors art exhibitions, lectures, and other events, some open to the public

The Players at 16 Gramercy Park South (East 20th St between Irving Place and Gramercy Park West) was a simple Gothic Revival brownstone house (1845) until actor Edwin Booth bought it and hired Stanford White to remodel it (1888) as an actors' club. The drip moldings on the upstairs windows remain from its earlier days. At the end of his sad and rootless life, Booth, one of the finest actors of his time, lived on the top floor of the club overlooking the park. The fine iron railings and lanterns and the two-story porch based on an Italian Renaissance prototype are known to be

White's personal work. Inside the park is a statue of Booth in the character of Hamlet (1918; Edmond T. Quinn).

The **former Stuyvesant Fish House** at 19 Gramercy Park South (East 20th St at Irving Pl), five stories of red brick built in 1845 and updated with a mansard roof in 1860, was built by an obscure Whig politician. In 1887, it was bought by the financier Stuyvesant Fish, whose business interests included railroads, insurance, and banking. After Fish moved uptown near the turn of the 20th century, the house declined, until public relations counsel Benjamin Sonnenberg bought it in 1931 and restored it to its former glory, both as a house and as a center of the city's social life.

Once threatened with demolition, the former Friends' Meeting House, 144 East 20th St (corner of Gramercy Park South and Gramercy Park East), an austere Italianate building (1859) whose severity is broken only by the arched pediment above the doorway, has been renovated as the **Brotherhood Synagogue** (1975; James Stewart Polshek). On its east side is the Garden of Remembrance, a memorial (dedicated 1982) to Jews who perished in the Holocaust.

Irving Place

Irving Place was named (1831) by Samuel Ruggles for his friend Washington Irving, writer and diplomat. The block of East 19th St between Irving Place and Third Avenue is known as **"The Block Beautiful"** for its charming 19th-century houses and converted stables. During the 1930s a small artists' colony flourished here, its residents including muckraker Ida Tarbell (*The History of Standard Oil*) and painter George Bellows.

The building containing Pete's Tavern, 129 East 18th St (Irving Pl), dates to 1829, but the tavern dates either to 1864 or 1899, when it became Healy's Café. Its most illustrious client, writer O. Henry (William Sydney Porter), lived at 55 Irving Place and described the café, which he called Kenealy's, in his story "The Lost Blend." The tavern survived Prohibition as a speakeasy disguised as a flower shop

THE FLATIRON DISTRICT

Map p. 581, D2. Subway: N, R, W or 6 to 23rd St. Bus: M2, M3, M5, M6, M7.
The neighborhood around the Flatiron Building, once known for its concentration of photographers' studios and camera shops, and for its wholesalers of toys and gifts, has in recent years become a trendy residential area, its older commercial buildings converted to condos, their ground floors housing restaurants, clubs, and shops.

The limestone **United Synagogue of America Building** at 153–57 Fifth Ave (21st and 22nd Sts), originally the Scribner Building (1894), is small and classically elegant, the first commercial work by the Scribner family's architect, Ernest Flagg, who also obliged his employers with a printing plant, an uptown store, and two private houses. Admired for its elegant metal and glass storefront, the building once had a salesroom reminiscent of a library in a private house, and a metal and glass entrance canopy.

The Flatiron Building

The Flatiron Building (175 Fifth Ave at 23rd St), which fills the elongated triangle where Broadway joins Fifth Avenue, was the world's tallest building (285ft) when completed in 1902, and one of the first to be supported by a steel skeleton. Dramatically sited and radically constructed (architect Daniel H. Burnham), the Flatiron is nonetheless conservatively garbed in limestone and terra cotta molded in ornate French Renaissance detail. The rounded corner turning (only six feet wide at the north end), and the eight-story undulating bays in the mid-section of the side walls soften its severity. First called the Fuller Building after its developer, the Flatiron Building has enthralled such diverse observers as H.G. Wells (1906), who admired its "prow … ploughing up through the traffic of Broadway and Fifth Avenue in the after-noon light," and Edward Steichen, whose photos of it are famous.

Just west of the Flatiron Building at 186 Fifth Ave (23rd St) is the **former Western Union Telegraph Company Building** (1884). Small in scale, this red-brick building with limestone trim, a gabled roof, dormers, and an odd, octagonal chimney tower is an early work by Henry J. Hardenbergh, the architect of the Dakota Apartments and the Plaza Hotel.

MADISON SQUARE PARK

Map p. 581, D2–D1. For events info, T: 212 538 6667 or visit www.madisonsquarepark.org. The Shake Shack, near Madison Ave and 23rd St, is open 11–11 in summer; hours adjusted seasonally; T: 212 889 6600; www.shakeshack.com.

Located on 6.2 acres between 23rd and 26th Sts, Fifth and Madison Aves, this recently restored park is now a pleasant haven in the midst of a busy commercial district. It includes a refurbished playground for children, a run for dogs, and an environmentally "green" refreshment hut called the Shake Shack. A few sculptures recall the park's rich history.

Before the Commissioners' Plan of 1811 (*see p. 30*) set the land aside, the area that is now Madison Square was successively a marsh and a potter's field. In 1811 it became a parade ground for soldiers. In 1844 the city fathers reduced the park to its present size and named it after president James Madison; it opened officially in 1847. In 1870, when the Parks Department was created, Ignatz Pilat, who had previously worked on Central Park with Frederick Law Olmsted, and William Grant landscaped the area again and brought in the statuary. For a while thereafter Madison Square Park was the centerpiece of the city's most glamorous neighborhood, a garden of pleasure for the socially elite. This happy time came to an end in 1902, when the skyscraping Flatiron Building arrived, signaling in a grand way the arrival of commerce.

The park was restored in 2001, along with its gardens and statuary. There are programs of art and music, as well as events for children and adults that maintain the vitality of the park.

Daniel H. Burnham's celebrated Flatiron Building (1902).

Monuments in Madison Square Park

At the southern end of the park is a statue (1876) of **William Henry Seward**, US senator and secretary of state under Lincoln and Andrew Johnson, best known for purchasing Alaska from Russia. The bronze figure by Randolph Rogers, admired when installed, drew scorn when a rumor (untrue) suggested that Rogers had recast the body from a figure of Lincoln made earlier and simply attached Seward's head to Lincoln's neck. Further along, a bronze statue commemorates **Roscoe Conkling** (1893; John Quincy Adams Ward), a US senator and presidential candidate who died of exposure after trying to walk home from his downtown office in the Blizzard of 1888.

Visible outside the park on the traffic island between Fifth Avenue and Broadway is a 51-ft granite obelisk which marks the grave of **Gen. William Jenkins Worth** (1857; James Goodwin Batterson), hero of the Mexican War, whose mortal remains lie virtually beneath the roaring traffic. The 19th-century cast-iron fence of swords embedded in the ground is also handsome.

Toward the north end is the finest work in the park, the **Admiral David G. Farragut Monument** (1880; Augustus Saint-Gaudens; pedestal design by Stanford White). The bronze figure of the admiral stands whipped by an imaginary wind, and gazing off at the horizon from his pedestal (a replica of the original), on which two low-relief female figures, *Courage* and *Loyalty*, emerge from a swirl of ocean currents. Saint-Gaudens and White collaborated to integrate all the elements of the monument—its pedestal and inscriptions, the siting and landscaping—into a satisfying whole. In the northeast corner is a statue of **Chester A. Arthur** (1898; George E. Bissell), 21st president of the United States.

The Museum of Sex

Open to adults (18+) Sun–Fri 11–6:30, Sat 11–8; last tickets 45mins before closing. Closed Thanksgiving and Christmas; T: 212 689 6337; www.museumofsex.com.

This small museum at 233 Fifth Ave (27th St) opened in 2002. Despite its avowedly educational mission statement—to document, study and display all aspects of human sexuality—it was denied not-for-profit status by the state, and the exhibits are sufficiently hard core to have ignited the fire of the Catholic League for Religious and Civil Rights. The permanent collection, begun when the museum was founded, now has some 15,000 objects, which range from erotic art to devices for enhancing (or deterring) sexual activity, to historical documents such as a *Guide to the Harem, or Directory to the Ladies of Fashion in New York and Various Other Cities* for the years 1855–56. Recent changing exhibits have focused on such topics as sex and disability; 2,500 years of sex in China; fetishes; and the evolution of pinup photography.

EAST OF MADISON SQUARE PARK

The **New York Life Insurance Company** (1928) at 51 Madison Ave (26th and 27th Sts) rises from an Italian Renaissance limestone base to a brightly gilded pyramidal tower, a feature architect *Cass Gilbert* also designed into his Woolworth Building and

Federal Courthouse at Foley Square. The grandiose lobby, with its imposing scale, coffered ceiling, bronze appointments, and great staircase, suggests the wealth of the institution that commissioned the building.

THE FIRST & SECOND MADISON SQUARE GARDENS

In the 1870s P.T. Barnum leased an unused railroad depot from the New York and Harlem Railroad, and opened the building as the Barnum's Monster Classical and Geological Hippodrome, a hall for spectacles that ranged from chariot races to waltzing elephants. In 1879 William Vanderbilt, who had become head of the railroad, took back the former depot, changed the name to Madison Square Garden, and reopened it primarily as a sports arena.

The second Madison Square Garden replaced the first, which had become "a grimy, drafty, combustible old shell" that was no longer making money for Vanderbilt. The architect, Stanford White, well-connected to the wealthy supporters of a new garden, constructed a pleasure palace that housed a restaurant, theater, and roof garden as well as a sports arena. The walls were of yellow brick and white terra cotta; the sidewalks were arcaded; and the roof was ornamented with six open cupolas, two small towers, and a large tower modeled after the Giralda in Seville. On top of the tower stood Augustus Saint-Gaudens's gilded *Diana*, a statue whose nudity distressed the city's more proper citizens even though the goddess's anatomical charms could be glimpsed only remotely since she stood some 250ft above the sidewalk.

Ironically, the new Madison Square Garden was the site of Stanford White's death. In June 1906 he was fatally shot (an unusual death for an architect) in the roof garden by Pittsburgh millionaire Harry K. Thaw, whose young wife, the former showgirl Evelyn Nesbit, had in earlier days enjoyed a well-publicized affair with White.

The Appellate Division of the New York State Supreme Court

The courthouse of the Manhattan Appellate Division (*27 Madison Ave at East 25th and East 26th Sts; open weekdays 9–5; T: 212 340 0400*), built in 1900 under the influence of the City Beautiful movement, is noteworthy inside and out for its sculpture and lavish decoration. Architect James Brown Lord was handed a then-astonishing $700,000 for the building, and he chose America's most renowned sculptors and decorators to embellish his work.

Built of white marble with a Corinthian portico facing 25th St and four more columns along Madison Avenue, the courthouse ultimately cost $633,768 of which more than one-third went for statuary and murals. The interior is lavishly decorated with murals, beaded chandeliers, marble, and wood paneling. In the courtroom is a fine stained-glass skylight bearing the names of famous American lawyers.

The exterior decoration

Along 25th St: Flanking the steps are *Wisdom* and *Force* (Frederick Wellington Ruckstuhl). The pediment above the main doorway bears a sculptural group, *The Triumph of Law* (Charles H. Niehaus). The central group on the roof balustrade is *Justice Flanked by Power and Study*, by Daniel Chester French.

Along Madison Avenue: At the third-floor level four caryatids by Thomas Shields Clarke represent the seasons. Karl Bitter's *Peace Flanked by Wisdom and Strength* is the central group on the balustrade.

Along both streets the roof balustrade supports large figures of famous lawgivers, including Moses, Solon (Athenian reformer and one of the Seven Sages of ancient Greece), and Lycurgus (lawgiver of Sparta and founder of its military might), each by a different sculptor. A statue of Mohammed was removed and destroyed (1955) at the request of the city's Islamic community, because religious law forbids such portraiture.

Annex: On the last bay is Harriet Feigenbaum's *Memorial to the Victims of the Injustice of the Holocaust*, a 38-ft, six-sided pilaster with a relief of flames; at eye level is an incised plan of Auschwitz, based on an aerial reconnaissance photo from 1944. The inscription reads "Indifference to injustice is the gate to hell."

Metropolitan Life Insurance Company Buildings

The blocks along Madison Avenue between 23rd and 25th Sts are occupied by buildings of the Metropolitan Life Insurance Company, MetLife for short. The limestone Art Deco North Building, 11–25 Madison Ave (25th and 24th Sts), is best seen from the park. Its high vaulted entrances and elaborate, angled setbacks have been praised for lightening the apparent mass of the building. In 1928 Harvey Wiley Corbett left the Rockefeller Center architectural team to design this building, which was completed in 1932. It was intended as the base of a 100-story skyscraper, which would have brought Corbett fame as architect of New York's tallest building. The Depression curtailed plans and the tower was never built.

When completed in 1909, the Metropolitan Life Tower at 1 Madison Ave (24th and 23rd Sts) surpassed the Flatiron Building as the world's tallest building, only to be topped by the Woolworth Building four years later. The tower, designed by Napoleon Le Brun & Sons (700ft high, 75ft wide on Madison Ave, 85ft wide on 24th St), was inspired by the campanile of St. Mark's in Venice, but is more than twice as tall. The clock on the four sides of the tower of is one of the world's largest, each face 26.5ft in diameter, each minute hand weighing half a ton, each numeral four feet high. In 1964 the original marble and much of the exterior ornament were removed during a renovation. In 2005 the building was sold for conversion to condominiums.

The Armory

The former 69th Regiment Armory on Lexington Avenue (25th and 26th Sts) was built (1904–06) by Hunt & Hunt for New York's "Fighting 69th" regiment of the National

Guard. It is the only armory in the city not designed to look like a medieval fortress; behind the Lexington Avenue façade, with its copper-framed windows and mansard roof, is an imposing barrel-vaulted drill hall. The building is famous as the site of the Armory Show (1913), officially known as the International Exhibition of Modern Art, where Marcel Duchamp's *Nude Descending the Stairs* stunned the New York art world.

THE ARMORY SHOW

The Armory Show is generally credited with introducing the American public to modern European art, and is considered the most important exhibition ever mounted in the US. It opened on Feb 17, 1913 and was seen by as many as 75,000 people in New York before it traveled to Boston and Chicago, attracting a significantly larger audience than most art exhibitions of the day.

Those who went to the show saw a broad survey of modern art, at least 1,250 works by 300 artists. The oldest piece was a miniature by Goya; the newest were created within the year of the show. About two-thirds of the pieces were American, but it was the European Modernists who provoked the most intense response.

Two artists in particular drew scorn. The first was Marcel Duchamp, whose Cubist-Futurist *Nude Descending a Staircase* (1912) depicted a moving figure as a series of fractured planes, painted with a restricted palette whose brownish and reddish tones intentionally simulated wood. It was parodied as "Rude Descending a Staircase: Rush Hour in the Subway" or "Food Descending a Staircase," and likened by one critic to an "explosion in a shingle factory."

The second object of derision was Henri Matisse, condemned, for example, by students at the Chicago Art Institute for "artistic murder, pictorial arson, artistic rapine, total degeneracy of color, criminal misuse of line, general aesthetic aberration, and contumacious abuse of title." Perhaps because Matisse's work was less abstract than Duchamp's it drew the stronger response. Even the sculptor William Zorach confessed that he was especially disturbed by Matisse's *Luxe II*, in which one of the nudes has only four toes.

Nonetheless, the Armory Show brought modern art into major collections. A California dealer purchased Duchamp's *Nude* sight unseen; Lillie P. Bliss bought paintings by Cézanne, Redon, and Vuillard among others (works that ended up in the MoMA); and the Metropolitan Museum bought Cézanne's *Hill of the Poor* (*View of the Domaine Saint-Joseph*). Other collectors began to buy Impressionist, Post-Impressionist, and 20th-century European art at an accelerated pace; some of these works now contribute to the core collections of major museums.

The achievement of the show was not so much that it taught individual artists the mystique of Cubism, but that it made Modernism attractive to a wider audience of collectors and gallery owners. By creating a market, the Armory Show laid the foundation which allowed American Abstraction to replace American Realism.

THE MEATPACKING DISTRICT
& CHELSEA

Map p. 580, B3–A3. Subway: A, C, E to 14th St; walk south to 13th St and west along Gansevoort St. Bus: M11, M14D.

The history, architecture, and demography of the Far West Side have been shaped by its closeness to the Hudson River. The low-rise commercial architecture of the small Meatpacking District remains from its 19th-century market, where meat and produce were brought by boat and rail. Chelsea is more complex, embracing early 19th-century piers; industrial sites (some now filled with glossy art galleries); and housing that ranges from tenements and urban renewal projects, to gracious Greek Revival and Italianate town houses built for a genteel middle class, to sleek modern high-rise apartments.

THE MEATPACKING DISTRICT

The Meatpacking District, formerly known as the Gansevoort Market, runs from about Gansevoort St to West 15th St along the Hudson River. Though a remnant of the wholesale meatpacking industry remains and still gives the neighborhood its working-class edge, it gentrified rapidly during the 1990s with stylish bars and restaurants, high-concept clothing and design stores, and art galleries spilling south from Chelsea.

A young meatpacking worker, photographed in 1999.

The district's original name honors Peter Gansevoort (1749–1812), an officer in the American Revolution and later brigadier general in the US Army. The Gansevoort Market is descended from two major 19th-century markets: the West Washington Market at the foot of West 12th St, through whose buildings and piers passed cargoes of produce from southern and Caribbean ports as well as much of the city's oyster supply; and the old Gansevoort Market across from it, a large paved area where New Jersey and Long Island farmers drove their wagons to await the pre-dawn beginning of the workday. Herman Melville, author of *Moby-Dick*, his literary career apparently in ruins, worked as a customs inspector on the former Gansevoort dock for 19 years from 1866.

Later, in the late 1920s when the Ninth Avenue El was torn down, the city decided to restructure the Gansevoort area as a meatpacking and distribution center. In 2003, the Gansevoort Market was landmarked to preserve its historic buildings.

There are no grand sights in the Meatpacking District. Its daytime pleasures—aside from the shops and restaurants—lie in its commercial architecture: the Belgian block streets; the loading platforms, overhung by metal canopies that once protected the meat and produce on the sidewalks; the old Greek Revival row houses, many with ground-floor shops; the aerial walkways between buildings; the High Line railroad viaduct (*see p. 188 below*).

CHELSEA

Map p. 580, B2. Subway: 1 to 18th St; A, C, E to 14th St. Bus: M11.
Chelsea runs from about West 14th St through the West 20s, and from the Hudson River to Sixth Avenue or (some say) Broadway. It owes its name and approximate boundaries to Captain Thomas Clarke, a retired British soldier who bought a tract of land in 1750 and named the estate after the Royal Hospital, Chelsea, in London, a refuge for old and disabled soldiers. Chelsea owes its most attractive streets to Clarke's grandson, Clement Clarke Moore, who developed it as a residential neighborhood. Moore (1779–1863), a professor of Classics at Columbia, compiled a Hebrew lexicon and published on subjects ranging from history to agriculture, but is remembered for his poem "A Visit from St. Nicholas" (which begins "'Twas the night before Christmas .."). Moore lived in Greenwich Village but summered in Chelsea until it became clear that the pressures of the city's northward growth would engulf its rolling hills and meadows. He astutely gave a plot of land to the General Theological Seminary (*see p. 187 below*), thus guaranteeing himself a genteel neighborhood, and began selling building lots with design and use controls attached: no alleys, no stables, no "manufactories," and a mandatory ten-foot setback for all houses.

Western and eastern Chelsea have developed differently through the years. The Hudson River Railroad, later absorbed by the New York Central, laid tracks down Eleventh Avenue (c. 1847), attracting breweries, slaughterhouses, and glue factories, which in turn attracted job-hungry immigrants. The overhead tracks of the Ninth

Avenue El (1871) plunged the avenue below into shadow, further depressing the area. Although the El was dismantled before World War II, the western part of Chelsea did not recover for many years.

Eastern Chelsea fared better. During the 1870s and 1880s a theatrical district flourished on West 23rd St, with an opera house and several legitimate theaters. Although the theater district moved uptown later in the century, Chelsea enjoyed a brief artistic revival around World War I as the center of early moviedom, before a better climate and more space lured the industry to California.

Like the Meatpacking District, Chelsea has undergone rapid change in the past decade, its western reaches transformed from an industrial neighborhood once blighted by both street-level and elevated railroads to the city's new SoHo, its streets enlivened by art galleries (more than 200 of these) and chic shops. Ethnic groups who have settled here include one of the city's oldest Spanish communities; the once-predominant Irish; a French colony; a Greek enclave on Eighth Avenue; and, after World War II, a Puerto Rican population.

Chelsea Market

Map p. 580, B3–B2 (bounded by West 15th and West 16th Sts, Ninth and Tenth Aves). Open Mon–Fri 7am–9pm, Sat–Sun 7am–8pm; individual businesses may have different hours.
In 1995 the former Nabisco (National Biscuit Company) factory reopened as the Chelsea Market, whose ground floor is filled with shops offering high-quality food, wine, kitchen wares, and flowers. There are industrial artworks here and there, a waterfall belching from a metal pipe, and sculpture made from cast-off machinery; the overhead piping and brickwork are handsomely exposed.

In the 1920s the baking company occupied all or part of five blocks in the market district and was the biggest baking factory in the world, turning out its signature Fig Newtons, Barnum's Animal Crackers, and Vanilla Wafers. Oreos and Mallomars were invented here. When the High Line was constructed, the company responded by routing a siding from the railroad to a second-story viaduct, still visible. In 1958 Nabisco moved to New Jersey.

West 18th to West 20th Streets

At 555 West 18th St, on the site of a former garage, stands Frank Gehry's only completed New York building, overlooking the Hudson River (his other, incomplete, project is the controversial Atlantic Yards development in Brooklyn; *see p. 26*). The **InterActiveCorp Building** (2007), a ten-story glass-clad office block whose sharp-edged yet billowing surfaces suggest a ship under full sail, is unmistakable from the West Side Highway, glowing at night, shining in the sunlight, and almost disappearing into the mist on cloudy days. It houses a media and internet conglomerate.

In the far west of Chelsea, **The Kitchen** (*512 West 19th St between Tenth and Eleventh Aves; T: 212 255 5793; www.thekitchen.org*) is a center for interdisciplinary and experimental art: video, music, dance, performance, and film. It was founded in 1971, in the former kitchen of the now defunct Broadway Central Hotel.

The **General Theological Seminary**, which occupies a full city block between Ninth and Tenth Aves, West 20th and West 21st Sts, was founded in 1817 and is the oldest Episcopal Seminary in the United States. (*Entrance on Ninth Ave. Self-guided tour available daily 9–5; closed on religious holidays and when school is not in session; T: 212 243 5150; www.gts.edu.*) Clement Clarke Moore (*see p. 185 above*), who taught Hebrew and Greek here, donated the land on which the seminary stands. With the exception of the Gothic Revival West Building (1836), most of the college was built 1883–1900. Especially attractive is the central Chapel of the Good Shepherd with its 161-ft tower and bronze doors by J. Massey Rhind.

Chelsea Row Houses

The block of West 20th St between Ninth and Tenth Aves has gracious Greek Revival and Italianate row houses. No. 402 West 20th St (1897; C.P.H. Gilbert) is remarkable for the concave façade that curves back from the corner tenement to meet the ten-foot setback of the adjoining row of older houses. The letters DONAC above the door commemorate Don Alonzo Cushman, not a Spanish grandee but a dry-goods merchant, friend of Clement Clarke Moore, parish leader, and developer who made a fortune building in Chelsea. **Cushman Row**, which includes nos. 406–18 West 20th St, is named after him. Completed in 1840, these brick, brownstone-trimmed Greek Revival houses still have many original details: fine cast-iron wreaths around small attic windows, paneled doors, iron stoop railings and areaway fences, and pilastered doorways with slender sidelights. Nos. 416–18 still have their pineapple newel posts. Further west are some exceptional Italianate houses (nos. 446–50) built in 1853, with round-headed ground-floor windows and doorways as well as unusual trim beneath the cornices. Arched windows and doorways, exemplifying the Italianate style's attraction to circular forms, appeared only on expensive houses, since they were relatively difficult to execute.

7,000 OAKS

Joseph Beuys's installation *7,000 Oaks*, along West 22nd St between Tenth and Eleventh Aves (*map p. 580, A2*), consists of 23 basalt columns each accompanied by a tree (not all of them oaks), each pair thus having a part that grows and changes, and a part that remains stable in its form and mass. Beuys, who was also an ecologist, was obsessed with the transformative powers of art, and for him the installation of the original 7,000 trees, begun in Kassel, Germany, in 1982, was the beginning of a worldwide tree-planting project to effect social and environmental change. The Dia Art Foundation, which funded the project in Germany, planted trees here (next to its former building) in 1988 and 1996.

The **London Terrace Apartments**, filling an entire block (West 23rd to West 24th Sts, Ninth to Tenth Aves), are an early modern apartment project (1930) named for a row

(i.e. terrace) of 19th-century colonnaded town houses torn down to make way for the present 14 buildings. Such amenities as a central garden, swimming pool, solarium, gymnasium, and doormen dressed as London bobbies attracted tenants to the 1,670 apartments. On the top level was a clubhouse and the Marine Roof, fitted out like the deck of a transatlantic liner, complete with lifebuoys and folding deck chairs.

THE HIGH LINE

Built in the mid-19th century, the New York Central Railroad used to run at street level down Eleventh and, further south, along Tenth Avenue. The streets were clogged with traffic, the trains were dirty, and the tracks were dangerous. "West Side Cowboys" mounted on horseback preceded the engines waving flags, but accidents happened and Eleventh Avenue became known as "Death Avenue."

The High Line, a 13-mile viaduct for freight trains, was constructed in the 1930s to solve these problems. It was built not directly over the avenue but mid-block, between buildings or right through them. Freight cars shunted into the elevated loading bays of the warehouses along the line could then roll out, and head straight up the New York Central tracks to Albany and beyond.

During the 1950s rail freight gave way to trucking, and the last train, with its consignment of frozen turkeys, journeyed to Gansevoort St in 1980. Because no one wanted to pay the demolition costs, the High Line was left to rust. As time passed, weeds sprouted from the rail bed giving the viaduct the beauty of a Piranesi ruin. Beginning in the late 1990s, a local advocacy group defeated proposals for demolition, and at the present time, a park is being constructed over the 1.6 miles between West 16th and West 30th Sts. The luxury buildings by celebrated architects that are being designed and constructed along the route will alter the humble Chelsea skyline.

The Chelsea Piers

The original deep-water Chelsea Piers, piers 54–62 (1902–07; *map p. 580, A3–A2*), stretched from about West 12th to West 20th Sts, and were designed by Warren & Wetmore, the architects of Grand Central Terminal, specifically to accommodate the large transatlantic liners built around the turn of the 20th century. These 800-ft finger piers were finished just in time to receive the *Mauretania* and the *Lusitania* (both 790ft), then the pride of the Cunard Line. The ships of the White Star and Grace lines also berthed nearby. When the *Titanic* sank, the passengers rescued by the Cunard steamship *Carpathia* docked at the Chelsea Piers. The *Lusitania* left from here on its fatal last voyage to England in 1915. The rusted metal arch at Pier 54 (near the foot of West 13th St) is all that remains of the Cunard pier house.

The Depression debilitated the Atlantic trade, but the piers were used as an embarkation point in World War II, and later, during the late 1950s and early 1960s, for

handling cargo. With the decay of New York as a port in succeeding decades, this segment of Chelsea's economy atrophied and the piers closed in 1968. Many of the Irish-American dockworkers who once lived here moved to New Jersey, where the piers are still active. In the 1990s, after gradually deteriorating, the Chelsea piers were converted to their present use as an entertainment and sports center.

West 26th to West 28th Streets

The 19-story **Starrett-Lehigh Building** (1931), at 601 West 26th St (Eleventh and Twelfth Aves) is an imposing Modernist industrial building, admired for its dramatic exterior—horizontal bands of glass, concrete, and brown brick wrapped around curved corners—and its innovative concrete column-and-slab construction.

Built over a spur line of the Lehigh Valley Railroad, the building was intended for freight handling and warehousing, and was equipped with powerful elevators that could lift loaded boxcars from the tracks to the warehouse above. But rail freight, which had to be ferried across the Hudson on railroad-car floats, could not complete with government–supported highways. The upper-story railroad tracks inside the building were never built and those at street level were torn out, but the elevators still hoist 15-ton trucks into the vast interior. It has been refurbished and has corporate tenants in communications and design.

The massive fortress between West 27th and West 28th Sts (Eleventh and Twelfth Aves) is the **Central Stores of the Terminal Warehouse Company** (1891), originally 25 storage buildings with 24 acres of warehousing walled into one space. The great arched doorway at one time admitted locomotives on a spur line of the New York Central Railroad, while the west façade opened onto the deepwater Hudson River piers. Cool cellars running beneath the entire structure were used to store wines, liquors, gums, and rubber.

The Protestant Episcopal **Church of the Holy Apostles**, at 296 Ninth Ave (West 28th St), a small, brick, country-style church (1848, Minard Lafever; transepts 1858, Richard Upjohn & Sons) with a copper-covered, slate-roofed spire and bracketed eaves, is an anomaly in a neighborhood of overscaled modern housing projects. The windows are by William Jay Bolton, one of America's earliest stained-glass artists, and his brother John. Simpler than much of Bolton's work, the windows have round sepia-toned oculi with biblical scenes, which are said to have been drawn from the Bolton family Bible.

CENTRAL CHELSEA

Third Shearith Israel Graveyard (*West 21st St between Sixth and Seventh Aves*) is a tiny cemetery that served the city's earliest Jewish congregation (*see p. 54*) from 1829–51, as it moved its synagogue uptown. **St. Peter's Church** (Protestant Episcopal) at 346 West 20th St (Eighth and Ninth Aves) is a modest early Gothic Revival fieldstone church (1836–38), constructed from designs by Clement Clarke Moore (*see p. 185*). At the west end of the tract is the rectory (1832), which first served as the church, and is built in the Greek Revival style, though with brick pilasters instead of the usual

freestanding columns. According to legend, the foundations for the present church had already been laid when a vestryman returned from England, so enthralled with the Gothic parish churches there that he persuaded his colleagues to redesign the new church. The resulting structure is Gothic more in its details than in its proportions and materials.

The **Joyce Theater** (1941), at 175 Eighth Ave (19th St), was once the Elgin Theater, which by the 1970s was reduced to showing pornography. In 1982, the firm of Hardy Holzman Pfeiffer gutted the building, rebuilt the interior especially for dance performances, and dramatically restored the exterior, including its elaborately patterned brickwork. The Joyce is now one of the principal venues for modern dance in the city.

The Rubin Museum of Art

Map p. 580, C2. 150 West 17th St (Seventh Ave). Open Mon 11–5, Wed 11–7, Thur 11–5, Fri 11–10, Sat and Sun 11–6. Closed Tues, New Year's Day, Thanksgiving, Christmas Day. Free Fri 7pm–10pm; T: 212 620 5000; www.rmanyc.org.

The only museum in the Western Hemisphere devoted to the art of the Himalayas, the museum showcases the private collection of Donald and Shelley Rubin. It occupies the well-known former Barney's clothing store, re-designed by Beyer Blinder Belle (2004), who preserved the dramatic central staircase.

THE HIMALAYAN REGION & ITS ART

The Himalaya mountain range straddles the border region of India and Tibet, extending from Pakistan in the northwest through Nepal to Bhutan and China in the east. Dominant cultural influences include Tibetan Buddhism in the north, and Hinduism from the Indian subcontinent. Islam thrives in the contested area of Kashmir, and varieties of shamanism have survived in more isolated areas.

The art of the Himalayas is steeped in religious traditions, and features iconography that may be unfamiliar to Westerners. Works created in the northern regions draw on teachings of Tibetan Buddhism, a mingling of native Bön shamanism and Buddhism, which arrived in the 2nd century AD. Tibetan art features a panoply of sacred figures such as the Bodhisattvas (enlightened beings who defer Nirvana until they have led all beings to buddhahood) and the Dharmapala (defenders of Buddhism often depicted as dark-skinned, ferocious creatures).

In the southern region of Nepal, Hindu deities and their Buddhist derivations are depicted in gilded casts. Among them are Shiva, god of destructive and regenerative power; Vishnu, the god of mercy who protects the universe; and Indra, god of thunder, lightning and war.   K.H.

The permanent collection comprises some 2,000 objects, shown in rotating exhibits. Its particular strength is *tangkas*, banners created for Buddhist altars and temples.

Painted with mineral or vegetable pigments on stretched canvas, prepared with a ground of chalk and glue and polished with a shell, these banners feature motifs such as the wheel of life, encompassing the stages that humanity passes through—from birth to death and rebirth—before attaining Nirvana. Other *tangkas* have mandalas (ornate geometric designs with a deity in the center, used in meditation), or portraits of buddhas or monastic scholars. The collection also offers bronze casts of buddhas, documents featuring Sanskrit and Tibetan calligraphy, small altars, and ritual objects. On the second floor there is a long-term installation that guides the viewer through the basic precepts of Himalayan art.

Tibetan *tangka* of peaceful and wrathful deities (18th–19th century).

The Chelsea Hotel

The Chelsea Hotel (1884; *map p. 580, C2–B2; 222 West 23rd St*) is an architectural and literary landmark, notable for its cast-iron balconies with interlaced sunflowers stretched row upon row across the long façade. As a hotel, it is known more for its legendary hospitality to all kinds of creative people than for its creature comforts.

The Chelsea started as a grand apartment building—the first apartment to reach 12 stories and to feature a penthouse. It was converted into a residential hotel in 1905. Writers Mark Twain and O. Henry lived here in the early days, but its artistic heyday came after the 1930s, when Thomas Wolfe, Mary McCarthy, Arthur Miller, Brendan Behan, Vladimir Nabokov, John Sloan, Sarah Bernhardt, Yevgeny Yevtushenko and many, many other writers, composers, and painters enjoyed its hospitality. Dylan Thomas lapsed into a fatal coma in room 205 (*see p. 143*); Andy Warhol portrayed it as a wild and impetuous place in his movie *Chelsea Girls*. The Chelsea's reputation grew when Sid Vicious, bass player of the punk rock band the Sex Pistols, was indicted in 1978 for murdering his girlfriend with a hunting knife, allegedly in the hotel. (He died of a heroin overdose before standing trial.) The hotel's most eccentric resident, perhaps, was George Kleinsinger, a composer who wrote a children's musical called *Tubby the Tuba* and who is said to have been fond of composing at the piano with his pet boa constrictor encircling his body. Christo and his wife Jeanne-Claude, now famous for their mega-scale installation art projects, stayed there in the 1960s, sometimes borrowing money for dinner when they ran short. In 2007 the management changed hands, and the new incumbents have announced that they will upgrade the hotel.

THE GARMENT DISTRICT
& HERALD SQUARE

Map p. 580, B1–C1. Subway 1 to 28th St (for Garment Dist.); B, D, F, V, N, Q, R, W to 34th St-Herald Sq. Bus M 10, M20 (for Garment Dist.); M2, M3, M4, M5, M6, M7 (Herald Sq).

The street signs for Seventh Avenue as it passes through the Garment District are subtitled "Fashion Ave," a name imposed with some bravado on an area that still houses one of the city's most important industries but is faced with significant problems. The American garment industry as a whole is shrinking in the face of cheaper imported goods, and the New York sector is further threatened with transportation difficulties and high labor costs. Nonetheless, the Garment District, which moved uptown from the sweatshops of the Lower East Side around the time of World War I, following the northward progress of the major department stores, is vital to New York. Until recent decades the entire industry—from designers to cutters, button makers, seamstresses, to marketing professionals—crowded within the borders of the district. Nowadays, with gentrification encroaching and an increasingly Asian labor force, many of the manufacturing operations (including illegal sweatshops) have moved to cheaper quarters elsewhere in the city or have been outsourced overseas, but many of the showrooms remain here.

The Garment District used to be subdivided according to specialties, and the old lines of demarcation can often still be discerned. What is left of the fur industry centers around the blocks from West 27th to West 30th Sts, Sixth to Eighth Aves, though only a few buildings are occupied entirely by furriers. Children's-wear firms cluster around 34th St; north of 36th St are businesses dealing in women's apparel. On the fringe of the Garment District are allied industries: firms dealing in millinery, hosiery, buttons, thread, trimmings, and fabrics.

THE GARMENT WORKER

Near 555 Seventh Ave (West 39th and West 40th Sts), Judith Weller's statue *The Garment Worker* (1984) sits on the sidewalk at a bronze treadle machine. Though the bronze Jewish sewing-machine operator is a composite of several people, it was inspired by Weller's father, a tailor. Weller exhibited a 24-inch model of the statue in an exhibition in 1978, where a member of the International Ladies' Garment Workers Union saw it and, working with the artist, raised money from Garment District companies to create the present version.

The Fashion Institute of Technology and the Museum at FIT
Map p. 580, C1. Seventh Ave at West 27th St; open Tues–Fri noon–8, Sat 10–5; closed Sun, Mon, legal holidays. Free. T: 212 217 4558; www.fitnyc.edu/museum.

The Fashion Institute of Technology is a prestigious professional school for people seeking careers in the clothing industry—including fashion design, computer animation, fragrance and cosmetic marketing, and toy design. In the plaza facing Seventh Avenue and 27th St is Robert M. Cronbach's hammered brass *Eye of Fashion* (1976).

The Museum at FIT mounts stylish exhibits, which should not be missed by anyone with an interest in fashion, textiles, or design. The permanent collection began with a research facility developed in conjunction with the Brooklyn Museum during World War I, when American designers were isolated from developments in Europe. Among the articles of dress are both men's and women's clothes, furs, foundation garments, lingerie, and an outstanding selection of work by 20th-century American designers and major European couturiers. The collection also contains selected costumes from the stage and screen and period costumes ranging back to the mid-1700s.

HERALD SQUARE & GREELEY SQUARE

Herald Square (*map p. 580, C1*) is the northern triangle formed by the intersection of Sixth Avenue and Broadway at West 34th St (and also the name given to the surrounding neighborhood). Greeley Square is the southern of the two triangles. Formerly a center of the newspaper and garment industries, the area remains a major shopping district, with the flagship Macy's department store its star attraction.

Before the arrival of the newspapers in the late 19th century, the neighborhood was part of the Tenderloin district, a vice-ridden area that stretched between 20th and 40th Sts, east and west from Fifth to Seventh Aves. Brooklyn reformer T. DeWitt Talmadge called it "Satan's Circus," but police inspector Alexander S. ("Clubber") Williams, whose nickname described his favored means of dispensing justice, gave the place its usual name: transferred to this precinct from quieter streets he remarked, "I've had nothing but chuck steak for a long time, and now I'm going to get a little of the tenderloin." He supplemented his modest salary with protection money extorted from the proprietors of saloons, gambling houses, and brothels, eventually owning a city home, a Connecticut estate, and a yacht. Through the efforts of reformers, the involvement of public officials in vice and crime became a source of general indignation; Williams was retired "for the good of the force."

Herald Square takes its present name from the *New York Herald*, a newspaper whose coverage of crime and scandal earned it a huge circulation. Its first publisher, James Gordon Bennett, was notoriously hostile to most reform movements (especially abolitionism). The editorial offices occupied a McKim, Mead & White *palazzo* on the northern side of 35th St. The bell and clock that once adorned the building have been installed as a memorial to Bennett and his son James Gordon Bennett Jr. Two muscular bronze figures nicknamed Stuff and Guff (or alternatively Gog and Magog) seem to hammer out the hours on the Meneely bell (actually the bell is struck from within), while a bronze Minerva and her owl observe the proceedings (1894; Jean-Antonin Carles).

Greeley Square contains Alexander Doyle's disappointingly bland statue (1892) of *New York Tribune* editor Horace Greeley (*see p. 83*). Unlike Bennett, Greeley was a reformer, and his paper was intellectual and high-minded. The eagles on the gateposts recall those on the *Tribune's* masthead.

Macy's

Map p. 580, C1. Broadway and 34th to 35 Sts. Open Mon–Sat 10–9:30, Sun 11–8:30; T: 212 695 4400; www.macys.com.

R.H. Macy & Company, occupying a square block and containing 2.2 million square feet of selling space, bills itself as the world's largest department store. Its moderate to upscale clothing, housewares, gourmet foods, and accessories make the store a shopping destination for New Yorkers as well as visitors. The building facing Broadway dates from 1901, while those along the side streets were added in 1931.

HISTORY OF MACY'S

Rowland Hussey Macy, a Nantucket Quaker, went to sea at the age of 15 and returned four years later with $500 and a red star, now Macy's logo, tattooed on his hand. After six failures in merchandising and additional disappointments in real estate and the stock market, Macy founded (1858) his New York store on Sixth Avenue near 14th St, an enterprise he developed to the point where he could bill it as "the world's largest store."

In 1887, a decade after the founder's death, the store passed to Isidor and Nathan Straus, who had leased space in the basement (1874) to run a china-and-glassware department. Macy's moved to its current Herald Square flagship location in 1902. Isidor Straus and his wife Ida perished together in the sinking of the *Titanic*, but the Straus family remained associated with Macy's for generations.

Macy's was long known for the variety of its merchandise, stocking furs and diamonds, caviar and raspberries, as well as more ordinary products. Among its spectacular past sales have been plumbing fixtures for Liberia's presidential palace and a length of silk to outfit a Saudi Arabian harem.

Between West 32nd and West 33rd Sts on Broadway stood the legendary **Gimbel Brothers Department Store**, long famous as Macy's competitor. Adam Gimbel, a Bavarian immigrant who started his career in this country as a pack peddler, founded Gimbels in 1842 in the Midwest. The store arrived in New York in 1910 and rose to fame for its "feud" with Macy's, romanticized in the film *Miracle on 34th Street*. The rivalry was generally profitable to both stores, but Gimbels fell on hard times in the 1970s and was bought out and closed in 1986.

The **Hotel Pennsylvania** at 401 Seventh Ave (West 33rd St) is famous for its telephone number. Financed by the Pennsylvania Railroad and designed by McKim, Mead

& White (1918), it was immortalized by big-band legend Glenn Miller in his song "Pennsylvania 6-5000" (the phone number in the days when telephone exchanges had names). During the 1930s the hotel was a center for big bands as well as a gathering place for out-of-town Garment District buyers who arrived at Pennsylvania Station.

PENNSYLVANIA STATION

Until it was destroyed in 1963, Pennsylvania Station (1906–10; *map p. 580, C1*) was McKim, Mead & White's masterpiece, a symbol of the power of the Pennsylvania Railroad, and a happy union of history and technology. The façade, with its imposing Doric colonnade, and the General Waiting Room, with its vaulted ceiling, were modeled on the Baths of Caracalla in Rome, while the steel and glass arches, domes, and vaults covering the concourse belonged to the tradition of crystal palaces and glass exhibition galleries. Novelist Thomas Wolfe called it "vast enough to hold the sound of time."

In 1962, the financially troubled Pennsylvania Railroad sold the air rights above the station for a new Madison Square Garden, which would rise above a smaller station underground. The demolition of the old station was considered a monumental act of vandalism and spurred the enactment of landmark preservation laws across the nation. Architectural historian Vincent Scully lamented that in McKim, Mead & White's grand building "one entered the city like a god," while in the present subterranean station "one scuttles in like a rat." Among the glories of the former station were

Pennsylvania Station, triumphant achievement of McKim, Mead & White (demolished 1963).

a row of 22 granite eagles on the cornice and a great stone clock framed by two classical figures, which were carted off and dumped in Secaucus, New Jersey.

The current Penn Station, underground beneath Madison Square Garden, still gives access to the old tracks laid down when its predecessor was completed. The city subway system, two commuter lines (the Long Island Railroad and New Jersey Transit), and the long-distance Amtrak line all pass through the station, making it the busiest passenger station in the country, used by some 570,000 passengers every weekday.

The present (rather graceless) **Madison Square Garden** (1968; Charles Luckman Assocs.) rises where Pennsylvania Station once stood. The complex includes a 20,000-seat arena enclosed in a precast concrete-clad drum, a theater (up to 5,600 seats), and an office building (29 stories). The New York Rangers (ice hockey) and the New York Knicks (basketball) call the garden home.

The General Post Office (1913, McKim, Mead & White; Eighth Ave at West 31st to West 33rd Sts; *lobby open every day 24hrs; T: 212 967 8585*) is also known as the James A. Farley Post Office to honor a former postmaster general. Its two-block colonnade of 53-ft Corinthian columns was intended to match that of the former Penn Station. Around the frieze marches the postal workers' motto, loosely adapted from Herodotus: "Neither snow nor rain nor heat nor gloom of night stays these couriers from the swift completion of their appointed rounds." There have been plans to convert this grand building to a new railroad station, which will replace the present Penn Station.

The Thirtieth Street Yards and Javits Convention Center

Before the diesel truck supplanted the locomotive as America's prime freight hauler, the **Thirtieth Street Yards** of the New York Central Railroad were the hub of the city's freight distribution system. They stretched more or less from West 30th to West 37th Sts, between Eleventh and Twelfth Aves, receiving trains from a railroad that stretched far into the hinterlands. Additional rail yards at 60th St were connected to this facility by a freight line down Eleventh Avenue, known as "Death Avenue" until the 1930s, when the tracks were dropped beneath street level. To the south, an elevated rail viaduct (the High Line; *see p. 188*) led to the St. John's Park Freight Terminal (1934) between Charlton and Clarkson Sts west of Washington St.

The northern portion of the yards has become the site of the **Javits Convention Center** (*map p. 578, A4*), one of the country's most popular trade-show venues. This five-square-block complex (1986; I.M. Pei & Partners) is named for a former senator from New York State, who died the year the building was completed. Though unprepossessing by day, at night when illuminated from within, it gleams like a many-faceted jewel. It incorporates some 16,000 glass panels and 100,000 square ft of skylights.

THE EMPIRE STATE BUILDING, MORGAN LIBRARY & BRYANT PARK

THE EMPIRE STATE BUILDING

Map 580, C1. Subway: 1, 2 or 3, A, C or E to 34th St-Penn Station; 6 to 33rd St; B, D, F, N, Q, R to 34th St-Herald Square. Bus: M1, M2, M3, M4, M5, M6, M7, M10.

Open daily 8am–2am. Last elevator at 1:15am. Visiting can be a major undertaking since more than 10,000 people go there on average each day. There are three lines (security check, ticket purchase, elevators), which may take hours to negotiate, especially in peak season and on weekends. Consider going early or late, or purchase tickets online at www.esbnyc.com. You can either print out your tickets or have them delivered by mail. There are limited Express Pass Tickets, for a hefty surcharge, which allow you to go to the head of the lines; if you haven't bought an Express Pass online, explain your wish to a guard. You can call in advance to check on visibility and the expected waiting time; T: 212 736 3100 or toll-free, 877 692 8439.

Observatories are located on the 86th and 102nd floors, with a small surcharge for visiting the higher one; tickets to the 102nd-floor observatory are sold only at the Observatory Ticket Office, located on the second floor. The 86th-floor observatory has both indoor and outdoor viewing areas; the higher one is only outdoor. During lightning storms and severe weather, the outdoor deck may be closed. Also on the second floor is the New York Skyride, a big-screen, motion-simulated aerial ride through the city, which probably appeals most to younger visitors (open daily 10–10; T: 212 279 9777; www.newyorkskyride.com). There are several family-style restaurants on the ground floor.

At 1,250 ft (1,472 ft to the top of the spire), the Empire State Building (1931; Shreve, Lamb & Harmon) is no longer the world's tallest building, surpassed first in 1972 by the Twin Towers of the World Trade Center, and later by several newer skyscrapers. Since the destruction of the Twin Towers, however, it is the tallest in the city once again, and for many people the Empire State Building has always been the quintessential skyscraper. On a clear day visibility reaches 80 miles and the view is spectacular, by day or night.

HISTORY OF THE EMPIRE STATE BUILDING

The concept of the Empire State Building, the world's tallest skyscraper budgeted at $60 million, was a product of the optimistic 1920s, but the building itself was a child of the Depression, clearance of the site beginning in 1929 just two months before the stock market crash. Remarkably, it was finished ahead of schedule and under budget, setting construction records still unrivaled, rising an average of 4½ stories a week and 14 stories during the ten peak working days. Steel was set in place as little as 80 hours after leaving the furnaces of Pittsburgh, and the supply and delivery of other materials were superbly co-ordinated with the building schedule. Lewis Hine's landmark photographs pay tribute to "skyboys" at work on the high steel. Because of the Depression, actual costs came only to $40,948,900, but the economic climate prevented full occupancy until almost the beginning of World War II, a period during which the building was nicknamed the Empty State Building. The building became profitable only in 1950.

The building's most famous visitor in the early years was King Kong; in the classic 1933 film, the mythical giant ape climbed the tower and battled a squadron of army planes. The building has also known its share of tragedy: in 1933 a woman named Irma Eberhardt became the first suicide to leap from the top; since then about 30 more people have succeeded. On a foggy July 28, 1945, after threading its way among the pinnacles of Midtown, an Army B-25 crashed into the 79th floor, killing 14 people.

The façade consists of a limestone curtain wall trimmed with vertical strips of stainless steel running the height of the building, a design chosen after 15 discarded attempts, in part because it would facilitate rapid construction. Everything possible—windows, spandrels, steel strips, even slabs of stone—was fabricated at the site of origin and shipped to be installed without further handfitting or stonecutting. Originally the building was to end at the 86th floor, but one of the backers determined that it needed a mast for mooring zeppelins, which added more than 150ft to the projected height. Several zeppelins attempted to dock there, but the mast was never a successful mooring place, though a Navy blimp managed to dock long enough in 1931 to dump its ballast—water—on pedestrians several blocks away.

Lewis Wickes Hine: *Icarus* (1930–31). A "skyboy" at work on the Empire State Building.

Since 1976 the façade has been illuminated with colored lights to commemorate holidays, the city's ethnic communities, important victories by New York sports teams, causes or events such as World Diabetes Day (blue) or the death of Frank Sinatra (also blue, for Ol' Blue Eyes), and such oddities as National Angel Food Cake Day (white). To honor Queen Elizabeth's Golden Jubilee, the building was bathed with purple and gold; to honor the death of actress Fay Wray, who played the woman loved by King Kong, the lights were dimmed for 15mins.

The lobby, three stories high, is lined with marble imported from France, Italy, Belgium, and Germany. A marble panel with an aluminum relief of the skyscraper superimposed over New York State faces the main entrance. Next to it is a 1938 scale model ($\frac{1}{16}$ inch = 1ft) of the building. Along the north corridor are colorful illuminated panels (1963) by Roy Sparkia and Renée Nemerov depicting the Eight Wonders of the World—the traditional seven plus the Empire State Building.

MORGAN LIBRARY & MURRAY HILL

Map p. 579, D4. 225 Madison Ave (36th St). Subway: 6 to 33rd St; 4, 5, 6, 7 to Grand Central; B, D, F, Q to 42nd St. Bus: M2, M3, M4, Q32 to 36th St. Open Tues–Thur 10:30–5, Fri 10:30–9, Sat 10–6, Sun 11–6. Closed Mon, Thanksgiving, Christmas Day, and New Year's Day; T: 212 685 0008; www.morganlibrary.org. Admission charge except Fri 7pm–9pm. Admission to the Morgan's study and personal library free during the following times: Tues 3–5, Fri 7–9, Sun 4–6. Pleasant dining room and café.

The Morgan Library and Museum, formerly the Pierpont Morgan Library, is one of the great repositories of culture in the Western Hemisphere. The nucleus of the world-class collection was gathered by financier J. Pierpont Morgan (1837–1913); his son, J.P. Morgan Jr., established the museum in 1924 according to the wishes of his father's will. Morgan's personal study and library remain much as they were during his lifetime and parts of the stunning collection are always on view in changing exhibitions.

THE BUILDINGS

The original library: exterior

The best view of the building is from East 36th St, between Madison and Park Aves.

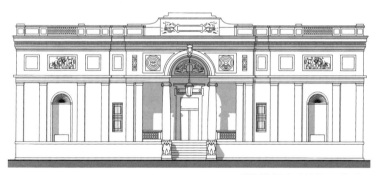

THE ORIGINAL MORGAN LIBRARY

In 1902 Morgan, then 65 years old, hired Charles Follen McKim of the firm of McKim, Mead & White to design a "little museum building" to house his books and collections, which had outgrown his large brownstone home on the northeast corner of East 36th St and Madison Avenue. The library was completed in 1906, and though its modest proportions were consistent with the residential scale of the neighborhood, the building is often considered the pinnacle of McKim's career. He and his partner Stanford White were leading exponents of the American Renaissance style, an architectural movement that sought models in the monuments of the past and embodied the notion that America had inherited the spirit of the Renaissance and its intellectual and material energies. Morgan, unsurprisingly, subscribed to these notions.

This small Neoclassical building is faced with marble blocks fitted closely together without mortar. Knowing that money was no great object for Morgan, McKim confessed his desire to construct such a building to realize a dream apparently born when, touring the monuments of ancient Athens, he had tried without success to insert his penknife into the cracks between the stones of the Erechtheion. The additional expenditure for the library's exquisitely accurate stone-cutting added only about $50,000 to the total construction cost of $1,154,669.

The library is faced in pinkish Tennessee marble and adorned with a Palladian-style loggia. Sculptured panels (Adolph A. Weinman) below the frieze represent (right to left) *Truth with Literature, Philosophy, History, Oratory, Astronomy*, and *Music Inspiring the Arts*. The marble lionesses guarding the doorway are by Edward Clark Potter, who later placed a more famous pair in front of the New York Public Library.

The Annex

J. Pierpont Morgan died in 1913, and in 1924 the Morgan Library opened to the public. As the years passed and the collections continued to burgeon, the "little museum building" no longer sufficed, and the Annex was added to the museum complex, at the corner of Madison Avenue and East 36th St. The building (1928; Benjamin Wistar Morris) stands on the site of Morgan's former brownstone home. Also Neoclassical in inspiration, and also faced in Tennessee marble, it has been described variously as "harmonious" or "dull," but it was never intended to compete, architecturally, with McKim's original library.

J.P. Morgan Jr.'s brownstone

In 1988 the Library purchased the former home of Morgan's son, J.P. Morgan Jr., on the southeast corner of Madison Avenue and 37th St. Built in 1852 for copper king Anson Phelps Stokes, the 45-room brownstone (with its 2,000-bottle capacity wine cellar) had been acquired (1904) by Morgan for his son, for a million dollars. Morgan had already bought the house between his own more modest dwelling and the Phelps Stokes house for a mere half million dollars; this middle house was torn down to make space for a garden. Today the Renzo Piano entrance stands in the former garden, while the bookstore and restaurant occupy part of J.P. Morgan Jr.'s home.

The expansion: exterior

An exhibit on the basement floor explains the expansion, with an architectural model and photographs.

Renzo Piano's expansion (2006) links the three existing buildings with glass and steel. The windowless "cube" between the Annex and the original library is used to display some of the Morgan's medieval and Renaissance treasures. The entrance facing Madison Avenue opens into a 50-ft glassy atrium with glass-walled elevators and ficus trees sprouting through the floor. A new concert hall and storage vaults have been drilled into bedrock below the building, keeping the above-ground scale appropriate to the neighborhood.

J. PIERPONT MORGAN AS COLLECTOR

At a time when other millionaires found themselves attracted to French landscapes or Old Master paintings, J. Pierpont Morgan used his fortune to amass (in the true sense of that word) not only paintings and sculpture, but rare books and manuscripts, porcelains, majolica, faïence, fine gold-work and enamel, Mesopotamian cylinder seals, cuneiform tablets, even Egyptian, Greek, and Latin papyrus rolls. Morgan's passion for collecting began early: at age 14, he asked President Millard Fillmore for an autograph and received it in an envelope personally franked by the president. As a student in Switzerland and Germany, Morgan began collecting bits of stained glass from the yards of old churches and cathedrals; some of these shards are now embedded in the windows of his study.

However, it was not until his father died in a carriage accident on the Riviera in 1890 and left J. Pierpont Morgan $15 million (equivalent to about $225 million today) that Morgan's collecting activities began in earnest. During the next decade he purchased a Gutenberg Bible on vellum, the 1459 Mainz Psalter, the famous 9th-century Lindau Gospels with their spectacular jeweled binding, four Shakespeare Folios, and original autograph manuscripts by Keats and Dickens, among others. In the last 20 years of his life he spent an estimated $60 million on his collections (equivalent to $900 million today), buying individual works, collections, and sometimes entire estates, and later selling off what he did not want.

Some of Morgan's motivation may have been personal, but larger forces were also at work. New York had become the center of world finance. European aristocrats, whose pedigrees were assured but whose cash flow was not, began to sell artworks to the cash-rich, culture-poor American market. Encouraged by new authentication techniques, the great American collectors of the period—Benjamin Altman, Henry Clay Frick, and Morgan—became more adventuresome in their choices, looking beyond Salon painting to other periods and media.

At first Morgan concentrated on autographs. Later he was advised in his choices by his scholarly nephew, Junius Spencer Morgan, who loved books and manuscripts, which may account for the emphasis on objects that document the history of the printed book: Egyptian, Greek, and Latin papyri; medieval works printed on vellum; incunabula (including three of the 49 known Gutenberg Bibles), and later examples of beautifully printed and bound books. Morgan's interest in cuneiform seals was unusual, and his collection is one of the finest in the world.

THE GALLERIES

The expansion: interior

On the right of the atrium is the Thaw Gallery, inside the "cube," a rather sterile exhibition space where some of the riches of the collection are on display. To the left of the

entrance is the **Stavelot triptych** (mid-12th century), a portable altar intended as a reliquary for fragments of the True Cross. It was commissioned by Wibald, abbot of Stavelot Abbey (in present-day Belgium). Opulent with enamels, gems, and metalwork, the wings of the triptych are decorated with roundels that tell the legend of the True Cross.

Within the gallery are the **Lindau Gospels** (back cover late 8th century, front cover c. 880), Morgan Manuscript 1. This marks the beginning of Morgan's career as the country's greatest collector of medieval manuscripts. The metal covers encrusted with jewels and the beautifully illuminated manuscript are outstanding examples of Carolingian book arts. Also here is the beautiful copper gilt and enamel **Malmesbury ciborium**, also called the Morgan ciborium (c. 1160–70).

The original library: interior

On view are three rooms from Morgan's original library, restored to their early 20th-century opulence.

Mr. Morgan's study: This was once called "the most beautiful room in America" and even now, though it seems dim and heavy (the velvet curtains are kept drawn to protect the wall coverings), it must be one of the most sumptuous. At one end is Morgan's custom-made desk, on whose surface weighty transactions in finance and art were consummated. The red silk damask on the walls replicates the original armorial pattern that once hung on the walls of the Chigi Palace in Rome. Morgan purchased the antique carved ceiling in Florence and had it reassembled and installed here. Displayed in the room are some of Morgan's favorite paintings and *objets d'art* in bronze, faïence, and metalwork, many of them notable for their intricate workmanship. They suggest Morgan's preference for small,

precious objects. Among the paintings are Hans Memling's *Portrait of a Man with a Pink* and two panels by Lucas Cranach.

The Rotunda (vestibule): The room has richly colored marble decoration and a domed ceiling with murals by H. Siddons

"The most beautiful room in America," J. Pierpont Morgan's study, with its original Florentine ceiling and red silk damask walls.

te deū laudam’

Eus in adiutozium meum t
tende. Domine ad adiuuandū
me festina. Gloria patri et fi
lio et spiritui sancto. Sicut e
rat in principio et nunc et sē
per: et in secula seculox Amen.
Ominus regnauit ps.
decorem indutus est:

Mowbray, whose inspiration came from Raphael. The lunettes over the main entrance and the doors to the east and west rooms represent the great ages of poetry. The marbles on the floor were brought from ancient quarries in Africa and Italy. Morgan especially liked the deep purple of Imperial porphyry, and had the large disc in the center of the room carefully delivered by Wells Fargo. The columns include beautifully veined grey-green columns of an Italian *cipollino* marble, whose striations may indeed suggest the rings of an onion.

Mr. Morgan's library: The triple tiers of rare books rise to a high, elaborately decorated ceiling. Treasures on display here always include a Gutenberg Bible (Mainz, c. 1455). The 16th-century Brussels tapestry above the mantelpiece depicts *The Triumph of Avarice*, perhaps an unintended ironic comment on the life of a man who accumulated such astonishing wealth. The Latin inscription warns that as Tantalus is ever thirsty in the midst of water, so the miser is always desirous of riches. It belongs to a series of the Seven Deadly Sins, designed by the great Flemish tapestry master Pieter van Aelst, father-in-law of Pieter Brueghel the Elder.

The zodiacal signs in the ceiling decoration, again by H. Siddons Mowbray, refer to important dates in Morgan's life. Flanking the door are his birth sign, Aries, and that of the date of his second marriage in May 1865: Gemini, with Mercury signifying Wednesday as the day of the week. Directly across is Aquarius with the Muse of Tragedy, an emblem that marks the death of Morgan's young first wife in February 1862, an event from which Morgan, prone to depression, never fully recovered.

Highlights of the collection

Belle da Costa Green, the first director of the Morgan Library, remarked that "It [the Library] apparently contains everything but the original tablets of the Ten Commandments," and while this statement is exaggerated, the range and scope of the Library's holdings are astonishing. The main areas of collecting include medieval and Renaissance manuscripts, prints and drawings, autograph manuscripts and letters, printed books, music manuscripts, and ancient cylinder seals.

Among the illuminated manuscripts are the Farnese Hours (1546) by Giulio Clovio, probably the last great Italian illuminated manuscript. The Hours of Catherine of Cleves (c. 1440), a masterpiece of Dutch illumination, is remarkable for showing humble scenes from daily life, for example the Holy Family at supper, with Joseph sitting by the fire eating porridge. The Reims Gospel Book, the collection's finest Carolingian manuscript, was written in gold (c. 860) at the Abbey of St-Rémi, and bought by J.P. Morgan Jr. Among the early printed books, in addition to the three Gutenberg Bibles, are works by Gutenberg's associates, Fust and Schoeffer; England's first printer, William Caxton; and the great Italian Renaissance printer Aldus Manutius. Later works include the First

From the Hours of Catherine of Cleves (Netherlands, Utrecht, c. 1440), illuminated by the Master of Catherine of Cleves, with a design of peas around the Latin text of the Verses and Responses for Lauds (morning prayer): "Incline unto my aid, O God; O Lord, make haste to help me."

Folio edition (1623) of Shakespeare's collected plays; the first printing, first state, of the American Declaration of Independence; and William Morris's *The Works of Geoffrey Chaucer* (1896), printed by the Kelmscott Press.

Master drawings include work by artists from Leonardo and Michelangelo to Degas and Matisse. The Library owns eight drawings by Albrecht Dürer, including *Adam and Eve* (1504), a celebrated work made in preparation for the engraving *Fall of Man*. William Blake is represented by a series of watercolor illustrations for the Book of Job as well as illustrations for Milton's *L'Allegro* and *Il Penseroso*. There is also an outstanding collection of etchings and drawings by Rembrandt, including two drawings of his wife Saskia asleep.

Among the musical manuscripts are autographs of Brahms's First Symphony and Mahler's Fifth Symphony, Beethoven's Violin Sonata in G major (op. 96), four Schubert Impromptus, the *Winterreise*, Offenbach's operetta *Robinson Crusoe*, and Stravinsky's *Perséphone*.

Highlights among the autograph manuscripts include Charles Perrault's *The Tales of Mother Goose* (1695) and Charles Dickens's *A Christmas Carol* (1843). In 2004 the Morgan acquired watercolor studies and drafts from Jean de Brunhoff's *The Story of Babar*, including the earliest plan for the Babar book (9$^1/_2$ inches by six inches) with 44 pages of pencil and watercolor sketches and the original text. John Milton's autograph manuscript of *Paradise Lost*, Book I, in the hand of various amanuenses, is the sole remnant of the manuscript from which the first edition was printed, and one of the most important British literary manuscripts in America. The collection of American manuscripts includes Twain's *Pudd'nhead Wilson*, Thoreau's *Journal*, and Steinbeck's *Travels with Charley*. There are letters autographed by Elizabeth I, Napoleon, George Washington, Thomas Jefferson, and an eclectic array of artists from Piranesi to Picasso.

In 1992 the Library received the Gilder Lehrman Collection, one of the finest private collections of American historical manuscripts in the world, whose treasures include a letter written by George Washington, a 1493 printing of Columbus's letter announcing his discovery, signed copies of the Emancipation Proclamation and the Thirteenth Amendment, and a signed copy of Gerald Ford's pardon of Richard Nixon.

MURRAY HILL

The Morgan Library lies in the upscale neighborhood of Murray Hill, bounded roughly by 34th St, Third Ave, 42nd St, and Madison Ave. The area is named after Robert Murray, who had a country home here (at the present East 37th St and Park Ave) during the Revolutionary War. In the mid-19th century real estate values soared as the upper crust—Morgans, Havemeyers, Phelpses, Delanos, Belmonts and Tiffanys—built brownstone mansions along Fifth, Madison, and Park Avenues. Although most have been torn down or stripped of detail, a few homes, clubhouses, and carriage houses remain to suggest Murray Hill in its glory days.

The Protestant Episcopal **Church of the Incarnation** (*map p. 579, D4; 205 Madison Ave at East 35th St; open weekdays 11:30–2, Wed also 5–7:30, Sat 1–4, Sun 8–1; T: 212 689*

The Pilgrim: stained-glass window by Louis Comfort Tiffany in the Church of the Incarnation.

6350; www.churchoftheincarnation.org). Founded as a mission of Grace Church (Broadway at 10th St), the building (1864; Emlen T. Little, rebuilt and enlarged after a fire in 1882) is English Gothic in style with a brownstone front and a corner tower. The interior is noteworthy for stained-glass windows by Louis Comfort Tiffany (*The Pilgrim*, south side of chancel); the Tiffany Glass Company (*Angel of Victory over Death* and *The 23rd Psalm*, both in the north wall); and John La Farge (*Calling of Peter and Paul* and *God the Good Vintner*, south wall). Other windows are by the William Morris Company, and from designs by Burne-Jones. The altar rail has carved oak angels by Daniel Chester French.

The **Consulate General of the Polish People** at 233 Madison Ave at East 37th St (1905; C.P.H. Gilbert) was originally built as the Joseph Raphael De Lamar mansion. De Lamar, a Dutch emigrant, started out in the marine salvage business but went west and made a fortune in gold- and silver-mining. The house has been described as one of the grandest Beaux-Arts mansions in the city, crowned with a staggering mansard roof, ornamented with copper cresting, extravagant in every detail.

THE NEW YORK PUBLIC LIBRARY & BRYANT PARK

Map p. 579, D4. Open Mon–Sat 11 until at least 6pm; Sun 1–5. Closed holidays. Hours vary for special collections. Guided tours Mon–Sat at 11, Sun at 2. Also exhibition tours. T: 212 930 0800 for general information; T: 212 592 7730 for recorded information on events and exhibitions; www.nypl.org. The website includes digitized images of rare materials in the collections.

The building generally known simply as "the New York Public Library" stands on the west side of Fifth Avenue between 40th and 42nd Sts. It is officially the Humanities and Social Sciences Library of the New York Public Library, one of the NYPL's four major research facilities, world famous for its collections and much admired for the architecture of its building (1911; Carrère & Hastings). The library mounts exceptional exhibitions on literary, artistic, and historical subjects in Gottesman Hall on the ground floor, and upstairs in special smaller galleries.

The building

The building sits on a wide terrace running the length of the Fifth Avenue façade. The steps, which have long attracted tourists, pigeons, footsore shoppers, and office workers at lunch, are flanked by two famous **marble lions** by Edward C. Potter (1911). Originally criticized as mealy-mouthed, complacent creatures, they seemed undeserving of the nicknames Mayor Fiorello La Guardia would later give them—*Patience* (south side) and *Fortitude* (north side)—virtues the mayor thought important for New Yorkers struggling economically during the Depression. In niches behind the fountains against the façade are two statues (1913; Frederick W. MacMonnies): *Truth* (a man leaning against a sphinx), and *Beauty* (a woman seated on the winged horse Pegasus). Above the entrance on the frieze are six allegorical figures: left to right they are *History*, *Romance*, *Religion*, *Poetry*, *Drama*, and *Philosophy* by Paul Wayland Bartlett. The pediment figures at the ends of the façade are *Art* (south) and *History* (north) by George Grey Barnard.

The **entrance hall** is finished in white Vermont marble, with an elaborate vaulted ceiling, heroic marble candelabra, and wide staircases. Behind it is **Gottesman Hall**, used for major exhibits of objects from the collection. To reach the **Rotunda**, take the elevator (end of the right corridor) to the third floor, or walk up the marble stairs that crisscross back and forth under marble barrel vaults. Visible from the stairway are the large interior courts that provide natural light for the catalogue and reading rooms. The Rotunda is decorated with murals (1940) by Edward Laning depicting the story of the recorded word. The Public Catalogue in Room 315 formerly held more than 10 million cards, which have been recorded electronically in the library's computerized catalogue system, CATNYP. (The catalogue for the branch libraries is called LEO.)

Beyond is the monumental **Main Reading Room**, with a shelf collection of some 30,000 reference books. The beautifully decorated ceiling, tall, arched windows, and the furniture designed by Carrère & Hastings make it one of the city's great interiors.

The collections

The collections developed from the consolidation of two privately endowed libraries (the Astor and Lenox Libraries) and the Tilden Trust, a bequest of $2 million and 15,000 books from Samuel J. Tilden, lawyer, governor, and unsuccessful presidential candidate. John Jacob Astor, not himself a bookish man, was persuaded by Joseph Green Cogswell, bibliographer for the Astor Collection, to establish a public library as a testimonial to his adopted country instead of the huge monument to George Washington he had earlier favored. Astor bequeathed $400,000 and a plot of land for its foundation (*see p. 159*). The books, largely chosen by Cogswell, were in the fields of greatest public interest including the "mechanic arts and practical industry," and languages, since Cogswell saw the American nation coming "into near relation with countries formerly the most remote." James Lenox, on the other hand, was a scholar whose particular interests are reflected in his collection: American literature and history, the Bible, Milton, Shakespeare, Bunyan, and Renaissance literature of travel and discovery. Lenox built his own library (1875) on the site of the present Frick

Collection but at his death in 1880 left his 85,000 peerless books and an endowment of $505,000 to the New York Public Library. The gift of bachelor Samuel J. Tilden, a bequest reduced from $4 million to $2 million by his relatives (who contested the will), was sorely needed as by 1886 the Astor and Lenox libraries already lacked funds for new books and maintenance. In 1895 the three gifts were united as the New York Public Library, Astor, Lenox, and Tilden Foundations.

In 1901 Andrew Carnegie, realizing that the city had nothing comparable to the public circulating systems of other American cities, gave $52,000,000 for the building of branch libraries. Today the library has 87 branches and four research libraries. The circulating collections are publicly supported while the research libraries depend upon endowment and contributions.

Among the collections are the Berg Collection with printed books and manuscripts mainly on the subjects of American and English literature, ranging from William Caxton's 1480 edition of *The Chronicles of England* to the countercultural poets of New York's Lower East Side (1960–80). Among the rarities in the Prints Collection is an engraving by Paul Revere of the British landing in Boston in 1768. The Arents Collection focuses on books published in serial form and on documents (1507–present) concerned directly or tangentially with tobacco. Holdings of the Rare Book Division include a Gutenberg Bible, the only known copy of the original folio edition (in Spanish) of Christopher Columbus's letter describing his discoveries (dated 1493), the first full folio of Shakespeare (1623), and a Bay Psalm Book (1640) from Cambridge, Massachusetts, the first book printed in America in the English language.

BRYANT PARK

Map p. 579, D4. There are two restaurants in the park, the more formal Bryant Park Grill (T: 212 840 6500) and the casual Bryant Park Café, open seasonally April–Nov, depending on the weather (T: 212 840 6500).

Directly behind the library is Bryant Park, named after William Cullen Bryant (1794–1878), editor, writer, abolitionist, and proponent of such projects as Central Park and the Metropolitan Museum of Art. Before 1844, these 9.6 acres were called Reservoir Park after the Croton Reservoir (1837–1900), which stood where the library is now, a walled and buttressed mass of gray granite with a wide promenade on top. In June 1842 the first water poured into the reservoir from man-made Lake Croton behind a dam in the Croton River, a tributary flowing into the Hudson north of Ossining, N.Y. Leaving Lake Croton, the water coursed along 33 miles of aqueduct, across the Harlem River on High Bridge, through pipes in the Manhattanville Valley, and into a tunnel that emptied into the reservoir. A jubilant crowd listened to speeches and a 38-gun salute as water filled the two basins within the aqueduct to a capacity of 150 million gallons. The opening of the reservoir ended a period of more than 200 years when the city, dependent on shallow wells and springs, was subject to frequent outbreaks of cholera and uncontrollable fires. The Croton system, enlarged, updated, and supplemented by the Catskill system, is still operative.

In 1853 a world's fair, complete with a Crystal Palace, opened in the park behind the reservoir, with exhibits on technology: pumps, hardware, and sewing machines. The Crystal Palace burned in 1858, and the reservoir was moved in the late 1890s.

After deteriorating into a haven for drug dealers and muggers in the 1970s and '80s, the park has been restored, redesigned, and re-landscaped—without the hedges that formerly concealed the interior from the streets. It reopened in 1992; today its kiosks, restaurants, and a full schedule of events draw people to its pleasant open spaces.

Monuments in the park

Statues in the park include a statue of William Cullen Bryant (1911; Herbert Adams), depicted as an elderly sage (just behind the library); a bronze statue (1922; Jo Davidson) of a ponderous Gertrude Stein sitting cross-legged, and a bronze bust of Goethe (1932; Karl Fischer) near the carousel. Facing Sixth Avenue the statue of José Bonifacio de Andrada commemorates a scholar, poet, and patriarch of Brazilian independence. The statue, by José Lima, was cast from an original (1889) and presented to the US in 1954 as a gift from Brazil. The Josephine Shaw Lowell Memorial Fountain (1912; Charles Platt) is the city's first public memorial dedicated to a woman. Shaw, born to a wealthy Boston family, became a reformer who sought social justice and improved working conditions, especially for women.

A WALK AROUND FIFTH AVENUE

Subway: B, D, F, N, Q, R to 34th St-Herald Square. Bus: M2, M3, M4, M5.

North of the Empire State Building, Fifth Avenue begins to show why it is still the most famous promenade in the city, the route of grand processions and grander stores. Several of the neo-palazzi that once housed famous department stores now hold educational institutions, but Lord & Taylor and Saks Fifth Avenue remain, along with other historic buildings.

At 365 Fifth Ave, the former **B. Altman & Company store** (1906; Trowbridge & Livingston) fills the entire block between Fifth and Madison Aves, East 34th and East 35th Sts. It now houses the New York Public Library's Science, Industry and Business Library and Oxford University Press, as well as the CUNY Graduate Center (entrance on Fifth Ave). Altman's was the first department store to intrude on a previously residential area and was modeled on an Italian *palazzo*, perhaps to soften the blow to disgruntled neighbors.

Benjamin Altman (1840–1913)
Founder Benjamin Altman, son of a Lower East Side milliner, opened his first shop on Third Avenue near 9th St and worked his way uptown via a stylish store in Ladies' Mile (Sixth Avenue and 19th St). He was a savvy businessman, who bought the first parcel of land on this block in 1896, but hastened to buy the entire block when Grand Central Terminal and Pennsylvania Station announced their new locations. Although Altman seems to have been a humorless workaholic, apparently he was also a compassionate man, installing rest rooms for the employees, providing funding for their children's education, and inaugurating a shorter work week. When Altman died unmarried in 1913, he left his art collection to the Metropolitan Museum of Art and $20 million in Altman's stock to a philanthropic foundation. The store was known through the years for its high-quality conservative clothing, home furnishings, dishes, and glassware; it went out of business in 1989.

Walk north on Fifth Avenue. Nearby are the former homes of several more fine stores that arrived at about the same time as Altman's. **No. 390 Fifth Ave** (1906; McKim, Mead & White) was built for the Gorham Company, jeweler and purveyor of table silver; the lower façade has been unfortunately altered. No. 402 Fifth Ave, with its fine terra-cotta decoration, was for a while the **A.T. Stewart Building** (*for the original A.T. Stewart store on Broadway and Chambers St, see p. 89*) built (1914) by Warren & Wetmore, the architects of Grand Central Terminal. At **409 Fifth Ave** is the former home of Tiffany's, (1906; McKim, Mead & White), modeled after the Venetian Palazzo Grimani.

Between 38th and 39th Sts is the only remaining department store on this stretch of the avenue, **Lord & Taylor**

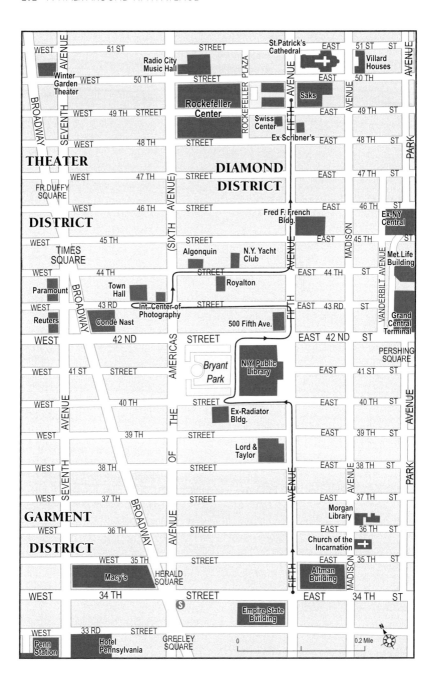

(1914; Starrett & Van Vleck), a conservative and gracious store, known for emphasizing American designers and traditional women's sportswear. Samuel Lord arrived in New York in April 1826 (when he was 22) on the packet *Constitution*, which listed his occupation as "iron moulder." He set up a dry goods shop on Catherine St and three months later invited his wife's cousin George W. Taylor into the business, each man contributing $1,000. They sold "heavy plaid silks for misses' wear" and "superior quality men's and women's silk hose," among other things, "at fair prices as usual."

Around the corner, the **former American Radiator Building** (1924; Hood & Fouilhoux), at 40 West 40th St, is a striking black brick and gold terracotta tower with a Gothic crown, now the Bryant Park Hotel. When the building opened, the gold top was illuminated to suggest the glow of a hot radiator, while the black brick was thought by some to suggest a heap of coal. The building is the work of Raymond Hood, later a senior architect for Rockefeller Center's design team.

Walk through **Bryant Park** (*see p. 209*) to the north, and then walk east on 42nd St toward Fifth Avenue. On the northwest corner of the intersection, **500 Fifth Ave** (1931) was designed by Shreve, Lamb & Harmon, who also designed the Empire State Building. At the time this corner was considered the second most valuable in Manhattan, behind the southeast corner of Broadway and Wall St.

The steel and glass box at the corner of West 43rd St (510 Fifth Ave) is the former Manufacturers Hanover Trust Co. (1954; Skidmore, Owings & Merrill). It was considered architecturally innovative in 1954 when banks still resembled *palazzi* or ancient temples. While the building was designed expressly so that it could be turned to other uses, the 30-ton Mosler safe in the window identifies it as a bank.

At 7 West 43rd St is the **Century Association** (1891; McKim, Mead & White). Founded by William Cullen Bryant, the club has long been known for its intellectual and cultural orientation. Members Charles Follen McKim and Stanford White here designed one of their first neo-Italian Renaissance clubhouses, notable for its mixture of materials (terra cotta, granite and yellow brick) and its second-floor ironwork beneath a Palladian window once part of an open loggia. The original plan was to have 100 members, but the roster has expanded to more than 20 times that number.

Continue west to Sixth Avenue. The **W.R. Grace Building** at 1114 Sixth Ave (corner of 43rd St), large and white with a self-important swooping façade, is the work of Gordon Bunshaft of Skidmore, Owings and Merrill (1974). The school of the International Center of Photography is located here. Across the avenue the corner of Sixth Ave and 43rd St (1133 Avenue of the Americas) is the **International Center of Photography** (*open Tues–Sun 10–6, until 8 on Fri; closed Mon, holidays; T: 212 857 0000; www.icp.org*), founded in 1974 by photographer Cornell Capa to preserve the memory of four photographers who died pursuing their work. One of them was his older brother, Robert, a photojournalist killed in Vietnam. Today the center is New York's foremost exhibitor of photography, and maintains a school and center for photographers, editors, artists, and others interested in the medium. The permanent collection contains more

than 100,000 photos, including the Robert and Cornell Capa Collections, and the Roman Vishniac and Weegee (Arthur Fellig) Archives and the Life Magazine Collection.

Down the block to the west is red-brick **Town Hall** (113–23 West 43rd St between Sixth Ave and Broadway; *box office, T: 212 840 2824; www.the-townhall-nyc.org*). Still one of the city's more important performance spaces, Town Hall was designed by McKim, Mead & White (1921) as a concert auditorium and a meeting place where people from all walks of life could participate in discussions on contemporary issues. The democratic ideals of the League for Political Education, who commissioned the building, are reflected in the absence of box seats. Margaret Sanger spoke here on family planning (she was arrested because the audience contained both men and women); Eleanor Roosevelt spoke in behalf of the New Deal; Andrés Segovia, Bob Dylan, and Leontyne Price enjoyed the hall's superb acoustics, and many hopeful musicians have given debut recitals here, hoping for favorable reviews from New York critics.

Return to Sixth Avenue and walk north to 44th St. The **Algonquin Hotel** (1902) at no. 59 is famous as a literary hangout. Frank Case, manager (1907) and later owner (1927), enjoyed rubbing elbows with literary and theatrical celebrities, and over the years the Algonquin hosted writers Gertrude Stein, James Thurber, Sinclair Lewis, F. Scott Fitzgerald, Tennessee Williams, Graham Greene, and many others. Beginning in 1919, Robert Benchley, Dorothy Parker, and Robert Sherwood, all of whom worked at nearby *Vanity*

Fair magazine, and other literary lights gathered for lunch in the hotel, amusing one another with clever conversation. The press referred to the group as "The Round Table," but members called it the "Vicious Circle." Harold Ross, founder of *The New Yorker* magazine, belonged to the coterie and created his magazine partly to enshrine the sophisticated, incisive humor of his friends.

The **Royalton Hotel** (1898) across the street at no. 44 was also a literary hotel, where *Smart Set* editor George Jean Nathan maintained an apartment for 50 years and Robert Benchley lived in a suite furnished with Victorian red draperies and appointed with two portraits of the queen. More recently (1988) hotelier Ian Schrager had the Royalton refurbished as a conspicuously high-style luxury hotel, starting the fad for "design hotels."

Further down on the other side (no. 37) is the **New York Yacht Club** (1901; Warren & Wetmore), on land donated by J.P. Morgan (commodore 1897–99). This wonderfully eccentric Beaux-Arts clubhouse is festooned with ropes and pulleys, anchors and hooks, and adrip with limestone seaweed. Truly astonishing, however, are the three windows fashioned like the sterns of ships plowing through ossified seas whose stony waves curl over the sidewalk. The keystone above the main entrance represents Poseidon. Until the 1983 defeat of its entry, *Liberty*, by the Australian challenger *Australia II*, the club housed the America's Cup, the ultimate prize in yachting, given in 1851 by Queen Victoria.

Further east, at 27 West 44th St, is the **Harvard Club** (1894; McKim, Mead & White), one of several university clubs in the neighborhood. Harvard's clubhouse,

neo-Georgian with a restrained brick and limestone façade, recalls the early architecture of the college itself.

Continue to Fifth Avenue again. On the corner of 45th St is the 38-story **Fred F. French Building** (1927; John Sloan and H. Douglas Ives), probably the city's first flat-topped skyscraper and certainly one of the best skyscrapers of the 1920s. Unusual faïence polychromy delineates the upper-story setbacks and the top of the building. The panels concealing the water tower on the roof are decorated with symbolic motifs chosen by Ives: on the north and south are the rising sun (Progress) amid winged griffins (Integrity and Watchfulness) and golden beehives with bees (Thrift and Industry); on the east and west are heads of Mercury, god of commerce.

Unimposing though it may be, the block of West 47th St between Fifth and Sixth Aves is the city's **Diamond District**. In the 1920s and early 1930s the diamond business centered around the Bowery and Canal St, but the refugees who fled the ghettos of Amsterdam and Antwerp ahead of Hitler settled uptown and were joined by jewelers who moved north from the Bowery. The glittering ground-floor shops are for the tourist trade, while the real business is transacted in trading clubs or upstairs in old buildings equipped with ultra-sensitive cameras and sophisticated alarm systems. Until recently virtually all the brokers and diamond-cutters were Jewish, using skills passed down the generations from as far back as the 16th century, when stonecutting was one of the few trades open to Jews. Recently jewelers and stonecutters from Cuba, Puerto Rico, Russia, and East Asia have arrived. Ninety percent of the diamonds that enter the US are said to go through New York, and most of those through the 47th St Diamond District.

Continue north on Fifth Avenue. After more than seven decades in this location the **former Charles Scribner's Sons bookstore**, 597 Fifth Ave (48th and 49th Sts), closed in 1989. The building (1913; Ernest Flagg) still remains, protected inside and out by landmarking. The black iron and glass storefront is reminiscent of *fin de siècle* Paris, and the dignified vaulted interior suggested a private library.

On the west side of the avenue, no. 604, painted a garish bright blue, is a T.G.I. Friday's restaurant, oddly enough designed by William Van Alen (1925), who also produced the Chrysler Building. The **Swiss Center**, next door at no. 608, built as the Goelet Building (1932), has fared better, its beautiful Art Deco lobby still intact.

On the east side of Fifth Avenue, between 49th and 50th Sts, is **Saks Fifth Avenue** (1924; Starrett & Van Vleck), a department store known for its high-fashion boutiques, luxury goods, and excellent service. There are 54 Saks Fifth Avenue outlets nationwide, but 20 percent of the total sales are provided by this flagship store. The business was founded in 1902 when Andrew Saks, who had begun his career as a peddler in Washington, D.C., established Saks Thirty-Fourth on 34th St near Herald Square. In 1923 Saks's son Horace, a Princeton graduate, sold the less exclusive 34th St store to the now-extinct Gimbels for $8 million in order to follow the carriage trade uptown. The next year he opened the present Saks with show windows offering a pigskin trunk ($3000), raccoon coats ($1000), and chauffeurs' livery.

WEST 42ND STREET & THE TIMES SQUARE THEATER DISTRICT

Map p. 578, C3. Subway: 1, 2, 3, 7, N, R to Times Square-42nd St. Bus: M6, M7, M10, M20, M27, M42, M104.

At the north end of Father Duffy Square is TKTS (the Times Square Ticket Center), a ticket service for discounted day-of-performance theater tickets. It opened in a "temporary" structure in 1973, and is currently being redesigned. NB: While the permanent TKTS is under construction, discounted tickets are available in a ground-level kiosk in the Marriott Hotel; entrance on West 46th St, about a third of a block west of Broadway. For evening performances, open Mon–Sat 3–8 and Sun 3 until 30mins before the latest curtain time being sold; for matinées Wed and Sat 10–2 , Sun 11–3 (no tickets for evening performances sold until 3pm).

View of Times Square in 1959.

The Times Square Information Center, housed in the refurbished former Embassy Theater, offers citywide information, as well as maps, brochures, ticket purchase for Broadway shows, an ATM, sightseeing tours, and Internet access. 1556–60 Broadway (West 46th and 47th Sts). Open daily 8–8; www.timessquarealliance.org.

Times Square is not a square at all. Geometrically it is two triangles created by the intersection of Broadway and Seventh Avenue (the "Crossroads of the World"), as the avenues merge, cross, and diverge. As a neighborhood Times Square stretches from about West 40th to West 53rd Sts between Sixth and Eighth Aves. It is the center of the city's theater district, a glitzy Mecca for tourists, and a symbol of urban renewal. Crowded and chaotic by day, it is spectacular after dark, illuminated by lighting displays famous the world over.

History of Times Square

Before 1904 Times Square, then known as Longacre Square, was dominated by horse exchanges, carriage factories, stables, and blacksmiths' shops. John Jacob Astor owned a large plot of land in the area, and enlarged his fortune selling off lots for hotels and other real estate ventures. In 1904 the subway arrived along with the *New York Times*, whose publisher persuaded the city to rename the area for his newspaper, perhaps in competition with Herald Square to the south, named for the *New York Herald*, then the dominant newspaper.

O.J. Gude, an advertising man, is said to have coined the name "the Great White Way" in 1901, when he realized the commercial potential of electrically enhanced billboards. Through the years electric billboards have given way to splashy animated neon and then to giant LED screens. Viewers have marveled at a gigantic smoker exhaling real smoke rings, a shower of golden peanuts cascading from an illuminated bag, and a giant electric Kleenex made of some 25,000 light bulbs.

The city's theater district developed around Times Square during the first three decades of the 20th century. First came a few pioneers, creeping up Broadway from Herald Square: Charles Frohman's Empire Theatre (1893) on Broadway at 40th St, and the former Metropolitan Opera House (1883) between 39th and 40th Sts. Oscar Hammerstein—opera impresario, composer, cigar-maker, and grandfather of the famous lyricist—was the first to forge north of 42nd St; and while his Olympia Theatre (1895) on Broadway between 44th and 45th Sts lasted only two years, Hammerstein rebounded from bankruptcy and resiliently built three more theaters in Times Square, earning himself the reputation of "the man who created Times Square."

As advances in transportation made the district widely accessible and investors realized the profits of theaters as real estate, Times Square flourished. Theaters were built either by speculators aware that a hit show could gross a million dollars in a single year—roughly the price of building a theater in the 1920s—or by financial backers working with independent producers like Charles Frohman and David Belasco. Times Square began attracting agents, producers, theatrical publications, restaurants, hotels, and theatrical clubs. New York's best season came in 1927–28, when 80 theaters were in operation. (Today there are 39 Broadway theaters.)

The Depression devastated Broadway. The Federal Theater Project kept some actors and writers in work, but the Times Square theater district embarked on a long process of attrition, abetted by rising land values and the inroads of the movies and, later, television. Many legitimate theaters were converted to burlesque theaters or to movie houses whose offerings deteriorated from Hollywood hits, to second-run movies, to X-rated pornography. By the 1970s, the area was known for crime, drug dealing, and prostitution. Times Square was no longer famous for its theaters and its neon, but notorious for its sleaze.

The turnaround began in the late 1980s, with new commercial real estate development in the West 40s and 50s. In the early 1990s, a combination of governmental, non-profit, and commercial organizations began to pull the neighborhood from its morass. In 1990 the state took over several historic theaters on 42nd St and formed The New 42nd Street, a non-profit organization, to oversee their redevelopment. The Walt Disney Company came into town in 1993, refurbishing the New Amsterdam Theatre for Disney entertainment. The Times Square Alliance, a business improvement association, was founded in 1992 to promote the area, improve public safety, bolster economic development, and deal with quality-of-life issues.

Today Times Square is cleaner, safer, more profitable, and more visitor-friendly (as many as 20 million tourists visit annually) than it was a decade ago. While no one wishes for the return of crime and squalor, some observers lament what has become of the neighborhood—its increasing corporate homogeneity and loss of individuality, its bland lineup of chain-stores (albeit grandly scaled and beautifully illuminated), and its sense of being for tourists, not New Yorkers.

THEATER DISTRICT: SEVENTH–TENTH AVENUES

NB: Many of the theaters have been landmarked, so that their façades may not be significantly altered. Unfortunately giant marquees often obscure the original architectural features, so the best views are from a distance.

42nd Street

The New Amsterdam Theatre: This theater building (1903, Herts & Tallant; restored 1997, Hardy Holzman Pfeiffer Associates) is a grand Art Deco hall where once the showgirls of the *Ziegfeld Follies* strutted. Like most of the other Broadway theaters, it suffered during the Depression, became a movie theater, and eventually closed. The Walt Disney Company returned the New Amsterdam to its former splendor for about $40 million, restoring its terra-cotta ornament, elaborately painted proscenium, and ornate woodwork. Now a venue for Disney's theatrical productions, the theater hosted a long and successful run of *The Lion King* as well as other family fare. *214 West 42nd St (Seventh/Eighth Aves). For information on guided tours, T: 212 282 2952.*

The New Victory Theater: This began as the Republic (1900; J.B. McElfatrick &

Co.), built by Oscar Hammerstein, who sold it to impresario David Belasco, who quickly renamed it after himself and added his own decorative touches. In 1931 it became a burlesque house. In 1942, renamed the Victory Theater in a burst of patriotic enthusiasm, it tried for a new life as a movie house, eventually sinking to XXX-rated films. Restored in 1995 (Hardy Holzman Pfeiffer Associates), it is now a center for children's and family entertainment, with puppet shows, circus performances, and educational offerings. *207 West 42nd St (Seventh/Eighth Aves)*.

Hilton Theatre Center: With its main entrance (1997; Beyer Blinder Belle) on West 43rd St, the Hilton opened as the Ford Center for the Performing Arts in 1998. The former Lyric and Apollo theaters, both of which had deteriorated badly, were demolished to make way for the present theater, which preserves the proscenium arch and dome from the Apollo, and the façades from the Lyric. *213 West 42nd St (Seventh/Eighth Aves)*.

American Airlines Theatre: The former Selwyn Theatre (1918; George Keister) was renamed for its corporate supporter, who paid $8.5 million to resuscitate its fortunes. It is the first permanent home of the highly regarded Roundabout Theatre Company. The theater was built by Edgar and Arch Selwyn, behind their six-story office building. George Keister, who designed the Belasco Theatre and several movie palaces, decorated the auditorium with large murals and elaborate plaster-work, much of which has been restored. On top is a penthouse lobby where patrons can relax and enjoy a snack or a drink. During restoration, part of the old Selwyn office building collapsed and has

been replaced by a new structure that houses the Roundabout box office, the 42nd Street Rehearsal Studios, and The Duke, a small experimental theater.

Established in 1965, the Roundabout Theatre Company offered its first produc-tions in the basement of a Chelsea super-market, and then spent almost four decades moving from place to place in search of a permanent home. It is New York's largest not-for-profit company, recognized for its exceptional productions of classic dramas and musicals. *227 West 42nd St (Seventh/Eighth Aves). For ticket information, T: 212 719 1300.*

Ripley's Believe it or Not! Odditorium: This throwback to old-style midway entertainment returned to Times Square in 2006 (an earlier version opened in 1939), sharing an address with Madame Tussaud. As its name amply sug-gests, the Odditorium offers peculiar and eccentric exhibits. *234 West 42nd St (Seventh/Eighth Aves). Open daily 9am–1am (last tickets midnight); T: 212 398 3133; ripleysnewyork.com.*

Port Authority Bus Terminal: Built in 1950 and twice expanded, the station has become the world's largest, covering two city blocks. Vast, confusing to the unin-itiated, and drab, it serves about 200,000 passengers every workday. Its ramps feed directly into the Lincoln Tunnel, some-what alleviating street congestion. The terminal has long been a refuge for the homeless, and while the problem has eased, it still exists. *Eighth to Ninth Aves (West 40th to 42nd Sts). For automated bus information, T: 212 564 8484.*

The new New York Times Building: This (2007; Renzo Piano) is the third home for the august newspaper, and the first new headquarters since 1913, when

it moved from Times Square to West 43rd St. Renzo Piano, famous for co-designing the Centre Pompidou in Paris and reconstructing the Potsdamer Platz in Berlin, was chosen as architect in a design competition. The *Times* unveiled the plans in Dec 2001, at a time when the city was still feeling vulnerable from the terrorist attacks, and many corporations were leery of tall buildings. Piano, who spoke of the design in terms of transparency and visibility, described his building as one "that will disappear in the air." The tower is clad in transparent glass that brings daylight into the building. Arrayed in screens in front of the glass, 250,000 ceramic rods reflect light and change color throughout the day, while reducing the building's cooling loads. The building extends the Times Square redevelopment project westward to Eighth Avenue. More than 50 businesses, from sex shops to third-generation hatters and fabric dealers, were displaced by the tower. *620 Eighth Ave (West 41st to West 42nd Sts).*

The former McGraw Hill Building: Best seen from West 42nd St between Seventh and Eighth Aves, this was a revolutionary skyscraper in its day (1931; Raymond Hood, Godley & Fouilhoux). Because the building originally contained printing presses, it was relegated to the fringes of midtown by the Zoning Resolution of 1916, which prohibited light industry further inland. The building is much admired for its blue-green terra-cotta sheathing, which helps it blend with the sky and makes it appear less bulky, as well as its horizontal bands of strip windows, which were needed to illuminate the loft and factory floors. *330 West 42nd St (Eighth/Ninth Aves).*

Theatre Row: The strip of West 42nd St between Ninth and Tenth Aves houses small Off- and Off-Off-Broadway theaters and studios. The original Theatre Row opened here in 1978, with several pioneering theater companies seeking to reclaim the then-derelict west end of 42nd St. The physical theaters were dreary, with primitive air conditioning and minimal amenities for audience and actors. The 42nd Street Redevelopment Corporation invested some $12 million, sold the air rights to the apartment tower that rises above the theaters, and reopened the present Theatre Row building (410 West 42nd St) in 2002, which houses audition and rehearsal studios as well as theaters, all equipped with state-of-the-art stage technology. Also on the block are Playwrights Horizons (416 West 42nd St), a not-for-profit company devoted to supporting contemporary American playwrights, composers, and lyricists since 1971; and the Little Shubert (422 West 42nd St), built by the Shubert organization for developing large-scale works. *Ticket Central, the box office for all Theatre Row productions, is at 416 West 42nd St (Ninth/Tenth Aves); open daily 12–8; T: 212 279 4200; www.theatrerow.org.*

Times Square

One Times Square: This eminent building, originally the Times Tower, overlooks the scene from the north side of the lower triangle made by Broadway and Seventh Avenue. When the *New York Times* moved in on Dec 31, 1904, the building had a granite base, a marble lobby, and 25 floors sheathed in ornamental terra cotta, as well

as space for the presses in the basement. Its unusual trapezoidal shape made it an instant visual landmark. In the 1960s, long after the *Times* had moved to West 43rd St, a featureless slick marble surface replaced the terra cotta and granite. Today the marble is barely visible, as the building serves mainly as a skeleton on which to hang advertisements and a platform from which to drop the famous ball on New Year's Eve. Three floors up is the "zipper," a wraparound moving sign that first announced the presidential electoral results of 1928 (Herbert Hoover won) and still informs passers-by of breaking news and sports scores. *West 42nd St (Broadway and Seventh Ave).*

NEW YEAR'S EVE IN TIMES SQUARE

The Times Square New Year's Eve celebrations have been a feature of city life since 1904, when *Times* publisher Adolph Ochs celebrated the paper's arrival (and that of the new year) with an all-day festival and a street-level fireworks display. Two years later the police banned the fireworks, so Ochs responded by lowering a wooden and iron ball illuminated with 100 25-watt light bulbs from the building's flagpole. Since then the ball-drop has been repeated every year, except in 1942–43, when it was changed to the ringing of church bells and moments of silence because of the wartime "dim out." During the 1980s, the ball was converted into a Big Apple, with the addition of red light bulbs and a green stem. The present crystal ball, built like a geodesic sphere, was inaugurated in 2000, when an estimated two million people crowded into Times Square for the coming of the new millennium.

The former Knickerbocker Hotel: The only survivor of several elegant hotels that graced the area at the turn of the 20th century, this red-brick Beaux-Arts building (1902) was commissioned by John Jacob Astor, whose family had long owned the land. The exterior is elaborated with terra-cotta and limestone pediments and a copper mansard roof. Inside were marble-floored dining rooms that could seat 2,000 guests. Enrico Caruso stayed here when he was performing in New York. *1466 Broadway (West 42nd St).*
Condé Nast Building: This is the headquarters (1999; Fox & Fowle) of one of several media giants to arrive in Times Square in recent years. (Condé Nast pub-lishes *The New Yorker, Vanity Fair,* and *Vogue,* among other stylish magazines.) The building faces commercial West 42nd St with a sober gray granite façade, and Broadway with a glassy neon-lit wall. On the northwest corner, a seven-story rounded tower with a high-tech electronic billboard provides stock market infor-mation and financial news along with ads. At street level, TV studios and a sports bar attract crowds of passers-by. On top is a giant antenna built to accommodate broadcasters whose facilities were destroyed with the World Trade Center. The building is also remarkable for its "green" construction, with increased insu-lation, solar collectors, and hydrogen-fuel

cells to generate hot water and electricity. *4 Times Square (Broadway between West 42nd and 43rd Sts)*.

Reuters Building: Across the street is the North American headquarters of the Reuters news and financial data agency (2001; Fox & Fowle). Like the nearby Condé Nast Building (by the same architects), the Reuters tower has a façade of stone (facing the Paramount Building), a wall of curved glass, and a giant neon marquee. *3 Times Square (Seventh Ave between West 42nd and 43rd Sts)*.

Paramount Building: This is a Times Square skyline landmark (1927; Rapp & Rapp), its setbacks converging on a clock-tower and an illuminated glass globe. Built as a palatial space for movies and live entertainment, the Paramount Theater hosted such famous performers as Benny Goodman, Tommy Dorsey, and Frank Sinatra. Though the theater is long gone, the original lobby (north of the reconstructed marquee) is theatrical in the old-fashioned way, with a heavily ornate ceiling, black marble-faced walls, opulent chandeliers, and paneled bronze elevator doors. A Hard Rock Café occupies the ground floor. *1501 Broadway (West 43rd and 44th Sts)*.

West 44th Street

Belasco Theatre: Built for playwright and producer David Belasco as a showcase for his technical innovations (1907; George Keister), it included an elevator stage, a sophisticated lighting system, and a studio for developing special effects, as well as a grandly furnished apartment for Belasco himself, which sits on top of the theater at its eastern end. Belasco, who wrote many forgettable plays, is perhaps best known for *Madame Butterfly* and *Girl of the Golden West*, both transformed into operas by Giacomo Puccini. *111 West 44th St (Sixth Ave and Broadway)*.

One Astor Plaza: The building occupies the territory of the once-splendid Astor Hotel (1904). Architecturally the current building (1969; Kahn & Jacobs) is recognizable at some distance by the concrete fins adorning its upper stories, suggestive to one critic of an Edsel crashing into it from outer space. It was the first building in the specially designated Times Square Theater District to take advantage of zoning bonuses that allow extra floor space to a building that includes a new legitimate theater (the Minskoff). Viacom, another mega-media company, is the major tenant, with its Paramount and MTV divisions here. The MTV studios overlooking Broadway sometimes draw crowds of screaming teenagers. *1515 Broadway (West 44th and 45th Sts)*.

Sardi's: The restaurant is known primarily as the one-time haunt of actors, writers, and theater people, who traditionally held opening night celebrations here while awaiting the newspaper reviews. Caricatures of famous faces adorn the walls. *234 West 44th St (Broadway and Eighth Ave)*.

Shubert Theatre: Along with its companion the Booth, this theater (1913; Henry B. Herts) has had a resoundingly prosperous career, beginning with its opening production, *Hamlet*, and including *A Chorus Line*, which won the Pulitzer Prize in 1976 and ran until 1990. Lavishly built, perhaps because it was a memorial to Sam Shubert (*see box opposite*), the

theater is unusual for the Venetian-style *sgraffito* decoration on the façade, apparently architect Herts's response to a stipulation in the building code that allowed no part of the theater to project beyond the building line. A medallion of Herts looks down from above the main entrance. The interior, including its elegant plasterwork and murals by J. Mortimer Lichtenauer, was restored in 1996. *225 West 44th St (Broadway and Eighth Ave).*

The Shubert brothers

The flagship Sam S. Shubert Theatre is named after the eldest Shubert brother, who with his younger siblings Lee and Jacob (known as J.J.) founded a theatrical empire. The brothers, children of a Syracuse, New York, peddler, came to the city around the turn of the 20th century. Beginning with a single theater, they took on and bested the ruling monopoly of the day, the Klaw and Erlanger Syndicate, emerging as the most powerful force in the American theater. Sam died at 26, from injuries sustained in a train wreck in 1905, and his brothers named the theater in his memory. In their heyday the Shuberts controlled the production, booking, and presentation of shows, dominating the try-out circuits through their ownership of theaters outside New York and forcing producers to book exclusively through their organization. A decree issued in 1956 as the result of an antitrust action brought by the federal government required them to stop their restrictive booking practices and to sell 12 theaters in six cities. Nevertheless, the Shubert Organization is still Broadway's most powerful landlord, controlling 16½ Broadway theaters (Irving Berlin's estate owns a half interest in the Music Box), more than twice those owned by the Nederlander Organization, its nearest rival.

Shubert Alley, now a promenade for theatergoers and formerly a gathering place for singers, actors, and dancers who hoped to be cast in Shubert-produced plays, was built because fire laws stipulated that there must be space for fire equipment behind the former Astor Hotel, now replaced by 1 Astor Plaza. At the north end of the alley is the **Booth Theatre** (1913; Henry B. Herts), built as a companion to the Shubert, also with *sgraffito* decoration. Less opulent than the Shubert, it was intended for intimate drama or small-scale musicals. It is named for actor Edwin Booth (1833–93), whose brother John Wilkes Booth assassinated Abraham Lincoln. *232 West 45th St (Broadway and Eighth Ave).*

West 45th Street

Marriott Marquis Hotel: This was an early arrival in the "new" Times Square. In 1982, despite public protests, the historic Helen Hayes and Morosco Theatres, as well as the Gaiety, the Bijou, and the Astor, were demolished for the hotel (1985; John C. Portman), whose presence, it was hoped, would help revitalize

this part of Times Square. In return the developer had to build a theater (the 1,600-seat Marquis) within the hotel. *Broadway (West 45th and 46th Sts)*.

Lyceum Theatre: This is the oldest surviving legitimate New York theater, and still one of the grandest (1903; Herts & Tallant). Now a part of the Shubert Organization, whose archives occupy the one-time apartment of entrepreneur Daniel Frohman, the building stands out for its glorious Beaux-Arts façade, its undulating marquee, its elaborate banded Corinthian columns, and its high mansard roof pierced with oval windows. At the turn of the 20th century, Herts & Tallant, both of whom had studied at the École des Beaux-Arts, were New York's premier theater designers. *149 West 45th St (Broadway and Seventh Ave)*.

West 46th Street

Former I. Miller Building: High up on the building (1929) and almost obscured by signs, four niches display marble statues of onetime ladies of the theater: Ethel Barrymore (drama), Marilyn Miller (musical theater), Mary Pickford (film), and Rosa Ponselle (opera)—all sculpted by Alexander Stirling Calder, father of Alexander Calder. Israel Miller, a shoemaker who arrived from Poland in 1892, got his start making shoes for Broadway productions. His work soon became popular with the vaudeville actresses of the day, and in 1911 Miller opened his own shop. He eventually expanded, had the façade redesigned, and organized a vote to pick the leading ladies. *West 46th St (northwest corner of Seventh Ave)*.

Statue of George M. Cohan: On the traffic island near the intersection of West 46th St and Broadway, this bronze memorial (1958; Georg Lober) commemorates Cohan (1878–1942), a song-and-dance man best known for writing "Give My Regards to Broadway," "Over There," and "I'm a Yankee Doodle Dandy." The statue was unveiled in a ceremony with Oscar Hammerstein II presiding, George Jessel acting as master of ceremonies, and a crowd of 45,000 attending. At the conclusion, everyone broke into "Give My Regards to Broadway."

West 47th Street

Father Duffy Square: The northern part of the traffic island is named for Father Francis P. Duffy (1871–1932), the "Fighting Chaplain" of the 69th Regiment during World War I. A figure of Duffy (1937; Charles Keck) stands near West 47th St in the middle of the traffic island. As pastor of nearby Holy Cross Church (at 333 West 42nd St), Father Duffy served a parish that embraced the slums of Hell's Kitchen, the burlesque houses and dance halls of Times Square, and the legitimate theaters of Broadway. When the statue was unveiled, a crowd of 30,000 including prize fighters, political figures, and Broadway characters came to pay him tribute, joining the 69th Regiment and the military bands which struck up "Onward Christian Soldiers." Father Duffy is depicted wearing his World War I uniform and holding the New Testament, his back to a granite Celtic cross. *(West 46th*

to 47th Sts, Broadway to Seventh Ave).
Palace Theatre: Barely visible beneath its signage, this was once Broadway's most illustrious vaudeville house (1913; Kirchoff & Rose). Among the performers who "played the Palace" (i.e. were at the top of their game) were Sophie Tucker, Jack Benny, and Bob Hope. After a stint as a movie house, the Palace again became a legitimate theater, showcasing Disney productions and other large-scale musicals, including *La Cage aux Folles* and *Beauty and the Beast. 1564–66 Broadway (West 46th and 47th Sts).*

West 49th–West 51st Streets

Brill Building: Constructed in 1931 by Abraham E. Lefcourt, a clothing manufacturer who had turned to real estate development in the 1910s, the building is named for the Brill Brothers, who ran a clothing business on the ground floor and bought the building from Lefcourt during the Depression. The bronze bust above the door is believed to represent Lefcourt's son Alan, who died in a car crash; the larger stone bust in the 11th-floor recess is Lefcourt himself. During the Depression, the owners rented to anyone who could pay, including music publishers; the Brill Building is famous for the music written there during the early 1960s by a group of young singer-songwriters (Carole King, Neil Diamond, and others), who blended the new sound of rock 'n' roll with the older Tin Pan Alley tradition of sophisticated popular music (written by such composers as Irving Berlin, Jerome Kern, and the Gershwin brothers). The "Brill Building sound" emanated from several buildings along Broadway from 49th to 53rd Sts, but the Brill Building was considered the most prestigious place to work. *1619 Broadway (between West 49th and 50th Sts).*
Winter Garden Theatre: Back when the neighborhood was the center of the horse-and-carriage district, the Winter Garden Theatre began as a horse exchange owned by William K. Vanderbilt, inheritor of Vanderbilt wealth, founder of the Jockey Club, and breeder of racehorses. The Shubert brothers took a 40-year lease from Vanderbilt in 1911 and converted the exchange to a theater, decorating it with a garden theme and changing the show ring into the auditorium. During its first decade the showgirls could walk out into the audience on a special runway from the stage, called the "Bridge of Thighs" by admiring observers. Many Shubert musicals enjoyed long runs here, including *West Side Story* and *Peter Pan*, all of them topped by *Cats*, which made Broadway history, playing 7,485 performances. After *Cats* closed, the auditorium, which had been gutted for the junkyard setting of the musical, was restored to its 1920s beauty. *1634 Broadway (West 50th and 51st Sts).*
Worldwide Plaza: The blockbuster office and residential complex (1989; residential tower Skidmore, Owings & Merrill) stands on the site of the third Madison Square Garden (*see box overleaf*). The first tall building to intrude into Hell's Kitchen, its presence probably nudged the area toward its current rapid gentrification. (*Eighth/Ninth Aves, West 49th to 50th Sts).*

THE THIRD MADISON SQUARE GARDEN

The third Madison Square Garden (1925; Thomas Lamb), undistinguished as a building, was developed as an institution by John Ringling, a circus entrepreneur, and Tex Rickard, sometime gambler, cattleman, and promoter of prizefights. The garden's staple offerings were boxing matches, ice hockey and basketball games, ice shows, the circus, rodeos, and expositions. Its social peak came with the annual horse show, for which a box cost $315 in 1939; its social nadir was probably the Six-Day Bicycle Race, for which in the same year a one-week admission cost a dollar.

HELL'S KITCHEN

Hell's Kitchen (*map p. 578, A3–B3*) is also known as Clinton, a dichotomy that suggests both the neighborhood's past as a low-scale, blue-collar district and its present as a gentrifying part of the far West Side of Midtown. The neighborhood stretches from the Hudson River to Eighth Avenue, from about West 34th to West 57th Sts.

During the mid-19th century Hell's Kitchen attracted large groups of immigrants, particularly the Irish, who lived in some of the city's worst tenements and worked in some of its least desirable industries. The proximity of the Hudson River and the railroad of that name (later the New York Central Railroad) on Eleventh Avenue attracted slaughterhouses, gas plants, and glue and soap factories, which provided jobs for the immigrants who were willing to work in them.

Local gangs preyed on the railroad yards and so terrorized the neighborhood that policemen from the nearby 20th Precinct would venture out only in groups larger than three. Bearing such colorful names as the Hudson Dusters, the Gophers, the Gorillas, and Battle Row Annie's Ladies' Social and Athletic Club, the gangs gave Hell's Kitchen a reputation as one of the most dangerous spots on the American continent. An urban legend, probably apocryphal, suggests that two policemen watching a street fight on a muggy summer night gave the district its name. Said one, "This neighborhood is hot as hell." "Hell is cool," corrected the other, "This here's Hell's Kitchen."

After 1910, when the New York Central Railroad hired a strong-arm squad who clubbed, shot, arrested, and otherwise incapacitated most of the old-style gangsters, life in the area mellowed for a while, only to resume its former violence with the arrival of bootleggers during the 1920s.

Although the waterfront flourished after World War II, containerized shipping sapped the economic vitality of the Hudson River piers. The Italians and Greeks who had worked as stevedores along with the Irish could no longer find jobs. In the 1950s new immigrant groups, blacks from the South and Puerto Ricans, moved to the neighborhood. Racial tensions from that era served as the inspiration for Leonard

Bernstein's *West Side Story*, whose Jets and Sharks contested turf in the West 60s where Lincoln Center now stands.

Plagued by drugs and crime in the 1970s, Hell's Kitchen began to gentrify in the 1980s. Today the process is accelerating, as large rental and condominium towers with upscale amenities and prices to match are changing both the appearance and the demographics of the neighborhood. It is also attracting young professionals working in the corporate towers of Times Square, and a gay population moving north from Chelsea. Ethnic restaurants still line Ninth Avenue, the site of the annual Ninth Avenue International Food Festival (usually in mid-May) when as many as a million people wander up and down the avenue, from West 57th to West 37th Sts, sampling on food from around the globe.

RETURNING TO THE WATERFRONT

The Intrepid Sea Air Space Museum, on the aircraft carrier *Intrepid*, was due to return to Pier 86 (near Twelfth Ave at West 46th St) shortly after press time of this guide. On board are historic aircraft and exhibits on the history of the ship and naval warfare. (*T: 212 245 0072; www.intrepidmuseum.org.*)

Hearst Tower

At 959 Eighth Ave (West 56th and West 57th Sts; *map p. 578, C2*), the Hearst Tower (2006; Norman Foster Partners) rises above the former Hearst Magazine Building (1928; Joseph Urban), whose theatrical façade is worthy both of its designer and its original owner. Viennese-trained architect Joseph Urban was famous for designing theaters and stage sets for companies as serious as the Metropolitan Opera and as frivolous as the *Ziegfeld Follies*. Here Urban embellished the façade with Art Deco sculptural figures: *Comedy and Tragedy* (left) and *Music and Art* (right) flank the entrance; *Sport and Industry* decorate the corner at West 56th St with *Printing and the Sciences* on the building's major corner at West 57th St. William Randolph Hearst gained fame and notoriety for building a nationwide chain of newspapers known for sensational journalism. The Hearst corporation owns only 12 newspapers today, but is still an important publisher of monthly magazines, including *Cosmopolitan*, *Good Housekeeping*, and *O, The Oprah Magazine*.

Financial difficulties during the Depression scuttled any attempt to build the tower Hearst had originally planned. Almost 80 years later Sir Norman Foster's triangulated 46-story tower arose behind the Urban façade. The bold form of the tower, its crossed steel braces, and soaring ground-level atrium have won the admiration of architectural critics. Its eco-friendly design has been widely applauded by environmentalists: under the floor of the atrium, water circulates through polyethylene tubing for cooling and heating; rainwater collected on the roof is used in the cooling system; the triangular external frame used about 20 percent less steel than a conventional building.

GRAND CENTRAL TERMINAL
& PARK AVENUE

Map p. 579, D4. Subway: 4, 5, 6, 7, S to 42nd St-Grand Central. Bus M1, M2, M3, M4, M101, M102, M103, M104. Every Wed at 12:30pm a free tour of the building sponsored by the Municipal Arts Society meets at the information booth on the Main Concourse; T: 212 935 3960. Every Fri at 12:30pm a free tour of the neighborhood including Grand Central, sponsored by the Grand Central Partnership, meets on 42nd St in front of the Altria Building across from Grand Central; T: 212 883 2420.

Grand Central Terminal (1903–13; Reed & Stem and Warren & Wetmore) stands proudly athwart Park Avenue at 42nd St. Though rail travel has declined in scope and grandeur since the terminal was built, Grand Central remains one of the world's great railroad stations, and an enduring symbol of the city. Visually less exciting outside than those other emblems of New York's preeminence—the Empire State Building, the Brooklyn Bridge, and the Statue of Liberty—it is still a fine building and a marvel of engineering and urban planning, bringing the railroad into the heart of the city while enhancing surrounding property. The concourse is one of the city's great interiors.

History of Grand Central Terminal

By 1869 Cornelius Vanderbilt, known as the Commodore because of his beginnings as a ferryboat entrepreneur, had seized control of all the railroads into New York by a series of bold financial maneuvers. He determined to consolidate the lines physically by erecting at Fourth Ave and 42nd St a Grand Central Depot—ambitiously named, since at the time 42nd St was in the hinterlands. He then acquired sufficient land along Fourth Avenue for storage and marshaling yards, land that constitutes practically all of the present Grand Central complex. A station designed by John B. Snook rose between 1869 and 1871, a "head house," whose trains either backed in or backed out. Never really adequate, the original station and its sheds and yards were enlarged and rearranged, including an 1898 remodeling in which a waiting room for immigrants was created in the basement so other passengers might not have to mix with them.

When the city demanded that the railroad electrify its lines or move the terminal to the outskirts, William J. Wilgus, the brilliant chief engineer, submerged the tracks, introducing the two present levels of trackage and electrifying the lines as far as the southern Bronx. He also suggested a new terminal that used the air rights over the tracks (Madison to Lexington Aves, 42nd to 50th Sts) for new, revenue-producing office and apartment buildings. A competition for the design of the station produced the innovative plan of architects Reed & Stem (Reed was Wilgus's brother-in-law) that wrapped Park Avenue around the station on viaducts. Later the firm of Warren & Wetmore (Warren was a cousin of William K. Vanderbilt, then chairman of the board of the New York Central Railroad) was brought into the project. Though Warren & Wetmore seem to have won the power struggle between the two firms, the basic

design premises, including the elevated driveway around the station and the placement of piers for future office buildings along Park Avenue, come from Reed & Stem.

The station covers three city blocks—42nd to 45th Sts between Vanderbilt and Madison Aves—and beneath it are electric power facilities, steam, water, sewage, and electric mains, and loops of track where trains can turn around without backing out of the station. At one time it was the terminus for two major railroads, the New York Central, which reached to the Mississippi River, and the New York, New Haven, and Hartford, which served New England. Today it is largely a commuter station.

It is not surprising that many assaults have been made on the architectural integrity of the terminal, sitting as it does on a prime Midtown site. Fortunately most have come to naught, with the exception of the MetLife Building (formerly the PanAm Building), which towers above the terminal from the north (*see p. 232*). Among the more unpleasant of these schemes was a plan (1960) to divide the main waiting room horizontally into four 15-ft stories, the upper three to contain bowling alleys. This proposal surely hastened designation of the terminal as a landmark in 1965, a status the Penn Central Railroad, then operating Grand Central Terminal, soon came to resent. The railroad, recognizing the inflation in surrounding real estate, proposed a 54-story tower over the waiting room, a design rejected by the Landmarks Commission. After several other plans to circumvent the designation failed, the railroad sued to have the landmark status withdrawn on the grounds of economic hardship, but in 1978 the Supreme Court upheld the city's right to protect architecturally or historically valuable buildings by this means.

The building

The best view of the terminal is from Park Avenue, south of the station. Whitney Warren, primarily responsible for the south façade, saw the station as a gateway to the city and designed it with three great arched windows framed by pairs of columns to recall the triumphal arches of the cities of antiquity. Jules-Félix Coutan created the sculptural group (1914) that crowns the façade. Entitled *Transportation*, it depicts Mercury (Commerce) flanked by Hercules (Physical Energy) and Minerva (Intellectual Energy). Directly beneath the clock (13ft in diameter) stands a heroic bronze figure of Cornelius Vanderbilt, commissioned by the Commodore himself (1869), designed by Albert De Groot, one of Vanderbilt's ship captains, and moved here from the former Hudson River freight station in 1929. The statue of a bald eagle over the Lexington Avenue entrance originally perched on the roof of the earlier Grand Central along with perhaps ten others. It was replaced here in 1999.

The station interior was beautifully restored and refurbished between 1994 and 1998, when the escalators, air-conditioning, and Grand Central Market were added, as was the staircase at the east end of the concourse—planned in the original design but never built. The quarry which supplied the marble from the western staircase was reopened so that the two staircases would match perfectly.

Directly behind the Main Waiting Room is the famous **Main Concourse** (120ft wide; 375ft long). Sheathed in marble and simulated Caen stone, it rises to a cerulean

elliptical vault (125ft high), decorated with the constellations of the zodiac designed by Whitney Warren with Paul Helleu and Charles Basing. The constellations are reversed, north to south, a fact discovered by an angry commuter in 1913. Various explanations have been given: that the painters made the mistake because the diagram was placed on the floor; or that the painters were using a medieval manuscript that showed the stars from a point beyond the heavens. The patch of grime in the darkened sky in the northwest corner has been left to show how the ceiling looked before the restoration. Worked into the ornamentation throughout the Main Concourse, even into the periphery of the cosmos, are clusters of oak leaves, chosen by the Vanderbilts as their family emblem.

FOOD IN GRAND CENTRAL

Grand Central Market, between the Main Concourse and Lexington Avenue, is a foodie's delight, with a beautiful display of edibles from top-of-the-line suppliers. On the balcony above the Main Concourse are restaurants for fine dining. On the level below is a food court, with casual eateries and takeout. **The Oyster Bar** (accessible from the staircase at the west end of the concourse) is architecturally interesting for its Guastavino tiles supporting a vaulted ceiling, and gastronomically appealing for its 20-some varieties of oysters. It opened in 1913 and has been serving seafood ever since. (*Open for lunch and dinner; closed Sun and holidays; T: 212 490 6650; www. oysterbarny.com.*)

Just off the Main Concourse, in the Shuttle Passage, is an **annex of the New York Transit Museum** (*open Mon–Fri 8–8; Sat–Sun 10–6; closed major holidays; T: 212 878 0106*), with changing exhibitions on the art and history of public transit.

VANDERBILT TERRITORY

Once the neighborhood around Grand Central was the focal point of the New York Central Railroad's vast real estate empire. Handsome, staid hotels rose around the station: the former Hotel Biltmore (1914; Warren & Wetmore) on Vanderbilt Avenue, named after Cornelius Vanderbilt's chateau in North Carolina, has been converted to office space, though the famous old clock still remains in an unobtrusive corner of the lobby (Madison Avenue side); the former Commodore Hotel, named after the railroad's founder, was stripped to the bones and refleshed as the Hyatt Regency on 42nd St at Lexington Ave; the Yale Club (1915; James Gamble Rogers), stands at 50 Vanderbilt Ave, welcoming students and alumni of the university which was attended by several Vanderbilt offspring.

EAST 42ND STREET

Across the street from Grand Central at 110 East 42nd St is the **former Bowery Savings Bank**, now a catering hall. This grand neo-Romanesque palace, with its dramatic deep arched entrance, was designed (1923) by York & Sawyer, among the city's finest bank architects. The former banking hall (*not open to the public*) is noteworthy for its monumental scale. The carvings in the frieze below the beamed and coffered ceiling suggest the building's origins: the squirrel for thrift, the rooster for punctuality, the bull and bear representing Wall Street.

The **Chanin Building** (1929), at 122 East 42nd St, is an Art Deco delight, decorated with geometric and floral bas-reliefs. René Chambellan, best known for his work at Rockefeller Center, collaborated on the design of the interior, including the lobby, whose theme is "City of Opportunity." The bas-reliefs and grillwork express, respectively, the active and the intellectual life of the individual, with the geometric patterns, in Chambellan's conception, also symbolizing emotions and abstractions of thought. The whole design tells the story of a city where a man, through the exertion of his mind and hands, could rise from a humble state to wealth and power. The theme was especially applicable to Irwin Chanin, one of the city's first real estate developers. In 1919 Chanin borrowed $20,000 to build two houses in Bensonhurst, Brooklyn. Ten years later he had created 141 buildings in the city, including hotels and several Broadway theaters.

THE CHRYSLER BUILDING

The beautiful Chrysler Building at 405 Lexington Ave (East 42nd St; *map p. 579, E4*) was built by automobile manufacturer Walter P. Chrysler to express both the luxury and mechanical precision of the automobile in its Jazz Age incarnation. Designed by William Van Alen and completed in 1930, it is one of New York's finest Art Deco buildings.

History of the building

The building was undertaken by William H. Reynolds, a former state senator with ties to Tammany Hall (*see p. 171*), and one of the developers of the Dreamland amusement park at Coney Island in 1904. Like other ambitious men reaching back to the builders of the Tower of Babel, Reynolds aspired to erect the world's tallest tower, and hired maverick architect William Van Alen to design it. Chrysler bought the lease and the plans in 1928, by which time the race for height had become a bitter rivalry between Van Alen and his former partner H. Craig Severance, then at work on the headquarters of the Bank of Manhattan (now 40 Wall St). Van Alen announced plans for a Chrysler Building of 925ft. Severance in 1929 topped off triumphantly at 927ft, having added a 50-ft flagpole and a lantern above the 60 stories and ten penthouses of his building. Meanwhile a team of steelworkers inside the fire shaft of the Chrysler Building was secretly constructing its 185-ft spire. When Severance declared himself the victor, they pushed the spire through a hole in the roof, bringing the building's height

to 1,048 ft, 64ft higher than the Eiffel Tower, previously the world's tallest structure. One year later, however, the Empire State Building soared above them all to 1,250 ft.

Architecture of the building

The Chrysler Building's slender tower rises to the shining stainless-steel spire above concentric arches pierced by triangular windows. There is probably more stainless steel on the façade of the Chrysler Building than on any other building in New York, since stainless steel—sleek, mirror-like, and vastly appealing to Art Deco designers— was too expensive for all but the most lavish builders. Below the spire, winged gargoyles resembling hood ornaments stare off in four directions and a brickwork frieze of wheels studded with radiator caps encircles the building.

The lobby is one of the city's most beautiful interiors. The walls are veneered with sensuously veined Moroccan marble in warm tones of buff and red. Overhead a mural by Edward Trumbull depicts two favorite Art Deco motifs—transportation and human endeavor. Its theme is "Energy and man's application of it to the solution of his problems." The beautiful elevator doors and walls are inlaid with African woods in intricate floral designs, and the elevator cabs are marquetried, no two alike.

Former Socony Mobil and Daily News buildings

The **former Socony Mobil Building**, at 150 East 42nd St (Lexington and Third Aves), was built (1955) by Harrison & Abramovitz, a firm with ties to the Rockefeller family and its interests. Socony (Standard Oil Company of New York) Mobil was a successor to the original Standard Oil, broken up in 1911 by the Supreme Court. At the time of the building's completion it was the world's largest metal-clad office tower. The *AIA Guide to New York City* calls it "the ultimate architectural tin can."

Further east between Third and Second Avenues (220 East 42nd St) is another fine Art Deco skyscraper, the **former Daily News Building** (1930), designed by Raymond Hood, often considered the quintessential architect of the Age of Commerce. The water tower and other machinery atop the roof are concealed within a vertical extension of the building—a radical notion at a time when such fripperies as temples usually served as camouflage. Handsome brickwork and a bas-relief around the entrance form the only decoration of this severe, cubistic building, which appeared in the 1970s "Superman" movies as the home of the mythical *Daily Planet*. Inside the lobby are meteorological displays including a two-ton revolving globe set into a floor recess, though the publisher at one point thought the public would prefer "murder charts," maps of the city with the location of crimes indicated.

North of Grand Central

Just north of Grand Central is the **MetLife Building** (*map p. 579, D3*), originally the PanAm Building (1963; Emery Roth & Sons, Pietro Belluschi, and Walter Gropius), at 200 Park Ave. It is big (59 stories, on a 3.5 acre site) and intrusive (spoiling the

Elevator doors in inlaid African wood, in the lobby of the Chrysler Building (1930).

former vista down Park Avenue to the terminal). The Helmsley Building, originally the **New York Central Building** (1929; Warren & Wetmore), at 230 Park Ave (45th and 46th Sts), once served as headquarters for the railroad and was a visible reminder of its power. The central lobby is finished with marble and bronze. Burgundy and gold were the Vanderbilt colors, and the oak leaf was one of the chosen family emblems—all much in evidence here. When the building opened, the architectural critic of *The New Yorker* magazine compared its dark red marble trim to "the red meat of a vigorous period when kings were kings and architects were princes." Two vehicular portals pierce the northern façade to carry traffic on ramps around the railroad terminal.

PARK AVENUE

Map p. 579, D3. Subway: 4, 5, 6, 7, S to 42nd St-Grand Central. Bus: M1, M2, M3, M4, M5, M101, M102, M103, M104. Walk north through Grand Central, the MetLife and Helmsley buildings to 46th St.

Park Avenue, which began as Fourth Avenue on the 1811 grid, long remained undeveloped because a granite ridge ran its entire length. When the New York and Harlem Railroad requested a right of way for its tracks and permission to run its steam engines above 14th St (1832), the city granted it Fourth Avenue. The railroad then blasted out the granite and laid the tracks in a cut from which coal smoke and noise polluted the neighborhood. In 1857 the city set 42nd St as the southern limit for steam engines and the trains were then pulled by horses downtown to their terminal. Fourth Avenue was renamed in sections, with the final portion up to the Harlem River receiving the name Park Avenue in 1888.

The avenue north of the New York Central Building is now in its third stage of urban development. Before 1900, when the railroad yards ran above ground, the street attracted modest dwellings and factories. The avenue began its upward swing when the Fourth Avenue Improvement Scheme (1872–74) submerged the tracks below street level as far as 56th St, although the neighborhood remained humble until the tracks were completely decked over during the construction of Grand Central Terminal (1903–13). By the 1920s, all air rights over the tracks had been acquired by apartments and hotels, and luxury dwellings began appearing along both sides of the avenue up to 96th St, where the tracks emerge from the tunnel. Land values soared, increasing over 200 percent between 1914 and 1930. After World War II, however, the drop in passenger revenues led the railroad to re-examine the potential of its real estate empire and to take advantage of the enormously increased land values along Park Avenue. Starting in the 1950s, Park Avenue began changing from a fine residential neighborhood to a desirable commercial area, for a while the heartland of corporate America.

On the northwest corner of 47th St is J. Seward Johnson's *Taxi!*, a lifelike sculpture of a businessman, briefcase in hand, who has been hailing a cab since 1983.

THE WALDORF-ASTORIA HOTEL

The Waldorf-Astoria Hotel (1931; Schultze & Weaver), at 301 Park Ave (*map p. 579, D3*), is still architecturally and socially one of the city's finest hotels, and an Art Deco landmark. Faced in brick and limestone over a granite base, the hotel rises to two chrome-capped, 625-ft spires, the Waldorf Towers, whose private apartments, reached from a separate entrance on 50th St, once attracted such tenants as the Duke of Windsor, President Herbert Hoover, and General Douglas MacArthur. Facing Park Avenue above the main door, a figure by Nina Saemundsson symbolizes the "Spirit of Achievement," though it is uncertain whether this applies to the clientele or the hotel management.

The first Waldorf-Astoria (1894) stood on the site of the Empire State Building, replacing two Astor mansions, which were torn down as the result of a family feud. The ambitious Caroline Schermerhorn Astor, in a struggle for social supremacy, offended her nephew William Waldorf Astor, who had inherited the southern mansion; in revenge William Waldorf tore down his house and built the Waldorf Hotel, named after the family's ancestral home in Germany. Caroline, offended by the towering hotel, moved uptown, leaving her house to her son, John Jacob IV, who tore it down and built the Astoria part of the Waldorf-Astoria, named after an Oregon trading post of the original John Jacob Astor's fur empire. In 1929 the hotel moved uptown to its present location.

The interior

Inside, the lobby is half a flight up, since like other Park Avenue buildings the hotel (1,800 rooms) stands over the railroad yards and needs space above ground for mechanical equipment. While the tracks may have been irksome for the architects, they were a convenience for former guests arriving in private rail coaches, who could be shunted onto a special siding, bypassing the terminal altogether. When the hotel opened during the Depression, President Hoover lauded it as an "exhibition of … confidence to the whole nation," and surely its exquisite Art Deco interiors with marble, bronze, and matched woods suggested that the management foresaw better times. The centerpiece of the lobby is a clock made for the Chicago Columbian Exposition in 1893. On it are likenesses of George Washington, Abraham Lincoln, Queen Victoria, and other notables, as well as bronze plaques representing various sports.

The names of some public rooms recall the hotel's grand past. The Starlight Roof once had a ceiling that could be rolled back on balmy evenings. Oscar's, today a casual brasserie, bears the name of Oscar Tschirky, a *maître d'hôtel*, who is said to have invented Waldorf Salad and whose collection of menus now belongs to Cornell University.

THE VILLARD HOUSES

The public rooms of the luxury New York Palace Hotel (455 Madison Ave, near 50th St; *map p. 579, D3*) are housed in part of the extraordinary Villard Houses (1886), a U-shaped group of six sumptuous neo-Renaissance dwellings built by McKim, Mead & White for railroad baron Henry Villard, an immigrant from Bavaria. At the peak of

his power in early 1883, Villard began construction on a group of houses that would convince the most casual passer-by of his success. By Christmas, however, he had lost his fortune (perhaps $5 million) and the presidency of the Northern Pacific Railroad. The unfinished houses were transferred to trustees to be completed and sold. Their buyers included Villard's lawyer Artemas Holmes, and Whitelaw Reid (editor of the *New York Tribune*) and his wife Elisabeth, who bought Villard's own house for $350,000 in 1886 with wedding money from her father, millionaire Darius Ogden Mills.

The houses remained residential until after World War II, when social and economic changes eroded the style of life implied by their grandeur. Commercial firms and the Archdiocese of New York all used the buildings as offices, fortunately leaving them more or less intact. When the archdiocese no longer wanted the property, exhaustive negotiations led to the present project. One of the stipulations of the conversion of the houses to a hotel was the preservation of the most important interiors.

The architecture

Finished in warm Belleville (New Jersey) brownstone, the façade is modeled after the Palazzo Cancelleria in Rome (1489–96), and was designed by Joseph Morrill Wells, first assistant in the office of McKim, Mead & White, and known for his dry humor as well as his talent. Once when White boasted that one of his own drawings was as good "in its way … as the Parthenon," Wells, eating breakfast, replied, "Yes, and so too, in its way, is a boiled egg."

In the center of the complex is a courtyard, once used as a carriage turnaround. On the left is the **Urban Center**, a group of organizations dedicated to historic preservation, architecture, and urban planning. One of them, the Municipal Art Society, was founded (1892) during the City Beautiful movement by architect Richard Morris Hunt, among others, to embellish the city with sculpture, fountains, and other forms of public art. Today the organization keeps a watchful eye on the urban environment, its design, preservation, and maintenance; it also offers changing exhibitions. The society's superbly stocked store, Urban Center Books (*T: 212 935 3595*) specializes in books on architecture and city planning.

In the Grand Lobby is a red fireplace mantle with marble figures above it representing Joy, Hospitality, and Moderation, designed by Augustus Saint-Gaudens, who with Stanford White also designed the zodiac clock near the top of the stairs. The hotel's upscale restaurant occupies Villard's landmark rooms, whose decoration includes a barrel-vaulted ceiling (30ft high) gilded according to instructions by Stanford White; murals (1888) by John La Farge representing Music and Drama; and plaster casts of Luca della Robbia's marble *cantoria* (an organ loft designed for the cathedral in Florence; 1431–48); and a ceiling supported by Corinthian columns with gilt-bronze capitals.

ST. BARTHOLOMEW'S CHURCH

St. Bartholomew's Church (Protestant Episcopal), between 50th and 51st Sts (1919; Bertram G. Goodhue), is one of the oldest buildings along Park Avenue (*map p. 579,*

D3). The congregation bought the site for $1.5 million in 1914 from the F. & M. Schaefer Brewing Co., which had been making beer by the railroad tracks since 1860.

The exterior

The ornate carved portico comes from the previous St. Bartholomew's Church (1902) on Madison Avenue, designed by Stanford White, who styled it after a Romanesque church at St-Gilles-du-Gard in southern France, and hired Daniel Chester French and Philip Martiny, among others, to execute the figures. Connecting the three arches of the portal is a frieze depicting events from the Old and New Testaments. The tympanum over the center doors contains a representation of the coronation of Christ.

On the south side of the church is the Community House (1927), added by Goodhue's successor firm after his death. The garden (1971) along with the Community House converts the church into an L-shaped complex whose pleasing proportions and open space provide a moment of grace along an avenue that is becoming increasingly an unrelieved wall of skyscrapers. (*Café St. Bart's on the terrace in warm weather and indoors otherwise is open Mon–Fri and Sun 11–2:30; closed Sat; T: 212 593 3333; www.cafestbarts.com.*)

The interior

The mosaics on the ceiling of the narthex by Hildreth Meière tell the story of the Creation. The narthex opens into the three aisles of the nave, built facing east in the traditional cruciform shape with a barrel-vaulted ceiling. The structural elements are stone and marble veneered over concrete, and much of the wall surface has been covered with rough-textured Guastavino acoustic tiles. The west window, made of stained glass given as memorials for the earlier Madison Avenue church, has figures of the Evangelists and scenes from the New Testament. Dominating the interior is a mosaic of glass and gold leaf (also by Hildreth Meière) filling the ceiling of the apse. It represents the Transfiguration, with Christ in the center flanked by Elijah and Moses standing on the mountain and the disciples Peter (north side), James, and John (south side). The five tall windows in the apse below are filled with thin sheets of amber onyx and covered with grilles of the same material.

General Electric Building

Providing a dramatic background to the church is the reddish-orange brick and terra cotta of the former General Electric Building (1931; Cross & Cross) at 570 Lexington Ave (southwest corner of 51st St). Its wonderful spiked Art Deco crown suggests the fantasies of science fiction, appropriate to the original tenant, the RCA Victor Company, which was wooed away to Rockefeller Center. The lobby, with terrazzo floors, pale purple marble panels, aluminum light sconces, and silvery barrel-vaulted ceiling openings, is as coolly elegant as anything in the city.

Along East 51st St near Park Avenue, Robert Cook's bronze *Dinoceras* (1971) suggests a struggling animal and is named after a horned mammal of the Eocene period (21 million years ago).

THE SEAGRAM BUILDING

The Seagram Building at 375 Park Ave (52nd and 53rd Sts; *map p. 579, D3–E3*) is an iconic skyscraper (1958), the only New York work of Ludwig Mies van der Rohe (working with Philip Johnson). This elegant metal and glass curtain-wall building is set back 90ft from the building line, and rises about 500ft on square columns. All the materials—from the wall of custom-made amber glass and bronze, to the green Italian marble seating around the fountains on a plaza of pink Vermont granite, to the brushed aluminum and stainless-steel hardware—were chosen for their quality and are meticulously deployed. The excellence of the building stems largely from the interest and sophistication of Phyllis Lambert, architect daughter of Seagram board chairman Samuel Bronfman, who persuaded her father to erect a monumental, not just a serviceable, building. Bronfman had already hired Charles Luckman, a successful business executive (Lever Brothers) turned less successful architect (the present Madison Square Garden and underground Penn Station were his biggest project). Bronfman fired Luckman and allowed his daughter to head the search committee, which chose Mies van der Rohe as architect.

The 38-story tower is thought to be the finest International Style skyscraper in the last half-century and is one of the most recently built of all landmark buildings. Inside is the **Four Seasons restaurant** (1959; Philip Johnson & Assocs). Its intentionally modern decor created a stir which has since subsided into enduring admiration. On display in the restaurant are a sculpture of gold-dipped brass rods by Richard Lippold and a stage backdrop for *Le Tricorne* (1929) by Picasso.

Ludwig Mies van der Rohe: Seagram Building (1958).

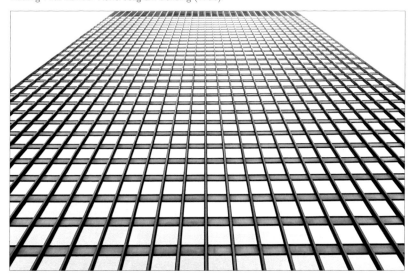

THE ROTHKO MURALS

The Four Seasons' art collection is famous also for what it does not have: a series of paintings by Mark Rothko, who was commissioned in 1958 to paint 600 square ft of murals for the restaurant. He was selected in part on the recommendation of Alfred Barr (*see p. 260*).

Why Rothko, left-wing and intellectual, accepted the commission for a restaurant that would cater to the rich and powerful, is not quite clear. He later said, perhaps disingenuously, that he had thought the works would be exhibited where working-class people could see them. At any rate he told a friend that he considered the commission as a challenge, that he wanted to create "something that will ruin the appetite of every son-of-a-bitch who ever eats in that room."

After accepting the commission, Rothko and his wife traveled to Europe. Among the places they visited was Michelangelo's narrow, claustrophobic vestibule to the Laurentian Library in Florence, which, said Rothko, "achieved just the feeling I am after—he [Michelangelo] makes the viewers feel that they are trapped in a room where all the doors and windows are bricked up, so that all they can do is butt their heads for ever against the wall."

When Rothko returned, he and his wife booked a table at the Four Seasons. Apparently he did not like what he experienced. That evening he called a friend to say he was returning the money and keeping the paintings. He gave some of them to Tate Modern; others are in the National Gallery in Washington, D.C., and in Japan's Kawagawa Memorial Museum of Art.

Across the street from the Seagram Building at 370 Park Ave (52nd and 53rd Sts) is the **Racquet and Tennis Club** (1918; McKim, Mead & White), designed after White and McKim were dead and Mead had retired. Beneath the cornice of this brick-and-limestone club, a terra-cotta frieze depicts racquets and netting.

Lever House, at 390 Park Ave (53rd and 54th Sts), seems modest today. It was the first commercial structure (1952) on this formerly residential avenue, and the first steel and glass building in a file of stolid masonry apartment houses. The building, designed by Skidmore, Owings & Merrill, takes its form from two slabs, one stretched out horizontally along the street, the other rising vertically. Lever House, once considered the ultimate corporate headquarters, is impressive today partly because it is smaller than it legally had to be, an act of restraint on the part of the builders which elicited proposals from developers to tear it down and replace it with something bigger.

THE CITIGROUP CENTER & CENTRAL SYNAGOGUE

The CitiGroup Center (1978) at 153 East 53rd St (Lexington Ave; *map p. 579, E3–E2*), a Midtown office tower, is as representative of 1970s architectural values as Lever House

The CitiGroup Center (1978), a tower supported at its midpoints instead of at the four corners.

and the Seagram Building were of the values of the 1950s. The building (Hugh Stubbins & Assocs), sheathed in gleaming white aluminum, rises 915ft from the street, resting on four 127-ft columns, which support it at the midpoints of the sides, not at the corners. The top of the building slants at a 45-degree angle; the large plane surface facing south was originally intended as a solar collector and is now a conspicuous form on the skyline among the flat tops of the previous generation and the domes, crowns, and spires of earlier skyscrapers.

On the northwest corner of the site, under the tower, is **St. Peter's Church** (Lutheran), founded in 1861, which has existed here since 1904. The church allowed CitiGroup to buy its old building (and, more importantly, the site) with the understanding that it would erect a new church. Inside is the beautiful Erol Beker Chapel of the Good Shepherd (*open for meditation during the day, Mon–Fri*), enhanced by Louise Nevelson's wall sculptures: north wall, *Cross of the Good Shepherd* and three columns, *Trinity*; east wall, *Frieze of the Apostles*; west wall, *Sky Vestment—Trinity*; south wall, *Grapes and Wheat Lintel*; southwest wall, *Cross of the Resurrection.*

Between 53rd and 54th Sts at 885 Third Ave is the "**Lipstick Building**" (1986; John Burgee with Philip Johnson), an elliptical building on a rectangular site.

The Central Synagogue
Map p. 579, E2. Tours Wed at 12:30; T: 212 838 5122; www.centralsynagogue.org.
The Central Synagogue (1872) at 652 Lexington Ave (corner of 55th St) is the oldest synagogue in continuous use in the state. It was designed by Henry Fernbach, the first Jew to practice architecture in New York, now known chiefly for his cast-ironwork in

CENTRAL SYNAGOGUE

SoHo. While Judaism has never had an architectural heritage similar to the Gothic tradition in Christianity, the Moorish style with its allusions to Judaic roots in the Middle East became the dominant style of synagogue architecture in the mid-19th century, and the Central Synagogue is generally considered the finest example of Moorish Revival architecture in the city, inspired by—but not precisely modeled on— the Dohány Street Synagogue (1854–59) in Budapest. The onion-shaped green copper domes rise to 122ft. The interior stenciled decorations in red, blue, and ochre were repainted after a 1998 fire, and are now bright and clear. The geometric designs are said to come from Owen Jones's influential *Grammar of Ornament* (1856).

The congregation was founded on Ludlow St as Ahawath Chesed ("Love of Mercy") by 18 men, most of them immigrants from Bohemia. The congregation moved

northward gradually, acquiring the present site in 1870. The building represents the spirit of optimism of the 150 families of the congregation at that time, who built a synagogue whose sanctuary can accommodate more than 1,000 worshipers.

THE SONY BUILDING & IBM

The Sony Building at 550 Madison Ave (*map p. 579, D2*), built for AT&T (1984; Philip Johnson & John Burgee), raised eyebrows when its design was announced in 1979. It stands on a 131-ft masonry base of rose-gray granite and rises to a huge broken pediment, which prompted jokes and questions about the architect's seriousness. Today the building (648ft tall) elicits praise for its monumental proportions, its beautiful materials and its public spaces, including a row of shops and a covered colonnade. Historians have pointed to the architects' rejection of the stark glass and steel of the International Style in favor of classic principles articulated in its materials and forms, such as the split pediment on top and the Renaissance-inspired arcaded base. Inside is the Sony Wonder Technology Lab (*under renovation at the time of writing. When open, admission free, but reservations advised to avoid waiting; T: 212 833 8100; www.wondertechlab.sony.com*), a hands-on museum geared to families and children, emphasizing Sony products.

The former IBM Building and Fuller Building

More conservative than the Sony Building, the block-long **former IBM Building** (1983; Edward Larrabee Barnes, Assocs at 590 Madison Ave and 56th/57th Sts is distinguished by its shape (a five-sided prism, like a right triangle with two points sliced off), its color (a dark gray-green), and its public spaces (an enormous, glass-enclosed garden atrium and an exhibition gallery). Although the IBM Building did not break radically from recent skyscraper design, it was hailed as a dignified addition to Midtown. The granite which sheathes this 403-ft skyscraper, chosen to harmonize with the greenish glass of the windows and the greenhouse park, was quarried in Quebec. The windows, set in strips around the building, are sealed shut but have 4-inch slots beneath them that can be opened to provide fresh air.

At the corner of 56th St and Madison Ave is a sculptural fountain, *Levitated Mass* (1982) by Michael Heizer, under which sluices a torrent of water. At the 57th St corner, also on Madison Ave, is Alexander Calder's bright *Saurien* (1975). Inside the IBM building is one of the city's better public spaces, the 68-ft atrium covered with a saw-toothed glass roof and brightened with seasonal displays of flora. The tall stands of bamboo, several sculptures, the fountain, tables and chairs, and the kiosk for snacks (*closed weekends*) make it a favorite Midtown rest stop.

The slender Art Deco **Fuller Building**, at 45 East 57th St (Madison Ave), is an important Uptown gallery building. The clock and sculptural figures above the main doorway are by Elie Nadelman. The building (1929) was designed by Walker & Gillette and built by the Fuller Company, at the time one of the nation's largest construction firms, best known for a building that for a while officially bore the Fuller name but now is known by its shape—the Flatiron Building.

ROCKEFELLER CENTER

Map 579, D3. Fifth to Seventh Aves (West 48th to West 51st Sts). Subway: 6 to 51st St; B, D, or F to 47th–50th Sts-Rockefeller Center. Bus: M1, M2, M3, M4, M5, M6, M7, M27; www.rockefellercenter.com. There are several kinds of tours available: NBC Studio tours (about 1hr 10mins) visit TV studios and control rooms; Rockefeller Center tours (1hr 15mins) visit buildings and artworks; T: 212 664 7174 for either tour. The Art and Observation Tour combines a tour of the buildings with a visit to the Top of the Rock Observation Deck. These tours leave from the NBC Experience Store, located in the GE Building (see plan on p. 246).

Rockefeller Center, a complex of commercial buildings, theaters, plazas, underground concourses, and shops developed principally during the Depression, is the world's largest privately-owned business and entertainment center. The first architecturally coordinated development in New York City, and a milestone in urban planning, it became a National Historic Landmark in 1987. Once steamship lines, airlines, tourist bureaus, and shipping firms, as well as representatives of the broadcasting and newspaper industries, tenanted its buildings, giving the center an aura of cosmopolitan glamour. Today, it remains a visual icon and a major tourist destination, embracing 19 buildings on 21 acres, offering shopping, restaurants, and other pleasant diversions.

History of Rockefeller Center

In 1927 the Metropolitan Opera, seeking to replace its outmoded house on Broadway and 40th St, became interested in the 12 acres of land owned by Columbia University between Fifth and Sixth Aves and West 48th and West 51st Sts. The land had blossomed briefly (1801–11) as the Elgin Botanic Garden, but now held speakeasies, rooming houses, and brothels. The opera company approached John D. Rockefeller Jr. (1874–1960) as a possible benefactor, hoping he might donate land for a plaza in front of the new opera house. Rockefeller in turn began exploring the possibilities of leasing the land himself, making the central portion available to the opera, and then subleasing the rest to commercial interests who would construct their own buildings. Since real estate experts led him to believe that he could realize as much as $5.5 million dollars annually on the property, he signed a contract with Columbia University in Oct 1928 to lease the property for a 24-year period with renewal options to 2019, later extended to 2069.

Then the stock market crashed (1929) and the Metropolitan Opera abruptly dropped its plans for a new house, leaving Rockefeller with a lease under which he owed more than $3.8 million a year on property that brought in only about $300,000. Rockefeller's only real choice was to develop the property without the opera house. He directed his planners to design a commercial center "as beautiful as possible consistent with maximum income," and work began on the city's first integrated commercial center, where skyscrapers could be planned in relation to one another with due consideration of open

space, light, and traffic control. Largely responsible for the early project were developers Todd, Robertson & Todd, and three principal architectural firms: Reinhard & Hofmeister; Corbett, Harrison, and MacMurray; and Hood & Fouilhoux, who all worked under the name of The Associated Architects, making it impossible nowadays to assign specific credit for individual buildings in the original development.

Between 1931 and 1940, 228 buildings were demolished and 4,000 tenants were relocated to make way for 14 new buildings; 75,000 workers were employed on the job. Architect Raymond Hood proposed that the Radio Corporation of America (RCA), still prospering during the Depression, should become the center's major tenant. For years most radio programs of NBC, a subsidiary of RCA, were produced here, and Rockefeller Center became known popularly as "Radio City."

Although Rockefeller drove the "last rivet" into the "last building," the United States Rubber Co. Building (now the Simon & Schuster Building at 1230 Sixth Ave) in 1939, development continued after World War II and again during the 1950s and '60s, when Rockefeller Center expanded west to Sixth Avenue, replacing low buildings and small business tenants with stiff, ponderous office towers. In 1985 Columbia University sold its land under the center to the Rockefeller Group for $400 million, the largest price ever paid at the time for a single parcel of city real estate. On the 11.7-acre plot sit Radio City Music Hall, the skating rink, the GE Building (formerly the RCA Building), and the other landmarked buildings of the original development. In 1989 the real estate arm of the Mitsubishi Group bought the center, provoking widespread indignation over what was seen as the sale of a prime piece of the American heritage to the Japanese. But when a recession squeezed profits, Mitsubishi walked away from its investment. In 2000 the real estate firm Tishman Speyer bought the property, and has improved both the appearance of the landmarked buildings, which have been returned to their former beauty, and the quality of the tenants. The Rockefellers are no longer directly involved with the landmarked office buildings, Radio City Music Hall, or the Rainbow Room.

Art Deco façades on Fifth Avenue

The most dramatic approach to Rockefeller Center is from Fifth Avenue between West 49th and West 50th Sts. (The façades facing Fifth Avenue can best be seen from the east side of the avenue.) Flanking a central promenade are two low buildings, both completed in 1933: on the north, the British Empire Building and on the south, La Maison Française, buildings whose modest scale reflects an earlier Fifth Avenue. By placing these low structures here, the developers gained rights to build the towering RCA Building in the center of the block, simultaneously preserving neighborhood property values by leaving the side streets unshadowed.

Over the main door of **La Maison Française** an elaborate bronze panel designed by Alfred Janniot depicts Paris and New York joining hands above three female figures: *Poetry*, *Beauty*, and *Elegance*. Above the panel soars an Art Deco version of the traditional symbol of the French Republic, a woman holding the flaming torch of Liberty.

Paris and New York link bronze fingers in Alfred Janniot's 1934 panel on La Maison Française.

ROCKEFELLER CENTER

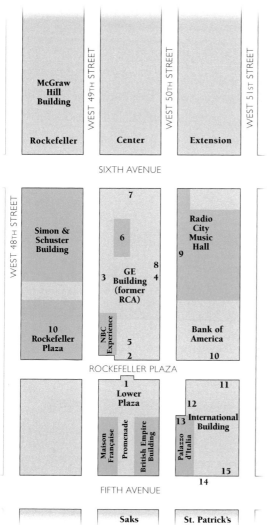

1 *Prometheus*
2 *Wisdom* relief
3 *Friedlander sculptures*
4 *Friedlander sculptures*
5 *American Progress* mural (in the lobby)
6 Rainbow Room
7 *Intelligence Awakening Mankind*
8 Entrance to Top of the Rock
9 Hildreth Meière plaques
10 *News*
11 *Workers* panels
12 "International" screen
13 *The Immigrants*
14 *Atlas*
15 *Youth Leading Industry*

Over the main entrance of the **British Empire Building** figures on a bronze panel (1933) by Carl Paul Jennewein represent nine major industries of the British Commonwealth. At the bottom a bronze sun symbolizes the empire on which the sun was expected never to set. Above the panel a cartouche bears the British coat of arms and the mottoes of the British monarch and the Order of the Garter.

A bronze strip in the sidewalk near the building line at the entrance to the **Promenade** marks the boundary of the property formerly owned by Columbia University. The Promenade (1933) was dubbed the "Channel Gardens" because it separates the British and French buildings; the walkway (60ft wide and 200ft long) is embellished with granite pools, exceptional seasonal floral displays, and spurting fountains. The bronze fountain heads (1935), designed by René Chambellan, represent tritons and nereids riding dolphins. They symbolize (east to west) Leadership, Will, Thought, Imagination, Energy, and Alertness—qualities chosen by the earnest designers of the center's arts program as those contributing to human progress. Most of the themes of the artwork were chosen by Professor Hartley Burr Alexander of the University of Southern California, hired to impose unity on the whole development. Professor Alexander's general topic, "New Frontiers and the March of Civilization," resulted in artworks sometimes illustrating technology and often encumbered with unwieldy titles.

THE LOWER PLAZA & SKATING RINK

The Promenade opens into the **Lower Plaza**. At the top of the stairway leading to the lower level is a commemorative plaque inscribed with John D. Rockefeller Jr.'s personal credo: "I believe in the supreme worth of the individual ... every right implies a responsibility, every opportunity an obligation ..." The plaza is dominated by an 18-ft **figure of Prometheus (1)**, designed by Paul Manship (1934). The eight-ton gilded bronze statue, resting on a gilded mountain peak, is encircled by a ring containing the signs of the zodiac. The red granite wall behind it offers a quotation from Aeschylus: "Prometheus, teacher in every art, brought the fire that hath proved to mortals a means to mighty ends." During the Christmas season, a large tree on the sidewalk behind the plaza is illuminated by thousands of lights, accounting in part for the spectacular crowds who pack the area during the holidays. The **Skating Rink** (*skating season usually begins in Oct; skate rental available; for information, T: 212 332 7654*) is probably the most famous in the world. The crowds make it less than perfect for serious skating, but the ambiance is without equal. During the summer it doubles as an outdoor café.

Rockefeller Plaza, a three-block private street which pleasantly breaks up the long east–west block, separates the Lower Plaza from the GE Building. Rockefeller Plaza remains one of the few private streets in the city, now furnished with seating for footsore visitors, who can enjoy the spectacle of the roughly 200 flags that surround the rink flapping in the breeze, their halyards clanking against the metal poles.

10 Rockefeller Plaza was completed in 1939 and intended for Dutch commercial and cultural interests. When Germany invaded Holland in 1940, those plans were abandoned, though the building did briefly house the Dutch government-in-exile.

Today Christie's auction house is the major tenant. In the northeast corner at street level is NBC studio 1A, where *The Today Show*, a popular news and talk program, is broadcast weekday mornings 7am–10pm, drawing crowds of onlookers.

The GE Building

The first building constructed at Rockefeller Center is still its most famous and imposing: the GE Building, originally the RCA Building (1933). Major tenants are the conglomerate General Electric, and NBC, one of its divisions. The building is roughly rectangular, with its narrow edge facing east–west, and broad slab-like walls on the north and south. It owes its disproportionate length to Rockefeller's desire to include within its walls some potentially unprofitable lots he owned on Sixth Avenue, which were at the time darkened by the elevated railway. Skillfully designed setbacks give the building the impression of soaring height. An 11-story wrap-around structure houses television studios, constructed free from the rest of the building to minimize vibrations. Over the east entrance is a stone relief by Lee Lawrie **(2)**, which glories in the following title: *Wisdom, Which Interprets to the Human Race the Laws and Cycles of the Cosmic Forces of the Universe, Making the Cycles of Light and Sound*. Wisdom, a giant with a remarkable Art Deco beard, spreads a compass above a glass screen made of 240 blocks of Pyrex, cast in relief in 84 different molds. Only when the work was well underway did the art committee notice the embarrassing similarity between Lawrie's work and William Blake's frontispiece to *Europe: A Prophecy* (1794).

Flanking the 49th St entrance two limestone pylons bear sculptures by Leo Friedlander **(3)**: *Transmission Receiving an Image of Dancers and Flashing it Through the Ether by Means of Television to Reception, Symbolized by Mother Earth and Her Child, Man*. Above the marquee at the 50th St entrance two more pylons, also sculpted by Friedlander **(4)**, represent *Transmission Receiving Music and Flashing It Through the Ether by Means of Radio to Reception*. Rockefeller, whose taste was generally conservative, found these works "gross and unbeautiful"; critics generally concur.

Directly in front of the main entrance is a large mural by Catalan artist José María Sert **(5)**, originally entitled *Triumph of Man's Accomplishments Through Physical and*

The "Cycle of Sound," part of Lee Lawrie's famous *Wisdom* relief (1933).

Mental Labor, now called *American Progress*. In the mural Abraham Lincoln, standing, represents the "Man of Action," while Ralph Waldo Emerson, seated, represents the "Man of Thought." Sert's painting (1937) is famous primarily for replacing the controversial Diego Rivera fresco destroyed by the Rockefellers (*see box below*). The massive ceiling painting, again by Sert, is entitled *Time*, while the murals against the elevator banks in the north and south corridors by Sert and English painter Frank Brangwyn illustrate themes of progress against such obstacles as disease, slavery, and crushing physical labor.

THE DIEGO RIVERA FRESCO

Commissioned to paint a mural illustrating the theme of "man's new possibilities from his new understanding of material things," Rivera submitted a sketch acceptable to his patrons—but then produced a fresco that included a portrait of Lenin, a crowd of workers near Lenin's tomb carrying red flags, and a scene of rich people playing cards while venereal disease germs hover over them. When asked to substitute another face for Lenin's, Rivera replied that he would prefer to destroy the painting, at least preserving its integrity. The fresco remained shrouded in canvas during the opening ceremonies and eventually Rivera's wish was granted: the Rockefellers had the mural destroyed. In the recriminations that followed, cowboy humorist and sage Will Rogers "advised" Rivera that he "should never try to fool a Rockefeller in oils."

The Rainbow Room

The elevator banks, down the corridor, contain the city's first high-speed elevators, including those to the Rainbow Room **(6)** on the 65th floor. The nightclub opened in 1934—the first dining spot at the top of a skyscraper—and was through the years celebrated for its view and handsome decor. Noel Coward and Cole Porter came on opening day; the great dance bands of the '30s and '40s played there. Built as a two-story cylinder with no internal columns, and called the Stratosphere Club, the place was renamed the Rainbow Room for its "color organ," which threw colored lights corresponding to musical pitches on the domed ceiling.

The Rainbow Room, now largely a catering hall, is open sometimes for dining and dancing and regularly for Sunday brunch. The Rainbow Grill, on the same floor, caters to those with slightly less ample wallets.

The Concourse

Underground there are more than two miles of passages, lined with shops (generally more modest than those on the ground floor) and restaurants. The passageways reach to Sixth Avenue and connect to every building in the complex.

The Sixth Avenue entrance

The entrance to Rockefeller Center at the Sixth Avenue side is less opulently decorated than the east façade. A glass mosaic by Barry Faulkner (7), made of about one million pieces of colored glass, shows *Intelligence Awakening Mankind*. Four limestone panels by Gaston Lachaise higher on the façade depict *Genius Seizing the Light of the Sun, Conquest of Space, Gifts of Earth to Mankind*, and *Understanding—Spirit of Progress*.

THE EXTENSION TO SIXTH AVENUE

On the west side of Sixth Avenue loom four later additions to the center, known as the Rockefeller Center Extension. Built during the 1960s and '70s by the successors of the Associated Architects (Harrison, Abramovitz & Harris), the buildings have been criticized for lacking sympathetic human scale, their developers opting to use maximum permissible space at the expense of light and air and pleasing proportions. Eminent critic Vincent Scully called them "an incoherent splatter of skyscrapers" marching along the west side of Sixth Avenue. The small mid-block park behind the McGraw Hill Building (1221 Sixth Ave), along West 49th St between Sixth and Seventh Aves, provides some relief from the overbearing architecture; its walk-through waterfall is a favorite with visitors.

The Top of the Rock

The Top of the Rock Observation Deck offers spectacular panoramic views from on high. (*Entrance on West 50th St.* (8) *Open 8:30am–11:30pm; T: 212 698 2000 or 1 877 NYC ROCK (1 877 692 7625); www.topoftherocknyc.com. Timed tickets may be purchased in advance. The combination MoMA/Top of the Rock ticket, which can be also purchased at the Museum of Modern Art, offers discounted admission to both sites.*) The observation deck was originally opened in 1933. Furnished with Adirondack chairs and a telescope, the deck was intended to give something of the feeling of being on an ocean liner. The quaint, Gothic-style cast-iron perimeter fence was apparently a sop to Rockefeller's fondness for historic details. The deck re-opened in 2005 after a major restoration. It now has three levels with indoor and outdoor viewing spaces, as well as historical exhibits.

Radio City Music Hall

1260 Sixth Ave. You can visit the interior by attending a performance or joining a Radio City Stage Door Tour (about 1hr). Same-day tickets for tours available at the Radio City Avenue Store (between West 50th and West 51st Sts on Sixth Ave); open Mon–Sat 10–6, Sun 11–6; T: 212 485 7149. For advance tickets, call TicketMaster, T: 212 307 7171. Online tickets at www.radiocity.com or www.ticketmaster.com. Box office information, T: 212 247 4777.
Radio City Music Hall was the world's largest theater when it opened in 1932, and, though overtaken since, remains a masterpiece of Art Deco decoration. Every holiday season since 1933 the theater has presented the Radio City Christmas Spectacular,

which entertains more than a million visitors with hundreds of lavishly costumed performers, over-the-top high-tech special effects, and a chorus line of leggy Rockettes, the famous women's precision dance team. The Music Hall's co-ordinator was Edward Durell Stone, who went on to design the Museum of Modern Art.

HISTORY OF RADIO CITY MUSIC HALL

Samuel Lionel Rothafel (1882–1936), better known as Roxy, began his career showing movies in the back room of a bar and rose to become a show business mogul, producing radio programs and stage shows and managing several New York theaters, including the opulent Roxy. His reputation of knowing infallibly what the public wanted earned him broad powers as director of the Music Hall. He contributed to the design of the theater and shaped its general policies, intending to revive vaudeville and produce spectacular variety shows.

Unfortunately Roxy's variety shows lost $180,000 in the first two weeks, and the format was changed. Until television began to pose a significant threat, the Music Hall hit upon the successful formula of presenting wholesome movies paired with stage shows, drawing five million patrons a year at the end of 1967. By 1977 attendance had fallen to fewer than two million and the theater lost $2.3 million. In 1978 Rockefellers announced they would demolish the Music Hall, but a wave of public support resulted in its interior being designated a landmark. In 1999, the hall was beautifully restored (Hardy Holzman Pfeiffer Associates).

The interior

The interior of the Music Hall, with its great auditorium, is one of the high points of American theater design and one of the city's grandest and most sophisticated displays of Art Deco styling. The unity of the hall's decorative features—carpets, wall coverings, statues, murals, and furniture—was coordinated by Donald Deskey, who had been influenced by the Exposition Internationale des Arts Décoratifs in Paris. Deskey had attracted the attention of Abby Aldridge Rockefeller by the Braque-like abstractions he used in his Saks Fifth Avenue store windows, and had designed art galleries in the Rockefeller town house on West 54th St.

The Grand Foyer (140ft long, 45ft wide, and 60ft high) is decorated in warm, dark colors, and ornamented with brass and chrome. The carpet, designed by Ruth Reeves, who had studied with Fernard Léger in Paris, is executed in red, brown, gold, and black with abstract forms of musical instruments. Over the imposing staircase at the north end is a mural by Ezra Winter, *The Fountain of Youth*, its subject suggested by Professor Alexander (*see p. 247 above*) and drawn from an Oregon tribal legend. It depicts an old man gazing at a gleaming inaccessible mountaintop on which bubbles the fountain of youth; across the sky marches a cloudy procession representing the vanities of life. Gold mirrored panels reflect the light from two 29-ft glass chandeliers (two tons apiece). After

the restoration, Stuart Davis's Modernist mural *Men Without Women* (1932) was returned to its original home after being sequestered for a almost a quarter century in the Museum of Modern Art.

The most impressive space in the Music Hall is the **auditorium**, which seats about 6,200 people. The ceiling is egg-shaped, a form Roxy demanded for its supposed acoustic superiority. The great proscenium arch (60ft high, 100ft wide) compels attention. Rising outward and forward from it are the successive overlapping bands of the ceiling, painted with perpendicular rays, whose effect has been compared to the aurora borealis, a sunburst, and the rays of dawn. Roxy liked to assert that a sunrise he had witnessed at sea inspired the design, but the model of the auditorium, complete with ceiling, had been photographed six days before he embarked on the inspirational voyage.

The stage machinery includes sections that can be raised or lowered on elevators, a revolving central turntable, and a moveable orchestra pit. The stage can support 12 grand pianos, three Roman chariots with horses, or six elephants.

THE MIGHTY WURLITZER

Adding to the grandeur of Radio City Music Hall Spectaculars is the "Mighty Wurlitzer" pipe organ. As the show opens, two organ consoles (each weighing 2.5 tons, the weight of a luxury sedan) roll out from curtained alcoves on either side of the stage. The original plans called for elevators to lower the consoles into the basement for storage after the organists had finished; when this proved unfeasible, the consoles were placed in alcoves, covered by the electrically operated curtains. The organ operated by the consoles was built specifically for this theater, and draws its huge and varied sound from more than 4,000 pipes in 58 ranks; the pipes range from the size of a pencil to 32ft and are housed in 11 separate rooms.

ALONG WEST 50TH STREET

On the wall of the Music Hall facing West 50th St are plaques designed by Hildreth Meière **(9)** symbolizing Dance, Drama, and Music. Further east, at the corner of West 50th St and Rockefeller Plaza, is the former Associated Press Building (1938), now the **Bank of America Building** (*50 Rockefeller Plaza*). Above the main entrance is Isamu Noguchi's stainless-steel panel *News* (1940) **(10)**, depicting five men with the tools of the reporter's trade: pad and pencil, camera, telephone, wirephoto, and teletype. It is arguably the best piece of public art in the center.

Across from this panel, on the west side of the International Building, are Gaston Lachaise's panels depicting workers **(11)**, a tribute to the builders of Rockefeller Center.

The International Building

The International Building at 630 Fifth Ave was built in a hurry in 1935, requiring only

136 working days of construction once the excavation had been completed. The early tenants were steamship lines—the French Line, the Grace Line—travel agencies, and a US Passport Office.

Over the side entrance, at 25 West 50th St, a limestone screen by Lee Lawrie **(12)** symbolizes the international purpose of the building. The four figures in the central rectangle on the bottom row represent the four races of mankind; above them are a trading ship; figures representing art, science, and industry; and Mercury, messenger of trade. The upper side panels represent regions of the Earth (whale's fluke, palm trees, mosque, and Aztec temple), while the lower ones symbolize the old order (Norman tower and lion) and the new industrial, republican age (smokestacks and eagle). Two other panels by Lawrie are *Swords into Ploughshares* (over the doorway at no. 19), and (at no. 9) *St. Francis of Assisi*, with a halo of golden birds.

Lee Lawrie: *St Francis of Assisi* (1937). Relief panel on the West 50th St elevation of the International Building.

The main entrance is on Fifth Avenue, where a central doorway is flanked by two projecting wings. The south wing is known as the **Palazzo d'Italia** (1935), and like the British and French buildings demonstrates the developers' desire to attract foreign tenants at a time when American ones were not readily available. Its primary decoration is a relief panel by Giacomo Manzù depicting entwined wheat stalks and grapevines, symbolizing fruitfulness. A second panel by Manzù, *The Immigrants*, showing a barefoot peasant woman and her child with their belongings tied to a stick, has been moved around the corner to a site near the 50th St entrance **(13)**. These works, installed in 1965, replace Piccirilli's *Sempre Avanti Eterna Giovinezza*, a muscular youth energetically spading the earth, which was removed in 1941 when war with Italy was looming, because its imagery was considered fascistic.

In front of the central entrance a muscular bronze *Atlas* (1937) **(14)** shoulders an armillary globe studded with signs of the zodiac. Designed by Lee Lawrie, this giant (height of figure, 15ft; diameter of sphere, 21ft; weight, 14,000 lb) impresses by his sheer size. The relief of *Youth Leading Industry* **(15)** above the north wing of the International Building (636 Fifth Ave) is by Attilio Piccirilli, the companion piece to *Sempre Avanti Eterna Giovinezza* formerly above the door of the Palazzo d'Italia.

The interior

The central escalators, dominating the room like the grand staircases of 18th- and 19th-century public buildings, recall the fondness of Art Deco designers for machinery as a stylistic motif. It is worth a trip up and down to see the view through the rings of Atlas's sphere to the rose window and Gothic arches of St. Patrick's Cathedral across the street.

ST. PATRICK'S CATHEDRAL, MoMA, & FIFTH AVENUE TO 59TH STREET

Map p. 579, D3–D2. Subway: B, D, F, V to 47th–50th Sts-Rockefeller Center; N, R, or W to 49th St; 6 to 51st St. Bus: M1, M2, M3, M4, M5, M6, M7, M27.

St. Patrick's Cathedral (*open daily 6:30am–8:45pm; T: 212 753 2261; www.saint-patrickscathedral.org*) is the seat of the Roman Catholic Archdiocese of New York, a famous city landmark and a symbol of the success in New York of its immigrant Irish Catholic population. Designed by James Renwick (1879; towers, 1888) with William Rodrigue, whose contribution seems to have been minimal, it draws on the Decorated Gothic style of the 13th century. It is the largest Catholic cathedral in the US and the eleventh largest in the world.

HISTORY OF ST. PATRICK'S

In 1828 the two major Catholic churches of New York, St. Peter's and St. Patrick's—then at the corner of Prince and Mott Sts—bought the plot where the cathedral now sits, intending it as a burial ground. Unfortunately, the buyers neglected to examine the land, which turned out to be far too rocky for its intended purpose. In 1850 Archbishop John Hughes announced his intention to build a new cathedral on the site. Hughes had arrived in America from Ireland in 1817, an uneducated 20-year-old eager to become a priest. He arrived in New York 19 years later a bishop, a skillful administrator, and a flamboyant orator. By 1858, Hughes had raised the money to lay the cornerstone and begin construction (1858); in 1879 the cathedral was dedicated, having cost twice as much as estimated and taken four times as long to build (including an interruption during the Civil War). It was consecrated, debt free, in 1910.

The exterior

The general plan is a Latin cross with traditional east–west orientation. The façade is marble. Because the interior vaulting is brick and plaster, not stone, flying buttresses were not needed, but the pinnacles of the buttresses exist, perhaps because Renwick originally called for stone interior vaulting supported by flying buttresses. The bronze doors (added 1949) at the west entrance were designed by Charles Maginnis with figures by John Angel. The figures on the doors represent (top to bottom, left to right): St. Joseph, patron of this church; St. Isaac Jogues, first Catholic priest in New York; St. Frances X. Cabrini, founder of the Missionary Sisters of the Sacred Heart and "Mother of the Immigrant"; the Blessed Kateri Tekakwitha, an Indian maiden called the "Lily of the Mohawks," and St. Elizabeth Ann Seton, the first American-born saint.

The interior

Two rows of clustered columns divide the nave. Above the arches runs the triforium, divided into four sections by the arms of the cross. Above the triforia rise clerestory windows. The ceiling is groined with (plaster) ribs.

Chapels and aisle windows in the south aisle include a modern Shrine of St. Elizabeth Ann Seton (1975; sculptor Frederick Shrady) with the window above dedicated to St. Henry, 11th-century Holy Roman Emperor.

The Stations of the Cross in the south transept were designed by Peter J.H. Cuypers in Holland. Over the entrance is a window devoted to St. Patrick, depicting 18 scenes from his life, given by Old St. Patrick's Cathedral (*see p. 117*). In the west wall of the transept is another St. Patrick's window, this one given by architect Renwick, who appears in the lower panels. In the south

St. Elizabeth Ann Seton, the first American-born saint, by John Angel.

ambulatory beyond the sacristy is a marble *Pietà* (1906; William O. Partridge), styled after Michelangelo's famous work in St Peter's in Rome, but much larger.

The Lady Chapel at the east end of the church, begun in 1901 and completed in 1906, was designed by Charles T. Matthews and is based on 13th-century French Gothic architecture. The stained-glass windows (Paul Woodroffe) over this altar and the two flanking it depict the mysteries of the rosary. Directly opposite the Lady Chapel is the entrance to the crypt (*closed to visitors*), in which are buried the remains of Archbishop Hughes, the other cardinals of New York, and several rectors of this church, as well as Archbishop Fulton J. Sheen.

In the north ambulatory, adjacent to the Lady Chapel on the north side, is the altar of St. Michael and St. Louis, designed by Charles T. Matthews and executed by Tiffany & Co. Beyond the usher's office and bride's room are the altar of St. Joseph and the chancel organ (1928) with 2,520 pipes. In the north transept, in front of the altar of the Holy Family, is the marble Baptistery. The focal point of the sanctuary is the high

altar with its baldachin designed by Charles D. Maginnis, made of bronze and rising to a height of 57ft. Suspended from the ceiling of the sanctuary above the altar are the *galeros* or ceremonial hats of all the cardinals of New York.

From the crossing there is a good view of the west or rose window, 26ft in diameter and filled with stained glass in geometric patterns. In the loft beneath it is the Great Organ (1930), with 9,000 pipes, ranging from three inches to 32ft in length.

F. Scott Fitzgerald and Zelda Sayre were married in the sacristy in 1920. When Robert F. Kennedy's funeral mass was held here in 1968, lines of mourners stretched around the block. Andy Warhol's service (1987) filled the cathedral with a congregation of artists, writers, and designers, as well as his wealthy, social admirers. Funerals for many police officers and firefighters who died at the World Trade Center took place at the cathedral during the autumn of 2001.

FIFTH AVENUE IN THE 50s

THE VANDERBILTS ON FIFTH AVENUE

In the 1880s Fifth Avenue in the low 50s was Vanderbilt territory; the family built 15 buildings there—mansions on the avenue and lesser houses and stables on the side streets. William Henry Vanderbilt (1821–85) built three grandiose brownstones for himself and his two daughters on the west side of the avenue between 50th and 51st Sts. The socially ambitious Alva Smith Vanderbilt, first wife of his second son, William Kissam Vanderbilt (1849–1920), wanted something better than brownstone, and commissioned Richard Morris Hunt to design a limestone palace based on the château of Blois in the Loire Valley. It occupied the lot on the northwest corner of 52nd St. All these eventually succumbed to the northward march of commerce.

On the east side of the street, at 647 Fifth Ave, is the sole remaining Vanderbilt home, built as part of a family effort to keep commercial establishments out of "their" part of town. The sons of Richard Morris Hunt built it in 1905 for George W. Vanderbilt (1862–1914), who later leased it to Robert Goelet, his wife Elsie, and their son Ogden (who lived there with 14 servants; his sister married Cornelius Vanderbilt). The Vanderbilt holding action failed: businesses encroached from downtown, and the house was altered to become a store for art dealers Rene Gimpel and Nathan Wildenstein. The current tenant is Versace.

Meanwhile, William K. Vanderbilt, alarmed by the northward creep of commerce, sold the corner lot, 653 Fifth Ave, to millionaire banker Morton F. Plant on the condition that the site remain residential for 25 years. Plant, Commodore of the New York Yacht Club, obliged with a five-story neo-Italian *palazzo* of marble and granite (1905) but by 1916 he found the area too commercial and built a new mansion further uptown. Vanderbilt bought Plant's *palazzo* for a million dollars and quickly rented it to Cartier's for $50,000 a year. Cartier is still the tenant.

"Swing Street"

Between Fifth and Sixth Aves, 52nd St has been designated "Swing Street" to commemorate its place in the history of jazz. Known simply as "The Street" among jazzmen, it attracted attention beginning in the late 1930s with its nightclubs, many of them former speakeasies, where the great innovators and performers of the period worked: Art Tatum, Dizzy Gillespie, Thelonious Monk, Lester Young, Kenny Clark, and of course Charlie Parker, for whom Birdland would later be named. In particular the street has been identified with bop, a style that emerged in Harlem between 1940 and 1944 and came downtown when black musicians began working in the clubs of the area. The best known were the Onyx, the Spotlight, the Three Deuces, the Royal Roost, and Bop City. The period was a golden age for jazz and for 52nd St, but by 1948, when heroin abuse was widespread among jazz musicians, the street had become the territory of prostitutes, strippers, and drug pushers.

At 21 West 52nd St is **The 21 Club** (1872), a speakeasy during Prohibition and a power lunch spot today that nonetheless retains some of its former clandestine atmosphere. It is famous for its wine cellar and for the cast-iron jockeys above the entrance, said to be painted with the racing colors of patrons who donated them.

The Paley Center for Media

Map 579, D3. 25 West 52nd St. Open Tues–Sun 12–6, until 8 on Thur; closed Mon, New Year's Day, July 4, Thanksgiving, and Christmas. T: 212 621 6800 for daily information on scheduled activities; T: 212 621 6600 for other information; www.mtr.org.

Formerly known as the Museum of Television and Radio, and originally as the Museum of Broadcasting, the Paley Center has a permanent collection of some 140,000 TV and radio programs and advertisements, which visitors can select from the library and watch on individual consoles or at television screenings or radio presentations. In addition, the center offers seminars and discussions that explore the impact of the media on modern lives.

The center was launched in 1975 by William Paley, a pioneer in radio and television, and its three name changes reflect the development of broadcast media. The collection dates back to the dawn of radio, when station KDKA sent out its first signals over the airwaves in Pittsburgh in 1920. Documentary programs include decisive moments in 20th-century history, the earliest a 1920 broadcast by Franklin D. Roosevelt, then running for vice-president. The list includes an eyewitness account of the crash of the *Hindenburg*, Adolf Hitler's address to the Reichstag in 1939, the Hiroshima news bulletin, President Truman's dismissal of General Douglas MacArthur, and coverage of the ticker tape parade that followed. The TV collection begins with such early pieces as an excerpt from a 1936 drama called "Poverty Is Not a Crime" and continues to the present.

At 5 East 53rd St is small, serene **Paley Park** (1967), planted with ivy and a dozen honey locust trees. The white noise of the "waterfall" obliterates the whine of traffic. Before William S. Paley donated the park in memory of his father Samuel, the site was occupied by the Stork Club, a nightclub beloved of café society and gossip columnists.

ST. THOMAS CHURCH

Map 579, D3. Open 7–6 weekdays, Sat 10–3:30, Sun 7–3:30; T: 212 757 7013; www.saint-thomaschurch.org. There is a guided tour of the church after the 11am Sunday service.

On the corner of 53rd St and Fifth Ave (1 West 53rd St) is Protestant Episcopal St. Thomas Church—picturesque, asymmetrical, and French Gothic in antecedents. It was originally built (1914) without steel, following the principles of Ralph Adams Cram (also architect of St. John the Divine), who believed that if a church were Gothic in style it should be Gothic in construction, its columns supporting its weight. However, eleven years after completion, with the unbuttressed north wall bulging dangerously, steel beams were placed across the columns above the ceiling. Later, during blasting for the subway under 53rd St, a steel beam was installed under the altar.

The exterior

Bertram G. Goodhue (architect of St. Bartholomew's on Park Avenue) planned the limestone façade, which is notable for its single corner tower. Above the double entrance doors a gilded relief depicts the four different buildings in which the congregation has worshiped, two on Houston St and Broadway and two here. The central figure between the two doors is St. Thomas, and above the left-hand door are depictions of his Despair and Doubt. Left of the main portal is the Bride's Entrance; above the doorway some observers have discerned a stylized dollar sign, whose presence recalls medieval times when carpenters and stoneworkers left tokens of social comment in obscure parts of their cathedrals.

The interior

The remarkable 80-ft reredos of ivory-colored Dunville stone (from Ohio) is pierced by three deep blue stained-glass windows and decorated with more than 60 statues of saints, apostles, churchmen, divines, and political leaders. Lee Lawrie, known for his work at Rockefeller Center, and architect Goodhue designed it, though the central portion of kneeling angels adoring the Cross was copied from a smaller reredos by Augustus Saint-Gaudens in the previous church on this site (burned 1905). Below the Cross, in the central carved canopy immediately above the altar, is a kneeling figure of St. Thomas.

In the chancel, the carved panels on the kneeling rail in front of the choir stalls have designs representing important historical events and fields of human endeavor. From the left they are: Christopher Columbus's ship, Theodore Roosevelt, Lee Lawrie (between the steamship and the telephone), a radio, and representations of Finance (with the initials of J.P. Morgan) and Medicine.

Detail of the great reredos of St. Thomas Church, by Lee Lawrie and Bertram G. Goodhue. In the center, Christ the King is flanked by the Virgin and St. John.

THE MUSEUM OF MODERN ART

Map p. 579, D2. Subway: E or V to 5th Ave-53rd St; B, D, or F to 47–50th Sts-Rockefeller Center. Bus: M1, 2, 3, 4, or 5 to 53rd St. 11 West 53rd St (5th and 6th Aves). Open Sat–Mon and Wed–Thur 10:30–5:30, Fri 10:30–8; closed Tues, Thanksgiving, and Christmas Day. T: 212 708 9400; www.moma.org.

The Museum of Modern Art (MoMA) is one of the city's premier cultural institutions, one of the great repositories not only of modern painting and sculpture, but also of drawing, design, photography, and film. The historic building, expanded and reconfigured by Yoshio Taniguchi, re-opened to considerable fanfare in 2004, drawing 2.67 million visitors in the next year to gaze at the Picassos and Matisses, the van Goghs and Cézannes, and the huge splattered canvases of Jackson Pollock that have made West 53rd St a destination for lovers of modern art.

History of MoMA

In 1929, when modern art was not considered art at all in many quarters, Abby Aldrich Rockefeller (1874–1948) and two wealthy, well-connected, and socially committed friends, Lillie P. Bliss (1864–1931) and Mary Quinn Sullivan (1877–1939), founded a small museum in rented space in what is now the Crown Building on Fifth Avenue near 57th St. Their first exhibit was *Cézanne, Gauguin, Seurat, van Gogh*, a choice more daring then than it seems today. Despite the fact that the stock market had crashed a few days earlier, the show was a wild success with 47,000 visitors, including 5,300 on the last day, crowding into the six-room rented apartment. The initial collection—donated by one of the trustees in 1929—was less impressive, consisting of eight prints and one drawing, but two years later the museum got a major boost when Lillie Bliss bequeathed her collection, including masterworks by Cézanne, Gauguin, Matisse, Modigliani, Picasso, Seurat, and Degas.

The first director was Alfred H. Barr Jr., who developed the concept of a museum that would include not just painting and sculpture but other visual arts—film, industrial design, prints, drawings, photography, and printed books. Barr quickly shaped the museum into a major force. In 1932 the exhibit *Modern Architecture: International Exhibition* was influential in introducing the International Style to the American public, and in 1935 an exhibition of van Gogh proved, in the words of the *WPA Guide to New York City*, that "art can attract as many people as a prize fight."

In 1932 MoMA moved to the present site, leasing a brownstone from John D. Rockefeller Jr. (Abby Aldrich Rockefeller's husband), who later donated the land on which the house stood. Throughout the 1940s and '50s the museum continued to blaze new territory, increasing its photographic collection, mounting exhibitions on Matisse, Nolde, Rodin, Magritte, Turner, Pollock, de Kooning, and Oldenburg, and sending abroad the influential exhibition *The New American Painting*, devoted to Abstract Expressionism.

As its collection increased, the museum gradually became more conservative: its strengths became those of conserving the past and offering a historical view of art

from Post-Impressionism to relatively recent times. To counteract this trend, MoMA merged in 1999 with P.S.1 in Long Island City, whose focus is avant-garde contemporary art (*see p. 495*).

The building

The building has evolved along with the museum and now has a long pedigree. Five days after the Wall Street crash of 1929, the Museum of Modern Art opened in temporary quarters in the Heckscher Building (now the Crown Building) on Fifth Avenue at 57th St. After three years in the temporary quarters and five in the leased Rockefeller brownstone at 11 West 53rd St, the museum put up its first building in 1939, an austere exemplar of the International Style designed by Philip L. Goodwin and Edward D. Stone.

The façade with its aluminum shell and canopied entrance featured a new insulating material, Thermolux, whose two sheets of clear glass enclosed a layer of spun glass. The first sculpture garden, designed by John McAndrew, was installed behind the museum on land also donated by John D. Rockefeller Jr., and quickly became the urban oasis it remains today.

By the 1960s the museum had outgrown its space, and new wings, designed by Philip Johnson (1964), were attached east and west of the 1939 building; at the same time Johnson redesigned the sculpture garden, which was renamed to honor Abby Aldrich Rockefeller. A decade later, as the collections and visitors increased, the museum again found its facilities inadequate, and in 1976 announced that it would again expand. To develop new sources of revenue, the museum sold the air rights over its prime Midtown location to a developer for a condominium apartment tower, and engineered a trust arrangement with the City so that the museum receives the benefits of most of the municipal real estate taxes generated by the tower. Designed by Cesar Pelli & Associates, the expansion (1984) was admired more for the revenue scheme than for its interior spaces.

Twenty years later that expansion proved inadequate, and, in 2004, the museum reopened after a two-year sojourn in Queens. The $858-million expansion by Japanese architect Yoshio Taniguchi has met with mixed critical reviews. The restored Goodwin and Stone façade (right down to the Thermolux panels formerly covered to provide hanging space inside), the mid-block passageway between 53rd and 54th Sts, and the revived sculpture garden have met with approval. But while the building was acclaimed for its serenity and its urbanity before the art was re-installed, the gallery space has met with less enthusiasm.

The collections

MoMA's outstanding collection of 19th–20th-century painting and sculpture—the reason most people come to the museum—is installed on the fourth and fifth floors, with the older works on the fifth floor.

(*NB: It is best to start on the fifth floor and work downwards. Works on view are sometimes rotated.*)

Fifth floor

Twelve galleries present painting and sculpture from the formative period of modern art, 1880–1940. In the hallway near the café is Henri Rousseau's *The Dream* (1910).

Gallery 1: Post-Impressionism and Fauvism. Works by Paul Cézanne: *The Bather* (c. 1885) is an important early painting, whose central figure was described by director Alfred Barr as "rising like a colossus who has just bestrode mountains and rivers—for Cézanne, adapting a landscape from another painting, has again fumbled his naturalistic scale while achieving artistic grandeur." Also by Cézanne are *Still Life with Apples* (1895–98) and *Pines and Rocks, Fontainebleau* (c. 1897). Georges Seurat is represented by *Grandcamp, Evening* (1885); *The Channel at Gravelines, Evening* (1890); *Port-en-Bessin, Entrance to the Harbor* (1888). Vincent van Gogh's *Portrait of Joseph Roulin* (1889) is one of five portraits of Roulin, the postman at Arles, who with his wife obliged the painter by sitting as models. Van Gogh was impressed by Roulin's socialism and also by his warm domestic life as father of a large family. *The Starry Night* (1889), a visionary painting with a tumultuously radiant night sky, is one of the most popular pictures in the museum. Van Gogh intended *The Olive Trees* (1889) as a daylight complement to *The Starry Night*. Henri de Toulouse-Lautrec's *La Goulue at the Moulin Rouge* (1891–92) shows one of the artist's favorite figures from the *demi-monde*; "La Goulue" ("the Glutton") was the nickname of dancer Louise Weber, whose substantial appetite eventually led her to become grossly fat.

Paul Gauguin is represented by *The Moon and the Earth* (1898) and Henri Rousseau by *The Sleeping Gypsy* (1897); when Rousseau offered this painting to his home town, his generosity was refused, but Rousseau's work was appreciated by other artists long before the public valued it. Also on view are Fauve landscapes by André Derain and Georges Braque.

Gallery 2: Early Cubism. This gallery contains early examples of what is commonly called Analytical Cubism, a radical style developed largely by Picasso and Braque, in which forms were analyzed into geometrical components and rendered, for the most part, in subdued colors. The focal point of the gallery is Picasso's **Les Demoiselles d'Avignon** (1907), one of the most important paintings in the museum. The painting was bought by MoMA in 1939 at the time of its first Picasso show, in part in exchange for works by Degas included in the Lillie Bliss Bequest. Picasso had first imagined the work as a narrative brothel scene including a sailor and a medical student as well as the naked female figures, but gradually the work evolved into its present form, where the five prostitutes stare frontally at an unseen (and presumably male) viewer. *Les Demoiselles* is generally considered a seminal work in the history of modern art for its flattening and fracturing of conventional pictorial space, its

Cézanne: *Bather* (c. 1885): "a colossus who has just bestrode mountains and rivers…"

inclusion of disjunctive elements—Egyptian, Iberian, African, European—and its expressionistic, even savage, rendering of the prostitutes, particularly the threatening masklike faces of the two women on the right. Picasso, who had visited the museum of African art at the Trocadéro while working on *Les Demoiselles*, referred to the painting as his "first exorcism picture."

Other Cubist works here are Picasso's *Ma Jolie* (1911–12) and Braque's *Man with a Guitar* (1911–12). Complementing these paintings are earlier works by Picasso: *Boy Leading a Horse* (1905–06) and *Acrobats with Dog* (1905), and two works in bronze: Picasso's *Woman's Head (Fernande)* (1909) and *The Serf* (1900–04) by Henri Matisse.

Gallery 3: Cubism: 1912 through the Beginning of World War I. Here is Picasso's famous sheet-metal *Guitar* (1912–13), a startling break from previous sculptural traditions. Also, *Glass of Absinthe* (1914), which combines Cubist notions of dismantled objects viewed simultaneously from different perspectives with the Cubist practice of including found objects in a sculptural composition.

Marcel Duchamp saw in his *The Passage from Virgin to Bride* (1912) a personal transition from the formal analysis of Cubism to his own intellectual concept of painting, which he thought of as "reduction" rather than abstraction. This painting, executed in warm organic colors, has its own esoteric symbolism, which has given rise to considerable explication. Also in this room are paintings by Fernand Léger, Kazimir Malevich, and Juan Gris.

Gallery 4: Italian Futurists. In the center of the room is Umberto Boccioni's *Unique Forms of Continuity in Space* (1913), a windswept figure in brightly polished bronze. Along with Boccioni, Gino Severini and Giacomo Balla, both represented here, were the outstanding figures in the Futurist movement, which used Cubist techniques of spatial dislocation to render motion.

Gallery 5: German and Austrian Expressionism. Outstanding here is Wilhelm Lehmbruck's *Standing Youth* (1913). Some observers find in Lehmbruck's elongated figures a precursor of Giacometti; the downward gaze and vaguely defensive posture suggests the theme of alienation common to many German Expressionists. Marc Chagall's *I and the Village* (1911) is a Cubist vision of the Hasidic community outside Vitebsk, where Chagall was born. Gustav Klimt's ornamental, oriental stylization and the frequently erotic nature of his images, even allegorical ones like *Hope II* (1907–08), have made him the embodiment of *fin-de-siècle* Vienna. Also here are works by Oskar Kokoschka, street scenes by Ernst Ludwig Kirchner, and large panels by Vasily Kandinsky.

Gallery 6: Matisse. Many of the paintings beloved by MoMA visitors hang in this gallery: *The Red Studio* (1911), *The Blue Window* (1913), *Bather* (1909), *The Moroccans* (1915–16), *Still Life after Jan Davidz de Heem's "La Desserte"* (1915), *Woman on a High Stand (Germaine Raynal)* (1914). The museum also owns *The Piano Lesson* (1916), and several much later works including *The Swimming Pool* (1952), Matisse's largest

cut-out, a 54-ft frieze of blue bathers silhouetted against a rectangle of white.

Gallery 7: Works from the 1910s and 1920s. Notable here are Picasso's *Three Women at the Spring* and *Three Musicians* (both 1921). The latter picture is said to epitomize Picasso's "Synthetic" or decorative Cubism; the flat, rectilinear quality of the figures has reminded some observers of a jigsaw puzzle or of the Cubist technique of collage. The year before this picture was painted, Picasso designed costumes for Stravinsky's *Pulcinella*, a ballet based on the *commedia dell'arte*, from whose tradition the figures of the harlequin and Pierrot (playing the clarinet) are drawn.

Examples of the Metaphysical art of Giorgio de Chirico are *Gare Montparnasse (The Melancholy of Departure)* (1914); and *The Song of Love* (1914), with its strange juxtaposition of objects: the surgical glove, the Greek statue, the train passing in the distance. Also on view in this gallery is a group of statues by Constantin Brancusi: *The Cock* (1924), *Bird in Space* (1928), *Endless Column* (1918), *Mlle Pogany* (1913), and *Blonde Negress* (1933).

Gallery 8: Dada and Russian Constructivism. Highlights in this gallery include an icon of the 1910s, Kazimir Malevich's *White on White* (1918), one of his Suprematist compositions, a series of geometrical abstractions. He explained that the artist became a creator "only when the forms in his picture have nothing in common with nature." His ideas reached their conclusion in a series of paintings of white squares on a white background. Marcel Duchamp's *Bicycle*

Wheel (1951, after a lost original of 1913), is one of the artist's celebrated "readymades," common objects exhibited as art that challenge accepted notions of the nature of art.

Gallery 9: Monet, Water Lilies. Three panels of Monet's *Reflections of Clouds on the Water-Lily Pond* (c. 1920) stretch across one wall of this gallery. Between the early 1890s and the end of his life in 1926, Monet was preoccupied with several series of paintings of the pond in his garden at Giverny. His intention was to render the surface of the water, the water lily blossoms and pads, and the reflections of the trees and sky as faithfully as possible under different conditions of light, weather, and season. The museum's triptych and additional panel are the largest holding of the *Water Lilies* outside France. Also on view are *The Japanese Footbridge* (c. 1920–22) and *Agapanthus* (1918–26).

Gallery 10: Mondrian. The museum has a fine collection of the works of Piet Mondrian, which outlines the development of his painting over most of his career, from his early land- and seascapes to *Broadway Boogie Woogie* (1942–43), the last painting he completed. It attempts to abstract the frantic energy of the urban scene (Mondrian came to New York during World War II). Mondrian also theorized that American jazz, with its de-emphasis of traditional melody and stress on rhythm, was the musical equivalent of what he was trying to achieve visually.

Gallery 11: Paul Klee. One of his aims as an artist, Klee said, was to "make secret visions visible." *Around the Fish*

(1926) is a painting filled with Klee's personal symbolism, including the sun and moon, even the atomic constituents of matter. Also here are *Cat and Bird* (1928); *Mask of Fear* (1932), a dome-headed, blank-faced shield walking on four tiny feet; and *Heroic Strokes of the Bow* (1938), whose thick black lines may refer to the path of a violin bow zigzagging back and forth across the strings; Klee was a fine amateur violinist.

Gallery 12: Surrealism. Here are such iconic works of the Surrealist movement as Salvador Dalí's *The Persistence of Memory* (1931), Joan Miró's *The Birth of the World* (1925), and Meret Oppenheim's fur cup, *Objet (Le Déjeuner en fourrure)* (1936). On one side of the room, on a low pedestal, is Alberto Giacometti's sprawled, insectivorous, *Woman with Her Throat Cut* (1932).

Gallery 13: In the small room leading to the exit are paintings by Charles Sheeler, Edward Hopper, and Andrew Wyeth's well-known *Christina's World* (1948), which show's the artist's neighbor who was crippled by polio, pulling herself through an apparently desolate Maine landscape toward a distant farmhouse.

Gallery 14: On the staircase landing is Matisse's joyous *Dance (I)* (1909). MoMA's painting is a study for a commission from the Russian merchant Sergei Shchukin, who wanted two panels, *Dance* and *Music* (now in the Hermitage Museum, St. Petersburg). The final version of *Dance* was to hang on a staircase landing in Shchukin's Trubetskoy Palace, in Moscow.

Fourth floor
The galleries on this floor offer works from the late 1940s to the late 1960s.

Gallery 15: New York Painters, 1940s. Works by American and ex-patriate painters: Arshile Gorky, Willem de Kooning, Robert Motherwell, Lee Krasner.

Gallery 16: European Painters, 1940s. Alberto Giacometti is represented by *The Chariot* (1950), an attenuated female figure standing precariously on a large-wheeled chariot; also *City Square* (1948).

Gallery 17: Jackson Pollock. This is perhaps the best single gallery anywhere to observe the development of Jackson Pollock from his early works to his classic "drip" paintings to work created in the 1950s. Among the earlier works are *Stenographic Figure* (1942) and *The She-Wolf* (1943), a spattered and washed canvas whose subject may refer to the wolf who nurtured Romulus and Remus, or perhaps to some personal mythological iconography. *Full Fathom Five* (1947), one of Pollock's first "drip" paintings, appears to have been executed on top of a previous painting of a standing figure with its legs apart; the extraneous matter—cigarette butts, coins, a key, buttons—embedded in the paint seem to be related to the figure beneath the surface. *Number 1A, 1948* (1948), one of the largest of the drip paintings, and *One: Number 31, 1950* (1950), both

Mark Rothko: *No. 3/No. 13* (1949).

exemplify Pollock's classic style, in which labyrinthine arcs of paint were dripped, poured, and flung at the canvas. After about 1951, Pollock re-

introduced some figurative elements: *Echo: Number 25, 1951* (1951); *Easter and the Totem* (1953).

Galleries 18 and 19: New York School.
Here are paintings by Pollock's contemporaries including Barnett Newman, Mark Rothko, and Clyfford Still. These painters, though known collectively as Abstract Expressionists, illustrate a variety of approaches. Willem de Kooning's *Woman, I* (1950–52), an aggressive, predatory, but nonetheless humorous image, marked the painter's transition from earlier work to a less figural style. The figure reminded him of a landscape "with arms like lanes, and a body of hills and fields … a panorama all squeezed together." Sometimes on view here with contemporaneous painters working outside New York is Matisse's late paper cut-out *Memory of Oceania* (1952–53). Also on view are paintings by Robert Motherwell, Helen Frankenthaler, Morris Louis, and Hans Hofmann.

Galleries 20–22: Mid-1950s–early 1960s. Works here, by painters reacting to Abstract Expressionism, show a return to representational art, sometimes incorporating imagery or found objects. Included here are Robert Rauschenberg's *Bed* (1955) and Jasper Johns's *Flag* (1954–55), both landmark works from this period. In Gallery 22 is Marcel Broodthaers's *White Cabinet and White Table* (1965), an early Conceptual work.

Gallery 23: Pop Art. Iconic paintings here are Andy Warhol's *Gold Marilyn Monroe* (1962) and *Campbell's Soup Cans* (1962), and Claes Oldenburg's comical *Giant Soft Fan* (1966–67).

Gallery 24: Minimalist and Post-Minimalist Art. The final gallery on this floor offers Carl Andre's *144 Lead Square* (1969) and Donald Judd's *Untitled, Stack* (1967), both illustrating the Minimalists' interest in non-art materials, especially machine-made or industrial ones. Among the Post-Minimalists are Eva Hesse and Bruce Nauman.

Third floor
On this floor are changing selections from the collections of **architecture and design**, **drawings**, and **photography**, as well as special exhibitions. The design collection focuses on mass-produced utilitarian objects created to serve a specific need, while the architectural archives include models and photographs of buildings as well as architectural drawings, including the Mies van der Rohe Archive.

Objects in the design collection include pillboxes, nylon tents, vacuum cleaners, Tiffany lamps, self-aligning ball bearings, and an entrance arch to the Paris Métro. Among the chairs are the Gerrit Rietveld "Red and Blue" chair and the Le Corbusier tubular steel armchair. One of the most memorable objects is a Bell-47D1 helicopter, which hangs in the main stairwell.

The museum owns 6,000 works on paper, with drawings in pencil, ink and charcoal, as well as watercolors, gouaches, collages, and works in mixed media. The photography collection of more than 25,000 works dates from about 1840 to the present and includes work by artists, journalists, scientists, entrepreneurs, and amateurs.

Second floor
The **contemporary galleries**, whose 22-ft ceilings allow for the installation of large-

scale works, are devoted to artists working after about 1970. In the 110-ft high Atrium at the top of the stairs are shown such monumental works as Barnett Newman's *Broken Obelisk* (1963–69), a 24-ft sculpture of Cor-Ten steel. On the walls are Cy Twombly's *Four Seasons* (1993–94).

Works in the adjoining galleries are rotated every nine months. On view are painting and sculpture, film and video, installation, drawings, and interdisciplinary works by such artists as Rem Koolhaas, On Kawara, Jeff Koons, Jane and Louise Wilson, Gerhard Richter, Robert Gober, Bruce Nauman, Rachel Whiteread, Matthew Barney, Jeff Wall, and David Hammons.

Ground floor

Standing before the doors to the sculpture garden is Auguste Rodin's massive *Monument to Balzac* (1898, this casting 1954). Rodin explained that his aim in this 9-ft statue was less to capture Honoré de Balzac's physical appearance than his artistic vitality: "I think of his intense labor, of the difficulty of his life, of his incessant battles and of his great courage."

The Abby Aldrich Rockefeller Sculpture Garden is one of the city's beloved oases and a touchstone of American landscape architecture. Now restored to Philip Johnson's 1953 design, the 19,000 square-ft courtyard with reflecting pools, greenery, and seating, displays favorite examples of figurative and abstract sculpture, such as Picasso's *She-Goat* (1950, cast 1952), Gaston Lachaise's *Standing Woman* (1932), and Joan Miró's *Moonbird* (1966). The garden is closed during inclement weather, but the works can also be viewed from different points inside the museum.

IN THE NEIGHBORHOOD

The **American Folk Art Museum** (*45 West 53rd St between Fifth and Sixth Aves; open Tues–Sun 10:30–5:30, Fri until 7:30; closed Mon, national holidays; T: 212 265 1040; www.folkartmuseum.org*), founded in 1961, is the only New York institution devoted solely to traditional and contemporary American folk art. The architects, Tod Williams Billie Tsien and Assocs, compared the form of the building (2001) to an abstracted open hand, to make a quiet statement of independence on an architecturally busy street. The collection includes traditional folk art from the 18th and 19th centuries, as well as the work of modern self-taught "outsider" artists. Among the traditional works are paintings, trade signs, weather vanes, quilts, scrimshaw, and carvings. Ammi Phillips's *Girl in a Red Dress with Cat and Dog*, the *St. Tammany Weathervane* (c. 1890; *see p. 171*), and the well-known *Flag Gate* (c. 1876) are iconic pieces. The collection also includes work by Bill Traylor and other 20th-century American artists, as well as the nation's largest holdings of work by Henry Darger, a Chicago recluse who devoted much of his life to a fantastic 19,000-page epic illustrated with hundreds of watercolors.

The **Museum of Arts & Design** (*40 West 53rd St; open daily 10–6, Thur until 8, pay-as-you-wish 6–8; closed major holidays; T: 212 956 3535; www.madmuseum.org*), formerly the American Craft Museum, offers changing exhibits from its collections of

contemporary hand-made objects in glass, ceramics, fiber, paper, wood, and metal. The museum will move to 2 Columbus Circle (the former "Lollipop" building, by Edward Durell Stone; *see p. 391*), greatly enlarging its exhibition space.

The **CBS Building** (1965; Eero Saarinen & Assocs; 51 West 52nd St, Sixth Ave), the network's corporate headquarters, is the only skyscraper designed by Saarinen, who died in 1961. Known as "Black Rock" for its dark granite cladding, it is an elegant and understated building. Saarinen, who greatly admired Mies van der Rohe, is said to have made this building as different as possible from the latter's Seagram Building.

Art in corporate spaces: the AXA Equitable Center

Midtown corporate lobbies offer both permanent and rotating exhibits of significant art. All are free and open during working hours (*approx. Mon–Fri 8–5*).

The AXA Equitable Center complex (*map p. 578, C3*) comprises two office buildings that fill the entire block between Sixth and Seventh Aves and 51st and 52nd Sts: the AXA Equitable Tower (1984; Edward Larrabee Barnes and Assocs) and the UBS Building (1961; Skidmore, Owings & Merrill).

1290 Sixth Avenue: In the lobby are Thomas Hart Benton's murals *America Today* (1930–31), which were painted for the New School of Social Research and reflect life in rural and urban America during the Jazz Age. All but one of these muscular paintings are energized by an optimistic spirit that seems, with historical hindsight, at odds with Depression America, but as Benton pointed out, the Depression hit hard only when he had almost completed them. Several panels depict industrial prowess and lionize the American worker, envision technological progress, and depict American regions and their productiveness. Only one panel, perhaps painted as late as 1932, *Outreaching Hands*, suggests the effects of the Depression.

UBS Art Gallery: The exhibition space offers non-profit New York-area arts and cultural organizations prime Midtown space and the chance for wider audiences to see their exhibitions. Outdoors,

on West 52nd and West 51st Sts, is Scott Burton's granite furniture. *1285 Sixth Ave (West 51st and West 52nd Sts).*

Galleria: The Galleria runs between the UBS Building and the Equitable Tower to its west. Here are Barry Flanagan's wry *Hare on Bell* (1983) and *Young Elephant* (1985). Also on view is Sol LeWitt's *Wall Drawing: Bands of Lines in Four Colors and Four Directions, Separated by Gray Bands* (1984–85).

AXA Equitable Tower: The atrium is dominated by Roy Lichtenstein's *Mural with Blue Brushstroke* (1986), a 68-ft compendium of images from the artist's career, including Lichtenstein's own familiar motifs and visual references to the works of other 20th-century painters. The blue brushstroke is simultaneously a waterfall and a visual pun on the gestural style of the Abstract Expressionists. In the center of the atrium is Scott Burton's *Atrium Furnishment* (1985), a marble settee and table-fountain. Burton began

as a performance artist, and his chair sculptures evolved from performance works, though he was also inspired by designers such as Gerrit Rietveld and the artists of the Bauhaus. He once stated that art should "place itself not in front of, but around, behind, underneath (literally) the audience." Also on view is James Rosenquist's *Nasturtium Salad* (1984). *787 Seventh Ave (West 51st and West 52nd Sts).*

WEST 54TH–57TH STREETS

At 1 West 54th St, the **University Club** (1899) occupies a grand McKim, Mead & White neo-Italian *palazzo*. It was built during a time when clubmen like Cornelius Vanderbilt belonged to as many as 16 clubs (and spent in dues what the average worker earned in a year). Above the main door is a head of Athena modeled after a statuette owned by Stanford White. The interior (*not open to the public*) is remarkable for its opulent decoration: hallways paved with marble, ceiling paintings by H. Siddons Mowbray (of Morgan Library fame), pilasters of Italian walnut.

When St. Luke's Hospital vacated **West 54th St** in 1896, new dwellings began to rise on both sides. Five adjoining houses (nos. 5–14) from this period, designed by the city's most prestigious architects in styles ranging from Georgian Revival to French Beaux-Arts, have been landmarked (most now occupied by businesses). Financier Robert Lehman lived at No. 7; his art collection is now exhibited in the Metropolitan Museum of Art in a wing that replicates some of the rooms (*see p. 339*). The Rockefellers owned houses at nos. 13 and 15; governor Nelson Rockefeller installed his Museum of Primitive Art, now also part of the Metropolitan, at no. 15 and died in 1979 at no. 13.

Standing on the site of the senior John D. Rockefeller's town house at 17 West 54th St are the **Rockefeller Apartments** (1936), an experiment in middle-class housing financed by John D. Rockefeller Jr. The project, designed by Harrison & Fouilhoux, has two buildings running back to back (the other faces West 55th St) with a central garden between to admit light but not noise to the rear bedrooms. Because the cylindrical bays were designed as "dinettes," their windows face away from one another, insuring privacy.

55th–57th Streets

At 2 East 55th Street is the **St. Regis Hotel** (1904; addition, 1925), a venture of John Jacob Astor IV (1864–1912), who realized from his experience with the Waldorf-Astoria that expensive hotels in fine residential neighborhoods attracted a clientele eager for proximity to social splendor. Astor named it after the French monk and patron saint of hospitality to travelers. The Beaux-Arts exterior has stone garlands, a mansard roof with bull's-eye windows and copper cresting, and on 55th St, a brass and glass kiosk for the top-hatted doormen. Inside, Astor provided automatic thermostats in every room, a system for heating, cooling, moistening, or drying the air (predating air conditioning), 47 Steinway pianos, a service of gold-plated flatware, and other decorative touches that cost him $1.5 million. Once famous for its restaurants, including a palm room where

members of both sexes could smoke publicly at all hours, the St. Regis is now known for the King Cole Room, with Maxfield Parrish's mural of the king holding court (originally commissioned for another Astor enterprise, the Knickerbocker Hotel in Times Square).

At 718 Fifth Ave (56th St) is **Harry Winston**, the famous jewelry store. Winston (1896–1978) was the son of an immigrant who ran a modest jewelry sales and repair shop on Columbus Avenue. The younger Winston, who left school at 15 to go into business with his father, eventually owned some of the world's most famous jewels, including the 44.5-carat Hope diamond, which he donated to the Smithsonian Institution. He sent the diamond to the museum by registered mail. "If you can't trust the US mails," he asked, "who can you trust?"

Occupying most of the east side of Fifth Avenue between 56th and 57th Sts is **Trump Tower** (1983; 725 Fifth Ave), a project of the real estate entrepreneur Donald Trump. Designed by Der Scutt of Swanke Hayden Connell, the building, with its lavish six-story marble-faced atrium and its waterfall, provides an opulent setting for shops, though these are less upscale than when the building opened. The tower replaced Bonwit Teller, a women's apparel store that moved here in 1930.

At the southeast corner of 57th St is **Tiffany & Co** (727 Fifth Ave), one of the world's renowned jewelers. It was founded by Charles L. Tiffany (1812–1902), father of Louis Comfort Tiffany, the famous designer of stained glass, jewelry, enamels, and interiors. The firm moved to this modest granite *palazzo* from a fancier palace on 37th St and Fifth Avenue.

On the southwest corner of 57th St (730 Fifth Ave) is the **Crown Building** (1921; Warren & Wetmore), originally the Heckscher Building. It was the first tall building to invade upper Fifth Avenue, and the first office building constructed after the Zoning Resolution of 1916 (*see p. 68*). The Museum of Modern Art had its modest beginnings here in 1929, when its founders rented space on the 12th floor for loan exhibitions.

BERGDORF GOODMAN & THE PLAZA

Cornelius Vanderbilt II, father of Gertrude Vanderbilt Whitney, built his mansion on the west side of Fifth Avenue (57th and 58th Sts) where Bergdorf Goodman now stands. It was a 137-room castle, filling the whole block with peaks, gables, dormers, and other Victorian extravagances. Like so many of the city's other luxury stores, Bergdorf Goodman had humble beginnings. Herman Bergdorf, a tailor known for adapting men's suits to the female figure, founded the firm, but Edwin Goodman, who bought out Bergdorf in 1901, raised the store to its present heights, moving it in 1928 to this white marble building, initially built as seven distinct storefronts. The store is known for its luxury European clothing and accessories, its fur collection, and its service.

Grand Army Plaza

Grand Army Plaza, between 58th and 60th Sts on the west side of Fifth Avenue, and popularly known as "the Plaza," commemorates the Union army during the Civil War. The open square, one of the few deviations from the city's gridiron plan, provides a

site for the **Pulitzer Memorial Fountain** (Carrère & Hastings), built in 1916 with a $50,000 bequest from the will of newspaper publisher Joseph Pulitzer (1847–1911), who wanted fountains "as far as possible like those in the Place de la Concorde." The fountain is surmounted by Karl Bitter's statue of Pomona, Roman goddess of orchards and, by extension, abundance—an appropriate virtue for a neighborhood dominated by the Plaza Hotel and Bergdorf's. Bitter, a protégé of Richard Morris Hunt, was killed by a car in 1915 as he was leaving the Metropolitan Opera; his studio assistants completed the statue from Bitter's clay model.

On the northern half of the Plaza, on the west side of Fifth Avenue and north of Central Park South, is the **Sherman Monument**, a fine equestrian statue (1892–1903) of General William Tecumseh Sherman by Augustus Saint-Gaudens. The Civil War general is best remembered for his brutal, "scorched earth" sweep through Georgia. Victory walks before the conqueror, waving a palm branch; the fallen pine branch on the granite pedestal (Charles Follen McKim) signifies Georgia.

The Plaza Hotel

Facing the plaza between 58th and 59th Sts is the Plaza Hotel (1907), the second Plaza Hotel on this site. Architect Henry J. Hardenbergh has long been admired for his skill in manipulating the details of its French Renaissance design—dormers, balustrades, high roofs, and rounded corner turnings—to create a harmonious whole. In the past two decades this celebrated hotel has changed ownership several times and has recently undergone a $400-million renovation and the conversion of some of its rooms to condos. The hotel is as famous for its guests as for its site—with views of Central Park and Fifth Avenue—its architecture, and its luxury. The first to sign the guest register were "Mr. & Mrs. Alfred G. Vanderbilt and servant"; since that day Mark Twain, Groucho Marx, and the Beatles have enjoyed its hospitality. Frank Lloyd Wright maintained a suite there for five years—he called it Taliesin East—while he supervised construction of the Guggenheim Museum. Truman Capote held his famous Black and White Ball there in 1966; and the six-year-old fictional Eloise, whose portrait used to hang in the lobby, cavorted in its halls.

Doris C. Freedman Plaza

The northernmost extension of Grand Army Plaza is named Doris C. Freedman Plaza for the city's first Director of Cultural Affairs. The space frequently hosts exhibitions of contemporary sculpture. Freedman spearheaded Percent for Art legislation, whereby developers of certain city-owned buildings must allocate one percent of the capital budget to art.

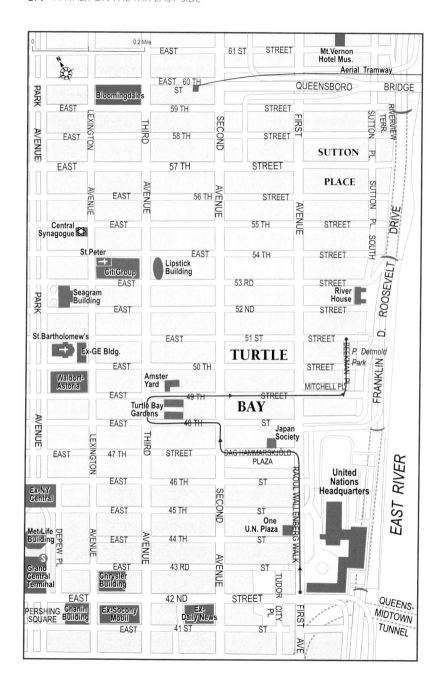

A WALK ON THE FAR EAST SIDE

Subway: 4, 5, or 6 to 42nd St-Grand Central. Bus: M15, M27, M42, M50, M104.

East of Fifth Avenue, the hustle and glitz of 42nd St around Times Square gives way to a more sedate form of commerce. Here are fine office buildings and important institutions—most important of all, the United Nations. North of 42nd St on the far East Side are several charming and exclusive residential enclaves.

On the east side of First Avenue (East 42nd–East 48th Sts), are the four principal **United Nations buildings**: the low General Assembly Building, the tall Secretariat Building, the Dag Hammarskjöld Library, and the Conference Building (not visible from First Ave). Le Corbusier established the original design of the complex: a tall slab with offices for the bureaucracy—a low horizontal building for conferences, and a functionally-shaped though imposing assembly building—all to be set on a landscaped site, a scheme, according to critic Lewis Mumford, that demonstrated architecturally that "bureaucracy ruled the world."

The visitors' entrance is located on First Ave at 46th St, on the north side of the General Assembly Building. Except for the Visitors' Center, the UN Headquarters can be visited only by guided tour. (*Tours last approx. 1hr, and are conducted seven days a week, except weekends in Jan and Feb, Thanksgiving, Christmas, New Year's Day, and during the opening week of the General Assembly in late Sept–beginning Oct. General tour hours Mon–Fri 9:30–4:45; Sat, Sun 10–4:30; but hours are subject to change; T: 212 963 TOUR (8687) Visitors must pass through a security check.*)

In a circular pool in front of the Secretariat Building is Barbara Hepworth's bronze sculptural abstraction *Single Form*

(1964), placed there to honor Dag Hammarskjöld, secretary-general of the UN killed (1961) in a plane crash on a peace mission in the former Congo.

On the northwest corner of East 44th St and First Ave stands **One United Nations Plaza** (1976; Roche, Dinkeloo and Associates), a 39-story, glass-walled tower with office space for the UN and a hotel for delegates and others. Because the UN Development Corporation charter forbids the construction of any building taller than the Secretariat, this building stops at 505ft.

Continue north on First Avenue. The west side of the avenue from 42nd–49th Sts was renamed (1985) **Raoul Wallenberg Walk** to honor the Swedish diplomat who saved thousands of Hungarian Jews during World War II. In 1945 he disappeared from Soviet-controlled Budapest and was never seen again. Hungarian-born sculptor Gustav Kraitz, who was studying art in Budapest in 1945, designed the *Hope* monument (1998), which stands on the traffic island at 47th St. A blue ceramic sphere symbolizing hope caps the tallest of the five black Swedish granite pillars. A bronze attaché case with Wallenberg's initials rests on a pavement of stones from the Budapest ghetto.

The Japanese-style building (1971; Junzo Yoshimura) at 333 East 47th St

serves as headquarters of the **Japan Society**, founded in 1907 to promote understanding through cultural exchange (*gallery open during exhibitions Tues–Thur 11–6, Fri 11–9, weekends 11–5; closed Mon and major holidays; T: 212 832 1155; www.japansociety.org*). The building contains indoor gardens, a reflecting pool and a waterfall, as well as tables, chairs, and benches designed by George Nakashima.

Café Milkshake at 342 East 47th St specializes in grilled cheese sandwiches, milkshakes, and malts, but also has a full-service bar for the lactose averse; outdoor seating in season (*T: 917 880 2393; www.nymilkshake.com*). The upscale Blair Perrone Steakhouse at 885 Second Ave (47th and 48th Sts) is an option for the more carnivorously minded; open for lunch and brunch as well as dinner (*T: 212 796 8000; www.blairperrone.com*).

Continue west to Second Avenue and walk north to 48th St. In the block between Second and Third Aves is the former **William Lescaze Residence** at 211 East 48th St. The house began as an ordinary 19th-century brownstone, but was aggressively transformed (1934) by architect Lescaze, who made dramatic use of his trademark glass blocks. The façade, pushed forward to the building line, is covered with smooth gray stucco (originally white), and is brilliant when illuminated at night. In its day the house caused such a stir that for a while Lescaze and his wife set aside an hour on Mondays for public visitation.

Along East 48th and East 49th Sts (Second and Third Aves) is the **Turtle Bay Gardens Historic District** (remodeled 1920), two rows of 19th-century brownstones. Unlike ordinary New York row-house back yards, described in an 1893 article as "a dreary monotone of gray board fences, ash and garbage barrels, slop pails and clotheslines," these yards are combined into a common garden inside the block. Wealthy Charlotte Hunnewell Martin, inspired by her travels in France and Italy, bought 20 deteriorating brownstones, filled in the swampy areas, shaved six feet off each backyard to create the common garden, and redesigned the houses so that they faced inward. Famous residents have included Leopold Stokowski, Katharine Hepburn, Stephen Sondheim and essayist E.B. White, for whom an old willow tree in the garden symbolized the city—life surviving difficulties, growth against odds.

Walk around the block to 49th St (Second and Third Aves). **Amster Yard** (1870, remodeled 1945) at no. 211–15 is another enclave almost entirely secluded from the street. Originally the yard held workshops and small houses built on the site of what may have been the terminal stop of the Boston–New York stagecoach route. After the Second Avenue El was demolished in 1942, James Amster, a designer, bought the property and developed it into an attractive group of shops, apartments, and offices, around a central courtyard. Today the yard is occupied by the Instituto Cervantes New York, a non-profit organization created by the Spanish government for the teaching of Spanish and the understanding of Hispanic-American culture (*T: 212 308 7720; nuevayork.cervantes.es*).

At 225–27 East 49th St stands the former Efrem Zimbalist House (1926), home of the violinist as well as his wife, diva Alma Gluck, their son, actor Efrem Zimbalist Jr., and Gluck's daughter from a previous marriage, novelist Marcia

Davenport. The cartouche over the door bears a violin, a staff with some unidentified musical theme, and an open-mouthed cherub. Later Henry Luce of Time-Life Inc. lived here, but between 1957 and 1960 the house was the 17th Precinct Police Station House.

Walk east now and then turn north into **Beekman Place**, which runs along a high bluff overlooking the river. Its controlled development by the Beekmans made it as socially desirable early in its history as it is now. Among those who have lived here are John D. Rockefeller III, Irving Berlin, Gloria Vanderbilt, and Rex Harrison. The Beekman mansion, Mount Pleasant (built 1765), stood near the river at about 51st St, and for a while during the Revolution served as British headquarters. In 1783 James Beekman got his house back and here entertained American officers and staff entering New York on Evacuation Day with punch made with lemons plucked from trees growing in the greenhouse. In 1874 the house was demolished.

THE SUTTON PLACE NEIGHBORHOOD

This neighborhood is far from public transportation. The M50 runs crosstown west on 49th St. Buses run north or south on the major avenues. The nearest subway is at Lexington Ave and 53rd St.

This is one of the city's quietest and most elegant neighborhoods. One of the more imposing prominences overlooking the water is **River House** (433–37 East 52nd St, east of First Ave). Completed the same year as the George Washington Bridge, the Empire State Building, and the Waldorf-Astoria Hotel, River House quickly became synonymous with privilege and wealth. The apartments in the tower were built on two or three floors with as many as 17 rooms (one had nine bathrooms), while those in the body of the building were only slightly more modest. The serenity of the setting was disturbed by the arrival of the Franklin D. Roosevelt Drive, begun downtown in 1936 and completed after World War II as a major artery linking the city with outlying highways.

Sutton Place, which runs between 53rd and 59th Sts, was formerly and less glamorously known as Avenue A. It was renamed after one Effingham B. Sutton, a dry goods merchant who developed the area around 1875 with a fortune he had made in the California gold rush of 1849, not by striking the motherlode but by selling picks, shovels, and provisions to prospectors who hoped to do so. His venture with Sutton Place was timed about 50 years too soon, and the street remained modest until Anne Morgan, daughter of J. Pierpont Morgan, and Mrs. William K. Vanderbilt (Anne Harriman; Vanderbilt's second wife) arrived in 1921.

No. 1 Sutton Place South (1927; Cross & Cross, with Rosario Candela) vies with River House as one of the city's premier apartments. Sutton Square, the block between 57th and 58th Sts, has a group of town houses sharing a common back garden, hence the name. At the foot of 57th St is a small park with a replica of Pietro Tacca's *Wild Boar* from the Straw Market in Florence, the model for which is in the Uffizi.

At East 58th St east of Sutton Place is another small park and north of it, parallel to the river, a small, cobbled, private street—Riverview Terrace—with 19th-century houses looking out from the top of the ridge. From the end of 58th St is a fine view of the Queensboro Bridge (1909; Gustav Lindenthal, engineer; Palmer & Hornbostel, architects) which joins Long Island City in Queens with 59th St in Manhattan.

THE QUEENSBORO BRIDGE (59TH STREET BRIDGE)

As early as 1852 some of Long Island City's most powerful families—Steinways and Pratts for example—began lobbying for a bridge, an enterprise furthered by Long Island Railroad tycoon Austin Corbin and later by a Dr. Thomas Rainey, who foresaw the bridge as an aid to tourism, freight handling, and the funeral business (there were 15 cemeteries on Long Island at the time). Political and financial problems delayed construction for some 40 years and the collapse of another partially built cantilever bridge, the Quebec Bridge, called in doubt the safety of this one.

The span is 1182 ft long and 135ft above mean high water. About 50,000 tons of steel were used in construction at a cost of $20.8 million. Bicycle riders and pedestrians can still cross the bridge but can no longer descend to Roosevelt Island. Beneath the Manhattan approach to the bridge are handsome vaults with Guastavino-tiled arches, now called Bridgemarket and used as retail space.

The **Roosevelt Island Aerial Tramway**, one of two ways to reach the island (*see p. 382*), offers spectacular views from high above the East River. (*Manhattan tram station on Second Ave between 59th and 60th Sts; tram runs about every 15mins, more frequently during rush hours, 6am–2pm. MetroCards accepted. NB: At the time of writing, the tram was scheduled to be closed for a major overhaul during much of 2009.*)

Mount Vernon Hotel Museum and Garden

At 421 East 61st St (First and York Aves) is the Mount Vernon Hotel Museum and Garden, a survivor from the early years of the American republic. (*Open Tues–Sun 11–4; closed Mon, New Year's Day, July 4, Thanksgiving, Christmas, month of Aug. T: 212 838 6878; www.mvhm.org.*) Set on a half-acre of landscaped grounds, the house has been painstakingly restored and refurnished with period furniture (1800–30) predominantly in the Federal style. Behind the house is a pleasant garden with herbs and plantings reminiscent of those popular around 1800. In 1795 the land was owned by Colonel William Stephens Smith and his wife Abigail Adams Smith, daughter of John Adams. In 1798 William T. Robinson bought it and completed what is now the museum building as a stable and coach house for the mansion. Later the mansion became the Mount Vernon Hotel, known for its turtle soup, and even later a female academy, which was destroyed by fire in 1926.

CENTRAL PARK

Open 6am–1am all year; park drives are closed to vehicular traffic on weekends, major holidays, and weekdays during non-rush hours.

Central Park is the heartland of Manhattan, 843 acres set aside for the recreation of New Yorkers and visitors alike. Although the park seems "natural," the largest surviving piece of Manhattan unencrusted with asphalt and masonry, its landscape and scenery are completely man-made, based on designs by Frederick Law Olmsted and Calvert Vaux.

Information and maps
A map of the park is given on pp. 282–83 below. For more detail, the not-for-profit Central Park Conservancy (www.centralparknyc.org) publishes an excellent map, available from their visitor centers at the Dairy (65th St, mid-park, T: 212 794 6564), Belvedere Castle (79th St, mid-park, T: 212 772 0210), and the Charles A. Dana Discovery Center (110th St near Fifth Ave, T: 212 860 1370). For park tours, T: 212 360 2726; for general park information, T: 212 310 6693. The New York City Department of Parks & Recreation offers information about park events on www.nyc.gov/parks. The information number is (from New York City), T: 311; (from outside New York City), T: 212 NEW YORK (639 9675). The Urban Park Rangers patrol the park, assist visitors, and offer park tours and nature programs; T: 212 628 2345.

Crime
Central Park has one of the lowest crime rates in the city. Nevertheless, it is unwise to wander in remote areas of the park or to visit the park at night alone except to attend scheduled events. Precinct policemen, urban rangers, and park enforcement personnel patrol the park; direct-line emergency call-boxes are located throughout; they require no dialing and are connected directly with the police. The Central Park Police Precinct is located on Transverse Road No. 3 (at 86th Street); T: 212 570 4820.

Finding your way
The first two digits on the metal plate attached to most park lampposts (some have been ripped off) tell the approximate cross street: thus 06413 means 106th St and 70235 means 70th St. The odd-numbered final digits are on the west side of the park, and the even ones on the east.

Refreshments and restrooms
Informal service year round at the Model Boathouse, Loeb Boathouse, the Merchants' Gate Plaza, and the Zoo. Full-service restaurants at Tavern on the Green, T: 212 873 3200, www.tavernonthegreen.com; and the Loeb Boathouse, T: 212 517 2233. In warm weather snacks are available from carts. Restrooms are located at the Heckscher Playground (62nd St/mid-park), the Sheep Meadow Café at Mineral Springs (mid-park/69th St, closed in

winter), Bethesda Terrace (mid-park, 72nd St, closed in winter), Model Boathouse Café (Conservatory Water, East 74th St), Loeb Boathouse (East 74th St/East Drive), Delacorte Theatre (80th St/Turtle Pond), North Meadow Recreation Center (mid-park/97th St), Dana Discovery Center (110th St/Malcolm X Blvd, formerly Lenox Ave).

Sports and activities

Bicycling: *Best on roadways when the park is closed to traffic, though there are also bike lanes available at other times. Bicycles may be rented at the Loeb Boathouse (northeast corner of the Lake at 74th St) March–Oct, weather permitting, 10–dusk, from 9am on weekends; must leave ID and credit card, or ID and significant cash deposit; call for information: T: 212 517 2233; www.thecentralparkboathouse.com.*

Boating: *Rowboats and kayaks for rent at the Loeb Boathouse (northeast corner of the Lake at 74th St), open daily beginning March, 10–5; modest cash deposit; call for exact hours and details, T: 212 517 2233, or visit www.thecentralparkboathouse.com. Gondola rides also available spring through fall, approx. 5–9pm weekdays and 2–9pm weekends during summer. Reservations needed; call or visit website for details (number and URL as above).*

Carousel: *Mid-park at 64th St. Summer open 10–6 or 7, every day weather permitting; winter (roughly Nov–April) open weekends and holidays 10am–dusk; T: 212 879 0244.*

Carriage rides: *Grand Army Plaza, 5th or 6th Aves at 59th St; T: 212 736 0680, www.centralparkcarriages.com.*

Ice Skating and Swimming: *Wollman Rink, mid-park, roughly Nov–March. Skate rental, T: 212 439 6900. Also at Lasker Rink, mid-park near 107th St; T: 917 492 3856. Lasker Rink becomes a swimming pool July–Labor Day; T: 212 534 7639.*

HISTORY OF CENTRAL PARK

In 1844 poet William Cullen Bryant (among others) began calling for a public park, observing that commerce was devouring great chunks of Manhattan and the population sweeping over the rest. Andrew Jackson Downing, an architect and the preeminent landscape designer of the period, added his voice as did several politicians, and in 1856 the city bought most of what is now the park for $5 million. The land was desolate, covered with scrubby trees, rocky outcroppings, and occasional fields where squatters grazed pigs and goats; a garbage dump, a bone-boiling works, and a rope walk added their own atmosphere. Egbert Viele, a graduate of West Point and a civil engineer, was hired to survey the land and to supervise its clearing; he was aided by the police, who forcibly ejected the squatters and their livestock.

The board of Park Commissioners (established 1857) arranged a design competition for the park in part because Andrew Jackson Downing—who probably would have been chosen—had recently drowned in a steamboat accident. Among 33 entries, the Greensward Plan (1858) by Olmsted and Vaux was chosen, a plan based on enhancing existing land contours to heighten the picturesque, dramatic

qualities of the landscape. During the initial 20 years of construction, 10 million cartloads of dirt were shifted; 4–5 million trees of 632 species and 815 varieties of vines, alpine plants, and hardy perennials were planted; and half a million cubic yards of topsoil were spread over the existing poor soil (some of it recovered from the organic refuse of the garbage dump). Sixty-two miles of ceramic pipe were laid to drain marshy areas and to supply water to lawns where hydrants were installed.

The Greensward Plan also incorporated the existing Arsenal and the Croton reservoirs, rectangular receiving pools for the aqueduct system that brought water from the Catskills. Curving drives, designed to keep would-be horse racers in check, carried traffic around obstacles, while straight transverse roads recessed below ground level took crosstown traffic unobtrusively through the park. North of the reservoir site (later filled in to become the Great Lawn as the present reservoir was created) the land was high and rocky with good views, and the designers chose to leave this area as wild as possible. South of the reservoir long, rocky, glacial ridges running north–south would be changed into open meadows, shady glens, and gently sloping hills. The formal element was to consist of a mall, an avenue of trees with a fountain at one end and statuary along its length.

Socially the park was intended for the relief of working people, whose daily lives were often confined to tenements and sweatshops, as well as for the amusement of the wealthy, who could display their clothing, carriages, and horses along the tree-lined drives. It was also a public works project employing a staff of several thousand laborers, though it unfortunately attracted politicians who saw in its labor-intensive landscape a golden opportunity for patronage (controlling immigrant votes) and for letting out lucrative contracts to cronies in the building trades.

Even before its completion the park was a target for unwanted encroachments, beginning with a racing track for horses, which Olmsted blocked. While an airplane field (1919), trenches to memorialize World War I (1918), an underground garage for 30,000 cars (1921 and frequently thereafter), and a statue of Buddha (1925) have not materialized, paved playgrounds, skating rinks, a swimming pool, a theater, and a zoo have taken park land. Robert Moses, zealous Parks Commissioner from the La Guardia era to 1960, advocated organized sports, accepted various buildings donated by philanthropists, and tore down structures of Olmsted's vintage, replacing them with boxy brick buildings. The present park environment represents therefore a compromise between the Olmsted vision of pastoral serenity and modern interests in active sports and recreation.

About 25 million people visit the park each year, which takes a toll on the landscape and facilities. The not-for-profit Central Park Conservancy, founded in 1980, now maintains the park under contract with the city. The Conservancy has raised more than $350 million to improve the park, and has restored major landscape areas—the Great Lawn, Harlem Meer, Reservoir, and Sheep Meadow—as well as buildings, bridges, and playgrounds.

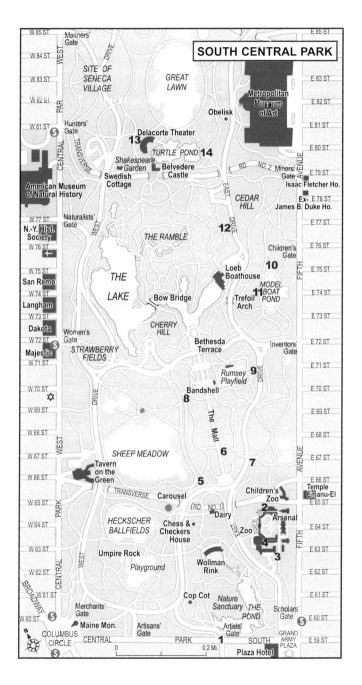

SOUTH CENTRAL PARK

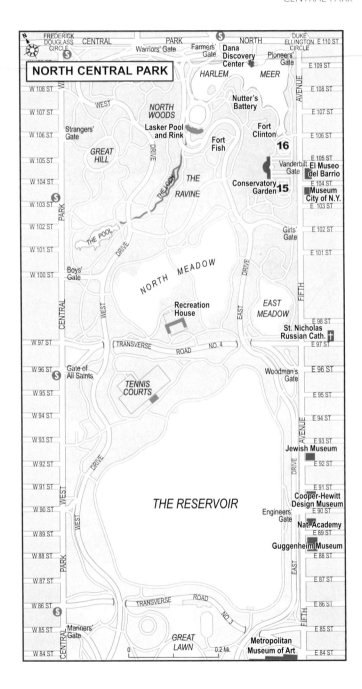

NORTH CENTRAL PARK

FREDERICK DOUGLASS CIRCLE

CENTRAL PARK NORTH

DUKE ELLINGTON CIRCLE

Warriors' Gate

Farmers' Gate

Dana Discovery Center

Pioneers' Gate

HARLEM MEER

Nutter's Battery

NORTH WOODS

Strangers' Gate

Lasker Pool and Rink

Fort Clinton

GREAT HILL

Fort Fish

16

Vanderbilt Gate

El Museo del Barrio

THE RAVINE

Conservatory Garden **15**

Museum City of N.Y.

THE POOL

Girls' Gate

Boys' Gate

NORTH MEADOW

Recreation House

EAST MEADOW

St. Nicholas Russian Cath.

TRANSVERSE ROAD NO. 4

Gate of All Saints

Woodman's Gate

TENNIS COURTS

Jewish Museum

THE RESERVOIR

Cooper-Hewitt Design Museum

Engineers' Gate

Nat. Academy

Guggenheim Museum

Mariners' Gate

TRANSVERSE ROAD NO. 3

GREAT LAWN

0   0.2 Mi.

Metropolitan Museum of Art

FREDERICK DOUGLASS CIRCLE
W 108 ST
W 107 ST
W 106 ST
W 105 ST
W 104 ST
W 103 ST
W 102 ST
W 101 ST
W 100 ST
W 97 ST
W 96 ST
W 95 ST
W 94 ST
W 93 ST
W 92 ST
W 91 ST
W 90 ST
W 89 ST
W 88 ST
W 87 ST
W 86 ST
W 85 ST
W 84 ST

E 110 ST
E 109 ST
E 108 ST
E 107 ST
E 106 ST
E 105 ST
E 104 ST
E 103 ST
E 102 ST
E 101 ST
E 98 ST
E 97 ST
E 96 ST
E 95 ST
E 94 ST
E 93 ST
E 92 ST
E 91 ST
E 90 ST
E 89 ST
E 88 ST
E 87 ST
E 86 ST
E 85 ST
E 84 ST

WEST DRIVE
THE LOOP
CENTRAL PARK
EAST DRIVE
FIFTH AVENUE
PARK DRIVE

Frederick Law Olmsted (1822–1903)

Olmsted had trouble settling on a career, but when he did, he changed the face of the urban landscape. As a young man he wandered from job to job: he sailed to China as an apprentice seaman, clerked in a store, tried his hand at scientific farming, and settled down (he thought) to a career as a journalist. Between 1852 and 1857, he traveled the South, reporting on the moral and economic effects of slavery for the precursor of the *New York Times*. By the time he embarked on his ultimate career, landscape design, his social views were well formed.

Olmsted's opposition to slavery extended to a belief in egalitarianism and faith in education as a tool for social equality. Education would not only give the "lower classes" the skills of reading and writing, but would teach "taste" as well, by which he meant civility and the attainment of a certain cultural level. This kind of education "to refinement and taste" would improve "the mental and moral capital" of the learners.

In 1850 he had traveled to England where he visited Birkenhead Park, the first public park developed with government funds. In a magazine article about his trip, he noted that the park was enjoyed "about equally by all classes … some who were attended by servants … and a large proportion of the common ranks, and a few women with children … [who] were evidently the wives of very humble laborers." He also commented that "in democratic America there was nothing to be thought of as comparable with this People's Garden."

The design of Central Park embodies this social consciousness, and the belief in a common green space accessible to all, a novel idea at a time when most parks were either estates that had been given to a city or gardens of the wealthy to which the public was sometimes allowed entrance. Olmsted had noted the dehumanizing effects of the "modern" city, where many people were forced to live "with heart-hardening and taste-smothering habits." He saw the park as a counterpoise to the artificiality of the built-up city, a restorative to the stress of urban life, and an educational force.

CENTRAL PARK: 59TH–72ND STREETS

Subway: 4, 5, 6 to 59th St; N, R to 5th Ave. Bus: M1, M2, M3, M4, M30, M57.

Central Park South

Spaced out along the southern edge of the park (Central Park South at Sixth Ave) stand three **equestrian statues of South American liberators (1)**. Nearest Fifth Avenue is a statue of Simón Bolívar (1919; Sally James Farnham), who fought Spanish domination in South America. Facing straight down Sixth Avenue is Anna Hyatt Huntington's 1959 rendering of José Julián Martí, completed when the sculptor was 83 years old. Martí, a Cuban poet and intellectual (his "Versos Sencillos" were adapted as the popular song

"Guantanamera"), organized Cuba's liberation from Spain while exiled in New York and returned to his homeland in 1895, where he was mortally wounded in a skirmish that marked the opening of Cuba's war for independence. He is shown dressed in civilian attire, clutching his wound, about to topple from his horse. To the west is José de San Martín (c. 1950; Luis J. Daunas), who led the revolt of Argentina, Chile, and Peru against Spain. The intersection of Central Park South and Sixth Avenue (officially renamed The Avenue of the Americas in 1945) is known (also officially) as Bolívar Plaza.

THE PARK ENTRANCES

In 1862 the Central Park Board of Commissioners issued a report that outlined a program for naming the park's 18 entrances after the industrial and intellectual pursuits of the day, giving the gates meaning and identity. The Inventors' Gate (72nd St and Fifth Ave), Mariners' Gate (85th St and Central Park West), Engineers' Gate (90th St and Fifth Ave), and one additional gate not planned in the original draft, the 76th St Gate (now the Children's Gate at 76th St and Fifth Ave), were the only ones inscribed until recently. During the fall and winter of 1999–2000, the Conservancy and city inscribed the remaining 14 blank entrances with the names originally proposed in 1862, including Merchants' Gate (59th St and Eighth Ave), Miners' Gate (79th St and Fifth Ave), Pioneers' Gate (110th St and Fifth Ave), Farmers' Gate (110th St and Lenox Ave) and others.

The Pond and Wollman Rink

The **Pond**, at the southeast corner of the park, was transformed by Vaux and Olmsted from swampland inhabited by a few impoverished immigrant families to a peaceful miniature lake. Real swans once glided across the waters, along with swan boats until 1924. The swans have largely been replaced by ducks, occasionally geese and egrets, and on the periphery, plenty of pigeons. Hallett Nature Sanctuary (*open only for special tours*) is a rocky landscape filled with shrubs, wildflowers, trees, and birds.

In the winter **Wollman Rink** (1951) is a magical place to skate, with great views of the skyline and park landscape. The rink was restored in 1987 by real estate developer and TV celebrity Donald Trump, to the embarrassment of the city government. Trump, unshackled by city regulations, renovated the skating surface and rebuilt the rink building in five months for less than $3 million after the city had spent six years and $12.9 million without completing the job. The Trump Organization now manages the rink (*www.wollmanskatingrink.com; T: 212 439 6900*).

Central Park Zoo

Although park designers Olmsted and Vaux disapproved of caging animals in zoos and made no such plans for the park, gifts of animals began to arrive as soon as construction began: a bear cub was left in the custody of a park messenger boy. The park

commissioners, deluged with donated animals, including white mice, cattle, and deer, established a menagerie in the Arsenal that remained there until 1934. The Central Park Zoo, which opened in 1935, originally had both large and small animals, most confined to barred cages; a renovation in 1988 (Roche, Dinkeloo and Associates) made the exhibits more suitable to the small scale of the zoo, retaining the popular sea lions and polar bears, but concentrating on smaller animals.

Animal statuary near the zoo includes *Honey Bear* **(2)** and *Dancing Goat* **(3)** (c. 1935) by Brooklyn-born Frederick George Richard Roth, known for his animal sculptures, several of which grace Central Park; and *Tigress and Cubs* **(4)** (1866) by Auguste Cain, a prominent French sculptor whose commissions included a similar work for the Jardins des Tuileries in Paris.

At the north entrance to the Children's Zoo is the **Delacorte Clock** (1964–65; Andrea Spadini), commissioned by publisher George T. Delacorte, who admired the animated clocks of Europe. Every hour a parade of bronze animals circles the clock, brandishing musical instruments and playing nursery tunes and such seasonal favorites as "Younger than Springtime," and "Winter Wonderland." A shorter performance takes place on the half-hour. At the **Children's Zoo**, young animal lovers can pet and feed goats, sheep, and a pot-bellied pig. Paul Manship, most famous for his *Prometheus* at Rockefeller Center, sculpted the boys, goats, and tendrils of curling vegetation that decorate the gates.

The Arsenal

Beyond the zoo toward Fifth Avenue is the Arsenal (1848; Martin E. Thompson), an ivy-covered, eccentrically charming brick building surmounted by eight crenellated octagonal towers. The newel posts of the central staircase represent cannons, while the balusters supporting the railing resemble rifles.

Although it was constructed to replace an older ammunition depot downtown on Centre St whose decrepitude made it an easy mark for thieves, the remoteness of the present building (in 1848) rendered it only dubiously effective as a place for stockpiling arms and ammunition. One critic complained that the cannons in the Arsenal, four and a half miles from the previous depot, would be utterly useless, since a mob could riot before the troops could drag the artillery into action. The building later housed the Eleventh Police Precinct, the Municipal Weather Bureau, the American Museum of Natural History, and the menagerie that predated the Central Park Zoo, before finally becoming home to the city's Parks and Recreation Department in 1934.

On the third floor is the **Arsenal Gallery** (*open Mon–Fri 9–5; T: 212 360 8163; free*), whose changing exhibitions focus on nature, urban space, New York City parks, and park history. Also on view is the original Greensward Plan, Frederick Law Olmsted and Calvert Vaux's winning entry in the competition for the design of Central Park.

The Dairy

North of Wollman Rink is the Dairy (1870; Calvert Vaux; *open Tues–Sun 10–5, earlier closing in winter; T: 212 794 6564*), built as a refreshment stand and resting place for

mothers and children, now one of the park's three visitor centers. The Gothic Revival building is said to combine features of a country church (the pointed-arch windows), a mountain chalet (the steep pitched roof and open-air loggia), and a barn (the framing of the beams and gambrel ceilings). Inside are displays on park history, information about daily programs, and a shop with maps, books, and gift items.

Olmsted and Vaux set aside for children and their parents the southern portion of the park, the part most accessible to the city, which was then sparsely developed this far north. At a time when milk—much of it produced on farms within the city—was unregulated and often contaminated, the Dairy was more than just a romantic pastoral feature. The park's herd of cows grazed in a field between the Dairy and what is now Wollman Rink.

Also part of the Children's District were the Children's Cottage (demolished), the Carousel, two rustic shelters, and a playground. One of the shelters, replaced by the Chess and Checkers House in 1952, stood on the Kinderberg ("Children's Mountain"), a nearby rocky outcrop. The other shelter, the **Cop Cot**, is a close replica (1984) of the original rustic summerhouse placed here when the park opened; it is built of tree limbs and trunks constructed where possible with such traditional joinery techniques as mortise and tenon instead of nails and bolts.

Calvert Vaux (1824–95)
Born in England, Vaux co-designed the Greensward Plan (the winning entry in the competition to design Central Park) with Frederick Law Olmsted, and is also responsible for most of the built environment in the park. In addition to his talents as an architect, Vaux was a skilled draftsman. An exhibition of his landscape watercolors in a London gallery attracted the attention of Andrew Jackson Downing—America's leading landscape architect, a proponent of the Gothic Revival style, and an influential editor. Downing invited Vaux to join his firm in Newburgh, New York, and later introduced him to Olmsted.

Vaux was quiet, perhaps shy, and though his personality was overshadowed by Olmsted's charisma, he was an equal partner in the ventures the two shared: Central Park and Morningside Park in Manhattan, Prospect Park and Fort Greene Park in Brooklyn, and other projects outside New York City. Among his other commissions in New York, Vaux designed the American Museum of Natural History and the rear façade of the Metropolitan Museum. He designed most of the original buildings and bridges in Central Park.

The Carousel

The Carousel, with its 58 beautiful horses, delights more than 250,000 riders every year. According to legend, the first park carousel (1870) was turned by a blind mule and a horse in the basement, who were trained to respond to one or two knocks on the floor over their heads. When the predecessor to the present carousel was destroyed

by fire, the Parks Department found this one in a trolley warehouse in Coney Island. The horses were hand-carved in 1908 by artists Sol Stein and Harry Goldstein, who worked for a carousel-manufacturing company in Williamsburg, Brooklyn.

Heckscher Ballfields and Playground

The recently restored playground west of the Carousel occupies the site of a 19th-century playground, which Vaux and Olmsted designed without slides, swings, or other aids to juvenile enjoyment. The "playground" was simply a meadow designated for field sports. Adults were not allowed, and even the children needed permits for all sports except sledding, a measure designed to protect the landscape. In 1927, compelled by overwhelming pressure for adult sports, the park managers installed five permanent fields with backstops. The playground to the south was donated by August Heckscher, who also established the Heckscher Children's Foundation (now home of El Museo del Barrio) and sought to eradicate slum housing.

Between the ballfields and the playground is a large outcropping, **Umpire Rock**, a hunk of Manhattan schist, the bedrock that underlies much of Manhattan, grooved and striated by the Wisconsin glacier that covered the city some 30,000 years ago.

At the pretty brick-and-tile Ballfields Café (note the baseball ball motif along the frieze) you can sit out in warm weather and admire the treetops and Manhattan skyline.

The Mall and Literary Walk

The Mall (1212 ft long) is a formal *allée*, based on European precedents, and bordered by a stand of mature American elm trees. Most American elms in the nation were destroyed by Dutch elm disease, which struck first in the 1930s, and these trees have survived only because they are closely monitored. The Mall is the only area Olmsted and Vaux considered appropriate for statuary; memorials elsewhere in the park result mainly from the passion for commemorative objects that gripped the city during the last half of the 19th century.

The Indian Hunter **(5)** (1866) by John Quincy Adams Ward is one of the best sculptures in the park, the fruit of months spent by the sculptor in the Dakotas sketching Native Americans. Other statues nearby commemorate major and minor poets—from Shakespeare to Fitz-Greene Halleck **(6)**, a 19th-century poet who also served as John Jacob Astor's private secretary. Beyond the Willowdell Arch on the right is *Balto* **(7)** (1925; Frederick George Richard Roth), leader of a team of heroic huskies that carried diphtheria serum across 600 miles of stormy Alaskan wasteland to Nome in 1925. The dog's back and tail have been worn shiny by affectionate petting.

Further up the Mall on the west is Christophe Fratin's *Eagles and Prey* **(8)** (c. 1850), a bronze group of two ferocious eagles sinking their claws into a goat trapped between rocks. Fratin belonged to a group of French sculptors whose renderings of wild animals expressed a fascination with violence and terror; some 19th-century critics found this work too violent for the tranquil beauty of the park.

To the east are the Naumburg Bandshell, with its coffered interior vault, and the Wisteria Pergola, covered by Chinese wisteria. The **Rumsey Playfield** (1936) behind

the bandshell replaced the Casino, an expensive night spot for adults, including former Mayor James J. ("Beau James") Walker, who entertained lavishly and is alleged to have occasionally skipped out on his bills. The statue of *Mother Goose* **(9)** (1938) at the eastern edge of the playfield is by Frederick George Richard Roth.

Bethesda Terrace and Fountain

At the top of the Mall the **Bethesda Terrace Arcade** leads under the car road to Bethesda Terrace. The walls are decorated with ornamental stonework, some now very worn, by Jacob Wrey Mould (*see box below*).

Jacob Wrey Mould (1825–86)
Responsible for much of the decorative stonework and many small structures in Central Park, Mould was recognized by his contemporaries as a man of many gifts. Born in England, Mould trained with Owen Jones, an architect known for his interest in decoration and for his studies of the Alhambra in Spain. Mould apparently visited Spain, and what he saw at the Alhambra may have informed his later decorative work, much of which suggests Moorish influences. He came to New York when he was 27, with a commission to design the All Souls Unitarian Church (no longer standing). The church, faced with red Philadelphia brick and light yellow Caen stone set in broad alternating stripes, earned the nickname, "The Church of the Holy Zebra." A contemporary described Mould as "bold as a lion in the selection of his colors."

Mould was also a linguist who translated opera libretti, and a musician who played the piano and composed songs. He worked easily in stone, metal, and wood. He designed houses as well as churches, and earned the praise of his colleagues for his skill in decoration. Likeability, however, was not among Mould's gifts. Diarist George Templeton Strong, a lawyer and vestryman of Trinity Church, called Mould "ugly and uncouth but very clever … [an] architect and universal genius." The architectural critic Montgomery Schuyler, while admiring Mould's way with color, called him "that strange genius" and an "irresponsible bohemian," apparently because Mould flouted convention by living openly with a woman. He also earned a reputation for dishonest business dealings. In 1875 he left his job as an assistant architect for Central Park and went to Lima, Peru, for five years. Biographical sources are unclear as to the motive for this sudden uprooting.

When he died in 1886 he had few friends, but an acquaintance noted that "a woman he called his wife stuck with him to the last." He is buried in Green-Wood Cemetery, in Brooklyn (*see p. 491*).

In the underpass, the blind arches of the lateral walls are adorned with marble panels painted with *trompe l'oeil* designs. The ceiling is covered with 15,876 fine hand-crafted Minton tiles, also designed by Mould. The arcade reopened in 2007 after a

painstaking restoration of the tiles by Maw and Company, like Minton a British firm specializing in tiles. (Nowadays Minton produces only tableware.)

At the center of the terrace is the **Bethesda Fountain** and its statue, *Angel of the Waters* (1868), by Emma Stebbins, one of the few works especially commissioned for the park. It depicts the biblical angel who stirred the waters of the Bethesda pool in Jerusalem, conferring healing powers on it, and was commissioned to commemorate the opening of the Croton Aqueduct in 1842. In an era when the public water supply was often contaminated and cholera epidemics were frequent, Stebbins equated the pure Croton water with the healing waters of Bethesda. On the column beneath the angel, four plump cherubs represent the virtues of Temperance, Purity, Health, and Peace.

Emma Stebbins (1815–82)
Born to a wealthy and influential New York family, Stebbins was one of America's first important woman sculptors. She was the only woman hired to create a work of art for Central Park, but the fact that her brother headed the park commissioners surely influenced the choice. Stebbins was a feminist, a bohemian, and a lesbian who had a long relationship with Charlotte Saunders Cushman, one of the great actresses of the day. Cushman underwent years of treatment for breast cancer, with Emma Stebbins remaining at her side and nursing her. After Cushman died in 1876, Stebbins never made another sculpture. The *Angel of the Waters* is her most famous work, but she is also represented in New York by a figure of Columbus in front of the New York State Supreme Court Building in Cadman Plaza, Brooklyn.

The terrace is, and has been since it opened, prime territory for people-watching. During the 19th century the well-to-do displayed their horses, carriages, and stylish clothing along Terrace Drive, now the 72nd St vehicular road. Today chic clothing and stylish pets are still on display here, though the carriages are long gone.

West of the Bethesda Terrace is **Cherry Hill**, originally a turnaround for carriages; the decorative fountain, designed by Jacob Wrey Mould, was intended as a watering trough for horses.

Strawberry Fields

The 2.5-acre area near Central Park West and the 72nd St park entrance is called Strawberry Fields to honor John Lennon, the songwriter, singer, and member of The Beatles, who was assassinated in the courtyard of the nearby Dakota Apartments in 1980. "Strawberry Fields Forever," one of Lennon's most popular songs, took its title

The Bethesda Fountain with its statue, *Angel of the Waters* (1868), by Emma Stebbins.

from the name of a Liverpool Orphanage, though the lyrics in fact have hallucinogenic overtones. The title of another famous song, "Imagine," is inscribed in the center of a black and white pavement mosaic—a reproduction of a mosaic from Pompeii and a gift of Naples, Italy. The garden, landscaped and set aside as a meditative Garden of Peace, was donated by Lennon's widow, Yoko Ono.

Strawberry Fields opened in 1985 after its planners overcame some unusual obstacles beginning with the wish of conservative City Council members to name the area for Bing Crosby instead of the politically controversial Lennon. When Yoko Ono ran an advertisement in the *New York Times* requesting rocks and plants from nations around the world, many countries sent plants suitable to other climates or offered gifts inappropriate to the park—a totem pole, a tile bench, and a large amethyst. Eventually 150 nations sent plants to create the Peace Garden. The site is now one of the most popular destinations for visitors, a shrine where fans from all over the world leave flowers and other tokens of remembrance.

Tavern on the Green

West Drive runs south from Strawberry Fields to the Tavern on the Green (West 66th St at Central Park West), a large, elaborately decorated restaurant popular as much for the glitter as for the food. Built as a sheepfold (1870; Jacob Wrey Mould) that stood here until 1934, it sheltered a flock of Dorsets and Southdowns who grazed in the Sheep Meadow. Commissioner Robert Moses re-assigned the sheep to Prospect Park in Brooklyn and converted the Sheepfold to a restaurant, with doormen in top hats, riding boots, and hunting coats; cigarette girls in court costumes; and a 12-piece orchestra dressed in forest green.

CENTRAL PARK: 72ND–84TH STREETS

Subway: 4, 5, 6 to 72nd St. Bus: M1, M2, M3, M4, M30, M72.

Model Boat Pond (Conservatory Water)

The **Model Boat Pond**, formally known as the Conservatory Water, gets its name from an unbuilt glass conservatory for the exhibition of tropical plants. Included by Olmsted and Vaux in the original plans for the park, it was abandoned after the foundations were laid because money ran short. The area planned as a flower garden near the conservatory was reconfigured as a pond. In its waters sail radio-controlled and wind-driven model yachts, some luxurious enough for model moguls.

At the north end of the pond an 11-ft bronze statue of *Alice in Wonderland* **(10)** (1959) by José de Creeft sits on a giant mushroom, surrounded by the Mad Hatter, the Dormouse, the Cheshire Cat, and the March Hare and (usually) a crowd of children, who scramble over the mushrooms. Publisher George T. Delacorte commissioned the statue to honor his wife, who read the classic story to their children.

On the west shore of the pond an eight-foot seated bronze **statue of Hans Christian Andersen (11)** (1956; Georg Lober) reads to a two-foot, 60-lb Ugly Duckling waddling

in front. In 1973 a thief sawed the duckling off its base and stole it, but it was recovered undamaged several weeks later in a paper bag near a Queens junkyard.

The Lake, Bow Bridge, and Ramble

From the boat pond a path leads west under the Trefoil Arch. The brownstone arch, trefoil on one side only and with a wooden ceiling, designed by Vaux, who planned the original park architecture, is part of a scheme that separated different modes of transportation within the park, an innovative notion in the 19th century, as were the sunken transverse roads across the park carrying city traffic.

In front of the **Loeb Boathouse** (1954), donated by philanthropists Carl and Adeline Loeb, a small bronze statue, *The Rowers* (1967; Irwin Glusker), commemorates the donors. The gondola that plies the waters was built in Venice and donated in 1986, replacing one given in 1862 by the city of Venice. The original New York gondolier, a former mail sorter, was trained by two Venetian gondoliers who traveled here to teach him the art.

A walkway follows the shore of the lake past the Bethesda Terrace (*see p. 289 above*) to the beautiful cast-iron **Bow Bridge** (1859; Calvert Vaux), which crosses the Lake to the **Ramble**, a heavily planted glen with intricately winding paths and carefully organized cascades in a meandering brook, the Gill. In designing the park, Vaux and Olmsted studiously avoided straight paths, and in the Ramble they outdid themselves, so it is easy to get lost here. The wilderness of the Ramble attracts birds and their watchers, nature lovers, and walkers. (*NB: While the Ramble's reputation as a place for drug deals and anonymous sex has declined since the 1970s, the woods can be deserted and it is unwise to go there alone after dark.*)

East of the Ramble along East Drive is Edward Kemeys's site-specific ***Still Hunt*** **(12)** (1881–83), a bronze panther crouched on a natural rock as if to pounce on the runners who jog obliviously along the road. In the late 1860s Kemeys wielded an axe for the engineering corps that cleared the grounds for Central Park, earning two dollars a day.

Belvedere Castle and Turtle Pond

North of the Ramble is Vista Rock (elevation 135ft), site of **Belvedere Castle** (1869), used as a weather station since 1919, now one of the park's visitor centers. Built as a Victorian folly, its three terraces offer great views of the surrounding landscape. North of the castle is Turtle Pond with the **Delacorte Theater** on its western shore. Near the entrance are bronze statues by Milton Hebald **(13)** representing *The Tempest* (1966) and *Romeo and Juliet* (1977) dedicated to Joseph Papp, the theatrical producer (*see p. 159*) who brought Shakespeare to the park.

The **Shakespeare Garden** (east of West Drive, between the theater and the Swedish Cottage at the latitude of 80th St) contains plants mentioned in the Bard's works. The **Swedish Cottage**, a replica of a Swedish schoolhouse made for the 1876 Philadelphia Centennial Exposition, houses the Swedish Cottage Marionette Theater (*for information, T: 212 988 9093*).

Turtle Pond is the last trace of the old Croton Receiving Reservoir (drained 1931), which once filled the site now occupied by the 55-acre **Great Lawn**. Over the years the lawn has been a popular venue for large-scale events, including a papal Mass with John Paul II that attracted 350,000 people, and a concert by Paul Simon that attracted 600,000. Compacted by heavy use, the Great Lawn became a dustbowl until a two-year restoration by the Central Park Conservancy brought it back to its former health and beauty; today events are carefully selected and monitored, but the New York Philharmonic and the Metropolitan Opera do give summer performances here.

SENECA VILLAGE

Between about 81st and 89th Sts, the Great Lawn, and Central Park West, an African-American community known as Seneca Village existed until the inhabitants were uprooted to make way for the park. The origin of the name is unknown. African-Americans began owning land here from about 1825, building houses, churches, a school, and establishing burial grounds. In the 1850s they were joined by German and Irish immigrants, and by 1855 the population had reached at least 254 people. In 1853, the state legislature authorized the use of eminent domain to take land for Central Park. As ground was broken for the park, the media began characterizing the residents of the future parkland as squatters, "insects," and "bloodsuckers." Although many residents of Seneca Village resisted through the courts, their efforts were futile; they were told to leave in the summer of 1856. By 1857 the community had disappeared.

Near Turtle Pond, a bronze **statue of King Wladyslaw Jagiello (14)** (1939; Stanislaw Kazimierz Ostrowski) honors a warrior under whom Poland became a major power. Wladyslaw, Grand Duke of Lithuania, married the heiress to the Polish crown in 1386. The union made Poland the largest kingdom in Europe; nevertheless, it lacked an outlet to the Baltic, a region controlled by the Teutonic Knights, against whom Wladyslaw fought long and hard. The statue shows him holding above his head the crossed swords of his adversaries, whom he finally defeated at the battle of Grunwald in 1410. The statue stood in front of the Polish Pavilion at the 1939 World's Fair; when World War II broke out, the statue remained in the United States, and was given to the City in 1945 by the Polish government in exile.

North of this statue behind the Metropolitan Museum of Art is New York's oldest piece of outdoor sculpture, the 71-ft, 244-ton **Obelisk**, erected as one of a pair in the 15th century BC by Tuthmosis III at Heliopolis on the Nile. It stood there a thousand years until toppled by the Persians, and thereafter lay on the ground until the Romans set it up in Alexandria (16 BC) not far from a temple built by Cleopatra (who had died in 30 BC), thus giving it its nickname, "Cleopatra's Needle." In hopes of stimulating trade, the khedive of Egypt gave it to New York a few years after the Suez Canal

The obelisk known as "Cleopatra's Needle" (15th century BC), presented to New York in the 19th century AD by the khedive of Egypt.

opened (1869), but it didn't arrive in the city until 1881, after William H. Vanderbilt paid the $100,000 shipping bill. Part of the expense went toward constructing a trestle to drag the pink granite statue across town from the Hudson. At the four corners of the obelisk are replicas of the giant bronze crabs the Romans had used to support the stone, whose lower corners had been broken off during the trip from Heliopolis to Alexandria. The second obelisk of the pair, also called Cleopatra's Needle, was given to Britain in 1819 and today stands on the Thames embankment in London.

CENTRAL PARK: THE RESERVOIR

Subway: 4, 5, 6 to 86th St. Bus: M1, M2, M3, M4.

The Reservoir occupies the midline of Central Park, from about 86th to 96th Sts. The main entrance, at East 90th St, is through the Engineers' Gate, familiarly known as the Runners' Gate, where runners enter the park during the New York Marathon. Near the gate a granite monument (1926; Adolph A. Weinman) honors John Purroy Mitchel, a political reformer who served a term as mayor (1914–17). Another monument (1994; Jesús Ygnacio Domínguez) honors Fred Lebow (1932–94), who organized the New York Marathon in 1970 and developed it from a race with 127 participants to one that attracts more than 35,000 runners every year.

Thousands of pedestrians round the 1.58-mile track every day—walking, jogging, running, bird watching, or simply enjoying the skyline views across the water. The stretch of road along Fifth Avenue between about East 86th and East 94th Sts is the longest straightaway in the park.

From 1862 until 1993, the billion-gallon reservoir supplied drinking water to the city as part of the Croton system, but nowadays its water fills the three bodies of water in the northern park: the Loch, the Pool, and the Harlem Meer. After Jacqueline Kennedy Onassis died 1994, the Reservoir was renamed to honor her commitment to the city. Three ornamental bridges cross the bridle path, and two stone gatehouses (designed by Calvert Vaux) contain equipment for treating the water and controlling its flow.

CENTRAL PARK: 96TH–110TH STREETS

Subway: 4, 5, 6 to 96th St; 6 to 103rd St. Bus: M1, M2, M3, M4.

Less studded with attractions than the southern part of Central Park, the northern reaches offer the beautiful Conservatory Garden, the Harlem Meer, and several sites that played a role in the Revolutionary War.

The **Vanderbilt Gate** at Fifth Ave and 105th St formerly kept the riff-raff away from the Cornelius Vanderbilt II mansion, where Bergdorf Goodman now stands (58th St at Fifth Ave). Made in Paris (1894), the wrought-iron gates were donated to the city in 1939 by Gertrude Vanderbilt Whitney, daughter of Cornelius II and founder of the Whitney Museum.

The Burnett Memorial Fountain by Bessie Potter Vonnoh. The children are based on the characters of Mary and Dickon in Frances Hodgson Burnett's *The Secret Garden*.

Conservatory Garden

The six-acre **Conservatory Garden**, the park's only formal garden (*open 8am–dusk*), is named for an elaborate greenhouse (1898) torn down in 1934 during the Depression as a cost-cutting measure.

The present garden (opened 1937) began as a Works Progress Administration project, providing employment during the Depression. By the early 1970s the garden had fallen into disrepair, its broken fountains running dry, its hedges and trees growing unpruned. In 1982 Lynden B. Miller, a painter and garden designer, took over, and the following year the Central Park Conservancy began restoring the perennial beds and planting wildflowers and bulbs. Today the Conservatory Garden, with its magnificent displays of blooms and fine collections of perennials, draws people to admire the plants, contemplate nature, and even get married.

The garden is divided into three sections. The **Center Garden** is Italian in style with a thick lawn bordered with flowering quince, yew hedges, and symmetrical rows of crab apples. On the hillside a wrought-iron arbor supports a beautiful mature Chinese wisteria. The **South Garden** contains the Burnett Memorial Fountain **(15)** (1936; Bessie Potter Vonnoh), whose statues represent two of the children in Frances Hodgson Burnett's classic *The Secret Garden*. The beds have been designed in a modern American mixed-border style. Around the periphery is the Woodland Slope, whose shrubs and plants thrive in a shady environment. The **North Garden**, formal and French in style, centers around the Untermeyer Fountain **(16)** with its bronze *Three Maidens Dancing* (1947; Walter Schott). Circular beds surround the fountain, the outer ones planted with spectacular seasonal displays of tulips and chrysanthemums.

The Harlem Meer

The Harlem Meer (completed 1866), once a swamp, now an artificially filled lake, is the largest body of water in the northern park. On its northern shore stands the **Dana Discovery Center** (1993), which offers exhibits, family programs, and seasonal events (*open Tues–Sun 10–5; T: 212 860 1370*).

Steps lead down to the water's edge, planted with roses, hydrangeas, and irises. Impressive, mature trees surround the Meer. The water has been stocked with some 50,000 fish so that local children can try their luck at catch-and-release fishing.

At the southwest edge of the Meer is the shallow Lasker Pool and Rink, where thousands splash or glide in season. The pool is generally considered an ill-chosen intrusion in the park and has been derided as the "Lasker sitzbath," and "the park's most disastrous 'improvement.'" Nevertheless it remains extremely popular with local children.

CENTRAL PARK IN TIME OF WAR

The Albany Post Road, built over an old Indian trail, once ran northward approximately along the course of East Drive from 103rd to 106th Sts, threading its way between two jutting hills where the scanty remains of Fort Clinton and Fort Fish now stand. During the Revolutionary War the pass became an escape route for Colonel William Smallwood's Marylanders, covering the retreat of the colonial troops after the British invasion at Kip's Bay (about the level of East 35th St) on Sept 15, 1776; and for the rest of the war British troops and German mercenaries were garrisoned there to protect the city from a northerly invasion. About 30 years later, during the War of 1812, the pass again gained strategic importance as New Yorkers realized, following the bombardment of Stonington, Connecticut, that their city was vulnerable to a land attack from the north. A volunteer force that included gentlemanly Columbia College students as well as butchers, Freemasons, and tallow chandlers worked by day and night to strengthen the old line of Revolutionary forts from Third Avenue to the Hudson. In the McGowan's Pass area were Fort Clinton, named after Mayor DeWitt Clinton; Fort Fish, named after Nicholas Fish, chairman of the defense committee; and Nutter's Battery.

Duke Ellington Circle

Duke Ellington Circle at Fifth Ave and East 110th St honors the jazz giant—composer, pianist, and band leader—who died in 1974. The monument (1994; Robert Graham) shows an eight-foot figure of Ellington standing by an open grand piano, supported by three ten-foot columns, each topped off by three nude female caryatid figures representing the Graces. The monument has been controversial; at the time of unveiling some viewers found it sexist, others found it ugly. Most of the money for the statue was raised from private donations solicited by the great cabaret singer-pianist Bobby Short (1924–2005).

THE FRICK COLLECTION

Map p. 579, D1. 1 East 70th St (Fifth Ave). Subway: 6 to 68th St. Bus: M1, M2, M3, or M4. Open Tues–Sat 10–6, Sun 11–5. Closed Mon and holidays. Admission charge; pay-as-you-wish Sun 11–1. T: 212 288 0700; www.frick.org.
NB: Because few ropes or cases are used to protect fragile objects, children under ten are not admitted; those under 16 must be accompanied by an adult.

The Frick Collection, housed in one of the few remaining great Fifth Avenue mansions (1914; Carrère & Hastings), is a monument to the passion for acquiring European art that beset many wealthy men around the turn of the 20th century. The interplay between the superb paintings and sculpture, the opulent house itself, and the fine collection of decorative arts provides an experience unique in New York. The house remains much as it was when the Fricks lived there, so that a visit to this museum, considered one of the great small collections in the world, also gives insight into the lives of the great industrialists and financiers around the turn of the 20th century.

History of the collection

Henry Clay Frick began collecting art seriously around 1895 and continued for the rest of his life, at first indulging a penchant for French works by Daubigny, Bouguereau, and the painters of the Barbizon School. As he matured, he sold earlier acquisitions and began buying the Flemish, Dutch, Italian, and Spanish paintings which presently grace the collection, aided by English dealer Joseph Duveen, whose taste he admired. When J. Pierpont Morgan died in 1913, Frick purchased paintings (including Fragonard's *Progress of Love*), porcelains, and small bronze sculptures from Morgan's estate.

When Frick died, he bequeathed the house and the works of art to a board of trustees to make the art available to the public. Since his death the collection has been increased by about a third. The Frick Art Reference Library, with some 75,000 auction catalogues, 300,000 books, and more than a million study photographs ranks as one of the nation's finest libraries documenting the history of art and of collecting in America.

The building

In 1905 Frick abandoned plans for a new house and gallery in Pittsburgh: he felt that pollution from the steel mills would be hazardous to his collection. Instead he bought the former Lenox Library, which stood on the only complete blockfront facing Fifth Avenue available as a single parcel. He commissioned architect Thomas Hastings (of Carrère & Hastings) to build a home that would suitably display his collection and eventually become a museum. After several false starts, Hastings came up with the design for this grand limestone mansion with a front portico in the style of Louis XVI and a Beaux-Arts axial plan. Frick, by now estranged from his former business

partner Andrew Carnegie, was aware of Carnegie's mansion at Fifth Ave and 90th St, and, according to legend, remarked that his own mansion would make Carnegie's look like a miner's shack.

Attilio Piccirilli, best known for the *Maine* monument at Columbus Circle (*see p. 393*), sculpted bas-reliefs on the tympana of the pavilion at the north end of the building. Sherry Fry, who had studied at the American Academy in Rome, one of Frick's philanthropies, designed the reclining nude over the East 70th St doorway. Interior details were planned by Sir Charles Allom, an eminent London designer, who had redecorated Buckingham Palace for George V. In his correspondence, Frick repeatedly advised Allom to "avoid anything elaborate" and to make sure "the ceilings are almost plain." Upstairs furnishings and accoutrements were chosen by Elsie de Wolfe, a tastemaker who parlayed her sense of style into a career as a decorator and an international hostess, eventually marrying into the English aristocracy. Wadley & Smythe, the landscape architects, carted tons of soil onto the property and planted 13 mature chestnut trees along the avenue. The trees, alas, did not survive, but today three magnificent magnolias bloom each spring in the garden.

The permanent collection

NB: Not all works of art are on display all of the time, and only the Living Hall remains just as it was when Henry Clay Frick was alive. Only a selection of the works on display is discussed here; those purchased by Frick himself are given in bold. The description reflects the status quo at the time of writing.

(3) East Vestibule: Displayed here is an oil sketch of **Perseus and Andromeda** (1730) by Giovanni Battista Tiepolo, the greatest Venetian artist of the 18th century. The sketch was produced as a preliminary study for a ceiling fresco in a Milanese *palazzo* (since destroyed). In it we see reflected all Tiepolo's innate sense of theater and drama. The strong axiality of the composition and the bold use of color make it capable of standing alone as a finished work of art.

Also here is a bronze bust by the great French Baroque portrait sculptor Antoine Coysevox, one of a number of works by him in the museum. The subject is Louis XIV's chief architect Robert de Cotte, who completed the Grand Trianon and chapel at Versailles.

(5) South Hall: The museum has three works by the Flemish artist Jan Vermeer. Two hang here. **Officer and Laughing Girl** (c. 1655–60) is the earliest; the exaggerated size of the officer in the foreground may have resulted from Vermeer's use of a *camera oscura*, a sort of pinhole camera that threw the image onto a sheet of paper so that the outlines could be traced. The scene is seemingly an everyday one, but the sense of enigma is strong. We cannot see the officer's face, and have no idea what is making the girl smile. In **Girl Interrupted at Her Music** (c. 1660) Vermeer presents another enigmatic scene, possibly with erotic undertones, as suggested by the portrait of Cupid on the wall.

Also here is François Boucher's *A Lady on her Day Bed* (1743), a delec-

THE FRICK COLLECTION

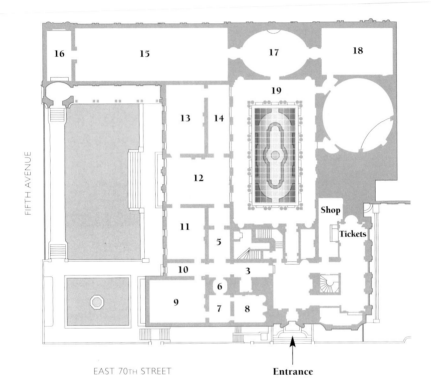

FIFTH AVENUE

Shop

Tickets

EAST 70TH STREET

Entrance

table portrait of Boucher's wife in their charmingly disordered apartment.

Agnolo Bronzino's portrait of **Lodovico Capponi** (c. 1550–55) depicts a page at the court of Cosimo I de' Medici in Florence, where Bronzino worked as court painter for most of his career.

(6) Octagon Room: Of particular interest in this small room is Francesco Laurana's **Bust of a Lady** (c. 1470s). This smoothly abstract marble portrait of an unknown woman is typical of the

hieratic style of this Dalmatian-born sculptor, whose work must surely have influenced Brancusi.

(7) Anteroom: Hans Memling's *Portrait of a Man* (c. 1470) is a superb early example of the portrait genre. Also here is the **Purification of the Temple** (c. 1600), instantly recognizable as by the hand of El Greco from its mannered, elongated figures, the almost Expressionist choice of colors and highlighting of the drapery, and the wispy, wraith-like figures in the background.

Henry Clay Frick (1849–1919)
Henry Frick rose from humble beginnings in rural Pennsylvania to wealth and power as a pioneer in the coke and steel industries. From childhood Frick made it clear that he did not intend to remain poor. He left school to clerk in a grocery store and then become a bookkeeper in various local businesses, including the whiskey distillery of his successful maternal grandfather, Abraham Overholt. While he was still a young man, an appraiser of his prospects remarked that Frick worked industriously all day and did the book-keeping in the evenings, but might "be a little too enthusiastic about pictures but not enough to hurt."

During his 20s Frick laid the foundations for the industrial empire he would build, founding the H. Frick Coke Company and taking advantage of the low prices during the depression that followed the Panic of 1873 to buy out competitors. Since coke, a coal-based fuel, was essential to the blast furnaces of the burgeoning steel industry, Frick soon attracted the attention of steel baron Andrew Carnegie. The two merged their interests and profited handsomely, dominating steel manufacture in Pennsylvania.

As an industrialist, Frick was far-sighted, daring, and ruthlessly competitive. He is best remembered for his role in the Homestead Steel Strike of 1892. For two years before the strike, the price of steel products had dropped more than 35 percent. Frick, ever hostile to unions, was determined to lower workers' wages and to crush the Amalgamated Association of Iron and Steel Workers, who in more prosperous times had negotiated a favorable contract. To do so Frick used increasingly harsh tactics—slashing wages, locking out workers, refusing to negotiate with the union but only with individual workers, and ultimately hiring mercenary soldiers from the Pinkerton detective agency to confront the striking steelmen.

When the Pinkerton guards arrived at the plant on barges towed up the Monongahela River, they were met by thousands of strikers and townspeople, many of them armed. In the battle that followed, nine strikers and seven Pinkertons were killed; most of the other Pinkertons were injured together with many strikers. The strikers had won the day, but they lost the battle when the governor intervened with 8,000 state militia. Strikebreakers were brought in on sealed trains, many not even knowing their destination. Protected by the militia, the strikebreakers reopened the plant.

Andrew Carnegie, who professed sympathy for the labor movement but had conveniently taken his summer vacation in Scotland during the strike, thoroughly approved of Frick's plans and perhaps even helped draft them. Nevertheless, Carnegie tried to put the blame for the Homestead massacre on Frick's shoulders.

Public sympathy, which had swung to the strikers because of Frick's relentless suppression of the strike, swung back when Alexander Berkman, an anarchist, attempted to assassinate Frick in retaliation for his actions. Berkman attacked Frick in his office, shooting the industrialist twice and stabbing him four times in the leg before he was pulled away by Frick's employees.

There was, however, another side to Frick. In business he was an intensely private man, guarded in his relationships and capable of enduring anger, but to his family, he was affectionate and devoted.

(8) Boucher Room: The walls of this small sitting room are decorated with panels by François Boucher entitled *The Arts and Sciences* (c. 1750–52). Madame de Pompadour, mistress of Louis XV and patroness of the arts, may have originally commissioned them as designs for chair coverings, but the designs were later painted as decorative panels in the library of her château at Crécy. They were formerly installed in Mrs. Frick's second-floor boudoir, which was reassembled here after her death. The delicate Rococo walls and furnishings throw the plainness of the ceiling into stark relief. The panels show plump, rosy-cheeked children playing at adult occupations: *Fowling and Horticulture, Fishing and Hunting, Architecture and Chemistry, Comedy and Tragedy, Astronomy and Hydraulics, Poetry and Music, Singing and Dancing,* and *Painting and Sculpture.* Boucher's sense of humor saves the ensemble from being sickly sweet: the children are bungling their jobs. The mini-architect has a badly leaking roof; the astronomer is looking through the fat end of his telescope.

Among the period furniture are a **desk by Jean-Henri Riesener**, one of the pre-eminent cabinetmakers during the reign of Louis XV, and a **bed table by Martin Carlin**. They were acquired for Mrs. Frick by Elsie de Wolfe (*see p. 300 above*). The *Bust of a Young Girl*, made in the 19th century after a model of 1750 by François-Jacques-Joseph Saly, appears in Boucher's figure of *Painting and Sculpture* on the west wall of the room. Antoine Coysevox was one of the favored sculptors of Louis XIV; his portrait bust of *Louis XV as a Child of Six* (1716) shows the child-king who would rule France for a further 58 years, conferring fame on many artists such as Boucher and Fragonard, bringing notoriety to more than a handful of courtesans, and making the monarchy dangerously unpopular.

(9) Dining Room: If the Boucher Room shows Frick's taste for 18th-century France, the Dining Room demonstrates his affection for the same period in England. Adorning the walls is a gallery of aristocratic 18th-century English portraits. The stunning **portrait of Miss Mary**

Edwards (1742) by William Hogarth depicts the artist's wealthy patron wearing a richly brocaded red dress set off with lace and jewelry. She inherited a large fortune, married secretly, and later repudiated the marriage because her husband's recklessness with her fortune would have consumed her son's inheritance. The portrait of General John Burgoyne painted (probably 1766) by Sir Joshua Reynolds show the general posed dramatically before a stormy sky; Burgoyne is known best in this country for his efforts in the Revolutionary War and his defeat at the crucial battle of Saratoga in 1777, but this romantic portrait probably celebrates earlier victories. One of Thomas Gainsborough finest paintings, *The Mall in St. James's Park* (1783), shows London's fashionable set on a *rus in urbe* promenade. Also in this room are **portraits by John Hoppner and George Romney**, as well as examples of English silver and Chinese porcelain.

(10) West Vestibule: The four panels by Boucher represent *The Four Seasons* (1755) and were painted for Madame de Pompadour.

(11) The Fragonard Room: Decorated with paintings (1771–73 and 1790–91) by Jean-Honoré Fragonard, a master of Rococo art, this room demonstrates Frick's taste toward the end of his collecting career. The four largest panels (*The Pursuit*, *The Meeting*, *The Lover Crowned* and *Love Letters*) are known collectively as *The Progress of Love* and were commissioned by Madame du Barry, who eventually succeeded Madame

de Pompadour as chief mistress of Louis XV. Fragonard, a student of Boucher, had the ill luck to outlive the taste for the style he had perfected; he was never able to adapt to the more severe Neoclassical taste associated with the French Revolution, and died in poverty. Though these paintings are often considered his masterpieces, Madame du Barry rejected them (she was notoriously capricious in this regard, and often left painters and cabinetmakers with unpaid bills). Fragonard complemented the panels with *Love the Avenger* (over south mirror facing Fifth Avenue), *Love the Sentinel* (over the next mirror), *Hollyhocks*, *Love the Jester* (over door to Living Hall), *Reverie*, *Love Triumphant*, and *Love Pursuing a Dove* (over door from West Vestibule). Frick bought them in 1915 from the estate of J. Pierpont Morgan, who had them in his London house.

Sculpture includes Jean-Antoine Houdon's *Comtesse du Cayla* (1777) and two terra-cotta groups by Clodion: *Satyr with Two Bacchantes* (1766), and *Zephyrus and Flora* (1799). Their stylistic differences suggest that Clodion, unlike Fragonard, successfully made the transition from the Rococo to the Neoclassical style.

Among the porcelains is a rare **Sèvres pot-pourri vase** (c. 1759) in the form of a ship: the "port-holes" along the side and the holes in the "rigging" allowed the aroma of dried petals to escape. Another fine example of such a vase is held in the Metropolitan Museum. Note the furled banner hanging from the "mast," emblazoned with the *fleur de lys* of royal France.

Fragonard: *The Meeting* (1771–73).

The gilt-bronze two-tier **tripod table** with Sèvres porcelain plaques painted with a bouquet and a hanging basket of flowers (c. 1783) has been attributed to Martin Carlin. It is an extremely fine example of its genre.

(12) Living Hall: Every painting in this wood-paneled room is a masterpiece. Flanking the fireplace are two works by Hans Holbein the Younger. To the left is an exceptional portrait of *Sir Thomas More* (1527), the author and statesman who served as Lord Chancellor to Henry VIII. More resigned that office over Henry's divorce from Catherine of Aragon, and later refused to subscribe to the Act of Supremacy, which made the King head of the Church of England; for this he was accused of treason and executed. Various versions of this painting exist, but this one is believed to be the original. On the other side of the fireplace hangs *Thomas Cromwell* (c. 1532–33), the portrait of an opportunist of obscure origins who rose to high office under Henry VIII. He helped Henry dissolve the monasteries, obtain his divorce from Catherine of Aragon, marry and then behead Anne Boleyn. His brokering of Henry's marriage to Anne of Cleves was his downfall. The union was a failure; and when it was whispered that Cromwell was a traitor, he was arraigned and executed without any royal opposition.

Over the mantel is El Greco's *St. Jerome* (c. 1590–1600), the ascetic saint (c. 342–420) who translated the Bible from Greek and Hebrew into Latin; his translation, the Vulgate, remained in use by the Catholic Church for centuries. Several versions of this painting exist, including one at the Metropolitan Museum of Art and another at the National Gallery in London.

In the center of the other long wall is Giovanni Bellini's *St. Francis in Ecstasy* (c. 1480), a wonderful work by this genius of Venetian painting. Among Bellini's skills were a mastery of perspective and color and a facility for capturing details of the everyday world. Flanking the Bellini are two portraits by Titian, who was not only Bellini's greatest, but also his most innovative pupil, abandoning forever the medium of egg-tempera on wood for the new and exciting possibilities offered by oil on canvas. The work on the right, *Pietro Aretino* (c. 1550), depicts Titian's friend and patron, a satirical writer and indefatigable lover, also hailed as the founder of the modern press. To the left is *Portrait of a Man in a Red Cap* (c. 1516), an early work.

Also in this room are examples of the **small Renaissance bronzes** which Frick began to collect toward the end of his life, purchasing many from the estate of J. Pierpont Morgan (d. 1914), who himself had swept up large numbers from European collections.

(13) Library: This room contains further examples of Frick's interest in 18th-century British portraiture, Chinese porcelains, and Renaissance bronzes. Here are portraits by Thomas Gainsborough, Sir Joshua Reynolds, Sir Henry Raeburn, and Sir Thomas Lawrence, as well as George Romney's likeness of the young **Emma Hamilton**, future mistress of Lord Nelson.

J.M.W. Turner's *Mortlake Terrace: Early Summer Morning* (1826) shows the Thames river west of London, painted from the lawn of an estate belonging to a friend of the artist.

Gilbert Stuart's **George Washington** (1795) is an early copy of Stuart's likeness of Washington as president painted for John Vaughan of Philadelphia. Stuart executed three types of Washington portraits—the Vaughan type, the Lansdowne type (a standing figure), and the Athenaeum type (which appears on the dollar bill)—all of which he copied repeatedly. Though he spent much of his early career in Britain, Stuart is considered the creator of a specifically American style of portraiture.

(14) North Hall: In this hall is Antoine Watteau's *The Portal of Valenciennes* (1709–10); Watteau is best known for his rather melancholy depictions of love in idealized pastoral settings, but he painted several small military scenes while he was in his 20s; this is the only one in the United States. Here also are a ballet scene by Degas and landscapes by Monet, Corot, and Théodore Rousseau. Jean-Auguste-Dominique Ingres's elegant *Comtesse d'Haussonville* (1845) was painted over a period of three years, occasioning more known studies and sketches than any of his other portraits. Louise, Princesse de Broglie, was the granddaughter of Madame de Staël and, like her grandmother, a woman of independent intellect.

Sculpture includes another bust by Francesco Laurana, this one of Beatrice of Aragon (1470s), the daughter of the King of Naples. As queen to Matthias Corvinus of Hungary, she brought art, craftsmanship—and, it is reputed, fine cuisine and table-manners—to a hitherto barbarous land. Currently on view here is Houdon's beautiful *Bust of Mme His* (1775), whose luminous marble surface almost glows with life. Mme His, a friend of the sculptor, was married to a German banker.

(15) West Gallery: This long room, illuminated in part by natural light, was planned by Frick as a setting for the major part of his collection and designed to permit the kind of interesting juxtaposition of paintings he enjoyed. The paintings here reveal the general contours of Frick's interests: the majority are tranquil scenes or portraits. On the south wall are fine landscapes by Ruisdael, Hobbema, Constable and Corot; a harbor scene by Aelbert Cuyp; and superb portraits by van Dyck and Frans Hals, a painter whose work was much in demand at the time Frick was gathering his collection.

Flanking the arched doorway at the west end of the gallery are two large works by the Venetian artist Paolo Veronese: **Allegory of Virtue and Vice** and **Allegory of Wisdom and Strength** (both c. 1580). The first of these shows Hercules arrayed as a Venetian nobleman, in white satin with a neatly trimmed beard, fleeing the clutches of Vice, who is depicted as a Venetian courtesan and whose talons have torn his stocking. In the second panel, garbed in the skin of the Nemean Lion (his first labor), he gazes down at the crown and jeweled orb scattered on the ground, while a female personification of Divine Wisdom encourages him to look upward, away from worldly wealth.

On the north wall is Gerard David's **Deposition** (c. 1510–15), one of the earliest known works painted in oil on canvas, rather than tempera on wood. The technique is thought to have been

brought to Italy from the Lowlands.

Vermeer's **Mistress and Maid** (c. 1665–70) is the third Vermeer in the collection, and was the last purchase of Frick's career, bought in 1919. Once again, the scene presented is an enigmatic one. Has the mistress just finished writing the letter? Is the maid delivering it? Which of the two, if either, knows its contents?

(16) Enamels Room: This beautifully paneled room, beyond the large arch, was originally Frick's home office, rebuilt as a cabinet gallery after he bought a collection of **Limoges enamels** from the estate of J. Pierpont Morgan. Dominating the room is Piero della Francesca's magisterial *St. John the Evangelist* (1454–69). Duccio di Buoninsegna's superb *Temptation of Christ* (1308–11) is one of the panels from his great altarpiece of the *Maestà*, painted for Siena cathedral. Duccio was one of the earliest medieval masters to begin lifting painting away from the static forms of Byzantine art towards a new, Humanist approach.

(17) Oval Room: This was added during the remodeling in 1935 when the

Symphony in Flesh-Color and Pink (Mrs. Frederick R. Leyland), 1872–73, by Whistler.

house was adapted to its role as a museum. It contains **portraits by van Dyck and Gainsborough**, as well as Renoir's *Mother and Children* (mid-1870s). The

identically-dressed little girls look lonely and rather wistful; the very young "mother" more wistful still. They take no part in the sociable gaggle behind them. It has been suggested, in fact, that the group shows a nanny taking her two small charges for a mandatory walk in the park.

(18) East Gallery: Along with fine portraits by Goya, Sir Anthony van Dyck, and Jacques-Louis David, are four large works by James Abbott McNeill Whistler, stunning elements in a collection not otherwise noted for its American art. All four have titles which powerfully suggest how Whistler viewed them: not simply as portraits, but as "compositions." Whistler's portrait of the dandified, even effete, Robert, Comte de Montesquiou-Fezensac (***Arrangement in Red and Gold***; 1891–92) is one of the last paintings he completed and the most recent painting acquired by Frick himself. Montesquiou is said to be one of the sources for the Baron de Charlus in Proust's *Remembrance of Things Past*. Mrs. Frederick R. Leyland (***Symphony in Flesh-Color and Pink***; 1872–73) was the wife of one of Whistler's chief patrons, a wealthy Liverpool ship-owner. Mrs. Leyland wears a dress the artist himself designed; its appliqué flowers echo the spray of cherry blossom on the left, an orientalist touch very typical of the era, when many artists were influenced by Japanese prints. Also here are Whistler's *Lady Meux* (***Harmony in Pink and Grey***; 1881), a portrait of an actress who married a wealthy industrialist but who never quite fitted in with polite society—as her bright red lips and (almost) vulgar dress gently suggest; and *Miss Rosa Corder* (***Arrangement in Black and Brown***; 1875–78), which shows the self-assured profile of a woman who was herself an artist and bohemian.

(19) Garden Court: This coolly pleasant space, filled with the sound of splashing fountains, was designed by architect John Russell Pope on the site of the original Frick carriage court when the house was remodeled as a museum. With its colonnade, its greenery and its sculpture, the Court is one of the most pleasant spots to sit and think about art or anything else. In the central part is a lovely bronze *Angel* by Jean Barbet; the left wing bears the inscription: "le xxviii jour de mars / lan mil cccc lx + xv jehan barbet dit de lion fist cest angelot" (on the 28th day of March in the year 1460 + 15 Jean Barbet, called of Lyon, made this angel). Barbet seems to have been the cannon-founder who cast the figure rather than the sculptor who designed it.

THE FRICK ART REFERENCE LIBRARY

10 East 71st St. Open to researchers Mon–Fri 10–5, Sat 9:30–1. Closed Sun, holiday weekends, Sat in June and July, and during Aug. First-time researchers must bring photo ID and arrive at least 2hrs before scheduled closing. T: 212 547 0641.
The Frick Art Reference Library (1931–35; John Russell Pope) is a memorial to Henry Clay Frick from Helen Clay Frick, his youngest child. It is a leading site for research on art, especially in determining provenance and studying the history of collecting.

Helen Clay Frick (1888–1984) never married. She and her father were increasingly close, as her mother, grief stricken by the death of two of her children, retreated into depression. After Frick's death, Helen inherited the largest share of his fortune and became the caretaker of his legacy. As a trustee of the collection she struggled against other trustees, notably John D. Rockefeller Jr., to keep the public rooms intact, with the furnishings more or less as they had been during her father's lifetime.

Touring Europe in 1920, she visited Sir Robert C. Witt, a trustee of the National Gallery in London, who had an impressive and exquisitely organized photo archive of European and American paintings. Inspired to emulate him, she took over the basement bowling alley in the mansion and soon made the library her life's work. In less than a year her library had expanded beyond the bowling alley and soon needed a home of its own.

For the expanded library Miss Frick bought two neighboring houses and tore them down; she hired John Russell Pope, who also designed the Garden Court and made other appropriate changes when the Frick mansion went public as a museum.

The collection, which contains some 300,000 books, 75,000 auction catalogs, and more than a million photographs (as well as an increasing number of electronic resources), is a tribute to Miss Frick's energy and ingenuity. She gained access to private collections using her connections with art dealers and others. During the 1920s she sent out teams of photographers to record European and American paintings that were largely undocumented, sometimes even having the researchers knock on doors when they had heard a valuable painting was in the neighborhood.

FIFTH AVENUE IN THE 60s
(SOUTH OF THE FRICK)

Map p. 579, D1.

Along the north side of East 70th St are four landmarked homes of the Fricks' well-to-do neighbors. All were built between 1909 and 1918 in Neoclassical or Renaissance styles. Two are now occupied by respected art galleries.

A **memorial to Richard Morris Hunt**, one of New York's great Eclectic architects (1898; Daniel Chester French), stands at the edge of Central Park at East 67th St. Hunt's architectural achievements include the pedestal of the Statue of Liberty, part of the Metropolitan Museum of Art, and many former mansions for Astors, Vanderbilts, and their ilk. The memorial faces the site of the former Lenox Library (1870), one of Hunt's finest buildings. Frick bought the library and tore it down for his mansion, though he offered to have it dismantled piece by piece and rebuilt in Central Park on the site of the Arsenal (the city refused). Architect Bruce Price, a student of Hunt's, planned the granite monument on which rests a bust of his mentor flanked by two classically draped women: *Sculpture and Painting* (left) with a mallet and palette, and *Architecture* (right). The figures, six feet tall and weighing in at 600 pounds apiece, were stolen in 1962 and almost melted down in a belt buckle factory before they were recognized and returned.

ECLECTICISM ON FIFTH AVENUE

The period during which the mansions of Frick and his fellow millionaires rose on Fifth Avenue coincided roughly with the Eclectic period in American architecture. As the new moguls, many of whom had made their fortunes during the post-Civil War boom, arrived on the social scene desirous of building suitably impressive homes, they turned for advice to the city's influential architects, who controlled the canons of taste. What the established architects—notably Richard Morris Hunt, Charles Follen McKim and Stanford White—offered was Eclecticism, a self-conscious selection of styles from the established orders of the past. The new "classical" architecture depended on the availability of cheap, skilled labor, supplied by the influx of immigrants, many of whom were experienced in masonry, ironwork, stone carving, painting and gilding, and ornamental plasterwork. Eclecticism died after the end of World War I, when changing economic patterns and new building technology dictated the end of sumptuous masonry construction and ushered in the era of the skyscraper and the high-rise apartment.

Although Eclecticism made itself felt in other parts of the city, the greatest concentration of such buildings in residential uses was here in the vicinity of Fifth Avenue. So much so that novelist Edith Wharton, whose well-to-do background and judicious eye made her a keen commentator on social developments of the period, once described this wide-ranging selection of detail a "complete architectural meal." Some of the mansions have become museums, others have been taken over by charitable or educational institutions.

Also in Central Park, on Fifth Ave at East 67th St, is the **One Hundred Seventh Infantry Memorial** (1927; Karl Illava), a memorial to the men of that regiment who died in World War I. The larger-than-life-sized bronze foot-soldiers are posed as if charging into battle from the wooded park. The sculptor, a sergeant in the regiment, modeled the soldiers' hands on his own.

The **Permanent Mission of the Federal Republic of Serbia to the United Nations** (1905; Warren & Wetmore), at 854 Fifth Ave between East 66th and East 67th Sts, occupies what was once the town house formerly belonging to R. Livingston Beekman, whose lineage includes two prominent New York families. Designed to reflect 18th-century French architecture of the Louis XV period, the house, crowned by a steep copper-covered mansard roof with two stories of dormers, maintains an air of dignity and monumentality, despite being hemmed in by two large apartment buildings.

Ulysses S. Grant bought the house at 3 East 66th St in 1881 with money raised by J. Pierpont Morgan and other wealthy men. Because he lost his military pension when he became president, a position without a pension, he was in dire financial circumstances. He invested most of his assets with a Wall Street firm in which his son

was partner. Ferdinand Ward, the other partner, defrauded the investors, and in 1884 the firm went bankrupt, as did Grant. In the same year he was diagnosed with throat cancer. Desperate to provide his wife and children with financial security, Grant started to write his war memoirs, which were published by a firm partly owned by his friend Mark Twain. Grant died in 1885, shortly after finishing the memoirs, which were both critically and financially successful.

The **Lotos Club** at 5 East 66th St is one of the oldest literary clubs in the country, founded in 1870. Mark Twain, who joined in 1873, called it the "The Ace of Clubs." The house was built in 1900 in the French Renaissance style as a wedding present for a granddaughter of William H. Vanderbilt. Architect Richard Howland Hunt was the son of Richard Morris Hunt, who earlier had built Vanderbilt houses along Fifth Avenue (now gone); in Newport, Rhode Island; and North Carolina.

Temple Emanu-El

1 East 65th St (Fifth Ave). Open every day 10–5 for meditation; www.emanuelnyc.org. Bernard Museum of Judaica open Sun–Thur 10–4:30; T: 212 744 1400, ext. 259.
Established in 1854, Temple Emanu-El is the oldest Reform Jewish congregation in New York. The building (1929; Robert D. Kohn, Charles Butler, and Clarence Stein) is the largest Jewish house of worship in the world.

Congregation Emanu-El was founded by 33 German immigrants, who came with a wave of Jews fleeing western Europe during the early decades of the 19th century. The group met first in a rented room on the Lower East Side, and moved northward as they become more prosperous—first to a former Methodist church on Chrystie St (still on the Lower East Side), then to a former Baptist church on West 12th St, then north to

Fifth Ave and 43rd St, where for the first time the congregation built its own building. Services were conducted in German until 1873, when the congregation hired its first English-speaking rabbi.

Congregation Emanu-El merged with Temple Beth-El in 1927, and two years later built the present imposing synagogue. Architecturally, the building incorporates Romanesque, Byzantine,

Circumcision knife (Italian, 18th century) and prayer book for the circumciser (German, 1744). From the collection of the Bernard Museum of Judaica, Congregation Emanu-El of the City of New York.

Photograph by Malcolm Varon.

Moorish, Gothic, Art Nouveau, and Art Deco architectural styles, drawing on the decorative motifs of synagogues of earlier eras and suggesting the mingling of Eastern and Western cultures. Symbols of the 12 tribes of Israel decorate the arch. The wheel window has at its center the six-pointed star or Star of David.

The sanctuary seats 2,500 people. In accordance with the Jewish restriction on visual images, sanctuary decorations are limited to a few traditional designs: the six-pointed Star of David seen in the mosaics and stained glass windows, the Lion of Judah, and the crown, a traditional Torah ornament. The mosaics are by Hildreth Meière.

In the **Beth-El Chapel**, set back from the avenue north of the main building, is a stained-glass window (over the ark) by Louis Comfort Tiffany, brought from Temple Emanu-El's earlier building at 43rd St and Fifth Ave.

MRS. ASTOR'S MANSION

The temple replaced the mansion of Mrs. Caroline Webster Schermerhorn Astor (wife of William Astor), also known as *the* Mrs. Astor, who dominated New York society in the closing years of the 19th century. Her mansion, designed by Richard Morris Hunt, resembled a French Renaissance château. It featured a two-ton bathtub cut from a single block of marble, and a ballroom, the capacity of which was said to correspond to the number of acceptable people in New York society, the "Four Hundred."

Brick and limestone

The 14-story apartment building at **834 Fifth Ave** and East 64th St (1931; Rosario Candela and James Carpenter), is considered one of the city's finest addresses. Candela, a Sicilian-born immigrant, became the most sought-after architect of luxury apartments during the 1920s and '30s. He arrived when he was 19, barely speaking English, and graduated from the Columbia School of Architecture three years later, in 1915. Not unaware of his talent, he is reputed to have roped off his drafting table at Columbia so the other students could not copy his work. The building is clad in limestone, decorated with a few Art Deco touches, and topped off with a 20-room triplex that once belonged to Laurance Rockefeller, son of John D. Rockefeller Jr. The apartment was sold in 2005 for $44 million.

The **former Edward Berwind mansion** at 2 East 64th St (1896; N.C. Mellen), a brick and limestone Italianate *palazzo*, has been converted to apartments. Berwind was at one time reputedly the largest owner of coal mines in the nation and for many years served as the chief executive officer of the IRT (Interborough Rapid Transit) subway line. Described as Prussian in appearance, and as dour, close-mouthed, and acquisitive in business dealings, he was apparently socially charming and belonged to about 40 clubs and societies.

At 3 East 64th St stands **New India House** (1903; Warren & Wetmore), home of the Indian Consulate and one of the few remaining buildings of modest scale designed by Warren & Wetmore, most famous for Grand Central Station. The house originally belonged to Mrs. Marshall Orme Wilson, neé Caroline Schermerhorn Astor, socialite daughter of the dowager Mrs. Astor (also named Caroline Schermerhorn Astor; *see box on previous page*). The mansion of molded limestone with a slate and copper roof, arched drawing-room windows, and small oval dormers, exemplifies the Beaux-Arts style.

The opulent house on the **corner of East 63rd St** (no. 2) was built for William Ziegler Jr. (1920; Sterner & Wolfe), heir to the Royal Baking Powder fortune. He lived there for only five years, perhaps because he and his first wife divorced. A proposal to convert it to a hospital for actors and actresses came to nothing (perhaps to the relief of the neighbors), and Norman B. Woolworth, a distant cousin of the founder of the five-and-dime chain, bought it in 1929. Woolworth donated it to the New York Academy of Science 20 years later. In 2005, the building was sold to a private individual for $31,250,000. (The Academy is now located at 7 World Trade Center.)

Although the majority of nearby buildings in the Eclectic style reflect French or Italian originals, the **Knickerbocker Club** at 2 East 62nd St (1915; Delano & Aldrich) recalls a town house of the Federal period, with fine brickwork, marble lintels, and wrought-iron window gratings. The club was founded downtown in 1871 by several members of the Union Club who felt that admission standards were becoming too lax.

At 1 East 60th St is the **Metropolitan Club**, in an imposing Italian Renaissance *palazzo* (1892–94; McKim, Mead & White). The club is another offshoot of the Union Club, founded (1891) for reasons quite different from those that gave birth to the Knickerbocker Club. J. Pierpont Morgan and other disgruntled members of the Union Club bolted after the board of governors blackballed John King, president of the Erie Railroad, whom Morgan had proposed for membership. One of the participants in the rejection allegedly remarked that Morgan's protégé had been voted down because, figuratively at least, he ate with his knife. Morgan is alleged to have called Stanford White into his presence and said, "Build a club fit for gentlemen. Damn the expense." The clubhouse, which set the members back about $2 million, is resplendent with marble walls, stained-glass windows, a coffered ceiling, and a grand staircase leading to a second-story loggia.

FIFTH AVENUE IN THE 70s
(NORTH OF THE FRICK)

Map p. 577, D4.

The former **home of Joseph Pulitzer** at 11 East 73rd St (1903) was modeled by McKim, Mead & White on two Venetian *palazzi*, with a wide façade, arched windows, and colonnades. It stood empty much of the time Pulitzer owned it, because the publisher's illness, near-blindness, and extreme sensitivity to sound made the house

unattractive to him, despite the fact that it had been provided with a special room with double walls, to minimize noise and vibrations.

The Commonwealth Fund, at 1 East 75th St, makes its headquarters in the **former Edward S. Harkness house** (1909). The house provides a remarkable example of the superb craftsmanship available at the turn of the century to those who could pay for it. Protected by a spiked iron fence and a "moat," the building, with its beautifully carved marble, resembles an Italian *palazzo*, elegantly detailed from the elaborate cornice to the iron ground-floor gates. The fund was started by Anna Harkness, wife of one of the original partners of Standard Oil, who was charged by her husband to "do something for the welfare of mankind"; it supports improvements to the health-care system, with particular regard to society's more vulnerable population.

A well-preserved patrician block

The **former James B. Duke mansion** at 1 East 78th St (1912) is now preserved as the New York University Institute of Fine Arts. Built of white limestone so fine that it looks like marble, the building was modeled after an 18th-century mansion in Bordeaux. James Buchanan ("Buck") Duke rose from humble beginnings on a North Carolina farm to dominate the tobacco industry, becoming president of the American Tobacco Co. in 1890 and maintaining his position of power even after the Supreme Court found his company in violation of the antitrust laws. The architect, Horace Trumbauer, was already known in Philadelphia for his grand houses; this is his first New York work, and perhaps the best of his urban mansions. Duke lived here until his death in 1925; his daughter, Doris Duke, and his widow donated the property to New York University in 1957.

The Cultural Services of the French Embassy, on Fifth Ave between 78th and 79th Sts (972 Fifth Ave) are located in the **former Payne Whitney House** (1906) by McKim, Mead & White, one of the earliest Italian Renaissance mansions north of 72nd St. It is notable for its gracefully curved and elaborately carved façade of light gray granite, a material not generally favored because of its extreme hardness. The house belonged first to Payne Whitney, philanthropist, financier, and aficionado of horse racing who kept stables in Kentucky and on Long Island. His estate was calculated at a quarter of a billion dollars. His elder brother married Gertrude Vanderbilt (*see p. 317*); his wife, Helen Hay Whitney, was a daughter of John Hay, secretary of state under Presidents William McKinley and Theodore Roosevelt. Their daughter, Joan Whitney Payson, was the principal owner of the New York Mets baseball team from its beginnings in 1962 until her death in 1975, and their son, John Hay (Jock) Whitney, was publisher of the *New York Herald Tribune* and ambassador to Great Britain. The **former Cook mansion** next door at 973 Fifth Ave (1902–05) is by McKim, Mead & White.

Looming up on the southeast corner of Fifth Ave and 79th St is the home of the **Ukrainian Institute of America**. The house (1899), designed by C.P.H. Gilbert for Isaac D. Fletcher, is a picturesque French Gothic mansion, with high slate roofs, pinnacled dormers, gargoyles, and a "moat" protected by an iron fence. It maintains a collection of contemporary Ukrainian art and mounts occasional exhibitions.

THE ISAAC D. FLETCHER HOUSE

Isaac D. Fletcher, a broker and banker, died in 1917, leaving his art collection and $3 million in stocks to the Metropolitan Museum. The collection included a *Head of Christ* attributed to Rembrandt or a pupil, several Corots, and Millet's *Autumn Landscape with a Flock of Turkeys*, as well as many minor works, including a picture of the Fletcher mansion and a portrait of Fletcher himself.

After Fletcher's death, the house was sold to Harry D. Sinclair, founder of the oil company that bore his name. Sinclair was implicated in the Teapot Dome scandal during the administration of President Warren G. Harding, and was indicted for bribery and conspiracy to defraud the government of lucrative oil leases. Sinclair spent six months in jail for contempt of court (he had hired a detective agency to shadow each of the jurors), and thereafter sold the house, his reputation but not his fortune in tatters.

The next owner was Augustus Van Horn Stuyvesant, who lived here with his sister Anne. The pair, both unmarried, had sold their town house on 57th St to move north, ahead of the onslaught of commerce. Augustus, the last direct male descendant of the irascible one-legged Dutch governor Peter Stuyvesant, was a successful real estate dealer. After Anne's death in 1938, Augustus spent his declining years in the house, eventually becoming a complete recluse, attended only by his butler and his footman.

THE WHITNEY MUSEUM
& ITS NEIGHBORHOOD

Map 577, D4. Subway: 6 to 77th St. Bus: M1, M2, M3, M4.

The Whitney Museum of American Art, known simply as "the Whitney," holds a special place in the New York art world as a museum devoted to contemporary American art. Since its inception in 1931, the museum has championed innovative work and unknown artists in accordance with the vision of its founder.

945 Madison Ave (East 75th St). Open Wed–Thur 11–6, Fri 1–9 (Fri 6pm–9pm pay-as-you wish), Sat–Sun 11–6; closed Mon–Tues, Thanksgiving, Christmas Day, New Year's Day; T: 1 800 WHITNEY (944 8639), or 212 570 3676; www.whitney.org.

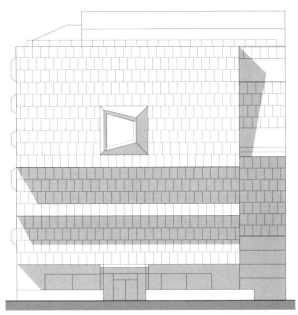

THE WHITNEY MUSEUM OF AMERICAN ART

Gertrude Vanderbilt Whitney and the history of the museum

Gertrude Vanderbilt (1875–1942), the great-granddaughter of Cornelius "Commodore" Vanderbilt, was heir to fortunes in both shipping and railroads. When she was 21, she married Harry Payne Whitney, whose own wealth rested on oil, tobacco, and banking. Though she could have lived a life of ease and self-indulgence, Mrs. Whitney established herself early as a sculptor and a patron of the arts.

Oil on canvas, 127 × 182.9 cm (50 × 72 in). Whitney Museum of American Art.

Robert Henri: *Gertrude Vanderbilt Whitney* (1916). Henri (1865–1929) was one of the artists whose career Whitney helped to further by her patronage.

In 1907 she opened a studio at 19 MacDougal Alley in Greenwich Village and began receiving public commissions for monumental sculpture. Surviving examples include a statue of Peter Stuyvesant in Stuyvesant Square (*map p. 581, E2*). She also began to buy work of radical painters including John Sloan and Robert Henri, who were working in her neighborhood, and organized shows of emerging artists. It was during this period that she met Juliana Rieser (later Juliana Force), an executive secretary and self-made woman who would become her lifelong associate in curatorial matters, ultimately serving as the founding president of the Whitney Museum.

At a time when European painting dominated American galleries, Mrs. Whitney took American art seriously and directed her patronage towards unrecognized artists whom she admired. In 1914 she opened the Whitney Studio gallery at 8 West Eighth St, in a Neoclassical row house adjacent to her studio (it is currently the home of The New York Studio School; *see p. 144*). Four years later she purchased neighboring properties and established the Whitney Studio Club, an exhibition gallery and gathering place for artists. The club also funded living quarters, studio space, and life-drawing sessions for artists who could not otherwise afford them. In 1929 she offered her collection to the Metropolitan Museum of Art, which turned down her offer.

When she opened the Whitney Museum in 1931, Mrs. Whitney had accumulated a collection of 500 works, including pieces by Edward Hopper, Stuart Davis, Reginald Marsh, George Bellows, Thomas Hart Benton, and Charles Sheeler. In 1954 the

museum moved to a new building next to the Museum of Modern Art, a move that vastly increased its attendance. Eventually overshadowed by MoMA and already in need of larger quarters, the Whitney opened its present building at Madison Avenue and 74th St in 1966.

Today the Whitney continues in its commitment to contemporary artists, showcasing new or recent works in its continuously rotating exhibits and famed (and often controversial) Biennials. While this dedication to new art brings unexpected delights to the visitor, it can be a mixed blessing for those hoping to find old favorites, since pieces from the museum's permanent collection are not always on display. While the first four floors are given over to temporary exhibitions, only the fifth floor and the mezzanine below show works from the museum's holdings, approximately one percent of the total at any given time.

The building

The museum's present building (1966) was designed by Marcel Breuer, one of the pioneers of Modernism. Born in Hungary, educated in part at the Bauhaus, Breuer joined the Harvard faculty in 1937 along with Walter Gropius, where the two of them influenced the next generation of American architects.

The building is sheathed in dark gray granite and overhangs a sunken sculpture court, which is spanned by a concrete bridge. The upper three floors are cantilevered outward, creating maximal gallery space and also throwing the sculpture court into shadow. The trapezoidal windows, irregularly spaced and sized, are angled so that light does not fall on the works of art within. Because the Whitney's philosophy emphasized changing exhibitions rather than showcasing a permanent collection, the interior spaces were arranged to provide flexibility. Three floors have large, open gallery spaces in which moveable wall panels can be arranged and rearranged for new shows.

At the time it was built, before the emergence first of SoHo and then Chelsea as hot spots for viewing contemporary art, the museum was squarely in the heart of the gallery district, a neighborhood with pleasant low-rise buildings and occasional taller post-war apartments. Intended to stand out, perhaps brazenly, from its neighbors, the building's architectural power was recognized immediately. "At the top of the list of must-be-seen objects in New York," noted the architect-authors of the *AIA Guide to New York City* (American Institute of Architects); *New York Times* critic Ada Louise Huxtable found it harshly handsome, a "disconcertingly top-heavy inverted pyramidal mass [that] grows on one slowly, like a taste for olives or warm beer." Some critics objected to its brutalism, but gradually the building has won widespread if occasionally grudging admiration. As the collection has increased, the Whitney has again outgrown its space, and for the past two decades has been seeking ways to expand, first at the present location, more recently in the Meatpacking District.

The collection

Gertrude Vanderbilt Whitney favored the work of then-revolutionary artists from the

Ashcan School, urban realists who included John Sloan, George Luks, and Everett Shinn. She was a friend of Arthur B. Davies and Robert Henri, the most influential members of The Eight (a group of American painters who together challenged the traditions of the National Academy), and bought four of the seven paintings sold at their initial show (in fact their only group exhibition) at the Macbeth Gallery in 1908. She collected works of American Regionalist painters John Steuart Curry and Thomas Hart Benton. Her initial gift also included works by Edward Hopper, whom she helped financially, exhibiting and purchasing his paintings. The widows of Edward Hopper and Reginald Marsh made substantial donations to the museum in recognition of the Whitney's continuing support of their art, and today the Whitney has unparalleled holdings in the works of both these artists. Mrs. Whitney also bought paintings by early Modernists, including Stuart Davis, Charles Demuth, and Charles Sheeler.

The museum has increased its collection by purchasing the work of artists shown in the Biennial exhibitions, which date back to 1932. Works by Arshile Gorky, Philip Guston, and Jasper Johns came from these shows. A group of wealthy collectors and benefactors acquired some significant works from the mid-20th century, particularly abstractions: Willem de Kooning's *Door to the River*, David Smith's *Lectern Sentinel*, and Franz Kline's *Mahoning*. A gift in the 1960s brought many sculptures to the collection, including those by Donald Judd, Claes Oldenburg, and Louise Nevelson. The Whitney owns the largest body of work by Alexander Calder of any museum; Calder's *Circus* remains a favorite among visitors. The museum has in-depth holdings of Marsden Hartley, Georgia O'Keeffe, Gaston Lachaise, and Agnes Martin. John Marin is well-represented by both oils and watercolors.

IN THE NEIGHBORHOOD

St. Jean Baptiste Church (1913; Nicholas Serracino), whose towered and domed silhouette anchors the intersection of Lexington Avenue and East 76th St (*map p. 577, E4*), was built to serve a Yorkville parish of French Canadian Catholics founded in 1882. Thomas Fortune Ryan, whose wealth derived from streetcars, tobacco investments, and eventually insurance (as well as some allegedly shady deals), funded the building. According to legend, Ryan arrived late for Mass one Sunday in 1910 and had to stand throughout the service; afterwards he asked the priest the cost of a new, more commodious church; the priest tossed off the figure of $300,000 without much reflection, and Ryan immediately offered to pay for the building, which turned out to cost twice the priest's guess.

Architectural historians have noted that around the turn of the 20th century American Catholics were searching for an architectural identity for their new churches; since the Gothic style had been pre-empted by the Protestants, Catholics experimented with Romanesque, Renaissance, and other styles. This church has Italian Renaissance precedents, especially in its soaring dome, open towers, and Corinthian portico.

THE ASIA SOCIETY & MUSEUM

Map p. 579, D1. 725 Park Ave (East 70th St). Open Tues–Sun 11–6, Fri until 9 (except July 4 through Labor Day); closed Mon, July 4, Thanksgiving, New Year's Day; T: 212 288 6400; www.asiasociety.org.

In 1951, John D. Rockefeller 3rd made a trip to Japan that awoke his interest in the Far East. One of the fruits of that trip is the Asia Society, which he founded five years later to deepen and enrich American understanding of Asian cultures—the arts, history, and contemporary affairs of a diverse group of peoples. Today the Society has become a global institution with offices elsewhere in the US and in Asia.

The New York branch of the society occupies a building (1981; Edward Larrabee Barnes Assocs) which was expanded and redesigned in 2001 (Voorsanger and Assocs). On the original Park Avenue façade, incised in the red Oklahoma granite, is the society's logo, a lion adapted from an 18th-century bronze Nepalese guardian lion. Buddhist temples in Asia are traditionally protected by images of fierce beasts at the four entrances, their ferocity symbolizing a defense against evil forces. The expansion doubled gallery space, adding a two-story garden court and connecting the floors of the building with a dramatic swooping staircase.

The collection

The society's exhibitions of Asian art are of the greatest interest. They range from ancient to contemporary art, and include work from private collections in Asia and the West, as well as masterpieces from the society's own permanent collection, the core of which was given by Mr. and Mrs. Rockefeller. The collection is small and personal in scale but of uniformly high quality, with pieces from Japan, Korea, China, India, and Southeast Asia. It includes Chinese bronze ritual vessels dating to the early 10th century BCE, and Ming Dynasty (early 15th century) ceramics including Ching-te-chen blue and white ware; Indian sculpture from the Kushan period (late 2nd–3rd centuries); manuscript pages from the Rajput School (16th–19th centuries in northern India); Buddhist sculptures from Thailand (7th–8th centuries), Indonesia (8th–12th centuries), and Burma (11th–15th centuries); and Japanese woodcuts and ceramics, ranging from the Jomon period (c. 10,500–300 BCE), through 16th-century stoneware, to elegant porcelains of the Edo period (1615–1867).

DOMESTIC ARCHITECTURE ON EAST 70TH STREET

The rich and/or famous began moving east of Fifth Avenue around the turn of the 20th century, building town houses on this quiet and much-admired street. Some not-for-profit organizations have moved into former residences, but the houses that remain residences still draw the rich and/or famous, selling (at the time of writing) in the $20-million range.

The **Explorers' Club** (46 East 70th St, near Park Ave), founded in 1904, includes on its roster famous explorers past and present: Sir Edmund Hillary, Tenzing Norgay, Neil

Armstrong, and Reinhold Messner. The club (*not open to the public except for occasional lectures*) owns rare books, manuscripts, and paintings of historical value as well as memorabilia of famous explorers. The building (1912; Frederick J. Sterner) was originally the home of Stephen C. Clark, younger son of Singer Sewing Machine magnate Edward Clark, who built the Dakota Apartments.

The **Visiting Nurse Service of New York** (107 East 70th St) occupies the former Thomas W. Lamont residence (1921; Walker & Gillette), a grandiose Tudor Revival home with leaded-glass windows and a heavy, detailed wooden door. Lamont was chairman of the board of J.P. Morgan & Company and worked to protect American financial interests abroad during the 1920s and '30s.

The neo-Georgian house at **118 East 70th St**, with its attractive fanlight and side-lights, was designed (1900) by Trowbridge & Livingston, who also built (1903) the Beaux-Arts town house across the street (123 East 70th St) for architect Samuel Trowbridge himself. The undistinguished modern house at **124 East 70th St** was built in 1941 for Edward A. Norman, an heir to the Sears, Roebuck fortune. Architect William Lescaze, who earlier had built his own, more successful, town house on East 48th St (*see p. 276*), was one of the pioneers of the International Style in New York.

The **former Paul Mellon House** (125 East 70th St), built for the philanthropist, art collector, and horse breeder, is one of the few town houses built after World War II (1965; H. Page Cross). It is neo-French Provincial in style and remarkable for its 40-ft width (two town houses were torn down to make way for it) and its garden.

China Institute and Gallery

The China Institute in America (*map p. 579, E1; 125 East 65th St. Gallery open daily 10–5; closed holidays and between exhibitions; T: 212 744 8181; www.chinainstitute.org*) is a non-political, non-profit organization (founded 1926) by American educational philosopher John Dewey and Chinese educator Hu Shih (who later became the Chinese ambassador to the United States). The institute promotes the understanding of traditional and contemporary Chinese culture, and offers language courses and workshops for travelers headed for China and for business people interested in understanding Chinese business culture. There are classes in painting, calligraphy, and tai-jiquan (tai chi), and an exhibition program.

In 1944 the building, designed by Charles A. Platt in 1905, was given to the Institute by the Henry R. Luce Foundation in memory of Luce's father, who had been a missionary to China where Luce, who became editor of *Time* magazine, was born. The building served as a gathering place for the almost 2,000 Chinese students stranded in the United States by World War II. China House Gallery presents high-quality, wide-ranging exhibits of Chinese art, from Neolithic to modern.

PARK AVENUE IN THE 60s

The **Union Club** (1932; Delano & Aldrich; 101 East 69th St at Park Ave) is the city's

oldest social club, dating back to 1836. The architects were best known for their red-brick Georgian-style designs, which inform the Knickerbocker Club (*see p. 314*), the Colony Club (for women, on Park Avenue at East 62nd St), and the former Willard Straight house (1130 Fifth Ave), so this imposing limestone-clad building with its big mansard roof is a departure from their usual style. When the club chose not to expel its Confederate supporters during the Civil War, some members, offended, resigned and formed the Union League Club, now on Park Avenue at East 38th St.

Occupying the west side of the block of Park Avenue between East 68th and East 69th Sts is a stylistically related group of houses built in the years after the turn of the 20th century, when the railroad tracks beneath Park Avenue were covered over. In 1965 a developer wanted to demolish three of them for an apartment building, but Margaret Rockefeller Strong de Larraín, Marquesa de Cuevas, a granddaughter of John D. Rockefeller, bought the endangered houses and turned them over to their present owners, most of them cultural institutes.

The present **Consulate General of Italy** occupies the second house built on this block front (1917; Walker & Gillette; 690 Park Ave at East 69th St), formerly the home of Henry P. Davison and his wife. Davison was a banker and partner in J.P. Morgan & Company. The Italian Cultural Institute at 686 Park Ave and East 68th–69th Sts (*T: 212 879 4242; www.iicnewyork.esteri.it*) occupies the one-time home of William Sloane and his wife. Sloane was the president of the formerly top-drawer W. & J. Sloane furniture company. The firm of Delano & Aldrich designed the house in 1919, in the Colonial Revival style preferred by many of their clients. The neo-Federal town house at 684 Park Ave (1926) was built by McKim, Mead & White for Percy Pyne's daughter on land that was formerly the garden of Pyne's house. Like several of his neighbors, Percy Pyne was a financier and philanthropist. The building is now home to the Queen Sofía Spanish Institute for Spanish and Latin-American culture (*T: 212 628 0420; www.spanishinstitute.org*).

The **Percy and Maud H. Pyne House** at 680 Park Ave at East 68th St (*gallery open Tues–Sun 12–6; T: 212 249 8950; www.americas-society.org*), the earliest of the brick town houses on this block (1912; McKim, Mead & White), is now the Americas Society, whose mission is to educate the people of the United States about the cultures, societies, and art of its Western Hemisphere neighbors. Since 1967, the Americas Society Art Gallery has presented exhibitions of the art of Latin America, Canada, and the Caribbean, from pre-Columbian times to the present.

The red-brick former **Seventh Regiment Armory** (1880; Charles W. Clinton) fills the entire block of Park to Lexington Aves (East 66th to 67th Sts) with its machicolated bulk. Inside are a huge drill hall (187ft by 290ft) and private rooms decorated by Louis C. Tiffany and Stanford White, among others. The armory was built with private funds raised by the National Guardsmen themselves, a socially prominent and well-heeled group, nicknamed the "silk-stocking regiment." Their social status gave them access to John Jacob Astor and William H. Vanderbilt and their peers, who donated generously after expected city funds totaling $350,000 didn't materialize. Architect Clinton was a regiment veteran. The armory now hosts antiques shows and other large-scale events.

Sara Delano Roosevelt Memorial House

This double house at 47–49 East 65th St, Park and Madison Aves (*map p. 579, D1*) was commissioned (1908; Charles A. Platt;) by Sara Delano Roosevelt as a Christmas gift, half for herself and the other half for her son Franklin and his bride Eleanor (a layout not mentioned in the letter describing the gift). Not only do the two halves share a front entrance, but they are connected by interior doors, something any bride might not look upon with pleasure, especially Eleanor, whose mother-in-law wanted to continue dominating her only child's life.

When FDR was struck by polio he recuperated here, close to the centers of political power, a decision Eleanor supported. Since Sara had wished her son to retire from politics and live the life of a country gentleman at Hyde Park, the family estate, Eleanor's support for Franklin's political career, and her rejection of Sara's wishes, started the couple on the political partnership they ultimately shared. The house is now owned by Hunter College, part of the City University of New York.

Museum of American Illustration

The Museum of American Illustration (*128 East 63rd St, Park and Lexington Aves; map p. 579, E2. Open Tues 10–8, Wed–Fri 10–5, Sat noon–4; closed Sun, Mon, month of Aug, legal holidays. Free. T: 212 838 2560; www.societyillustrators.org*), located in an 1875 carriage house, is the exhibition space for the Society of Illustrators and offers changing exhibitions designed to encourage interest in the art of illustration.

The society dates back to 1901, when its monthly dinners attracted such famous artists as Maxfield Parrish, Frederic Remington, and N.C. Wyeth. The museum, however, dates from 1981 and now has a collection of about 2,500 works. Exhibitions include solo and group shows, historical and thematic exhibitions, and the Illustrators' Annual Exhibition which showcases the best book, editorial, advertising, and institutional illustrations of the year.

Bloomingdale's

Bloomingdale's (*Lexington to Third Aves, East 59th to East 60th Sts; map p. 579, E2*), the mid- to upscale department store, now has branches across the United States, but its New York flagship is *the* Bloomingdale's. It is known as "Bloomies" to its habitués, who can be seen toting its trademark "Small," "Medium," and "Big" brown bags around the city.

Lyman Bloomingdale, who with his brother Joseph founded the store in 1872, learned the retail business as a clerk in Bettlebeck & Co. Dry Goods in Newark, N.J., a firm with an all-star sales staff that also included Benjamin Altman (later of B. Altman & Co.; *see p. 211*) and Abraham Abraham (later of Abraham and Straus). Unlike the other 19th-century department stores, which began downtown and migrated uptown, Bloomingdale's started at 938 Third Ave, only a few blocks from its present location. In both its arrival and its demise, the Third Avenue elevated railway was a blessing to Bloomingdale's, first bringing so many shoppers from downtown when it opened (1879) that within seven years the store had to move to larger

quarters on the northwest corner of Third Ave and 59th St, a block it now completely occupies. Then, when the El was torn down (1954), the Upper East Side, its real estate formerly depressed by the dark and dirty railway, began a swift climb to respectability and affluence. Fortunately Bloomingdale's management had already begun upgrading the inventory from its former good-quality-but-sensible merchandise to more stylish gear. In the 1970s, Bloomingdale's was a destination, so much so that Queen Elizabeth visited in 1976, and though its star may have faded somewhat, it remains an iconic store, known worldwide.

SHOPPING IN THE NEIGHBORHOOD

The Upper East Side, one of Manhattan's wealthiest neighborhoods, was built up in the early decades of the 20th century by the well-to-do and has remained their territory for a century. In its most elite commercial precincts—Madison Avenue between about 57th and 86th Sts, the shopping opportunities are commensurate with the general economic scale.

Flagship boutiques of European and American designers, and shops glittering with all kinds of luxury goods line Madison Avenue. Here you can buy French crystal, Italian shoes, Chinese export porcelains, American leather handbags, and Swiss watches. You can eat hand-made chocolates, buttery pastries, and perfectly ripened cheese. You can have your nails done, your shoes fixed and your clothes dry-cleaned, and your hair styled. You can resell your wedding dress, or buy a designer gown that belonged to someone else. You can also buy more ordinary things, but that is not what this patch of pavement is known for.

Both Madison Avenue and East 57th St have many art galleries, whose shows are sometimes of museum quality. In general the uptown galleries are traditional rather than cutting edge, though there are always surprises. Saturday is the conventional gallery-hopping day. Stores usually open Mon–Sat 10–6. Some stay open late on Thur and are open on Sun. Many art galleries are closed Mon and have restricted summer hours.

THE METROPOLITAN MUSEUM OF ART

Map p. 577, D3. Subway: 4, 5 or 6 to 86th St. Bus: M1, M2, M3, or M4. Open Tues–Thur and Sun 9:30–5:30, Fri and Sat 9:30–9pm. Closed Mon except Mon federal holidays (Martin Luther King Jr. Day, Presidents' Day, Memorial Day, Independence Day, Labor Day, Columbus Day); closed New Year's Day, Thanksgiving, Christmas Day. Suggested donation. T: 212 535 7710; www.metmuseum.org. NB: At the time of writing a number of galleries were closed for renovation. Visitors wishing to see particular collections should phone or check the website before their visit.

The Metropolitan Museum of Art, generally called simply The Met, is the largest, most comprehensive art museum in the world. The building occupies 1.5 million square feet (roughly 31 times the size of an American football field or 47 times the footprint of Westminster Abbey) and its collections include more than two million objects, whose range includes the whole world and the entire sweep of human civilization. Every year more than five million people visit.

There is far too much to see in a single visit; even two or three won't suffice to see everything of interest in the vast collections. If this is your first time, you might enjoy the guided Highlights Tour, which departs from the Tour Kiosk in the Great Hall. Otherwise it is probably wise to confine yourself to a few departments.

The building

The museum building has grown from modest Ruskinian Gothic beginnings to its present size and complexity, with additions reflecting the reigning architectural styles of the past century. The original building (1874–80; Calvert Vaux and Jacob Wrey Mould) faced Central Park; its brick and limestone walls are visible from the Lehman Wing and European Sculpture Court. Richard Morris Hunt designed the central Fifth Avenue façade (1902); the north and south wings (1911 and 1913) are by McKim, Mead & White. The uncarved blocks above the columns of Hunt's façade were to have allegorical groups representing major periods in the history of art, but funds never materialized.

During the 1970s and '80s Roche, Dinkeloo and Associates redesigned the Fifth Avenue stairs and added glass-walled wings on the other façades: the Lehman Wing (1975) to the rear, the Sackler Wing (1979) to the north and the Rockefeller Wing (1982) to the south. Conservationists criticized the expansion, echoing sentiments of park designer Frederick Law Olmsted, who regretted allowing the museum a toehold in his territory. More recently the museum has refined its interior spaces, for example filling former courtyards with gallery space and reclaiming the former restaurant for the new galleries of Roman and Hellenistic art, which opened in 2007.

The grand staircase from Fifth Avenue leads into the Great Hall, with imposing floral displays, and, often, formidable crowds, which are thinnest just after opening, and grow steadily through the morning and early afternoon.

THE VIRTUAL MET

The Met has an outstanding website, which you can use both to plan your visit and to deepen your understanding of what you have seen. The site includes images and detailed discussions of a great many objects in the collection (including 2,200 works of art in the department of European paintings), and a useful timeline of art history with links to thematic essays. You can browse recent acquisitions, or listen to audio files of curators and artists talking about exhibitions or works in the collection, and to recordings of musical instruments from the collection being played.

GREEK & ROMAN ART

The collection of Greek and Roman art and antiquities spans several millennia, several civilizations, and several thousand miles—from the Bronze Age cultures of the Aegean to the farthest-flung colonies of the Roman Empire. The earliest pieces come from the Cycladic civilizations of the 2nd and 3rd millennia BC, and the most recent from the Roman Empire at the time of Constantine (emperor AD 306–37), whose conversion to Christianity marked a turning point in the history of the ancient world.

In 2007 the museum completed a 15-year renovation of the galleries for Greek, Hellenistic, Roman, and Etruscan art. The central focus of the new installation is a two-story peristyle court, originally designed by McKim, Mead & White to hold Classical art but which long languished as a cafeteria and restaurant. The glass roof above the barrel-vaulted gallery was uncovered during the renovation, and natural light now floods the statuary.

Greek art

(1) Central Gallery (Greek Art, 6th–4th centuries BC): This gallery, one of the city's great interior spaces, is now used for displaying large-scale sculpture and vases. Here are examples of Athenian prize amphorae, large vases which were filled with olive oil and presented to the victors in athletic contests held to honor Athena, patron goddess of Athens. The athletic event is pictured on one side of the vase; on the other is an image of the goddess. In the center of the gallery are large-scale Roman marble copies of bronzes made in Greece during the 5th–4th centuries BC. Except for temple decorations, votive *kouroi* and grave reliefs, most Greek sculpture was executed in bronze; very few of these sculptures have survived except in later marble copies, many made by admiring Roman sculptors. Marble is a less tensile material than bronze, and it is often possible to tell a copy by its strategically placed support, in the form of a tree trunk, column or urn. Among the finer works in the Met's collection are a Roman marble copy of a

METROPOLITAN MUSEUM
(FIRST FLOOR)

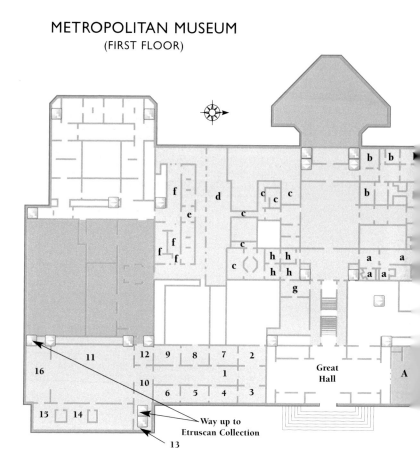

statue of the Greek warrior Protesilaos, the first Greek to set foot on Trojan soil at the beginning of the war; and a *Wounded Amazon* (c. 450–425 BC), whose serene classic face betrays no pain. The *Diadoumenos*, (1st century AD) depicts a young man tying a fillet around his head after an athletic victory; this is a Roman copy of a Greek bronze original believed to be by Polyclitus.

(2–3) Belfer Court: These rooms display the earliest works in the collection.

The western room (2) contains Neolithic and Cycladic marble sculptures, monumental vases from the Geometric period (1050–700 BC), and small-scale bronzes. Notable are a marble Cycladic statuette of a seated harp player (c. 2800–2700 BC), and a small bronze group of a man engaged in combat with a centaur. Mycenaean pottery includes a stirrup jar (12th century BC) decorated with fish and an octopus (a common pattern for such jars),

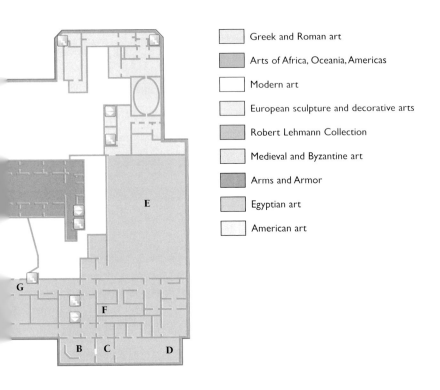

Greek and Roman art

Arts of Africa, Oceania, Americas

Modern art

European sculpture and decorative arts

Robert Lehmann Collection

Medieval and Byzantine art

Arms and Armor

Egyptian art

American art

whose tentacles surround the swelling body of the jar. Traders probably used such vessels for transporting oil or wine.

The eastern gallery (3) documents the art of Archaic Greece (c. 700–480 BC). Here are works in stone, bronze, terra cotta, and gold. Included are an ivory plaque (c. 650–600 BC) of two women driven insane by Dionysus, whom they have offended; in their madness they have unpinned their gar-

ments. Also on display are beautifully decorated pieces of bronze armor from Crete.

(4) Greek Art, 6th century BC: Outstanding is a fine marble *kouros* or nude male figure, the earliest Greek marble statue in the museum, which dates from the end of 7th century BC. The traditional appearance of the *kouros*—frontal pose, left foot slightly forward, blocky form, stylized wiglike hair—shows the influence of Egyptian art. Also in this

METROPOLITAN MUSEUM
(SECOND FLOOR)

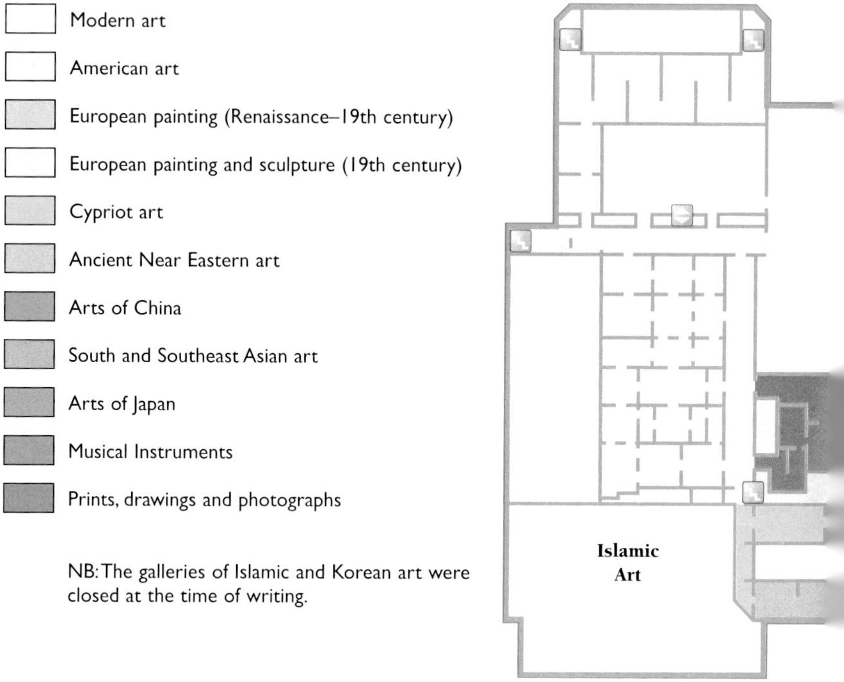

Modern art

American art

European painting (Renaissance–19th century)

European painting and sculpture (19th century)

Cypriot art

Ancient Near Eastern art

Arts of China

South and Southeast Asian art

Arts of Japan

Musical Instruments

Prints, drawings and photographs

NB: The galleries of Islamic and Korean art were closed at the time of writing.

Islamic Art

gallery are funerary monuments including a grave stele from the Archaic period (c. 540 BC) showing a boy and girl in low relief guarded by a sphinx; it was erected by a father who lost his son, here shown as an athlete with an oil bottle (*aryballos*) strapped to his wrist.

(5) Greek Art, 5th century BC: Here are displayed ceramics and grave markers from the time when Athens became dominant in the arts. The most famous relief here, *Girl with Doves*, conveys the idealized beauty and sweetness of the child, although the figure of the girl has been made more mature; actual children or old people do not appear in Greek sculpture until much later. There is also a fine family monument (c. 360 BC) with a group of three adult figures and a child and a partial figure of a woman facing them. Since the accompanying inscription has been lost, it is unclear who has died and who is mourning.

(6) Greek Art, 4th century BC: A collection of Macedonian jewelry, as well as lively terra-cotta statuettes (known as *Tanagra* figures from the town of Tanagra in central Greece, where they were

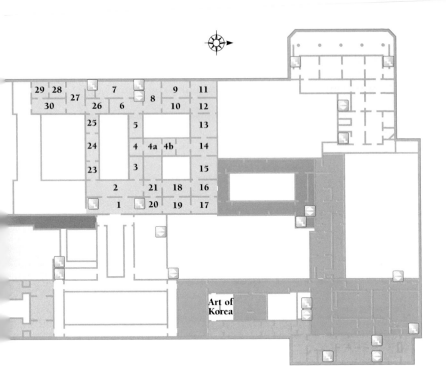

made) that represent fashionable women. They were almost certainly secular, not votive, pieces, probably used as ornaments.

(7–9) Greek vase-painting, 6th–early 4th centuries BC): Greek vases of the 6th century BC include much fine black-figure ware, a style of pottery that evolved in Athens, placing the human figure and narrative at the center of the decorative scheme. The figures are black (often decorated with red) against a natural, clay-colored ground. Details were incised into the black glaze. It is at this period that we first begin to learn the names of some of the artists. Lydos, for example, one of the leading painters in this style, is credited with an imposing krater (a mixing bowl for wine and water) whose decoration shows *The Return of Hephaistos*, a procession with Hephaistos, satyrs, maenads, and Dionysus. The neck amphora (storage jar) from c. 540 BC with a wedding procession with a chariot is attributed to the famous painter Exekias (who was also his own potter).

From about 530 BC, the red-figure style came into its own. Figures were drawn in

black outline and the spaces between them filled with a black slurry. After firing, the figures showed up red, and details could be added with a paintbrush, a technique which offered more expressive possibilities than incision. An early example of the style is a vase painted with Heracles and Apollo in the struggle over the Delphic tripod, attributed to the Andokides painter. Other fine pieces from this period include an amphora by the Berlin Painter (c. 490 BC) showing a youth singing and playing the kithara, and a plate painted by Epiktetos depicting a boy on a rooster, an unusual subject.

Fifth- and early 4th-century pieces include *lekythoi* (vases for pouring libations), typically painted with scenes of farewell.

Roman and Hellenistic art

(10) Sardis Gallery: The Sardis column is a gracefully scrolled Ionic capital with parts of a deeply fluted column from the Temple of Artemis in Sardis (capital of ancient Lydia, near modern Izmir in Turkey), found during excavations in 1911–14 and dating from the 4th century BC. Nearby is an idealized marble head of a Ptolemaic queen (3rd century BC), member of a royal family of Macedonian Greeks who ruled Egypt from the death of Alexander the Great (323 BC) until Rome annexed Egypt in 30 BC after defeating Cleopatra.

(11) Atrium: This is the centerpiece of the recent re-installation of Hellenistic and Roman art. In the center are Roman sculptures from the 1st century BC. The *Old Market Woman* portrays a recognizable person in an ordinary situation—an old woman bent by age, carrying her chickens and produce to market. Two Roman statues of Hercules depict him as a muscular youth and as a mature man, bearded and garbed in his familiar lion skin.

Portrait heads, arrayed chronologically along the east wall of the court, include emperors, whose depictions reveal traditions in portraiture as well as individual characteristics; they include Augustus (idealized, dignified), Caligula (proud), Antoninus Pius (benign, philosophical), and Caracalla (scowling). Among the sarcophagi are the Marble Garland sarcophagus (c. AD 200–25), the first object offered to and accepted by the Met (1870). Much more elaborate is the Badminton sarcophagus, carved from a single block of marble and lavishly decorated with a procession of Dionysus and his support group of satyrs and maenads and four winged figures representing the Four Seasons. It is named after Badminton House in England, which it adorned after the Duke of Beaufort bought it (1728).

(12) Greek art from southern Italy, 4th–1st centuries BC: Painted vases and other objects attest to the connections between the Greek mainland and her colonies in south Italy (*Magna Graecia*). A calyx-krater from c. 400–390 BC shows three comic actors performing in a play.

(13) Hellenistic Treasury: Among the small, luxurious objects here is a stunning pair of gold armbands (c. 200 BC) with male and female tritons, each holding a tiny figure of Eros. Also in this room is a much-admired dark bronze

statuette of a veiled and masked dancer (3rd–2nd century BC), whose fluted drapery and rhythmic pose convey the motion of the dance.

(14) Roman wall paintings: The Met has the finest collection of Roman wall paintings outside Italy. The three panels from Boscoreale, the luxurious country villa of a wealthy Roman named P. Fannius Synistor, are probably intended to celebrate a dynastic marriage. The panels were painted in about 40–30 BC and were preserved by the eruption of Vesuvius in AD 79; the fact that they were not painted over as styles changed during the intervening century suggests an early recognition of their high quality.

In the next room are frescoes from a bedroom (*cubiculum*) at Boscoreale, decorated with *trompe l'oeil* architectural vistas. The twisted mullions of the metal window frame, warped by the heat of the eruption, give a sense of the power of the cataclysmic event. The paintings in the Boscotrecase Bedroom came from a villa built by Agrippa (friend of the emperor Augustus and commander of the fleet which defeated Antony and Cleopatra), and were painted by artists of the imperial household. They depict ornamental landscapes and mythological scenes. Their dark, greenish background brought a sense of coolness to the bedroom.

(15) Roman Imperial art, 1st century AD: Here are luxurious objects from Augustan Rome, including cast and mold-blown glass. A sardonyx cameo, only an inch and a half in height, shows the emperor Augustus, outfitted as a semi-divine being, crowned with a laurel wreath. Also here are busts, pottery, and an elaborate bed or couch.

(16) Art of the later Roman Empire, 3rd century AD: This period was marked by political upheaval and an increasing distance between the wealthy elite and ordinary citizens. The gallery contains portraits of two emperors. The larger-than-life nude bronze portrait statue of Trebonianus Gallus, his brow lined with anxiety, his torso grotesquely thickened, dates from AD 251–53. A similarly anxious expression, typical of portraits of the 3rd century AD, strains the features of the irascible emperor Caracalla. Considering the rapid turnover of 3rd-century Roman emperors and the fates of these two, both murdered, their anxiety seems well-founded. In the corner of the room, the blocky, colossal head of Constantine (c. 325) with its uplifted eyes, possibly to indicate the spirituality of the emperor who first embraced Christianity, shows a further movement away from naturalism and back towards the idealization of the Augustan age.

Etruscan art (mezzanine level)

Overlooking the skylit court is a mezzanine (access marked on the plan) containing the Study Collection and Etruscan Art. The Etruscans, who controlled central Italy west of the Apennines from the Arno Valley to the Tiber delta, reached the height of their power in the 6th century BC. Etruscan skill in metalwork is apparent in this gallery, whose most spectacular object is a reconstructed bronze chariot (late 6th century BC), found in a tomb near Spoleto. Its repoussé reliefs illustrate episodes from the life of the Greek hero Achilles. By the 6th century the Etruscans no longer used chariots to wage war, so this vehicle was probably used ceremonially. The Etruscan

collection also contains gems, notably the Morgan amber, a five-inch chunk of amber carved to depict a reclining man and woman. One of the most important pieces of pre-Roman amber, it came to the museum through the bequest of J. Pierpont Morgan. Nearby are bronze mirrors, tripods, cauldrons, pails, and other utilitarian objects, as well as examples of Etruscan pottery and a fine display of jewelry.

THE ARTS OF AFRICA, OCEANIA, & THE AMERICAS

The architecturally dramatic Michael C. Rockefeller Wing (1982; Roche, Dinkeloo and Associates) was given by former New York State governor Nelson A. Rockefeller in memory of his son Michael, who died in a rafting accident (1961) while on a collecting expedition in Papua New Guinea. It houses the collection of the former Museum of Primitive Art, privately founded by Nelson Rockefeller, as well as his own personal collection, supplemented by gifts and other museum acquisitions.

African art: The two galleries devoted to African art offer beautiful wooden sculptures from Western, Central, and Equatorial African cultures. In the section devoted to the Guinea Coast is an extraordinary early 16th-century ivory pendant mask and a collection of bronze and brass objects from the Court of Benin (Nigeria).

Art of the Americas: The galleries devoted to art of the Americas offer ferocious Aztec and Toltec stone sculptures and ceramics from several cultures. Olmec artifacts include jade ornaments, and a "baby" figure, possibly representing a god. The 6th-century Seated Figure is one of the few Maya wooden objects that have survived time, moisture, and infestation. In the Treasury are pre-Columbian and later objects of gold and silver, including nose and ear ornaments, vessels, and pendants.

Arts of Oceania and Native American art: Highlights of this collection are an impressive group of objects from New Guinea, including nine tall Asmat memorial poles, reclining two-headed ancestor poles, and a remarkable 48-ft

H. 13⅜ in (34cm). The Michael C. Rockefeller Memorial Collection.

Olmec "baby" figure from Mexico (12th–9th century BC). Ceramic, cinnabar, red ocher.

Asmat canoe capable of carrying up to 20 people. A new gallery is devoted to the arts of peoples of Island Southeast Asia; others display Native American Art, from Arctic ivory carvings to archaeological objects from the Mississippian era (Lower Carboniferous; c. 300 million years ago).

MODERN ART

The Metropolitan awakened to the 20th century rather late, establishing a department of 20th-century art only in 1967, although earlier gifts, for example Georgia O'Keeffe's bequest from the estate of Alfred Stieglitz, had nudged the museum toward modernity. The collection includes paintings and sculpture by major European figures, but its strength lies in American art, particularly The Eight, the Alfred Stieglitz circle, and the Abstract Expressionists, groups which had strong ties to New York City.

The first-floor galleries are arranged in a square, with a special exhibitions gallery and a design gallery. The exhibit continues upstairs to the mezzanine (large-scale works and temporary exhibitions), the second floor, and finally the roof, which is used for exhibits of large-scale sculpture during warm weather. Also on the roof is a café with beverage and sandwich service (*open May–Oct 10am until closing, including Fri and Sat evenings*). Along with the sandwiches come wonderful views of the skyline and Central Park.

First floor

Rooms 1–4: Works by European painters at the turn of the 20th century, including Bonnard, Utrillo, Kandinsky, and Vuillard. The second room has Pablo Picasso's *Portrait of Gertrude Stein* (1906), painted when the artist was 24 and Stein was 32. When someone told Picasso that Stein did not look like her portrait, he replied, "She will." Henri Matisse's *Nasturtiums with the Painting "Dance"* (1912) includes *Dance* leaning against the wall in Matisse's studio; one version of *Dance* belongs to the Museum of Modern Art (*see p. 266*). In the third room is Balthus's *The Mountain* (1936), a monumental early painting, as well as work by the seminal Metaphysical artist Giorgio de Chirico and the Surrealist Joan Miró.

Sculpture in the fourth gallery includes work by Umberto Boccioni and Constantin Brancusi's *Bird in Space* (1923), a marble abstraction intended, according to the sculptor, "to catch the essence of flight."

Rooms 5–8: In 1998 the Met inherited the collection of Jacques and Natasha Gelman (he produced the immensely successful films starring Cantinflas). In the first gallery are Fauve artists, including André Derain and Maurice de Vlaminck. In the second, paintings illustrate developments in Cubism between 1911 and 1924. The next section is devoted to Modigliani, Braque, and Bonnard, including Braque's *Still Life with a Guitar* (1924) and two paintings by Bonnard featuring Marthe Boursin (later his wife): *After the Morning Bath* (1910) and *The Dining Room at Vernonnet* (1916). The section on Surrealism includes works by two important Catalans: Salvador Dalí's *Accommodations of Desire* (1929) and paintings by Joan Miró, including *The Potato* (1928), in which a gigantic white woman casts her arms across a blue sky, a brown potato with three roots growing in the center of her forehead.

Rooms 9–12: The rooms beyond the Gelman Collection are dedicated to

American 20th-century painting, with a rotating selection of favorite works. Thomas Hart Benton, *July Hay* (1943) and Grant Wood, *The Midnight Ride of Paul Revere* (1931) are outstanding examples of American Regionalism. Edward Hopper's *Tables for Ladies* (1930) depicts a waitress and cashier in solitude, one of Hopper's frequent themes. Also on view are works by Georgia O'Keeffe, Milton Avery, George Bellows, Florine Stettheimer, and Lyonel Feininger. Members of The Eight shown here include John Sloan and William Glackens.

Second floor

The second-floor galleries contain works by American (and a few European) painters working after World War II. To see the galleries more or less chronologically, begin at the east end near the entrance from 19th-century paintings and sculpture.

The Lila Acheson Wallace Gallery, its windows overlooking the park, is dominated by Max Beckmann's autobiographical and fantastic triptych *Beginning* (1949), and Chilean painter Roberto Matta's enormous mural-size canvas *Being With (Être Avec)*, painted in 1946 while he was living in New York. Further along are works by Alexander Calder, Robert Motherwell, Arshile Gorky, and William Baziotes, as well as Willem de Kooning's garishly colored *Woman* (1944).

Dominating the next section is *Autumn Rhythm (Number 30)* (1950) by Jackson Pollock; dribbled, splashed, and poured, it is considered a masterpiece from his most important period, admired for its balance of control and spontaneity. His earlier *Pasiphaë* (1943) was originally entitled *Moby-Dick*, but the name was changed when James Johnson Sweeney (an art critic and onetime head of the Guggenheim) saw in it the iconography of the Minotaur story (Pasiphaë, wife of King Minos, became mother to the Minotaur after consummating her passion for a bull).

The Color Field painters are well represented, with work by Clyfford Still, Mark Rothko, Hans Hofmann, and Barnett Newman. David Smith's large-scale stainless steel *Becca* (1965) exemplifies his late work. Jasper Johns is represented by *White Flag*, (1955), the largest of his flag paintings and the first one painted monochromatically. Here also are Ellsworth Kelly's large, hard-edged color paintings, as well as Morris Louis's soft-edged stripes, Andy Warhol's multiple images of Jacqueline Kennedy, and Roy Lichtenstein's iconic *Stepping Out* (1978).

EUROPEAN SCULPTURE & DECORATIVE ARTS

The Metropolitan's collections, more than 50,000 objects strong, contain sculpture from the Renaissance to 1900, and a rich variety of ceramics, glass, metalwork and jewelry, woodwork and furniture, tapestries, textiles, clocks, and mathematical instruments. The galleries are organized geographically and chronologically to show the development of these arts throughout Europe, but there are so many objects on display in so many galleries that the collection can be overwhelming. Ceramics, clocks, goldsmiths' work, and other small objects are usually shown in changing exhibitions, as are fragile works, including textiles.

(a) Italian decorative arts: The display of Italian decorative arts begins just to the north of the Medieval Galleries. Period rooms in this section include the small *studiolo* from the Ducal Palace in Gubbio, a room for study and inspiration. It dates from c. 1479–82 and belonged to Duke Federico da Montefeltro, whose intellectual interests decorate the *trompe l'oeil* "cabinets," executed in wood inlay. The Farnese table, a monumental marble piece inlaid with alabaster and semi-precious stones, was made for a powerful papal family. A corridor gallery with two gondola prows from Venice serves as an antechamber to the bedroom from Palazzo Sagredo, an 18th-century palace that overlooked the Grand Canal. Such niceties as the ceiling painting and the 32 fluttering stucco cupids were created for more eyes than those of the home owner, since it was a custom of the time to receive formal visits in bed.

(b) English decorative arts and period rooms, 17th–18th centuries: English furniture and decorative arts of the 17th and 18th centuries are displayed in a group of ten galleries and period rooms. The rooms include the dining room from Lansdowne House (1768), London, decorated by Robert Adam; the Tapestry Room from Croome Court (1760), near Worcester, with remarkable Gobelins tapestries; and the dining room from Kirtlington Park (c. 1748), north of Oxford, notable for its carved wood doors and Rococo plaster decoration. Another room is dominated by a large and lavish state bed (c. 1698), hung with blue-black silk and decorated with a fringe. There is also a wonderfully carved staircase from Cassiobury Park, a former country house in Hertfordshire, dating from about 1674. Silver, some by the great Huguenot silversmiths active in London during the 18th century; Chelsea and Bow porcelains; needlework; and several galleries of furniture round out the display.

(c) French decorative arts and period rooms, 18th century: The French 18th-century period rooms recreate the luxury and elegance of the reigns of Louis XV and XVI. Among the rooms are the only Parisian shopfront (c. 1775) remaining from the reign of Louis XVI, and a reception room from the Hôtel de Cabris in Grasse, with magnificent painted and gilded paneling. Furniture includes Louis XV's writing table, sometimes described as the most important piece of 18th-century French furniture ever to have crossed the Atlantic; a mechanical table of adjustable height used to serve Marie Antoinette her meals in bed after the birth of her first child; and prime examples of upholstered, lacquered, and gilded furniture. The collection also contains Savonnerie carpets, gold snuff boxes, rare examples of French silver, small-scale sculpture, and Sèvres porcelains.

(d) European Sculpture Court: This skylit garden court, with its air of repose and formality, looks out into Central Park through large windows that bring daily and seasonal changes of light into the galleries. Sculptures are arranged in chronological order from east to west (the Central Park side). Two of the earliest pieces, *Flora* and *Priapus* by Pietro Bernini, father of the more famous Gian Lorenzo Bernini, symbolize spring and fall and were made for Cardinal Scipione Borghese. Across the entrance (the

original carriage entrance from Central Park) is one of the most important pieces in the group, Jean-Louis Lemoyne's *Fear of Cupid's Darts* (1739–40), given by Louis XV to Mme de Pompadour's brother. Closer to the park *Ugolino and his Sons* (1865–67), by Jean-Baptiste Carpeaux, dramatically depicts an incident in Dante's *Inferno*, in which the traitor Ugolino della Gherardesca is imprisoned with his children in a tower and left to starve. The most dramatic piece in the room is Auguste Rodin's *The Burghers of Calais* (1885–95), anatomically distorted and psychologically intense depictions of six citizens of Calais who volunteered for martyrdom at the hands of England's Edward III to spare Calais from destruction. (Another casting of the group is in the Brooklyn Museum; *see p. 475.*)

(e) French and Italian terra cotta and marble, 18th–19th centuries: The square gallery leading from the middle of the Sculpture Court contains Clodion's *Balloon Monument*, a terra-cotta model for a work planned to commemorate the first balloon ascent in 1783. It shows *putti* stoking a fire whose heat inflates a balloon. In a nearby case is Jean-Antoine Houdon's *Sabine* (1788), a tender portrait of his year-old daughter.

(f) 18th–19th-century decorative arts: The two nearby Gould Galleries offer examples of Neoclassical, Baroque, Rococo, and Empire styles in France, Britain, Germany, Italy, and northern Europe. The adjacent Cantor Galleries for 19th-century sculpture and decorative arts contain works that span the period from the restoration of the Bourbon dynasty in France in 1815 to the Art Nouveau period at the beginning of the 20th century.

(g) 16th–17th-century bronzes: The museum has an outstanding collection. Among the works are a figure of *Paris* by Pier Jacopo Alari Bonacolsi, known as Antico for the many scaled-down versions of ancient works that he produced. *Paris*, however, a youth with gilded hair holding a gilded apple, seems to have been his own creation. The Paduan Andrea Briosco, known as Il Riccio, created numerous mythological figures, including the imposing *Striding Satyr* (c. 1506–08).

(h) The Jack and Belle Linsky Galleries: The Linsky collection of European paintings, sculpture, and decorative arts was donated to the museum in 1982 with the stipulation that it be kept together. Among the Italian medieval and Renaissance paintings in the **Red Room** are works by Carlo and Vittorio Crivelli, Giovanni di Paolo, and Andrea del Sarto. A wonderful small panel by Juan de Flandes shows the marriage feast at Cana (c. 1500–04); the figure outside the columns is thought to be a self-portrait.

The still life by Luis Egidio Meléndez, *La Merienda*, in the **Beige Room**, is one of the artist's largest and most elaborate paintings. Meléndez, largely neglected in his own time, is now recognized as the greatest Spanish still-life painter of the 18th century, remarkable for his skill with composition and his ability to depict texture and volume.

In the blue-gray **Rotunda** is the earliest dated painting by Peter Paul Rubens, *Portrait of a Man* (1597); the sitter might have been an architect or geographer, since he holds the tools of those trades. In the **Gold Room** are 17th-century Dutch paintings, notably Jan Steen's *The Dissolute Household* (c. 1665).

THE ROBERT LEHMAN COLLECTION

Among the great collections donated to the museum, the Robert Lehman bequest is perhaps the most conspicuous, since a condition of the gift was that the collection remain permanently intact and that seven period rooms from the Lehman town house on West 54th St be recreated within the museum. The Metropolitan's institutional architects, Kevin Roche, John Dinkeloo and Associates, designed the pyramidal glass and concrete wing that houses the collection; the red-brick and gray granite east wall is the back wall of the original Metropolitan, designed by Calvert Vaux and Jacob Wrey Mould.

Robert Lehman, investment banker and collector

In 1925 Robert Lehman succeeded his father as head of the Lehman Brothers investment bank, which had originated before the Civil War as a commodities trading firm. The younger Lehman invested early in such fledgling businesses as retail chains, airlines, and television, and brought the firm to eminence. He once remarked that the key to success in investment banking was to "put your money in the right place at the right time." It was advice Lehman applied also to the art market, about which he had encyclopedic knowledge.

Lehman's father Philip had started collecting in 1911, purchasing Italian, Spanish, and French paintings, as well as decorative arts. As the available supply of Old Masters dried up, Robert Lehman began to purchase in other areas, buying Impressionist paintings, illuminated manuscripts, and a large number of exquisite drawings. He also bought a few Old Masters, as they became available, including Rembrandt's *Gérard de Lairesse* and Ingres's *Princesse de Broglie*.

Among the artists of the Italian Middle Ages and Renaissance, painters of the Sienese School are well represented; the collection includes works by Ugolino da Siena, a *Madonna and Child* by Simone Martini (c. 1326) in a transitional style from the Byzantine to the Giottesque, the superbly dramatic *Creation of the World and Expulsion from Paradise* by Giovanni di Paolo (1445), and the mysterious Osservanza Master's *St. Anthony Abbot Tempted by a Heap of Gold* (c. 1435), which depicts the saint in an almost surrealistic landscape. Outstanding among the Florentine painters is Sandro Botticelli, whose *Annunciation* (c. 1490), a small painting, was probably intended for private devotion. The beautifully drawn figures of the Virgin and angel curving toward one another, the complexity of the composition, and the transparent colors make this one of the most attractive of several Annunciations Botticelli painted at this time.

Among the northern Renaissance paintings are works by Hans Memling, Petrus Christus, and a portrait of Erasmus of Rotterdam (c. 1530?) by Hans Holbein. The portrait of Margaret of Austria (c. 1490) by the Master of Moulins (Jean Hey) shows a richly dressed, unhappy child.

There are fine Dutch paintings, including Rembrandt's portrait of Gérard de Lairesse (1665). Among the Spanish paintings are El Greco's *Christ Carrying the Cross* (c. 1580) and *St Jerome as Cardinal* (c. 1610–14), as well as Goya's *Condesa de Altamira and her Daughter, María Agustina* (1787–88).

There are French masterworks of the 19th and 20th centuries, including a glorious portrait of the Princesse de Broglie (1851–53) by Ingres; the engaging *Two Young Girls at the Piano* (1892) by Renoir; and paintings by the Post-Impressionists and the Fauves. Balthus's *Nude Before a Mirror* (1955) is one of the most recent works in the collection.

MEDIEVAL ART

NB: Medieval art is also on display at The Cloisters, the Metropolitan's only branch museum, in Fort Tryon Park at the upper tip of Manhattan; see p. 449.

The collection here contains Byzantine silver, enamels, glass, ivories, jewelry, metalwork, stained glass, sculpture, enamels, and tapestries. The works were created from the 4th–early 16th centuries, roughly from the time of the fall of Rome to the beginning of the Renaissance. Financier J. Pierpont Morgan, whose collections focused on books and decorative arts, died in 1913 and left the museum a trove of objects which form the nucleus of the more than 4,000 works presently here. (The accession numbers for objects in the Morgan gift begin with 17.190.)

The galleries are arranged more or less chronologically, with an introductory section on Byzantine art, two large galleries devoted to Romanesque and Gothic art, and a Medieval Treasury with small, richly decorated enamels, ivories, and examples of metalwork—jeweled or not.

Byzantine galleries: The three galleries around and under the Grand Staircase showcase works from AD 330 (when the capital of the Roman Empire moved to Constantinople) to 1453 (when Constantinople fell to the Ottoman Turks). Important works include the Syrian Attarouthi Treasure (6th–7th centuries), which includes silver and silver-gilt chalices, censers, a wine strainer, and a silver dove representing the Holy Spirit; and a set of silver plates depicting biblical scenes, the largest of which shows David's victory over Goliath. An important secular piece is a delicate ivory diptych announcing Justinian's appointment as consul; Justinian, who became emperor six years later, had it

made as a presentation gift to celebrate this major career step.

Sculpture: Important pieces of sculpture in the collection include a mutilated limestone head of King David (c. 1150), a rare survivor of many that once decorated the portals of Notre Dame in Paris. The statue was decapitated during the French Revolution, but the head has been identified from engravings made of the doorway before the Revolution.

Central Gallery: In the large central gallery are tapestries and sculpture. The beautifully carved alabaster mourners from the tomb of the Duc de Berry represent relatives and allies of the duke, whose full-size effigy lay on top of the sarcophagus. An imposing eagle lectern

(c. 1300) carved from marble by one of the finest Gothic sculptors, Giovanni Pisano, once stood in the cathedral of Pistoia in Tuscany. Tapestries include *The Annunciation* (c. 1410–30), probably woven in Arras; and the famous Rose Tapestries (c. 1450), a set depicting courtiers and ladies, woven for Charles VII of France.

There are many smaller devotional objects. One of the most unusual is a small crib of the Infant Jesus; these little cribs were venerated during the Christmas season; there would have been a figure of the infant Jesus beneath the silk coverlet. One beautiful work represents the *Visitation* (c. 1610), the visit of the Virgin Mary to St. Elizabeth, who was also expecting a child; the crystal ovals probably covered tiny images of the infant Christ (Mary's baby) and John the Baptist (Elizabeth's).

The Medieval Treasury: To the right of the large gallery, this has delicately carved ivory plaques, including one with the *Journey to Emmaus* and a *Noli Me Tangere* (c. 1115–20). A gilded and bejeweled silver processional Cross from Spain (late 11th–early 12th century) with the figure of Adam rising from his grave at the bottom, shows the skill of artisans from a small medieval Spanish parish. Also on view, in the next gallery, are humble everyday objects—locks, game boards and pieces, combs—as well as ceramics including early Spanish lusterware.

ARMS & ARMOR

The collection of arms and armor contains weapons that range from simple arrowheads to elaborate ceremonial jewel-encrusted swords. The centerpiece of the galleries is the **Equestrian Court**, where fully armed and armored men and their horses "parade" beneath colorful banners. Among the finer pieces are suits of English armor made at the royal workshops in Greenwich, established by Henry VIII.

Among the earliest objects in the collection of **European armor** is an early 6th-century gilded Germanic *spangenhelm*, a style probably brought to the West during the invasion of Europe by the Huns; it is the only such helmet in the Western Hemisphere. Another important piece is a parade helmet (1543) signed by the Milanese master armorer Filippo Negrolo. Also on view are rapiers, daggers, swords, and a collection of firearms, both European and American.

The collection also contains astonishing examples of **Japanese armor**. On view are ferocious face masks from the Edo period (1615–1868), armor from the Kamakura period (early 14th century), and helmets in shapes ranging from an eggplant to a crouching rabbit. The collection also includes **Islamic arms**, notably spectacular jeweled daggers and sabers, helmets, and firearms.

EGYPTIAN ART

The Met owns the finest collection of Egyptian art in the United States; its 36,000 objects date from the Paleolithic era to the Byzantine occupation during the reign of the emperor Justinian (c. 30,000 BC–AD 641). The galleries are organized chronologically

beginning with the prehistoric material just north of the Great Hall on the east (Fifth Ave) side of the building; they continue in a U-shape, reaching the Temple of Dendur and then doubling back to the Great Hall. There are many beautiful objects in every gallery, accompanied by explanatory texts.

Highlights of the collection include wonderful tomb models illustrating aspects of everyday life, collections of royal jewelry, and the Archaeological Room with its superb groups of funerary objects (painted coffins, canopic jars, etc.) illustrating burial customs. The Temple of Dendur and the Tomb of Pernebi are notable architectural monuments.

ART OF THE DEAD

Egyptian art, which conveys such a vigorous picture of life in ancient Egypt, is fundamentally the art of the dead. While other cultures have assumed survival after death, the ancient Egyptians provided for their future with unrivaled diligence, setting aside the favorite possessions of the deceased and artistically recreating the minutiae of their daily lives to be enjoyed beyond the grave. The dead took with them all the comforts of home: phalanxes of servants either painted on tomb walls or fashioned as statuettes; food and drink; jewelry, clothing, and even entertainments. Most of the objects in the collection, therefore, are funerary objects and many were uncovered by museum archaeologists during a series of important excavations that began in 1907 and continued for 35 years.

(A) Tomb of Pernebi: This *mastaba*, built c. 2450 BC, for an official of Dynasty 5 of the Old Kingdom, is an architectural highlight of the collection. The central room is a chapel, decorated with images of Pernebi, who is shown at a table receiving food offerings from servants and relatives. At the rear of the chapel a false door allowed Pernebi's spirit to emerge from a subterranean burial chamber to enjoy offerings which were arranged on a slab in front of the door.

(B) Gallery 4: Here is a marvelous set of Middle Kingdom wooden models from the tomb of Meketre at Thebes (c. 1990 BC; *see box opposite*). Meketre was a powerful administrator who began his career under Nebhepetre Mentuhotep of Dynasty 11. The models—human figures, boats, scenes from daily life in the stable, granary, brewery and bakery—assured perpetuation of the activities they depict: Meketre could be eternally sure of his beer and bread. The statuette of a woman with an offering of food, with its graceful bearing and exquisite detail, is the finest figure in the collection. The feather pattern on her dress was sometimes associated with goddesses.

(C) Royal portraiture statuary of the 12th Dynasty (c. 1991–1783 BC): Another strength of the collection, royal statuary includes a quartzite portrait of Senwosret III (c. 1878–1841 BC), whose heavy-lidded eyes and lined cheeks give the face a somber, careworn expression not usually found in portrayals of other rulers. Also from Dynasty 12 is the blue

faïence statuette of a Hippopotamus, which has become a symbol for the Met's Egyptian collection. The figure may have been sculpted as a protective amulet since the ancient Egyptians, armed with first-hand experience, considered hippos menacing, not cute. The surface decoration refers to river plants; three of the legs have been restored, as the originals were broken to prevent the animal from wreaking havoc in the afterlife.

Other important artifacts from this dynasty include the jewelry of Princess Sit-Hathor-yunet. The outstanding piece is a cloisonné pectoral, made of 372 precious stones, precisely cut and set into metal cells, showing two falcons, representing the sun god Re; from the two cobras above the falcons hang two ankhs (the symbol of life); the central cartouche encircles a hieroglyph with the throne name of Senwosret II.

THE DISCOVERY OF MEKETRE'S TOMB MODELS

By 1920 when museum archaeologists visited Meketre's tomb, it had completely collapsed, leaving a dark, gaping cave. The museum's chief excavator, Herbert Winlock, who was having the tomb cleared in order to make an accurate floor plan, discovered a small hidden chamber filled with these beautifully preserved models. Although the rest of the tomb had been robbed in Antiquity, the chamber and its contents had remained hidden for nearly 40 centuries. The models were divided between the Egyptian Museum in Cairo and the Metropolitan, which received six boats, four models of food production, an enclosed garden, a procession of three offering bearers led by a priest, and a tall offering figure.

(D) Likenesses of Hatshepsut: The Met has remarkable works portraying the female pharaoh Hatshepsut (18th Dynasty; c. 1473–1458 BC). Hatshepsut, the sister and wife of Tuthmosis II, produced no male heir; her successor, Tuthmosis III, a son of the same king by a lesser wife, was therefore both her nephew and her stepson. When Tuthmosis II died young, Hatshepsut became regent for her stepson-nephew, a position that apparently gave her a taste for power. She therefore declared herself Pharaoh and continued to rule, using the authority of powerful advisors, in particular the chancellor Senenmut. It is uncertain whether Tuthmosis III killed

Hatshepsut or simply waited for her to die, but on her death he saw to it that all her memorials were destroyed. Hatshepsut's funerary temple in western Thebes was adorned with some 200 statues of her; 26, all broken, stand in this gallery. The most appealing of the museum's works, known as the *White Hatshepsut* (29.3.2), is a limestone seated figure which shows her in masculine clothing but with a female body.

(E) The Temple of Dendur: The temple (c. 23–10 BC) was built on the banks of the Nile by the Roman emperor Augustus in part as a public relations gesture to appease a conquered people; some 19 centuries later it came to the United States

as a good will gesture for contributions to preserve Nubian monuments endangered by the Aswan Dam. The temple honors Osiris, a god associated with the Nile and its fertility, as well as two brothers who drowned in the sacred river during military campaigns.

A gateway leads to the temple; the winged disk on the lintel represents the god Horus, who ascended to the sky in this form. Reliefs on the gateway show the Pharaoh (Augustus) making offerings to local divinities, a theme repeated both inside and outside the structure. Beyond the gateway, the temple (*closed to the public*) has three rooms: an entrance room, an undecorated chamber probably used for storing offerings, and a sanctuary where the images of the chief temple gods would normally be kept and attended by priests. On the exterior rear wall a beveled block can be removed to reveal a hidden chamber (9½ ft by 6ft by 2ft) where the drowned brothers might have been entombed.

(F) Archaeological Room: Displayed in this properly claustrophobic gallery are superb tomb groups from Dynasty 26, as well as funerary objects from Dynasties 19–26 (c. 1320–525 BC) illustrating the development of burial customs in Thebes during this period. Included are decorated coffins, canopic chests, *shawabtys*, figures with the form and attributes of Osiris (god of the dead), and mummies.

(G) Facsimile paintings: A lounge area contains reproductions of tomb and temple paintings, many from Thebes, most from the 3rd–11th Dynasties. Copied (1907–39) by museum staff members, they provide an archive of Egyptian art (many of the temples have since been destroyed) and a source of information on daily life that would be available otherwise only in texts.

(H) The final galleries: Here are works from the Macedonian–Ptolemaic periods (332–30 BC). The objects, which date from the time of Alexander's conquest of Egypt (332 BC) to the death of Cleopatra (30 BC), show the influence of the West upon Egyptian art. One gallery features Roman art from the time of Augustus (ruled 27 BC–AD 14) to the 4th century AD. The faces in the "Fayum Portraits" represent people who lived 18 centuries ago, but look as if they could be seen today. Found in 2nd-century Greco-Roman cemeteries in the Fayum district (south of Cairo), where the customs of the large Greek community merged with the traditional Egyptian ways, the panels, painted in the Greek style, were placed over the faces of mummies wrapped and buried according to Egyptian rites. The artifacts in the final gallery, Roman and Coptic periods (30 BC–AD 641), show the influence of Christianity and may seem closer to the Byzantine or the Western tradition of the early Middle Ages than to their Egyptian antecedents.

THE AMERICAN WING

The American Wing holds a superb collection of American painting, sculpture, and decorative arts from the late 18th–early 20th centuries. Because of the historical development of the wing, which opened in the 1920 and was enlarged in 1980, the floor plan is convoluted, with newer galleries wrapped around a core of period rooms.

Highlights include important works by John Singleton Copley, Winslow Homer, Thomas Eakins, John Singer Sargent, and the Hudson River School of landscape painters. The *Panorama of Versailles* by John Vanderlyn is a remarkable, room-filling view of Versailles. The new Greek Revival galleries on the ground floor offer outstanding examples of decorative arts from about 1810–40.

First floor

Garden Court: This is the centerpiece of the wing, with its expansive windows, fountains, greenery, and views of Central Park. In this tranquil setting are usually displayed examples of reigning 19th- and early 20th-century sculpture and architectural elements. On one end is the staid marble façade (1824) of the United States Branch Bank, once located on Wall St; at the other is an ornamental loggia (c. 1905) with ceramic capitals, glass tiles, and lanterns by Louis Comfort Tiffany, America's foremost master of the Art Nouveau style. The subtle gradations of color in the stained-glass window *View of Oyster Bay* (c. 1905) show Tiffany's technique at its most dazzling.

Period rooms of the Federal Period (1790–1820): The doorway of the United States Branch Bank leads from the Garden Court into the Federal Gallery with distinguished examples of furniture from Boston, New York, Philadelphia, and Baltimore. The era was marked by the influence of British Neoclassicism, especially the work of Robert and James Adam. Included are works by Duncan Phyfe and Charles-Honoré Lannuier, both immigrant craftsmen who brought with them their knowledge of continental styles. Nearby period rooms feature original architectural elements from Maryland, Massachusetts, and Virginia.

Neoclassical Galleries (1810–40): North of the Federal Gallery, these galleries are arranged in room-like settings with examples of furniture, ceramics, glass, and silver that imitate antique Classical forms. There are paintings by members of the very artistic Peale family: James Peale's *Still Life: Balsam Apple and Vegetables* (1820s) with a feathery Savoy cabbage and other finely colored and textured vegetables; and Rembrandt Peale's portrait of his two youngest children, *Michael Angelo and Emma Clara Peale* (c. 1826). At the end of the corridor the Shaker Retiring Room from New Lebanon, New York, is furnished in the simple, utilitarian manner associated with this austere religious sect.

Vanderlyn's Panorama: Across the corridor John Vanderlyn's *Panorama of the Palace and Gardens of Versailles* (1818–19), the largest painting in the museum, fills an oval room. The panorama was originally exhibited in a specially-built rotunda in City Hall Park to suggest the sensation of actually standing on the grounds of Versailles surrounded by its buildings and gardens. At one of the palace windows stands a figure of Louis XVIII, King of France at the time. In an age when travel was arduous, these panoramas of faraway places were a popular form of entertainment, painted on great canvases, rolled up and carried from city to city. Vanderlyn hoped to make his fortune with this rendering of Versailles, but the painting failed to

attract the public, possibly because of its formality and emptiness.

19th-century Revival styles: Galleries on the other side of the Panorama contain groupings of furniture and period rooms—ornate, extravagant, and sometimes amusing to contemporary tastes—that reflect 19th-century Revival styles: Greek, Gothic, Rococo, Renaissance, and Egyptian.

Frank Lloyd Wright Room: This re-creates a living room (1914) from the Francis W. Little house in Wayzata, Minnesota. Wright's "prairie houses," were low structures with open interiors, whose ornamentation avoided embellishment aside from the natural colors and textures of the building materials. Henry James called one of the prairie houses "all beautiful with omissions."

Second floor

American decorative arts: Galleries on the balcony above the Garden Court usually contain American decorative arts from the 17th–20th centuries, with outstanding examples of pewter, silver, glass, and ceramics that range from simple utilitarian wares to opulent presentation pieces. A reduced copy of Daniel Chester French's grave memorial *Mourning Victory* (1908; this replica 1915) is mounted against the south wall. Also known as the Melvin Memorial, the monument commemorates three brothers who died in the Civil War. It was commissioned by the surviving brother, who also ordered this replica for the museum, sculpted by the Piccirilli brothers (*see p. 393*).

Period rooms of the late Colonial Period (1730–90): Period rooms on this floor include a Pennsylvania German room with furnishings made by German-speaking immigrants who settled in southeastern Pennsylvania, bringing with them their colorful decorative traditions. Other period rooms include a parlor from Philadelphia (c. 1765); a gentleman's bedroom from Maryland; and the Alexandria Ballroom, an assembly room from a tavern in Virginia.

American painting and sculpture: 18th-century portraits include works by John Singleton Copley, the most gifted of the American colonial painters, noted for his skill at suggesting characterization and his rendering of textures—and his willingness to portray his subjects as they might wish to be seen. Charles Willson Peale, John Trumbull, James Peale, and Gilbert Stuart are all represented. George Caleb Bingham's *Fur Traders Descending the Missouri* (c. 1845), remarkable for its luminous mist, was painted by an artist whose professional training was scanty, but whose experience of the American West was extensive.

One strength of the collection is painting from the **Hudson River School**, a native tradition of landscape painting that developed in the mid-19th century and focused on the natural beauty of the still-unspoiled continent. Thomas Cole was generally acknowledged the founder of the school. His *View from Mount Holyoke, Massachusetts, after a Thunderstorm—The Oxbow* (1836) is considered a masterpiece of American landscape painting. Here also are works by Asher B. Durand, Cole's friend, an engraver-turned-painter.

Sculpture from about this period includes several works by Hiram Powers, notably his bust of a worn and toothless Andrew Jackson (c. 1838–44). Works by the second generation of Hudson River School painters include Martin Johnson Heade's *The Coming Storm* (1859) and works by John Frederick Kensett, Fitz Hugh Lane, and others deeply interested in effects of light and atmosphere. Albert Bierstadt's *The Rocky Mountains, Lander's Peak* (1864) and Frederic Edwin Church's *The Heart of the Andes* (1859) exemplify the interest in large-scale, dramatic landscapes.

The collection contains works by Winslow Homer, from his early Civil War paintings to his late seascapes. Emanuel Leutze's *Washington Crossing the Delaware* (1851), a romantic reconstruction of history, inaccurate in many details, is nonetheless deeply imprinted on the American consciousness.

Examples of Western art include paintings and bronzes by Frederic Remington, chronicler of cowboys, Indians, and army troopers; as well as works by visionary painters Albert Pinkham Ryder and Ralph Albert Blakelock.

Among the works by late 19th- and early 20th-century Realists is an impressive group of paintings by Thomas Eakins, who with Winslow Homer was one of the outstanding painters of the

George Caleb Bingham: *Fur Traders Descending the Missouri* (1845).

period; *Max Schmitt in a Single Scull* (1871), with Eakins himself rowing in the middle distance, is as much a study of perspective and light as it is of the champion rower working out on the Skuylkill River. Also in the collection are works by Mary Cassatt, part of whose importance to the museum lies in her influence on her wealthy compatriots (particularly Mrs. H.O. Havemeyer) to whom she introduced the paintings of the French Impressionists. Among the American Impressionists is John Twachtman, whose masterpiece is

Arques-La-Bataille (1885), painted in subdued tones of gray and green; the dark green reeds in the foreground suggest his attraction to Japanese prints. John Singer Sargent's, *Madame X* (1884) was a scandalous portrait in its day, both for the real-life behavior of its subject and for her depiction in the painting, wearing a dress with a plunging neckline and a wandering shoulder strap, later painted over. Sargent moved to England in 1885 after the exhibition of the portrait, and ended his career as a portraitist in Paris.

Third floor

Period rooms of the early Colonial Period (1630–1730): These include a meeting house gallery, with early American furniture—chests with Tudor and Jacobean motifs, cupboards, and several pieces in the William and Mary style. The Hart Room from Ipswich, Massachusetts (before 1674) is the earliest period room in the collection and is

furnished with 17th-century oak and pine furniture. Later rooms include one from a home on Long Island whose furnishings and tiles surrounding the fireplace show the Dutch influence on that area; and a room from Portsmouth, Rhode Island, near Newport, whose formal furnishings recall the elegance of Georgian England.

EUROPEAN PAINTING: RENAISSANCE–19TH CENTURY

For many visitors, these galleries are the prime attraction of the museum. The collection includes many paintings known to every art lover. The galleries, at the top of the Grand Staircase, are organized chronologically and geographically.

Gallery 1: Dominating this large room are heroic paintings by the 18th-century Venetian master Giovanni Battista Tiepolo, including *The Triumph of Marius* (1729), which depicts the victorious Roman general Gaius Marius preceded by his captive, the African king Jugurtha. Tiepolo painted himself at the left of the painting in front of the torchbearer. Also here are *The Battle of*

Vercellae and *The Capture of Carthage* (both 1725–29).

Gallery 2: In this second large gallery are French Neoclassical works by Jacques-Louis David, including *The Death of Socrates* (1787) and a great double portrait of *Antoine-Laurent Lavoisier and his Wife* (1788). Also works by Élisabeth-Louise Vigée Le Brun, Adélaïde Labille-Guiard, and Jean-Baptiste Greuze.

Italian painting

The right-hand row of galleries is devoted primarily to the Italian Renaissance. The rooms are numbered and labeled, though the painters mentioned on the placards do not exactly correspond to the contents of the rooms.

Gallery 3 (13th–14th centuries): The Byzantinesque *Madonna and Child* is one of three securely attributed paintings by Berlinghiero, a Tuscan painter of the early 13th century. Giotto is represented here by a rendering of *The Epiphany* (c. 1320). Also here are works by the Sienese artists Sassetta, Giovanni di Paolo, and Paolo di Giovanni Fei, whose *Madonna and Child* retains its original frame with cabochon gems and glass medallions. *St. Andrew* by Simone Martini is part of an altarpiece to which *St. Ansanus* in the Lehman Collection belongs.

Gallery 4 (15th century): Sassetta's *Journey of the Magi* (c. 1435) is the upper half of a panel showing the Three Kings bringing their gifts to the Christ Child, whose manger (in the lower panel, now in Siena) lies below the golden star on the hill. Here also are works by Giovanni di Paolo, and the Florentines Lorenzo Monaco and Fra Angelico.

Gallery 4a (15th-century secular painting): Filippo Lippi's *Portrait of a Woman with a Man at a Casement* (c. 1440), probably commissioned for a wedding, is the earliest known Italian portrait in a domestic interior. Domenico Ghirlandaio's *Francesco Sassetti and his Son Teodoro* (1487) depicts a banker who worked for the Medici banks abroad and also served as an advisor to the heads of the family.

Gallery 4b (Italian Renaissance art from the Benjamin Altman Collection): *The Holy Family with St. Mary Magdalene* (1490–1506) by Andrea Mantegna, painted on canvas instead of the more commonly used wood, was probably intended for private devotion. The *Last Communion of St. Jerome* (early 1490s) is by Botticelli. Also here is Antonio Rossellino's delicately carved marble relief of the *Madonna and Child with Angels*.

Gallery 5 (15th century, Venice and Northern Italy): Giovanni Bellini's *Madonna and Child* (late 1480s) is a mature work with a luminous background landscape said to anticipate Giorgione and Titian. Andrea Mantegna's *The Adoration of the Shepherds* (c. 1450) is an early work, painted when the artist was only about 20 years old. Also here are Vittore Carpaccio's *Meditation on the Passion* and a superb *Madonna and Child* by Carlo Crivelli, filled with all his typical symbolic imagery: the goldfinch which the Christ Child clasps protectively to His bosom stands for the human soul, to be redeemed from evil, symbolized by the large housefly on the parapet.

Gallery 6 (late 15th century, Northern Italy): In this spacious gallery are larger works, most of them by Florentine painters. Domenico Ghirlandaio's *St. Christopher with the Infant Christ* (c. 1475) is a large fresco possibly from a church façade. Note the fish, visible in the translucent water. Piero di Cosimo's *A Hunting Scene* is typical of the work of this original and uncategorizable artist. Man in his primitive, bestial state is shown with satyrs engaged in acts of abominable carnage against the animal kingdom.

Gallery 7 (16th century, Florence, also Raphael): Agnolo Bronzino's *Portrait of a Young Man* (c. 1540) is typical of his elegant portraits; the arrogant, self-consciously posed subject in his fashionably slashed doublet is dressed in aesthete's black and holds a book. Raphael's *Madonna and Child Enthroned with Saints* (c. 1504) is part of an altarpiece for a convent in Perugia, painted when Raphael was about 20 years old. *The Agony in the Garden* was painted as part of the predella (small painting or series of paintings below the main panel) of the same altarpiece. Andrea del Sarto's *Holy Family with Infant St. John* (c. 1530) is a late work, painted in soft, rich colors; John the Baptist, patron saint of Florence, offers Christ a globe possibly symbolizing Christian dominion.

Gallery 8 (16th-century Venice): Works here include paintings by Titian, Lorenzo Lotto, Veronese, and Tintoretto. Titian's renowned *Venus and the Lute Player* (1565–70) is one of several paintings by the master depicting Venus in a musical setting symbolic of love; the head of Venus and the curtain behind her were probably completed by an assistant. Paolo Veronese's *Mars and Venus United by Love* (1570s) is a work of the painter's maturity. Though the allegorical meaning has not been unanimously agreed upon, the painting seems to show exhausted War collapsed at the feet of bounteous Love, while one *putto* binds their legs together with a length of pink cloth and another holds Mars's warhorse at bay.

Gallery 9 (16th century, Northern Italy): Here are works by Correggio, a fine portrait by Moretto da Brescia, and Giovanni Battista Moroni's unsparing portrayal of the elderly Abbess Lucrezia Agliardi Vertova (1556).

Gallery 10 (18th-century Rome): Giovanni Paolo Panini was the first painter to specialize in painting ruins. His *Ancient Rome* and *Modern Rome* depict the ancient and 18th-century buildings of Rome as objects in an architecturally elaborate art gallery. Also on view are works by Pompeo Batoni, who executed many commissions for fashionable young men on the Grand Tour.

Dutch and British painting

Gallery 11: This room is devoted to 17th-century Dutch landscapes.

Gallery 12 (Dutch painting, 17th century): Here, along with paintings by Jan Steen, Nicholas Maes, and Pieter de Hooch, are four paintings by Vermeer. Fewer than 40 universally accepted paintings by this artist have been known to survive; the Metropolitan has five examples (four here and one in the Altman Gallery). *Young Woman with a Water Jug* (c. 1662) is a wonderful rendering of light and color. *Study of a Young Woman* (late 1660s) is one of Vermeer's few "portraits," though its intention was not so much to capture a likeness as to suggest character. Also on view are *Woman With a Lute* (early 1660s) and the least successful of Vermeer's extant works, *Allegory of the Faith* (early 1670s)—though the rendering of the glass sphere above the allegorical figure is masterful nevertheless.

Gallery 13 (Rembrandt and Hals): The display includes some several fine portraits of prosperous Dutch burghers by

Frans Hals, whose slashing brushwork impressed later painters. Van Gogh said that Hals had no less than 27 varieties of black, useful for painting somber Dutch garb. Also here is a stunning collection of works by Rembrandt. *Aristotle with a Bust of Homer* (1653) depicts Aristotle resting his right hand on Homer's head; his left hand fingers a gold chain with a medallion of his pupil, Alexander the Great. The museum bought this exceptionally fine work in 1961 for the then-astronomical price of $2.3 million. Other works by Rembrandt here include: *Bellona, Flora* (probably a portrait of his mistress, Hendrickje Stoffels), and several other portraits of anonymous sitters.

Gallery 14 (Dutch painting from the Benjamin Altman Collection): Altman

bought fine landscapes by Cuyp and van Ruisdael, two of which are on display here: Aelbert Cuyp, *Young Herdsman with Cows* (1650s); Jacob van Ruisdael, *Wheatfields* (1670s). He purchased two genre scenes by Frans Hals: *Young Man and Woman in an Inn* (1623) and *Merrymakers at Shrovetide* (c. 1615). But it was Rembrandt who captured his imagination, and he bought more paintings by that master than any other American collector. Many of these paintings were of the highest quality. He almost bought the *Aristotle with a Bust of Homer*, but the dealer sold it to Mrs. Collis P. Huntington. Altman was sometimes misled as to attribution, and some of the paintings he bought as Rembrandts have been downgraded to "School of Rembrandt."

Benjamin Altman as Collector

Benjamin Altman, founder of the now-defunct department store B. Altman & Company, which from 1906–89 occupied a Renaissance-style *palazzo* on Fifth Avenue (*see p. 211*), was a bachelor who devoted himself totally to his work and his art collection. On his death in 1913, he left a $15-million collection of paintings and porcelains to the museum on condition that the collection be maintained intact in two adjoining rooms—one for the paintings, statuary, Limoges enamels, and rock crystals, a second for the Chinese porcelains. Although the museum has not adhered strictly to this request (the porcelains line the galleries around the Great Hall Stairway), his paintings are grouped in adjacent galleries.

Altman began collecting around 1900, first fastening his attention on porcelains from the Chinese Qing Dynasty (1644–1912). Soon he turned to painting, and like his wealthy contemporaries bought works by painters of the Barbizon School. His eye matured swiftly, however, and he began to purchase works by Italian Renaissance and 17th-century Dutch painters. Unlike J. Pierpont Morgan, another great collector of his day, Altman was slow to decide on a painting, often vacillating for weeks. But when he decided, he did not haggle about price.

Included in Altman's Rembrandts on view are a self-portrait (1660), *The Toilet of Bathsheba* (1643), *Man with a*

Magnifying Glass (mid-1660s), and *Woman with a Pink* (1662–65). Here also is Vermeer's *A Maid Asleep* (1656–57), the

earliest known Vermeer with the kind of domestic interior now recognized as his hallmark. Some commentators, influenced by the untidy table, suggested the painting was an allegory of sloth, but x-ray studies have revealed a man in the background, and the painting may depict a social encounter that has just ended. **Gallery 15 (18th-century British portraits):** Here are pictures of well-to-do patrons and their families by the pre-eminent portraitists of the time: Reynolds, Gainsborough, Raeburn, Romney, and Hoppner. Especially appealing is Sir Thomas Lawrence's *Elizabeth Farren* (1790), the work of a young virtuoso; the subject was a popular actress who retired from the stage and married the Earl of Derby.

Spanish painting

Galleries 16 and 17 (17th–18th centuries): Among the works in these two galleries are Diego Velázquez's superb portrait of his assistant Juan de Pareja (1650), who was of Moorish descent. Goya is represented by several portraits including *Don Sebastián Martínez y Pérez* (1792) and (attrib. to Goya) *Majas on a Balcony*. Also here are works by Zurbarán and Murillo. The museum has two celebrated paintings by El Greco: *Portrait of a Cardinal* (probably Cardinal Don Fernando Niño de Guevara; c. 1600), unforgettable for his severe spectacles; and his extraordinary, eerie landscape, *View of Toledo*.

French painting

Gallery 18: Works by Boucher, Chardin, Fragonard, and Watteau.

Gallery 19 (17th century): Featured here are works by Nicolas Poussin with mythological and literary themes. *The Blind Orion Searching for the Rising Sun* (1658) is a haunting picture painted late in Poussin's career. Orion, a mighty hunter blinded by the king of Chios for trying to rape his daughter, was told by an oracle that the rays of the rising sun would restore his sight. *The Abduction of the Sabine Women* (c. 1633?) shows Romulus, ruler of Rome, signaling his men to seize the Sabine women, needed to populate the newly founded city.

Claude Lorrain came to Rome as an adolescent, apprenticed to a pastry cook. He is known for his idealization of the Italian landscape, as seen in *View of La Crescenza* (c. 1649). Also on view here is Georges de la Tour's *The Penitent Magdalene* (1638–43). De La Tour is known for his handling of light, particularly candle light; this is one of four pictures he painted of the repentant saint.

Gallery 20 (Tiepolo, Watteau, and Chardin): Outstanding among the preparatory works for ceiling paintings by Tiepolo is the *Allegory of the Planets and Continents* (1752), a large oil sketch for the decoration of the staircase ceiling in a palace in Wurzburg. Here also is Jean-Baptiste Chardin's *Boy Blowing Bubbles* (c.1734); the 17th-century Dutch masters influenced both the subject and style of this painting. Antoine Watteau's fine *Mezzetin* (1718-20) depicts a stock character in the *commedia dell'arte*, a

Bequest of Mrs. H. O. Havemeyer, 1929 (29.100.6).

El Greco (1541–1616): *View of Toledo.*

sympathetic figure troubled by unrequited love, here wistfully depicted serenading an unseen lover; even the marble statue turns her back.

Gallery 21: This gallery contains fantasy landscapes by Hubert Robert, usually on display in the galleries of European decorative arts.

Northern European painting

Gallery 23 (Netherlandish painting, 15th century): Although artists had been painting with oils as early as the 12th century in Northern Europe, it was the technical brilliance of such early 15th-century Netherlandish painters as van Eyck and

van der Weyden that led to oils eventually becoming the major painting medium in Europe. Jan van Eyck's *The Crucifixion* and *The Last Judgment* (c. 1430) are remarkable not only for the acutely observed detail, especially in the Crucifixion scene, but also for the masterful handling of paint to achieve effects of rippling waves and fleeting clouds. Also in this gallery is *Portrait of a Carthusian* (1446), a fine work by Petrus Christus, van Eyck's chief follower. Another arresting portrait is Rogier van der Weyden's *Francesco d'Este* (c. 1460), a cool and aristocratic rendering of the illegitimate son of the Duke of Ferrara in front of an unusual white background. Hans Memling's wonderful portraits (probably 1470) of Tommaso di Folco Portinari and Maria Portinari (Maria Maddalena Baroncelli) probably commemorate a wedding. Tommaso managed a branch of the Medici banking house in Bruges and arranged loans to the dukes of Burgundy to fund their wars. The two paintings probably flanked a central panel of the Virgin and Child.

Gallery 24 (Netherlandish painting, 15th–16th centuries): Gerard David's *Rest on the Flight into Egypt* is a beautiful and original treatment of the subject. The three panels of Joachim Patinir's *The Penitence of St. Jerome* (after 1515) depict St. Jerome in the center, the baptism of Christ and the temptation of St Anthony on the interior wings. Patinir was known for his landscapes, which sometimes dominated the religious subjects; here the panorama continues across the panels.

Galleries 25–26 (Netherlandish and French painting, 16th century): Quentin Massys, painter of *The Adoration of the Magi* (1526) is known for his interest in extreme, almost caricatured faces,

considered by him to reveal character. Jean Clouet's *Guillaume Budé* (c. 1536) is his only documented work. The dour-looking Budé was France's greatest Greek scholar, admired by Erasmus for his erudition. Also in this gallery is *The Harvesters* (1565) by Pieter Brueghel the Elder; the painting is part of a cycle representing the months. Brueghel, who typically painted peasants and energetic outdoor scenes, was an Antwerp intellectual who included a cardinal among his patrons.

Gallery 26 (German painting, 16th century): Lucas Cranach the Elder is represented here not only by his charming mythological *The Judgment of Paris* (c. 1528) but by a court portrait of John, Duke of Saxony (c. 1537) and two biblical scenes: *Judith with the Head of Holofernes* and *Samson and Delilah*. A fine portrait by Hans Holbein the Younger, *A Member of the Wedigh Family* (1532), possibly depicts a London merchant; the line on the paper in the book is from Terence and is translated "Truth breeds hatred." The portrait is distinguished by its precise drawing and fine characterization. Albrecht Dürer's *Virgin and Child with St. Anne* (1519) shows the Virgin Mary and her mother adoring the sleeping Christ Child; the picture was painted the year after Dürer's conversion to Lutheranism.

Galleries 27–28 (Flemish painting, van Dyck and Rubens): Anthony van Dyck, who lived in England during the 1630s, was much in demand by the aristocracy and influenced several generations of English painters; *James Stuart, Duke of Richmond and Lennox* is a flattering portrait of a cousin of Charles I. Peter Paul Rubens's *Venus and Adonis* (?mid-1630s) was influenced by Titian's treatment of the

same subject; the color and technique are indicative of Rubens's maturity. *Rubens, his Wife Helena Fourment, and their Son, Peter Paul* (c. 1639) is a full-size portrait of Rubens and his second wife, whom he married (1630) when he was 53 and she was 16.

Later Italian painting

Gallery 29 (Italian painting, 17th century): Caravaggio is represented by an early allegorical painting, *The Musicians* (c. 1595), and by a late one, a dark and brooding psychological study, *The Denial of St. Peter* (?1610). Also in this gallery is Artemisia Gentileschi's *Esther before Ahasuerus* (1628–35), which depicts the Jewish queen who pleaded for her people. Legend has it that Esther fasted three days before the interview, and so she is usually depicted swooning from hunger. Gentileschi was the most admired female artist of her day and one of the most successful followers of Caravaggio.

Gallery 30 (Italian painting, 17th century): In this gallery are works of the Bolognese classicist Guido Reni, as well as Roman and Neapolitan artists. Guido Reni's *Charity* (c. 1630) is typical of his influential late style, with its soft colors and depictions of gentle emotions. Also represented are Mattia Preti, Guercino, Ludovico Carracci, and Salvator Rosa.

19TH-CENTURY EUROPEAN PAINTINGS & SCULPTURE

Within the collection of European paintings, the galleries of 19th-century paintings are rightly a great favorite with visitors. The collection spans several styles: Neoclassicism, Romanticism, Salon Painting, Impressionism, and Post-Impressionism.

Among the Neoclassical painters are works by Jacques-Louis David and Jean-Auguste-Dominique Ingres, represented by a portrait of the industrialist Joseph-Antoine Moltedo (c. 1810) and another of Jacques-Louis Leblanc (1823). Major works by painters of the Romantic persuasion include Eugène Delacroix's *The Abduction of Rebecca* (1846) and works by Jean-François Millet and Honoré Daumier, as well as others by members of the Barbizon School including Théodore Rousseau. There are landscapes and figure paintings by Camille Corot, and works by J.M.W. Turner. The museum has one of the world's largest holdings of the work of Gustave Courbet.

There are works—paintings and sculpture—by Degas, many collected by Mrs. H.O. Havemeyer, one of the museum's major benefactors. Through her friendship with Mary Cassatt, Louisine Havemeyer knew the Impressionist painters and was especially captivated by the work of Degas. On exhibit is his most famous sculpture, *Little Fourteen-Year Old Dancer*, the only piece exhibited during the artist's lifetime. Paintings include *The Dance Class* (1874), *A Woman Seated Beside a Vase of Flowers* (1865), and *The Collector of Prints* (1866).

Édouard Manet is well represented by *A Young Lady in 1866* (1866), *Mlle V... in the Costume of an Espada* (1862), *The Spanish Singer* (1860), *Young Man in the Costume of*

a *Majo* (1863), *Boy with a Sword* (1861), *A Matador* (1866–67), and *The Dead Christ with Angels* (1864). The museum owns almost 40 works by Claude Monet that span his long career: *The Green Wave* (1865), *Garden at Sainte-Adresse* (1867), *La Grenouillère* (1869), *Poplars* (1891), as well as painting from his series depicting the Houses of Parliament, Rouen Cathedral, and haystacks.

Among the works by Paul Cézanne are *The Gulf of Marseilles Seen from L'Estaque* (c. 1885), *Mont Sainte-Victoire and the Viaduct of the Arc River Valley* (1882–85), *Mme Cézanne in a Red Dress* (c. 1890), *The Card Players* (1890), and several still lifes. Renoir's elegant portrait of *Mme Charpentier and her Children* (1878) is a world away socially from *A Waitress at Duval's Restaurant* (c. 1875).

The museum owns the well-known *Ia Orana Maria* (1892) by Paul Gauguin and Henri Rousseau's *The Repast of the Lion* (c. 1907). Paintings by Vincent van Gogh include *Cypresses* (1889), *Mme Ginoux (L'Arlésienne)* (1889), *Shoes* (1888), *The Potato Peeler* (1885) with *Self-Portrait with a Straw Hat* (?1887) on the other side, and *Irises* (1890). There are several paintings by Seurat, including the mysteriously illuminated *Circus Sideshow* (1887–88). Also here are works by Paul Signac and Odilon Redon.

CYPRIOT ART

The Metropolitan has the best collection of ancient Cypriot art outside of Cyprus, much of it gathered by Luigi Palma di Cesnola (1832–1904), first director of the museum. An immigrant from Italy with a military background, Cesnola fought valiantly in the American Civil War and was rewarded by being made consul on Cyprus. Once there, he was overcome by a mania for archaeology, and devoted his considerable energy and money to unearthing thousands of works and having them shipped to New York.

The collection is installed chronologically. In the first room are prehistoric pieces including ceramics and bronze tripods. Among the highlights from the Geometric and Archaic periods (second room) is a silver-gilt bowl (c. 725–675 BC) whose decoration shows a mix of Mesopotamian and Egyptian motifs—an Assyrian winged god wrestling with a lion in the center and Egyptianized animals in the borders. The most outstanding work in the Cypriot collection from the Classical period (third room) is the monumental limestone Amathus sarcophagus, whose decoration shows Greek, Cypriot, Egyptian, and Persian influences. The basic shape and architectural ornaments (for example the sphinxes on the lid) are Greek, while the figures on the short sides show the influence of Egyptian and Phoenician art. The final room contains works from Hellenistic and Roman Cyprus.

ANCIENT NEAR EASTERN ART

The galleries of Ancient Near Eastern Art contain pre-Islamic works that date from the 6th millennium BC until the Arab conquest of the Near East in the mid-7th century AD. Geographically the collection extends across Mesopotamia, Syria, Iran, Anatolia, and other regions bounded by the Caucasus in the north, the Gulf of Aden in the

south, the western borders of modern Turkey in the west and the valley of the Indus River, now in central Pakistan, on the east.

The history of the Ancient Near East unlike that of Egypt, unified by the physical presence of the Nile, is fragmented into different political and cultural areas. In southern Mesopotamia alone were the capital cities of the Sumerians, Akkadians, Babylonians, Seleucids, Parthians, and Sasanians. Yet despite their chronological and cultural remoteness, the objects from these cultures have a immediacy that often speaks across time and distance.

Assyrian art: The most impressive monuments are large stone reliefs and imposing carvings taken from the palace of King Ashurnasirpal II (reigned 883–859 BC) in Nimrud (now northern Iraq) on the upper Tigris. Two enormous winged creatures, a bull and a lion, both with human heads (and originally supporting an arch above), defend the entrance to the other galleries. Their mere bulk and weight convey power, but to ancient observers their horned caps would have symbolized their might and divinity. In the adjacent galleries are objects from the excavations at Nimrud—bowls, clay figurines, and delicately carved ivories in Assyrian, Phoenician, and Syrian styles.

Mesopotamian art (5th–1st millennium BC): The focus is on works from the earliest urban societies through the Sumerian, Akkadian, and Babylonian periods. Along the north wall are cylinder seals with geometric symbols, human and animal shapes, and cuneiform inscriptions. One of the most famous objects in the collection is a wide-eyed gypsum statue of a bearded Sumerian worshiper (c. 2750–2600 BC) wearing a long sheepskin skirt with a tufted border. Mesopotamian gods were believed to dwell within their images, which were ritually fed and tended every day. Also on display is jewelry including a headdress ornament (c. 2600–2500)

with gold pendants shaped like poplar leaves. Sculpture includes a neo-Sumerian statue of Gudea (c. 2150 BC), governor of the city-state of Lagash, with a cuneiform inscription explaining that the statue was placed in a temple to show Gudea praying before the gods.

Anatolian and Syrian art: In the case with the golden objects from Mesopotamia is a bronze foundation figure of a snarling lion, buried to commemorate the construction of a building; its form was intended to frighten off evildoers. The yoked long-horned bulls (c. 2300–2000 BC) served as a finial, maybe for a ceremonial standard or chariot pole; the exaggerated length of their horns is characteristic of ancient Near Eastern art.

Pre-Islamic antiquities from Iran: Known from biblical stories for his wickedness, Nebuchadnezzar II (reigned 604–562 BC) was also a great builder, constructing royal palaces, gateways, and roads. The glazed and molded brick panels on the east wall depict lions, symbol of Ishtar, the Mesopotamian goddess of love and war. Civilizations of the 5th and early 4th millennia BC are represented by pottery with geometric and animal designs, for example a large ceramic storage jar (central case) decorated with silhouettes of mountain goats. The modeled stone mountain goat or mouflon (Indus valley, second half of the

3rd millennium BC) may have been a religious object, ceremonially buried to ensure a plentiful supply of game. A bronze head of a man (late 3rd millennium BC), whose inherent dignity and power led scholars to believe the figure represented a ruler, is considered a masterpiece of ancient art. A lovely gold cup dating from about 1000 BC shows four gazelles executed in delicate detail. **Achaemenid, Parthian, and Sasanian art:** The Achaemenid dynasty was founded by Cyrus the Great (c. 559–530 BC), who led a revolt of the Persians against their Median rulers and then went on to conquer neighboring lands, establishing ceremonial centers in Iran and Mesopotamia. The Achaemenids were noteworthy for their skill in metalwork and in this art they influenced the Greeks who eventually conquered them. Noteworthy are a gold horn-shaped cup ending in the head of a lion made of seven pieces joined

almost invisibly, and a silver cup in the shape of a horse's head decorated with a gold foil bridle.

The Sasanians ruled northwest Iran from the 3rd–mid-7th century AD and extended their empire both east and west. Among the Sasanian artifacts are many silver and silver-gilt objects, some decorated with banquet or hunting scenes, for example a plate with a king hunting rams (late 5th–early 6th century AD).

The period that stretched from the last few centuries before Christ until the Islamic conquests in the 7th century witnessed almost continuous warfare between the great empires of Byzantium and Sasanian Iran. The two powers consumed their resources trying to dominate the trade routes and the wealth of Syria and Anatolia, so that by the mid-7th century Sasanian Iran as well as half the Byzantine empire had succumbed to Arab armies from the west, followers of Islam.

ASIAN ART

The collection of Asian art is organized geographically, with separate sections devoted to China, Japan, South Asia, Korea, and Southeast Asia. The works—paintings, lacquer work, calligraphy, textiles, sculpture, and ceramics—date from the 2nd millennium BC to the present. Examples from the museum's fine collection of Asian ceramics are displayed on the northern part of the balcony overlooking the Great Hall.

NB: At the time of writing, the Korean galleries were closed for re-installation.

Arts of China

To the north of the balcony is the Sackler Gallery of large-scale Chinese stone sculpture from the 5th and 6th centuries. Beyond the arch are galleries of the arts of ancient China, which contain works from the Neolithic period (4000–1500 BC) through the T'ang Dynasty (AD 618–906). The scope of the other galleries is outlined below.

Neolithic Gallery: Among the objects in the collection are painted grain jars and pottery vessels from the Yellow River

region of northwestern China; and examples of carved jade (nephrite), especially in the form of perforated disks (*bi*),

important ceremonial objects dating from 2700–2200 BC. They may have been used in burials to help the soul of the departed rise to heaven.

Bronze Age Gallery: Among the artifacts from about 1500–2000 BC is a Tuan Fang altar set with ritual vessels. From the Shang dynasty (11th century BC) come a bronze lobed tripod cauldron decorated with an animal mask and a ritual vessel in the form of a bird, used for pouring wine. Also here are decorated weapons, hooks for closing garments, jade ornaments, and small sculptures.

Han Dynasty Gallery (206 BC–AD 220): Here are ceramic tomb figurines, which appeal to modern sensibilities for their depiction of human activities. A pair of men play a game, one clearly happier than the other with the outcome. A dancing woman with a long robe and hanging sleeves is captured in an expressive movement. Architectural models, houses, and farm buildings (complete with livestock) suggest the domestic side of Han life. Here are also vividly painted animal-shaped containers and vases, rare outside China.

Gallery of the Six Dynasties (AD 220–618): The focus is on a collection of early Buddhist sculpture from northern China created at a period after the collapse of the Han Dynasty when Buddhism became a significant intellectual and religious force in China. Prominently displayed is a Maitreya altarpiece (AD 524) from the Northern Wei Dynasty. Its central figure is Maitreya, the Buddha of the Future, whose return to earth was anticipated during this period.

T'ang Dynasty Gallery (AD 618–906): These objects were created during an era when China enjoyed political and cultural influence and its capital (modern Sian) at the end of the Silk Road was among the most technologically advanced cities on earth. Gold and silver vessels and ornaments and jade belt plaques illustrate the wealth and cosmopolitan spirit of the age. Also in this gallery are several T'ang tomb figures. These ceramic objects, decorated with "three-color" glazes, which melted and flowed with the heat of the kiln, are one of the hallmarks of T'ang culture. Hundreds of such figures representing soldiers, grooms, servants, tomb guardians, camels, and horses, were placed in tombs to serve the needs of the dead.

Galleries of Chinese paintings: Works from the Sung, Yuan, Ming, and Qing dynasties are shown on a rotating basis along with sculpture and objects from the same dynasties, important loans, and special exhibitions.

Chinese Garden Court: Modeled on a 12th-century court from Suzhou, west of Shanghai, built by a public official who retreated there from the burdens of his job, the courtyard was constructed in China and assembled here (1980) according to traditional methods by Chinese engineers and craftsmen. The garden is carefully designed so that contrasting principles—light and dark, hard and soft, high and low, crooked and straight, dynamic and static—balance and complement one another. The garden is the center of an implied architectural whole; in China many rooms would have been built around the courtyard. Here in the museum are three typical garden structures: the viewing pavilion or *ting*, the winding walkway, and the small main hall (called the Ming Room), with formally arranged furniture. Against the south wall

stands a fantastically shaped Taihu rock, one of several in the courtyard harvested from the bottom of Lake Tai, whose waters and sands give these rocks their characteristic forms. A connoisseur would savor the proportions of the rock, which should appear lean and bony, be broader at the top than at the base, have holes so that it rings when struck, and have "walkable" passages through its surface where the mind could wander and climb.

South and Southeast Asian art

These galleries, which opened in 1994, allowed visitors for the first time to see a permanent display of works from several great artistic cultures. The beautiful galleries, with their varied floor paving, lighting, and architectural details, harmonize with the art on display. The first seven galleries are devoted to the arts of South Asia, from 3000 BC until the 16th century.

Gallery 1 (Early India; c. 3000 BC–1st century BC): Among the statues are those of nature gods and goddesses, dwarfish male figures called *yakshas* and female figures called *yakshis*. Also on view is a beautiful pair of gold earrings dating from the 1st century BC, the most elaborate pieces of early Indian jewelry known to exist.

Room 2 (Kushan and Ikshavaku periods; 1st–4th centuries AD): The Kushans, nomadic warriors who conquered much of northwest India, including Gandhara (parts of present-day Pakistan and Afghanistan), controlled the trade routes from the Mediterranean to China. Their art reflects contact with Western cultures. The torso of a standing bodhisattva, for example, shows the influence of Greek art in its idealized features and the execution of the robe. Bodhisattvas are enlightened beings who help others achieve salvation.

Room 3 (Gupta period; 4th–7th centuries): The arts flourished under the generous patronage of the politically powerful Gupta rulers of northern India. A sandstone standing Buddha is one of the most important pieces in the collec-

tion: the flowing lines of the robe and the posture of repose suggest the spirituality achieved by the god. *Krishna Battling the Horse Demon Keshi* (5th century), the only large Gupta terra cotta in the collection, depicts Krishna's body with the rounded limbs typical of the Gupta style.

Room 4 (Kashmir and contiguous regions; 5th–11th centuries): The artistic traditions of northwest India were influenced by the art of Central Asia, Iran, and the Greco-Buddhist art of Gandhara. The *Padmapani Lokeshvara Seated in Meditation* (7th century) shows the deity Lokeshvara, a form of the Bodhisattva of Infinite Compassion; the lotus (*padma*) is a symbol of transcendence. Near the right wall is a white marble *linga*, a phallic emblem for the generative force of the universe, with the face of the god Shiva emerging from its shaft.

Room 5 (Kingdoms of northeast India, Pala and Sena periods; 7th–12th centuries): The *Goddess Durga Killing the Buffalo Demon*, a small intricate sculpture from India or Bangladesh, depicts the 16-armed warrior as she severs the head of a buffalo inhabited by a demon, who emerges from the buffalo's headless body.

Rooms 6–7 (South India): A huge seated four-armed Vishnu is one of the few examples of art from the Pandya Dynasty (8th–9th centuries), which ruled southernmost India. The god is depicted seated on a lion throne; his raised front right hand would have been posed in the "fear allaying gesture." In the next room, devoted to the dynasties of the 8th–14th centuries, are fine bronze images from the Chola period (880–1279); the standing Parvati depicts the Hindu goddess, consort of Shiva, in the graceful traditional "thrice bent" pose. The iconography of *Shiva as Lord of the Dance* (11th century) shows the god as creator, preserver, and destroyer. Also on display are a delightful figure of Hanuman, leader of the monkey clan, and a beautiful copper *Yashoda and Krishna* (14th century), showing the god being nursed by his foster mother.

Rooms 8–9 (Medieval sculpture and Sri Lankan art): In the Medieval Sculpture Gallery are examples of the arts that flourished from the 8th–13th centuries, derived from the styles of the Gupta period. *Loving Couple*, a 13th-century stone temple sculpture, shows a bejeweled couple embracing, symbolic not only of physical pleasure but of the soul's longing for union with the divine. A doorway at the right of the façade leads to a small room of Sri Lankan art.

Room 10 (Jain Temple): Overhead rises a carved wooden dome along with its supporting structure which belonged to a meeting hall of a 16th-century Jain temple in Gujarat. The elaborate wood carvings inside the dome represent the splendors of the heavenly realms. Seated in front of it is a white marble *tirthankara*, an enlightened being.

Rooms 11–13 (Indian miniatures, Nepali and Tibetan art): Here (mezzanine level) are examples of Indian miniature painting and decorative arts (15th–18th centuries), Nepali art (6th–17th centuries), and Tibetan art (11th–18th centuries) including *tangkas* (paintings on cloth). One fine work in the Nepali room (12) is a standing Bodhisattva Maitreya, a gilded figure standing in the "thrice bent" pose, characteristic of Indian sculpture.

Room 14 (Southeast Asia: Thailand, Vietnam, and Indonesia; Bronze Age–3rd millennium BC): Among the ceremonial vessels is an imposing bronze object in the shape of an ax head; it probably dates from 500 BC–AD 300, but neither its place of origin nor its use are known. Also here are pre-Angkor sculptural works from Cambodia and Vietnam.

Room 15 (Indonesia; 5th–15th centuries AD): Indian culture was transported to the Indonesian archipelago by maritime traders who stopped at the islands en route to China. In a freestanding case is a bronze figure of Krishna on Garuda, the half-god, half-bird figure in the Hindu pantheon, who symbolizes the power of the sun. Also here are other small bronze sculptures and gold ornaments.

Room 16 (Thailand, Cambodia, and Vietnam, pre-Angkor period; 6th–9th centuries): Like the Indonesian archipelago, the culture of mainland Southeast Asia was influenced by contacts with Indian traders. Cambodian and Vietnamese sculpture reflects Indian traditions, but is remarkable for its undecorated simplicity and sense of physicality. The four-armed

Avalokiteshvara, the Bodhisattva of Infinite Compassion (8th century), is distinguished from the more usual imperial images found elsewhere in Asia by his simple clothing and lack of jewelry.

Room 17 (Khmer Courtyard, Angkor period; 9th–13th centuries): The Khmer kings controlled Cambodia, Vietnam, and Thailand for five centuries, during which artistic traditions remained relatively constant. Among the fine bronzes in this quiet courtyard is a kneeling female deity (2nd half of 11th century), believed to be a goddess making a gesture of adoration; she wears a pleated sarong and a great deal of jewelry.

Room 18 (Later Thailand and Burma; 12th–16th centuries): Ceramics and other objects include a bronze standing Buddha (12th–13th century).

Arts of Japan

The Japanese galleries contain painting, sculpture, ceramics, lacquer, textiles, metalwork, and woodblock prints spanning more than 4,000 years, from the third millennium BC up to the present. Prints, textiles, and other fragile works are shown in rotation. While the installation is roughly chronological, it also offers insights into the Japanese aesthetic sensibility, which unlike Western taste traditionally made no distinction between the fine arts and the decorative arts. The galleries also conform to the Japanese sense of appropriateness, displaying objects in settings similar to the temples, houses, and palaces for which they were created.

The scope of the main galleries is described below. The remaining galleries offer changing selections of Japanese ceramics and other decorative arts. Works from the late Edo period include textiles with painstaking embroidery, elegant lacquer ware, and woodblock prints.

Pre-Buddhist and Shinto art: On the left side of this small gallery are objects from the nomadic Jomon (cord marking) culture (10,000–c. 250 BC) and the subsequent Yayoi period (c. 250 BC–AD 300) including rare Jomon tools and pottery, as well as *haniwa* figures (cylindrical clay sculptures). In the years from c. 300 BC–c. AD 300, enormous tomb mounds were built for the military aristocracy and these *haniwa* figures were placed around the mounds, possibly to serve as guardians. On the other side of the gallery is a fierce bronze image of Zao Gongen (11th century), a tutelary deity who became the object of a cult incorporating both Buddhist and Shinto beliefs.

Buddhist art: Different schools of Japanese Buddhism, first imported from China in the 6th century, are reflected in the images of this room. Dominating the room is a 12th-century Dainichi Buddha, seated upon a lotus pedestal in a contemplative posture; the dais supporting him represents Mt. Sumeru, the mystic center of the Buddhist universe. Nearby is a ferocious standing 12th-century Fudo (the name means "immovable"), a protective deity who warded off Buddha's enemies with his sword.

Kamakura narrative painting: (Paintings rotated because of light-sensitivity.) During the Kamakura period (1185–1333), as power shifted from the

aristocracy to a class of landed warrior chieftains (shoguns), a native realistic style of Japanese narrative painting developed. Important illustrations from the Kamakura period are the *Kitano Tenjin Engi*, illustrating the legendary origins of the Kitano Shrine of the Tenjin cult, and the *Miracles of Kannon*, which describe the mercies of the compassionate bodhisattva Kannon.

Muromachi period: The Muromachi period (1392–1568) saw the re-introduction of Chinese art, particularly monochromatic landscape paintings and screens of the type shown in this gallery. Chinese monks of the Zen sect brought to monasteries near the new capital at Kamakura their native art and culture. The Japanese Zen Buddhist monasteries became spiritual havens in a period of feudal warfare.

In the center of the galleries is Isamu Noguchi's sculptural *Water Stone*, a contemporary evocation of Japan's tradition of symbolic, spiritual gardens. The basalt boulder, sliced and polished to reveal a contrast between the rough, natural exterior and the smooth, shiny core, is hollowed into a basin from which water wells up and slides down into a bed of smooth, white stones taken from the Ise River, site of a sacred Shinto shrine.

Shoin Room: Adjacent to the sculpture is a replica of a Momoyama period (1568–1615) *shoin*. The *shoin* originated in 14th-century Zen temples as a place of study for monks and later was adopted by the Ashikaga shoguns as an area for the display of prized art objects. The mid-17th century *Ancient Plum*, attributed to Kano Sansetsu, is usually displayed on the sliding doors.

Edo paintings and objects: Works from the long Edo period (1603–1867) are among the most famous of the collection. Ogata Korin's *Eight Plank Bridge* (also called *The Irises*), with its brilliant colors, is often considered the artist's masterpiece. Known for his sensitivity to landscape, Katsushika Hokusai introduced a dramatic era of printmaking with his *Thirty-Six Views of Fuji*. *The Great Wave at Kanagawa*, with its towering breaker and distant view of the mountain, was said to have inspired Debussy's *La Mer*. *The Battles of the Hogen and Heiji Eras*, by an anonymous artist, shows a panoramic view of Kyoto peopled by warring figures.

MUSICAL INSTRUMENTS

The musical instruments in the museum's collection were chosen for their sound, appearance, and social and technical importance. Collected from six continents, they date from about 300 BC to the present. The audio tour gallery includes musical selections from the instruments in the collection.

Highlights include the world's oldest piano, made by Bartolommeo Cristofori, who invented the instrument (c. 1700); simple and austere in form, it is still playable. At the opposite end of the design spectrum is a grand piano from Erard et Cie (c. 1840), whose elaborate gilding and marquetry show its function as a status symbol; not surprisingly it was seldom played. A Venetian *spinettino* made (1540) for the duchess of Urbino has an inscription that warns off the morally and musically unworthy: "I am rich in gold and rich in tone; if you lack goodness, leave me alone."

Among the reed instruments are saxophones and sarrusophones (double-reeded saxophones), shawms, oboes, and bassoons. Bagpipes include folk versions of fur, leather, and wood with goats' heads carved on them as well as the familiar Scottish variety with plaid air bags. Pre-eminent among the stringed instruments is a group of Baroque violins, three by Antonio Stradivari, one of which is unique in having been restored to its original appearance and tone.

In the galleries of the Americas, Asia, and Africa are instruments as simple as pottery whistles and as elaborate as an Indian *mayuri*, a fretted lute-like instrument with a tail of peacock feathers. One of the most visually beautiful of the percussion instruments is a *Goqing* (or sonorous stone) from 19th-century China, a large piece of dark jade carved and incised to resemble a drooping lotus leaf. Among the Tibetan instruments are trumpets made from the thigh bones of priests and executed criminals, which were expected to call up fearsome magical powers. Indian instruments include sitars in many forms, as well as drums, trumpets, and other bowed and plucked stringed instruments.

PRINTS, DRAWINGS, & PHOTOGRAPHS

The collection of prints and drawings is known for works by Italian and French artists from the 15th–19th centuries, including drawings by artists whose paintings are rare, for example Michelangelo, Leonardo, Pontormo, and Altdorfer. Also important are northern Gothic and Renaissance prints, and those from 18th-century Italy and 19th-century France.

Photographs are shown in nearby galleries. The collection is noteworthy for European and American photographs, dating from the 1830s to the present. Especially important are the holdings in 19th-century British photography; the Alfred Stieglitz Collection (masterpieces of the Photo-Secession movement, 1902–17, as well as Pictorialist photography); American and European photography between the World Wars; and the personal archive of the American photographer Walker Evans.

THE COSTUME INSTITUTE

The Costume Institute (on the ground floor) contains a collection of more than 75,000 costumes and accessories from seven centuries and five continents. The clothing includes bullfighters' capes, a bridal robe from Korea, and tribal headgear from Central Africa. Among the urban garments are American and European dresses from the late 17th century to the present time, lingerie, accessories, and notable examples of elegant couturier clothing. The collection is shown in two yearly themed exhibitions, mounted (not surprisingly) with great style.

MUSEUM MILE

Map p. 577, D3–D1. Subway 4, 5, 6 to 86th St; 6 to 96th St or 103rd St. Bus M1, M2, M3, M4, M79, M86, M96, M106.

Museum Mile, the section of Fifth Avenue between 82nd and 105th Sts, has more museums—nine, planned to rise to ten—than any other stretch in the city. The encyclopedic Metropolitan Museum dominates the group (*see p. previous chapter*), but the eight other institutions form a vital part of the city's cultural life. Several occupy the palatial former homes of industrialists and bankers, built at the turn of the 20th century, when this stretch was known as "Millionaires' Row."

FROM TOWN HOUSE TO APARTMENT

At the turn of the 20th century the blocks facing Fifth Avenue between 81st and 83rd Sts remained an enclave for the very rich, with a row of grandiose town houses staring haughtily across the avenue toward the Metropolitan Museum. Apartment houses were just beginning to encroach on this moneyed territory, for example the building at 998 Fifth Ave (1910; McKim, Mead & White) on the northeast corner of 81st St. Its elegant good taste and spacious apartments (a typical one-story apartment had 17 rooms) helped the wealthy succumb to the advantages of living under the same multi-occupancy roof as their neighbors. Among the first tenants was Elihu Root, secretary of state and Nobel Peace Prize winner, to whom the rental agent reputedly offered a cut rate, hoping (successfully) to lure his social peers into the building.

A few town houses remain from this transitional period. The one at the southeast corner of 82nd St (1009 Fifth Ave), a Beaux-Arts beauty built on speculation in 1901 by Welch, Smith & Provot, is handsomely ornamented with wrought iron and limestone. It was first sold to Benjamin N. Duke, brother of the tobacco king James B. Duke, and remained in the Duke family until 2006, when a private buyer bought it for $40 million. The Goethe Institut cultural institute of Germany at 1014 Fifth Ave occupies another town house by the same firm (1907), first owned by a banker and broker. (*Gallery open weekdays 10–5, Sat 12–5; T: 212 744 8310.*)

THE NEUE GALERIE

Map p. 577, D3. 1048 Fifth Ave. Open Sat, Sun, Mon, Thur 11–6, Fri 11–9; closed Tues, Wed, Jan 1, Memorial Day, July 4, Labor Day, Thanksgiving, Christmas, Dec 31. T: 212 628 6200; www.neuegalerie.org. Subway: 4, 5, 6 to 86th St. Bus: M1, M2, M3, M4 to 86th St.

Situated in one of the most elegant mansions along the avenue, the Neue Galerie is devoted to early 20th-century Austrian and German art and design. Its name recalls an earlier Neue Galerie, which opened in Vienna in 1923 and showed the work of Klimt, Schiele, and other artists associated with the Secession, the revolt against 19th-century academic art. The museum was founded by Serge Sabarsky (1912–96), an art dealer and collector, and Ronald S. Lauder (b. 1944), philanthropist, collector, and heir to the Estée Lauder cosmetics fortune. The two became friends about the time Sabarsky opened his New York gallery (1968), and bought the present building in 1994. Lauder opened the museum in 2001, as a tribute after Sabarsky's death.

The building

William Starr Miller, a minor railroad baron and banker, commissioned the house in 1914 from Carrère & Hastings, the architects of the New York Public Library at Fifth Ave and 42nd St. Built of red brick and limestone, crowned with a slate mansard roof, the mansion is reminiscent of the 16th-century houses in the Place des Vosges in Paris—not surprisingly perhaps, since the architects had studied at the École des Beaux-Arts. In 1944 Grace Wilson Vanderbilt, widow of Cornelius Vanderbilt III, bought the house, which she referred to as the "Gardener's Cottage," since despite its 28 rooms, it was a comedown from the 58-room *palazzo* she had previously occupied further down the avenue. Nevertheless, she entertained lavishly. After her death in 1953, the YIVO Institute for Jewish Research occupied the building, until it was purchased by Lauder and Sabarsky. Fortunately, YIVO could not afford to re-model it, and so left the moldings, ceilings, and other architectural details intact.

The collection

Second floor: The second-floor galleries are filled with examples of art from early 20th-century Vienna, notably by Klimt, Schiele, and Kokoschka. Klimt's gold-flecked portrait of Adele Bloch-Bauer (1907), the wife of a Jewish sugar magnate and a leader of salon society, is considered one of the artist's finest works, and indeed is the finest in the collection. It was looted by the Nazis when they invaded Austria; Lauder bought it at auction in 2006 from Bloch-Bauer's niece, who had successfully sued the Austrian government for its return; the price, $135 million, was at the time the highest price ever paid for a painting.

Also on view are examples of furniture designed by Viennese architects Otto Wagner, one of the greatest exponents of Jugendstil, who later turned to Functionalism; and the Functionalist Adolf Loos, author of the famous essay "Ornament is Crime." Decorative arts by Josef Hoffmann and Koloman Moser, co-founders of the Wiener Werkstätte, are also on display.

Third floor: These galleries feature early 20th-century German art from several schools or movements: the Brücke, the Blaue Reiter, Neue Sachlichkeit, and the Bauhaus. There are several paintings by Max Beckmann, including a portrait of himself holding an imposing horn.

Rational, functional Bauhaus design is visible in furniture and household objects by Mies van der Rohe (architect of the Seagram Building) and the Hungarian Marcel Breuer (architect of the Whitney Museum).

THE SOLOMON R. GUGGENHEIM MUSEUM

Map p. 577, D3. 1071 Fifth Ave (88th St). Open Sat–Wed 10–5:45, Fri 10–7:45. Closed Thur, holidays; T: 212 423 3500; www.guggenheim.org. Subway: 4, 5, 6 to 86th St. Bus: M1, M2, M3, M4, M86.

The Solomon R. Guggenheim Museum is Frank Lloyd Wright's masterpiece—his only significant building in the city—and the repository of some 4,000 paintings, sculptures, and works on paper from the Impressionist period to the present. More than that of any other New York museum (with perhaps the exception of the Whitney), the Guggenheim's collection reflects the tastes of a few individuals. Its exhibitions of modern and contemporary painting and sculpture are shown in one of the world's most remarkable Modernist buildings, which itself is the jewel of the collection. Crowds of tourists usually fill the Rotunda, photographing one another in front of the cantilevered ramps or aiming their cameras at the fractured geometric spaces of the great oculus.

HISTORY OF THE GUGGENHEIM

Like so many other millionaires of the time, Solomon R. Guggenheim (1861–1949), whose fortune was based on mining and smelting, started out collecting traditional European paintings. This focus changed entirely in the late 1920s after he met Baroness Hilla Rebay von Ehrenwiesen, an intense, highly opinionated artist who introduced him to her artist friends (including Robert Delaunay, Fernand Léger, Vasily Kandinsky), and to her taste for Abstract art. In 1939 the Solomon R. Guggenheim Collection of Non-Objective Painting was shown in rented quarters at 24 East 54th St, with the Baroness in charge.

James Johnson Sweeney followed Rebay as museum director in 1952, and under his guidance the Guggenheim Museum became less narrowly ideological, purchasing Picassos and Cézannes, for example, which Rebay would have outlawed on the grounds that they were Figurative. A gift of Impressionist and Post-Impressionist work from Justin K. Thannhauser, a noted dealer and collector, further enriched and broadened the collection. The bequest of Peggy Guggenheim (Solomon's niece) put her entire collection of Cubist, Surrealist, and postwar painting and sculpture in the custody of the Guggenheim Foundation, though that collection remains in Venice, and is shown in New York only on occasional exchanges. In recent years the Guggenheim Foundation has (not without controversy) opened branches in Bilbao, Las Vegas, and Berlin.

The building

The idea of building an architecturally remarkable museum and of hiring Frank Lloyd Wright to design it apparently came from Rebay; and since Guggenheim died long before plans came to fruition, the realization of the building was left to her and to Harry Guggenheim, Solomon's successor. The result is one of the city's most controversial and distinctive buildings: a spiral with a ramp cantilevered out from its interior walls sitting above a horizontal slab. The ramp, about a quarter of a mile long, rises 1.75 inches per 10ft to a domed skylight 92ft above the ground. The ramp diameter at ground level is 100ft; at the top, 128ft. Wright called the building "organic" architecture, imitating the forms and colors of nature, while his critics called it a "bun," a "snail," and an "insult to art."

Between the time of Wright's original design and the completion of the building 16 years elapsed, many of them spent in arguments with the city Department of Buildings, whose ideas on construction differed from Wright's, and in quarrels with former museum director Sweeney, who argued that Wright's design would create serious problems in storing and hanging the collection (reservations that proved well-founded).

Today, however, the building is greatly admired—so much so that a rectilinear expansion (1992; Gwathmey Siegal & Assocs), which allows more of the permanent collection to be shown, was hotly controversial and derided as an insult to Wright's masterpiece. In 2005 the museum began a multi-year restoration of the exterior of Wright's dome, removing 12 coats of paint and repairing cracks that developed shortly after the building opened. Restoration was still in progress at the time of writing.

Highlights of the collection

Since works are rotated through the galleries, or may be displaced by major exhibitions, you can never be sure what you will see on a given visit, so the following description outlines the general holdings of the collection.

Impressionist and Post-Impressionist painters: The Thannhauser Gallery on the first level above the gift shop always includes selections from Justin K. Thannhauser's significant holdings. Camille Pissarro's *The Hermitage at Pontoise* was painted before his Impressionist works and is the earliest (c. 1867) picture in the collection. Vincent van Gogh's *Mountains at Saint-Rémy* (1889) is a turbulent landscape painted from the asylum where van Gogh was a patient. Among the paintings by Paul Cézanne are *Man with Crossed Arms* (c. 1899), a still life, and several landscapes.

Paul Gauguin's *In the Vanilla Grove, Man and Horse* (1891) evokes the lush Tahitian landscape, though the pose of the man and horse comes from the frieze on the Parthenon. Pablo Picasso's *Le Moulin de la Galette* (1900) was painted when Picasso was 19 years old and still under the influence of Toulouse-Lautrec. The collection also contains Picasso's *Woman Ironing* (1904), whose angular, distorted pose and flat monochromatic colors typify the end of the artist's Blue Period. *Fernande with a Black Mantilla* (1905–06), a portrait of Picasso's mistress, suggests the painter's movement toward Abstraction.

Camille Pissarro: *The Hermitage at Pontoise (Les Coteaux de l'Hermitage)* (c. 1867). The earliest painting in the collection.

Early 20th-century works: Paintings from the first decades of the 20th century may include (not necessarily from the Thannhauser bequest) *Reclining Nude* (1917) and *Jeanne Hébuterne with a Yellow Sweater* (1908–19) by Modigliani, Henri Matisse's *The Italian Woman* (1916), and Pierre Bonnard's *Dining Room on the Garden* (1934–35).

Pioneers of Modernism: Among the artists who fell within the canons of Rebay's taste were Georges Braque, represented by *Violin and Palette* and *Piano and Mandola*, both analytical, monochromatic studies painted around 1909–10, as well as the later *Guitar, Glass, and Fruit Dish on Sideboard* (1919). Picasso is represented by *Accordionist*, painted (1911) when he and Braque were together in the Pyrenees,

and by *Mandolin and Guitar* (1924), a more colorful, lively painting whose surfaces are less fractured. Fernand Léger's *The Great Parade* (1954) is considered by many to be the definitive work of his career, but the Guggenheim also owns works from the opening decades of the 20th century when he was experimenting with non-objective, Cubist forms, and from the 1920s when he was creating streamlined, machine-like forms.

Albert Gleizes, Robert Delaunay, Ernst Ludwig Kirchner, Emil Nolde, Oskar Kokoschka, Egon Schiele, Gino Severini, Kazimir Malevich, Piet Mondrian, Theo van Doesburg, Joan Miró and Paul Klee are all present in the collection. The Guggenheim owns a trove of paintings by Vasily Kandinsky, a particular favorite of

Oil on canvas, 37½ × 59⅛ in (95.2 × 150.1 cm). Solomon R. Guggenheim

Vasily Kandinsky: *Group in Crinolines* (1909), from the Solomon R. Guggenheim Founding Collection.

Rebay's. His work is well represented from its early Post-Impressionist and Fauve roots through his later, symbolic formal paintings of circles.

Postwar painters: Among the works are canvases by Willem de Kooning, Jackson Pollock, Mark Rothko, Franz Kline, and Richard Diebenkorn. Andy Warhol is represented (among other works) by a silk screen with multiple images of an electric chair, *Orange Disaster* (1963); and Roy Lichtenstein by *Preparedness*, which he called "a muralesque painting about our military-industrialist complex." There are also color field paintings by Morris Louis and Ellsworth Kelly.

Sculpture: Although Hilla Rebay envisioned a collection of painting only, the museum began to purchase sculpture after her departure as director. Alexander Archipenko's *Médrano II*

(1913–14), assembled from metal, wood, glass, and painted oilcloth, represents a circus dancer. Constantin Brancusi, Alberto Giacometti, Henry Moore, Jacques Lipchitz, Isamu Noguchi, Louise Nevelson, and David Smith are all represented in the collection.

Recent acquisitions: In 1990 the museum acquired (not without controversy) the Panza di Biumo collection of American Minimalist art from the 1960s and '70s, with such works as Carl Andre's *Alstadt Copper Square* (1967) and *Fall* (1968), a modular arrangement of 21 large pieces of rolled steel. In 1993, the Robert Mapplethorpe Foundation gave the Guggenheim nearly 200 photographs and other works, introducing photography into the collection and inaugurating a photography gallery.

THE NATIONAL ACADEMY

Map p. 577, D3. 1083 Fifth Ave (89th–90th Sts). Open Wed–Thur 12–5; Fri–Sun 11–6. Closed Mon, Tues, major holidays. T: 212 369 4880; www.nationalacademy.org.

The National Academy, a block north of the Guggenheim, is an artists' honorary association, with a museum and an art school attached.

The town house facing Fifth Avenue (1914; Ogden Codman Jr.), where the academy holds its exhibitions, was donated (1940) by Archer M. Huntington, whose wife, sculptor Anna Hyatt Huntington, was an academy member. The academy is a conservative institution, its members drawn from the ranks of the nation's established painters, sculptors, and graphic artists. Founded in 1825 as the National Academy of Design by painters Samuel F.B. Morse and Rembrandt Peale, among others, it strove to promote the arts through its art school and exhibitions.

Over the years the academy has amassed a collection of more than 5,000 works of art, in part the product of a ruling that members must supply a representative sample of their work. The holdings represent a summary of most established 19th- and 20th-century styles in American art. There are idealized landscapes from Hudson River School painters, examples of American Impressionism, Fauvism, Abstraction, and Photo-Realism. The exhibition program includes loans, works drawn from the collection, and an annual juried show.

CARNEGIE HILL

The neighborhood from Fifth to about Third Avenues, from about East 86th to East 96th St, is known as Carnegie Hill. It is quietly residential and upscale, with elegant town houses, occasional mansions, fine apartment buildings, and prestigious private schools. Carnegie Hill is remarkable for still having a gradient, since many of New York's geographical features were leveled or filled as the street grid made its way inexorably northward.

En passant: in Central Park at Fifth Ave and 91st St is the William T. Stead Memorial (1913; George James Frampton), a bronze tablet commemorating this British journalist who died on the *Titanic* after helping other passengers into lifeboats.

COOPER-HEWITT NATIONAL DESIGN MUSEUM

Map p. 577, D2. 2 East 91st St (southeast corner of Fifth Ave). Open Mon–Thur 10–5, Fri 10–9, Sat 10–6, Sun noon–6. Garden entrance on 90th St open May–Sept (weather permitting). Closed Thanksgiving, Christmas, and New Year's Day; T: 212 849 8400; www.cooperhewitt.org. Subway: 4, 5, 6 to 86th or 96th St. Bus: M1, M2, M3, M4, M86, M96.

The Cooper-Hewitt National Design Museum, part of the Smithsonian Institution, offers exhibitions drawn from its stupendous collections that include everything from antique wallpaper to sand toys and Asian porcelains. The museum, which presents the annual National Design Awards for the best in American design, presides over its well-heeled neighborhood from a mansion constructed by steel baron and philanthropist Andrew Carnegie (*see box below*).

Andrew Carnegie.

Andrew Carnegie and his Fifth Avenue Mansion

Andrew Carnegie (1835–1919), an immigrant from Scotland, amassed a fortune in iron, coal, steel, steamship and railroad lines. In 1898 he announced his intention to build "the most modest, plainest, and roomiest house in New York." For this plain and roomy house, he chose a rocky, semi-rural plot far north of the trophy houses of his more fashionable financial peers. His architects, Babb, Cook & Willard, finished the house in 1901. It was remarkably comfortable and technically advanced for its time, well-suited for his domestic needs and for the philanthropic projects he administered from his first-floor office. The most advanced and sophisticated pumps and boilers available filled the sub-basement, two of each major piece so that a spare was always available. If city water or electricity were interrupted, an artesian well and generator would relieve the family and servants of any inconvenience. Up in the attic great fans pulled air through cheesecloth filters over tanks of cool water in a primitive system of air-conditioning. The house was the first private residence in the city with a structural steel frame, an Otis passenger elevator, and central heating.

The decoration is opulent. Over the main door, on 91st St, hangs an ornate copper and glass canopy. The marble vestibule leads to the Great Hall, paneled in Scottish oak, a token of Carnegie's affection for his homeland, to which he returned yearly. At the east end of the hall stood the organ, its pipes in a shaft now used for the elevator. The doorways to Carnegie's study and library, on the west end, are appropriately scaled to his height (he was 5ft 2in tall). Along the south side of the first floor, facing the garden, were public rooms—the music room on the west with a large crystal chandelier and musical motifs, including a Scottish bagpipe, in the ceiling moldings. In the garden vestibule, next to the music room, are leaded-glass windows by Louis Comfort Tiffany. Across the garden facing 90th St is a town house formerly belonging to Carnegie's daughter, now used for administration. Unfortunately the present configuration of the museum obscures many of these architectural details.

The collection

Sarah, Eleanor, and Amy Hewitt, granddaughters of industrialist Peter Cooper, founded the museum in 1897 as part of the Cooper Union for the Advancement of Science and Art. During their travels, the three had been impressed by the South Kensington Museum (now the Victoria & Albert) in London, and the Musée des Arts Décoratifs in Paris. Helped by their friends (for example J. Pierpont Morgan, who donated European textiles) they began amassing decorative objects, prints and drawings, and assorted items that appealed to them as good design—napkins, gloves, cookie tins.

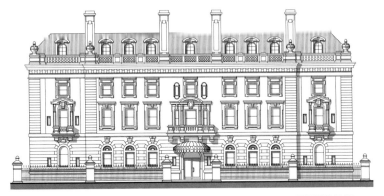

COOPER-HEWITT MUSEUM: 91ST STREET FAÇADE

Among their first acquisitions were Italian architectural and decorative drawings that had belonged to the curator of the Borghese collection. Later came 1,500 drawings, sketches, and paintings by American landscapist Frederic Edwin Church, and the contents of Winslow Homer's studio. The Hewitt sisters admired both European culture and the kind of American industrial savvy represented by their grandfather (who along with his other accomplishments had designed the first American locomotive), and their acquisitions reflect these preferences.

The museum was first installed at Cooper Union, an educational institution founded by Peter Cooper in the East Village (*see p. 162*). The collection grew in size and quality over the years, broadening its focus after the last Hewitt sister died in 1930, until by 1963 Cooper Union could no longer maintain the museum financially, and supporters engineered its adoption by the Smithsonian Institution.

The collections today include more than 250,000 objects, divided into four curatorial departments: Product Design and Decorative Arts; Wall Coverings; Textiles; and Drawings, Prints and Graphic Design. The collections are shown in changing exhibitions and to researchers by advance appointment. In 2002 on a visit to the Cooper-Hewitt, Sir Timothy Clifford, then director of the National Galleries in Scotland, discovered in an old storage box a drawing of a candelabrum, which has since been attributed to Michelangelo. The museum had bought the drawing in 1942 from a London dealer along with other decorative designs, the whole batch for $60.

THREE RECYCLED MANSIONS

The **Convent of the Sacred Heart** (1918; C.P.H. Gilbert & J. Armstrong Stenhouse) at 1 East 91st St (Fifth Ave) occupies the former mansion of Otto Kahn (1867–1934), financier, philanthropist, and patron of the arts. One of the largest and most restrained neo-Italian Renaissance mansions in the city, the house has unusual arched carriage entrances. Kahn, a member of the German-Jewish elite known as "Our Crowd," was chairman of the board of the Metropolitan Opera, which he saved from artistic mediocrity by hiring Giulio Gatti-Casazza as manager and Toscanini as conductor, and from financial bankruptcy by personally donating an estimated $2.5 million.

The former **James A. Burden House** (7 East 91st St), now also part of the Convent of the Sacred Heart, was built in 1902 by W.D. Sloane (heir to a high-end furniture company) and his wife Emily Vanderbilt Sloane for their eldest daughter, Adele. Adele married James A. Burden, who was heir to an ironworks in Troy, N.Y. The Burden ironworks produced most of the horseshoes for the Union Army during the Civil War (at a peak rate of 3,600 per hour) and eventually developed into the American Machine and Foundry Company, making James a brilliant match for Adele, by reputation a beautiful and spirited woman.

The architects, Warren & Wetmore, who stood in the good graces of the Vanderbilts (they also built Grand Central Terminal), built a house that has been described as a modern French interpretation of an Italian *palazzo*: Italian in its massing and the simplicity of details, French in the inventive ornament and the presence of a service floor between the ground floor and what in a less imposing building would be called the parlor floor.

The nearby **John Henry Hammond House** (1909; Carrère & Hastings) at 9 East 91st St was built for Adele Sloane's younger sister, also named Emily Vanderbilt Sloane. Emily married John Henry Hammond, who was educated at Yale and Columbia Law School but was not sufficiently socially secure to accept with equanimity a house of such proportions: "I'm going to be considered a kept man," he is said to have told his wife when shown the plans. Their son, also named John Henry Hammond (1910–87), spent a lifetime discovering, nurturing, and promoting musical talent, a career that shaped the direction of American popular music from the early years of the Depression until his death. Hammond was passionately committed both to music and to civil rights. He promoted, among others, Billie Holiday and Count Basie. He fostered the early career of Benny Goodman, and urged him to hire black musicians Teddy Wilson and Lionel Hampton. Hammond, who did not care for bebop, which came along in the mid-1940s, faded from prominence for a while, but during the 1960s and '70s nurtured the careers of Aretha Franklin, Bob Dylan, and Bruce Springsteen.

THE JEWISH MUSEUM

Map p. 577, D2. 1109 Fifth Ave (92nd St). Open Sat–Wed 11–5:45, Thur 11–8. Closed Fri, major Jewish holidays, Martin Luther King Day, Thanksgiving Day, New Year's Day. On Sat the shop, restaurant, children's exhibition, and interactive exhibits are closed, but the galleries are open. T: 212 423 3200; www.jewishmuseum.org. Subway: 4, 5, 6 to 86th St, or 6 to 96th St. Bus: M1, M2, M3, or M4.

Founded in 1904, the Jewish Museum is operated under the auspices of the Jewish Theological Seminary of America. The museum houses a collection of some 28,000 artifacts, works of art, ceremonial objects, and antiquities and is considered to be the most important collection of Judaica in the Western Hemisphere. In addition to its permanent exhibition, the museum offers changing exhibitions.

The permanent exhibition, *Culture and Continuity: The Jewish Journey*, occupies the top two floors and explores Jewish culture from its archaeological beginnings to the present. The first part, "Forging an Identity" (c. 1200 BCE–c. 640 CE), illuminates the early evolution of the Jews as a people with their own customs and rituals. On view are archaeological objects, vessels, implements, and a selection from the museum's collection of Hanukkah lamps.

The second section, "Interpreting a Tradition" (640–1800 CE), explores the cultures of Middle Eastern, Sephardic, and Ashkenazi Jews. Here are objects as diverse as a portion of a synagogue wall from 19th-century Persia showing the artistic influence of Islam, a metalwork Hanukkah lamp from 18th-century Frankfurt, and a 20th-century Torah crown of silver and pearls designed by Moshe Zabari in 1959.

The third section, "Confronting Modernity" (c. 1800–1948), deals with the choices confronting Jews in modern times: assimilation or nationalism, religious orthodoxy or reform, capitalism or socialism. Works on view include Louis Goldman's photo of Independence Day in Tel Aviv, sculpture by Elie Nadelman, and painting by Ben Shahn.

"Realizing a Future" contains contemporary art, painting, sculpture on such themes as the interaction between Jews and those around them, and Jewish ritual and spirituality. The plaster model of George Segal's *The Holocaust* (the bronze cast is in San Francisco) uses his familiar technique of casting live models using hospital bandages.

The building

The former Felix Warburg Mansion forms the core of the museum. Warburg admired the Isaac Fletcher House (72nd St and Fifth Ave; *see p. 316*) and hired its architect, C.P.H. Gilbert, to design something in the same French Gothic style. The mansion remained in the family until 1944, when the financier's widow, Frieda Schiff Warburg, donated it to the Jewish Theological Seminary for a museum. In 1990–93 the museum restored and expanded the building, doubling the exhibition space and replicating along Fifth Avenue its intricately carved limestone façade, using stone from the original quarry.

THE MUSEUM OF THE CITY OF NEW YORK

Map p. 577, D1. 1220 Fifth Ave (East 103rd St). Open Tues–Sun 10–5; closed Thanksgiving, Christmas Day, New Year's Day, and Mon except Mon holidays. T: 212 534 1672; www.mcny.org. Subway: 6 to 103rd St. Bus: M1, M3, M4 or M106 to 104th Street, M2 to 101st St.

The Museum of the City of New York offers exhibitions that explore the city's complex history from its early days as a Dutch colony to its present eminence. Founded in 1923, the museum's collections contain more than three million artifacts—real and toy fire engines, maps and prints, ship models, portraits of prominent New Yorkers, and even stripper Gypsy Rose Lee's hand-embroidered garter belt. The museum building (1932; Joseph H. Freedlander) is unprepossessing, but the collections are unrivaled for anyone interested in the history of the city.

Several ongoing exhibits document the theater in New York and the city's importance as a port; a 25-min film gives an overview of the city's growth from its beginnings as a struggling settlement to the present. Period rooms recreate interiors from the homes of prominent New Yorkers, notably John D. Rockefeller Sr.

Paintings in the collection include portraits of prominent New Yorkers and cityscapes by Childe Hassam, Asher B. Durand, and Reginald Marsh. The collection of American silver offers examples of restrained work by 18th-century New York silversmiths, as well as florid 19th-century pieces from such firms as Tiffany & Co. The toy collection has more than 100,000 dolls, books, soldiers, trains, boats, and puppets from the colonial period to the present. The crowning glory of the dolls' house exhibition is the Stettheimer Dollhouse, whose meticulously executed interiors include miniature reproductions of works by Gaston Lachaise and Marcel Duchamp, as well as dolls representing Gertrude Stein, Virgil Thomson, and Edward Steichen.

EL MUSEO DEL BARRIO

Map p. 577, D1. 1230 Fifth Ave (104th St). Open Wed–Sun 11–5; closed Mon, Tues, Thanksgiving, Christmas Day, New Year's Day. T: 212 831 7272; www.elmuseo.org. Subway: 6 to 103rd St. Bus: M1, M3, M4.

El Museo del Barrio is one of the city's outstanding small, sharply-focused museums; the only museum in the city devoted to Puerto Rican, Caribbean, and Latin American culture. El Museo's permanent collection, its schedule of highly-regarded changing shows, and its community programs make it a leading institution of Latino culture.

Located at the edge of Spanish Harlem or *El Barrio* (literally "the neighborhood"), El Museo was founded in 1969 by community activists, teachers, and artists, mainly Puerto Ricans. It operated first from a classroom in a public school, and then moved to several storefronts until it found a long-term home in the present building, originally a settlement house for the Heckscher Foundation for Children and now owned by the city. At first El Museo focused on the culture of its Puerto Rican neighborhood, but as New York's Latino population has grown and diversified, the museum has

expanded its programs. Important exhibitions have brought wide attention to El Museo, whose attendance has increased dramatically in the past decade. In addition to art exhibitions, the museum runs festivals and outreach programs. A new, glassy entrance pavilion with a café and meeting spaces is under construction.

The collection

El Museo's permanent collection includes pre-Columbian artifacts, traditional Caribbean and Latin American arts, 20th-century prints, drawings, paintings, sculptures and installations, as well as photography, documentary films, and video. The museum has an outstanding collection of *santos de palo*—wooden saints and religious figures, most made by self-taught Puerto Rican carvers. The Taíno collection of pre-Columbian artifacts, shown in the only permanent exhibit, showcases ceremonial and domestic objects from the Taíno, Carib and Igneri cultures. Examples of traditional Latin American arts include musical instruments, miniature houses, dolls, and a wonderful group of masks.

COMING TO THE MILE

The Museum for African Art is scheduled to move to a new permanent home on Fifth Avenue at 110th St; in the meantime exhibitions are presented at various venues throughout the city. The museum focuses on the art of sub-Saharan Africa, with changing exhibitions that explore the continent's rich artistic and cultural heritage, or showcase contemporary African art.

YORKVILLE & THE
EAST RIVER

Map pp. 579, F1–577, F2. Subway: 6 to 77th St. Bus: M15, M18, M72.

Formerly a neighborhood of Germans, Hungarians, Czechs, and Slovaks, Yorkville today is similar to other middle-class locales that attract the young and well-to-do to its high-rise towers.

HISTORY OF YORKVILLE

In the late 18th century Yorkville was a small hamlet between New York and the village of Harlem, its country estates owned by wealthy families of Germanic origin—Schermerhorns, Rhinelanders, and Astors. When the New York and Harlem Railroad arrived in 1834, Yorkville quickly became a suburb drawing middle-class Germans, among them people like the Rupperts, who operated a brewery. Less wealthy Germans usually settled first on the Lower East Side, notably around Tompkins Square in a neighborhood called "Kleindeutschland." By 1900, as waves of eastern European and Italian immigrants poured into downtown Manhattan, many Germans began moving to Yorkville, a migration hastened in 1904, when the *General Slocum*, an excursion steamer jammed with Kleindeutschland women and children, burned and sank in the East River. More than a thousand people died, making it too painful for many surviving husbands to remain in the old neighborhood.

Though Yorkville was never rich, it remained a solid neighborhood through the years of the Depression, a place where people worked close to home—either in small businesses or for the brewery—and enjoyed themselves at local restaurants, Bavarian beer gardens, or cafés modeled after those in Vienna. In the years before World War II, Yorkville was a center of both Nazi and anti-Nazi activity. After World War II, the area saw a last wave of German immigration. Until the recent arrival of the well-to-do, ethnic newcomers were largely Hispanics filtering down from Spanish Harlem on the northern edge of Yorkville.

As elsewhere, immigrant groups clustered together. Little Bohemia, with Czechs and Slovaks, lay at the southern end of Yorkville around First Avenue from the upper 60s to the mid-70s. North of the Czech quarter was Little Hungary, which centered around Second Avenue in the upper 70s and low 80s. The abortive Hungarian Revolution (1848) touched off the first wave of immigrants, lasting until just before World War I; Hungarians began moving uptown from the Lower East Side around 1905. A new wave arrived after the Soviet Union's invasion of Hungary in 1956.

Sotheby's

Sotheby's, at 1334 York Ave near 72nd St (*map p. 579, F1*), is the American branch of the world's oldest firm of fine arts auctioneers, founded in London in 1744. Sotheby's is open for viewing before some auctions (*T: 212 606 7000; www.sothebys.com*).

In 1964 Sotheby's merged with the American company Parke-Bernet, creating a wide-reaching international auction house. Among Sotheby's record sales have been the highest-priced single work of art—Picasso's *Garçon à la Pipe* ($104 million)—sold in 2004; the most expensive contemporary work—Mark Rothko's *White Center (Yellow, Pink and Lavender on Rose)*—sold in 2007 for $72.8 million (offered by David Rockefeller); and the most ever paid for a sculpture and an antiquity at auction—$57.2 million for the Guennol Lioness, a tiny limestone figurine from ancient Mesopotamia, believed to be at least 5,000 years old (sold in 2008).

Cherokee Apartments

Stretching across Cherokee Place from 507–23 East 77th St to 508–22 East 78th St (*map p. 577, F4*) are the Cherokee Apartments (1911), a six-story complex formerly known as the Shively Sanitary Tenements because they incorporated Dr. Henry Shively's notions for treating tuberculosis with fresh air and sunlight. The buildings have small balconies accessible from triple-hung windows, along with Guastavino-tiled tunnels leading to central courtyards. There, corner stairways rise to upper floors, roofed against the rain with iron and glass. All these features were designed to produce a healthful environment.

Henderson Place and the Asphalt Green

The well-preserved Henderson Place Historic District (along East End Ave and Henderson Place, East 86th and East 87th Sts; *map p. 577, F3*) was once part of John Jacob Astor's country estate. John C. Henderson, who made his fortune in furs and fur hats, built the houses for people of moderate means, though they seem upscale today. Twenty-four of the original 32 two-story Queen Anne row houses (1882) remain. Built of brick and rough stone, they are glorified with the usual appurtenances of the Queen Anne style: bays, oriel windows, dormers, and gables. The buildings are set back with front yards, which is atypical for Manhattan.

Further north is the **former Municipal Asphalt Plant** (1944; Kahn & Jacobs) at 555 East 90th St (east of York Ave). This was the first American parabolic arch built in reinforced concrete over a steel frame. Abandoned by the city in 1968, it has been converted to a not-for-profit center for fitness and sports, known as the Asphalt Green.

GRACIE MANSION

Map p. 577, F3. Open by guided tour Wed 10, 11, 1, and 2; for reservations call T: 311 or, from outside the city, 212 NEW YORK (212 639 9675); http://www.nyc.gov/html/om/html/gracie.html.

Gracie Mansion.

The mayor's official residence, Gracie Mansion (1799, later additions), faces the East River from Carl Schurz Park (East End Ave at 88th St). Restored in 2002, and fitted out with period furniture, it is one of Manhattan's oldest residences, now used for official gatherings and to host visiting dignitaries. (The present mayor does not live here.) With its 16 rooms and fine detailing—leaded glass sidelights and a semicircular fanlight above the main doorway, railings around the roof and above the main floor—the mansion exemplifies Federal domestic architecture at the elegant end of the scale.

The present Gracie Mansion began as the country home of wealthy merchant Archibald Gracie, who had a Downtown town house on State St across from Battery Park. Gracie's business foundered during the War of 1812 (*see p. 30*) and he sold the house in 1823. In 1896 the city bought it, and for years used it as a concession stand and restrooms for nearby Carl Schurz Park. After housing the Museum of the City of New York (1924–32), it became the mayor's residence in 1942 when Fiorello La Guardia rejected industrialist Charles M. Schwab's 75-room now-demolished neo-château at Riverside Drive and 73rd St. "What," exclaimed the fiery, 5-ft 2-in mayor, a man of modest tastes, "me in that?"

Carl Schurz Park

Gracie Mansion sits in Carl Schurz Park (on the East River between 84th and 90th Sts), which provides beautiful views of the river. The park is named for the most prominent German-American of the 19th century. Schurz (1829–1906), a hero of the German revolutionary movement of 1848, arrived in America in 1852 and became a

brigadier general during the Civil War, a US senator, and secretary of the interior. He moved to New York in 1881 and lived in Yorkville. A promenade, John Finley Walk, honors John Huston Finley (1863–1940), president of the City College of New York, associate editor of *The New York Times*, state commissioner of education, and an unflagging pedestrian, who on several occasions walked the 32 miles around Manhattan Island. From the promenade Mill Rock, Hell Gate, the Triborough Bridge, and the Hell Gate Arch are visible.

THE EAST RIVER

Mill Rock and Hell Gate

Mill Rock, 2.5 acres of undeveloped land, lies about 1,000 feet offshore opposite about 96th St. Fortified during the War of 1812, it protected the eastern entrance to New York harbor. The US Army Corps of Engineers used it at the end of the 19th century to experiment with explosives for clearing obstacles in the river. Today Mill Rock belongs to the Parks Department.

East of Mill Rock is **Hell Gate**, the channel leading to the protected waters of Long Island Sound. Ever since explorer Adriaen Block sailed the *Tyger* through it in 1612, Hell Gate has had a reputation for treachery. Hell Gate is 22.5 miles from the open sea via New York Bay but more than 100 miles via Long Island Sound, which accounts for three hours' difference in the tides at the two ends of the East River. These conflicting tides along with reefs and rocks in the water once made Hell Gate so tortuous that hundreds of ships are said to lie beneath its waters. The most famous wreck, the Revolutionary frigate *Hussar*, went down in 1780, carrying—according to legend—gold and silver coins worth $500 million as payroll for British troops. Neither the ship, nor the coins have ever been found. Today Hell Gate, still difficult to navigate, is tamer than it was when the *Hussar* sank. In the mid-19th century, the Army Corps of Engineers blasted away such colorfully named rocks as Hen and Chickens, Hog's Back, Frying Pan and Bald-Headed Billy. On Oct 10, 1885 the corps detonated 150 tons of explosives reducing to rubble nine-acre Flood Rock, a major navigational hazard; it was the largest intentional man-made explosion until the atomic bomb was dropped 60 years later.

The Triborough Bridge and Hell Gate Arch

The Y-shaped Triborough Bridge (1936; Othmar Ammann, chief engineer) links Randall's and Ward's Islands (now joined together by landfill) to the Bronx, Manhattan and Queens. The Bronx arm crosses the Bronx River and the Harlem Kills and can be converted into a lift bridge if the Kills, now a ditch, is ever made navigable. The Queens arm, running from Randall's Island to Astoria (Queens) above Hell Gate, is a 1,380-ft suspension bridge. The Manhattan arm begins at East 125 St and crosses the Harlem River.

The second bridge crossing these islands is Hell Gate Arch (1917; Gustav Lindenthal, engineer, and Henry Hornbostel, architect), a 1,017-ft span carrying four

railroad tracks across the East River over Ward's Island. This structurally beautiful and imaginatively engineered bridge is considered the peak of Lindenthal's career. The bridge is also a monument to Alexander Cassatt, the turn-of-the-20th-century president of the Pennsylvania Railroad, who planned a direct rail link between New England and the northeast corridor cities—Philadelphia, Baltimore, and Washington. The arch's design is unusual in that the upper arc curves upward at the ends, a pleasing visual effect, which also allows overhead clearance for locomotives and aids the bridge's rigidity by allowing deeper stiffening trusses. The handsome granite-faced towers with their arched openings reminded early observers of the portico to a mammoth temple. Among Lindenthal's engineering feats were the bridging of an underwater fissure in the bedrock beneath the Ward's Island foundation and his construction of the arch without using scaffolding to support the unfinished span, since that would have closed Hell Gate to navigation. When the final steel section was hoisted in place at the center, an adjustment of only $5/16$ of an inch was needed to close the arch.

ROOSEVELT ISLAND

Roosevelt Island (map p. 579) is accessible by subway (F train) and by cable car (Manhattan tram station Second Ave at 60th St). Visitor Center at the Roosevelt Island Tram Plaza (open weekends from noon–5pm).

Roosevelt Island, its northern tip visible in the East River from Carl Schurz Park, is a two-mile slice of land that was long used as a place of exile for madmen, criminals, and incurables. It emerged in the 1970s as a planned community for people of varying economic backgrounds.

In the island's mid-section rise the towers of the original new town, whose housing, schools, transport, and even rubbish removal were all planned by urban strategists according to a master plan by Philip Johnson and John Burgee. Down the midline runs a modern Main Street; girding the shoreline is a promenade, designed for its views. At the ends of the island are newer residential developments, some of them upscale, as well as monuments of older, less orderly times—a ruined smallpox hospital designed by James Renwick on the south and a lighthouse built by inmates (or perhaps a lunatic) on the northern tip.

LINCOLN SQUARE TO COLUMBUS CIRCLE

Map p. 578, B1–C2. Subway: 1 to 66th St-Lincoln Center; A, B, C, D, 1 to 59th St-Columbus Circle. Bus: M5, M7, M11, M20, M66, M104.

Lincoln Square, the neighborhood from Columbus Circle at West 58th St, stretches north along Broadway and Columbus Avenue to West 70th St. It is a thriving residential area, an educational hub with schools and colleges, and a cultural center, whose major institution is Lincoln Center for the Performing Arts. Here also are restaurants, an upscale shopping district along Columbus Avenue, and several corporate headquarters including the Time Warner Center.

LINCOLN CENTER FOR THE PERFORMING ARTS

62nd to 66th Sts, Amsterdam to Columbus Aves; T: 212 8751800; www.lincolncenter.org. Underground concourse to all buildings. You can see the interiors of individual theaters during performances and on guided tours; T: 212 875 5350 for tour reservations and information. NB: Lincoln Center is engaged in a $750-million redevelopment. Artwork in the construction area is in storage.

Lincoln Center for the Performing Arts is North America's pre-eminent cultural center. Occupying an area of over 16 acres, its 12 performing arts organizations present thousands of events every year and play a major role in the city's intellectual life, while its travertine-clad, colonnaded buildings have become recognizable icons. Five million people visit Lincoln Center every year, of whom 3.8 million buy a ticket to an event.

Architecturally Lincoln Center usually evokes the image of its three largest halls—the Metropolitan Opera House, Avery Fisher Hall, and the New York State Theater—which surround the central plaza, the most engaging public part of the site. The three halls were designed to complement one another: all are classical in inspiration; all face the plaza with large expanses of glass; all have colonnades; all are finished with travertine, a creamy white marble from ancient quarries near Rome. (Unfortunately the marble has not stood up well to New York's winter weather.) The fountain (1964) and its pavement design of concentric circles and spokes were designed by Philip Johnson. The fountain's 88 lights and 577 water jets can be set to spray as many as 9,000 gallons of water per minute in different patterns. Johnson had hoped, in vain, that artists—for example, Leonard Bernstein or George Balanchine—would program it.

In the summer the plaza is enlivened with music and dance events, while at Christmas there is a ceremonial tree-lighting. At any time of the year it draws passersby, who sit by the fountain and people-watch. After dark, the white marble building façades, the giant plate-glass windows, and the waters of the fountain are brightly illuminated against the night sky.

HISTORY OF THE LINCOLN CENTER

Two major factors paved the way for the development of Lincoln Center. In 1955, Lincoln Square, the then-dingy neighborhood around Broadway and Amsterdam Avenue at 65th St, was designated for urban renewal. And the Metropolitan Opera needed a modern opera house, to replace the "Old Met" which had opened on Broadway at 38th St in 1893. City planner Robert Moses picked the site, wanting to upgrade the neighborhood. John D. Rockefeller 3rd directed the fundraising, while Wallace K. Harrison (who had a long personal and professional relationship with the Rockefeller family) headed the board of architects.

In 1959, President Dwight D. Eisenhower dug up the first shovelful of earth beginning a period of construction that ended with the opening of the Juilliard School in 1969. Architects for the individual buildings and spaces included such luminaries as Harrison, Gordon Bunshaft (Skidmore, Owings and Merrill), Eero Saarinen, Pietro Belluschi, and Philip Johnson. In 1962 Philharmonic Hall (now Avery Fisher Hall) opened, with a gala performance led by Leonard Bernstein, conducting the New York Philharmonic, 200 black-robed choristers, and 13 big-name soloists. By 1987, however, most of the companies had outgrown their facilities and the trustees broke ground once again. The Rose Building (1991; Davis Brody Inc) on West 65th St opened four years later.

At present, the center is undergoing another renewal after years of sub-par maintenance and changing artistic needs. The overpass that darkened West 66th St has been removed; Alice Tully Hall will be given a new entrance, the approach to the central plaza from Columbus Avenue is being redesigned, as are the plaza between Avery Fisher Hall and the Beaumont Theater. The designers for the project are Diller, Scofidio + Renfro, in collaboration with FXFowle Architects.

Despite its obvious successes, or perhaps because of them, Lincoln Center has not escaped controversy. Social critics initially decried the destruction of a lower-income neighborhood rebuilt for the affluent: 1,647 families had to find new homes when their buildings were demolished to make way for the center. Acoustics in several buildings have been troublesome. Though time and familiarity have mellowed its big, glossy marble buildings, architectural critics never liked Lincoln Center, at worst citing it for slick, mediocre Classicism or even "monumental Modernism," a term usually reserved for Fascist architecture. At best critics faintly praised the scale of the buildings and their relationships to plazas and open spaces. Artists have sometimes found Lincoln Center too institutional, too rich, too powerful, too elitist. The undeniable fact remains, however, that Lincoln Center, despite its initial cost overruns, ongoing budgetary struggles, and perpetual attraction of criticism, is a vital cultural institution for both the city and the country, and one that has helped revitalize a neighborhood.

Tickets to Lincoln Center events

Alice Tully Hall: During renovation, tickets for Chamber Music Society of Lincoln Center and New York Film Festival events are available from Avery Fisher Hall (see below).

Avery Fisher Hall: 10 Lincoln Center Plaza. Mon–Sat 10–6, Sun noon–6; T: 212 875 5030.

Frederick P. Rose Hall, home of Jazz at Lincoln Center, Rose Theater and the Allen Room: Broadway at 60th St. Mon–Sat 10–6, Sun noon–6.

The Juilliard School–Peter Jay Sharp Theater, Drama Theater, Paul Recital Hall, Morse Recital Hall: 60 Lincoln Center Plaza. Mon–Fri 11–6; T: 212 769 7406.

Metropolitan Opera House: 30 Lincoln Center Plaza. Mon–Sat 10–8, Sun noon–6; T: 212 362 6000.

New York State Theater: 20 Lincoln Center Plaza. Mon 10–7:30, Tues–Sat 10–8:30, Sun 11:30–7:30; T: 212 870 5570.

Vivian Beaumont Theater and Mitzi E. Newhouse Theater: 150 West 65th St. Mon–Sat 10–8, Sun noon–6. T: 212 362 7600.

Walter Reade Theater: 165 West 65th St. Open daily 12:30 until 15mins after the last screening or performance; T: 212 875 5600.

By phone

CenterCharge, open daily 9–9; T: 212 721 6500. For Big Apple Circus tickets; all events in Alice Tully Hall, Avery Fisher Hall, New York State Theater, Rose Theater and the Allen Room; All Lincoln Center Presents, Chamber Music Society of Lincoln Center, Jazz at Lincoln Center, Juilliard School ticketed events, New York City Ballet, New York City Opera, New York Philharmonic events.

Dizzy's Club Coca-Cola, Jazz at Lincoln Center (at Time Warner Center, see p. 392); T: 212 258 9595.

Met Ticket Service, Mon–Sat 10–8, Sun noon–6; T: 212 362 6000; all Metropolitan Opera and American Ballet Theatre events.

TeleCharge, open 24hrs; T: 212 239 6200; all Lincoln Center Theater events.

Online

www.lincolncenter.org.

THE METROPOLITAN OPERA

The 10-story Metropolitan Opera House (*map p. 578, B1; www.metopera.org*), the centerpiece of Lincoln Center (1966; Wallace K. Harrison), faces Broadway from the west side of the plaza. The Metropolitan Opera is known for the grandeur of its productions, most chosen from the traditional repertoire, and for its star-studded casts.

The Metropolitan Opera was founded by a group of "new" capitalists—i.e., Goulds, Whitneys, J. Pierpont Morgan, and the occasional Vanderbilt—who were denied boxes at the Academy of Music on 14th St because the "old nobility" held title to them all. The first house (1883; J.C. Cady and Louis de Coppet Bergh) on Broadway at 39th St had an auditorium whose deep "diamond horseshoe" gave box holders an unrivaled opportunity to look at one another—but it had disastrous sightlines, with some 700 seats having a partial or obstructed view of the stage. The present house opened

on Sept 16, 1966, with the premiere performance of Samuel Barber's *Antony and Cleopatra*, whose title roles were sung by Justino Diaz and Leontyne Price.

The main façade has five marble arches separated by columns, while the long side walls reach back the equivalent of 45 stories. At night when the house is illuminated, the two murals by Marc Chagall (*see below*) gleam through the windows. (They are sometimes protected by curtains during the day.)

The interior

Finished in red plush, gold leaf, and marble, the lobby recalls the color scheme of the old Met, attempting to reconcile the splendor of traditional opera houses with a more contemporary approach, an attempt that some critics felt failed on the side of over-decoration and timidity. The concrete forms for the sweeping curves of the Grand Staircase were executed by boat builders. Chagall's predominantly red mural on the south side, *Le Triomphe de la Musique*, contains references to opera, folk music, and jazz, as well as images of the New York skyline. The charismatic Metropolitan general manager from 1935–72, Sir Rudolf Bing, appears in gypsy costume (the central figure in the group of three on the left). Originally from Vienna, Bing was also one of the founders of the Glyndebourne Festival in England. The yellow mural, *Les Sources de la Musique*, with a King David-Orpheus figure holding a lyre, and a Tree of Life afloat in the Hudson River, also has visual references to Wagner, Verdi, Bach, Beethoven's *Fidelio*, and Mozart's *The Magic Flute*. The crystal sunburst chandeliers were donated by the Austrian government.

The auditorium, also decorated in red, has 3,788 seats arranged in the traditional manner, though with a widened horseshoe to improve sightlines. Large by European standards (c.f. Covent Garden's 2,268 seats), it offers only a single row of boxes. Otherwise the seating is "democratic," in contrast to the old Met, which provided segregated elevators and less comfortable seats for patrons of the less expensive levels. The free-form sculpture for the proscenium arch (1966) is by Mary Callery.

THE NEW YORK STATE THEATER

On the south side of the plaza stands the New York State Theater (1964; Philip Johnson & Richard Foster), home to the New York City Opera and the New York City Ballet. The resident New York City Ballet, founded in 1948 by general manager Lincoln Kirstein and artistic director George Balanchine, became famous for its performances of Balanchine's abstract, Neoclassical ballets. The New York City Opera is a company of predominantly young, predominantly American singers, who perform an adventurous repertoire as well as standard operatic favorites.

Over the glass front wall rises a colonnade of paired square columns, interrupted by an outdoor balcony used as a promenade during intermissions.

Art inside the hall includes work by Lee Bontecou and Jasper Johns, as well as two large, curvaceous statues at either end, one pair representing *Two Nudes*, the other, *Two Circus Women* (originals 1930 and 1931; Elie Nadelman), which were duplicated in Carrara marble at twice the original size by Italian artisans. They are perhaps the

most controversial artworks in the theater: detractors have called them "absolutely pneumatic," likening their polished whiteness to yogurt, while admirers have found them to combine "high style, sly levity, and swelling monumentality."

The auditorium (seats 2,713), designed without a center aisle for better sightlines, is decorated in a garnet color, with big jewel-like lights studding the tiers of balconies and a central chandelier that resembles a colossal, many-faceted diamond. The stage, engineered specifically to meet the demands of dancers, features a sprung floor with air spaces between its layers. The theater's acoustics have never been friendly to singers, however, and in 1999 a "sound enhancement system" (i.e. amplification) was installed, arousing consternation among many opera fans.

AVERY FISHER HALL

AVERY FISHER HALL

Facing the New York State Theater is Avery Fisher Hall, originally Philharmonic Hall (1962; Max Abramovitz), a glass box caged behind 44 tapered travertine columns. Renamed (1973) after Avery Fisher, manufacturer of hi-fi components and donor of $10 million to Lincoln Center, the hall is the home of the New York Philharmonic. The auditorium seats 2,738.

The Philharmonic Hall was planned to be a miracle of modern acoustic science. Originally designed in a shoe box shape (like Boston's acoustically successful Symphony Hall), the auditorium was altered to accommodate more seats even before building began. From its opening (Sept 23, 1962), the hall's acoustics proved distressing to musicians, audiences, and its designers. Musicians complained of being unable to hear one another, while trained listeners in the auditorium were troubled by a lack of low-frequency sounds, a strident quality in the upper registers, and an echo. When small adjustments failed to improve the acoustics, engineers resorted to increasingly radical measures, changing wall contours, replacing heavily upholstered seats with thinly padded, wooden-backed chairs, and filling in the space between the "clouds" with plywood. Even so, in 1974 the Boston and Philadelphia Orchestras, still dissatisfied, went back to Carnegie Hall (*see p. 393*) for their New York appearances. Finally in 1976, using half of Avery Fisher's gift, architects Philip Johnson and John

Burgee with acoustical guidance from Cyril Harris, consultant for the Metropolitan Opera House, had the hall completely gutted and rebuilt. Though improved, the hall has never been entirely successful and will be rebuilt once again beginning in 2010.

In the entrance foyer at ground level are (west end) Seymour Lipton's *Archangel* (1964), an abstract sculptural work of bronze and Monel metal (a nickel-based alloy); and Dimitri Hadzi's tall, dark bronze work *K. 458—The Hunt* (1964), whose title refers to a Mozart string quartet. In the main foyer (up the escalator) a two-part hanging work by Richard Lippold entitled *Orpheus and Apollo* is constructed of 190 strips of polished Muntz metal (a copper alloy) suspended from the ceiling by steel wires.

Between Avery Fisher Hall and the Vivian Beaumont Theater, a reflecting pool harbors Henry Moore's two-piece bronze *Lincoln Center Reclining Figure* (1965). Moore described the piece as "a leg part and a head and arms part." Near the library entrance is Alexander Calder's *Le Guichet* (1965), a stabile of blackened steel (22ft long, 14ft high). The name means "the ticket window."

OTHER LINCOLN CENTER LANDMARKS

The Vivian Beaumont Theater: Named for a generous donor (the heiress of a department store fortune), the theater (1965; Eero Saarinen) has been praised as the center's visually most successful building. Situated west of the reflecting pool, the main façade appears as a horizontal slab of travertine projecting over a glass wall. The stage, designed when thrust stages were in vogue, was conceived as a compromise between a traditional proscenium arch and a thrust stage, with complex machinery for converting it from one to the other. The auditorium is arranged as an amphitheater. With 1,080 seats, it is the only theater large enough to qualify as a "Broadway theater" outside the Times Square Theater District. Also in the building is the **Mitzi E. Newhouse Theater**, a small house for more intimate and experimental drama. Since 1985, operated by the non-profit Lincoln Center Theater, it has enjoyed great success including the presentation of new dramas, classics, and revivals. *150 West 56th St (Broadway and Amsterdam Ave); www.lct.org.*

The New York Public Library for the Performing Arts: To the left of the theater and wrapped around it is the New York Public Library for the Performing Arts (1965; Skidmore, Owings & Merrill). The library has circulating collections of some 250,000 items including books, music, audio and video recordings, and music. Highlights of the superb collection (*open Tues–Sat 12–6; closed Sun, Mon; T: 212 870 1630; www.nypl.org*) include manuscripts of Mozart and Bach, diaries of Nijinsky, correspondence of John Barrymore and Tennessee Williams, and rare cylinders of Metropolitan Opera performances dating to the turn of the 20th century. *111 Amsterdam Ave (West 62nd and West 65th Sts); or enter through the Lincoln Center Plaza.*

The Juilliard School: Juilliard (1969; Pietro Belluschi), one of the country's premier performing arts conservatories, was founded in 1905 as the Institute of Musical Arts by Frank Damrosch and James Loeb, and endowed in 1920

through a bequest from merchant and philanthropist Augustus D. Juilliard.

Of all the buildings at Lincoln Center, this is the most complex, housing **Alice Tully Hall** (seats 1,096), home of the Chamber Music Society of Lincoln Center, as well as the school itself, which offers performance training in music, dance, and drama. (Alice Tully was being refurbished at the time of writing).

Also on site are the **Juilliard Theater** (seats 1,026); a small recital hall; a drama workshop theater; and 82 soundproof practice rooms, three organ studios, some 200 pianos, 35 teaching studios, and 16 two-story studios for dance, drama, or orchestral rehearsals. *60 Lincoln Center Plaza (West 65th St between Amsterdam and Columbus Aves); www.juilliard.edu.*

The Rose Building: Visible above the Juilliard building is the newest addition to Lincoln Center, the Samuel and David Rose Building (1992; Davis Brody & Assoc. and Abramovitz Kingsland Schiff), with the Meredith Willson Residence Hall rising above it. The building is sheathed in Minnesota stone, a cream-colored material similar to the travertine of the original Lincoln Center buildings. The 28-story tower contains office space, living quarters for Juilliard and American Ballet School students, rehearsal studios, and the 300-seat **Walter Reade Theater** for the Film Society of Lincoln Center. On the tenth floor of the 28-story tower is the Kaplan Penthouse, a small venue with a big view, sometimes used for concerts and recitals. *165 West 65th St (Broadway and Amsterdam Ave).*

3 Lincoln Center: This dark condominium tower (1991; Harman Jablin Architects) is a private development built with some of Lincoln Center's air rights. In return for the air rights, the rights to the prestigious Lincoln Center name, and $48.5 million, the developer agreed to put up the basic structure of the Rose Building, from whose base the two towers rise. The bronze glass and the chamfered corner facing the Rose Building, according to one architectural critic, make the apartment tower "as deferential as a 60-story skyscraper can be" to Lincoln Center's Rose Building.

IN THE NEIGHBORHOOD

The southern triangle created by the intersection of Broadway and Columbus Avenue at 63rd St is known as Dante Park (*map p. 578, B1*). It contains a bronze statue of Dante Alighieri (1921; Ettore Ximenes), erected to commemorate the 600th anniversary of the poet's death. Originally the New York chapter of the Dante Alighieri Society had hoped for something larger in Times Square to celebrate the 50th anniversary of Italian unification, but fundraising fell short and the society settled for this compromise. *Time Sculpture* by Philip Johnson, made in 1999 when he was 93, a 28-ft bronze pylon with four clock faces, is an updated version of the traditional pedestrian street clock.

In **Richard Tucker Park**, the northern of the two triangles, near West 66th St, is a bronze portrait bust of the tenor Richard Tucker (1913–1975). The statue, by Milton Hebald, sits on granite pedestal inscribed with the names of 31 operas that Tucker performed. A native New Yorker, Tucker appeared in 499 performances in 21 seasons with

the Metropolitan Opera and was one of the company's most popular singers, as well as the only person to have his funeral held at the present opera house.

Nearby at 2 Lincoln Square is a branch gallery of the **American Folk Art Museum** (Columbus Ave between West 65th and West 66th Sts; *open Tues–Sat 12–7:30, Sun 12–6:30; free; T: 212 265 1040; www.folkartmuseum.org*), with a changing selection of items drawn from the permanent collection on West 53rd St (*see p. 269*).

The former **Kent Automatic Parking Garage** at 47 Columbus Ave (West 61st and West 62nd Sts) is a much admired Art Deco building (1930; Jardine, Hill & Murdock), constructed as one of the city's first high-rise "automatic" (i.e. elevator-equipped) parking garages. Later it became the Sofia Brothers Warehouse, and was recycled (1985) as the luxury Sofia Apartments

Fordham University

Fordham University (*map p. 578, B2*) is a Jesuit institution founded in 1841 with its original campus in the west Bronx. Its Lincoln Center campus was built as part of the Lincoln Center urban renewal project. The campus has two main buildings: the Fordham Law School (1962; Voorhees, Walker, Smith, Smith & Haines) on the south, and the Leon Lowenstein Center (1969; Slingerland & Booss). Facing Columbus Avenue at 61st St in front of the Law School is Lila Katzen's *City Spirit* (1968), whose curved forms signify, according to the sculptor, the interlocking elements of the city. Closer to 62nd St is *Circle World #2* (1969; Masami Kodama), a cube of black granite inserted in a broken circle of pink granite. In the plaza of the Lowenstein Center is a 28-ft bronze statue, *Peter, Fisher of Men* (Frederick Shrady; 1965), casting a 14-ft bronze net across the plaza's reflecting pool.

Museum of Biblical Art and Bible House

1865 Broadway (West 61st St), second floor. Open Tues–Sun 10–6, Thur until 8; closed Mon and public holidays. Suggested admission charge. T: 212 408 1500; www.mobia.org.

Bible House (1966, Skidmore, Owings & Merrill; glass entrance and stairs 1998, Fox & Fowle) is the headquarters of the American Bible Society, founded in 1916 to make the scriptures available to every literate person in a language each can understand. One the second floor is the **Museum of Biblical Art** (MOBIA), a small scholarly museum which presents changing exhibitions of art inspired by the Bible.

The society maintains an extensive collection of scriptures, with volumes written in 1,900 languages. Among the books are rare and unusual Bibles: a first edition of John Eliot's Massachusetts Indian Bible (1661–63), 15th-century Latin Bibles from European printers, 16th-century Luther Bibles, and a 1440 Wycliffe New Testament. Also in the permanent collection are Helen Keller's Braille Bibles and a Chinese Torah scroll made for a community of Chinese Jews who lived in Honan in the 13th–15th centuries.

Church of St. Paul the Apostle

Map p. 578, B2; Columbus Ave at West 60th St. Open weekdays 7:30–end of 5:30 Mass, Sat 8:30–end of 5:15 Mass, and Sun 8–8.

The Roman Catholic church of St. Paul the Apostle (1885; Jeremiah O'Rourke) was founded in 1858 by Father Isaac Thomas Hecker to spread Catholicism in the then-largely Protestant US and Canada. It is the home of the Paulist Fathers or Missionary Society of St. Paul. The bas-relief by Lumen Martin Winter on the neo-Gothic façade depicts the conversion of St. Paul and contains 50 tons of travertine fixed against a mosaic background of Venetian glass tiles in 15 shades of blue. Stanford White designed the high altar and the altars at the ends of the aisles. The *Angel of the Moon* mural (high on the south wall of the sanctuary), the Connemara marble altar of St. Patrick in the north aisle (second bay from the main entrance), the east window, and the two blue windows at the west end were designed by John La Farge.

COLUMBUS CIRCLE

Map p. 578, C2. Subway A, B, C, D, 1 to 59th St-Columbus Circle. Bus: M1, M5, M10.
Park designer Frederick Law Olmsted included a nameless circle at the southwest corner of Central Park in his original plan. The circle acquired its present name after a monument was erected there to commemorate the 400th anniversary of Columbus's "discovery." The monument, donated by Italian-Americans, consists of a 77-ft granite column on top of which a marble statue of Christopher Columbus (1894; Gaetano Russo) looks south down Broadway. At the base of the column a winged allegorical figure represents Discovery; two bronze tablets depict the explorer's departure from Spain and his arrival in the New World. The column itself sports three pairs of bronze rostra—the beaky prows of ancient warships, intended for ramming enemy vessels.

Until recently Columbus Circle was a traffic nightmare and crossing the street to the central fountain was a hazardous undertaking. In 2005 it was redesigned with an enlarged central circle, pedestrian walkways, new plantings and seating, and bigger and better fountains. From the center of the circle, there is a panorama of all the important surrounding buildings.

2 Columbus Circle

The smallish, boxy building south of the circle, presently known as 2 Columbus Circle, will become the new home of the **Museum of Arts & Design**, currently located on West 53rd St, across from the Museum of Modern Art (*see p. 269*).

A & P Supermarket heir Huntington Hartford commissioned the original building (1965; Edward Durell Stone) to house his art collection. What he got was a ten-story marble-clad tower pierced with portholes, topped off with a loggia, and raised above the ground on curved "legs," which were also pierced with round holes. Its northern façade followed the arc of the traffic circle. Critics hated it. The influential Ada Louise Huxtable called it a "die-cut Venetian *palazzo* on lollipops," and 2 Columbus Circle was often thereafter referred to as the Lollipop Building.

Huntington Hartford's museum lasted five years, and thereafter the building fell on hard times, changing occupants and enduring periods of vacancy. In 2002 the city

Economic Development Corporation designated the Museum of Arts & Design to redevelop the site. Three years later the museum got permission to alter the formerly maligned façade. Efforts to have the building landmarked were unsuccessful, and amidst demonstrations, accusations, and lawsuits, the museum has gone ahead with its planned alterations.

Time Warner Center

Map p. 578, B2.

The Time Warner Center (2003; Skidmore Owings & Merrill, David Childs, design partner) is a mixed-use skyscraper whose base curves around Columbus Circle and whose two towers rise 750ft above it. The lower floors constitute a vertical shopping mall, with a large upscale grocery store below street level and four floors of chic shops above. On the fifth floor several even more upscale restaurants open off a large lobby, whose gray Indian granite, Australian green marble, Russian black granite, and snowy Italian marble give the premises a cool, formal tone. Above that are stacked offices, the headquarters of Time Warner, studios for CNN (the TV station is owned by Time Warner), a luxury hotel, condominiums, and penthouses.

Jazz at Lincoln Center, the offsite location of Lincoln Center's jazz programs, occupies the fifth–seventh floors of the northern tower (*entrance by elevator from the ground floor of the shops. For ticket information, see p. 385*). Designed by Rafael Viñoly, its three elegant performance spaces host large and small performance groups. Largest is the 1,200-seat Rose Theater, the first theater acoustically designed especially for jazz; the 550-seat Allen Room has a 50-ft plate-glass window overlooking Central Park and the East Side skyline. Dizzy's Club Coca-Cola seats about 140 people in a cabaret setting. The Jazz Hall of Fame (*open Tues–Sun 10–4; free*), a multimedia installation, celebrates the history of jazz and its most famous players, and inaugurates a new class every year.

Trump International Hotel and Tower

1 Central Park West (Columbus Circle).

The Trump International Hotel and Tower occupies the former Gulf + Western office building (1969; Thomas E. Stanley). Real estate developer Donald Trump bought the building and had architect Philip Johnson and others redesign it during the 1990s, cladding it with bronze glass. Trump also commissioned the 40-ft stainless steel *Unisphere* (1997; Kim Brandell).

The Maine Memorial

Map p. 578, C2. Central Park West at Central Park South (West 59th St).

The *Maine* Memorial commemorates the sinking of the US battleship *Maine* (Feb 15, 1898), an incident that helped trigger the Spanish-American War. The memorial (1913; sculptor Attilio Piccirilli; architect H. van Buren Magonigle) consists of a blocky granite stele (43$\frac{1}{2}$ft) with bronze and marble sculptures. The group on the top, with *Columbia Triumphant* standing in a shell pulled by three sea horses, is made of bronze recovered from the guns of the *Maine*. At the base facing the circle, a boatload of marble figures

includes *Victory* (a youth kneeling in the prow), accompanied by *Courage* (a male nude), and *Fortitude* (a mother comforting a weeping child). Behind them stands a robed figure representing *Peace*. Another group, facing the park, includes *Justice*, *History*, and a Warrior, whose upraised hand once clenched a bronze sword. The reclining youth on the side of the stele facing downtown represents the *Atlantic*, while the *Pacific*, facing uptown, appears as an aged man. The allegorical conception of the memorial suggests America's perception of itself in 1898 as a dominant world power.

Attilio Piccirilli (1866–1945)

Attilio Piccirilli was born in Massa Carrara in Tuscany, near the veins of white Carrara marble used for Trajan's Column in Rome, Michelangelo's *David*, and Marble Arch in London. The family immigrated to New York when Attilio was eleven years old, eventually opening a studio in the Mott Haven section of the Bronx. Attilio and his five brothers all followed in their father's footsteps and became stonecutters; Attilio and Furio also became sculptors, designing their own works as well as executing the designs of others. Attilio developed a close friendship with mayor Fiorello La Guardia, who called him Uncle Peach. The Piccirillis' most famous work is Daniel Chester French's statue of Abraham Lincoln in the Lincoln Memorial in Washington, D.C., but they also contributed to the streetscape of New York City.

Among their works are the lions by Edward Clark Potter and pediment statues at the New York Public Library (Fifth Ave near 42nd St); *The Four Continents* by Daniel Chester French and the pediment statues by various artists at the Custom House (near Bowling Green Park); the pediment figures by John Q.A. Ward and Paul Wayland Bartlett at the New York Stock Exchange (on Wall St); the two figures of George Washington by Alexander Stirling Calder and Hermon A. MacNeil on the arch at Washington Square; more than 600 sculptures at Riverside Church (Riverside Drive and West 122nd St); and the Fireman's Memorial by H. van Buren Magonigle (Riverside Drive and West 100th St).

Other works are *Youth Leading Industry* (1935) at the Rockefeller Center (*see p. 253*); the figures of *Manhattan* and *Brooklyn* by Daniel Chester French and pediment statues at the Brooklyn Museum (Eastern Pkwy at Washington Ave), originally at the Manhattan Bridge; and the simple funeral monument in the Bronx's Woodlawn Cemetery for Fiorello La Guardia's wife and infant daughter, who died in 1921, as well as several more elaborate funerary works there.

CARNEGIE HALL & ENVIRONS

Map p. 578, C2. During the season, tours given Mon–Fri 11:30, 2, 3; Sat 11:30 and 12:30; Sun 12:30. Tickets at the box office from 11am Mon–Sat and 12 on Sun. Each tour lasts

approx. 1hr and departs from the main lobby; T: 212 903 9765; www.carnegiehall.org. Box office, T: 212 247 7800. Rose Museum open 11–4:30 daily during concert season; closed July 1–Sept 14.

Carnegie Hall at 154 West 57th St (Seventh Ave), built in 1891, was financed by Andrew Carnegie partly as a venue for the Oratorio Society, whose board he headed, and partly as a $2-million investment. Designed by architect (and cellist) William B. Tuthill, the building is not visually outstanding—a bulky brownish neo-Italian Renaissance hall with a high square corner tower—but it is a musical landmark. The Rose Museum (1991) on the first tier level offers an exhibition on the history of the hall and changing thematic shows drawn from the hall's archives and those of other institutions.

The acoustics of the original auditorium were legendary, delighting both audiences and performers, beginning with Tchaikovsky, who appeared as guest conductor during opening week. Even so, the hall came close to demolition in the early 1960s when its owners began yearning for larger profits (Andrew Carnegie didn't make much money on his investment either); but preservationists headed by violinist Isaac Stern saved it. Although the New York Philharmonic, which first made Carnegie Hall its home and appeared here under the batons of Toscanini and Leopold Stokowski, now resides at Lincoln Center, major orchestras and soloists are still booked into the hall.

Art Students League of New York

The Art Students League of New York at 215 West 57th St (Seventh Ave) enjoys a dignified French Renaissance building (1892) by the architect of the Plaza Hotel (Henry J. Hardenbergh). The League was founded in 1875 as an alternative to the more rigid and formal National Academy, whose curriculum demanded ten weeks of "painting from the antique" before students could paint from life, their main interest. The school has long been known for its outstanding teachers, many of whom in the early days had studied in Europe, for example William Merritt Chase. The teachers in turn were fortunate to have many outstandingly talented (though not necessarily like-minded) students: Chase taught Georgia O'Keeffe; Thomas Hart Benton taught Jackson Pollock; George Grosz and Hans Hofmann taught Louise Nevelson.

New York City Center

At 135 West 55th St (Sixth and Seventh Aves) is the elaborate, neo-Moorish City Center for Music and Drama (1924), built as a temple for the Shriners (Ancient Order of Nobles of the Mystic Shrine) when they outgrew their clubhouse on West 45th St. The hall never succeeded financially, and the city took it over in 1943, converting it to a theater. It is a major dance venue and is also known for its *Encores!* series of classic American musicals.

THE AMERICAN MUSEUM OF NATURAL HISTORY & CENTRAL PARK WEST

Map p. 576, B4. Subway: 1 to 79th St-Broadway; B (weekdays only) or C to 81st St. Bus: M7, M10, M11, M79, M86, M104.

The American Museum of Natural History, along with the Rose Center for Earth and Space, should delight anyone interested in the natural sciences, from astronomy to zoology. The collection contains some 36 million specimens (not all, fortunately, on display) ranging from the famous dioramas of animal habitat groups and the dinosaur exhibits to the world's largest cut gem. There is also a stunning new hall on human origins.

HISTORY OF THE MUSEUM

Founded in the 1868 by Albert Bickmore, a scientist and student of Louis Agassiz, one of America's first leading naturalists, the museum opened in Central Park's Arsenal (1869) and moved to its present building in 1877. The remote uptown location attracted few visitors, and the museum soon fell into debt. Morris K. Jessup, the museum's third president and a successful securities broker, boosted attendance by keeping the museum open on Sunday (a more radical innovation than it seems now) and encouraged programs in paleontology, anthropology, and zoology. His successor, the wealthy and aristocratic Henry Fairfield Osborn, a paleontologist originally hired to update the fossil collection, captured attention by sponsoring trips to Mongolia and Africa to search for human ancestors. In 1935, the Hayden Planetarium opened.

The museum has pioneered new exhibit techniques and is generally credited with being the first to mount animal skeletons in natural poses and to create habitat exhibits. While most other institutions collected whatever specimens were available, the museum sent scientists into the field to gather specific items. American Museum of Natural History scientists also pioneered the use of photographs and tape recordings.

Through the years the museum has evolved to keep up with changes in scientific theory and in public perception. In the 1940s and '50s exhibits on ecology and cultural anthropology opened (Margaret Mead, a pioneering American cultural athropologist, headed the anthropology department). Exhibits that reflected Osborn's racist views were replaced. New halls, for example the Hall of Biodiversity, reflect present-day ecological thinking, and the re-installation in the 1990s of the beloved dinosaur halls incorporates contemporary scientific insights. In 1995 a new Hall of Human Origins opened, to be replaced only 12 years later by a newer one, incorporating the latest findings in genomics and paleontology.

The building

The museum occupies the equivalent of four city blocks (West 77th to West 81st Sts, Central Park West to Columbus Ave), an area formerly called Manhattan Square and intended by the designers of Central Park as a park annex. The first building (1877) is now almost walled in by the wings and additions that have made the present complex an architectural hodge-podge of some 22 buildings.

The oldest visible part of the façade (1892; J. Cleveland Cady & Co) facing West 77th St is also the most attractive. This wing (60ft by 110ft), Romanesque in style, is faced with pink granite, flanked by two round towers, a seven-arched arcade, and a central granite stairway that sweeps up over what was once a carriage entrance. (At the time of writing, this façade was undergoing restoration.) The façade facing Central Park West (1922; Trowbridge & Livingston) is faced with smooth blocks of the same granite. The central portion is the Theodore Roosevelt Memorial, its triumphal arch framing a 16-ft statue of Theodore Roosevelt (1940; James Earle Fraser), depicted as an explorer; the flanking guides symbolize Africa and America.

Visiting the museum

Central Park West at 79th St. T: 212 769 5600 or 212 769 5100 for recorded information; www.amnh.org. Open every day 10–5:45. Closed Thanksgiving and Dec 25. For planetarium information, see p. 408. There is far too much to see in one, two, or even three visits. The box opposite outlines the main highlights. Guided tours are available to the most popular exhibits.

Relief of wolves on the entrance façade of the American Museum of Natural History.

MUSEUM HIGHLIGHTS

Fossil halls: These contain arguably the world's best dinosaur exhibits, including such favorites as the *Tyrannosaurus rex* (mounted in a scientifically accurate low-slung posture) and the *Apatosaurus* (formerly known as *Brontosaurus*), *Stegosaurus* and *Triceratops*, dinosaur eggs, a partial skull of a *Velociraptor*, and several dinosaur "mummies" with fossilized skin and soft tissues (*fourth floor*).

Hall of Biodiversity: Includes a walk-through rainforest and a stunning display of some 2,500 models and specimens (*first floor*).

Animal Habitat dioramas: World-famous for their beauty, workmanship, and accuracy. Most of the mounted specimens have been placed in habitat groups in environments carefully simulated down to the last leaf (*North American groups first floor; African groups second floor*).

Hall of Human Origins: This exhibit (opened 2007) incorporates the newest theories in genomics and paleontology to explain evolution. Four startling dioramas show our hominid ancestors in their prehistoric habitats (*first floor*).

Hall of Minerals: Displays some 6,000 of the museum's 120,000 specimens, including a half-ton copper block with malachite and azurite crystals, a giant topaz crystal (597lbs or 1,330,040 carats), the Star of India sapphire and the Patricia emerald (*first floor*).

First floor

(1) Theodore Roosevelt Memorial Hall: The barrel-vaulted lobby in the Roosevelt Memorial wing is known as the Rotunda. The short end walls are finished in Scottish Renfrew marble containing fossils of colonial sponge-like animals; the long side walls are faced with Portenelle marble, a Portuguese limestone with fossils of oyster-like bivalves. The murals depict scenes from Theodore Roosevelt's life: the building of the Panama Canal, the signing of the treaty at the end of the Russo-Japanese War, and Roosevelt's explorations in Africa.

In the center of the room a 55-ft skeleton of a *Barosaurus*, one of prehistory's largest creatures, towers toward the ceiling, defending its young from an attacking *Allosaurus*. The 150-million-year-old fossilized skeleton of the *Barosaurus* was found in the southwestern US; the exhibit, the tallest free-standing dinosaur exhibit in the world, is a resin-and-foam replica since the original bones are too fragile to be mounted vertically. On the hoof the *Barosaurus* weighed an estimated 25 tons; it is seen about to drop down onto the *Allosaurus*, attempting to crush it with its massive forelimbs.

(2) Hall of North American Mammals: Here are remarkable dioramas of habitat groups of musk oxen, Osborn caribou, mountain goats, bison, Alaska brown bears, grizzly bears, mountain lions, wolves, coyotes, and lynxes. The back-

AMERICAN MUSEUM OF NATURAL HISTORY
(FIRST FLOOR)

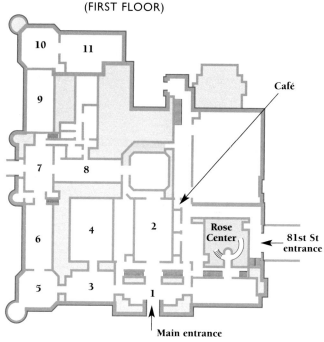

1   Theodore Roosevelt Memorial Hall
2   Hall of North American Mammals
3   Hall of Biodiversity
4   Hall of Ocean Life
5   Hall of North American Forests
6   Hall of New York State Environment

7   77th St Foyer (Grand Gallery)
8   Hall of Northwest Coast Indians
9   Hall of Human Origins
10 Hall of Meteorites
11 Hall of Minerals and Gems

ground paintings are by recognized masters of the genre, for example James Perry Wilson and Charles Shepard Chapman. Wilson created the background to the bison diorama in 1938 from a locale in Wyoming, where he made color sketches and photos, and collected specimens. His diorama paintings are known for the way the real objects in the foreground blend with the painted background, creating the illusion of a three-dimensional whole.

(3) Hall of Biodiversity: The exhibit here is one expression of the museum's efforts to alert the public to this important ecological issue. The walk-through Dzanga-Sangha diorama reconstructs a rainforest in the Central African Republic. On one wall is *The Spectrum of Life*, a stunning display of some 2,500 models and specimens: bacteria, fungi, plants, and animals. The extraordinary blown-glass protozoa on one wall of the hall, created as educa-

tional models, were made by Herman O. Mueller, whose family had been glass-blowers in Germany for generations. Mueller spent 40 years working on the models, completing the series in 1943.

(4) Hall of Ocean Life: Hanging over-head in this dimly-lit hall is a 94-ft model of a female blue whale, molded from polyurethane, supported by steel, and coated with fiberglass. The upper level gallery contains displays on biology (adaptation to environment, feeding, defense, etc), as well as plaster and plastic casts of sharks. Across the room the evo-lutionary tree of fishes classifies them according to shared characteristics, begin-ning with fossil fish and including jawless and jawed fish, cartilaginous fish, and bony fish. The lower level contains dio-ramas of fish and marine mammals.

(5) Hall of North American Forests: In the entrance corridor here is a display, 24 times larger than life, populated with out-sized creatures of the forest floor: gigantic earthworms, millipedes and weevils, mycorhizae. The exhibit illustrates the process of decomposition, by which natural debris is broken down into soil nutrients. Other dioramas reproduce the primary North American forest environ-ments: giant cactus forest (Arizona), mixed deciduous forest (Tennessee), piñon-juniper pine forest (Colorado), and others.

(6) Hall of New York State Environment: Just before you enter is a cross-section of a giant sequoia (harvested 1891), 16ft 5in in diameter and cut from a 1,300-year-old tree that weighed 6,000 tons. Displays focus on such topics as soil

use, the water cycle, glaciation, and the relation of plants to soil, with special ref-erence to the geological history of New York State.

(7) 77th St Foyer: Hanging from the ceiling is a 63-ft seagoing war canoe, probably made from a single Western red cedar around 1878, burned and cut with iron adzes, and steamed into its present shape. Until 2006, 17 plaster Northwest Coast Indians "paddled" the canoe, but when the canoe was cleaned, the painted decoration (a killer whale and an eagle) became so clear that it was decided to hang the boat from the ceiling to make them more visible.

(8) Hall of Northwest Coast Indians: This, the oldest hall in the museum, has an outstanding collection of artifacts from Indian tribes of the Pacific coast from southeastern Alaska to Washington state. Many of the objects were gathered during the museum's first major field expedition (1897–1902), which studied the cultural and biological links between people on both sides of the Bering Strait. The goal of the undertaking was to determine whether America was populated originally by Asians who migrated across the strait.

Two towering rows of extraordinarily carved totem poles range down the center of the room. Also on display are sculp-ture, clothing, tools, and ceremonial objects of the Nootka, Kwakiutl, Chilkat, Tlingit, Coast Salish, and other tribes. Tlingit body armor is covered with Chinese coins, which the Tlingit received from the Boston merchants in the China trade. Sailing a triangular route, the traders exchanged metal tools and goods with the Tlingit for sea-otter pelts, which

they then exchanged in China for spices, which were brought back to Boston.

(9) Hall of Human Origins: This is the newest exhibit (2007) in the museum, and the first anywhere to combine genomic research with the study of fossils in explaining the theory of evolution. At the entrance, skeletons of a modern human, a chimpanzee, and a Neanderthal invite comparison of their similarities and differences. On the right side of the hall, the fossil evidence includes some 200 casts of human and pre-human fossils, which show evolving physical character-istics. Four life-size dioramas depict possible scenes in the lives of human predecessors: *Homo ergaster*, Neanderthal, Cro-Magnon and *Homo erectus* (depicted in the moments before he falls prey to a hyena). In a freestanding case is a lifelike reconstruction of "Lucy," a three-million-year-old fossil found in Ethiopia in 1974, a stunning discovery because her skeletal development showed that she walked upright. Near Lucy and her companion a cast of the famous Laetoli footprints, found in Tanzania, shows two hominids walking upright side by side. Exhibits toward the back of the hall show human developments in language, music, art (a replica of the Lascaux cave drawings), and the use of tools. A replica of a 75,000-year-old piece of ochre decorated with geometric patterns, recently discovered in South Africa, is an early example of sym-bolic thinking.

On the left side of the room, the DNA exhibits explore the genetic similarities between humans and their nearest non-human relatives. There is a sample of Neanderthal DNA, 38,000 years old, donated by the Max Planck Institute, where genetic material was first extracted from Neanderthal bones.

(10) Hall of Meteorites: The centerpiece here is a 34-ton fragment of Ahnighito (the Eskimo name means "The Tent"), the Cape York meteorite discovered in 1897. This massive chunk was shipped back to New York from northern Greenland by explorer Robert Peary, who spent four Arctic summers digging it out of the frozen ground. The floor supports beneath it reach all the way down to the bedrock under the building.

Also in the hall are two other sections of the Cape York meteorite, called "The Woman" and "The Dog," worn smooth in places by Eskimos who scraped them for the iron, which they used for knives and weapons. In front of a photomontage of the far side of the moon stands a case containing three moon rocks, represent-ing the three major lunar types. Other displays include a meteorite studded with small diamonds, an array of tektites (glassy objects once thought to have fallen from the moon but now known to have a terrestrial origin), and the Brunflo fossil meteorite, which landed 460 million years ago in Sweden.

(11) Hall of Minerals and Hall of Gems: Some 6,000 of the museum's 120,000 specimens of minerals are hand-somely displayed here. A cylindrical case near the entrance contains large speci-mens of fluorite, hematite, and sulfur, among others, chosen to illustrate the nature of minerals. Along the left wall a display of systematic mineralogy classifies minerals by composition (native elements, halides, oxides, sulfates) and by structure (silicates). At the far end of the hall are

aesthetic stones, whose form or color makes them natural masterpieces. Elsewhere are spectacular geodes, a giant topaz crystal (597lbs or 1,330,040 carats), glittering azurite and gold crystals, and agates from Brazil and Uruguay.

Near the entrance to the Hall of Gems stands a 4,700-lb slab of nephrite (jade) from Poland. In the hall itself, a cylindrical case opposite the door contains diamonds and star sapphires including the world's largest blue sapphire, the Star of India (563 carats, mined 300 years ago in Sri Lanka) and donated to the museum in 1901 by J. Pierpont Morgan. Not quite so large but hardly less impressive is the Midnight Star (116.75 carats), also a gift from J. Pierpont Morgan. Equally dazzling are the rubies including the DeLong ruby (100 carats), and the emeralds including the Schettler engraved emerald and the twelve-sided uncut Patricia emerald (632 carats), found in the Colombian Andes in 1920 and named for the mine-owner's daughter. The array of "fancy" (i.e. not blue) sapphires includes the Padparadschah sapphire (100 carats), one of the finest on display anywhere.

Second floor

This floor contains the world-famous Akeley dioramas of African animals, collections of Asian animals, and major exhibits on Asian, African, and South American peoples.

(12) Akeley Memorial Hall of African Mammals: The dramatic dioramas here include habitat groups of gorilla, rhinoceros, lion, buffalo, giraffe, and zebra. Settings are recreated from photographs and sketches made on site, and vegetation is carefully simulated: a blackberry bush in the gorilla diorama, with 75,000 artificial leaves and flowers, took eight months to make and cost $2,000 (in the 1930s). Special efforts were made to present the animals in characteristic actions: hyenas and vultures devouring a dead zebra, giraffes browsing.

(13) Hall of African Peoples: The two introductory rooms are devoted to the origins of man and society in Africa and to river valley civilizations (Nile, Niger, Zambesi, and Congo). The main display is organized environmentally, treating Grassland, Forest-Woodland, and Desert cultures.

(14) Hall of Asiatic Mammals: This is considered the best collection of such mammals in the world. The display includes a group of Indian elephants and dioramas showing habitat groups of tigers, wild boar, rhinoceros, water buffalo, and lions, as well as a dramatic diorama of an Asian deer attacked by a pack of wild dogs.

(15) Hall of Asian Peoples: Exhibits of costumes, artifacts, paintings, and photographs document traditional Asia. The first part of the hall is organized historically and includes prehistoric development, archaeology, and the rise of civilization. The rest of the hall is organized geographically, with exhibits on Korea, Japan, China, India, Tibet, and the Islamic world.

(16) Birds of the World: The dioramas here are organized by environment:

AMERICAN MUSEUM OF NATURAL HISTORY
(SECOND FLOOR)

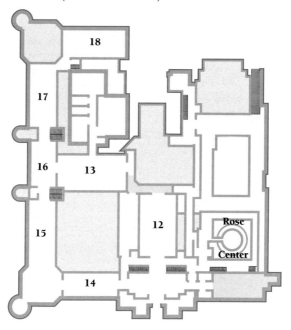

12 Akeley Memorial Hall of African Mammals	15 Hall of Asian Peoples
13 Hall of African Peoples	16 Birds of the World
14 Hall of Asiatic Mammals	17 Hall of Mexico and Central America
	18 Hall of South American Peoples

Canadian tundra, New Forest in the south of England, Alps, Gobi Desert, Japan, East African plains, and the south Atlantic region near Antarctica.

(17) Hall of Mexico and Central America: Exhibits here use archaeological finds (primarily pottery and stone carvings) as well as full-sized replicas of large monuments and architectural scale models to document the pre-Columbian cultures of Meso-

America. The rear of the room is devoted to Maya and Aztec cultures. Among the more spectacular objects are a cast of a large animal form and two 35-ft stelae, also casts, from the Maya site of Quirigua in eastern Guatemala, models of temples from the ruins at Palenque, Campeche, and Tikal, and casts of stelae and actual architectural elements from Uxmal brought back by John Lloyd Stephens, a principal discoverer of the ancient Maya ruins.

Dominating the Aztec section is a full-sized replica of a stone of the sun, sometimes mistakenly thought to be a calendar.

(18) Hall of South American Peoples: Here are artifacts of aboriginal cultures from Colombia to the southern tip of Chile. Highlights include brilliantly colored textiles, pottery, and carefully crafted gold and silver ornaments. An exhibition on metallurgy and mining includes the mummified body of the Copper Man (AD 500), a Chilean miner killed when the shaft collapsed on him. He lies on his side, surrounded by his tools. A display on ethnology uses films, artifacts, and mannequins to describe Amazonian cultures. Particularly impressive is a plaque used during an initiation ceremony of the Wayana Indians of the Guianas; during the ceremony the plaque filled with hundreds of stinging ants is strapped to the initiate's chest as a harrowing test of endurance.

Carl Akeley (1864–1926)

Born on a farm in upstate New York, Carl Akeley had only three years of formal schooling. Already famous when he began working for the museum for his innovations in taxidermy, he eventually won recognition also as a great field collector and explorer, an author and sculptor, and the inventor of a panoramic motion-picture camera and a cement gun, originally used in constructing animal models, but later used to patch deteriorated building concrete. In 1924, alarmed by hunters' slaughter of gorillas, Akeley persuaded King Albert of Belgium to set aside 250 acres for a gorilla sanctuary in what is now the Democratic Republic of the Congo near the Rwanda border.

Earlier taxidermists usually just skinned their specimens and stuffed them, but Akeley pioneered a technique of mounting that began with observing the living animal in its habitat and photographing it in motion. Akeley then copied the skeleton of the specimen and filled out the muscles and tissues with clay; from this he made a plaster cast and from that a *papier mâché* mould onto which the skin was glued.

The hall was completed in 1936, ten years after Akeley died of a fever during an expedition in the Belgian Congo, where he was buried, near Mount Mikeno—the volcano seen furthest to the right in the gorilla diorama.

Third floor

Favorite exhibits in the **Hall of Reptiles and Amphibians (19)** include the Komodo dragons (the world's largest and fiercest lizards), the Poison Dart frogs (among the world's most toxic animals), and a 25-ft reticulated python. The **Hall of Primates (20)** makes use of taxidermic specimens, skeletons, and diagrams to illustrate the relationships between different groups of primates, beginning with the lowly tree shrew (near the restrooms), and proceeding through lemurs, lorises, macaques, and mangabeys,

AMERICAN MUSEUM OF NATURAL HISTORY
(THIRD FLOOR)

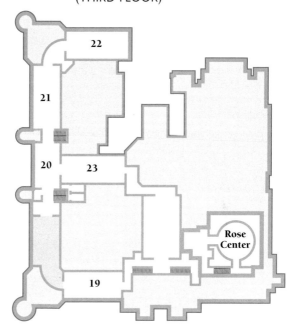

19 Hall of Reptiles and Amphibians
20 Hall of Primates
21 Hall of Eastern Woodlands and Plains
    Indians

22 Margaret Mead Hall of Pacific Peoples
23 Hall of North American Birds

to the higher primates and, finally, man. The **Hall of Eastern Woodlands and Plains Indians (21)** of the United States and Canada documents the arts and culture of these peoples from prehistoric times to the early 20th century.

The **Margaret Mead Hall of Pacific Peoples (22)**, named after the anthropologist who spent 53 years at the museum as a curator of ethnology, is the only hall of its kind in the world. It contains artifacts reflecting the Pacific cultures of Polynesia, Micronesia, Melanesia, Australia, Indonesia, and the Philippines; that is, the cultures of almost 70 separate tribal groups. Artifacts on display date from a carved stone representation of a god from 14th-century Java to pieces acquired after World War II.

The **Hall of North American Birds (23)** is named for Frank M. Chapman (1864–1945), a largely self-taught ornithologist and conservationist, who once said that birds were Nature's most eloquent expression of beauty, joy, and freedom. The diorama showing an adult peregrine falcon feeding its young recreates a scene

Chapman saw on the Hudson River palisades. The birds on display include the golden eagle, whooping crane, warblers, wading birds of the Everglades, boobies, the California condor, great horned owl, American egret, bald eagle, and wild turkey.

Fourth floor

The Fossil Halls are one of New York's premier attractions. The museum has the world's largest and finest collection of fossil bones (only about 5 percent is on display), including magnificent fossilized skeletons from the Jurassic period (180–120 million years ago), early reptiles of the Triassic period (225–180 million years ago), mammal-like reptiles of southern Africa, and fossil fish

As part of the reinstallation of the fossil halls, the museum restored the famous murals by Charles R. Knight, one of the first artists to use fossil remains in reconstructing the appearance of prehistoric animals and their environments. Four murals from Knight's series (1930s), titled the *Age of Mammals in North America*, are on display here. His dinosaur paintings, based on newly discovered material in Wyoming, were the first to show dinosaurs interacting in dramatic ways. Painted in the Impressionistic style and influenced by Japanese artists (although Knight suffered from very poor eyesight, and had to work with the aid of special spectacles), his artwork remains a magnificent example of early restorations of past life.

CLADISTICS

Unlike most fossil exhibitions, which are arranged chronologically, the exhibits here are organized in pathways that show evolutionary relationships, each animal grouped with its closest relatives. Taken together, these groups form a giant evolutionary diagram, or cladogram. A black stripe down the center of each gallery floor represents the "trunk" of the dinosaur family tree; many of the most spectacular specimens are shown along this midline. Branches lead off the main trunk to alcoves showing related groups of dinosaurs. To follow this evolutionary path in the correct sequence, you should enter from the Hall of Vertebrate Origins near the café. (A short film in the Orientation Center explains the arrangement of the rooms.)

(24) Hall of Vertebrate Origins: This explores the development of physical characteristics—the backbone, jaws, limbs, and the ability to reproduce without returning to the water—which were crucial to evolution. Here are displayed the first vertebrates to live entirely on land, and the first flying vertebrates. Highlights include *Buettneria*, a six-foot, four-limbed swimming predator; the massive armored early fish *Dunkleosteus*; the gigantic aquatic turtle known as *Stupendemys*; and *Pteranodon*, a flying reptile with a 23-ft wingspan.

AMERICAN MUSEUM OF NATURAL HISTORY
(FOURTH FLOOR)

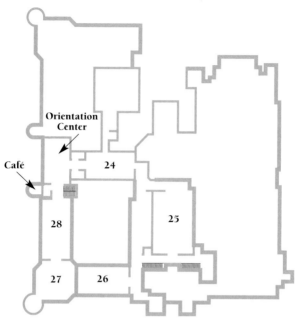

24 Hall of Vertebrate Origins
25 Hall of Saurischian Dinosaurs
26 Hall of Ornithischian Dinosaurs

27 Primitive Fossil Mammals
28 Advanced Fossil Mammals

(25) Hall of Saurischian Dinosaurs:
The display illustrates the idea of how dinosaurs developed from a common ancestor, whose salient evolutionary characteristic was a hole in its hip socket, a feature that allowed an upright posture (as opposed to the horizontal stance of turtles or lizards, whose legs sprawl out to the sides). Saurischian dinosaurs are further marked by a grasping hand or claw. The most famous specimen here is a 65-million-year-old *Tyrannosaurus rex*, with a four-foot jaw, six-inch teeth, and massive

thigh bones. *T-rex* was formerly mounted upright, with its tail dragging on the ground, but the present stalking pose reflects recent scientific thinking. This specimen has a couple of healed broken ribs and evidence of a facial abscess, as well as several fused vertebrae in its neck and lower back, all scars of the traumas of a fighting life.

Nearby is a predatory *Allosaurus*, feeding on the remains of an *Apatosaurus* (*see below*). The bones of the *Apatosaurus* are marked with grooves that may have been

caused by the teeth or claws of the 140-million-year-old predator; *Allosaurus* teeth found near the *Apatosaurus* bones inspired the idea for the mount.

Across the corridor from *Tyrannosaurus rex* is plant-eating *Apatosaurus*, the correct name for a dinosaur formerly known as *Brontosaurus*. The confusion dates to the 19th century when the eminent paleontologist Othniel Charles Marsh gave two names to different fossil assemblages that were in fact largely of the same species, though one had an incorrect head. The recent reinstallation added 20ft to the tail and rectified the skull. Near the *Apatosaurus* (climb the steps to the overlook) is the Glen Rose Trackway, part of a long series of tracks discovered in the Paluxy River in Texas. Once thought to contain the tracks of a single plant-eater pursued by a single carnivore, the trackway is now known to incorporate at least five trackways, perhaps made at different times. Other important exhibits in this hall are two cannibalistic *Coelophysis* skeletons with bones of young *Coelophysis* inside, the first *Velociraptor* skull ever found, and two recently discovered embryonic-sized dinosaur skulls that may be baby *Velociraptors*.

(26) Hall of Ornithischian Dinosaurs:

Ornithischian dinosaurs are characterized by a backward-pointing extension of the pubis bone. They include armored dinosaurs, duckbills, and horned dinosaurs. Near the entrance are the armored dinosaurs, including a splendid *Stegosaurus*, which came from the Bone Cabin Quarry in Wyoming, a site named after a sheep herder's hut built on a foundation of dinosaur bones. The mistaken notion that *Stegosaurus* had two brains

can be traced to the same O.C. Marsh who caused the *Brontosaurus* confusion. Describing the *Stegosaurus* in the 1890s, Marsh emphasized its small brain cavity and the expansion of the spinal column in the pelvis; this gave rise to the notion that *Stegosaurus* needed a second "brain" to drive its hindquarters. Also on view here are *Ankylosaurs*, creatures with clublike tails, some of them so completely plated that even their eyes could be shielded with bony curtains.

Further along are two robotic skulls (real fossils, not mock-ups), whose chewing actions show the difference between animals that crush and grind (duck-bills, for example) and animals that slice and dice (horned dinosaurs, for example). On the left of the central corridor are the horned dinosaurs (*ceratopsians*), beginning with a nest of dinosaur eggs originally believed to belong to *Protoceratops*, a primitive member of this group. Dinosaur eggs were first found (1923) in Mongolia by museum researchers, a stupendous discovery confirming the hypothesis that dinosaurs indeed did lay eggs.

Further along are *Triceratops*, well-known for its big, bony neck frill, and *Styracosaurus* (meaning spiked reptile), whose neck frill and nose are adorned with long spikes.

On the other side of the walkway are duck-billed dinosaurs (*hadrosaurs*) and their relatives. The "mummified" skeleton of *Edmontosaurus* (a reptile from the Edmonton Formation) is displayed lying on its back with its knees drawn up just as it was found; it is remarkable in having evidence of skin and other soft tissues. Two 30-ft duck-billed dinosaurs of the genus *Anatotitan* (giant duck) are mounted in standard postures, but now

paleontologists believe that they walked on all fours, stretching out their tails to counterbalance their necks. A skeleton of *Corythosaurus* retains fossilized impressions of skin with scales of different sizes and shapes. The exhibit ends with a display on dinosaur extinction.

(27) Primitive Fossil Mammals: Among the extinct relatives of modern mammals is *Dimetrodon*, a dramatic fossil with a large sail-like structure on its back. *Moschops capensis*, a near relative of mammals, had a skull almost four inches thick.

Other classes of mammal shown here are monotremes (egg-laying mammals); marsupials (pouched mammals); and edentates (toothless mammals, though actually they had teeth), including prehistoric sloths, armadillos, and anteaters. One spectacular fossil is the skeleton of *Panochthus frenzelianus*, an armadillo-like creature, completely covered with a shell of fused bony plates.

(28) Advanced Fossil Mammals: Early carnivores are displayed first. A fossil of *Smilodon necator*, a saber-toothed cat, has a broken upper canine, showing how fragile these imposing teeth really were. A

skeleton of *Ursus spelaeus*, a cave bear, shows the animal in a threatening posture, as it may have confronted early humans. Across the corridor are rabbits and rodents, insectivores, bats, and primates.

Further along (left side) are *artiodactyls* (animals with an even number of toes) including pigs, deer, and camels. Facing the central corridor a dramatic exhibit shows a bear-like *Amphicyon* ferociously pursuing an ancestral antelope. Nearby *Megaloceros*, the largest deer in history, displays huge, broad antlers, its heavy head supported by large neck bones. The horse display on the central corridor shows the evolution of this animal from a small Eocene *Hyracotherium*, the earliest known horse, to the modern *Equus*. In the alcove devoted to horses, rhinos, and tapirs, is a fossil of a mare, *Protohippus simus*, that may have died giving birth; the head and limbs of the foal are visible behind the mother's rib cage.

Concluding the exhibit are spectacular exhibits of *probosicideans* and *desmostylians* (mammoths and mastodons), including the mummified trunk, head, and leg of a baby mammoth, freeze-dried by the Alaskan tundra some 25,000 years ago.

THE ROSE CENTER FOR EARTH & SPACE

Map p. 576, B4. Direct entrance on West 81st St (Central Park West and Columbus Ave); also accessible from the American Museum of Natural History. Open 10–5:45 every day except Thanksgiving and Christmas Day, and until 8:45 on the first Fri of every month. Entrance is included with entrance to museum, but extra tickets (at the museum or by advance purchase, by telephone or at the planetarium) are required for the Space Show.
The $210-million Rose Center for Earth and Space (2000; Polshek Partnership), a new architectural setting with sophisticated new exhibits, replaces the former Hayden Planetarium (opened 1935). Visually stunning, this aluminum-clad sphere (87ft in diameter) within a cube of water-white glass (more transparent than ordinary glass) on a gray granite base took less than six years from conception to completion.

Inside the top part of the sphere, still called the Hayden Planetarium, is the Space Theater, whose custom-built Zeiss Mark IX Star Projector can virtually recreate the night sky and other dazzling simulations on the inner surface of the dome. Space shows change periodically.

Other exhibit areas include the Scales of the Universe walkway, which attempts to convey the relative sizes of objects in the cosmos, from astronomically large to sub-atomically small. The Cosmic Pathway, a descending circular ramp, shows how the universe has changed over the last 13 billion years. All of recorded human history appears as the thickness of a hair at the very end of the ramp. On display on the ground floor is the 15.5-ton Willamette meteorite (*see box below*).

THE WILLAMETTE METEORITE

Formed more than four billion years ago, this mass of iron and nickel is the oldest meteorite in the US. It was found in Oregon, where it had been carried by glaciers during the last ice age, probably from an impact site in Idaho. It was acquired by the museum in 1906. To the Clackamas, Native Americans of the Willamette Valley, Oregon, the meteorite is known as *Tomanowos* ("Heavenly Visitor") and is greatly revered. It is said that warriors would dip their arrowheads in rainwater that collected in pits in the meteorite's surface, believing that this would endow them with special power. In June 2000, the museum signed an agreement with the tribe that ensures members an annual ceremonial visit. As part of the pact, the tribe dropped its claim for return of the meteorite and the museum agreed to place a description of the meteorite's spiritual significance to the Clackamas alongside the description of its scientific importance.

THE NEW-YORK HISTORICAL SOCIETY

Map p. 576, B4. 170 Central Park West (West 76th and West 77th Sts). Open Tues–Sun 10–6; later closing on Fri; closed holidays; T: 212 873 3400; www.nyhistory.org.

The New-York Historical Society (1908, York & Sawyer; north and south wings 1938, Walker & Gillette) is the oldest museum in the city. The building is a paragon of Neoclassical severity, faced in hard gray granite and barely ornamented.

Founded in 1804 by business and civic leaders, the New-York Historical Society was originally conceived of as an exclusive private club and library, whose purpose was to preserve documents and artifacts relevant to the history of New York and the United States. That the organization retains the old hyphenated spelling of the city's name suggests the conservatism that has long characterized the society.

In 1868 the society refused the City's offer of land in Central Park, maintaining its commitment to support only from private individuals. (The Metropolitan Museum of

Art presently occupies the rejected land parcel.) After surviving a financial crisis in the early 1990s, the society now hopes to expand the landmark building and possibly to use the air rights above it to erect a 23-story luxury residential tower, a plan that meets with community opposition.

The collections

The society's collections include paintings by Hudson River School landscapists, portraits from the colonial period and later, John James Audubon's watercolors for *The Birds of America*, and extensive holdings of decorative arts. There are artifacts relating to New York's participation in local and global events, among them the slave trade, the American Revolution, and the terrorist attack on the World Trade Center. The Research Library, open to scholars, has half a million books, 10,000 newspapers, and every New York City directory printed since 1768. There is a rich trove of letters, manuscripts, and other documents pertaining to the founding of the Republic, as well as a collection of 10,000 dining menus.

Second floor

Gallery 3 (at the top of the stairs): Here are examples of Staffordshire pottery with American scenic views as well as paintings of the Hudson River valley, including views of steamers plying the river.

Negative #4260; accession #1952.80. Collection of the New-York Historical Society. Oil on canvas, 49 1/4 x 38 7/8 in.

Gallery 4: In this long gallery are examples from the society's fine collection of landscapes by the painters of the **Hudson River School** (occasionally rotated). Among the paintings are Asher B. Durand's *White Mountain Scenery: Franconia Notch, New Hampshire* (1857), and *The Solitary Oak* (1844). Albert Bierstadt is represented by *Black Mountain from the Harbor Islands, Lake George, New York* (1875), and *Donner Lake from the Summit* (1873), given by Archer Milton Huntington.

Unidentified woman (formerly thought to be Edward Hyde, Lord Cornbury, dressed in the garb of his sovereign, Queen Anne). Anon. early 18th-century artist.

John James Audubon: Watercolor of an Arctic tern. From *The Birds of America* (1827–38).

Sierra Nevada mountain range in California. Frederic Edwin Church's *Cayambe* (1858) depicts a lush Ecuadorian landscape with palm trees in the foreground and a snowy volcano in the distance. There are two views of Niagara Falls by John Trumbull, an unusual subject for an artist best known for his portraits and paintings of events in the American Revolution. Thomas Cole is represented by *Catskill Creek* (1845), *Autumn Twilight, View of Conway Peak [Mount Chocorua], New Hampshire*, and his five-part allegory *The Course of Empire*. These five paintings, executed between 1834 and 1836, present a romantic rendering of the rise and fall of a mythical civilization from its savage beginnings to its ruinous ending.

Huntington was the son of railroad magnate Collis P. Huntington, who commissioned the painting, which depicts the summit where the Central Railroad reaches its highest point crossing the

Gallery 3 (around the corner): These rooms contain studies by Asher B. Durand and Thomas Cole's *The Vale and Temple of Segestae, Sicily* (1844), as well as genre paintings and domestic scenes by Eastman Johnson and others.

Fourth floor

The Henry Luce III Center for the Study of American Culture offers a well-organized display of some 40,000 objects, about 70 percent of the collection. The objects are grouped in areas: paintings, Audubon watercolors and other drawings, textiles, furniture, historic relics and artifacts from 9/11, and so on.

Gallery 1: An especially arresting portrait here (*illustrated on previous page*) is thought by some to depict Edward Hyde, Viscount Cornbury, who served as governor of New York and New Jersey (1702–08). Hyde is depicted dressed as a woman, something he occasionally did, because, he said, he acted in the person of his cousin, Queen Anne. (Other experts, however, believe that the sitter is simply an unidentified woman.) Also here is an anonymous portrait of the freed slave Peter Williams (*see p. 76*) from c. 1815. There are also portraits by Gilbert Stuart, John Trumbull, Thomas Sully, Charles Willson Peale, and Rembrandt Peale.

Gallery 2: The collection of **Audubon watercolors** from *The Birds of America* was published (1827–38) by London engraver Robert Havel. The book became one of the most valuable ever printed, and the Historical Society is fortunate to own all but two of the original watercolors. These watercolors and other drawings are shown on a rotating basis.

Gallery 6: Contains sculpture by John Quincy Adams Ward, Augustus Saint-Gaudens, and Frederick MacMonnies, as well as a large collection of work by the American Victorian sculptor John Rogers.

Long gallery: In the center of this gallery at the top of stairs is the English-made Beekman family coach (c. 1770), one of a very few extant 18th-century vehicles. The Beekmans donated it to the society in 1911.

Gallery 8: Decorative objects include a large collection of American silver, much of which belonged to prominent New Yorkers including Roosevelts, Schuylers and De Peysters, or was made by such outstanding silversmiths as Cornelius Kierstede and Myer Myers.

Gallery 9: Examples of practically every type of lamp created by Louis Comfort Tiffany.

CENTRAL PARK WEST

Map pp. 576–B4–578, B2. Subway: 1 to 79th St-Broadway; B (weekdays only) or C to 81st St. Bus: M7, M10, M11, M79, M86, M104.

The extension of Eighth Avenue north of 59th St was renamed Central Park West after the opening of the park in 1876, to boost land values. The older buildings date back to the last decade of the 19th century, when the arrival of the Ninth Avenue elevated railroad in 1879 made the Upper West Side accessible to the middle class, and the area began to be developed. The newer buildings, with a few exceptions, date from before 1931—remarkable longevity considering the city's penchant for tearing down and building up. Among the newer buildings facing the park are several examples of Art Deco apartment architecture; among the older ones are fine masonry buildings. Along the side streets are long blocks of brownstone row houses dating to the late 19th century, many with imposing stone stoops and exuberant ornamentation.

Today the section from West 79th St down to Columbus Circle offers a walk along a pleasant avenue whose venerable institutions and stately apartment buildings serve the cultural and spiritual needs of many New Yorkers, as well as the domestic needs of a select few. Making their mark on the skyline here are three twin-towered apartments (best seen from Central Park), all of which have attracted celebrities as well as the anonymously wealthy. (The triple-towered Beresford at West 81st St, built in 1929, is considered one of the masterpieces of the architect Emery Roth; *see box below.*)

Between West 76th and West 73rd Streets

The Gothic **Fourth Universalist Society of New York** (1898; William A. Potter), originally called the Church of the Divine Paternity is one of the few non-Neoclassical buildings on Central Park West (*160 Central Park West at West 76th St. Visitors welcome during the day, except when special events are in progress; T: 212 595 1658*). It has decorative work by Louis Comfort Tiffany and Augustus Saint-Gaudens, as well as an exceptional Skinner organ. *New York Tribune* editor Horace Greeley, showman Phineas T. Barnum, and baseball star Lou Gehrig worshiped here.

At 145–46 Central Park West (West 74th and West 75th Sts) are the twin-towered **San Remo Apartments** (1930; Emery Roth), finished in Neoclassical garb with cartouches over the entrances and finialed temples on top. In 1929 the city passed the Multiple Dwelling Act, which, among other provisions, allowed residential buildings to be taller than formerly permitted, as long as the lot size exceeded 30,000 square ft and the builder provided large courtyards for light and air. The Beresford predated that law, and its towers contain water tanks and elevator machinery, but the twin-towers of Roth's buildings contain apartments with significant amounts of light. Celebrities have long gravitated to the San Remo: Stephen Spielberg, Steve Jobs, and Donna Karan, among other glitterati. Rita Hayworth spend her declining years here; Eddie Cantor, who was making about a half million dollars a year in the early 1930s, also lived here.

Emery Roth (1871–1948)

The firm of Emery Roth & Sons built more than 100 glass and steel skyscrapers after World War II (few of them with much distinction), but between 1903 and the late 1930s, Emery Roth *père* produced many fine masonry apartment buildings and hotels ornamented with Neoclassical detail. Among these buildings were three of the Central Park West twin towers: the San Remo, the Beresford, and the El Dorado. Roth, of Hungarian parentage, came to the US from what is now Slovakia in 1886 at the age of 13, and four years later began working as a draftsman on the Chicago World's Columbian Exposition. Like other conservative architects, he was deeply impressed by the dignity of the Beaux-Arts buildings that dominated the exhibition, a style later reflected in his own work. He came to New York on the invitation of Richard Morris Hunt, who had been impressed by the young man's skill at draftsmanship.

The Langham at 135 Central Park West (West 73rd and West 74th Sts; 1905, Clinton & Russell) stands on land bought—but later sold—by the Clark family at the time they developed the Dakota (*see below*). The Langham was intended as the finest apartment in the city, according to a 1904 account in *The New York Times*. Its apartments were nothing if not spacious (only four per floor), and the building offered other luxuries: a central refrigeration plant and a conveyor system for delivering mail to individual apartments. Famous residents have included Edward Albee (grandfather of the playwright and head of the Keith-Albee-Orpheum theaters), Isadore Saks, who founded Saks 34th Street, and Lee Strasberg, director and acting teacher.

The Dakota Apartments

The Dakota Apartments at 1 West 72nd St (1884; Henry J. Hardenbergh) are architecturally one of the city's finest apartment buildings and socially one of the pre-eminent West Side addresses.

In 1884 apartments were beginning to find favor with the well-to-do, so when Singer Sewing Machine heir Edward S. Clark undertook a magnificent apartment house on West 72nd St, he was not acting without precedent. His choice of location, however, was daring: uptown, surrounded by shanties and vacant land—so far north and west of civilization, in fact, that detractors called it Clark's Folly, one of them allegedly remarking that the building might as well be in the Dakota territory. Whether this story is true or not, the architect garnished the building with ears of corn, arrowheads, and a bas-relief of an Indian's head above the main gateway.

Hardenbergh is outstanding for his sense of composition, and the Dakota is generally acknowledged to be his masterpiece. Built around an open central courtyard, it is finished in buff-colored brick with terra-cotta and stone trim, and embellished with balconies, oriel windows, ledges, turrets, towers, gables, chimneys, finials, and flagpoles. The fence railings are decorated with griffins and heads of Zeus (others see them as sea monsters and heads of Poseidon). They were made by the Hecla Ironworks, a premier firm responsible for decorative work at Grand Central Terminal, the St. Regis Hotel, and the interior of the New York Stock Exchange.

Not surprisingly the building has attracted a striking clientele, notably people involved in the arts. Among them have been Boris Karloff, Zachary Scott, Leonard Bernstein, Lauren Bacall, Roberta Flack, and scientist Michael Idvorsky Pupin. Most famous of all was John Lennon, who was shot and killed in the courtyard by a deranged admirer on Dec 8, 1980.

The **Majestic Apartments** on the other side of West 72nd St are the second of the four double-towered buildings that give the skyline along Central Park its distinction. Stylistically related to the Century, nine blocks downtown (*see p. 416 below*), the Majestic was also built (1931; Jacques Delamarre) by the Irwin S. Chanin Company. René Chambellan, better known for the fountains at Radio City, designed the brickwork patterns. Corner windows were frequently used in Art Deco buildings, whose steel cage construction allowed corners to be opened up (unlike masonry construction, where corners were load-bearing).

BROWNSTONES

Both West 70th and West 71st Sts off Central Park West are fortunate in retaining rows of handsome brownstone houses.

Brownstone is a Triassic sandstone whose characteristic chocolate color comes from iron ore. A brownstone in the local dialect is a row house (built for a single family) faced with this material, usually dating from the late 19th century, usually four or five stories high and two or three windows wide, usually featuring a tall stoop and a cornice at the top. Most brownstones were built by masons or builders, but the one at 20 West 71st St enjoyed the talents of an architect (1889; Gilbert A. Schellenger), who designed a row of four houses here.

Brownstones were usually constructed in small groups, and their widths became fractions of the standard city building lot (25ft by 100ft). The most spacious are 25ft wide, while smaller varieties are 20ft (a fifth of four lots), 18¾

ft (a quarter of three lots) or 16⅔ ft (a third of two lots). Because these houses were built for prosperous middle-class families, the interiors were executed in fine materials, and the façades often elaborately decorated; note, for example, the cupids at the cornice of no. 24; the cartouches on nos. 26, 28, and 30; and the lions' heads on nos. 33–39.

As a child, novelist Edith Wharton lived in a brownstone on West 23rd St, but she was never sentimental about her childhood home. In *A Backward Glance* she opined that brownstone rendered New York "hide-bound in its deadly uniformity of mean ugliness." And in *The Age of Mirth*, she speaks of brownstone as the uniform hue that "coated New York like a cold chocolate sauce."

Shearith Israel Synagogue

99 Central Park West at West 70th St. Open during services; T: 212 873 0300; www.shearithisrael.org.

Also known as the Spanish and Portuguese Synagogue, this the newest home (1897; Brunner & Tryon) of Congregation Shearith Israel, the nation's oldest Jewish congregation, which dates back to 1654 when the first Jewish refugees arrived in New Amsterdam fleeing the Inquisition (*see p. 52*). The building's classical style was

influenced by the archaeological discovery of the ruins of the Second Temple in Jerusalem, built during the Roman occupation. Earlier synagogue builders in America often chose Moorish styles (for example the Central Synagogue; see *p. 241*) that reflected the Moorish heritage of Sephardic Jews.

Under Dutch rule Jews had to worship in secret, but in 1682, under a more tolerant British governor, they founded Congregation Shearith Israel ("Remnant of Israel") and held organized services, first in a rented room on Beaver St, then in the upper story of a flour mill on Mill Lane and South William St (*see p. 54*). The first synagogue building (1730) at what is presently 26 South William St is gone, but some of its artifacts and two large millstones from the Dutch mill are preserved in the Little Synagogue here, which reconstructs the original sanctuary.

Between West 67th and West 62nd Streets

West 67th St is a charming anomaly, containing several studio buildings constructed expressly for working artists. The most famous is the **Hotel des Artistes** (1915; George Mort Pollard) at no. 1, with large two-story windows and fanciful neo-Gothic statuary above the second story. Among its famous tenants have been Noel Coward, Isadora Duncan, Norman Rockwell, and Howard Chandler Christy, whose elegant murals still adorn the upscale ground-floor restaurant, Café des Artistes.

55 Central Park West, between 65th and 66th Sts (1940; Schwartz & Gross), is an Art Deco-inspired building with an ironwork marquee over the entrance, whose spiky finials echo those elsewhere on the building. The brickwork is shaded from red at the bottom to tan at the top—to give the impression, observers have said, of a ray of sunshine perpetually shining on the façade. Radio singer Rudy Vallee was an early resident.

The Prasada, at 50 Central Park West, was built in 1907 (Charles W. Romeyn & Henry R. Wynne), just as Central Park West was becoming a street of noteworthy apartment buildings. Massive two-story banded columns flank its entrance, though the origin of the building's name is not known. Oscar J. Gude, said to have introduced electric advertising signs to Times Square, once lived here. So did novelist Edna Ferber.

The **New York Society for Ethical Culture**, at West 63rd and West 64th Sts, was founded in 1876 by Felix Adler to further morality independently of organized religion. The Ethical Culture school system began with the city's first free kindergarten (1878), early establishing itself as a force in experimental education. Today the society operates the prestigious Fieldston Schools in the Bronx as well as the Ethical Culture School here, all known for their progressive outlook. The southern building (1902; Robert D. Kohn and Carrère & Hastings) houses the school; the limestone Art Nouveau northern building at 2 West 64th St (1910; Robert D. Kohn with Estelle Rumbold Kohn, sculptor) houses the meeting hall.

The Art Deco **Century Apartments**, at 25 Central Park West between West 62nd and West 63rd Sts (1931; Jacques Delamarre and the Irwin S. Chanin Construction Co.), take their name from the Century Theater (1909), a grandiose undertaking with national ambitions that turned out to be too large and too far uptown to make a profit, even when Florenz Ziegfeld staged spectaculars here.

MORNINGSIDE HEIGHTS

Map p. 574. Subway: 1 to 110th St-Cathedral Pkwy. Bus: M4, M11, M104 to 110th St-Cathedral Pkwy.

Bounded by Cathedral Parkway (110th St) on the south and the deep valley of West 125th St on the north, Morningside Heights sits on the rocky ridge that runs the length of Manhattan Island. Harlem lies on low ground to the east; on the west the terrain slopes down to the Hudson. The area is known for its educational and religious institutions, Columbia University and St. John the Divine among them.

HISTORY OF MORNINGSIDE HEIGHTS

Before the Revolutionary War much of Morningside Heights, like much of the rest of New York, was farmland. During the Revolution the Battle of Harlem Heights, fought in a wheatfield near Broadway and 117th St, was Washington's only significant victory in the campaign for Manhattan; his other efforts resulted in a series of lost battles followed by spectacularly successful retreats.

Morningside Heights remained isolated until the Ninth (Columbus) Avenue El opened in 1880. In its pastoral serenity dwelt the owners of small farms and houses and the squires of country estates, as well as the orphans of the Leake & Watts Asylum and the inmates of the Bloomingdale Insane Asylum. Riverside Drive also opened in 1880, touted as a new Fifth Avenue, a prophecy that was never quite realized, though by the end of the 19th century it seemed that the Heights would become a cultural, intellectual, and spiritual center of the city. The Cathedral Church of St. John the Divine, Columbia University, and St. Luke's Hospital would minister to the needs of spirit, mind, and body.

Major educational, religious, and service institutions dominate the social and economic tone of the area. They boast beautiful and impressive buildings and own much of the local real estate. Surrounding neighborhoods suffered during the Depression, and by the middle of the 20th century the area had deteriorated economically with attendant social problems.

The disparity between the wealth and power of the institutions and the struggles of the surrounding communities has engendered antagonism, especially apparent during the 1960s, when the institutions seeking to secure their frontiers and to expand tried to encroach on nearby park areas and residential space. Columbia's attempt (1968) to build a gymnasium in Morningside Park provoked protests from Columbia University students as well as the community. Tensions still exist as Columbia seeks to expand northward.

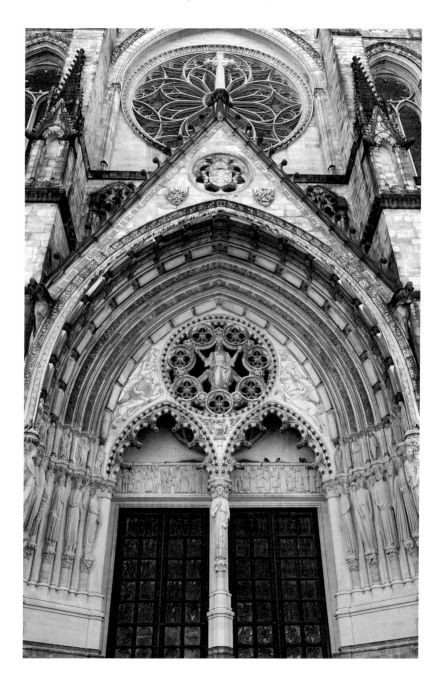

THE CATHEDRAL CHURCH OF ST. JOHN THE DIVINE

Map p. 574, B4. Amsterdam Ave at 112th St. Open Mon–Sat 7–6, Sun 7–7; you can wander at will except during services. Public tours Tues–Sat 11am, Sun 1pm. Grounds and gardens open during daylight hours; T: 212 316 7540; www.stjohndivine.org.
NB: Fire devastated the church in 2001. At the time of writing, the narthex and nave were closed for cleaning and restoration.

The Cathedral Church of St. John the Divine rises in uncompleted splendor on the heights above Morningside Park. The enormous stone arches erected to support the never-built dome and tower of the crossing stand exposed to the sky and to the eyes of passers-by, who have a rare opportunity to see a masonry cathedral under construction. St. John the Divine, sometimes irreverently called "St. John the Unfinished," is known also for its many social and cultural programs.

Building the cathedral

In 1887 a wooded plot of almost 13 acres belonging to the Leake & Watts Orphan Asylum was purchased for an Episcopal cathedral, for a momentous $885,000. The next year 68 entrants submitted designs in an architectural contest, from which the firm of Heins & La Farge emerged victorious. Like many of the other entries, the Heins & La Farge design, a Romanesque plan incorporating Byzantine elements, placed the long axis of the building along the spine of Morningside Heights. This would have given the church a spectacular flight of entrance stairs down to 110th St, but the tradition of building cathedrals with the nave running east–west eventually prevailed. In 1892 the cornerstone was laid.

Excavations for such a heavy building proved difficult, and J. Pierpont Morgan poured half a million dollars into an ever deeper hole before workers struck bedrock some 70ft down. George Heins died in 1907. In 1911, almost 20 years after the digging had begun, only the choir and the four stone arches to support the central tower were in place. Five years later the Heins & La Farge Romanesque plan was discarded, and Ralph Adams Cram (of the firm of Cram & Ferguson) redesigned the church on Gothic principles. Cram added about 80ft to the length of the nave, divided it into five aisles instead of the usual three, and proposed the use of alternate thick and slender piers to help in vaulting over its great width (twice as wide as Westminster Abbey). He also made several proposals for covering the crossing, whose size presented aesthetic problems as well as difficulties in engineering.

Ground was broken for the nave foundations in 1916; the nave itself was begun in 1925 and completed about 10 years later, but excavations for the north transept went slowly and the money raised for its construction ran out when the walls had reached a height of about 40ft. In 1939 the Romanesque choir was bricked up and remodeled

The main west portal of St. John the Divine (the "Portal of Paradise"), with St. John on the central column between the doors, and Christ in Glory above.

to conform to Cram's Gothic interiors. During World War II major construction was halted once again.

In the 1960s a plan for completing the crossing in a contemporary style with an unattached campanile was submitted but not approved. Then in 1967, during an era of intense national social awareness, the bishop announced that the building might never be completed; instead the church would devote its energies to relieving poverty in the community surrounding it. After a decade of social involvement, the trustees in 1978 announced a fund-raising campaign for completion of the crossing and the west façade, including the two towers.

Master masons were brought in to teach apprentice stonecutters, some from the local neighborhood, who cut enough limestone blocks for the southwest tower. The first stone was mortared into place in 1981. High-wire artist Philippe Petit, famous for walking the gap between the towers of the World Trade Center, opened the ceremonies, crossing Amsterdam Avenue 15 stories above the road with a ceremonial trowel for the bishop, who awaited him on the cathedral roof.

Construction ceased once more in 1993, with about 50ft added to the south tower, although the stone carving on the Portal of Paradise continued to completion (1997). To commemorate its centennial, the cathedral instituted an architectural competition for completion of the south transept, won by Spanish architect Santiago Calatrava, whose glass-enclosed biosphere was never built. In 2001 a fire devastated the unfinished north transept, filling the cathedral with smoke and damaging the Barberini Tapestries, two of them irreparably.

The exterior

Because towers on the west façade were never completed, the cathedral squats rather than soars. On the north, a chain-link fence encloses the former stoneyard. Urban grime and rust from steel scaffolding have darkened the stone of the façade. Nevertheless, the cathedral is impressive for its sheer mass.

The central doorway is known as the "**Portal of Paradise**." The bronze doors (sculptor Henry Wilson) were cast in Paris by Barbedienne, the firm that cast the Statue of Liberty. Their 60 panels depict scenes from the Old Testament (left-hand doors) and the New Testament (right-hand doors). The frieze above the doors shows the peoples of all nations standing before the Lamb. The figure on the central post, his eyes raised heavenward, is St. John the Divine, author of the Book of Revelation. The Four Horsemen of the Apocalypse are shown beneath this feet. Directly above him in the tympanum, a *Majestas* shows Christ in Glory surrounded by the seven lamps and the seven stars of St. John's revelation.

Surrounding the doors are statues of biblical figures, carved in 1988–97 by British master sculptor Simon Verity and others. Some of the figures are based on local personalities: Noah (upper rank figure furthest north) was modeled on the seventh dean of the cathedral, who holds the unfinished Ark and looks back toward the unfinished cathedral; his Welsh corgi lies at his feet. Some of the decorative sculpture on the column capitals offers wry contemporary interpretations of conventional iconography.

The prophet Jeremiah (third figure to the right of the portal), who foretold the destruction of Jerusalem, stands on a column whose capital depicts a mushroom cloud over a New York in which the Twin Towers were still standing. (*A pamphlet available at the Visitors' Booth explains the symbolism of all the portal sculpture.*)

The interior

NB: The description and plan that follow reflect the situation at the time of writing, when only the crossing and east end were viewable. These are described in detail. Other areas of the cathedral are described only briefly.

THE CATHEDRAL TAPESTRIES

(*NB: The tapestries are not on display during the restoration of the cathedral.*)
The cathedral owns two remarkable sets of tapestries. The **Mortlake Tapestries**, woven in England and based on a series of cartoons by Raphael, depict *The Acts of the Apostles*. Commissioned by Pope Leo X in about 1513, the cartoons, from which numerous sets of tapestries were woven, were dispersed throughout Europe and eventually lost. Sir Francis Crane, manager of the Mortlake tapestry works, rediscovered them in Genoa in 1623 and had them sent to England where a set was woven for Prince Charles (later Charles I) and others.

The twelve **Barberini Tapestries** were woven during the first half of the 17th century on the papal looms founded by Cardinal Francesco Barberini. Eleven depict scenes from the life of Christ; the other is a map of the Holy Land; the cartoons, by Giovanni Francesco Romanelli, are now in the Vatican. Two of the tapestries—*The Last Supper* and *The Resurrection*—which were on display in the north transept were severely damaged in the fire of 2001; what remains of them is being conserved in the cathedral's laboratories of textile conservation.

Areas closed at the time of writing

The nave: The piers of the nave are alternately massive and slender (16ft by 6ft), an arrangement reflected both in the exterior buttressing and in the design of the vaulting. The thick piers have an inner core of granite and are faced with limestone. The slender piers are made of solid granite. The outer aisle on each side of the nave is divided by an arcade into seven bays, illuminated by stained-glass windows. The bays in the aisles refer to the religious aspect of various professions and human activities: law, education, fatherhood and motherhood, the armed services, medicine, and so on. Some of them contain memorials: to firefighters, to victims of AIDS.

A general theme of the cathedral's iconography is internationalism, the cathedral as a house of prayer for all nations. This theme is reflected especially

ST. JOHN THE DIVINE

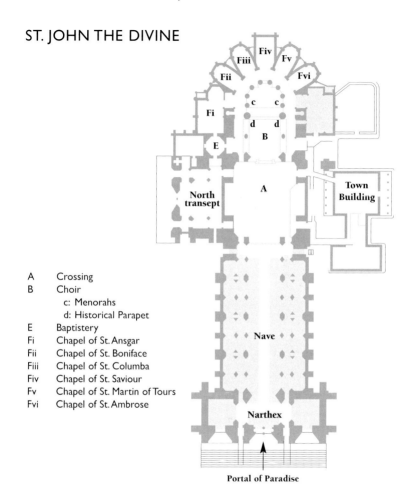

A   Crossing
B   Choir
      c: Menorahs
      d: Historical Parapet
E   Baptistery
Fi   Chapel of St. Ansgar
Fii   Chapel of St. Boniface
Fiii   Chapel of St. Columba
Fiv   Chapel of St. Saviour
Fv   Chapel of St. Martin of Tours
Fvi   Chapel of St. Ambrose

in the windows, in the decoration of the apsidal chapels, and in the Pilgrim's Pavement. Medallions in the pavement of the nave commemorate important people and sites in Christian history.

The original great organ (Ernest M. Skinner, 1910) was rebuilt in 1954; a new stop, the State Trumpet, was added, whose 61 silver pipes are directly under the rose window in the west front. The organ suffered smoke damage during the 2001 fire, and is currently being cleaned.

The rose window itself, best seen from the east end of the nave (*but sadly not on view at the time of writing*), was designed by Charles Connick and contains more than 10,000 pieces of glass. From the central figure of Christ radiate symbols representing the gifts of the Holy Spirit, the Beatitudes, and the heavenly choir. The lesser rose window below it, also by Connick, develops the symbolism of the

number seven: from a central monogram of Christ radiate seven fountains, seven growing vine forms, seven pairs of doves, and seven stars.

Areas open at the time of writing

(A) The crossing: Visible in the crossing are the imposing "bones" of the cathedral, the great granite piers, the uncompleted arches, and the remarkable "temporary" dome of tan Guastavino tile hastily installed in the summer of 1909. The dome, which was to be replaced by a tall central tower, was chosen as a cheap alternative to a flat wooden roof supp-orted by steel beams. The self-supporting tile served as its own scaffolding, and the masons worked from above, standing on the previous day's work to add a few more rows of tiles each day.

(B) The choir: The work of Heins & La Farge and Ralph Adams Cram can be seen here. The lower part (from the ground to the balustrade below the clerestory windows) remains from the original Romanesque plan (completed 1911); the work above (altered 1939–41) is Cram's Gothic remodeling. Dominating the choir are eight 52-ft granite columns from Vinalhaven, Maine, originally quar-ried as monoliths but cut in two after the first two columns cracked while being turned and polished on a special lathe. Because the land slopes sharply downhill at this end of the church, the foundations for the columns go down 135ft. Although the choir is relatively short (145ft), a kind of false perspective makes it seem longer: the arcades at the east end are closer together and the floor slopes upward in that direction.

Among the interesting objects in the choir are the two **menorahs (c)** near the altar. Designed after those in the Temple of Jerusalem depicted on the 1st-century AD Arch of Titus in Rome, they were donated (1930) by former *New York Times* publisher Adolph Ochs.

The **Historical Parapet (d)** at the ascent to the sanctuary (in two sections at either side) is carved with figures of notable men (and one woman) from the first 20 centuries of the Christian era, including St. Augustine of Hippo, St. Francis of Assisi, Shakespeare, and Abraham Lincoln. The statue of George Washington was decapitated by vandals in 2006, but a new head has been carved. The most recent group of statues (left end of the northern section of the parapet) represents Martin Luther King Jr., Albert Einstein, Susan B. Anthony, and Mohandas Gandhi.

(E) The baptistery: This octagonal chamber (1928; Frank Cleveland of Cram & Ferguson) was donated by the Stuyvesant family, whose Dutch origins are symbolized in the decoration of the room. Their coat of arms bearing a stag, dog and rabbit is in the spandrel of the ground-level arcade in the northeast wall. The marble font is modeled on that of the cathedral of Siena, Italy.

The **Chapels of the Tongues (F)** open from the ambulatory. Built between 1904 and 1918, the chapels represent different national or ethnic groups, in keeping with the international ideal of the cathedral. Each chapel is associated with a relevant

saint and most are constructed in styles appropriate to the groups they honor.

(Fi) Chapel of St. Ansgar (1918), named after a 9th-century Frankish missionary to Denmark, Sweden, and Germany. It is stylistically reminiscent of 14th-century English Gothic architecture and honors Scandinavian immigrants.

(Fii) Chapel of St. Boniface (1916), honors immigrants from Germany. St. Boniface was an English monk (c. 680–755) sent by Pope Gregory II to convert the tribes of Germany and martyred by a heathen mob while preaching in West Friesland. The 11-ft stiff-winged bronze statue of Michael the Archangel was made and donated (1963) by Eleanor M. Mellon.

(Fiii) Chapel of St. Columba (1911), commemorates the Irish saint (521–97) who founded the monastery of Iona and worked to convert the Celts. The statues flanking the entrance are by Gutzon Borglum, known for his huge sculptures of presidential faces on Mount Rushmore, and represent influential figures in English church history. Architects Heins & La Farge designed this chapel in the Romanesque style they chose for the cathedral as a whole. It is dedicated to immigrants from the British Isles.

(Fiv) Chapel of St. Saviour: The central chapel and the first one built (1904; Heins & La Farge) is dedicated to the Eastern Church, though its style is Gothic, not Byzantine. The 20 figures flanking the entrance represent the Heavenly Choir, and were designed by Gutzon Borglum, as were the figures of

scholars, bishops, and saints of the Eastern Church on either side of the window. The Heavenly Choir stirred up controversy when installed, since all the figures are female. Keith Haring's triptych, the *Life of Christ*, said to be based on a traditional Russian icon, was the artist's last work before his death from AIDS in 1990, and his only religious work.

In the ambulatory directly opposite the entrance to the chapel is the **tomb of Bishop Horatio Potter** (1802–87), designed after the tomb of Edward the Confessor in Westminster Abbey and occupying the spot behind the high altar traditionally reserved for a cathedral's founder.

(Fv) The **Chapel of St. Martin of Tours**, a 4th-century Gallic bishop, was designed by Ralph Cram (1918) in a style reminiscent of 13th-century French Gothic, and honors French immigrants. It is noteworthy for its beautiful windows (Charles Connick) depicting scenes from the lives of three French saints (left to right): St. Louis, St. Martin, and St. Joan of Arc. The statue of Joan of Arc (donated 1922) on the left wall is by Anna Hyatt Huntington and stands above a stone taken from the saint's cell in Rouen. A small chip of Reims Cathedral blasted away during World War I is embedded in the trefoil above the altar cross.

(Fvi) Chapel of St. Ambrose, named after the 4th-century bishop of Milan and patron saint of lawyers. It was designed (1914; Carrère & Hastings) in a style Cram called "purely Renaissance." Dedicated to Italian immigrants, it is decorated with several kinds of Italian marble.

The last chapel, the Chapel of St. James (1916), had not been cleaned and was not open at the time of writing. It is dedicated to the people of Spain.

The cathedral close

The grounds surrounding the cathedral cover about 11 acres. Near the sidewalk at 111th St, the bronze **Peace Fountain** (1985; Greg Wyatt) depicts the battle between Good and Evil as represented by the figures of Satan and the archangel Michael. The pedestal, formed like a double helix, suggests DNA, carrier of the genetic code. Figures in the sculpture include a smiling sun face, a moon face, some giraffes, and a giant crab. Various observers have described the sculpture as fascinating, repugnant, or "gnarly."

In the center of the lawn is the **Outdoor Pulpit on the Green**, a tall open-work Gothic spire, originally used for outdoor services. Buildings include **Synod House** to the right of this (offices of the Bishop of the Diocese of New York) and **Diocesan House** behind and beyond (once a training school for deaconesses, now used for offices, apartments, and the cathedral library). **Cathedral House** further east was originally the bishop's house, built like a Gothic château with money donated by J. Pierpont Morgan. Morgan defended its elegance by opining that bishops should live "like everyone else," though he probably had a rarefied view of how "everyone else" lived. Adjoining it is **Ogilvie House**, once the deanery, now home to the bishop. Beyond is the **Cathedral School**, formerly a day school for choirboys, and now a co-educational elementary and middle school, from whose enrollment the choir still draws its treble voices. The **Biblical Garden** is planted with flora mentioned in the Bible.

The **Town Building** (1843), adjoining the south transept, was designed by Ithiel Town, one of the country's first professional architects, for the Leake & Watts Orphan Asylum. It now houses the cathedral's social outreach programs and the Textile Conservation Laboratory.

IN THE NEIGHBORHOOD

Diagonally opposite the cathedral, at Amsterdam Ave and 111th St, is the **Hungarian Pastry Shop**, a small, old-fashioned café which serves traditional Central European coffee and cakes. The pumpkin pie is also particularly good. Further up Amsterdam Avenue, the small square building on the corner of 113th St is a **gatehouse** (c. 1890) that marks the end of a section of masonry aqueduct beneath the avenue. Most of the water supplied from the city's reservoirs is carried by pipes, but during the later years of the 19th century, when labor was cheap and pipe was expensive, the city built several masonry aqueducts. A second gatehouse stands at 119th St, where the pipes end and the masonry begins.

Although much of **St. Luke's-Roosevelt Hospital Center** (St. Luke's Division) on the north side of 113th St is new, part of the original central pavilion is still visible, though crowded and overshadowed by the modern wings. St. Luke's Hospital was founded in 1846 by the Episcopal Church, and merged with Roosevelt Hospital in 1979.

MORNINGSIDE PARK

Morningside Park occupies about 30 acres, including a rocky cliff of Manhattan schist, which plunges down to the Harlem Plain. In the mid-19th century the Parks Department took over these precipitous slopes, which were unsuitable for real estate development, and hired Frederick Law Olmsted and Calvert Vaux, already famous for their work in Central and Prospect Parks, to design a park. Realizing that the most attractive feature of the area was the view to the east, Vaux and Olmsted planned a walkway on top of the cliff, and studded it with balconies facing the Harlem Plain below. When their original design (1887) was rejected, Jacob Wrey Mould, who had worked with them on Central Park, planned the massive, buttressed masonry wall that supports the overlooks.

The park had a reputation for danger as early as the 1930s, but in 1981 some Columbia undergraduates founded the Friends of Morningside Park, which advocated returning the then overgrown and neglected park to its original design, and reclaiming its wilderness. Since that time crime has decreased, though has not altogether disappeared.

The Roman Catholic **Church of Notre Dame** at Morningside Drive and West 114th St (apse 1909–10, Dans & Otto; remainder 1914–28, Cross & Cross) was originally built as a mission church of the Church of St. Vincent de Paul (on West 24th St) and ministered to a congregation of French-speaking immigrants. The building, with its portico of Corinthian columns, was intended to recall churches of Napoleonic France. The interior is remarkable for its replica of the grotto at Lourdes. Today the pastor serves as chaplain to Catholic students at Columbia.

Just inside the park, at West 116th St, is the **Carl Schurz Memorial** (1913; sculptor Karl Bitter, architect Henry Bacon). Forced to flee Germany because of his revolutionary political sentiments, Schurz (1829–1906) emigrated to the US where he became a leader of the Republican party, a friend of Abraham Lincoln, a major general in the Union Army during the Civil War, a senator, and an editor. Bitter's bronze statue depicts Schurz as strong and idealistic; the low relief panels on the monument portray the liberation of oppressed peoples: Native Americans, Asians, and blacks. From the overlook to Morningside Park there is a sidelong view across the rockface of Jacob Wrey Mould's massive retaining wall.

COLUMBIA UNIVERSITY

Map p. 574, B4–A3. Amsterdam Ave and Broadway, West 114th–West 120th Sts. Subway: 1 to 66th St-Columbia University. Bus: M4, M11, M60, M104. The medical campus is near West 168th St and Broadway. For free campus tours, call the Visitors Center; T: 212 854 4900.

Columbia University, one of the oldest, wealthiest, and most respected of all North American universities, is known for its professional schools—medicine, law, business, education, journalism, and architecture—and for the School of General Studies, where adults of any age can work toward degrees. Undergraduate Columbia College is co-educational; affiliated with the university are Barnard College (women), Teachers College, the Jewish Theological Seminary, and Union Theological Seminary.

History of the University

Columbia was founded as a gentlemen's college to "instruct youth in the learned languages and in the liberal arts and sciences." By the mid-18th century it became apparent to contemporary observers that while New York outstripped its American rivals commercially, it lagged behind culturally, its populace (according to observers from Boston or Philadelphia) afflicted by ignorance, their lives dominated by a sordid thirst for money. Consequently a group of citizens set out to establish a center of learning that would lighten the intellectual gloom, in the process outshining Harvard, Yale, and the College of New Jersey (later Princeton). Among them were several vestrymen of Trinity Church, who arranged a transfer of five acres of church property to the proposed college—a plot not far from the World Trade Center site, bounded by Church, Murray, and Barclay Sts and the Hudson River. It was Columbia's first piece of valuable real estate.

The college was chartered by King George II in 1754 and named King's College, the fifth such institution in the colonies. The first president was Dr. Samuel Johnson, an Anglican pastor from Stratford, Connecticut; and the first class of eight men—who bore such resounding old New York names as Verplanck, Van Cortlandt, and Bayard—met in the schoolhouse of Trinity Church.

Among the early students were Alexander Hamilton (enrolled 1775), who later became the first secretary of the US Treasury; and John Jay, first chief justice of the US Supreme Court. After the Revolution the college, renamed Columbia, entered a period of intellectual dormancy that lasted well into the 19th century. In 1814 the trustees appealed to the state for financial aid, hoping for a share in the proceeds of a state lottery. Instead they received a plot of land between 47th and 51st Sts west of Fifth Avenue. Appraised by the state at $75,000, it seemed worth much less to the trustees since it was rocky, remote from the city, and overgrown with weeds. In the long run it turned out to be worth much more: today Rockefeller Center stands on that 11.5-acre parcel, which in 1985 the university sold to the Rockefeller Group for $400 million.

In 1857 the college moved uptown, not to the Rockefeller Center site but to buildings formerly owned by an asylum for the deaf and dumb between Madison and Fourth (now Park) Avenues, bounded by 49th and 50th Sts. The school remained there until its relocation to the Morningside Heights campus in 1897. In 1902 Nicholas Murray Butler became president; under his guidance Columbia achieved its high reputation.

MORNINGSIDE HEIGHTS CAMPUS

The university purchased the land from the Bloomingdale Insane Asylum in two parcels

(1892 and 1903) for a total of $3.9 million. The original campus, built on the first parcel north of West 116th St, contains the college's finest buildings, Low Library and St. Paul's Chapel. The Morningside Heights Campus was designed (1893) by McKim, Mead & White, but is principally the work of Charles Follen McKim, who envisioned a densely developed area with small side courtyards and a narrow central quadrangle. McKim's original intentions can be seen in the brick and limestone classroom buildings with green copper roofs on the periphery of the main quadrangles, and in the placement of St. Paul's Chapel, Low Library, Earl Hall, and University Hall. The only side courtyard actually built is the one bounded by Schermerhorn, Avery, and Fayerweather Halls, and St. Paul's Chapel (and it has been altered by the Avery Library extension). After McKim's death (1909) the university elected to retain the central open space and expand instead into surrounding city streets, a policy that has not been without repercussions.

Butler Hall and Buell Hall

College Walk is the pedestrian extension of West 116th St to the center of the campus. The principal building in the Lower (or South) Quadrangle is **Butler Hall**, the main university library (1934; James Gamble Rogers), named after Nicholas Murray Butler. The present Columbia collection, housed in several smaller libraries as well as Butler Hall, numbers more than five million volumes and is one of the largest in the nation.

Dominating the Upper Quadrangle (north of College Walk) is Low Library (*see below*). The picturesque three-story gabled brick building just east of it is **Buell Hall**, the only building remaining from the days of the Bloomingdale Asylum. In front of Philosophy Hall is a cast of Rodin's *The Thinker* (modeled 1880, cast 1930).

Low Memorial Library

Low Memorial Library (1895–97; McKim, Mead & White) dominates the quadrangle by virtue of its scale, its site at the top of three flights of stairs, and its imposing Classicism. Seth Low, president of Columbia from 1890–1901, donated the building to honor his father, Abiel Abbot Low (1811–93), a wealthy tea-merchant and China-trade pioneer, whose warehouses still grace the South Street Seaport area (*see p. 56*). The younger Low resigned his office to become mayor of New York (1901–03), a position he won not because of special political acuity but because his opponents were flagrantly corrupt. Low Library remained the main university library until 1934, when Butler Hall superseded it. Today it houses the Visitors Center and offices.

On its broad steps sits Columbia's most famous piece of sculpture, *Alma Mater* (1903; Daniel Chester French). The statue, originally covered with gold leaf, was regilded in 1962 to the dismay of students and faculty members, who demanded the removal of the gaudy gold in favor of the familiar gray-green patina. In 1970 the figure was slightly damaged by a bomb set off during student uprisings. *Alma Mater* sits on a throne flanked by torches implying enlightenment; her right hand holds a scepter topped with a crown, an emblem referring to Columbia's beginnings as King's College. An owl, symbolic of Athena and therefore wisdom, peers from the folds of her robe; a laurel garland wreathes her head; a book, signifying knowledge, lies open on her lap.

The architecture of Low Library has its stylistic origins in the Roman Pantheon; its general plan is that of a Greek cross with an octagonal transition to a saucer dome. The outer dome of solid masonry covers an inner dome of plaster on a steel frame, which forms the ceiling of the former reading room.

The interior of the former reading room, with its 16 polished granite columns capped by gilt bronze Ionic capitals and its domed ceiling rising above semicircular clerestory windows, exemplifies the most elegant work of McKim, Mead & White. At one time the sub-basement contained a large canvas tank and a stationary rowing rack for the Columbia crew.

St. Paul's Chapel

Just north of Buell Hall is **St. Paul's Chapel** (1904–07; Howells & Stokes), one of the campus's most beautiful buildings, originally affiliated with the Episcopal Church but now used for diverse religious services, concerts, and other events. Money for the chapel was donated by Olivia Egleston Phelps Stokes and Caroline Phelps Stokes as a memorial to their parents, with the stipulation that their nephew, Isaac Newton Phelps Stokes, design the building. St. Paul's Chapel was the first building at Columbia that was not designed by McKim, Mead & White.

Constructed of brick and limestone, the building is shaped like a short Latin cross with a vaulted portico on the west and a semicircular apse on the east. A dome covers the crossing. The capitals of the columns flanking the entrance are decorated with heads of cherubim by Gutzon Borglum.

The interior walls of the chapel are of tan brick, and the fine Guastavino tile vaulting is in warm tones of salmon and buff. The three apse windows (John La Farge) show St. Paul preaching to the Athenians on the Areopagus (the hill west of the Acropolis where the city philosophers had invited "the babbler" to explain his strange conduct and stranger god). The windows in the transepts show teachers of the Old Testament (north transept) and the New Testament (south transept).

SCULPTURE ON THE OVERPASS

Just beyond the chapel, an overpass crosses Amsterdam Avenue toward the east at West 117th St. On its plaza are several sculptures: *Three-Way Piece: Points* (1967; Henry Moore), a swelling, volumetric bronze abstraction resting on three points; *Tightrope Walker* (1979; Kees Verkade), an elongated aerialist with a second figure balanced on his shoulders, donated as a monument to William "Wild Bill" Donovan, a Columbia alumnus and head of the Office of Strategic Services during World War II; and *Flight* (1981) by Gertrude Schweitzer. Also visible is Jacques Lipchitz's *Bellerophon Taming Pegasus* (cast 1973, installed 1977), near the white high-rise Law School. According to the sculptor, the monumental statue symbolizes the control by law over the forces of disorder.

Avery and Uris

Avery Hall (1912: McKim, Mead & White) houses the School of Architecture and the nation's largest architectural library. On the eighth floor is the university's **Wallach Art Gallery** (*open during the academic year Wed–Sat 1–5; T: 212 854 7288*).

In front of **Uris Hall** stands a 3-ton, hollow, black-painted steel sculpture by Clement Meadmore, installed in 1968 and entitled *Curl*. Meadmore, an Australian sculptor who moved to New York in 1963, was known for his monumentally-scaled metal sculptures.

The School of Journalism and Mathematics Building

Between Low Library and Lewisohn Hall to the west reclines a statue of *The Great God Pan* by George Grey Barnard. Cast of bronze and weighing more than 3 tons, *Pan* was completed around 1898, intended for a fountain in the courtyard of the Dakota apartments. Barnard spent years in Paris and though he denied it, was influenced by Rodin. He also collected medieval architectural fragments and sculpture, some of which eventually formed the core of The Cloisters (*see p. 450*).

The **School of Journalism** (1912–13; McKim, Mead & White) was founded by publisher Joseph Pulitzer in 1912. Considered the most prestigious journalism school in the nation, it comes into the public eye each spring when it announces the Pulitzer Prizes.

On the wall of the **Mathematics Building** on the east side of Broadway at about 117th St is a large plaque depicting the Battle of Harlem Heights.

THE BATTLE OF HARLEM HEIGHTS

On Sept 15, 1776, the British Army landed at Kip's Bay (on the East Side near 35th St), routing the defenders, and trapping the main body of American forces in Lower Manhattan. The following day a force of American troops, encamped on Harlem Heights, moved south to encounter a British force in a buckwheat field in this vicinity. The Americans hoped to lure some of the British down into the valley where 125th St now runs, to outflank them and eventually to cut them off. The plan failed since the flanking party fired prematurely, revealing their whereabouts. Nevertheless, the Americans did hold off the British for several hours and forced them to retreat. While the battle had no great significance in the course of the war, it did bolster sagging American morale and demonstrated to Washington that his soldiers, despite several disastrous recent performances, were capable of standing up to the British.

Barnard College

The campus of Barnard College (for women) lies on Broadway between West 116th and West 120th Sts. The school was founded to provide an education for women

equal to that of the elite private men's undergraduate colleges, most of which until the 1960s admitted only men.

Frederick A.P. Barnard became president of Columbia in 1864, following a string of men distinguished more for their piety than their administrative abilities. Among his liberal innovations was the institution of a women's course, which the trustees grudgingly accepted in 1883. Since women were not allowed to enter the classrooms, and faculty members were not allowed to counsel or advise women outside class, the course was not notably successful. Nevertheless, it was due to Barnard's efforts that the women's college was founded in 1889. Columbia College (the undergraduate college of the university) began admitting women in 1983 after a decade of failed negotiations to merge with Barnard.

Pupin Laboratories and Teachers College

Columbia's **Pupin Physics Laboratories**, on the east side of Broadway (at West 120th St), were built in 1925 but named 10 years later after Michael Idvorsky Pupin (1858–1935), a Serbian immigrant who became one of America's foremost inventors in the field of electricity and a revered professor of electrical engineering. In this building in the late 1930s and early 1940s, Harold C. Urey, Enrico Fermi, and I.I. Rabi did the work in nuclear fission that won them the Nobel Prize.

The row of red brick buildings on the east side of Broadway between West 120th and 121st Sts houses **Teachers College**, an affiliate of Columbia University. Founded in 1889 by Nicholas Murray Butler, the college grew from humble beginnings as the Kitchen Garden Club of the Church of St. Mark's-in-the-Bowery, an organization for introducing manual training into the public school system and teaching working-class girls the elements of housekeeping and gardening. Since the days when John Dewey belonged to the faculty, Teachers College has earned a reputation for spearheading progressive causes in education. Most of the buildings date from around the turn of the 20th century. Halfway down the block on 120th St is Main Hall (1892; William A. Potter), the campus's earliest building, an elaborate composition of dormers, gables, pointed-arch windows, porches, and turrets.

Two theological seminaries and the Manhattan School of Music

Union Theological Seminary on the west side of Broadway (1910; Allen & Collens, altered 1952 by Collens, Willis & Beckonert), founded in 1836 as a graduate school for Protestant ministers, has long enjoyed a reputation for liberal religious thought and involvement in social action. Its library is outstanding, said to be second only to the Vatican in the breadth of its holdings. Among its faculty and graduates have been such luminaries as Reinhold Niebuhr, Norman Thomas, and Henry Sloane Coffin. The classroom and residential buildings are organized in a quadrangle around a central courtyard dominated by the Brown Memorial Tower on Broadway and the James Memorial Tower on Claremont Avenue. Constructed of rockface granite with limestone trim, the buildings belong to an era when American universities imitated the Gothicism of Oxford and Cambridge.

The **Jewish Theological Seminary** (Broadway, West 122nd to West 123rd Sts) is a center of Conservative Judaism and one of the important rabbinical seminaries of that movement. The building (1930; Gehron, Ross, Alley) is a large prosaic example of neo-Georgian architecture. Founded in 1886, it has become a major center of Jewish education and is affiliated with Columbia University. Its library has the most comprehensive collection of Judaica and Hebraica in the western hemisphere.

Across Broadway stands the **Manhattan School of Music** (West 122nd St between Broadway and Claremont Ave), one of the nation's leading conservatories, founded in 1917. It offers degrees in both classical music and jazz. The building (1910; Donn Barber) was constructed for the Institute of Musical Art; later it was the home of the Juilliard School of Music. Famous alumni include soprano Dawn Upshaw, composer Tobias Picker, and drummer Max Roach.

THE RIVERSIDE CHURCH

Map p. 574, A3. 490 Riverside Drive (West 120th St). Subway: 1 to 116th St. Bus: M104, M4, M5. Claremont Ave entrance open daily 7am–10pm. Guided tour Sun at 12:30 after worship. T: 212 870 6700; www.theriversidechurchny.org.

The Riverside Church occupies a commanding site overlooking the Hudson River. Originally affiliated with the Baptist Church, its membership is now interdenominational, interracial, and international; the church has long been known for its liberal appeal and community service. Martin Luther King Jr., Nelson Mandela, César Chávez, Desmond Tutu, Fidel Castro, and Reinhold Niebuhr have spoken here. Among its senior ministers have been Harry Emerson Fosdick and William Sloane Coffin Jr.

The church began as a small Baptist congregation meeting on the Lower East Side. As the immigrant population overwhelmed the Lower East Side, the Baptists moved uptown, first to 46th St, later to Park Avenue, and finally to the present location. The present church was built largely with money from John D. Rockefeller Jr., originally a Baptist and later a leader in the interfaith church movement.

The exterior

Despite its Gothic inspiration and particular indebtedness to the Cathedral of Chartres, the Riverside Church (1930, Allen & Collens and Henry C. Pelton; south wing 1960, Collens, Willis & Beckonert) is a modern, steel-framed building, its Gothicism relegated to surface details. Although criticized when completed for its disproportionately tall tower (392ft), for its aesthetic servitude to Europe, and for its eclecticism, the church is nonetheless distinguished for its fine stained glass, stonecarving, and woodwork, which represent the finest materials and craftsmanship available.

Faced with Indiana limestone, the building has its long axis parallel to Riverside Drive. The 22-story tower at the south end contains classrooms and offices as well as the carillon. The principal entrance on the west is elaborately carved and is clearly intended to recall the portals at Chartres. The tympanum depicts a seated Christ

surrounded by the symbols of the Evangelists. Above the tympanum are five archivolts, the first and fifth depicting angels, the middle ones portraying scientists, philosophers, and religious leaders drawn from the whole sweep of human history. The chapel door, just south of the West Portal, is thematically devoted to the Nativity. Near the cloister entrance on Claremont Avenue is a bronze *Madonna and Child* (1927) by Jacob Epstein.

The interior

Narthex: Here are two windows of 16th-century Flemish glass, the only windows not made specifically for the church. The small Gethsemane Chapel contains Heinrich Hofmann's painting of *Christ in Gethsemane*, donated by John D. Rockefeller Jr. Also accessible from the narthex is Christ Chapel, inspired by the 11th-century Romanesque nave of the Church of St-Nazaire at Carcassone, France.

Nave: The magnificent nave, 215ft long, is finished in Indiana limestone and divided into three aisles by an arcade, above which is a triforium gallery and a clerestory. The clerestory windows are copies of the famous 12th–13th-century windows at Chartres, while those on the aisle level present modern motifs as well as historical ones. The 51 colored stained-glass windows in the church were made by firms in Boston, Chartres, and Reims.

Chancel: The nine-ton pulpit is carved from three blocks of limestone; its niches (both upper and lower levels) contain figures of prophets; ten of the figures on the upper level stand beneath canopies representing the major cathedrals of France. In the center of the chancel floor a marble maze has been adapted from the labyrinth at Chartres, whose route medieval penitents traced out on their knees. The chancel screen portrays seven aspects of the life of Christ, shown in each panel, surrounded by people who have fulfilled the divine ideal, including Pasteur, Savonarola, Florence Nightingale, and J.S. Bach. The panels represent (left to right): Physicians, Teachers, Prophets, Humanitarians, Missionaries, Reformers, and Lovers of Beauty.

On the rear wall of the nave at the gallery level, but best seen from the chancel, is Sir Jacob Epstein's imposing *Christ in Majesty*, the original clay model, now gilded, for the aluminum statue at Llandaff Cathedral in Cardiff, Wales.

Carillon tower (*currently not open to the public*): Twenty stories above the ground, this has an open observation platform with spectacular views of Upper Manhattan and the rivers. The Laura Spelman Rockefeller Memorial Carillon, gift of John D. Rockefeller Jr. in memory of his mother, contains 74 bells, ranging from the 20-ton Bourdon (the largest tuned bell ever cast) to a 10-lb treble bell. Cast in three stages (1925, 1930, and 1956; Gillet & Johnston Foundry, England, and Van Bergen Foundry, Holland), it is the first carillon to exceed a range of five octaves.

GENERAL GRANT NATIONAL MEMORIAL

Map p. 574, A3. Riverside Drive at 122nd St. Subway: 1 to 116th St. Bus: M5. Open daily 9–5; free. Closed New Year's Day, Thanksgiving, Christmas Day, and during severe snow-storms (call ahead); T: 212 666 1640; www.nps.gov/gegr.

The General Grant National Memorial, familiarly known as Grant's Tomb, is the imposing resting place of the victorious commander of the Union forces in the Civil War. The massive granite sepulcher (1891–97; John H. Duncan) contains the remains of Ulysses S. Grant (1822–85) and his wife, Julia Dent Grant. It was intended to be unmistakably tomblike, despite objections that it would give a funereal tone to the neighborhood.

HISTORY OF THE TOMB

After an illustrious career as commander-in-chief of the Union Armies in the Civil War and a more tarnished period as president (1868–76), Ulysses S. Grant died in 1885. He had requested burial either in New York, or at the US Military Academy at West Point, or in Galena, Illinois, where he had lived before the Civil War. Because Galena seemed too remote and Mrs. Grant, a civilian, could not be buried at West Point, New York was chosen. In 1885, Grant's body was temporarily interred in a brick structure near the present tomb, and five years later John H. Duncan won the competition for a memorial to cost about half a million dollars (eventually 90,000 subscribers contributed about $600,000). Duncan's design was based largely on three famous works: the tomb of Mausolus at Halicarnassus (4th century BC), that of Hadrian in Rome (2nd century AD), and that of Napoleon in Paris.

Ground was broken in 1891, and the general's remains were quietly brought to the finished tomb in 1897. Despite the scandals that marred his administration, Grant himself remained a revered figure, and even while the tomb was under construction two attempts were made to claim his remains for other locales.

In the early years of the 20th century Grant's Tomb was a popular site of pilgrimage, more popular even than the Statue of Liberty; in 1906, the peak year, 607,484 people visited (about 100,000 come yearly now). The Grant Monument Association oversaw its upkeep until the 1950s, when the National Park Service took it over. In the 1970s and '80s the monument fell on hard times, despoiled by vandalism and neglect. In the 1990s, Frank Scaturro, a history major at Columbia, mobilized public opinion to restore it. The Park Service took action—cleaning up graffiti, repairing the leaking roof, replacing the cracked paving stones, and restoring the interior. The work was completed in time for the 1997 centennial.

Grant's Tomb has a cubelike base topped by a drum supporting a stepped conical dome. A broad flight of steps flanked by two large eagles leads to the Doric portico and

General Grant National Memorial.

entrance. The raised stone blocks above the portico were originally intended to support equestrian statues of Union generals. Above the cornice a tablet contains Grant's words, "Let us have peace," spoken upon accepting the presidential nomination of 1868. The stepped cone, derived from reconstructions of the tomb of Mausolus (died 353), was to have been crowned by a statue of Grant in a triumphal chariot.

The austere interior, inspired by Napoleon's tomb at the Hôtel des Invalides in Paris, is in the form of a cross and dominated by the sunken crypt directly below the dome. Above the windows, mosaics (1966; Allyn Cox) depict Grant's victories at Vicksburg (east) and Chattanooga (west), and the surrender of Confederate leader Robert E. Lee at Appomattox (north). Beneath the dome, sculptured women (by J. Massey Rhind) symbolize phases of Grant's life: birth and childhood, military career, civil career, and death. A double staircase in the north arm leads down into the crypt, which contains the imposing red granite sarcophaghi of General and Mrs. Grant. Niches in the wall at the crypt level contain bronze busts of Grant's generals: Sherman and Sheridan (by William Mues), and Thomas, Ord, and McPherson (by Jeno Juszko); all were installed in 1938 as part of a WPA project. Flanking the staircase are two reliquary rooms with painted maps of the Civil War theater and trophy cases with replicas of Civil War flags.

Originally the window panes were clear glass over which were drawn dark purple curtains, symbolizing mourning, but the curtains deteriorated and the windows were redesigned by the Tiffany studios and glazed with purple glass, which in its turn was found to be too somber. The present yellow color seems to be some sort of compromise.

Unlike other National Park sites, the memorial has no public restrooms. According to oral tradition, Mrs. Grant insisted that there never be a public toilet in her tomb.

GRANT CENTENNIAL PLAZA

The rather seedy park surrounding the monument, known as Grant Centennial Plaza, commemorates Grant's establishment in 1872 of Yellowstone, the first national park in North America. Directly behind the tomb a fence encloses the Commemoration Tree, a ginkgo given by China in 1897 to honor Grant. The free-spirited, free-form mosaic benches (1972–74; Phillip Danzig and Pedro Silva), created as part of a community project, bear little relationship to the character of the monument.

Across Riverside Drive to the west (about opposite the public restrooms in the park), a fence near the footpath encloses a small stone urn "Erected to the Memory of an Amiable Child," St. Claire Pollock, age 5, who died in a fall from the rocks on July 15, 1797. His uncle, George Pollock, a wealthy Irish linen merchant, had built his home at what is now Riverside Park and 123rd St, on high land commanding a view of the river. The house (c. 1783), called Strawberry Hill, stood at the north end of the landscaped oval behind Grant's Tomb. After the child's death, Pollock sold the house to Joseph Alston, husband of Aaron Burr's daughter Theodosia, and returned to Ireland, requesting that the child's grave remain untouched. In the mid-19th century the house became the Claremont Inn, popular with travelers and numbering among its illustrious guests the Morgans and Whitneys. It burned down and was demolished by the city in 1952.

HARLEM

Bounded by the East and Harlem Rivers, the cliffs of Morningside Heights and St. Nicholas Terrace, and by 110th and 168th Sts, Harlem is the most famous center of African-American life and culture in the US. African-American blacks make up most of the population, though the area east of Park Avenue and north of 96th St, with a large Puerto Rican and Latino population, is known as El Barrio or Spanish Harlem.

HISTORY OF HARLEM

The fertile soil and the strategic advantages of the Harlem plain attracted Dutch farmers, who in 1658 founded Nieuw Haarlem, ten miles north of New Amsterdam at the tip of Manhattan. Increasingly in the 18th and early 19th centuries, this beautiful outlying land attracted gentlemen farmers and wealthy merchants, who developed estates and built country mansions.

In 1837 the New York and Harlem Railroad reached out along Park Avenue from City Hall to the Harlem River, opening the area for development, but simultaneously raising a barrier between the east and west sides of Harlem and creating a strip of blight where factories, squatters' shacks, and tenements quickly sprang up. In successive years eastern Harlem became home to immigrants from Russia, Germany, Italy, Ireland, Hungary, Scandinavia, England, and Spain, as well as Eastern European Jews. Western Harlem, however, began to attract middle-class German-Americans, both Jew and gentile. Speculators, anticipating the full-blown arrival of the middle class from downtown, put up substantial apartment buildings and handsome row houses. Oscar Hammerstein had opened the Harlem Opera House at 205 West 125th St in 1889 expecting the same thing. When an affluent middle class did not arrive, the real estate market collapsed, leaving landlords with unrentable buildings. In 1904, black realtor Philip A. Payton stepped into the gap, taking over building management and guaranteeing high rents to landlords who would accept black tenants, making decent housing available to blacks for the first time in New York.

At the close of the Civil War, New York's black population, estimated at 15,000, had been concentrated in ghettos in Lower Manhattan, notably around Thompson St in Greenwich Village. By the end of the 19th century the black population was centered around the Tenderloin (west of Broadway between 32nd and 42nd Sts) and Hell's Kitchen (the 40s and 50s west of Seventh Avenue). As demolition for the construction of the old Penn Station displaced them, blacks moved up into the San Juan Hill neighborhood, north and west of Columbus Circle. The next move was to Harlem, and during the 1920s its black

population increased from 83,248 to 203,894 with a density of 236 people per acre, twice that of the rest of the city. White business and property owners fought bitterly to keep Harlem white, but failed simply because it was too profitable to rent to blacks, although the arriving blacks were barred from holding jobs in white-owned businesses.

Nevertheless, the 1920s were years of optimism and great artistic activity, as writers, artists, and intellectuals made the pilgrimage to Harlem, by then the capital of black America. The "Harlem Renaissance," usually considered the brief period from 1924 until the stock market crash of 1929, saw the flowering of black literature, art, music, and political thinking. Black authors—Zora Neale Hurston, Countee Cullen, James Weldon Johnson, Langston Hughes—were published with greater frequency than ever before. Marcus Garvey awoke black self-respect and militancy with his back-to-Africa movement, while black and white intellectuals still enjoyed cordial relations. Harlem also became famous for its music. Whites flocked uptown to enjoy the ballrooms and cabarets, and the jazz at famous nightclubs—the Cotton Club, Connie's, and Smalls' Paradise—many of which were white-owned and had white-only audiences.

The Depression devastated Harlem, revealing the poverty behind the glittering exterior. Throughout the city, the marginally employed were the hardest hit, and blacks, excluded from virtually all but menial jobs, were among the first to suffer. The 1930s were the years of "rent parties," where guests paid an entrance fee to hear the music, drink the bathtub gin, and help pay off the month's rent. Literary output dried up, housing deteriorated, and racial tensions heightened.

During the civil rights era of the 1950s and '60s, Harlem was a focus of political and social activity. Black Muslims founded the Temple of Islam at 116th St and Lenox Ave, and black civil rights leader Malcolm X worked there until he founded his own Organization of Afro-American Unity in 1964. After riots in 1964 and 1968, federal, state, and local money was channeled into Harlem to improve housing and education, and to solve social problems.

In the 1970s, as the city at large fell into fiscal difficulties, Harlem suffered even more. Its streets were pocked with abandoned buildings. Some landlords found it cheaper to walk away from their property than to pay delinquent taxes; arson began to look like an attractive alternative for many, who burned their own buildings to collect the insurance. During these years the city became the unwilling owner of 65 percent of Harlem's real estate, collected for delinquent taxes.

Since the late 1990s, the northward spread of gentrification in Manhattan has reached into Harlem. The population is increasing, as are property values. Middle-class families have moved in; there are brownstone renovations in Mount Morris Park, Striver's Row, Hamilton Heights, and other neighborhoods with fine housing stock. The city, state, and federal governments as well as private developers have invested hundreds of millions of dollars in Harlem.

HARLEM STREET NAMES

The major avenues take on different names as they pass through Central Harlem. Eighth Avenue is Frederick Douglass Boulevard. Seventh Avenue was named Adam Clayton Powell Jr. Boulevard shortly after the black congressman died in 1972. Sixth Avenue north of Central Park was renamed twice—first Lenox Avenue, after James Lenox who established the Lenox Library, now part of the New York Public Library, and later Malcolm X Boulevard, after the assassinated Black Muslim leader. Most people still call it Lenox Avenue. Officially, 125th St is Martin Luther King Jr. Boulevard, but it is generally known as 125th St.

MOUNT MORRIS PARK HISTORIC DISTRICT

Map p. 574, C3. Subway: 2, 3 to 125th St. Bus: M1, M101.

The Mount Morris Historic District (West 118th to West 124th Sts from Fifth Ave to Adam Clayton Powell Jr. Boulevard) was designated because of its rows of late 19th- and early 20th-century row houses and handsome churches, built during the period when Harlem saw its future as an upscale residential neighborhood. At 201 Lenox Ave (northwest corner of 120th St) is the **Mount Olivet Baptist Church** (1907), built for a German-Jewish congregation by Arnold W. Brunner, who also designed Shearith Israel's home on Central Park West (*see p. 415*). Architectural features recalling the origins of the building include Stars of David above the column capitals and in the stained glass. Today the congregation is sufficiently influential to be visited by presidential candidates and foreign leaders.

Marcus Garvey Park, straddling Fifth Avenue between 120th and 124th Sts, was established in 1839, mainly because its steep, rocky terrain was unsuitable for building. When the surrounding land was leveled, the central hill (called Snake Hill by the Dutch) achieved a prominence that made the park visually dramatic. Its dominant man-made feature is a cast-iron watchtower (c. 1855), the sole survivor of many that once served as fire lookouts and warning stations (even the 10,000-lb bell remains). Originally called Mount Morris Park, it was renamed in 1973 to honor Garvey, a charismatic black leader fond of titles and prerogatives, who arrived in Harlem from the West Indies in 1914, dedicated to the advancement of his race. He encouraged blacks to be proud of their color and to work toward their own social and political institutions, but his major interest was in leading his people back to Africa, of which he dubbed himself emperor and provisional president. To this end he formed two steamship companies, whose vessels, along with many others of the period, attempted to subvert Prohibition by carrying some $3 million worth of liquor from New York to Cuba, a voyage that ended with government confiscation of the cargo. Later Garvey, convicted of mail fraud and imprisoned, was deported to Jamaica; he died an exile in London in 1940.

On the west side of the park between 122nd and 123rd Sts is an impressive row of brownstones with high stoops, and, at the southern end of the block, an apartment building designed by John Duncan, more famous for Grant's Tomb.

The **Theresa Towers**, formerly the Hotel Theresa (1913), at 2000 Adam Clayton Powell Jr. Boulevard (West 120th St), was long Harlem's tallest building. Until 1940 blacks were excluded, but when that policy was changed the hotel drew black celebrities and became known as the "Black Waldorf." Fidel Castro stayed there while visiting the United Nations in 1960, meeting with Soviet leader Nikita Khrushchev at the hotel.

The Studio Museum in Harlem

Map p. 574, C3 144 West 125th St (Lenox Ave and Powell Blvd). Open Wed–Fri 12–6, Sat 10–6, Sun 12–6; closed Mon, Tues, major holidays. T: 212 864 4500; www.studiomuseum.org. Founded in 1968 to collect and exhibit the work of artists of African descent, the museum mounts exhibitions that feature emerging and established artists as well as, on occasion, traditional African art. The permanent collection embraces 19th- and 20th-century African-American art, 20th-century Caribbean and African art, and traditional African art, but the emphasis is on contemporary artists. The museum also owns the archive of historic photographs by James VanDerZee, whose work constitutes the best visual record of Harlem during the 1930s and '40s. The museum's Artist-in-Residence program has enhanced the careers of some 90 emerging artists, many of whom have gone on to substantial careers.

Apollo Theater

Map p. 574, C3. 253 West 125th St. For group tours, T: 212 531 5337; www.apollotheater.com. The famous **Apollo Theater** (1913; George Keister) opened as Hurtig and Seamon's New Burlesque Theatre, for whites only, when the neighborhood was white and largely German-Jewish. As the neighborhood changed, so did the Apollo. In 1934, Leo Brecher and Frank Schiffman, who had previously run the Lafayette Theater (now a church), took over the Apollo, changed its name, and opened it to black audiences. The same year the theater began offering its famous Amateur Nights, which launched the careers of Sarah Vaughn and Ella Fitzgerald, and served as a springboard to success for Stevie Wonder, Aretha Franklin, Billie Holliday, and Diana Ross.

The theater fell on hard times during the 1970s and became a movie theater. In 1991 the state of New York bought it, and the Apollo is now run as a not-for-profit foundation, drawing more than a million visitors each year, with Amateur Hour living on as a syndicated TV production, "Showtime at the Apollo." The building has been extensively restored inside and out, and has been garnished with a contemporary LED marquee.

STRIVER'S ROW & NORTHERN HARLEM

The two-square-block area of West 139th and 138th Sts, between Frederick Douglass and Adam Clayton Powell Jr. Boulevards, now designated as the St. Nicholas Historic

District, is also known as the King Model Houses and Striver's Row (*map p. 574, C1*). The houses were built on speculation in 1891 to appeal to people with moderate incomes, while offering good design.

Successful contractor David H. King Jr., who had become prominent as the builder of Stanford White's original Madison Square Garden, put up four sets of row houses (146 in all) on speculation; to avoid monotony, they were planned by three different prominent architects. On the north side of 139th St are White's Italian Renaissance buildings of dark brick with terra-cotta trim. On the south and north sides of 138th St are Bruce Price's Colonial Revival rows in yellow brick with terra-cotta and limestone trim. James Brown Lord's row, on the south side of 138th St, has neo-Georgian red-brick houses with brownstone trim

The project succeeded architecturally, but not financially, as only nine houses were sold. The depression of 1895 set in and the remaining houses reverted to the mortgager, the Equitable Life Assurance Company, who rented some (to whites) and kept the others back. In the 1920s and '30s, as Harlem became increasingly black, the houses were sold to black families, some of them successful professionals, but mostly working people, who had to strive mightily to maintain a middle-class style of living. By the 1930s the houses were known as "Striver's Row." Among the well-to-do who bought the houses were W.C. Handy, often called "Father of the Blues"; bandleader Fletcher Henderson; surgeon Louis T. Wright; and songwriter-pianist Eubie Blake. Among the less affluent, some of whom converted their homes into rooming houses, was one Anna Hames, who in 1925 housed 15 lodgers—railroad workers, elevator operators, dressmakers, and domestic servants.

The Abyssinian Baptist Church

One of Harlem's most influential religious institutions, the Abyssinian Baptist Church, at 132 West 138th St between Adam Clayton Powell Jr. and Malcolm X Boulevards (*map p. 574, C1*), is built of New York bluestone and was designed (1923) by Charles W. Bolton & Son, a firm of Philadelphia architects who specialized in Protestant church design.

The church was founded downtown on Worth St in 1808 and moved uptown in stages, following the black centers of population. Pastor Adam Clayton Powell Sr. took over in 1908 and moved the church to Harlem. His son, Adam Clayton Powell Jr., succeeded him in 1938. Powell Jr., a charismatic preacher, became the first black city councilman; four years later he was elected to Congress, where he sponsored legislation focusing on civil rights and education, the minimum wage, and segregation in the armed forces. He became a powerful figure both in Congress, where he was the first black chairman of a major committee (education and labor), and in Harlem. Always controversial, Powell was censured by the House for financial irregularities in 1967 and stripped of his office, although the Supreme Court reinstated him in 1969.

The Schomburg Center for Research in Black Culture

Map p. 574, C2. 515 Malcolm X Boulevard (West 135th St). Open Mon–Wed 12–8, Thur–Fri 11–6, Sat 10–5; T: 212 491 2200; www.nypl.org/research/sc/sc.html.

The Schomburg Center for Research in Black Culture, a research branch of the New York Public Library, is one of the world's finest facilities for the study of the experience and history of peoples of African descent throughout the world.

The nucleus of the collection was gathered by bibliophile and scholar Arturo Alfonso Schomburg, son of an unmarried black midwife and a white father of Puerto Rican and German heritage. Schomburg was inspired to begin his life's work by the remark of one of his schoolteachers that blacks had no history and no accomplishments. His personal collection was purchased by the Carnegie Corporation in 1926 and merged with the New York Public Library's own collection of black history and literature. Schomburg was curator from 1932 until his death in 1938; the center was named for him in 1940. Today the collections include works by authors of the Harlem Renaissance; a recording of a speech by Marcus Garvey; a first edition of the poetry of Phyllis Wheatley; paintings, including work by Horace Pippin, Faith Ringgold, Elizabeth Catlett, and Romare Bearden; films of early jazz and tap dance; sheet music; and artifacts, including some from Africa. The building, which formerly exposed a fortress-like brick wall to the street, was redesigned (2007; Richard Dattner) with a glass façade and more welcoming public spaces. In the reading room are Aaron Douglas's murals (1934), *Aspects of Negro Life*.

On the north side of this building is the **Countee Cullen Branch of the New York Public Library** (1941), at 104 West 136th St (Lenox Ave). Cullen, a poet, editor, and social critic, was an important figure of the Harlem Renaissance. The Countee Cullen Branch stands on the site of a mansion built in 1913 by Mme. C.J. Walker, a St. Louis laundress who discovered a hair-straightening process and reaped a fortune. Her daughter, A'Lelia Walker Robinson, was Harlem's outstanding hostess during the 1920s, and for a time established one floor of the mansion as a café and gathering place for black poets and intellectuals.

City University of New York

Along Convent Avenue between 130th and 135th Sts (*map p. 574, B1–B2*) is the South Campus of the City University of New York, originally the City College of New York. CCNY was founded in 1849 after the state legislature authorized the Board of Education to establish a free academy for qualified male students. Its policy of free admissions for city residents long made City College a stepping stone into the middle class. In 1903 more than 75 percent of the students were Jewish, and in 1910 almost 90 percent came from Eastern European families. Nowadays, though tuition is no longer free and the student body is more black and Hispanic than Jewish, CUNY still provides an educational outlet for the city's aspiring students.

The grounds are divided into a north and south campus. The **South Campus** originally belonged to the Academy and Convent of the Sacred Heart. At the southwest corner of West 135th St and Convent Ave, between the two campuses, is a brownstone and granite **gatehouse** (1890) for the Croton Aqueduct, marking the end of the masonry aqueduct leading into Manhattan from High Bridge. From here the water was piped underground to the next gatehouse at 119th St and Amsterdam Ave (*see p.*

425). The gatehouse has become a performance space for Harlem Stage. The original Gothic collegiate buildings of the **North Campus**, between 138th and 140th Sts, were designed in 1905 by George B. Post and executed in dark Manhattan schist excavated from this site and from nearby subway construction.

Our Lady of Lourdes

Just west of Convent Avenue at 467 West 142nd St is **Our Lady of Lourdes Church** (*map p. 574, B1*; 1904; O'Reilly Brothers), an astonishing exercise in architectural recycling. The Rev. Joseph MacMahon, formerly a priest at St. Patrick's Cathedral, who was put in charge of constructing Our Lady of Lourdes, had designs more ambitious than his budget. He was fortunate in the buildings then being torn down as New York moved ever northward. Father MacMahon salvaged some windows and some beams from the Catholic Orphan Asylum at 50th St and Madison Ave. He got the gray and white marble Ruskinian-Gothic façade from the National Academy of Design (1865), which stood at Park Avenue South and East 23rd St. The apse and parts of the east wall came from St. Patrick's Cathedral when the east wall there was altered to make way for the Lady Chapel. The pedestals flanking the main entrance were salvaged from department store millionaire A.T. Stewart's mansion (1867; John Kellum) on the northwest corner of 34th St and Fifth Avenue. The parish, now about 90 percent Latino and two to three percent African-American, is raising money to stabilize and repair the building.

Hamilton Grange, the former home of Alexander Hamilton, was being moved at the time of writing to the northwest corner of St. Nicholas Park (*www.nps.gov.hagr*).

UPPER MANHATTAN

Upper Manhattan, largely unknown to visitors except for The Cloisters, has some of the city's best scenery, two of its oldest houses, and the institutions of Audubon Terrace, including the interesting Hispanic Society of America. The area from 155th St to Dyckman St is known as Washington Heights; north of that it is called Inwood.

NB: The major points of interest in this part of Manhattan are indicated on the map on p. 573.

WASHINGTON HEIGHTS

Situated on two rocky spines of Manhattan schist, Washington Heights was fiercely— but futilely—defended during the Revolutionary War. Long the site of country estates, for example that of John James Audubon, it was developed in the early 20th century when the subway arrived. Thereafter it attracted successive waves of immigrants, with one ethnic group quickly replacing another. The Irish came in the early years of the 20th century, followed by European Jews escaping the Nazis in the 1930s and '40s, when the Heights were known as "Frankfurt on the Hudson." Along with the Jews came well-to-do African-Americans, migrating uptown from Harlem; among them Count Basie and other successful musicians. During the next two decades, a large population of Greeks arrived, and the Heights became "the Astoria of Manhattan," after the Greek enclave in Queens (*see p. 499*). At the same time Cubans and Puerto Ricans were beginning to come, only to be superseded in the 1980s and '90s by Dominicans, who are now being replaced by more affluent whites. For the last three decades Washington Heights has had the largest Dominican community outside the Dominican Republic.

AUDUBON TERRACE

Subway: 1 to 157th St. Bus: M4 or M5 to 155th St.
Between West 155th and West 156th Sts along the west side of Broadway, stand the imposing but underused classical buildings of Audubon Terrace, once the home of a cluster of museums. Today the artistic and intellectual institutions have departed for more central locations, except for the Hispanic Society of America (which has announced plans to move) and the American Academy of Arts and Letters.

The buildings of Audubon Terrace were financed largely by Archer Milton Huntington, son and heir of Collis P. Huntington, transcontinental railroad builder and steamship magnate. The younger Huntington's interests ran to poetry, archaeology, and scholarship, not railroads, and he is remembered more for the money he gave away to libraries and museums than for the money that he made. Huntington intended to build an American acropolis on the high ridge of Washington Heights, and in 1904 he

started buying up parcels of the former estate of ornithologist and painter John James Audubon. Huntington hired eminent architects and his cousin, Charles Pratt Huntington, to build a quadrangle of imposing buildings (1908–30) for cultural institutions that would serve scholars and also be available to the public. Since the neighborhood did not develop as Huntington had envisioned, the institutions increasingly found themselves marooned, far from the center of the city's intellectual life.

Statues by Anna Hyatt Huntington, already well known as a sculptor at the time of her marriage to Archer Huntington, dominate the plaza. The largest is a bronze equestrian statue of *El Cid Campeador* (1927), a piece that celebrates the legendary medieval hero who defended Spain against the Moors. Known for her animal sculptures, Anna Huntington also contributed several animal groups and the equestrian reliefs *Don Quixote* (1942) and *Boabdil* (1944), the last Muslim king of Granada; the inscriptions beneath them are taken from the poetry of her husband.

The Hispanic Society of America

Audubon Terrace. Open Tues–Sat 10–4:30, Sun 1–4; tours 2pm Sat; T: 212 926 2234; www.hispanicsociety.org. Free. In 2007, the society entered into a three-year collaboration with the Dia Art Foundation, which currently lacks a permanent exhibition space in the city.

For anyone interested in Spanish painting and architecture, the trip uptown to this museum is well worth the effort. The collection was gathered mainly by Archer M. Huntington, whose fascination with Spanish and Portuguese culture dated from his first youthful visit to Spain.

The Main Court, two stories high and illuminated in part by skylights, and with its archways of deep red terra cotta ornately worked in Spanish Renaissance style, is one of the city's most remarkable interiors. On view are examples of Spanish painting from the Middle Ages to the present, with works from the Spanish Golden Age (1550–1700), the 19th century, and the early 20th century. There are paintings by great painters: El Greco's *St. Jerome* (c. 1600); several portraits by Velázquez; and *The Duchess of Alba in a Black Mantilla* (?1797), one of Goya's finer portraits of his formidable mistress. Also on view are works by Zurbarán, Jusepe de Ribera, Murillo, and Juan Carreño de Miranda. In the Sorolla Room, murals by Spain's most celebrated artist at the turn of the 20th century, Joaquín Sorolla y Bastida, depict street scenes and regional Spanish festivals. Genre scenes such as *After the Bath* (1908) exemplify his vivid and characteristic use of light, a technique known as *luminismo*. Also on display are decorative arts: ceramics including exceptional examples of Hispano-Moresque lusterware, gold- and silverwork, wonderful tomb statuary, elaborate archaeological artifacts, sculpture, and textiles.

OTHER WASHINGTON HEIGHTS LANDMARKS

The Church of the Intercession and Trinity Cemetery

550 West 155th St. Open during services Thur at noon and Sun 8–2. If you wish to tour the church, T: 212 283 6200 to schedule an appointment. Cemetery open 9–4:30 daily; entrance to the western parcel on 155th St near Riverside Drive; T: 212 368 1600.

On Broadway at the southeast corner of 155th St is the Church of the Intercession (1914; Cram, Goodhue & Ferguson), formerly a chapel of Trinity Parish, built by the preeminent ecclesiastical architect Bertram G. Goodhue. The church complex, which includes a bell tower, cloister, parish house, and vicarage, has been praised for its site design, which recalls the time when the neighborhood was still rural and evokes the Gothic Revival ideal of the country church. Noteworthy in the interior are the wooden ceiling supported by stone piers, the woodcarving, the high altar inlaid with some 1,500 stones collected from the Holy Land and other shrines of early Christianity, and the wall tomb of its architect, decorated with reliefs of some of his buildings. Behind the church is part of the cemetery, including the burial plot of John James Audubon (1785–1851), who after long struggles achieved fame and financial security with his *Birds of North America* (*see p. 412*) The gravestone, a tall brown Celtic cross decorated with reliefs of animals and birds, rests on a pedestal with sculpted rifles and a powder horn, a palette, and paintbrushes.

The other parcel of Trinity Cemetery lies between Broadway and Riverside Drive, West 153rd and 155th Sts. Its hummocky topography sloping toward the Hudson River suggests the 19th-century landscape before developers exercised their leveling powers over northern Manhattan. Here lies Clement Clarke Moore, popularly thought to have written the verses beginning "'Twas the night before Christmas..." (northwest part of the cemetery, lower slope near the Riverside Drive retaining wall and 155th St). Higher up the slope is Eliza Bowen Jumel, whose former home is now a museum (*see below*).

The Audubon Ballroom

Malcolm X, the civil rights leader, was assassinated at the Audubon Ballroom (*3940 Broadway between 165th and 166th Sts*) in 1965. The Ballroom, which had opened in 1912 as a vaudeville and movie theater, closed in 1967 and was taken over by the city. Columbia-Presbyterian Medical Center bought the property in 1983, intending to raze it for a research facility. In light of the ensuing controversy, a compromise was reached, in which the Broadway part of the Ballroom was restored, and the Malcolm X and Dr. Betty Shabazz Memorial and Education Center was created, with exhibits on Malcolm X's life and teachings (*open Mon–Fri 9–4; T: 212 568 1341; www.theshabazzcenter.org*).

The Morris-Jumel Mansion

Subway: C to 163rd St. Bus: M2, M3, M18, M101. Open Wed–Sun 10–4; T: 212 923 8008; www.morrisjumel.org.

The Morris-Jumel Mansion (1765; remodeled 1810) is situated in Roger Morris Park at Jumel Terrace and West 160th St just east of St. Nicholas Ave. The house, fitted out with period furniture, is the oldest in Manhattan, and has a noteworthy history.

Built as the summer home of Roger Morris and his American-born wife Mary Philipse, the house still has its original Georgian hipped roof, wooden corner quoins, and wide-board façade. The two-story portico and octagonal room are unusual in a dwelling of this period. On view inside are 12 rooms with furnishings that include many Jumel family pieces, notably a mahogany sleigh bed in which Napoleon is said to have slept.

George Washington may have used the office on the second floor, which is furnished with 18th-century English and American furniture.

In 1765, Roger Morris, a wealthy landowner and retired colonel in the British army, bought a river-to-river site on high ground. The land had an orchard and views as far as Long Island, Staten Island, and New Jersey. When the war broke out, Morris remained loyal to the king, returning to England in 1775 for unknown reasons, leaving his wife in charge of the house. She left as the American troops advanced from the south. Washington used the house as his headquarters from Sept 14–Oct 21, 1776, leaving when his army was forced off Manhattan. After the war the house was sold, and the Morrises returned permanently to England. The building was later purchased by Stephen Jumel, a wealthy French wine merchant, for his wife, Eliza Bowen Jumel (*see box below*).

Across Jumel Terrace between West 160th and West 162nd Sts is **Sylvan Terrace**, once the carriage drive of the Morris-Jumel mansion. Two rows of modest wooden houses, built (c. 1882) for workers, face one another across a quiet street.

Eliza Jumel (?1775–1865)

Eliza Bowen Jumel was born in Providence, Rhode Island. Forced into prostitution by poverty, her fortunes improved when in 1804 she married Stephen Jumel, a wealthy French wine merchant. Wagging tongues said that the brilliant and beautiful Eliza, already Jumel's mistress, feigned a deathbed crisis to lure him into wedlock. In 1810 the Jumels bought the house and restored it, adding the portico and enlarging the doorway in the Federal style.

Mme Jumel had an imperious tongue and boundless social ambition, which remained unfulfilled in New York because of her dubious past. In 1815 the Jumels went to Paris, where they did find acceptance; she became an outspoken Bonapartiste, an unwise move in the first years after Napoleon's exile, and was asked to leave France. She brought back Empire furniture, an extensive wardrobe, and Francophilic tastes. Her marriage suffered when Jumel discovered her early history and she discovered that the Jumel fortune was in decline.

In 1832 Jumel was injured in a carriage accident and died. It was whispered that she let him bleed to death. A year later Eliza, then about 58 and one of the city's richest women, married 77-year-old Aaron Burr. He was apparently fortune hunting, and the marriage was predictably stormy and brief; Burr only lived in the house about a month before they separated. Eliza sued for divorce, which was granted in 1836, ironically on the day of Burr's death. She lived on in the mansion, becoming eccentric and reclusive, and died there in 1865 at the age of 90.

The George Washington Bridge

The George Washington Bridge (1931; Othmar H. Ammann and Cass Gilbert), crossing the Hudson River to Fort Lee, New Jersey, is another of Manhattan's great links to the

outer world. Like the Brooklyn Bridge, it represented a step forward in technology while becoming also an object of beauty and imaginative inspiration. Its 3,500-ft span doubled the record for suspension bridges, while its soaring steel towers and curving cables inspired Le Corbusier to call it "the only seat of grace in the disordered city."

A trans-Hudson Bridge had been contemplated as early as 1868, when the state of New Jersey authorized one at the southern boundary of Union Township, a move the state of New York ignored. Conflicting interests and difficulties in financing and engineering halted progress until the Port of New York Authority was formed in 1921 and brought the project to fruition. Chief engineer Othmar H. Ammann, who had emigrated from Switzerland in 1904 expressly to participate in American bridge projects, studied the political, financial, and structural problems surrounding previous attempts at a Hudson River crossing. It was he who proposed an automobile crossing, not a railroad bridge, thus cutting costs and anticipating America's romance with the internal combustion engine. The Port Authority funded the bridge ($59 million) by selling bonds, a difficult task in the years before 1929 when stock prices were booming.

Groundbreaking ceremonies took place in 1927 and four years later 5,000 people came to listen to speeches marking the completion of the project. The length of the bridge between anchorages is 4,760 feet, making it the world's longest suspension bridge at the time it was completed. When the bridge was opened to the public, the first to cross were two boys from the Bronx on roller skates.

The original plans called for sheathing the towers in masonry, for which Cass Gilbert produced appropriate designs, but by 1931 the Port Authority, having just bought the Holland Tunnel, was unwilling to spend money for cosmetic purposes. Between 1958 and 1962 a lower deck was constructed without disturbing traffic on the existing bridge, a feat accomplished by raising 76 steel sections from below, either from the shores or from barges. Snidely nicknamed the Martha Washington Bridge, the new deck brought the total cost to $215.8 million and took longer to build than the original structure—but increased its capacity 75 percent. The bridge carries over 108 million cars each year.

Just under the tower of the George Washington Bridge stands the **Little Red Lighthouse** (1921), whose light and foghorn warned ships of the shoals off Jeffrey's Hook until 1947. Moved here from Sandy Hook, New Jersey, the lighthouse was commissioned in 1921 at a time when barge traffic on the river was more important than it is now. When the navigational lights on the bridge took over its function, the lighthouse went up for auction (1951) but was saved by the pleas of admirers, many of whom had read Hildegarde Hoyt Swift's children's tale *The Little Red Lighthouse and the Great Gray Bridge* (1942). (*The interior of the lighthouse can be visited only during Urban Park Ranger tours, spring and fall; T: 212 304 2365. There is also an annual festival in Sept.*)

Bennett Park

Bennett Park, between 183rd and 185th Sts, Fort Washington and Pinehurst Aves, stands on the site of Fort Washington, a Revolutionary War fortification. The park contains the highest natural elevation in Manhattan, a rocky outcropping that reaches 265.05 ft above sea level.

INWOOD

Inwood is Manhattan's most northerly neighborhood, two-fifths greenbelt and the rest largely residential. Fort Tryon Park contributes to the open space, as does Inwood Hill Park further north, 196 acres stretching west to the Hudson and north to the Harlem River. The park is Manhattan's only true wilderness, with steep rock slopes and caves where Native Americans once sought shelter. Beyond the park flows the Harlem River, which was not navigable to the Hudson until 1895, when a channel was cut through a bulbous promontory that formerly extended north of where Columbia University's stadium, Baker Field, and Ninth Avenue are presently located. Before then the narrow Spuyten Duyvil Creek flowed in a looping curve marked by the present boundary of Manhattan. In 1895 the Harlem Ship Canal was cut (400ft wide and 15ft deep), straightening the shipping route to the Hudson. When it was finished, Spuyten Duyvil was filled, making the area now known as Marble Hill physically a part of the Bronx.

SPUYTEN DUYVIL

The origin of the creek's strange name is unknown. One explanation was offered by Washington Irving in his *Knickerbocker's History of New York*: Anthony Van Corlaer, sent by Peter Stuyvesant to warn the settlers north of the creek of an imminent British attack, reached the waterway in the midst of such a storm that he could find no one to ferry him across. Emboldened by a few swigs from his flask, Van Corlaer swore he would swim across "en spijt den Duyvil" (in spite of the devil), threw himself into the wild waters, and drowned. Others suggest that "spuyten" could refer to a cold spring that once spouted in the area presently covered by the ballfields, and "duyvil" could be a corruption of *duyvel*, a Dutch word for meadow.

To the west is the **Henry Hudson Bridge** (1936; Emil F. Praeger), spanning the Harlem River with a fixed steel arch 2000 ft long and at its highest point 142.5 ft above the river. The bridge (span 800ft), conceived and brought to fruition by Robert Moses, was built originally as a single-deck, four-lane structure, because the bankers underwriting the project would only authorize $3.1 million in bonds, unable to believe that commuters would choose a toll bridge over the nearby free bridge on Broadway. When the bridge quickly proved itself financially viable, the second deck was added.

THE CLOISTERS

Map p. 573 (in Fort Tryon Park). Subway: A to 190th St-Overlook Terrace. Exit by elevator and take bus M4 or walk up Margaret Corbin Drive. Bus: M4 marked Ft. Tryon Park/The Cloisters. Gray Line New York Sightseeing buses also travel to the park April–Oct; T: 212 445 0848. By

car: Henry Hudson Pkwy north to first exit after the George Washington Bridge (Fort Tryon Park). Some free parking around museum. Modest open-air café in Trie Cloister during warm weather; New Leaf Café in the park (see p. 459). Museum open Tues–Sat 9:30–5:15; closes 4:45 Nov–Feb. Closed Mon, New Year's Day, Thanksgiving, Christmas Day. Limited wheelchair access; call in advance or check with a security officer at museum entrance; T: 212 923 3700.
Standing on a rocky hill near the northern tip of Manhattan, The Cloisters is remote from the rest of the city both in its surroundings and in the contemplative atmosphere fostered by its art and architecture. This museum, the only branch of the Metropolitan, is named after the colonnaded medieval courtyards that form the architectural core of the building. On view along with elements of actual medieval architecture are more than 6,500 beautiful works of European art, most from the 11th–14th centuries. There are breathtaking views of the Hudson River from both in and outside the building, as well as three medieval gardens, recreated where possible from medieval sources.

History of the collection

George Grey Barnard (1863–1938), an American sculptor of some renown, gathered the nucleus of the collection. A self-taught medievalist and admirer of what he called "the patient Gothic chisel," Barnard lived in France for years while working on a commission for a public building in Pennsylvania. Needing extra income, he became a casual dealer in medieval art, and later a knowledgeable collector, scouring the countryside for abandoned monasteries and churches for examples of medieval art and architecture, which he bought up piece by piece. He found unrecognized treasures stowed away in barns, farmhouses, cellars, and, on occasion, pigsties; none of the objects he collected was still in its original location. Among the nearly 700 pieces Barnard brought to New York were large sections of the cloisters of four medieval monasteries—one Romanesque, three Gothic—and such treasures as the tomb effigy of Jean d'Alluye and a Romanesque wooden torso of Christ whose original polychromy was protected by layers of later gilding and gesso applied when it served as a scarecrow. Barnard was fortunate in his timing, sending his collection to New York in 1913, just as France was growing concerned about the dispersal of its national treasures. As a placating gesture Barnard donated a fine set of arches from the cloister at Cuxa to France, which perhaps ensured the safe departure of the rest of his collection.

In 1914 Barnard put his collection on display in a building he designed and called The Cloisters, located on Fort Washington Avenue. He then turned his attention to building a peace memorial showcasing the achievements of world architecture, a project that ate up so much of his capital that he had to sell his museum. In 1925, with money from John D. Rockefeller Jr., the Metropolitan Museum purchased Barnard's collection. Five years later Rockefeller, who had already donated 42 Gothic sculptures to the Met from his own collection, gave the city the land for Fort Tryon Park in exchange for the East Side acreage where Rockefeller University now stands. Rockefeller reserved space at the north end of the park for the present museum building and then, to ensure a perpetually unspoiled view, bought land across the river along the palisades and gave it to New Jersey for a park—a prudent piece of foresight.

The building

The Cloisters (1934–38; Charles Collens of Allen, Collens & Willis) was not copied from any single medieval original, but was built around medieval architectural elements with an effort to make modern additions as unobtrusive as possible. The exterior granite was quarried by hand near New London, Connecticut, according to the dimensions of building blocks in Romanesque churches, especially the church at Corneille-de-Conflent near Cuxa. The Italian limestone of the interior was hand-sawn to suggest weathering. The courtyards and ramparts are paved with Belgian blocks taken from New York streets and the grounds are landscaped with trees, especially apple and crab apple trees, intended to recall the plantings surrounding medieval monasteries (with allowances for New York's harsher climate).

The permanent collection

While the medieval collections in the Metropolitan Museum span the period from the barbarian invasions (beginning roughly AD 370) to the close of the 14th century, works in The Cloisters focus on the two principal styles of the late Middle Ages, the Romanesque and the Gothic. The display is organized more or less chronologically, beginning with the Romanesque Hall and ending with the Late Gothic Hall and the Froville Arcade. (The accession numbers beginning 25.120 on the labels indicate works purchased from the original Barnard collection.)

Main level

(1) Romanesque Hall: The Romanesque Hall incorporates three portals which illustrate the evolution of the sculptured church doorway in the 12th–13th centuries: the round-arched Romanesque French doorway (c. 1150); the late 12th-century Reugny door from the Loire Valley with its pointed, more deeply recessed, five-lobed arch; and the magnificent 13th-century Moutiers door from Burgundy, whose decoration shows the full flowering of the Gothic style. The freestanding figures of the two kings in the niches might represent David and Solomon, but in the 16th century they were identified as Clovis I, first Christian king of France, and his son Clothar I, who, according to legend, exempted the monastery of Moutiers-Saint-Jean from royal and ecclesiastical jurisdiction.

Although the monastery was sacked repeatedly, and ultimately almost destroyed during the French Revolution, the sculptures survived because they had been moved to a private garden.

In the center of the room is an enthroned Virgin and Child from the Auvergne. Sculptors of 12th-century France produced many such statues, known as *Sedes Sapientiae*, which show the Virgin with Christ seated in her lap: Mary symbolizes the Throne of Divine Wisdom, while the Christ Child holds a Bible, the repository of that Wisdom. Most of these statues are rigidly frontal, formal, and symmetrical, impressing with their remote, majestic calm.

(2) Fuentidueña Chapel: The mid-12th century apse here comes from the

church of San Martín in Fuentidueña, about 100 miles north of Madrid. The church was probably part of a castle complex, built by Christians struggling to regain the Iberian peninsula from its Islamic conquerors. By the 19th century all of the church except for the apse had fallen into ruins. In 1957 the Spanish government permanently loaned the apse to the museum; it has been installed here in a room that suggests the plan of the original church. Built of limestone blocks, the apse has a barrel-vaulted roof decorated with limestone sculpture including large pier figures of St. Martin (left) and an Annunciation group (right). The two large capitals supporting the arch depict the Adoration of the Magi (left) and Daniel in the Lions' Den (right). The fresco depicting the Virgin and Child with the three Magi and the archangels Michael and Gabriel comes from another Spanish church in the Pyrenees region (c. 1130–50) and is a true fresco, painted onto wet plaster.

The large 12th-century Spanish Crucifix of carved, painted white oak is one of the finest surviving examples of the Romanesque type. The open eyes and golden crown (instead of the later crown of thorns) mark it as a symbol of life triumphant over death.

(3) Saint-Guilhem Cloister: This cloister is built around a series of columns (before 1206) from the Benedictine abbey of Saint-Guilhem-le-Désert, founded near Montpellier in 804 by Guilhem, count of Toulouse and duke of Aquitaine. Guilhem was one of Charlemagne's paladins, and medieval legends tell of his exploits: how he smuggled his soldiers into a besieged city in wine casks; lost the tip of his nose

in a battle to free Rome from the pagans; and escaped a Saracen king with the help of the king's wife. This is the stuff of legend, but it is historical fact that Guilhem became a monk in the monastery he founded.

The columns, many with intricate drillwork, are medieval versions of Classical Corinthian columns, but unlike their Classical predecessors, the shafts of these medieval columns are decorated with all sorts of designs—one resembling a stylized acanthus tree, another incised with a chevron pattern, a third carved to resemble a palm tree. The capitals, too, have a variety of designs—traditional acanthus leaves, biblical figures including Daniel in the Lions' Den and Christ in the Temple. One of the most unusual is the "Mouth of Hell" capital, with its clovenhoofed demons forcing sinners into the flaming maw of Hell (represented by an upside-down monster). The cloister's central fountain was once a column capital in the church of Saint-Sauveur in Figeac.

(4) Langon Chapel: Incorporated in the walls of this chapel is stonework from the 12th-century Romanesque church of Notre-Dame-du-Bourg at Langon near Bordeaux. The two large crowned heads on the capital of the column nearest the altar (right side) may represent Henry II of England and his wife Eleanor of Aquitaine, who visited Langon in 1155. The marble ciborium over the altar is from the church of Santo Stefano near Rome. In the chapel is a statue of the Virgin and Child enthroned, from Autun in northeast Burgundy. The limestone angel on the left wall, with fluttering drapery and feathered wings, comes from a side portal of the cathedral of Saint-

THE CLOISTERS
(MAIN LEVEL)

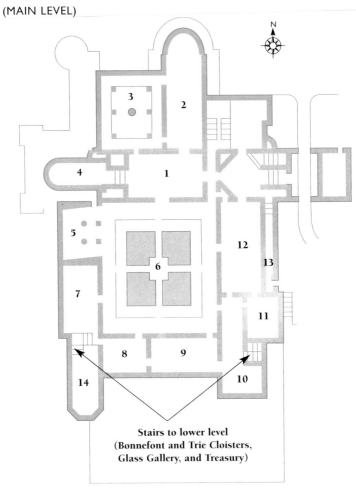

Stairs to lower level
(Bonnefont and Trie Cloisters,
Glass Gallery, and Treasury)

1	Romanesque Hall	8	Nine Heroes Tapestries
2	Fuentidueña Chapel	9	Unicorn Tapestries
3	Saint-Guilhem Cloister	10	Boppard Room
4	Langon Chapel	11	Spanish Room (Campin Room)
5	Pontaut Chapter House	12	Late Gothic Hall
6	Cuxa Cloister	13	Froville Arcade
7	Early Gothic Hall	14	Gothic Chapel

Lazare at Autun. The massive iron-bound doors, probably from the Pyrenees region, are unusual in size and condition.

(5) Chapter House from Pontaut:
With the exception of the plaster vaults and the floor, this is an architectural reconstruction, stone by stone and brick by brick, of the chapter house from the former 12th-century abbey of Notre-Dame-de-Pontaut in Gascony. It served as a meeting room where the monks gathered to discuss monastery business, and in its original setting it had a dormitory above. The windows in the west wall were never glazed but had hinges for shutters and holes for iron bars. The iron tethering rings on the two center columns date from the 19th century when the room was used as a stable. Architecturally, the room is transitional between Romanesque and Gothic styles, the arches round but the ceiling rib-vaulted.

(6) Cuxa Cloister: The Romanesque Cuxa Cloister, at the heart of the museum, comes from one of the most important abbeys in southern France, the Benedictine monastery of Saint-Michel-de-Cuxa, founded in 878. The stonework, with its mottled pink and white marble, dates from the 12th century. Cuxa suffered the fate of other monasteries—it was sacked in periods of hostility, deserted after the French Revolution, and left to fall into ruins, after which its architecture was dispersed. George Grey Barnard was able to purchase only part of the original stonework; it is known, however, that the original was approximately twice the size of the present reconstruction.

The simplest and perhaps the earliest of the marble capitals are undecorated; more elaborate ones depict pine cones, scrolled leaves, and a variety of lions, some in the company of apes, others devouring hapless people or gnawing their own forelegs; there are also eagles, monkeys, and a mermaid. Some of the designs may have been inspired by Near Eastern textiles, others by bestiaries, in which animal lore was allegorized to show the struggle between Good and Evil. The fantastic beasts on the Narbonne arch over the door in the northeast corner surely had such symbolic meanings. The lion, for example, who erased his tracks with his tail when hunting, symbolizes the Incarnation; the centaur represents a creature of intelligence still ruled by animal passions.

In the center is a garden with quadrants of grassy lawn, crab apple trees, and borders of herbs and flowers. In the winter the arcades are glassed in and the walkways are filled with pots of acanthus, wild daffodils, olive, and bay.

(7) Early Gothic Hall: Statues from the 13th and 14th centuries, paintings, and architectural elements (ceiling beams and stained-glass windows), and fine examples of stained glass are displayed in this hall. Among the sculptures is a pair of altar angels carved of oak. Originally polychromed, gilded, and winged, such angels often were placed on top of columns surrounding the altars of churches. The life-size sandstone Virgin from Strasbourg cathedral (c. 1250) is an important piece, expressing in its dignified grace the noble ideal of Gothic sculpture. Originally part of the church's choir screen, the Virgin stood with the Christ Child seated on a rosebush at her side; two angels held her veil while another two hovered above her head.

(8) Nine Heroes Tapestries: The door-way that leads from the Cuxa Cloister to a room displaying the Nine Heroes tapestries is from 15th-century France, designed in the flamboyant Gothic style, with flamelike double curves and stylized leaf forms. The room features the major part of a 14th-century set of French tapestries probably made for Jean, Duc de Berry, one of only two known existing sets from that period (the others are the Apocalypse tapestries in Angers). The Nine Heroes—Hector, Alexander, and Julius Caesar (pagan); David, Joshua, and Judas Maccabeus (Hebrew); and Arthur, Charlemagne, and Godfrey of Bouillon (Christian)—were a popular theme of medieval legend. The set, cut up and dispersed over the centuries, was reassembled from 95 fragments over a period of 20 years and now constitutes about two-thirds of the original work. Around the doorway from the Cuxa Cloister is the largest section, with Joshua and David seated on Gothic thrones and dressed in medieval costumes. Clockwise from here the tapestries depict Hector or Alexander, Julius Caesar, and King Arthur, the only Christian hero recovered. The figures around the heroes are members of a medieval court: bishops, knights and ladies, musicians, archers, and other courtiers.

(9) Hall of the Unicorn Tapestries: This room contains a superb series of six late medieval tapestries along with fragments of another which depict the Hunt of the Unicorn. While they were probably woven in Brussels—judging by the technique of the weaving and the style of the costumes worn—c. 1495–1505, it is not known who commissioned them or for what occasion. Scholars have investigated the bound "AE" monogram woven into the tapestries and have searched contemporary documents for clues, but without definitive success. It is known that they belonged to the Duc de la Rochefoucauld in the 17th century and were seized in 1793 during the French Revolution; for some years thereafter they were used to protect peasants' fruit trees and vegetables from frost, a period during which they must have sustained most of the damage. During the 1850s they were rediscovered lying in a barn and thereafter once again hung in the château.

According to medieval legend a unicorn could be caught only by a virgin, whose presence tamed the normally wild, swift, and powerful creature. This story was interpreted both as an allegory of human love and as an allegory of the Incarnation (with the unicorn a symbol of Christ). The subjects of the tapestries include: *The Start of the Hunt; The Unicorn at the Fountain; The Unicorn Tries to Escape; The Unicorn Defends Himself; The Unicorn is Captured by the Maiden; The Unicorn is Killed and Brought to the Lord and Lady of the Castle;* and *The Unicorn in Captivity*—one of the best-loved works in the collection—which shows the wounded Unicorn, subdued and docile, sitting chained inside a tiny corral, surrounded by flowers and fruiting plants. The image is said to symbolize both the Resurrection and the consummation of a marriage, which the tapestries were presumably woven to celebrate.

The Unicorn Tapestries are remarkable for their naturalism, range of color, and profusion of detail and incident. Over 100 different species of plants appear, of which 85 are recognizable.

The Unicorn Tries to Escape. One of the series of six exquisite tapestries (c. 1495–1505) showing the hunt of the Unicorn, in which the attacked animal tries to jump out of the stream to safety.

Woven of wool and silk, and colored from only three dye plants, they are works of such excellence that it is remarkable that their origin and the names of their designers should be unknown. They were donated to the Cloisters by John D. Rockefeller Jr.

(10) Boppard Room: The six stained-glass panels, from the second quarter of the 15th century, are perhaps the finest ensemble of late Gothic stained glass in this country. Made for the church of the Carmelite convent at Boppard on the Rhine, the windows depict (left to right) a bishop-saint trampling a dragon; the Virgin; another bishop-saint; and SS. Catherine of Alexandria, Dorothea of Caesarea, and Barbara. After Napoleon invaded the Rhineland, Church property was secularized and the glass was removed.

Behind the altar is an alabaster retable from Spain (mid-15th century) with scenes from the lives of St. Martin and St. Thecla. The central panel shows Pentecost, with the Holy Spirit descending upon the Apostles as tongues of flame. A six-foot Spanish paschal candlestick stands before the altar.

(11) Spanish Room: *NB: The Spanish Room was closed for restoration at the time of writing, but the Annunciation Triptych is on view in the Boppard Room.* The Spanish Room, also known as the Campin Room, with its 15th-century painted Spanish ceiling, has been arranged like a domestic interior with furnishings that serve as a backdrop to the masterful Annunciation triptych (also known as the Merode altarpiece) by Robert Campin (c. 1425). The work has three panels: two kneeling donors on the left, the Annunciation in the central panel, and St. Joseph in his workshop on the right. Campin is considered an early practitioner of Realism in Flemish panel-painting and one of the first painters to set the mysteries of religion, such as the Annunciation, in domestic bourgeois surroundings.

(13) Froville Arcade: The Froville Arcade, just outside the Late Gothic Hall, is constructed around nine pointed arches from the 15th-century Benedictine priory of Froville. The arches, grouped in threes and separated by buttresses as they were in their original setting, are typical of cloisters of that period, which depended for effect on their proportions rather than on great skill in decoration or stonecutting as did earlier Gothic and Romanesque arcades.

Lower level

(14) Gothic Chapel: The chapel displays stained glass and tomb sculpture. All the glass is from the 14th century, and includes windows from the church of St. Leonhard in southern Austria and the private chapel of the Ebreichsdorf castle south of Vienna. The limestone tomb effigy of Jean d'Alluye (d. 1248), a young man fully armed, his hands joined in prayer and his feet resting against a crouching lion (a frequently-used foot rest, symbolizing knightly courage), was one of George Grey Barnard's major acquisitions. Other important pieces in this room are tombs of the Spanish counts of Urgell in Catalonia, including are the effigy of an armored knight (possibly Ermengol X, d. 1314).

Bonnefont Cloister: The gray-white marble columns and capitals come from the former Cistercian abbey of Bonnefont-en-Comminges near Toulouse, founded in 1136, and used for burial of the counts of Comminges until the mid-14th century. Although the cloister, still standing in 1807, had virtually disappeared 50 years later, plundered by local inhabitants, Barnard recovered some 50 double capitals and a few shafts from scattered locations, including a stream where they had been used to dam up a drinking pond for cattle. The capitals (first half of the 14th century), over slender paired columns, are carved to represent natural and imaginary plants. The plants in the garden are all species mentioned in medieval herbals or monastic records, or suggested by archaeological evidence.

Trie Cloister: Next to the Bonnefont Cloister is the Trie Cloister from the Carmelite convent of Trie-en-Bigorre, southwest of Toulouse, destroyed (except for the church) in 1571 by the Huguenots. The capitals, probably carved

between 1484 and 1490, show scenes from the Bible, as well as saints' legends, grotesques, and coats of arms of local families. Where possible the biblical scenes are arranged in chronological order, beginning at the northwest corner near the entrance from the Bonnefont Cloister. In the south arcade is a fine Nativity capital. The capitals in the north arcade against the main part of the building are from the Bonnefont Cloister. The Stations of the Cross built into the south and west walls are from Lorraine (16th century). The plants in the garden are those native to European woodland and meadows, and which inspired medieval artists, who used them as backgrounds in tapestries and paintings.

Glass Gallery: This takes its name from the panels and roundels of silvered glass (15th–early 16th century) in the south windows. These panes were usually found in secular buildings, but often had sacred or moralizing subjects. Although not rare objects, the present examples are outstanding for the beauty of the drawing and the quality of the color. Among the wood carvings is a seated bishop carved by Tilman Riemenschneider, the most talented of a group of southern German sculptors working around 1500.

Treasury: In these two rooms are smaller objects of exceptional quality and value, many used for religious or state ceremonies. In the first gallery are the *Belles Heures of the Duc de Berry*, illuminated in the 15th century for Jean, Duke of Berry, the same collector who owned the Nine Heroes tapestries. Prominently displayed in the second gallery is the richly carved Cloisters Cross, one of the masterpieces of the collection, from the abbey of Bury St. Edmunds in England. On the front is a carving of Moses raising the brazen serpent in the desert, an Old Testament event that in medieval minds prefigured of the Crucifixion. (The central figure of Christ is missing from this side of the Cross.) On the back are figures of Old Testament prophets, and symbols of the Evangelists. The central plaque depicts an allegorical figure of Synagogue, piercing Christ with a lance. The Latin inscriptions accompanying this image reinforce the medieval Church view of the Jews' responsibility for the death of Christ.

MARGARET CORBIN DRIVE

The roadway into the park from the subway stop at 190th St and Fort Washington Ave is named after Margaret Cochran Corbin, a 26-year-old Revolutionary War heroine who fought beside her husband John in the Battle of Fort Washington (*see box overleaf*). When he was killed, she took over his gun and continued firing until she herself was severely wounded. After the war Corbin, known familiarly as Captain Molly, became a domestic servant, and was known to have an unbridled tongue and an indifference to the niceties of dress. She died in 1800 and was buried in modest circumstances until the Daughters of the American Revolution had her body exhumed and re-interred in the Post Cemetery at West Point.

FORT TRYON PARK

Map p. 573. New Leaf Café in the park; proceeds go to park maintenance; reservations advised on weekends; T: 212 568 5323.

Fort Tryon Park, 66 acres of hills and rocks, offers landscaped gardens, wooded slopes, and several miles of paths, some overlooking the Hudson River. The eponymous fort, the site of which is now marked by a plaque, was a Revolutionary War outpost intended to protect Fort Washington to the south. The outwork was then renamed after the British governor, Sir William Tryon (1729–1788), a major general and, as it turned out, the last British governor of colonial New York.

THE BATTLE OF FORT WASHINGTON

After defeats on Long Island and in Manhattan, General George Washington led his troops north, leaving a garrison at Fort Washington, a crudely fortified earthwork, under the command of Colonel Robert Magaw. On Nov 16, 1776, Hessian mercenaries fighting for the British, scaled the outworks on Long Hill (the ridge in what is now Fort Tryon Park) from the north and east, and attacked the Americans. General Cornwallis invaded Manhattan across the Harlem River at the present site of 201st St; the 42nd Highlanders crossed the Harlem River more or less where High Bridge now stands, and British troops led by Lord Percy marched up from downtown Manhattan, while warships bombarded the fort from the Hudson. The defenders of the outworks were killed or pushed back into the fort, which quickly surrendered after it became clear that the American troops were outnumbered. The loss of 54 lives and the capture of 2,634 of Washington's best-equipped troops were severe blows to the ragged, inexperienced American army.

The former Billings Estate

The contours of the park bear traces of the former estate of Cornelius K.G. Billings, a millionaire horseman, yachtsman, and later, aficionado of automobiles. Billings retired from a Chicago utilities company in 1901 and devoted himself to his hobbies, eventually becoming known as the American Horse King.

In 1903, Billings, who lived on Fifth Ave at 53rd St, bought land here for a stable, since he enjoyed racing his trotters on the nearby Harlem Speedway. He also built a country lodge to go with the 25,000-square-ft stable (near the site of the New Leaf Café). To celebrate the completion of these facilities, he threw a dinner for 36 of his friends at Sherry's restaurant, an affair known in the annals of New York society as the Horseback Dinner. Billings's companions were seated on real horses, which had been brought upstairs in the freight elevators; the meals were served on little tables attached to the saddles. Lest anyone snigger at the incongruity of it all, the walls of the restaurant were masked with painted woodland scenery and the floor was covered with grasses.

Billings enjoyed his lodge so much that he expanded it into a year-round home, a turreted and towered French-style mansion complete with a swimming pool, bowling alley, formal gardens, and a yacht-landing in the Hudson River. The original entrance was on 190th St, but when Riverside Drive was paved in 1908, the millionaire wanted a roadway up the hill from the river. The hill was so steep that one of the switchbacks would have had to swing out into mid-air, and the architects were obliged to build an arched structure to support the road (it is still visible from the northbound lanes of the Henry Hudson Parkway).

By 1917 Billings had tired of his hilltop home, and he sold it to John D. Rockefeller Jr. Nine years later, the house burned to the ground in a fire that attracted thousands of onlookers. In the early 1930s, Rockefeller hired the Olmsted brothers, sons of the famous co-designer of Central Park, to transform the rocky topography into a park that maintained the area's magnificent vistas. Frederick Law Olmsted Jr. worked for four years creating promenades and gardens, including the Heather Garden, intended as a place of rest and meditation.

Dyckman Farmhouse Museum

4881 Broadway (West 204th St). Open Wed–Sat 11–4, Sun 12–4; T: 212 304 9422; www.dyckmanfarmhouse.org.

This museum is a fine example of colonial domestic architecture. Built c. 1784, it resisted the ambitions of developers through the determination of two Dyckman descendants, who bought it in 1915, restored it, and donated it to the city. Once the center of the 300-acre Dyckman farm, whose meadows reached to the Harlem River, the present house replaces an earlier Dyckman homestead destroyed by the British during the Revolutionary War. It has the overhanging eaves and gambrel roof of the Dutch Colonial style. Inside are period rooms with early American furnishings and a winter kitchen, its staircase built around a slab of Inwood marble too large to dig out. Behind the house are a garden with a reconstructed smokehouse and a well. In another corner of the garden is the reconstruction of a military hut, similar to those used by the British in the Revolutionary War, when both British and Hessian soldiers camped on the farm.

BOROUGH OF BROOKLYN
(KING'S COUNTY)

Once a separate city, Brooklyn today still preserves a separate identity and an almost mystical hold on the hearts and imaginations of its admirers. Some of its aura derives from its past, illuminated by the radiance of memory and nostalgia for which the departed Brooklyn Dodgers are the most powerful symbol. It evokes fierce pride, even chauvinism, in some of its residents (past, present, and spiritual), who defend its populace as the most stalwart and its nurturing qualities as the most conducive to worldly success. People write books, songs, and poems about Brooklyn as they do not, for example, about Queens, the Bronx, or Staten Island.

To outsiders Brooklyn has been an alien country, whose natives speak a unique, comic dialect. Its stereotypical inhabitant is an aggressive, humorous, streetwise, and ambitious character, not precisely like any of the many famous people who were born or raised there but something like all of them: Walt Whitman, Mickey Rooney, Mae West, Jackie Gleason, Woody Allen, S.J. Perelman, Barbra Streisand, Al Capone, and Danny Kaye.

Geographically Brooklyn occupies the western tip of Long Island and is bounded by the East River, the Narrows, and upper New York Bay on the west and north, by the Atlantic Ocean on the south, and the borough of Queens on the east. Rocky ridges created by the Wisconsin glacier run east and west through its central and western portions, while the southern and eastern parts of the borough are largely coastal plain, created by the glacial outwash. Many neighborhood names describe local geography: Brooklyn Heights, Park Slope, Stuyvesant Heights (now part of the conglomerate Bedford-Stuyvesant), Crown Heights, Bay Ridge, Flatbush, Flatlands, and Midwood. Even the name "Brooklyn," first applied to the 17th-century village near the present intersection of Fulton and Smith Sts, refers to a topographically similar Dutch town, *Breuckelen* ("Broken Land").

As one would expect, the waterfront has attracted industry and shipping; the downtown area is focused around Fulton St; and the rest of Brooklyn is largely residential, the pattern of its settlement influenced by transit lines—first horse cars, then elevated railways, and eventually subways—fanning outward through the borough. Its area of 78.5 square miles makes it the second largest borough geographically, while its 2.5 million inhabitants make it the largest in population.

Bridges link Brooklyn to the rest of the city. The Brooklyn Bridge (*see p. 464*), the Manhattan Bridge (*see p. 110*), and the Williamsburg Bridge span the East River to Manhattan. Othmar H. Ammann's beautiful Verrazano-Narrows Bridge (1964) soars above the Lower Bay, joining the Bay Ridge section of Brooklyn to Staten Island and to the national interstate system. The name of the explorer was chosen in order to placate the Italian-American community in Bay Ridge whose homes were destroyed to build the bridge approaches. Its 4,260-ft main span made it the longest suspension bridge until 1997, when the Tsing Ma Bridge in Hong Kong surpassed it.

HISTORY OF BROOKLYN

The Dutch first settled Brooklyn in the 17th century, buying land from the Canarsie Indians and chartering five of its six original villages: *Breuckelen* (1657); *'t Vlacke Bos*, now Flatbush (1652); *Nieuw Utrecht* (1662); *Nieuw Amersfoort*, now Flatlands (1666); and *Boswijck*, now Bushwick (1660). The sixth charter, for *Gravensande*, now Gravesend, went in 1645 to Lady Deborah Moody, an Englishwoman. Dutch culture, agrarian and conservative, endured in Brooklyn long after the Revolution, especially inland, although New Yorkers, many of them of British origin, were attracted to the waterfront and northern districts. Steam ferry services to Manhattan began in 1814, on a small scale, doing what the Brooklyn Bridge would accomplish on a grand scale in 1883—linking this rural area to the big city, making it a desirable place to live and do business. From 1820–60, Brooklyn's population nearly doubled every decade. Brooklyn rejected overtures to join New York politically in 1833, and in the following year became an independent city. As the century progressed, Brooklyn gradually absorbed outlying towns: New Lots, Flatbush, Gravesend, New Utrecht, and Flatlands, and became known as the "City of Churches" for the countless houses of worship that had sprung up.

Francis Guy: *Winter Scene in Brooklyn* (c. 1819–20), in the Brooklyn Museum (see p. 485).

Oil on canvas, 58¼ x 75 in (149 x 190.5cm). Gift of the Brooklyn Institute of Arts and Science.

In 1898, its destiny dictated by short-term fiscal needs and geography, Brooklyn voted by a slim majority to join Greater New York. The turn of the last century was a golden age for Brooklyn, its cultural institutions (the Brooklyn Museum, the Academy of Music, the Botanic Garden, the Historical Society) finding fertile soil in which to flourish, its major industries (oil and sugar refining, brewing and distilling, publishing, glass and ceramics, cast iron) providing jobs for its large population. Major public works projects (Prospect Park, the Brooklyn Bridge, the development of the Atlantic Basin in Red Hook) as well as the construction of sound housing along the rapid transit lines testified to its economic health.

After the turn of the 20th century, however, Brooklyn's demography also began to change as immigrants poured in from Europe and, after the 1930s, from the American South, all seeking jobs in the great manufacturing and port center that Brooklyn had become. By 1930 half Brooklyn's adults were foreign born, most gravitating to ethnic neighborhoods: Brownsville, Bensonhurst, and Greenpoint. The Depression hit hard, and by the mid-1930s some of these areas had become slums. Established middle-class families moved further out to suburban neighborhoods. The borough's population kept growing—between 1890 and 1940, it soared from 1.2 million people to 2.7 million. Despite the setbacks of the Depression, Brooklyn remained economically sound through the end of World War II, when the exodus to the suburbs of much of the remaining middle class, governmental policies favoring other regions of the country, and changes in the structure of capitalism eroded Brooklyn's economic base. The port lost jobs, the breweries of Bushwick shut down, the Navy Yard was abandoned by the Defense Department, and large neighborhoods became derelict, most poignantly Brownsville, long a working-class Jewish area noted for its social and intellectual vitality. In 1955 the *Brooklyn Eagle* ceased publication, and two years later the Brooklyn Dodgers left for Los Angeles, both losses potent symbols of the borough's decline.

For the next three decades Brooklyn, at times along with the rest of the city, struggled with drugs, crime, the decay of the infrastructure, and other urban problems. Recently, however, Brooklyn's fortunes have risen. At the upper end of the economic scale, young professionals and families, priced out of Manhattan or seeking a less frenzied atmosphere, have moved to such neighborhoods as Park Slope and Cobble Hill, where new restaurants, shops, and other upscale businesses have followed them. Brooklyn has its own arts culture in Williamsburg, DUMBO (Down Under the Manhattan Bridge Overpass), and Red Hook. Recently Brooklyn Bridge Park and Empire State Fulton Park have opened on the waterfront near the bridge, the first phase in a park that will replace abandoned piers and car sheds with open space. In 2001 the minor league Brooklyn Cyclones opened at Coney Island's new KeySpan Park, bringing professional baseball back to Brooklyn for the first time since the Dodgers departed.

THE BROOKLYN BRIDGE

The Brooklyn Bridge is one of New York's great landmarks, certainly the best-known and most-loved bridge in the city. The view from the bridge is spectacular, day or night, up to the cables or down to the river.

Pedestrian access to the bridge on the Manhattan side is just outside City Hall Park at the corner of Centre Street and Park Row (*map p. 582, C2*). On the Brooklyn side, the walkway begins at the corner of Adams and Tillary Sts and can be accessed via a staircase on Prospect St between Cadman Plaza East and West (*map p. 470*). The boardwalk, elevated above the roadway, is divided into bike and pedestrian lanes.

History of the bridge

When the Brooklyn Bridge opened on May 25, 1883, it was justly considered one of the world's greatest wonders. It was the largest suspension bridge in existence, with a single span arching 1,595 ft across the East River, and massive granite towers that stretched 276ft above the water. Only the thin spire of Trinity Church stood taller, at 281ft. The bridge was also a public works project conducted on a scale never before seen in New York, employing approximately 4,000 people, taking 14 years, and ultimately costing $15 million dollars.

Before the Brooklyn Bridge, anyone wishing to cross the East River had to take the Fulton Ferry. Limited to small loads and idle in poor weather, the ferry system could not keep pace with the expansion of industry which took place in the mid-19th century. As the Civil War ended, a push began for a bridge that would accommodate the growing flood of goods and people crossing the river. In 1867 two leaders of the Brooklyn Democratic political machine inaugurated the movement for a bridge. One was contractor and self-made millionaire William C. Kingsley, who had built much of Prospect Park and who offered to fund the initial operations. The other was state senator Henry Cruse Murphy, who had founded the *Brooklyn Eagle* newspaper and served as King's County prosecutor, mayor of Brooklyn, and congressman. He penned the charter for a New York Bridge Company and shepherded it through Albany.

The company included some of Brooklyn's most prominent citizens, among them Civil War hero General Henry W. Slocum and James S.T. Stranahan, a former congressman known as "the Father of Prospect Park." Representing New York was a man known for less savory accomplishments: William M. Tweed, whose ring (*see p. 86*) had already stolen millions from the city through graft and who now saw boundless opportunities for financial gain in the bridge. In later investigations it emerged that Tweed's sanction on the enterprise had most likely been made with the understanding that he would be remunerated for his support; but the ring was cracked and Tweed was dead several years before the bridge was complete.

Once assembled, the company chose their engineer: the brilliant John A. Roebling. Inventor, manufacturer and engineer, Roebling had brought a group of pilgrims from Germany to America in 1831 with the intention of founding an agricultural community. Having established the city of Saxonburg in rural Pennsylvania, he then obtained

the post of engineer and state surveyor. While working in this capacity, Roebling first hit on the idea of manufacturing wire rope for industrial use, and he soon became the most successful producer in the country. Wire rope was not only profitable, it was also central to Roebling's designs for suspension bridges. With such works as his Cincinnati Bridge, a dramatic dual-level bridge spanning the Niagara River, and his suspension aqueduct over the Allegheny River, the engineer quickly established his reputation.

Roebling had already sketched out plans for a bridge over the East River in 1856, and he returned to the project with the conviction that his suspension bridge would be the greatest in the world. With the aid of his son, Colonel Washington Roebling, who had served as a surveyor and engineer in the Union Army, Roebling put forth a daring plan for the bridge. Two mammoth granite towers were to be built offshore on underwater foundations. Four huge cables would be hung over the towers and secured by huge anchorages at either end of the bridge. A single arching span would hang from the cables and a web of supporting stays. The span would further be supported by a truss system for an extra measure of safety. In short, the great towers would support the weight of the cables and roadway, and the anchorages would offset their pull. The entire bridge would be over a mile long and could accommodate 18,700 tons at a time. The engineer also planned a promenade on the upper level, tracks for a special steam-powered train system, and cavernous storage houses within the massive anchorages.

Important aspects of Roebling's design, like the giant steel suspension cables and underwater foundations, were relatively new and had never been tested on such a grand scale. The work would prove dangerous, and dozens of men died during the construction. Roebling himself would not live to see a single stone of his great bridge laid, for he contracted tetanus in a freak accident while surveying the site in 1869 and suffered an excruciating death two weeks later. The task then fell to Washington Roebling to build his father's great bridge.

Two of the bridge's most important features lie out of sight at the bottom of the riverbed. These are the gigantic caissons employed by Roebling to sink the foundations of the bridge. Like mammoth diving bells, these huge, inverted boxes of timber, iron, and cement (each roughly 170ft by 100ft) were built on the shores of the river, "inflated" with compressed air and floated into position. Once in place, heavy stones were piled on top of each box until it came to rest on the riverbed. Then, through a system of airlocks, men would descend into the caissons to excavate the muddy riverbed until they hit solid rock. Inside they toiled away by dim light, removing huge boulders that appeared in the muck and hauling river mud and gravel to large buckets which then hoisted the debris out of the caisson. After ten months of digging the Brooklyn caisson touched bedrock. The New York caisson was sunk in 8½ months. Both caissons were then filled with cement to form the foundations of the bridge.

Caissons had only been tried at a much smaller scale previously, and the hazards of working with compressed air were not well understood. A phenomenon called "caisson disease" began to plague workers as they went deeper into the ground. The symptoms were temporary paralysis, vomiting, nose bleeds, pain in the joints, and in some cases death; they resulted from the formation of nitrogen bubbles in the body during the rapid

drops in pressure which the men experienced as they ascended after their shifts. Washington Roebling himself fell victim to caisson disease, and developed a nervous disorder which for several years left him unable to visit the work site or communicate with anyone but his wife Emily. As the towers rose and the cables ran across the river, Roebling watched the proceedings with binoculars from his home in Brooklyn Heights, delivering detailed instructions to his engineers through his highly numerate wife.

The method for stringing the cables was equally brilliant. Roebling had developed a revolutionary system for fabricating heavy suspension cables in mid-air, and had used this previously on smaller projects. Two gigantic cable loops were hung between the towers, forming four pendant arcs. Small vehicles holding workers and spools of wire were then strung along these cables. The shuttles moved back and forth, spinning out wire like big spiders until the requisite number of wires had been strung. Then the bunch was girded with more galvanized wire from end to end.

One hundred twenty-five years later the bridge is still an important part of the city's transportation network, carrying approximately 145,000 cars per day and numerous pedestrians. Twice in recent years the bridge has also played a crucial role in evacuations of Manhattan. First on Sept 11, 2001 and again on Aug 14, 2003 during a severe blackout. On the second occasion, vibrations from shoulder-to-shoulder pedestrian traffic caused the bridge to sway so much that some felt seasick, while the huge cables jerked and groaned. Still the bridge remained stable, for Roebling's tripartite system of supports had been designed for such emergencies.

Today the Akashi-Kaikyo Bridge in Japan is the longest suspension bridge in the world and the Brooklyn Bridge has slipped to a respectable 66th place. Still it remains a testament to the optimism and determination of a great city.

BROOKLYN HEIGHTS

Map p. 470. Subway: 2, 3 to Clark St; A, C to High St; 4, 5 to Borough Hall.
Brooklyn Heights, bounded by the East River, Old Fulton St, Atlantic Ave, and Court St, is an old residential neighborhood. Sometimes called New York's first suburb, it also became its first designated Historic District (1965).

Part of the larger village of Brooklyn, Brooklyn Heights started thriving after 1814, when Robert Fulton's steam ferry began scheduled crossings to and from New York (Manhattan) across the river. Not long thereafter prominent landowners began dividing their farms into standard 25ft by 100ft building lots. As the area was developed, one architectural style followed another, summarizing the whole history of domestic architecture in 19th-century New York. Row houses were built, first in the Federal style (1820s and 1830s), later in the Greek Revival style (1830s and 1840s), Gothic Revival style (1840s), the Italianate (1860s), along with a few picturesque Queen Anne and Romanesque Revival houses in the 1880s and 1890s.

Victorian Brooklyn Heights, relatively isolated from Manhattan, was known for its fine families, its churches, and its clergymen. When the bridge (1887) and the sub-

way (1908) arrived, the Heights lost its patrician edge. In the early 20th century, many private homes had been converted to rooming houses; a few had become seamen's clubs, missions, and even brothels. The Heights remained in social limbo until the late 1950s and early 1960s, when young married couples willing to invest labor and money began redeeming the old houses, awakening the spirit of preservation. Today Brooklyn Heights is one of the city's most expensive and desirable neighborhoods.

BROOKLYN HEIGHTS IN THE REVOLUTION

After the disastrous Battle of Brooklyn, Aug 27, 1776, in which the American forces were surrounded and slaughtered, the remaining colonial army retreated to Brooklyn Heights. In a half day of fighting, some 1,200 Americans had been killed and an additional 1,500 wounded or captured; the British lost only 60, with an additional 300 wounded. Had General Howe pressed his advantage, he might well have been able to push the ragtag and demoralized American troops into the East River. Instead, he waited, for two days. After dark on Aug 29, Washington silently brought his troops down from the Heights to the ferry landing (near present Fulton St). Waiting there with commandeered boats was a regiment of fishermen from Massachusetts. The fishermen rowed back and forth all night, hidden by fog, evacuating Washington's entire force of 9,500 men by daybreak.

Plymouth Church of the Pilgrims

75 Hicks St, at Orange St. Tours by appointment Mon–Fri 10–4, and most Sundays after 11am worship; T: 718 624 4743.
This red-brick Italianate barn of a church (1849) is best known for its first minister, Henry Ward Beecher (*see box overleaf*), who thundered forth from its pulpit for 40 years, expounding on the great issues of the day: temperance, woman suffrage, and, most notably, slavery. (Beecher's sister was Harriet Beecher Stowe, author of the anti-slavery novel *Uncle Tom's Cabin*.) In the garden is a statue by Gutzon Borglum, sculptor of Mount Rushmore, depicting Beecher and two slave children. Borglum also executed the nearby bas-relief of Lincoln, who, as a presidential aspirant in 1860, trekked to Brooklyn to hear its eloquent preacher.

The sanctuary, intended as a setting for Beecher's oratorical skills, is arranged like an auditorium, without a central aisle. The opalescent stained-glass windows (c. 1915) designed by the Lamb Studios—the oldest known American stained glass studio, founded 1857)—are unusual in that they depict historical rather than biblical events. Hillis Hall, given by coffee merchant John Arbuckle, has windows from the Tiffany Studios, originally in the Church of the Pilgrims on Remsen St, which merged with Plymouth Church in 1934. The arcade between the church house and sanctuary contains a historical exhibit, with a fragment of Plymouth Rock, and the ring given to Pinky (*see below*), which as a mature, married woman she returned to the church.

Henry Ward Beecher (1813–87)

Henry Ward Beecher came to Brooklyn in 1847 to the Congregational Church of the Pilgrims, called by the founders, many of them New England abolitionists. When fire damaged the original building, the present one, large enough to hold Beecher's growing congregation, replaced it. Beecher was especially popular with the middle-class women in his congregation, and—perhaps through their influence—took an interest in women's rights. At the height of his popularity "Beecher boats" ferried throngs of New Yorkers across the river to hear him, while policemen reined in the crowds that gathered hours before services. Abraham Lincoln commented on Beecher's productive mind, but Mark Twain, a skeptic in religious matters, described him as "sawing his arms in the air, howling sarcasms this way and that, discharging rockets of poetry and exploding mines of eloquence."

Always theatrical, Beecher staged mock auctions at which he would "sell" slaves to the highest bidder; when he took bids on nine-year-old Sally Maria Diggs, called "Pinky," the congregation, outraged by Beecher's imitation of a slave auctioneer, purchased her freedom. One congregant threw her fire-opal ring into the plate; Beecher placed it on the child's hand, saying "With this ring I wed thee to freedom." The church became a stop on the Underground Railway, offering aid to runaway slaves, and it sent rifles, known as "Beecher's Bibles," to anti-slavery settlers in Kansas. A sensational trial for adultery, of which he was acquitted, damaged Beecher's later career, but when he died, Brooklyn declared a day of mourning.

The New York Transit Museum

Map p. 470, corner of Boerum Place and Schermerhorn St. Open Tues–Fri 10–4, Sat–Sun noon–5; closed Mon and major holidays; T: 718 694 1600; www.mta.info/index.html. Subway: A, C, or G train to Hoyt-Schermerhorn station.

This two-level subterranean museum, located in an unused subway station, was inaugurated in 1976 for the bicentennial celebrations and proved too popular to close thereafter. Run by the Metropolitan Transit Authority, it includes exhibits on buses, bridges, and tunnels, but the emphasis is on the subway. Exhibits on the history and construction of the subway system include historic photographs, maps, models and drawings, turnstiles, and collection boxes, but the real draw is the antique equipment. Lined up on the tracks of the former Court St station are examples of most of the subway cars that have traveled the tracks since the first line opened in 1904. Other exhibits include fare collection devices, from an early wooden ticket chopper to a full-body turnstile known as the "iron maiden" to mosaics from early stations (intended partly as decoration but also to assist riders who could not read English). On occasion the museum offers tours and special events, for example trips to the city's first subway station, locked away under City Hall Park (*see p. 83*).

A WALK THROUGH BROOKLYN HEIGHTS

Brooklyn Heights, quiet and tree-shaded, offers well-preserved 19th-century houses in all the reigning styles, as well as a few examples of church architecture. Here also are stunning views across the East River to the Manhattan skyline and the interesting Brooklyn Historical Society, whose museum examines the borough's past.

From Plymouth Church of the Pilgrims, walk east to Henry St and turn north. Until 1964 the Rome Brothers' Printshop stood a block to the east, approximately where the subway stop is on Cadman Plaza East; here in 1855 Walt Whitman's *Leaves of Grass* was first printed.

Continue on Henry St to Middagh St, where the former **Mason Au & Magenheimer Confectionery Company** building (1885) still stands. An old advertisement for Peaks and Mason mints remains visible at the top of the south wall. Turn left at Middagh St and walk west to Willow St. The house on the southeast corner, **no. 24 Middagh St**, is a well-preserved clapboarded house (1824) with fine carved Federal detailing around the door, dormer windows, and quarter-round attic windows visible from Willow St. The cottage behind it, now joined to it by a wall, was originally the carriage house. In 1848 Henry Ward Beecher lived at 22 Willow St, across the intersection.

While many Brooklyn Heights streets are named after prominent 19th-century families, five streets—Pineapple, Orange, Cranberry, Poplar, and Willow—have botanical names. Legend (probably apocryphal) attributes them to the ire of one Miss Middagh, who allegedly tore down street markers bearing the names of neighbors she disliked and substituted the present ones.

Walk south on Willow St to **57 Willow St** on the northeast corner of Orange St, a house (c. 1824) exemplifying the Federal style with dormers, pitched roofs, Flemish bond brickwork, tooled stone lintels, and a parapet between the chimneys concealing the roof gable.

Turn right on Orange St and walk a block to **Columbia Heights**. No. 124 is built on the site of the house (then called 110 Columbia Heights) from which Washington Roebling oversaw construction of the Brooklyn Bridge, after the effects of the "bends" confined him to his house (*see p. 466*).

Turn left on Clark St. The former **Leverich Towers Hotel** (1928; Starrett & Van Vleck) at no. 21 once glittered as one of Brooklyn's brightest social spots, its four corner towers spotlighted at night. Today it is one of the many residence halls belonging to the Jehovah's Witnesses, a religious group that moved their headquarters to Brooklyn Heights in 1909 and since has become the Heights's largest landholder.

On the next block, between Hicks and Henry Sts, is the former **Hotel St. George**, an eight-building complex named after an 18th-century tavern. Built in various stages between 1885 and 1930, it was for a while the city's largest hotel (2,632 rooms), famous during the 1920s for its Art Deco ballroom and the world's largest indoor saltwater swimming pool.

Double back now and and walk south down Willow St. **Nos. 108–12** (c. 1880) are Brooklyn's best examples of the offbeat

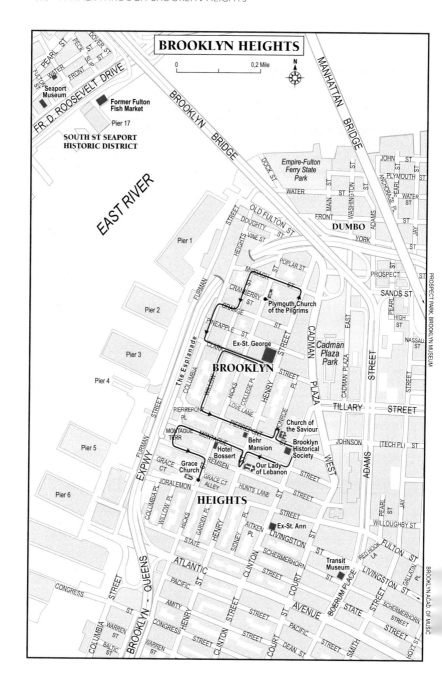

architectural style known as Queen Anne, which flourished in New York from 1880–1900, after its introduction from England at the Philadelphia Centennial Exposition (1876). The style combines medieval and Renaissance elements in a freehanded manner. The houses here form one visual unit, displaying a satisfying variety of forms (gables, bay windows, chimneys, dormers; round, square, and elliptical openings) and materials (brick, stone, terra cotta, ironwork, shingles).

Continue south to **no. 151 Willow St**, a red-brick carriage house set back from the street. Between nos. 151 and 155 is a towering **dawn redwood tree** (*Metasequoia glyptostroboides*), planted here in the 1950s. Until 1943, when a Chinese forester discovered one in a remote village, the species was known only from fossil records and was thought to have become extinct. The Brooklyn Botanic Garden and New York Botanical Garden have specimens. **Nos. 155–59 Willow St** are a trio of pristine small Federal row houses (c. 1829) with sidelights, leaded transoms, and paneled front doors flanked by colonnettes.

Turn left at **Pierrepont St**, which takes its name from Hezekiah Beers Pierpont, landowner and gin distiller, who early saw the advantages of opening Brooklyn Heights for suburban development. He backed the Fulton Ferry (1814) and by 1823 was offering 25ft by 100ft lots to "gentlemen whose duties require their daily attendance in the city." Hezekiah's children reverted to an earlier, fancier spelling of Pierrepont.

Continue east to no. 82, on the southwest corner of Henry St, the **former Herman Behr mansion** (1890), designed by Brooklyn architect Frank Freeman. Behr was a manufacturer of abrasives; his son was a tennis star and a *Titanic* survivor. With an addition in 1919, this handsome Romanesque Revival mansion became the Palm Hotel. It lost its luster, became a brothel, and was later redeemed by the friars of nearby St. Francis College, who took it over as a residence for novitiates. Converted to apartments, it was offered for sale in 2007 for $12 million.

No. 104 Pierrepont St (c. 1857) is a four-story brownstone with elaborately carved console brackets on the first and second stories. **No. 108–14 Pierrepont St** (1840) was once a Greek Revival double house with a central cupola; drastic remodeling has made it a strange hybrid, half Greek Revival, half Romanesque Revival. The doorway pediment and corner quoins on one half remain from the original façade. The other half was given its present Romanesque form for publisher Alfred Barnes by adding brownstone facing, terra-cotta ornament, a turret, and a rounded bay.

Walk east to Monroe Place, named after James Monroe, the nation's fifth President, who finished his life in straitened circumstances in New York. On the northwest corner of Monroe Place and Pierrepont St is the **Appellate Division of the New York State Supreme Court** (1938), stately but somewhat incongruous in this residential neighborhood. On the northeast corner stands Minard Lafever's (1844) **Church of the Saviour**, also called the First Unitarian Church. Some windows (the Low, Woodward, Farley, Frothingham memorials and possibly the other opalescent windows) are by the Tiffany Studios. **No. 46 Monroe Place** has Brooklyn Heights's only remaining iron-

work basket urn, topped with the traditional pineapple for hospitality.

At 128 Pierrepont St, at the southwest corner of Clinton St, is the **Brooklyn Historical Society** (1878; George B. Post), founded in 1863 as the Long Island Historical Society. The society maintains a library, a museum, and an educational center dedicated to Brooklyn history and culture. (*Open Wed–Sun 12–5; closed Mon, Tues, July 4, Thanksgiving, Christmas, New Year's; T: 718 222 4111; www.brooklynhistory.org.*) The permanent collection has photographs and paintings (of Brooklyn people and places), as well as newspapers, books, manuscripts, and other archival materials.

On the façade are terra-cotta heads of a Norseman and a Native American (over the main entrance) and busts of Johann Gutenberg, Benjamin Franklin, Michelangelo, Christopher Columbus, Shakespeare and Beethoven. All are by Olin Levi Warner, who had studied at the École des Beaux-Arts in Paris and returned to New York in 1872. Warner later went on sculpt the bronze doors of the Library of Congress, where he reused the Norseman and Native American motifs. He died after a bicycle accident in Central Park in 1896.

Turn right on Clinton St and walk one block to the neighborhood's main commercial street, **Montague St**, named after English writer Lady Mary Wortley Montagu, née Pierrepont. The final "e" in Montague is a misspelling. There are several cafés here, all with indoor and outdoor seating: *Caffè Buon Gusto*, 151 Montague St (*closed Sun; T: 718 624 3838); Armando's Ristorante*, 143 Montague St (*open until midnight seven days; 718 624 7167*) and the Heights *Café*, 84 Montague St (*open until midnight seven days, brunch Sat and Sun; T: 718 625 5555; www.heightscafeny.com*).

Walk west on Montague St. At Henry St turn left and walk south to the church on the corner of Remsen St (named after landowner Henry Remsen). Originally the Church of the Pilgrims (1846; Richard Upjohn), the first Congregational church erected in Brooklyn, this historic church has served Middle Eastern Catholics of the Maronite rite as **Our Lady of Lebanon Church** since 1944. The first round-arched, early Romanesque Revival ecclesiastical building built in the United States, it is faced with ashlar instead of the usual brownstone, and represents a brief departure from Upjohn's more familiar Gothic Revival style. The doors in the west and south portals contain medallions from the dining room doors of the luxury liner *Normandie*, which burned in 1942 and sank at its Hudson River berth. Purchased at auction by the pastor of the church in 1945, the medallions depict Norman castles, churches, and the SS *Ile de France*.

Return to Montague St. The **Hotel Bossert** at no. 98 on the southeast corner of Hicks St (1909) gets its name from founder Louis Bossert, a millwork manufacturer. In the 1920s and '30s the Marine Roof, decorated by theatrical designer Joseph Urban, afforded visitors a vista of the Manhattan skyline while they dined and danced. At the time of writing it was a residence for Jehovah's Witnesses.

Continue to the foot of Montague St and the waterfront. The **Esplanade**, known locally as the Promenade (1951), is a five-block walkway from Remsen to Orange Sts, providing spectacular views

of the Manhattan skyline as well as the Statue of Liberty and Ellis Island. It is cantilevered over the Brooklyn–Queens Expressway, which accounts for the constant whooshing sound of traffic below. A plaque at the entrance recalls the site of "Four Chimneys," where George Washington had his temporary headquarters and made the decision to withdraw his army across to Manhattan (*see box on p. 467*). Hezekiah Pierpont later bought the mansion.

Exit the promenade and look left to nos. 2–3 **Pierrepont Place**, two superb Renaissance Revival brownstones (1857) by Frederick A. Peterson, the architect of Cooper Union. An 1858 city directory lists the owners as Abiel Abbot Low (teas) and Alexander M. White (furs). Low, a Yankee from Salem, Massachusetts, got into the China trade early, made a fortune, and settled here with his family including son Seth, later mayor of Brooklyn and of New York City. From his opulent home—four stories elaborated with quoins, a heavy cornice, Corinthian pilasters at the entrance, and a conservatory added on the south end—Low could watch his ships setting out to sea. To the right of the Promenade entrance is **Montague Terrace**; follow it and turn left onto Remsen St, and then right onto Hicks St. Walk a short block to **Grace Court Alley** (on the left), once a mews for the horses and carriages of the Remsen and Joralemon St gentry; the stables converted to apartments now house the gentry itself.

Across the street is **Grace Church** (1847) by Richard Upjohn, who returned to his usual Gothic Revival manner a year after his experiment with the Church of the Pilgrims. A glorious old elm tree shades the courtyard to the south; three Tiffany windows adorn the sanctuary.

Terra-cotta head of a Native American, on the façade of the Brooklyn Historical Society.

THE BROOKLYN MUSEUM

Map p. 573. 200 Eastern Pkwy (Washington Ave). Subway: 2, 3 to Eastern Parkway-Brooklyn Museum. Car parking in lot accessible from Washington Ave. Open Wed–Fri 10–5; weekends 11–6; first Sat of each month open until 11pm. Closed Mon, Tues, Thanksgiving, Christmas Day and New Year's Day. Suggested contribution, except first Sats, when programs, mostly geared to families, are free 5–11; tickets distributed at the Visitor Center in the lobby. T: 718 638 5000; www.brooklynmuseum.org.
NB: At the time of writing some of the galleries of decorative arts were temporarily closed, and some of the period rooms had been dismantled.

Located near Prospect Park and Grand Army Plaza, two of the borough's best-known landmarks (*see p. 489 below*), the Brooklyn Museum harks back to the days when Brooklyn was a separate city, fired with ambitious plans to rival New York across the river. Today its rich collections (1.5 million objects), housed in a grand 19th-century building, make it one of the nation's finest art museums. Foremost among the reasons to visit is the dazzling collection of Egyptian art, including many pieces obtained during the museum's own program of excavations. The museum also has a large collection of American painting and decorative art, from the colonial period through the years after World War II. There are extensive holdings in both European and American landscape painting from the Romantic period through the early 20th century, and a fine display of Asian art.

The exterior

The imposing Beaux-Arts building (1897; McKim, Mead & White; later additions), complete with Ionic portico and an imposing pediment, represents only a quarter of the architects' original grand plan, which was to include four wings each surrounding a courtyard. Brooklyn's change in status from an independent city to a borough of Greater New York in 1898 curtailed these grandiose plans, and most construction halted in 1927. The most recent addition is a new entrance and pavilion by the firm of James Stewart Polshek Assocs (2004), which replaced an earlier grand staircase torn down in the 1930s.

The heroic sculptures on the frieze above the cornice include Mohammed, Praxiteles, Pindar, and Plato, personifying religion, art, poetry, and philosophy. On the pediment itself eight heroic figures by Adolph A. Weinman and Daniel Chester French represent the Arts and Sciences.

Daniel Chester French's statues of *Manhattan* and *Brooklyn* (1916), flanking the main museum entrance on Eastern Parkway, formerly stood near the Manhattan Bridge on the Brooklyn side, but were placed here when the bridge ramps were widened. In the 1960s Robert Moses, head of the Triborough Bridge and Tunnel Authority, whose obsession with ever larger and wider highways led to some of New York's finer arteries and some of its more blighted neighborhoods, proposed an expressway through Lower Manhattan. He asked the City Art Commission for permission to demolish the bridge approaches, claiming that removal of the sculpture

was necessary for bridge connections to the proposed roadway. Since it appeared that the road was inevitable and that the bridge approaches were doomed, the Commission sadly gave permission, under the condition that some of the sculpture be moved to other sites. The Brooklyn Museum volunteered to take these two sculptures and in 1963 they were moved here. Unlike many urban preservation stories, this one had a happy outcome, since the roadway project was defeated in 1969.

First floor

(1) Pavilion: Inside the steel and glass pavilion is an important group of sculptures by **Auguste Rodin**, given to the museum in the 1980s by Iris and B. Gerald Cantor. The gift included not only groups from the sculptor's best-known commissions (*The Gates of Hell, The Burghers of Calais*, and the monument to Balzac), but portraits, parts of figures, erotic groups, and mythological subjects, which suggest the entire scope of a long, prolific, and influential career. The museum owns 12 figures and studies from *The Burghers of Calais*, including *Eustache de St.-Pierre* (1886–87), *Andrieu d'Andres* (1886–87), and two figures of *Pierre de Wiessant* (1886–87 and 1886–88). The group was commissioned by the town of Calais in 1884 as a memorial to Eustache de St.-Pierre, one of six citizens who in 1347 volunteered to surrender to the English, virtually a sentence of death, to save the people of besieged Calais from starvation. Rodin proposed to sculpt all six of the burghers for the price of one and executed a number of studies of the figures, both singly and in groups. Recognized as one of his greatest works, the monument powerfully renders the conflicting emotions awakened by the heroic gesture of self-sacrifice (the English king spared their lives). The original casting still stands in Calais.

Other castings can be seen around the world from Copenhagen to Canberra, including another New York group in the Metropolitan Museum. The Brooklyn Museum also owns a large reduction of *The Age of Bronze* (1876), the "Helmet Maker's Wife" (1880s) from *The Gates of Hell*, and a monumental head and the "F" Athlete from the studies for the monument to Balzac.

(2) Arts of Africa: The museum began collecting African art as early as 1900, and today holds the largest collection of African art in any American art museum. Works are arranged by cultural and geographic groupings. Holdings are strong in the arts of Nigeria, the Democratic Republic of Congo, the Ivory Coast, and Mali. Highlights include Karanse masks of the Mossi people of Burkina Faso: with projections that tower six feet above the head, they are used in dances that honor ancestors. Also among the newly acquired objects are a finely carved wooden spoon whose handle incorporates the figure of a water buffalo, and a large equestrian figure from an altar shrine of the Yoruba people of Nigeria.

From the Democratic Republic of the Congo comes a Kuba mask of painted parchment, its face decorated with tiny shells and fringed with monkey fur;

THE BROOKLYN MUSEUM
(FIRST FLOOR)

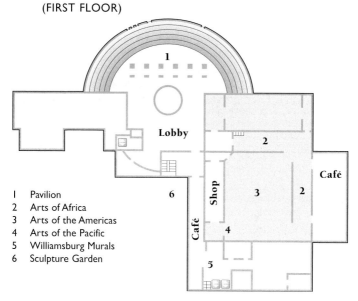

1 Pavilion
2 Arts of Africa
3 Arts of the Americas
4 Arts of the Pacific
5 Williamsburg Murals
6 Sculpture Garden

also on view is a collection of ivory ornaments. Because most objects of African art are created from perishable, organic materials, many of the works here date from the 19th or 20th centuries, but there are also a few earlier pieces. Outstanding are a terra-cotta head, which may date back as far as the 11th century. This representation of a sacred king from the Ife Kingdom of Nigeria is one of the oldest surviving sculptures from West Africa. A carved ivory gong or *sistrum* from the Edo people of Benin, dating from the 16th–17th century is another important survival. The wooden figure (early 18th century) of King Bom Bosh of the Kuba people is the earliest-known surviving example of a *Ndop*, a figure representing a king's spirit double.

(3) Arts of the Americas: A cavernous, boldly-colored gallery features arts of native peoples from North, Central and South America. From the Huaxtec culture of Mexico (northern Veracruz) is an almost life-size "Life-Death" figure, carved of stone. The front shows a young man wearing a conical hat and large ear ornaments; on the back is a skeleton with a grinning skull.

The collection of Native American Art is strong in works by the Northwest Coast Indians, including enormous totem poles and house posts, and wooden potlatch figures, ivory shaman's charms, and a detailed scale model of a Haida chieftain's house built for the World's Columbian Exposition held in Chicago in 1893.

South American art is represented by a stunning array of artifacts from Peru.

Among the Peruvian textiles, which include woven and feathered objects, is the most famous piece in the South American collection, the **Paracas Textile**. This rectangular mantle, which has been called the most exquisitely executed fabric ever produced in the Western Hemisphere, dates from between 300 BC and 100 AD. Bordering a central field of stylized faces are about 90 woven figures, believed to be celebrating some ancient Andean ceremony. The intricate and varied figures, knitted on small needles, include costumed humans, llamas, cats, and a profusion of plant forms.

Of particular historical interest is a 15th-century *khipe*, a hanging of knotted cords conveying a coded message. Such hangings were often worn as aprons by messengers who ran between the mountain courts of Inca rulers. The codes were closely guarded secrets, in case a runner was caught on his journey, and the meaning of the knots remains mysterious.

Also among the textiles (one of the most important forms of Andean art) are two vividly-colored embroidered mantles recovered from the Paracas necropolis, where between 200 BC and AD 400 more than 400 mummy bundles (all male, with artificially elongated skulls) were buried in the desert sand.

Ceramics include pots decorated in the early Nazca style, showing life-forms native to the south coast of Peru.

(4) Arts of the Pacific: A small gallery adjoining that of the Americas displays arts of the Pacific, with pieces from Indonesia, the Philippines, Polynesia and New Zealand. Tools, instruments of war, and religious objects are often carved from wood, embellished with shell and polished to a deep sheen with coconut oil. A gorgeous ancestral mask and zoomorphic treasure box were produced by the Maori people, original inhabitants of New Zealand. Not to be missed are two remarkable pieces of jewelry. One is a fantastic headdress from the Marquesas Islands composed of porpoise teeth. Clustered along a string of coconut fiber, the sharp little teeth somehow assume the delicacy of chrysanthemum blossoms for a lovely effect. Next, there is a necklace of human hair wound into a multitude of the finest braids imaginable, all clasped together with an ivory pendant.

Detail of the mantle known as the Paracas Textile (Peruvian, 300 BC–100 AD). Made of wool and cotton.

Early Intermediate South Coast Peru, Andes, John Thomas Underwood Memorial Fund.

(5) Williamsburg Murals: Located in a glass corridor leading to the elevators, the rediscovered Williamsburg Murals were executed by pioneer American Abstract artists Ilya Bolotowsky, Balcomb Greene, Paul Kelpe, and Albert Swinden. They were commissioned in 1936 by the New York Mural Division of the Works Project Administration. Burgoyne Diller, a painter deeply influenced by Mondrian, headed the Mural Division and selected the artists, a bold choice at a time when murals generally depicted American regional life or Socialist Realist subjects.

Originally the murals were installed in the public areas of the Williamsburg Housing Project in Brooklyn, a development designed by well-known New York architect William Lescaze. In time these public rooms became offices or storage space, and the murals were neglected; some were even painted over. Long believed to have been either lost or destroyed, they were recovered during the 1980s by the combination of a scholarly investigation of the records documenting their creation and a physical search of the building complex. Today, after restoration, they are on long-term loan.

(6) Sculpture Garden: Outside the glass corridor, the Sculpture Garden contains a collection of architectural ornaments and sculptures salvaged from demolished New York buildings, ranging from Pennsylvania Station to obscure tenements. Four pairs of Pegasus figures (1934), attributed to Harry Lowe, once cavorted before a Brooklyn fire-pumping station. Their majestic wings and curvy necks exude Art Deco elegance as they prance over rolling clouds.

Adolph A. Weinman's *Night* (c. 1910) was one of eight allegorical figures commissioned for the former Pennsylvania Station, designed by McKim, Mead and White. When the station was destroyed in 1963, the statues were broken up and buried in the New Jersey Meadowlands; only three have been retrieved.

The 47-ft replica of the Statue of Liberty by the parking lot formerly crowned the Liberty Storage Warehouse on West 64th St near Lincoln Center. The figure was commissioned by auctioneer William H. Flattau, apparently an immigrant, and cast probably either in Ohio or Pennsylvania. The statue was shipped to New York by rail on a flatbed car, sliced in half lengthwise because it was too large to fit through the railroad tunnels, welded together again, painted green, and installed atop the warehouse around 1902. The circular staircase inside was sealed by Flattau in 1912 because visitors were distracting his workers. When the warehouse was converted to apartments, the statue was placed here to honor fire, police, and other emergency workers for their heroism on September 11, 2001.

Second floor

The museum's fine collections of Asian and Islamic Art are installed here in a series of quiet galleries.

Islamic art: In the collection are ceramics, metalwork (including a Pakistani astrolabe dating from 1650), glass (including enameled and gilded mosque

lamps), carpets and textiles (including beautiful rugs from the McMullan collection). One of the earlier ceramic pieces is a bowl dating from the 9th or 10th century, excavated at Nishapur in northeastern Iran. Around the rim is an inscription in Kufic script whose meaning still partly eludes translators: "Peace is that which is silent and only his speech will reveal the [?] of the man with faults." Among the manuscripts and books are Islamic prayer books, which illustrate the beauty and importance of Arabic calligraphy, and illuminated manuscripts including beautifully illustrated poems from such Persian classics as the *Khamseh* or "Quintet" of the 12th-century poet Nizami. An exquisite watercolor rendering of a blue iris is the only known depiction of a single flower by 17th-century Iranian artist Muhammad Zaman.

Indian, Tibetan, and Southeast Asian art: Indian art includes Buddhist sculpture in stone and bronze. Particularly beautiful is a headless pale green limestone figure of a seated Buddha from the late 3rd century. The iconography of the throne upon which it sits suggests that the figure represents the historical Buddha, Sakyamuni, who gave his first sermon in the deer park at Sarnath. The large 9th-century granite *Buddha Meditating under the Bodhi Tree* shows the Buddha Sakyamuni attaining enlightenment. The museum owns a collection of Mughal paintings, including pages from the *Hamza-nama*, a cycle of stories about Amir Hamza illustrated during the reign of the emperor Akbar (1562–77).

A small selection of Tibetan and Southeast Asian art includes a sandstone head of Shiva from 10th-century Cambodia and a gilt copper seated Maitreya from Tibet. A lotus flanks his left shoulder and a stupa crowns his headdress.

Japanese art: The collection has been installed in galleries whose appointments suggest the austere serenity of a traditional Japanese room. Among the earlier pieces is a bell-shaped bronze ritual object or *dotaku* from the Yayoi period (2nd or 3rd century), which corresponds to Japan's Bronze-Iron Age. These objects were buried on hills overlooking the rice paddies to propitiate the spirits of nature. A hollow, earthenware figure of a shamaness from the Haniwa culture (5th or 6th century) was intended to guard a tomb. A painted screen (c. 1624–44) from the Edo period depicts a "Cherry Blossom Viewing Picnic," with a crowd of fashionable courtesans and their clients. Also here are selections from the museum's collection of woodblock prints and drawings, as well as contemporary Japanese ceramics.

Korean art: Ceramics include a celadon ewer from the first half of the 12th century, with the lid in the shape of a lotus blossom and the knob resembling a lotus bud. Celadon, a beautiful pale green glaze developed in China at the opening of the Sung Dynasty (960–1279), was imported to Korea by Chinese potters during the 10th and 11th centuries. A 17th-century dragon jar is decorated with the figure of a sinuous reptile, painted on with iron oxide. Such storage jars were humble, utilitarian ware intended for the lower classes of society.

Chinese art: Among the earliest pieces is a bronze ritual vessel from the Shang Dynasty (12th century BC) in the form of an animal; its surface is covered with designs suggesting dragons and other animal forms. An earthenware war horse from the T'ang Dyansty (7th or 8th century), glazed in brown, cream, green, and amber, was buried as a tomb figure, its appointed duty to serve its master in death as a real horse served him in life. One of the most beautifully shaped and decorated porcelain pieces is a blue and white jar with a design of fishes and water plants from the Yuan Dynasty of the 14th century. The technique of painting porcelain with blue cobalt oxide began in the 13th century with the Mongol conquests of Iran and Iraq. Among the landscape paintings, considered one of the highest art forms along with calligraphy, is a fine landscape showing an idealized view of trees and rocks by Lan Ying (1585), a major painter of the late Ming and early Qing dynasties.

Third floor

(1) European art

NB: At the present time, the European paintings are shown in a long-term, thematically organized exhibit of some 100 works, which visitors accustomed to geographic and stylistic groupings will possibly find unhelpful. The paintings are grouped in the discussion below by school and period. (The museum's outstanding collection of Italian Renaissance panels is on the fifth floor.) The bulk of the museum's European painting collection is arranged around the grand Beaux-Arts court, a large-pillared atrium topped with a splendid glass ceiling. The collection spans the beginning of Renaissance to the early 20th century. The holding of 19th-century French painting is particularly strong.

Italian art: The oldest work in this gallery is a small, gold-ground tempera panel, *Last Supper* (c. 1325–30), by Pseudo-Jacopino. The Apostles are depicted with an earthy humanism that heralds the early Renaissance. Davide Ghirlandaio's *Scene from the Tale of Nastagio degli Onesti in Boccaccio's "Decameron"* (after 1483) depicts the story of a knight's eternal punishment for committing suicide over rejected love; the painter's career was overshadowed by that of his more talented brother Domenico (master of Michelangelo), whom he assisted in many commissions. Three other standout works are *Portrait of a Lady as Mary Magdalene* (no date) by Bartolomeo Veneto; *St Sebastian* (late 15th century) by an anonymous painter; and a 15th-century portrait of a member of the Bentivoglio family by Lorenzo Costa, painter at the powerful Gonzaga court in Mantua.

Iberian and Latin American art: Portraits of the 18th–19th centuries all show the influence of the 17th-century Baroque in their rich hangings and heavy brocades. Works include two portraits of Doña María de la Luz Padilla y (Gómez de) Cervantes (c. 1735), one by Miguel Cabrera and the other attributed to Nicolás Enríquez. The centerpiece of

1 European art
2 Assyrian art
3 Egyptian art

THE BROOKLYN MUSEUM
(THIRD FLOOR)

this section is a stunning portrait in the Romantic style of the military leader Tadeo Bravo de Rivero by Goya (1806).

Dutch and Flemish still-life painting: The museum holds a few fine paintings in this genre: *Flowers in a Vase* (first quarter of 17th century) by Gaspar van den Hoecke; *Flowers, Snake and Butterflies* (not dated) "in the manner of" Otto Marseus van Schrieck; and *Flowers in A Figured Vase* (1670s), attributed to Jan Brueghel.

19th-century French painting: The museum's substantial collection includes fine works of the Barbizon School. Along with works by Antoine-Louis Barye and Narcisse-Virgile Díaz de la Peña are *Young Woman of Albano* (1872) and *Young Women of Sparta* (1868–70) by Corot, and *Shepherd Tending His Flock* (1866) by Millet.

Works by important painters from the Impressionist School through the later periods of Fauvism, Expressionism and Cubism include Degas, *Mlle Fiocre in the Ballet of "La Source"* (1867–68); Camille Pissarro, *The Climbing Path, Hermitage, Pontoise* (1875); Cézanne, *Village of Gardanne* (1885–86); Bonnard, *The Breakfast Room*; Matisse, *Flowers* (1906), *Nude in a Wood* (1906); Édouard Vuillard, *Thadée Natanson* (1897); Raoul Dufy, *The Regatta* (c. 1908–10); Chaim Soutine, *Gladiolas* (c. 1919); and Georges Braque, *Still Life* (1927).

Among the fine landscapes are Courbet's *Isolated Rock* (1862), *The Silent River* (1868), and *The Wave* (1869); Charles-François Daubigny's *Moonrise* (1877), *The River Seine at Mantes* (1856), and *A Bend in the River Oise* (1872); Henri-Joseph Harpignies's *A Meadow in the Bourbonnais, Morning* (1876); Monet's *Vernon in the Sun* (1894), *The Islets of Port-Villez* (1897), *Houses of Parliament—Effect of Sunlight* (1903), and *The Doge's Palace in Venice* (1908); Renoir's *Vineyards at Cagnes* (1906); and Alfred Sisley's *Flood at Moret* (1879).

(2) Assyrian art

Twelve spectacular Assyrian reliefs from the palace of King Ashurnasirpal II (9th century BC) dominate the Kevorkian Gallery of Ancient Middle Eastern Art. These feature huge winged genies, who anoint sacred trees with delicate grace. Running across each panel is cuneiform script relating the story of the king's lineage and his empire. In the shadow of these massive reliefs, a tiny leonine figure located in one of the freestanding display cases may seem to exhibit undue pride, until one learns that this Persian goddess is approximately 6,000 years old.

(3) Egyptian art

The museum's collection of Egyptian art spans a period of roughly 5,000 years, from the Pre-dynastic era through the age of Roman domination. Three vast galleries house antiquities from all major periods of Egyptian civilization. The central gallery introduces ancient Egypt through a variety of topics: the relationship of Egypt to surrounding societies, the place of women, farming and culture, and the importance of the River Nile. Two galleries on the right contain works from Pre-dynastic Egypt (6th–3rd centuries BC) through the early New Kingdom (2nd century BC). Galleries to the left contain artifacts from the early New Kingdom through the Roman Period (1st century BC and 1st century AD).

(a) Egypt Reborn (introductory gallery): This gallery gives an overview of Egyptian society and features works from the entire range of Egyptian history. Ceramics, jewelry, small ritual objects and utilitarian items (combs, cosmetic containers, and mirrors) all give a sense of daily life. Statuary indicates mastery of a wide range of materials, from stone and ceramics to painted wood. Varying styles of portraiture show the assimilation of different cultures which alternately subjugated Egypt or fell under its rule, including Persia, Nubia, Greece, and Rome.

Especially interesting are the head of a man with tight curly hair (marble, Ptolemaic period, c. 100 BC); the lyrical boy with a floral garland in his hair (tempera on wood, Roman period, AD 200–230); an engaging head and torso of a noblewoman (Middle Kingdom, c. 1844–1837 BC.); and a jar with boat designs (Pre-dynastic period, c. 3450–3350 BC). Pre-dynastic art begins on the gallery's right wall and continues in the adjacent chamber. Near the door stands one of the museum's oldest treasures, a terra-cotta "Bird Lady" of 3650–3300 BC, excavated during the first of the museum's many Egyptian expeditions.

(b–c) Egypt Reborn (early Egypt): A small chamber **(b)** displays objects from the Neolithic period, when farming communities dotted the shores of the Nile and Egypt had not yet been unified under one ruler. Vessels of carved stone, crude ceramics, and jewelry were found in Naqada, a river community in southern Egypt involved in the early gold trade. Diminutive zoomorphic figures and an offering table are associated with early religious practices. An extraordinary carved lion's head dates from 3200–3000 BC.

In the large chamber beyond **(c)** are objects from the earliest dynasties (2972–1540 BC). Here are alabaster vases from the burial site of Djoser, the king who raised the first pyramid; and a huge stone sarcophagus from Giza, site of the Great Sphinx and the largest pyramid of all, that of Khufu (Cheops). Old Kingdom sculptures in stone and painted wood depict early kings and court officials. There are also contemporary goods produced throughout the Aegean and Mediterranean region, including a spectacular Minoan jug decorated with octopi, aquatic plants and fishermen's nets (c. 1575–1500 BC).

The gallery ends with objects from the early 18th Dynasty of the New Kingdom, the beginning of Egypt's great cultural flowering. On display are a Middle Kingdom coffin for Mayet ("Kitty"), child bride of King Mentuhotep II; an elegant relief of Amunhotep I bearing the White Crown of Upper Egypt (New Kingdom, c. 1514–1493 BC); and the colorful tomb painting of a woman with offerings (New Kingdom, c. 1539–1425).

(d–g) Rubin Galleries (later Egypt):
Returning through the introductory gallery, the visitor finds a small chamber **(d)** with treasures from the reign of Akhenaten (14th century BC; Amarna period, 18th Dynasty), the revolutionary young pharaoh who established a monotheistic religion centered on the worship of Aten, a sun god of his own devising. Despite his radical impact on Egyptian religion, Akhenaten has been overshadowed in the modern imagination by his dazzling queen, Nefertiti (whose elegant bust sits in the Altes Museum, Berlin). This room allows an exceptional opportunity to become acquainted with an ancient pharaoh and his consort; for Akhenaten quickly established a new symbolic idiom focused on the daily life of his own family, which he imbued with mystical properties. After his death, Akhenaten became widely reviled as polytheistic practices were re-established, and many objects produced during his reign, including images of himself and the queen, were vandalized.

Just inside the main gallery **(e)** are spectacular works from the glittering reigns of Tutankhamun (ruled c. 1336–1327 BC) and Ramesses II (ruled 1279–1223 BC). On view are a gorgeous blue faïence necklace and other luxurious objects, important tomb reliefs, statuettes and papyri.

The gallery ends with the Ptolemaic period. In 332 BC Alexander the Great wrested Egypt from the Persians and established his seat of government at Alexandria. Upon his death in 323, Ptolemy, general of his legion, declared himself ruler and established a new dynasty which lasted until the reign of Cleopatra, ultimately defeated at Actium by Octavian (later Augustus Caesar) in 31 BC. Sculpture here shows the reigning influence of Hellenism, best seen in the famous Brooklyn Black Head (50 BC), a colossal head of a man whose strong features and curly hairstyle combine Egyptian artistic traditions with Greek influences.

The last galleries **(f–g)** are devoted to religion and burial traditions. The display includes funerary objects, sarcophagi, and depictions of major gods and goddesses. Shown are a wooden figure of Anubis, canine guardian of the dead (c. 664–30 BC) and mummies of sacred animals. A

large wooden coffin of a man named Kemy is from the New Kingdom (1539–1295 BC). Tomb statues, a small painted canopic chest, funeral stelae, offering basins, and many other objects provide a highly detailed overview of burial practices and beliefs about the afterlife.

The final chamber contains objects traditionally incorporated in burials. Reliefs from the tomb of Nespeqashuty (26th Dynasty) adorn two walls. Underneath are arranged the coffin and mummy of Thothirdes (Late Period, c. 564–525 BC), canopic jars for preserving organs (New Kingdom, reign of Ramesses II), and ritual statuettes. Faïence amulets of blue and green (Late period c. 664–after 30 BC) were intended to protect the soul and guarantee its resurrection in the afterlife.

Fourth floor

On this floor are the new (2007) Center for Feminist Art and selections from the decorative arts collection, including several period rooms.
NB: Many of the decorative arts galleries were closed at the time of writing.

Feminist art
Judy Chicago's iconic feminist mixed-media installation *The Dinner Party* (1974–79) occupies center stage in the Elizabeth Sackler Center for Feminist Art. Installed in a triangular exhibition hall, the work honors 39 women—from the Primordial Goddess to Georgia O'Keeffe—who, symbolically, have places at the triangular ceremonial banquet table. Each place setting consists of a goblet, a painted ceramic plate, and an embroidered runner, whose decoration signifies the woman being honored. The names of another 999 women are inscribed on the floor.

An adjacent biographical gallery presents exhibitions highlighting the women represented in *The Dinner Party*. There is also gallery space for a regular exhibition schedule of feminist art. In the corner gallery, facing the atrium, a long-term installation of ceramics by women artists in the museum's collection focuses on work from the 20th century, but also offers 19th-century examples of "china painting," and work by Native American artisans.

Period rooms
The John D. Rockefeller House at 4 West 54th St was purchased by the oil tycoon in 1864–65 from Arabella Worsham, who later married railroad magnate Collis P. Huntington. The opulent Near Eastern appearance of the Moorish smoking room reflects Worsham's taste.

The most recent of the period rooms is the Worgelt Study, a room from a Park Avenue apartment designed by the Parisian decorating firm of Alavoine in 1928–30. The Art Deco appointments of the room include the olive and palisander wood paneling, a metal Modernist window, and an abstract geometric panel behind the sofa. Behind a discreet door in the original apartment was a small walk-in bar, hidden because of Prohibition.

Several rooms of the Civil War era give the visitor a sense of the richness and luxury of Victorian decor, which is hard to glean from individual pieces of furniture.

Fifth floor

Luce Center for American Art
American painting, sculpture and decorative art are displayed in a series of galleries devoted to various aspects of the American experience. Although the recent redesign of the galleries and the Visible Storage study space does not serve the art well, the collection remains one of the greatest gatherings of American art and design in the US. The display is thematic, and is organized as follows:

A Brooklyn Orientation: This provides a cultural introduction to the borough. Two views of the Brooklyn Bridge by Georgia O'Keeffe and Samuel Halpert provide modern interpretations of its bold neo-Gothic form. William Glackens presents another modern perspective with his *East River Park* (1902). *Winter Scene in Brooklyn* (c. 1819–20; *illustrated on p. 462*) by Francis Guy lovingly depicts the puffing chimneys and stout clapboard houses of a bygone age. Daniel Huntington's *The Sketcher: A Portrait of Mlle Rosina, a Jewess* (1858) is a charming example of the neo-Renaissance style which flourished during the Beaux-Arts era.

Locally produced furniture and ceramics enhance appreciation of the borough as a vital center of craft production, especially during the Victorian era. A "century" vase, sporting a dizzying array of patriotic motifs—including buffalo head handles—is one of a pair designed by Karl Müller for the nation's Centennial Exhibition in Philadelphia (1876). (The other vase is at the High Museum of Art in Atlanta.) The manufacturer, Union Porcelain Works of Greenpoint, Brooklyn, was among the firms working to wean American consumers from fashionable European imports

From Colony to Nation: The first section of this gallery is devoted to art of the Colonial and Revolutionary periods. Isolated from the European spirit of Romanticism, some American artists forged a naïve style of folk painting—as seen in the two anonymously painted portraits *Woman with an Arrow* and *Woman with a Mirror* (both c. 1715). Other artists relied on older traditions of English painting. Further along are works of the Revolutionary period. Painting, including *Jonas Platt* (c. 1827–28) by Samuel F.B. Morse and pendant portraits of *Mr. and Mrs. David Leavitt* (c. 1820–25) by Samuel Lovett Waldo, shows the influence of the prevailing French style. The section culminates with two portraits of George Washington, one (1776) by Charles Willson Peale; the other (1796) a rendering of the standing figure known as the Lansdowne portrait, by Gilbert Stuart.

Inventing the American Landscape: During the post-Revolutionary period the spirit of Romanticism swept across America, inspiring exploration of the continent's natural beauty; the young nation was in an expansive mood and artists expressed all the optimism of the Great Experiment with a new subject: the

American landscape. The most dramatic work here is Albert Bierstadt's *A Storm in the Rocky Mountains—Mt. Rosalie* (1866), which depicts on an enormous canvas a mountain lake amongst verdant greenery, staggering cliffs, and luminescent clouds. Later landscapes by Arthur Dove, Marsden Hartley and Diego Rivera are highly imaginative examples of abstraction inspired by nature.

Everyday Life: This gallery reflects the development of American society during the 19th century, as represented in its painting and decorative art. Social customs, slavery, and the position of women are all examined.

Tracing American portraiture from the Revolutionary era to the dawn of the 20th century, the exhibit opens with the tender, naïve *Portrait of Jacob Anderson and His Sons* (c. 1812–15) by Joshua Johnson, a highly successful black painter active in the early 19th century. The informal mood of English Romanticism enters with Joseph Blackburn's *Portrait of a Woman* (1762) and a stunning portrait by Rembrandt Peale of his daughters, *The Sisters, Eleanor and Rosalba* (1826). Among the later works, a casually elegant *Lydia Field Emmett* (1892) by William Merritt Chase and Jane E. Bartlett's bold portrait of *Sarah Cowell LeMoyne* (1877) display the confidence of a new class of cultured women.

Several genre paintings by Thomas Cole, Asher Durand, and others depict the simple pleasures of rural life. Eldzier Cortor's *Southern Landscape (Southern Flood)* (1939–40) and *Louisiana Rice Fields* (1928) by Thomas Hart Benton present different views of the African-American experience.

Displays of china and an extravagant mantelpiece by the Herter brothers suggest the refinement of an established and acquisitive upper class.

A Nation Divided: This exhibit concerns slavery and the Civil War. A serious tone is set with two works by Augustus Saint-Gaudens: a bust of Lincoln (1922) and a figure of Victory from the Robert Gould Shaw Memorial, which honors Colonel Robert Shaw, commander of the first black regiment in the Union Army.

Dominating the room is a version of Hiram Powers's white marble nude, *The Greek Slave* (1869). Its subject is the Greek War of Independence, during which Christian Greeks were sold into slavery by the Turks. The first version of this Neoclassical sculpture was exhibited in 1844 and achieved such fame that Powers made six full-scale models. In time the piece became associated with anti-slavery sentiment.

Several paintings address the same theme. The dramatic *Ride for Liberty: The Fugitive Slaves* (c. 1862) by famed genre painter Eastman Johnson depicts a slave family racing towards liberty on horseback. Two men actively involved in the emancipation movement, Henry Ward Beecher and General Charles Frémont, are celebrated in portraits by George Baker and Charles Loring Elliott respectively. The most unusual object here is an 18th-century earthenware bowl inscribed with anti-slavery sentiments, which was excavated near Albany.

Expanding Horizons: This gallery considers exoticism in late 19th-century American art. During this period the establishment of the British Raj in India,

the opening of the Suez Canal, and the end of the Dutch monopoly on trade with Japan all encouraged interest in what was loosely called the "Orient." Advances in steamship technology also encouraged trade and travel, making a tour abroad essential for Americans seeking cultural sophistication.

Artists traveling through the Middle East developed the Orientalist style, featuring a romanticized view rendered in a sensuous brand of Realism. Paintings in this vein by Louis Comfort Tiffany, William Merritt Chase, and Frederick Arthur Bridgman all achieve a gemlike quality with careful attention to color and light.

Fascination with the Far East inspired *Japonisme*, represented here with stunning furniture, *objets d'art*, and a lovely portrait by William Merritt Chase: *Girl in a Japanese Costume* (c. 1890). The section ends with works by American artists traveling in Europe, among them Daniel Ridgway Knight, *The Shepherdess of Rolleboise* (1896); Frederic Edwin Church, *Tropical Scenery* (1873); Frank Duveneck, *Villa Castellani* (1887), and John Singer Sargent, *Paul Helleu Sketching with his Wife* (1889). This painting of an artist and his bride on their honeymoon shows Sargent's interest in French Impressionism, which he cultivated after he moved to England in 1885. Helleu, incidentally, painted the star-studded ceiling of the Great Concourse at Grand Central Station.

Artmaking: This exhibit covers American art from the Federal period through the early 20th century by two groups of artists: untrained artists working in naïve or folk traditions, and artists who attended art academies. Though this theme can create confusion, there are many fine pieces here.

Folk art on display includes work by two prominent self-taught painters: the Rev. Edward Hicks, *The Peaceable Kingdom* (1833–34), and Ammi Phillips, whose pendant portraits of Colonel Nathan and Betsey Beckwith (c. 1817) hang directly across the gallery.

Sculpture of the early 18th century includes an allegorical figure of Winter (1811) by William Rush, the son of a ship's carpenter, who came to be known as America's first sculptor. Important pieces of sculpture include Charles Dodge's wooden bust of his wife (1839–40), Elie Nadelman's *Dancing Figure* (1916–18), Malvina Hoffman's *Martinique Woman* (1927), and Augustus Saint-Gaudens's *Diana of the Tower* (c. 1895). At the end of the gallery are paintings by Thomas Eakins, Winslow Homer and Albert Pinkham Ryder.

Whimsical ceramics and simple furniture are indicative of a young nation isolated from European traditions, striving to forge its own cultural identity.

The Centennial Era: The Neoclassical spirit ran high during the late 19th century, and sculpture was central to the Beaux-Arts celebration of opulent splendor. Artists represented here often worked with the city's leading architectural firms, such as McKim, Mead & White, to embellish their imposing edifices.

Frederick William MacMonnies' bronze statuette of Nathan Hale was commissioned by the Sons of the Revolution of New York State for the Centennial. It honors the young school teacher and lieutenant of the Continental Army executed

for spying by the British (*see p. 82*). Another model sits in Fraunces Tavern Museum.

Augustus Saint-Gaudens's funerary panel *Amor Caritas* (1889) hangs nearby. The title may suggest a meditation on two types of love, the earthly (*amor*) and the spiritual (*caritas*). Saint-Gaudens executed 20 variants of this work, one of which is owned by the Metropolitan Museum of Art.

The lighter side of Beaux-Arts is captured in an ebullient *Bacchante* (1894), also by MacMonnies, who had studied under Saint-Gaudens. A bronze original was given by the sculptor to architect Charles McKim for his Boston Public Library. Though the work was soon removed from the library after opposition from the Woman's Christian Temperance Union, it was immensely popular and MacMonnies made several copies.

Seated Faun (1924) is by MacMonnies' first female student, Janet Scudder, whose ingenious garden sculptures often featured mythological figures or children at play. Inspired by the *putti*, the cherubic children who cavorted on the tombs and choir screens of the Renaissance, her work epitomizes the nostalgic character of the Beaux-Arts.

Modern Life: The last gallery offers a limited overview of modern painting and decorative art, with many other works scattered among other rooms, and more examples of modern design shown in the Visible Storage gallery nearby.

A chair and vase by Frank Lloyd Wright introduce the simplified lines inspired by the streamlining of Machine Age production. Wright minimized

ornament in his designs, allowing their functional elements to define their forms. This aesthetic was refined further during the Art Deco period; the furniture, sculpture, and metalwork on display are all redolent of an age captivated by technological innovation. Artists moved towards more organic forms in the mid-century, a trend exemplified by Isamu Noguchi's triangular wood and glass coffee table of 1944.

Painting of the era before World War II falls into three general categories. The theme of urban chaos is taken up in Everett Shinn's *Keith's Union Square* (c. 1902–06), John Sloan's *Haymarket* (1907), Walt Kuhn's *The Dressing Room* (1926), Reginald Marsh's *The Bowl* (1933), and Mark Rothko's *The Subway* (1936), all of which express defiance of social conventions in an age of turbulent economic growth. The industrial landscape is explored by Edward Hopper in *Macomb's Dam Bridge* (1935), in Charles Sheeler's *Incantation* (1946), Edward Dreis's *Gravel Silo* (c. 1930s), Luigi Lucioni's *Barre Granite Shed* (1931), George Bellows's *Morning Snow–Hudson River* (1910), and Maurice Kish's *Job Hunters* (1932–33).

Various forms of Abstraction appear in Marsden Hartley's *Painting No. 48 Berlin*, Gertrude Greene's *Construction in Ochre* (1941), Josef Albers's *Homage to the Square* (1957), three pieces by Stuart Davis, and a contemporary work by Ross Bleckner: *Green Hands and Faces* (1994).

Also here are paintings by Georgia O'Keeffe, and some small but noteworthy sculpture, including Isamu Noguchi's *My Uncle* (1934) and Robert Laurent's *The Wave* (1926).

PROSPECT PARK & ENVIRONS

Map p. 573. Subway: 2, 3 to Grand Army Plaza. The park and its sights are accessible Sat, Sun, and holidays 12–6 via the free Heart of Brooklyn Trolley. It leaves Wollman Rink in Prospect Park on the hour, circulates through the park, and stops at Grand Army Plaza (15mins past the hour), in front of the Brooklyn Museum (20 past), the Brooklyn Botanic Garden (25 past), and the bus stop near the newsstand in Grand Army Plaza again (30 past).
Prospect Park, 526 acres of meadows, woods, and lakes designed by Frederick Law Olmsted and Calvert Vaux, is the largest park in Brooklyn. Laid out by its designers (1866–67) after they had cut their teeth on Central Park, Prospect Park is thought by many to be their masterpiece. Today, in addition to Olmsted's beautifully enhanced landscape, there are picnic grounds, a bandstand for summer concerts and events, a small urban zoo, a nature center and nature trails, a carousel, and a skating rink.

Grand Army Plaza

Outside the northwestern gate of Prospect Park lies Grand Army Plaza (1867). Designers Olmsted and Vaux conceived of the area as a formal entrance to their magnificent park, finding inspiration in Baron Georges Haussmann's dramatic modernization of Paris, which emphasized grandeur and urban planning on a Roman scale. French Neoclassicism had informed the work of American artists since the Revolutionary period, and here its influence can be seen in urban design. The sweeping prospects and wide boulevards, patterned after Haussmann's Place de l'Étoile-Place Charles de Gaulle, are a welcome departure from the city's utilitarian grid pattern, allowing the visitor a panoramic view of the surrounding architecture, sculpture and greenery.

The addition of the **Soldiers' and Sailors' Arch** by John H. Duncan brought an overtly political element to the Beaux-Arts theme. This monument memorialized defenders of the Union in the Civil War, and its reference to Napoleon's Arc de Triomphe in Paris identified the Northern victory with the democratic French Republic and the true spirit of the American Revolution. Despite its heroic subject and grand proportions (80ft wide by 80ft high, with an arch attaining 50ft), the monument was considered artistically negligible at the time of its dedication in 1892, and its ornamentation was subsequently overseen by Stanford White. Sculptural groupings by Frederick MacMonnies (1863–1937) representing the Spirit of the Army and Spirit of the Navy were installed on either side of the arch. The figure of *Columbia*, a female allegory of the United States, appears on top of the arch, bearing a sword and flag and riding a quadriga, or Roman chariot drawn by four horses. Above the inner doorway to the arch are bas-reliefs of Lincoln and Ulysses S. Grant astride their horses. The men were sculpted by William O'Donovan (1894); the horses are by Thomas Eakins.

North of the arch is the **Mary Louise Bailey Fountain** (1932), surrounded by London plane and Callery pear trees. The fountain is a delightful hodgepodge of period styles. Art Deco allegories of *Felicity* and *Wisdom* stand above a neo-Baroque pedestal in the shape of a ship's prow. Neptune and sportive tritons splash and blow their conch-shell horns in a rocky basin reminiscent of Italian Renaissance grottos.

To the east and west of the central ellipse are earthen berms erected by Olmsted and Vaux to isolate the Plaza from traffic and noise. Sculptures of two prominent Brooklynites—pioneer gynecologist Alexander Skene (1905; J. Massey Rhind) and banker/philanthropist Henry Maxwell (1903; Augustus Saint-Gaudens)—are located northeast of the Plaza (Maxwell on the exterior side of the berm). Statues of Civil War figures Gouverneur Kemble Warren (1896; Henry Baerer) and General Henry Warner Slocum (1905; Frederick W. MacMonnies), both of whom led troops at Gettysburg, can be seen at the southern ends of the two berms.

The plaza's Beaux-Arts elegance was made complete with Stanford White's embellishment of the park entrance in the late 1890s. He installed four Doric columns, decorated at the base with axes and rams' heads and topped with soaring eagles; snake-handled urns (since replaced with replicas); and charming shelters for pedestrians in the manner of Chinese pagodas. Inside the entrance stands a statue of the "Father of Prospect Park" James Stranahan (1891; Frederick MacMonnies), whose tireless advocacy for public gardens in Brooklyn is largely responsible for the park we enjoy today.

The Brooklyn Botanic Garden

1000 Washington Ave (Eastern Pkwy). Other entrances from parking lot behind the Brooklyn Museum, and near the subway stop (trains 2, 3) at Eastern Pkwy. Open mid-March–Oct Tues–Fri 8–6, weekends and holidays 10–6. Restricted hours Nov–mid March. Closed Mon (except Mon holidays), Labor Day, Thanksgiving, Christmas Day, New Year's Day. Admission charge except Tues (unless a holiday) and Sat until noon. Free weekdays mid-Nov–Feb; T: 718 623 7200: www.bbg.org. Visitor Center on Magnolia Plaza, near Washington Ave.

Hedged around with asphalt and apartment houses, the Brooklyn Botanic Garden is an urban paradise of trees and flowers. A grand plot of 52 acres, the gardens offer plant enthusiasts and dedicated horticulturists a place of verdant beauty for education and enjoyment. Within the park are lawns dotted with fountains, trellises, and ornamental trees. Magnificent specimens of oak and pine soar above the perennial borders, duck ponds, and patches of spring flowers. Also within the grounds are small gardens devoted to different themes: gardens of herbs and native plants, a scent garden, a children's garden, and a rock garden with a bubbling waterfall. Highlights include the world-renowned Japanese garden, a Shakespeare garden featuring plants from the Bard's lexicon, and the glorious Cranford Rose Garden.

In the conservatories are rooms devoted to tropical forests, deserts, and temperate zones, each containing plants from all over the world. One gallery is dedicated to the evolution of plant life on earth. Nearby is a hothouse full of aquatic plants and orchids. The exquisite Bonsai Museum is one of the garden's finest features.

The Brooklyn Academy of Music (BAM)

Beyond map p. 470. Peter Jay Sharp Building, 30 Lafayette Ave (Ashland Pl and St. Felix St); Harvey Lichtenstein Theater, 651 Fulton St (Ashland Pl and Rockwell Pl); T: 718 636 4100, www.bam.org. Subway: B, Q, 2, 3, 4, 5 to Atlantic Ave; C to Lafayette Ave; D, M, N, R to Pacific St. The easiest way to attend a performance from Manhattan is to take BAMbus, which

travels between Manhattan and the academy before and after performances; reservations required 24hrs in advance; T: 718 636 4100.

The Brooklyn Academy of Music, the borough's most important performing arts venue, was founded in 1861 as the home of the Brooklyn Philharmonic. The building burned in 1902, replaced by the present neo-Italianate hall (1908), designed by Herts & Tallant, prominent theater architects. In its glory days, famous performers appeared here: Enrico Caruso and Geraldine Farrar, singing with the Metropolitan Opera, inaugurated the Academy with *Faust*; in 1920 Caruso suffered a throat hemorrhage onstage after the first act of *L'Elisir d'Amore*; he gave only three more performances and died within the year.

Brooklyn's decline after World War II pulled the academy down with it, until the organization was reduced to renting out studios for language and martial arts classes Beginning in 1967, Harvey Lichtenstein, a dancer-turned-arts administrator, brought it back from cultural limbo by dint of daring programming, broadening its offerings to include theater, opera, dance, and world music. He also established the Next Wave Festival, which drew crowds from Manhattan, breaking BAM's parochial isolation.

Green-Wood Cemetery

Map p. 573. Fifth to McDonald Aves, 20th–37th Sts. Subway: M or R to 25th St. Main entrance open 8–5 daily, weather permitting, extended hours in summer. Guided tours offered by cemetery historian; T: 718 768 7300; www.green-wood.com. Self-guided tour booklets for sale.

Green-Wood Cemetery, 478 acres rising to Brooklyn's highest point (216ft above sea level) was the chosen burial place of so many late 19th-century New Yorkers that the *Times* reported in 1866 that "it is the ambition of the New Yorker to live upon the Fifth Avenue, to take his airings in the [Central] Park, and to sleep with his fathers in Green-Wood." The cemetery offers both nature and art. The landscape takes advantage of the hills and valleys left by the glaciers that reached south into Brooklyn. The monuments in the cemetery, some of them extravagant, were created by prominent architects as well as anonymous sculptors. Architects Warren & Wetmore (Grand Central Terminal), Griffith Thomas (cast-iron buildings in SoHo), and Stanford White (Washington Square Arch, the second Madison Square Garden, and many other buildings) all left memorials here for wealthy clients. The Gothic Revival gates are by Richard Upjohn. Among those sleeping with their fathers in Green-Wood are politician William M. "Boss" Tweed (*see p. 86*), composer Leonard Bernstein, designer Louis Comfort Tiffany, artist William Merritt Chase, architect Jacob Wrey Mould, and newspaper editor Horace Greeley.

CONEY ISLAND

Map p. 5. Subway: D, F, Q, and N train to Stillwell Ave; the ride takes 45mins–1hr.

Coney Island is no longer the empire of the nickel, the great populist playground, where anyone who could afford the subway could bathe in the Atlantic and enjoy a midway with rides and sideshows. The frayed amusement strip along the boardwalk has been shrinking for decades, and its future is uncertain. Yet in the popular imagination Coney

Island survives as an archetype of American honky-tonk—the birthplace of the hot dog and home of the world's most terrifying roller coaster—a place remarkable for high energy and dubious taste.

Coney Island was settled by the Dutch, who named it *Konijn Eiland* after the rabbits they found there. Its history as a resort started with the Coney Island Hotel (1829), but its golden age began around the turn of the 20th century when three spectacular amusement parks opened: Steeplechase Park (1897), with a horserace ride, funhouse mirrors, and jets of air that sent women's skirts overhead; Luna Park (1903), tricked out with a million electric light bulbs; and Dreamland (1904). More sedate and less financially successful than Luna Park, Dreamland burned in 1911. The island was joined by landfill to the mainland early in the 20th century, so it is no longer an island, but a peninsula.

During the 1920s and '30s huge crowds thronged the boardwalk (opened 1923) or lay thigh to thigh on the sand. But by the 1940s the crowds were thinning, thanks to the rise of the automobile, the development of air-conditioning, and the policies of Parks Commissioner Robert Moses, who built parks and beaches that would lure people to more salutary forms of entertainment. In 1964 Steeplechase Park closed. In the following decades, urban renewal programs filled Coney Island's massive housing projects with the elderly, blacks, and Latinos. At present, Coney Island is once again in flux. Many of the amusements have been torn down or sold off, leaving empty buildings and vacant lots. However, three classic rides have been landmarked and cannot be destroyed: the Parachute Jump (*not operative*), the Cyclone roller coaster, and the Wonder Wheel. In 2007, the city announced a plan to rebuild the amusement area along the boardwalk, but past plans have come and gone without being implemented.

The non-profit **Coney Island History Project**, tucked away in a former souvenir shop under the Cyclone roller coaster (*Boardwalk at West 10th St; Fri–Sun 12–6; T: 718 265 2100; www.coneyislandhistory.org*), offers photos and artifacts highlighting the past. The exhibition includes the Coney Island Hall of Fame, among whose inductees is Charles Feltman, who allegedly invented the hot dog by putting the frankfurter into a bun (to avoid having to provide his customers with silverware). **Coney Island USA**, a second not-for-profit organization, strives to "defend the honor of American popular art forms" through programs and exhibitions that include Sideshows by the Seashore and the Mermaid Parade, held on the first summer weekend, a joyously garish procession with sea-themed costumes and some cheerful near-nudity. Coney Island USA also sponsors the small **Coney Island Museum** at 1208 Surf Ave (*open Sat and Sun all year 12–5; T: 718 372 5159; www.coneyisland.com*).

Coney Island once had a large Italian population; several restaurants remain from those days. Totonno's is a classic pizzeria that opened in 1924 (*1524 Neptune Ave between West 15th and West 16th Sts; T: 718 372 8606; www.totonnos.com*). Gargiulo's is even older (1907), a large restaurant offering large servings of southern Italian food (*2911 West 15th St between Mermaid and Surf Aves; closed Tues; T: 718 266 4891; www.gargiulos.com*).

Also in Coney Island are **Nathan's Famous**, the iconic hot dog stand founded in 1916 at 1316 Surf Ave (Stillwell Ave), and the **New York Aquarium** (T: 718 265 FISH), located at Surf Ave and West 8th St.

BOROUGH OF QUEENS
(QUEENS COUNTY)

The borough of Queens (*map p. 573*), the largest in the city, covers 112.2 square miles (about 35 percent of the city's total area) and is bounded by Brooklyn on the west, the East River on the north, the Atlantic Ocean on the south, and Nassau County on the east. Topographically it resembles the rest of Long Island, with a chain of hills created by glacial deposits running across the north and a low outwash plain in the south. The north shore is indented by Flushing and Little Neck Bays, while the Rockaway peninsula juts across the mouth of Jamaica Bay in the south to form a 10-mile ocean-front.

Queens is the second most populous borough (pop. 2,255,175), surpassed only by Brooklyn. About 48 percent of the population is foreign-born, making Queens by far the nation's most diverse county; more than 130 languages are spoken here. The number 7 subway train, from Times Square to Flushing, has been dubbed the "International Express" because it traverses so many different ethnic communities.

Queens is largely residential, with one- and two-family homes and apartment buildings of various heights, but it lacks the concentration of 19th-century brownstones and tenements that characterize Manhattan, Brooklyn, and the Bronx. Some of its wealthier neighborhoods—Kew Gardens, Forest Hills, Douglaston—are almost suburban in character, with detached houses, attractive gardens, and garages for that definitive suburban vehicle, the family car (or cars). At the other end of the economic scale are slums in South Jamaica, the Rockaways, and some older industrial areas. While Queens has earned its reputation as a bedroom community in the past half century, areas that developed earlier became industrial, with concentrations of factories in the vicinity of Long Island City, Maspeth and College Point, and along the right-of-way of the Long Island Rail Road. Commercial centers are scattered throughout the borough, usually located at the crossroads of earlier towns, established independently before the creation of Greater New York in 1898: the most important ones are Jamaica, Flushing, and Elmhurst.

Because of its former spaciousness and an 1851 law prohibiting further burials in Manhattan, Queens became the resting place of uncounted souls. Many lie in the belt of cemeteries that begins on the Brooklyn-Queens border and stretches eastward along the Jackie Robinson Parkway, an area known by the waggish as the "terminal moraine."

More than any other borough, Queens bears the stamp of Robert Moses, who as parks commissioner preserved acres and acres of forests, meadow, beaches, and marshes, while as master road builder he blighted equally large areas by lacing the borough with highways: the Grand Central Parkway, Interborough (now Jackie Robinson) Parkway, Clearview Expressway, Cross Island Parkway, Laurelton Parkway, Long Island Expressway, Brooklyn-Queens Expressway, and the Whitestone Expressway.

The presence of two of New York's major airports, John F. Kennedy and LaGuardia, make transportation-related industries critical to the borough's economy. Some manufacturing jobs remain, as well as service jobs in business and healthcare. TV and motion picture production studios have returned to Long Island City, across the river from mid-

town Manhattan. Two major sports venues are Shea Stadium, home of the New York Mets baseball team, and the United States Tennis Association National Tennis Center in Flushing Meadows-Corona Park, where the US Open is played.

HISTORY OF QUEENS

The first inhabitants of Queens were the Rockaway Indians, whose name lives on in the peninsula stretching across Jamaica Bay. The first settlers were Dutch, who arrived c. 1635, followed by the English some 20 years later. Gradually the Dutch staked out their claims to the western part of Long Island, while the English colonized the eastern part. In 1683, 19 years after the British took title to the former Dutch colony of New Amsterdam, the towns of Newtown, Flushing, and Jamaica were organized as Queens County, one of 12 making up the British province of New York. The name honors Catherine of Braganza, queen of Charles II. During the Revolution most residents of Queens were British sympathizers, and after the war many loyalists emigrated to Newfoundland.

Although a few industries, notably Steinway pianos, established manufacturing plants in Queens during the 19th century, the borough long remained rural and agricultural. As the railroads began pushing east across Long Island, the beaches began attracting summer residents: at the turn of the 20th century the land now occupied by LaGuardia Airport held an amusement park, and the Rockaways—whose remoteness is enshrined in the place name of its easternmost settlement, Far Rockaway—attracted the well-to-do to grand hotels or private estates.

In 1898 most of Queens joined Greater New York, although several of the eastern towns chose to remain independent. The population of 152,999 tripled in the next 20 years and doubled again between 1920 and 1930, as transit links opened Queens to development. In 1910 the Queensboro Bridge and the East River tunnel of the Pennsylvania Railroad allowed direct access to Manhattan, while during the next decades the subways reached the outer areas. The Triborough Bridge (1936), the Bronx–Whitestone Bridge (1939), the Queens–Midtown Tunnel (1939), and most recently the Throgs Neck Bridge (1961) made Queens readily accessible by car.

In 1939–40 the first of two world's fairs was held in Flushing Meadows, and several of these public works projects along with the development of LaGuardia Airport were undertaken to coincide with its opening. After World War II, Queens experienced its second great boom, one that took the form of suburban development as builders grabbed whatever open space remained and erected acre after acre of tract housing, small homes on small lots, monotonously repeated row upon row, block upon block. Despite the blandness of much of Queens's suburban development, its very newness has saved the borough from some of the problems of urban blight that afflict Manhattan, Brooklyn, and the Bronx.

Visiting Queens

A casual glance at a road map may make it appear that Queens is laid out in a regular rectilinear pattern, but it is deceptively difficult to find your way around. Numbered avenues generally run east–west (with the lower numbers on the north), but they are sometimes interspersed with Roads, Drives, and even an occasional Court bearing the same number. Streets generally run generally north–south, with lower numbers on the west. The pattern is further complicated by the vestiges of old roads dating from the colonial period, which often followed Native American paths, which in turn conformed to topographical features long erased by landfill or leveling. Modern highways have disrupted the continuity of street layouts as well as the social fabric of the neighborhoods they cross. Finally, developers have created special patterns arcs or crescents, for example—in communities such as Forest Hills Gardens that were developed all at once as planned communities or for real estate speculation. However, it's reasonable to assume that, say, 30–22 45th St is on 45th St between 31st and 32nd Aves.

LONG ISLAND CITY

In recent years Long Island City, a largely industrial neighborhood, has become a center for contemporary art, particularly sculpture, since its industrial architecture lends itself to the installation of large works. P.S.1 Contemporary Art Center and SculptureCenter are within walking distance of one another, as are the Noguchi Museum and Socrates Sculpture Park.

P.S.1 Contemporary Art Center

22–25 Jackson Ave (46th Ave). Open Thur–Mon 12–6; closed Thanksgiving, Christmas, New Year's Day; T: 718 784 2084; www.ps1.org. Subway: 7 to 45th Rd-Courthouse Sq; exit onto Jackson Ave and walk right one block.

P.S.1, which since 2001 has enjoyed a collaborative partnership with MoMA, is one of the best places in the city to see new and adventurous art, and its roomy, high-ceilinged galleries are well suited to showing site-specific and large-scale works. The center does not have a permanent collection, but there are several long-term installations, including James Turrell's *Meeting*, a "skyspace" in an upper room with shapes cut out of the ceiling to open it to the sky; as the sun sets, the choreographed light within the room changes quickly and sometimes dramatically (*installation open at sunset*).

SculptureCenter

44–19 Purves St (near Jackson Ave). Open Thur–Mon 12–6; T: 718 361 1750; www. sculpture-center.org. Subway: 7 to 45th Rd-Courthouse Sq; turn left onto Jackson Ave and walk three blocks; turn right onto Purves St.

Founded by a group of artists as The Clay Club in 1928, SculptureCenter moved to

Queens in 2002, settling into a former trolley repair shop redesigned by Maya Lin and David Hotson. Though distinguished artists (Isamu Noguchi, Louise Nevelson) have exhibited here, the focus remains on less established names. The 40-ft ceilings and an adjacent lot enclosed by a steel and glass fence allow for the exhibition of large-scale pieces.

Noguchi Museum

9–01 33rd Rd (Vernon Blvd). Open Wed–Fri 10–5, Sat–Sun 11–6; closed Mon, Tues, Thanksgiving, Christmas, New Year's Day. Pay-as-you-wish on first Fri of month. T: 718 204 7088; www.noguchi.org. Easiest access by shuttle bus (Sun only) from the Asia Society (see p 321) in Manhattan; bus leaves at 12:30, 1:30, 2:30, and 3:30. Subway: N (seven days) or W (weekdays) to Broadway in Queens. Walk ten blocks towards the Manhattan skyline. Turn left onto Vernon Blvd (not 11th St). Walk past the Socrates Sculpture Park offices and turn left. Walk two blocks further to 33rd Rd. Entrance at 9–01 33rd Rd, between Vernon Blvd and 10th St.

In the early 1960s Isamu Noguchi moved his studio to Queens from Manhattan, in order to be close to the marble suppliers on Vernon Boulevard. In 1975 he bought a small building, formerly a photo engraving plant, which he used for studio space and for storage; it is now part of the present museum. Over the years Noguchi nurtured the idea of creating a museum to display examples of his work that he had kept for himself, and in 1985 the museum opened. It now houses more than 250 works by the Japanese-born sculptor, whose work blends Modernism with a Japanese artistic sensibility. The collection includes work from all phases of Noguchi's career, from early brass sculpture of the 1920s that shows the influence of Brancusi (for whom he acted as a studio assistant) to his most mature and austere pieces sculpted from basalt and granite. His famous Akari light sculptures and furniture designs are also on view.

The garden, like a traditional Japanese garden, contains objects of both visual and aural pleasure, though the rocks have been chiseled and worked, in contrast to those in a classical Japanese garden, which remain in their natural forms. The well (1982) is a variant on the Japanese *tsukubai*, a hollowed stone into which water trickles, though in Noguchi's rendering the water rises to the surface and slides down the outside.

Socrates Sculpture Park

Vernon Blvd (Broadway). Open all year 10–dusk; T: 718 956 1819; www.socratessculpturepark.org. Subway: N (seven days) or W (weekdays) to Broadway in Queens; walk eight blocks along Broadway toward the East River. Follow directions for Noguchi Museum above. On Sun, you can also take the shuttle to the Noguchi Museum, which is only two blocks away.

Socrates Sculpture Park is an outdoor space for exhibitions of large-scale sculpture. Changing exhibitions by well-known and emerging sculptors are mounted in the spring and fall. Much of the work is created onsite, so visitors can watch art in process. The park is laid out in a four-acre windswept field facing the East River, leased from the city in 1985, and developed as a park largely through the efforts of sculptor Mark Di Suvero.

FLUSHING MEADOWS-CORONA PARK & FLUSHING

Flushing Meadows-Corona Park, girded by the Grand Central Parkway and the Van Wyck Expressway, occupies 1,255 acres running north–south along what was once the Flushing River, a navigable waterway to the old town of Flushing.

FROM DUMP TO PARK

The Flushing Meadows were once salt marshes, inundated by tides and therefore useless for housing. Saved thus from development, the marsh became the Corona Dump and the river an open sewer. By the 1920s trainloads of trash and garbage that arrived daily from Brooklyn smoldered nightly, giving the place a Dantesque aura and inspiring novelist F. Scott Fitzgerald to name it the "Valley of Ashes" in his novel *The Great Gatsby*. The swamp disappeared beneath tons of filth, one mound rising high enough to earn the name Mt. Corona. During the 1930s, Robert Moses converted the marshland into the grounds for the 1939–40 World's Fair, a project that involved channeling part of the Flushing River into a conduit as large as a tube of the Holland Tunnel, building sewage plants to decontaminate Flushing Bay, and removing hundreds of thousands of tons of garbage.

Surviving from the 1964–65 World's Fair is Donald De Lue's 45-ft statue *The Rocket Thrower*, a modestly draped, heavily muscular bronze athlete hurling a missile through a circle of stars. Straight down the mall is the *Unisphere* (1963–64; Gilmore D. Clarke), 700,000 lbs of stainless steel, 12 stories high and 120ft in diameter. Its theme was originally stated as "Man's Achievements on a Shrinking Globe in an Expanding Universe"; it has now come to represent the borough.

The Queens Museum of Art (QMA)

In Flushing Meadows-Corona Park. Subway 7 to Willets Point-Shea Stadium. Walk south past the stadium and tennis center (10–15 mins). Open Wed–Fri 10–5, Sat and Sun 12–5; closed Mon, Tues, and major holidays; T: 718 592 9700; www.queensmuseum.org.

The Queens Museum of Art occupies the former New York City Building (1939; renovated 1994, Rafael Viñoly), built for the city's exhibition in the 1939–40 World's Fair and later used by the United Nations General Assembly before its permanent headquarters was built. The museum has two long-term exhibitions, the Neustadt Collection of Tiffany Lamps, and the New York Panorama. Dr. Egon Neustadt—an immigrant from Austria, orthodontist, and real estate developer—bought his first Tiffany lamp in 1935 at a time when Tiffany designs had fallen from fashion. He became an avid collector, even purchasing 500 crates of glass left over when the company went bankrupt. The New York Panorama is an unforgettable architectural model of the city, commissioned by Robert Moses for the 1964 World's Fair and updated in 1992. It contains 895,000

buildings—every building constructed before 1992 in each of the five boroughs. In addition to its permanent galleries, the museum has an ambitious program of rotating exhibits, many of which focus on New York artists and the urban experience.

Louis Armstrong House

34–56 107th St, Corona. Subway: 7 to 103rd St-Corona Plaza. Walk two blocks north on 103rd St; turn right onto 37th Ave. Walk four short blocks, then turn left onto 107th St. The house is a half-block north of 37th Ave. Open Tues–Fri 10–5, Sat and Sun 12–5 (last tour every day at 4pm); T: 718 478 8274; www.satchmo.net. Guided 40-min tours leave every hour on the hour.

The great jazz trumpeter (1901–71) and his wife Lucille moved into this brick house in 1943 and lived here for the remainder of their lives. When Lucille died in 1983, she left the house to the City of New York to be made into a museum. Queens College, owner of the Louis Armstrong Archives, administers the house which opened to the public in 2003. The house and its furnishings remain much as they were during Armstrong's lifetime, and while the house is modest, there are occasional flamboyant touches: the turquoise kitchen and the mirrored bathroom with gold fixtures. Armstrong described his pleasure in the house in words as distinctive as his musical style: "The house may not be the nicest looking front … But when one visit the Interior of the Armstrong's home they see a whole lot of comfort, happiness & the nicest things. Such as that Wall to Wall Bed." Visitors can hear clips from his home-recorded tapes; changing exhibits chronicle such subjects as Armstrong's relationship with the civil rights movement or his preoccupation with food and weight control.

HISTORIC FLUSHING

Flushing today is an ethnic enclave with a large Chinese, Korean, Indian, and African-American population. Two historic buildings remain from the pre-Revolutionary period: the Friends' Meeting House and Bowne House, both with implications for freedom of religion in the US.

Friends' Meeting House

137–16 Northern Blvd (Linden Pl). Open for worship Sun at 11, tours at 12 or at other times by appointment; T: 718 358 9636; www.nyym.org/flushing. Subway: 7 to Main St, Flushing; walk north to Northern Blvd (four short blocks); turn right and walk half a block. The meeting house is on the right.

The Friends' Meeting House (1694), a simple wooden building with a steep hipped roof and very small windows, has changed little in the past three centuries. The back of the house faces busy Northern Boulevard while the front opens onto a garden and small graveyard, whose stones were unmarked until 1848, in accordance with the Quaker belief that death equalizes everyone. Except for a period during the British occupation (1776–83) when it served as a prison, hay barn, and hospital, the Meeting House has been used continuously for religious services since its construction.

Worship must have been uncomfortable during its first 50 winters, as iron stoves were not installed until 1760; central heating followed two centuries later (1965).

Bowne House

Bowne House (*37–01 Bowne St at 37th Ave. Closed for restoration at the time of writing; T: 718 359 0528; www. bownehouse.org*) is the oldest dwelling in Queens. It was built in 1661 by John Bowne, a Quaker convert born in England. His family and nine generations of his descendants lived here.

The Quakers' heretical beliefs, fanaticism, and ecstatic form of worship (hence their name, "Quakers") drew the wrath of conforming Christians, notably Governor Peter Stuyvesant, who particularly abhorred the sect, and arrested all those who allowed Quakers to meet in their homes. In 1657 he issued an edict declaring the Dutch Reformed Church the only permitted religion in the colony. Thirty Flushing farmers (or freeholders) responded with the Flushing Remonstrance, which rebuked Stuyvesant for curbing religious freedoms that had been promised them by the original charter of the town. Stuyvesant then arrested and fined several of the signatories. John Bowne subsequently let the Quakers meet in his kitchen, and in 1662 Stuyvesant fined Bowne and banished him to Holland. Bowne pleaded his cause with the Dutch West India Company, and the business-minded company directors advised Stuyvesant to moderate his antagonism, stressing that increased immigration to the underpopulated colony was more important than religious conformity.

ASTORIA

The Astoria section of Queens is still the place outside Greece with the largest number of people of Greek heritage, though today it also has growing Arab and Latino populations. Before World War II, Astoria was a center of the film-making industry, when the Famous Players-Lasky Corporation was one of the nation's most important studios. Gloria Swanson, Paul Robeson, the Marx Brothers, and Rudolf Valentino all worked there. During World War II, the US army took over the property, turning out training films and propaganda. After the government departed in 1971, the Astoria Motion Picture and Television Foundation was formed to restore the studios. The result is the most successful film-making property on the East Coast.

The **Museum of the Moving Image** (*35th Ave at 36th St. Open Wed and Thur 11–5, Fri 11–8 (free after 4), Sat and Sun 11–6:30; T: 718 784 0077; www.movingimage.us. Subway: N to Broadway in Queens; walk east to 36th St; turn right and walk two blocks to 35th Ave*) is one of the biggest tourist attractions in Queens. Its core exhibit, Behind the Screen, looks at the technical aspects of producing movies and TV. Tut's Fever Movie Palace, where classic serials are shown, is a tongue-in-check rendering of a 1920s movie palace, with Egyptoid figures of movie greats (Mae West standing behind the candy counter, James Dean laid out in a mummy case).

BOROUGH OF THE BRONX
(BRONX COUNTY)

Home of the Bronx cheer (or raspberry), the Bronx Zoo, and the Bronx Bombers (or New York Yankees), the Bronx (*map p. 573*) is the only borough of New York City attached to the mainland of North America, and even so it is surrounded on three sides by water: the Hudson River on the west, the Harlem and East rivers on the south, and Long Island Sound on the east. Its area of 43.1 square miles and population of approximately 1.36 million make it the second smallest borough in both categories.

The eastern Bronx is largely flatland, some of it originally salt marsh, sliced into long peninsulas by inlets and tidal rivers. Tons of garbage, euphemistically known as landfill, have been dumped onto the marshes since World War II, and the areas along Eastchester Bay are now densely populated. West of the flatlands three north–south ridges give the middle and western sections of the borough their hilly terrain. The westernmost ridge runs through Riverdale near the Hudson and west of Broadway, with Broadway following the lowland valley. The second ridge crosses Van Cortlandt Park and runs south to the Macombs Dam Bridge area with the Grand Concourse laid out along its spine. The third and lowest proceeds through the Bronx River Park and Crotona Park, falling away to the flatlands along the East River.

Most of the Bronx is residential, developed with apartment houses that range from onetime luxury Art Deco buildings along the Grand Concourse, and the finely kept high-rises overlooking the Hudson River, to the institutional towers of Co-Op City and the urban renewal housing projects of the southern Bronx. The strip along the East River has seen the rise and fall of various industries. Today an immense food distribution center, which includes the relocated Fulton Fish Market, dominates Hunts Point.

The most famous building in the Bronx is probably Yankee Stadium, home turf of the New York Yankees, major league baseball's most successful team. Founded in 1901, the team has been led by such famous players as Babe Ruth, Lou Gehrig, Joe DiMaggio, and Mickey Mantle. This historic sports field will be replaced by a new Yankee Stadium, presently under construction.

Though Sholem Aleichem and Edgar Allan Poe lived for a while in the Bronx, the artform most closely associated with the borough is hip hop, a largely African-American cultural movement that includes rapping, break dancing, and graffiti art.

HISTORY OF THE BRONX

In 1639 the Dutch West India Co. purchased from Native Americans the land that now constitutes the Bronx, and in 1641 Jonas Bronck, a Dane who arrived in the New World by way of Amsterdam, purchased 500 acres along the river, which soon was known as the Bronck's River. The borough takes its name from

this original settler. Among those arriving later was religious dissenter Anne Hutchinson, expelled as unfit for society by the theocrats of the Massachusetts Bay Colony who would tolerate neither her liberal religious views nor her quick tongue. After a stay in Rhode Island, she arrived at what is now Pelham Bay, where she settled in the early 1640s. Around the same time, John Throgmorton, an Anabaptist, arrived in the area with 35 families who shared his religious views. Soon after, Native Americans attacked both colonies, and though some of Throgmorton's followers were able to escape, Anne Hutchinson's colony was annihilated except for one of her daughters, Susannah, who was taken hostage. After two years with her captors, Susannah was returned, unwillingly, when the Dutch and Native Americans made a treaty to settle their differences. The place names "Throgs Neck" and "Hutchinson River" remain as evidence of these early sojourners. Other British settlers arrived, but both the Dutch and the Native Americans were (understandably) so entrenched that it was not until 1664, when the British took over, that settlement of the Bronx began in earnest. Still, the Bronx remained quietly rural, its land divided between modest farmers and large landowners whose style of life imitated that of the English landed gentry. Villages evolved along the post roads to Albany and Boston and later along the railroads.

After 1840, however, advances in transportation resulted in a population influx that ended with the Depression in the early 1930s. The first newcomers were the Irish, who started to arrive in the 1840s to labor on the railroads and on the Croton Aqueduct. After 1848 Germans followed, mostly farmers. In 1888 the Third Avenue elevated railway reached the hinterland of 169th St and a flood of newcomers began settling near it. Politically the Bronx joined New York in two sections: first the western towns in 1874, then, 20 years later, the eastern towns. The two areas officially became the Borough of the Bronx in 1898.

The golden age of the Bronx, as a stronghold of working-class families, lasted from about 1920 to the early 1950s, when it was a patchwork of tightly-knit neighborhoods, most dominated by one ethnic group. City services—education, transportation, parks—made life comfortable and attractive. The arrival of the automobile, however, and the construction of superhighways enabled the population, or at least the upwardly mobile part of it, a greater choice of where to live; the lure of Westchester County and Long Island attracted many. Public transportation began to deteriorate; the last trolley ceased running in 1948. Jobs became less plentiful. As middle-class whites left in the last half-century, much of the borough became increasingly poor.

Although the Bronx no longer has the acres of burned and abandoned buildings and rubble-filled lots that formerly evoked comparisons with Dresden at the end of World War II, it continues to struggle with problems that have plagued it since the 1970s and '80s. However, crime is down, real estate values are rising, and the borough's future looks promising.

The Bronx Zoo

Bronx River Pkwy at Fordham Rd. Open every day Nov–March from 10–4:30, until 5 in summer and 5:30 on summer weekends and holidays; T: 718 367 1010; www.bronxzoo.com. The zoo is most conveniently reached from Manhattan by the BxM11 express bus along Madison Ave; for schedule, T: 718 445 3100, or visit the zoo website.

The Bronx Zoo was one of the first great urban zoos, founded in 1899; today it offers modern outdoor and indoor habitat exhibits with more than 4,000 animals on a 265-acre preserve. A cable car ride, a monorail and shuttle (*extra fees*) cut down walking distances. Among the favorite exhibits is the Congo Gorilla Forest, with a small-scale rain forest and two families of primates. There are aerial bird feedings and keeper demonstrations with Siberian tigers. The zoo has an active wildlife conservation program (including some composting toilets outside the Bronx River Gate, which are projected to save the city one million gallons of water yearly).

The New York Botanical Garden

200th St and Kazimiroff Blvd. Open Tues–Sun 10–6, Mon federal holidays; earlier closings in Jan and Feb and for some events; free admission Wed and from 10–noon Sat; closed Thanksgiving, Christmas, and Mon except federal holidays. T: 718 817 8700; www.nybg.org. Metro-North Harlem local trains from Grand Central stop at the Botanical Garden station.

Included in the 250 acres of this historic garden are displays of seasonal bedding plants; gardens of herbs and perennials; a rose garden reconstructed after the designs of Beatrice Farrand; stands of magnolias, lilacs, and other flowering trees; thousands of naturalized daffodils; and 40 acres of uncut woodland, the only virgin forest remaining in New York City. The Conservatory, reminiscent of the Victorian glasshouses of the Royal Botanical Gardens in Kew outside London, has an important collection of palms, as well as habitat exhibits of tropical and desert flora, aquatic and insectivorous plants, extravagant seasonal displays, and an annual orchid show.

Wave Hill

Independence Ave at West 249th St. Gardens open April 15–Oct 14 Tues–Sun 9–5:30; July and Aug open until 9pm Wed; Oct 15–April 14 Tues–Sun 9–4:30; greenhouses open 10–noon & 1–4; closed New Year's Day, Thanksgiving, Christmas, and Mon holidays except Memorial Day, Labor Day, Columbus Day and Veterans Day; T: 718 549 3200; www.wavehill.org.

Train: Hudson Line local from Grand Central to Riverdale. Wave Hill is a safe but steep 15-min uphill walk. Walk up 254th St; turn right onto Independence Ave and continue two long blocks to the main gate at 249th St. On weekends from April–Oct, a free Wave Hill shuttle meets northbound trains at 10:45, 11:45, 12:45, 1:45, and 2:45. Return shuttles depart from the main gate at 1:20, 2:20, 3:20, 4:20 and 5:20 to meet Manhattan-bound trains (northbound passengers may wish to take the same free shuttle and wait 9mins).

Express bus: BxM1 and BxM2 routes operate from midtown Manhattan. BxM1 originates at Third Ave and 33rd St, running north along Third Ave. BxM2 originates at Sixth Ave and 35th St, running north along Central Park West. Wave Hill is a pleasant, 5-min walk from the Henry Hudson Pkwy-252nd St bus stop. Make a left off the bus onto 252nd St, cross over the

bridge, walk two blocks down 252nd St, turn left onto Independence Ave, and proceed one long block to the Wave Hill main gate at 249th St. When returning, catch the BxM1 or BxM2 on the southbound Henry Hudson service road at 252nd or 246th St. NB: Express buses are $5 each way payable with MetroCard, or exact change (dollar bills no longer accepted).

Subway (A, 1) and Bronx Bus (Bx7, Bx10): Wave Hill is a pleasant, 5-min walk down 252nd St from the Henry Hudson Pkwy-252nd St bus stop, served by the Bx7 and Bx10 buses. Take the A train to 207th St to connect to the Bx7 on Broadway, or take the 1 train to 231st St to connect to either the Bx7 or Bx10 on 231st St (northwest corner by Chase Bank). Alight at 252nd St and follow walking instructions above. When returning, catch the Bx7 or Bx10 on the southbound Henry Hudson service road at 249th St.

Wave Hill, formerly a country estate that hosted Charles Darwin, Thomas Henry Huxley, and Arturo Toscanini, is one of the most scenic spots in the city. Theodore Roosevelt lived here for a while as a child, and the beauty of the place surely contributed to his love of nature and the outdoors. Wave Hill's gardens today are justly famous; the views across the Hudson River to the palisades in New Jersey are beautiful at any time, but spectacular during the autumn leaf season. Among its charms are an aquatic garden with water lilies and lotus; mature specimen trees; and three small greenhouses with tender plants, cacti, and palms. Glyndor, one of the houses on the estate, hosts art exhibitions, exploring the relationships between people and nature.

Bronx Museum of the Arts

1040 Grand Concourse at 165th St. Open Thur–Mon 12–6, Fri until 8; closed Tues, Wed, Thanksgiving, Christmas, New Year's Day; T: 718 681 6000; www.bronxmuseum.org. Subway: B (anytime) or D (not during rush hours) to 167th St-Grand Concourse; exit at rear of station, walk south along Grand Concourse two blocks.

The museum has a small permanent collection of works by African, Latin American, and Asian artists and their American descendants, as well as changing exhibitions of living artists, usually of these ethnicities. Since its inception the museum has supported emerging artists with its highly regarded Artist in the Marketplace program, which has an annual exhibition. In 2006 the museum opened a dramatic extension, its shining surfaces symbolic to some of the revitalization of this part of the Bronx.

Edgar Allan Poe Cottage

2640 Grand Concourse (Kingsbridge Rd). Open Sat 10–4, Sun 1–5; closed mid-Dec through mid-Jan and major holidays; T: 718 881 8900; www.bronxhistoricalsociety.org. Subway: 4 to Kingsbridge Rd (walk three blocks east to Grand Concourse); D to East Kingsbridge Rd.

Edgar Allan Poe lived in several places in New York, stalked by poverty and his own bleak disposition; he came to this little house in 1846 hoping the country air would cure his wife Virginia's tuberculosis. She died during the first winter, but the poet stayed on to write "Ulalume" and "The Bells," and perhaps part of "Annabel Lee," a eulogy to his bride, whom he had married when she was just 13 years old. Poe rented out the cottage in 1849 and went south, dying in October of that year in Baltimore. The house has been converted to a simple museum, with a few period furnishings and memorabilia.

City Island

The BxM7B express bus runs on weekdays from Madison Ave, about 45mins in light traffic.
City Island, linked to the Bronx by a bridge from Pelham Bay Park, suggests a New England fishing village rather than an urban neighborhood. During the 19th century it was a famous center of boat-building, where the yachts of J.P. Morgan and his fellow financiers were constructed. Later the Minneford Boat Yard turned out America's Cup defenders, for which Ratsey and Lapthorn made sails, and during World War II its ship-yards manufactured landing craft and minesweepers. There are still several yacht clubs on the island, though the boat-building industry has gone elsewhere. Along City Island Ave are seafood restaurants, shops with antiques and collectibles, and a few galleries. Charming Victorian houses remain on the side streets (along with condos and some new houses). The City Island Historical Society operates a small museum at 190 Fordham St (*currently closed after a fire in 2007; T: 718 885 0507; www.cityislandmuseum.org*).

Van Cortlandt Park and Woodlawn Cemetery

Van Cortlandt Park (*entrance on Broadway at 246th St. Subway: 1 to 242nd St-Broadway*) occupies about two square miles along the ridges and valleys of the northern Bronx. The Parade Ground along Broadway attracts cricket players, mostly West Indian, on week-ends and holidays. The Old Croton Aqueduct hiking trail is punctuated with red-brick service towers; park rangers sometimes conduct tours (*T: 718 548 0912*). Also in the park is the Van Cortlandt House Museum (*open Tues–Fri 10–3, Sat and Sun 11–4; closed Mon, holidays, and the day after Thanksgiving; T: 718 543 3344; www.vancortlandt-house.org*), the Georgian rubblestone mansion (c. 1748) of the Dutch landowners who originally farmed the land. The house is furnished with English, Dutch, and colonial furniture, including pieces that belonged to the Van Cortlandts.

   Woodlawn Cemetery (*main entrance on Webster Ave at East 233rd St. Open daily 8:30–5; T: 718 920 0500 or, toll-free 877 496 6352; www.thewoodlawncemetery.org. Easiest access from Manhattan is via the Harlem line local from Grand Central to Woodlawn station. Maps available at the administration office or from the security guards at the main entrance. The Friends of The Woodlawn Cemetery gives tours Sun at 2pm; reservations recommended; T: 718 920 1470. Permit required for photography; apply online or at administration office, open Mon–Sat 8–5*) was founded in 1863, its location chosen in part by its proximity to the railroad: mourners from midtown Manhattan could reach it by train in only 35mins. Woodlawn is pleasantly landscaped and has its share of monumental funerary archi-tecture, but is most famous for the notable people buried here. Among them are F.W. Woolworth, Herman Melville, Robert Moses, and Fiorello La Guardia. Financier Oliver Hazard Perry Belmont and his wife Alva Vanderbilt Belmont hired Richard Morris Hunt to design a mausoleum modeled after the Chapel of St. Hubert at the Château d'Amboise in France. Perhaps the strangest epitaph in the cemetery belongs to one George Spenser (1894–1909): "Lost life by stab in falling on ink eraser, evading six young women trying to give him birthday kisses in office of Metropolitan Life Building."

BOROUGH OF STATEN ISLAND (RICHMOND COUNTY)

To the world at large Staten Island (*map p. 4*) is simply the end point of one of the greatest free rides in the domain of tourism, the Staten Island ferry, which runs for 5.2 miles across the bay. The island is 13.9 miles long and 7.3 miles wide in its largest dimensions, and is separated from Manhattan by Upper New York Bay, from Brooklyn by Lower New York Bay and the Narrows, and from New Jersey by the Kill Van Kull and the Arthur Kill (the word "kill" is a Dutch term for channel). It is the third largest borough in area (60.9 square miles) but the smallest in population (c. 477,000).

Down the center of the island runs a spine of rocky hills whose highest point, Todt Hill (409.2 ft), is also the highest point in the city and the highest point on the Atlantic seaboard south of Maine. Along the crest of these hills, around the turn of the 20th century, the wealthy built mansions, and today many still survive, though some have been adapted as schools or charitable institutions and others have surrendered part of their land to newer, often less imposing, homes. East of the central ridge lie low coastal plains, densely developed with back-to-back rows of tract housing and continuous commercial strips. The southern tip of Staten Island, once dominated by the sea, still retains some of its former charm, though the fishing villages and oystering communities no longer exist. The west, fronting the Arthur Kill, is lowland, much of it salt meadow: some has been filled and used for more tracts of housing, some has been put to commercial and industrial uses. The far north, site of several of the oldest settlements on the island, has industrial areas and housing, much of it old and battered, looking across the Kill Van Kull at the oil tanks in New Jersey. Inland are separate towns or neighborhoods, mostly with small, single-family houses or condominiums, but as development continues the communities are beginning to merge into one giant tract of suburban sprawl.

Staten Island was long infamous for a 2,200-acre dump, the Fresh Kills Landfill, where more than 10,000 tons of garbage from the five boroughs daily found their final resting place. The dump closed in early 2001, opening again for a while after September 11 to receive the wreckage from the World Trade Center site, which has since been dispersed elsewhere. The dump site will become a park.

HISTORY OF STATEN ISLAND

Both Giovanni da Verrazano (1524) and Henry Hudson (1609) made note of Staten Island during their explorations of the New World. Verrazano stopped off at a spring to refill his water casks and Hudson gave the borough its name, *Staaten Eylandt*, after the States General, governing body of the Netherlands. When the British took over New Amsterdam, Staten Island took the name of Richmond after the Duke of Richmond, illegitimate son of Charles II.

During the British colonial period, Staten Island continued to develop as an agricultural community with its less fertile areas devoted to raising stock, while its long coastline and protected waters made fishing, oystering, and shipbuilding important factors in the economy. Along the kills several tidal mills were built for grinding grist and sawing lumber. In the early summer of 1776, the arrival of some 30,000 British soldiers and Hessian mercenaries disrupted the agrarian quiet of the island, which soon became a vast military camp from which the British would stage operations on Long Island. Although the population was largely loyalist and welcomed the arrival of the British forces, the billeting of so many soldiers strained the resources of the 3,000 islanders and tensions inevitably developed. At the end of August the British attacked what is now Brooklyn and took the western end of Long Island, using barges built on Staten Island. In September the Billopp House at the southern tip of the island became the site of abortive negotiations to end the war. After the war Staten Islanders continued their way of life, largely unaffected by the heady changes across the bay, although the federal government did see the strategic importance of the island and fortified it during the War of 1812.

In 1829 teen-aged Cornelius Vanderbilt, born in northern Staten Island, started a regular ferry service to Manhattan, the first step in a business empire that would eventually make him the borough's wealthiest and most famous son. Staten Island burgeoned as a seaside resort, especially New Brighton where such hotels as the Pavilion attracted prominent New Yorkers and a large clientele from the South.

Garibaldi sojourned here for three years during his exile from Italy. Herman Melville frequently visited his brother Tom, governor of Sailors' Snug Harbor from 1867–84. And Frederick Law Olmsted tried his hand at farming in the southern part of the island before finding his life's work as a landscape architect.

Toward the end of the 19th century, Staten Island became less rural, but again changed more slowly than the other boroughs. Industries began to dot the northern and western shoreline: brick and linoleum factories, breweries, dye works, chemical plants. South Beach on the Lower Bay and Midland Beach, just south of it, became popular resort areas, the latter offering an amusement park with rides and pavilions. The first railroad (1860) was extended along both sides of the island linking formerly isolated communities, and charitable institutions aware of the growing shortages of land in Manhattan began buying sites for hospitals, orphanages, and schools. Nevertheless, in 1898, when Staten Island became part of Greater New York, it had only about 67,000 inhabitants, a population slightly larger than that of Manhattan in 1800.

Today Staten Island is struggling to maintain its heritage and preserve what natural beauty remains, while growing in an orderly fashion. Since the opening of the Verrazano Bridge, which brought the growth spurt long desired by some, the borough has seen large increases in crime and poverty. Rural and small-town Staten Island are virtually gone and the island has become another outpost of suburbia.

Visiting Staten Island

The sights described here can all be reached by local public buses that leave from the St. George ferry terminal, but most are more easily reached by car. Except for Historic Richmond Town and the Snug Harbor Cultural Center, most of the island's offerings are small in scale, yet worthwhile to anyone with a special interest in history or architecture. The ferry from Manhattan takes about 25mins, and is free.

The Staten Island September 11 memorial

Along the waterfront near the ferry terminal is a memorial honoring the 270 Staten Islanders who died in the fall of the Trade Center towers. Designed by architect Masayuki Sono and called "Postcards," the memorial (2004) consists of two asymmetrical resin wings that reach skyward and frame the point on the Manhattan skyline where the Trade Center once stood. Granite plaques bear the names, birth-dates, and facial profiles of the victims.

SNUG HARBOR CULTURAL CENTER

1000 Richmond Terrace (Tysen St). Grounds open daily dawn to dusk; hours for individual sites vary; T: 718 448 2500; www.snug-harbor.org. Café Botanica near Chinese Scholar's Garden. From the Staten Island ferry terminal, S40 bus (bus stop in front of the ballpark) to Snug Harbor (a 10-min ride). Tell the driver that you want to get off at Snug Harbor.

Snug Harbor Cultural Center, formerly Sailors' Snug Harbor, a haven for "aged, decrepit, and worn out sailors," is now Staten Island's center for the arts. Beautiful Greek Revival buildings as well as less imposing dormitories, laundries, and cottages have been recycled as exhibition and performance spaces, and artists' studios.

Sailors' Snug Harbor was established by the will of merchant Robert Richard Randall. His father, Thomas, had made a fortune at sea in activities that could charitably be described as "profitable commerce" or "privateering," but which with equal accuracy could be called piracy. Robert died in 1801, willing that his assets be used to construct a home and hospital for retired sailors on his Manhattan farm. During two decades of litigation with relatives, New York grew northward and the Randall farmland became valuable residential property, too valuable for a seamen's retirement home. Therefore Snug Harbor's trustees leased the farm (near present Washington Square) and bought land on Staten Island (1831). The first building was completed in 1833.

Sailing was a difficult and dangerous profession, and many older sailors had physical injuries, were without families, or were alcoholics. Of the original 37 who came to Snug Harbor, seven had lost a leg, two were blind, others had "rheumatism," probably arthritis. In 1900, Snug Harbor housed more than 1,000 sailors, but after social security took effect and sailors had other retirement options, the population dwindled; by the 1970s, fewer than 100 remained. The trustees of Snug Harbor wanted to demolish most of the buildings, but preservationists succeeded in getting them landmarked and eventually convinced the city to buy the land and its 28 buildings. Snug Harbor Cultural Center opened in 1976.

A SNUG HARBOR FOR THE SOUL

Among the original Snug Harbor trustees were the rector of Trinity Church and the minister of the First Presbyterian Church. They were, understandably, concerned with the spiritual welfare and social decorum of the "Snugs," whose lives had been spent under the authoritarian structure of shipboard rules, and who, in many cases, were not equipped emotionally for independence. Drunkenness and rowdy behavior were the main issues, reflected in the by-laws of the organization: *Any member … who shall bring in … ardent spirits or intoxicating liquors shall be forthwith expelled; Any member who shall be convicted of getting drunk, either on or off the premises of the Sailors' Snug Harbor, of quarrelling with or assaulting any of his fellow-inmates, or of using profane or obscene language, or of leaving the premises without permission from the Superintendent … shall be expelled; No person shall commence eating at the table before the blessing shall have been asked; Every member shall attend all the religious services of the Institution …*

Theodore Dreiser stayed near Snug Harbor for about a year and observed the sailors in local bars and on the waterfront. In *The Color of the Great City*, he wrote "this is a great institution and indeed a splendid benefaction, but it insists upon what is the bane and destruction of heart and mind: conformity to routine, a monotonous system which wears as the drifting of water … There is this material Snug Harbor for their bodies, to be sure. But where is the peaceful haven of the heart—on what shore, by what sea—a Snug Harbor for the soul?"

Snug Harbor architecture

The north gatehouse, Italianate in style, was built in 1873 to keep the sailors from smuggling liquor into the complex. The perimeter fence served the same purpose. The five Greek Revival buildings facing the Kill are the architectural centerpiece of Snug Harbor. The three middle buildings were designed by Minard Lafever, an influential architect whose work and publications helped disseminate the Greek Revival style in America. The Visitors' Center occupies the central building (1833), Lafever's earliest documented work, and the first building erected at Snug Harbor. The rotunda ceiling was decorated 50 years later with Victorian- style murals depicting nautical motifs. Veterans' Memorial Hall, now a theater, was originally the chapel for the sailors. The Music Hall (1892) is the city's second oldest theater behind Carnegie Hall.

The John A. Noble Maritime Collection

Open Thur–Sun 1–5; closed New Year's Day, Easter, July 4, Thanksgiving, Christmas; call for winter hours; T: 718 447 6490; www.noblemaritime.org.

Next to the Visitors' Center, Building D (Minard Lafever; 1840–41) houses this collection of maritime art. In 1928, while working on a schooner in the Kill Van Kull, Noble (1913–83) discovered the former Port Johnston coal docks, which had become a grave-

yard for wooden ships. The sight changed Noble's life. In the following decades he committed himself to documenting the history of the harbor, working from a floating studio on a houseboat which he had built "out of the small bones of larger vessels." Later Noble became one of the passionately committed activists whose work saved Snug Harbor from commercial development. Exhibitions focus on Noble's work and on the history of New York harbor. The museum has a re-creation of Noble's floating studio and a restored dormitory room.

The Staten Island Botanical Garden

Open April–Oct Tues–Sun 10–5, Nov–April Tues–Sun 10–4; T: 718 273 8200; www.sibg.org. Well worth a look if you are visiting Snug Harbor is the Staten Island Botanical Garden's Chinese Scholar's Garden. Its courtyards and pavilions, sparsely planted with plum, pine, and bamboo, are modeled after Ming Dynasty (1368–1644) precursors, intended for the serene contemplation of nature.

OTHER STATEN ISLAND POINTS OF INTEREST

The Alice Austen House

2 Hylan Blvd (Edgewater St). Museum open Thur–Sun 12–5; closed Jan, Feb, and major holidays; grounds open every day until dusk; T: 718 816 4506; www.aliceausten.org. Bus S51 from the ferry terminal to Hylan Blvd and Bay St (15mins). Walk one block east.
This charming Gothic Revival cottage (1691–1710, later alterations) is the former home of photographer Alice Austen (1866–1952), whose pioneering work depicts New York life at the turn of the 20th century. The house was purchased and modernized by Alice's grandfather John Austen in 1844. After Alice's mother was deserted by her husband, she moved back with her financially comfortable parents. Alice became one of the first female photographers in the nation to work outside the studio, her interests taking her beyond the boundaries of Staten Island and the restrictions of her upbringing. Her photos document the social customs of her generation, the influx of immigrants to New York City, and the workings of the former Staten Island Quarantine Stations. She lived in this cottage until illness and poverty forced her out at age 70. The house, furnished with Victorian period pieces, has a magnificent view of New York Harbor and a pretty garden replanted, following Austen's photographs, with weeping mulberry, flowering quince, and other shrubs.

The Garibaldi-Meucci Museum

420 Tompkins Ave (near Chestnut Ave). Open Tues–Sun 1–5; closed Mon and all major holidays, Christmas Eve, and New Year's Eve; T: 718 442 1608; www.garibaldimeucci museum.org. Bus S52 or S78 from ferry terminal to the corner of Chestnut and Tompkins Aves.
This small house-museum memorializes Italian freedom fighter Giuseppe Garibaldi, who lived here with his friend Antonio Meucci from 1850–53. Exiled from Italy after the fall of the Roman Republic in 1849, the impoverished Garibaldi sought refuge in the US. He was taken in by Antonio Meucci, who with his wife rented this simple Gothic

Revival house. The two men barely supported themselves hunting and making candles. Garibaldi left New York in 1853 and returned to Italy to continue the struggle for Italian unification and independence. The museum contains letters, photos, military artifacts, and other memorabilia of Garibaldi's life, including his red shirt. There is also an exhibit on Meucci, who was declared the first inventor of the telephone by the US Supreme Court in 1886, though by then it was too late for him to benefit from his invention.

Antonio Meucci (1808–89)
Born in 1808 near Florence, Antonio Meucci came to Staten Island in 1850 after a stint as a set designer and stage technician in Havana. While in Cuba, Meucci, an inveterate tinkerer and an avid reader of scientific literature, became curious about the therapeutic uses of electric shock, and one day while experimenting on a friend, heard the friend's exclamation transmitted over a copper wire from the next room. Realizing that he had discovered something significant, he spent the next ten years bringing his observation to a practical stage.

Meucci's lack of entrepreneurial skill, his inability to speak English, and his increasing poverty all worked against him. Although he filed a notice of intent to take out a patent on his invention in 1871, six years before Alexander Graham Bell filed for his patent, Meucci could not come up with the $250 necessary to register his invention officially. Through a series of Kafkaesque bureaucratic blunders (including the loss of his prototypes and repeated delays), Bell received credit for the invention of the telephone and the rights to the financial rewards that went with it. Although Meucci sued to regain his commercial rights, he was at a disadvantage in court, and not unexpectedly the court found in Bell's favor. Investigations eventually uncovered collusion between employees of the Patent Office and officials of Bell's company, and although the government in 1886 upheld Meucci's claim and initiated prosecution for fraud against Bell's patent, Meucci died in 1889, and the case was eventually dropped.

Jacques Marchais Center of Tibetan Art

338 Lighthouse Ave (past St. George Rd). Open Wed–Sun 1–5; closed holidays (call ahead); T: 718 987 3500; www.tibetanmuseum.org. Bus S74 or S54 from the ferry terminal to Lighthouse Ave (about 30mins). Walk up the (steep) hill (5–10mins) to the museum. Train: Staten Island Railway from ferry terminal to Great Kills, then S54 bus.

The Jacques Marchais Center of Tibetan Art (founded 1947), sitting high on the rocky spine of Staten Island, is the creation of a midwestern woman enamored of Eastern art. The museum's architecture recalls Tibetan mountain monasteries: sturdy buildings whose thick stone walls are pierced with small windows and overhung by cedar roofs.

Jacques Marchais (1887–1948), née Edna Coblentz, was born in Illinois. As a child she was captivated by a collection of 13 bronze Tibetan figures she had found stashed away in a trunk in the attic, apparently souvenirs her great-grandfather had brought

back from Asia. Edna Coblentz grew up to become a successful dealer in Asian art, and, using the professional name Jacques Marchais (her married name was Jacqueline Klauber), she ran a gallery on Madison Avenue and gradually built her personal collection. Though enthralled by Asian culture and religion, Marchais never went to the Far East, but enlarged her holdings by buying pieces from other collections at private sales or auctions, or by working closely with dealers. Among the pieces of sculpture in the museum here are the 13 bronze figurines that originally awoke her interest.

Historic Richmond Town

441 Clarke Ave (Richmond Rd and Arthur Kill Rd). Open July and Aug Wed–Sat 10–5, Sun 1–5; Oct–June Wed–Sun 1–5; closed Thanksgiving, Christmas, and New Year's Day. Tours at 2:30 on weekdays, and at 2 and 3:30 on weekends; T: 718 351 1611; www.historicrich-mondtown.org. Bus S74 from the ferry terminal to Richmond Rd and Court Pl, the middle of the restoration area (about 30mins). Train: Staten Island Railway to Great Kills, then S54 bus.
Historic Richmond Town is a 100-acre outdoor museum whose buildings trace the evolution of village life on Staten Island from the 17th–19th centuries. The village offers homes, shops, and public buildings, some restored inside and out, some relocated here from other parts of Staten Island. There are also demonstrations of cooking, blacksmithing, candle making, and other skills once necessary to daily life.

One of the most important buildings is the little frame Voorlezer's House (c. 1695), built by the Dutch Reformed congregation for its *voorlezer* (lay reader), who lived and also taught school there. It is the oldest surviving elementary school building in the nation. The oldest structure here, however, is the Britton Cottage (c. 1670, with later additions), whose original section is believed to have been the Town House where public meetings were held, thus becoming Staten Island's first government building.

Conference House (Billopp House)

7445 Hylan Blvd (Satterlee St). Open April–mid-Dec Fri–Sun 1–4; T: 718 984 6046; www.theconferencehouse.org. Bus S78 from the ferry terminal to the last stop on Craig Ave (1hr or more); buses run less frequently on weekends.
At the very southern tip of Staten Island, in a park overlooking Raritan Bay, is the Conference House, also known as the Billopp House after its first owner. Built around 1680, this stone manor house was the site of a failed peace conference during the Revolution. On Sept 11, 1776, when American prospects for victory looked bleak, the Continental Congress sent a group of delegates including Benjamin Franklin and John Adams to the Billopp House to meet with Admiral Lord Richard Howe. Howe offered to pardon those who had taken up arms against the Crown if the colonies would rescind the Declaration of Independence, which had been signed just two months earlier; the Americans replied that independence was not negotiable, and the talks broke off.

The house is built of local stone with ground seashells mixed into the mortar. Inside are an impressive basement kitchen and a vaulted root cellar. Most of the furnishings are from the 18th century, though a 17th-century sea chest remains as the sole Billopp family possession.

PRACTICAL INFORMATION

PLANNING YOUR TRIP

When to go

You can enjoy New York at any time of the year, but the most predictably pleasant seasons are spring and fall. Winter can be invigorating, though it can also be bleak, gray, and bitterly cold. January is the coldest month, with daytime averages of 38–25°F (3–4°C). Summer can be warm and pleasant, but there are usually periods in July and August when it is stiflingly hot and humid.

The cultural calendar is most crowded September–May. Attractions may be less crowded in summer, when New Yorkers vacation. Christmas, when the city is brilliantly decorated, draws thousands of visitors; expect crowds everywhere and high rates.

Useful and interesting websites on New York

www.nycvisit.com: Official City Tourism Bureau;

www.nyc.gov: city government site, with useful links to city events, parks, etc;

www.nycgovparks.org: Information about park events and activities, food service, park maps, and Wi-Fi access. Text of historical signs in the parks;

www.centralparknyc.org: Everything you need to know about Central Park: maps, history, events, activities;

www.mta.info: Subway and bus information, schedules, and maps;

www.nysonglines.com: Building by building walking tours of famous New York streets and avenues with interesting historical tidbits, well-written and researched by a city history buff;

www.forgotten-ny.com: Pictures and interesting descriptions of New York byways, by another aficionado of New York history;

www.nyc-architecture.com: Good photos of important buildings;

www.nytimes.com: The *New York Times* site, reviews of theater, art, music, along with the rest of the news that is fit to print.

Travelers with disabilities

New York is not totally accessible to disabled visitors, but it is manageable. The airports have accessible restrooms, telephones, and restaurants, as well as handicap parking spaces. The website of the Port Authority of New York and New Jersey has detailed information about airport facilities (www.panynj.gov; search "disabled traveler").

Public transit buses are wheelchair friendly. The subways, however, are not, though some stations now have elevators and other facilities. For information about a particular station, or for help routing a journey, call New York City Transit, T: 718 596 8585. The Mayor's Office for People with Disabilities (MOPD) also has information on accessible transportation; T: 212 788 2830; TTY: 212 788 2838; www.nyc.gov/html/mopd.

MOPD publishes *Access New York*, with detailed information. It is available as a PDF on the MOPD site. The NYC & Company website, www.nyc-visit.com, has a section for travelers with disabilities.

Taxis are not equipped to accommodate wheelchairs, but many drivers will help stow folding wheelchairs in the trunk.

Many public buildings, especially newer ones, are accessible to wheelchairs. Some Broadway theaters have induction loops for hearing-impaired people. Hospital Audiences, Inc., a non-profit organization dedicated to making cultural events accessible, maintains a hotline with accessibility information (T: 212 575 7676, toll-free: 888 424 4685; www.hospitalaudiences.org.)

Restaurants vary in accessibility, dining rooms may be accessible, restrooms may not. Hotels also vary widely. Call ahead.

Big Apple Greeters offers free neighborhood visits guided by volunteers. Visitors with disabilities are especially welcome; T: 212 669 8159; TTY: 212 669 8273; www.bigapplegreeter.org.

ARRIVAL BY AIR

John F. Kennedy Airport: Map p. 5; T: 718 244 4444. Most international and many domestic flights arrive here, about 15 miles from midtown Manhattan (60mins in moderate traffic).

LaGuardia Airport: Map p. 5; T: 718 533 3400. About 8 miles (30–45mins) from Midtown, serves primarily domestic flights.

Newark Liberty International Airport: Map p. 5; T: 973 961 6000. About 16 miles (45–60 mins) from Midtown. Both international and domestic flights originate and terminate here. Convenient for Manhattan's West Side.

Transportation to and from airports

NB: Prices given in this section were valid at the time of writing, but are subject to change, and are intended as a guide only.

The Port Authority of New York and New Jersey (www.panynj.gov) has detailed information about ground transportation to Manhattan and the suburbs. The Port Authority also offers a telephone hotline with similar information: T: 800 AIR RIDE (i.e. 247 7433). Live operator available Mon–Fri 8–6. Recorded information other times.

Taxis

Taxis to Midtown are available at all three airports. During peak hours uniformed dispatchers will direct you to a cab. Licensed taxis (the legal ones) are yellow and have a medallion shield on the hood. When uniformed taxi dispatchers are not on duty, you must hail your own cab; New Yorkers are assertive in this respect.

Ignore offers of transportation from people who approach you in the terminal; visitors unfamiliar with New York have been grossly overcharged and sometimes

intimidated by these taxi hustlers. Go to information counters, bus stops, or taxi dispatchers for safe and legitimate transportation.

Taxi drivers are required legally to stay inside their cabs except to help with luggage, etc. Drivers will expect a 15–20 percent tip.

Taxis from Newark and LaGuardia are metered. From LaGuardia you pay the meter amount (estimate $20–40) plus bridge and tunnel tolls, plus tip. From Newark, you pay the meter amount (estimate $50–75), plus $10, plus toll and tip. You can organize a shared group rate for up to four passengers from 8am–midnight; make arrangements with the taxi dispatcher before you start. To go to Newark Airport from Manhattan, you pay the metered rate plus the toll, plus tip.

Taxis from JFK are charged at a flat rate of $45 plus tolls, a blessing when you are stalled in traffic. One fare covers all passengers, but applies only to first destination.

Shuttles

Vans and buses run from the airports to locations in midtown, and are easy and cost effective. Ground Transportation Information counters are located on the baggage claim level of all terminals. Fares run $12–15.

New York Airport Service operates buses from JFK and LaGuardia to the Port Authority Bus Terminal (42nd St/Eighth Ave), Grand Central Terminal (Park Ave between 41st and 42nd Sts), Penn Station (34th St/Seventh Ave), Bryant Park (42nd St/Fifth Ave), and Midtown hotels between 31st and 60th Sts. Buses run from 5am–10pm to JFK, and from 5am–8pm to LaGuardia; coming from JFK buses operate 6.15am–11.10pm; coming from LaGuardia buses run 7:20am–11pm. Fare is $15 from JFK and $12 from LaGuardia. T: 718 875 8200; www.nyairportservice.com.

SuperShuttle runs blue and yellow vans to and from all three airports. They will stop at your hotel, office, or home, but they will also deliver others traveling at the same time to nearby destinations, so you may make several stops before your destination. Returning to the airport, you should reserve 24hrs in advance if possible. Since the van stops to pick up other passengers, allow extra time. Fare based on destination, about $16–23. (T: 212 258 3826, toll-free 800 258 3826; www.supershuttle.com.)

Olympia Trails-Coach USA provides express bus service between all terminals at Newark Airport and the Port Authority Bus Terminal in Manhattan (42nd St/Eighth Ave), Bryant Park (Fifth Ave/42nd St) and Grand Central Terminal (42nd St/Park Ave). Buses leave at intervals of 20–30 mins, less frequently after midnight. The fare is $14. T: 212 964 6233 or 877 863 9275, www.olympiabus.com.

AirTrain from JFK and Newark

AirTrain JFK is less expensive than other forms of transportation into Midtown, but it is far less convenient than the shuttle services and you will have to handle your luggage. It links the airport to the Howard Beach subway station (A train), and the Jamaica station of the Long Island railroad, with connections to Manhattan. T: 718 217 5477 or 877 535 2478; www.panynj.gov/airtrain or www.mta.info/lirr. The trip takes about an hour to Midtown under ideal conditions. Cost is $2 for the subway and $5 for the train.

AirTrain Newark connects the airport to the New Jersey Transit and Amtrak trains, via Newark Liberty International Airport Station. The train goes first to Penn Station in Newark (5mins); here you must change to a PATH train to Penn Station in New York (20mins). Trains run round the clock, with frequent service during the day and less frequent service from midnight to 5am. The fare to Penn Station in Manhattan is $14. For information, T: 888 397 4636; wwwpanynj.gov/airtrainnewark.com.

TOURIST INFORMATION

NYC & Company (www.nycvisit.com) is the motherlode of New York City information and maintains several kiosks and visitor centers. The visitor center at 810 Seventh Ave (52nd and 53rd Sts) is open weekdays 8:30–6, weekends 9–5; T: 212 484 1222. The center has brochures describing attractions, discounted theater tickets, subway and bus maps, lists of hotels and restaurants. NYC & Company also publishes the *Official NYC Guide*, with information about attractions, performing arts, nightlife, sports, and other events. Order by calling T: 212 397 8222, or outside New York 800 NYC VISIT (692 84748); you can also email from NYC & Company's website.

Other kiosks run by New York & Company are: NYC Heritage Tourism Center at the southern tip of City Hall Park on the Broadway sidewalk at Park Row (open seven days Mon–Fri 9am–6pm, Sat and Sun 10am–5pm); the Visitor Information Kiosk for Chinatown, located in the triangle where Canal, Walker and Baxter Sts meet (open Mon–Sun 10–6).

The Times Square Information Center in the former Embassy Theater, 1560 Broadway (46th and 47th Sts) is open daily 8am–8pm (www.timessquarebid.org). The center has information on events, theater tickets, sightseeing, Times Square walking tours, and area maps.

GETTING AROUND IN THE CITY

An atlas of Manhattan appears on pp. 574–83, with major sights covered in this book clearly marked. The outer boroughs are shown on p. 4 (Staten Island) and p. 573 (Queens and the Bronx), with major sights indicated. In Lower Manhattan the street plan, which reflects historical development, is irregular; you will probably need a map to get around. North of about 14th St a grid system makes it easier to find your way. An exceptionally good resource is the *New York Mapguide* by Michael Middleditch (Penguin Books), with monuments, cafés, shops and restaurants also marked.

Avenues run north–south and are named (Park, Lexington, West End), numbered (First Ave, Fifth Ave), or lettered (Avenue A, B, C, and D on the Lower East Side). Sixth Avenue, officially The Avenue of the Americas, is still Sixth Avenue to New Yorkers. Traffic on most avenues flows in one direction, with alternate avenues running north and south, though there are exceptions to this rule.

Streets run east–west and are numbered east or west of Fifth Avenue, with the smallest numbers closest to it; thus 12 East 72nd St lies east of Fifth Avenue but fairly near to it. Broadway, originally an Indian trail and the major exception to the grid, runs diagonally northwest–southeast.

Traffic generally flows east on even-numbered streets and west on odd-numbered ones, though again there are exceptions. Some major crosstown streets with two-way traffic are 14th St, 23rd St, 34th St, 42nd St, 57th St, and 72nd St. Transverses cross Central Park at 65th/66th St, 79th/80th St, and 96th/97th St. Uptown means north; downtown means south; crosstown means either east or west. Midtown is usually considered the part of Manhattan from about 34th–59th Sts (though Downtown lies south of 14th St; that leaves the Flatiron District, Chelsea, Gramercy Park, and Madison Square between Downtown and Midtown).

MANHATTAN ADDRESS FINDER

To find the nearest cross street on any avenue in Manhattan, take the address number, cancel the last digit, divide by two and add or subtract the key number below. Example: Where is 500 Fifth Ave? Cancel the last 0, and divide 50 by 2. To 25 add the key number 18 to get 43. 500 Fifth Ave is near 43rd St.

First, Second Aves: add 3.
Third Ave: add 10.
Fourth Ave: add 8.
Fifth Ave 63–108: add 11; 109–200: add 13; 200–400: add 16; 400–600: add 18; 600–775: add 20; 775–1286: eliminate the last digit, do not divide by 2, subtract 18; 1286–1500: add 45; above 2000: add 24.
Sixth Ave: subtract 12.
Seventh Ave: add 12; above 1800: add 20.
Eighth Ave: add 9.
Ninth Ave: add 13.

Tenth Ave: add 14.
Amsterdam Ave: add 59.
Broadway: subtract 30.
Columbus Ave: add 60.
Broadway: 756–846: subtract 29; 847–953: subtract 25; above 953: subtract 31.
Lexington Ave: add 22.
Madison Ave: add 27.
Park Ave: add 34.
West End Ave, Central Park West: divide number by 10, add 59.
Riverside Drive: cancel last digit and, up to 567: add 72; 568 and above: add 78.

PUBLIC TRANSPORTATION

Public transportation will take you most places you want to go. Subways are quick, fairly reliable, and reasonably easy to negotiate. Buses allow you to see the passing scene, though they can get stalled in traffic. During the rush hours, buses and sub-

ways are unpleasantly crowded. Fares are payable using a MetroCard (*see below*) or, on the bus, exact change (no dollar bills).

Official bus and subway maps, including bus maps of the outer boroughs, are available at the information booth on the main concourse in Grand Central Terminal. Subway maps are available at the token booths of subway stations and are posted inside the stations and in the trains; bus maps are available on buses. The Manhattan bus maps are useful for finding your way on foot. Maps are also available online at www.mta.info, or you can request a map from the NYC Transit Customer Assistance, T: 718 330 3322.

MetroCards

If you plan to use public transportation even minimally, buy a MetroCard, a prepaid fare card that can be read by the subway turnstiles and bus fare boxes. MetroCards offer both discounts and convenience. There are two types of cards: the Unlimited Ride MetroCard and the Pay-Per-Ride MetroCard. The Unlimited Ride MetroCard comes with 1-day, 7-day, or 30-day expiration dates. The Pay-Per-Ride MetroCard is available in increments (from $4 to $80 at the time of writing). Pay-Per-Ride cards can be shared; Unlimited Ride cards will work only once during an 18-min period in the same subway station or on the same bus route. Reduced fare cards (half price) are available for travelers with disabilities and the elderly (65 and older); T: 718 243 4999.

MetroCards allow you one free transfer from bus to subway or vice versa, and from one bus to another one crossing its route. When your card is swiped, the scanner automatically records a transfer, good for the next 2hrs. You can check your MetroCard balance when using the card on the bus or in subway stations at a MetroCard reader attached to the token booth.

MetroCards are sold at any subway station or any one of the participating neighborhood merchants (news centers, pharmacies, delicatessens and grocery stores, check-cashing centers, etc), and at the NY Transit Museum Gallery and Store at Grand Central Terminal. The larger MetroCard vending machines accept cash, credit cards or debit cards. The small MetroCard vending machines are for credit cards or debit cards only and do not accept cash. Single-ride tickets are available only at the larger MetroCard vending machines and must be purchased with cash and used within 2hrs of purchase.

Buses

Buses are relatively cheap and moderately reliable, though they can be crowded. They can slow to a crawl during rush hours, but are still the best way to travel short distances or east–west in Manhattan (subways run primarily north–south).

Pay the fare with exact change (no bills) or a MetroCard (the easiest way). If you pay with cash and wish to transfer to an intersecting bus line (free), ask the driver when you board; the paper transfer will enable you to change within 2hrs to a second bus on an intersecting route. If you pay with a MetroCard, the card will automatically enable you to transfer to another bus or a subway.

Most buses stop on demand about every two blocks going uptown and downtown, and every block crosstown. Buses marked "Limited" make fewer stops. Most buses run

on a 24-hr schedule with reduced service at night. Press the yellow or black tape on the wall to signal to the driver that you wish to stop.

For late-night safety, Request-A-Stop bus service (every day 10pm–5am) allows you to get off along the route between regular stops. Tell the driver where you want to get off and he or she will stop there or at the closest corner where it is safe to stop the bus.

Subways

Subways are the fastest but not always the most pleasant way to get around, as they can be very crowded. Avoid rush hours (7:30–9:30am & 5–6:30pm) if you can.

The trains run 24hrs a day in four boroughs (excluding Staten Island), serving around 5 million riders on an average weekday. Express trains make only certain stops; local trains stop at every station. Trains to widely different destinations often travel on the same track, so check the number on the front of the train before you board. Announcements are made over a public address system, but they are often garbled and impossible to understand.

The subway's reputation for crime is exaggerated but not entirely undeserved. Use common sense; be aware of your surroundings; stay with other people; avoid going down empty stairwells or riding in empty cars; don't lean over the edge of the platform. Panhandlers, pickpockets, and purse snatchers work the subways as well as the street.

If possible take a taxi or bus instead of the subway late at night, especially when you are alone. If you do take the subway during off-hours, ride in the car with the transit policeman, if there is one, or the conductor, who has a telephone. Avoid waiting on an empty platform; use the Off-Hours Waiting area.

Taxis

The city fleet contains about 12,000 cabs, a statistic difficult to believe during a rainy rush hour. Yellow cabs are licensed and regulated by the New York City Taxi and Limousine Commission and may be identified by their color and the medallion displayed on the hood. Rates, which cover up to four passengers, are posted on the door. A night surcharge from 8pm–6am is in effect on all cabs, as well as a peak surcharge for daytime rides between 4pm–8pm. Fares to destinations outside the city should be negotiated before you start. You must pay for bridge or tunnel tolls. Cab drivers will expect a tip of 15–20 percent. Credit-card readers are being installed in taxis; drivers, however, sometimes resist accepting anything but cash, so it is a good idea to carry small bills.

There are dispatcher-controlled taxi stands at major transportation terminals and elsewhere within the city, but most cabs cruise looking for passengers. Taxi drivers do not always speak or understand English perfectly, so speak clearly and make sure that you are understood. Have an idea of the cross street of your destination; that is, ask to go to Madison Ave at 61st St rather than 660 Madison Ave.

To inquire about lost property or to register complaints, T: 212 NYC TAXI (i.e. 692 8294). You must know either the taxi identification number from the lighted roof panel or the driver's identification number, posted inside the cab. Your receipt has the taxi ID number printed on it; keep it in case you wish to complain.

"Gypsy" cabs operate in the outer boroughs and in Manhattan outside the central districts; they are painted colors other than yellow and may have "livery" license plates. They are not recommended, since they are less regulated than medallion cabs.

Walking

Walking is one of the best ways to enjoy New York. There are 20 north–south blocks to a mile (crosstown blocks, except between Lexington and Madison Aves, are about three times as long).

Driving

Unless you plan excursions out of town, a car is no advantage in New York. Traffic can approach gridlock. Street parking is hard to find, parking garages are absurdly expensive, parking tickets are even more so. To the uninitiated, the city's alternate-side-of-the-street parking regulations (parking allowed on one side one day, on the other side the next day) may seem Byzantine. If you do have a car and are staying at a hotel, check with the doorman about parking facilities.

Cars parked illegally may be towed and impounded. It is expensive in time, emotional energy, and money to retrieve your vehicle. Theft, either of your car or its contents, is another possibility. If you park on the street, do not leave valuables in your car.

ADDITIONAL INFORMATION

Alcoholic beverages

Liquor stores are open daily except Sun, holidays, and election days while the polls are open. Beer is sold in grocery stores and delicatessens, as well as liquor stores, except on Sun mornings. The legal drinking age is 21; many bars will request photo ID. Bars are permitted to remain open until 4am.

Banking and business hours

Most New York banks are open Mon–Fri 9–4; some have extended hours; some are open Sat morning as well. Banks are closed on legal holidays. Business hours for most offices are Mon–Fri 9–5. Department stores and many specialty shops open at 10am; groceries, pharmacies, and other service shops may open earlier.

Crime and personal security

Although New York is safer than most other American large cities, it is wise to be cautious about personal security. Traditional, common-sense advice includes being alert to your surroundings and looking confident about where you are going. (No statistics exist, however, as to the effectiveness of this posture.) If your instincts tell you the neighborhood is unsafe, leave. Don't flash cash or jewelry on the street.

Walking is generally safe in New York. During the day you can go almost anywhere, especially in company, and at night you can certainly walk on busy streets. Avoid

deserted streets. Do not wander in the parks after dark unless attending a concert or other activity and even then stay with the crowds; do not walk alone in the isolated, remote parts of parks.

Hang on to your handbag. Shoulder bags are safer than backpacks. Put your wallet in a front pants pocket. Tourists are targets because they often carry a lot of cash. Use ATMs for small amounts, and be alert when using one.

A real pedestrian hazard is the corps of bicycle-riding messengers, most of them deeply committed to speed. Since these cyclists often ride against the flow of traffic and not infrequently run traffic lights, look both ways before stepping into the street.

Electrical current

Electricity in the US is 110–120V, 60-cycle AC current. Unless you have a dual-voltage appliance with flat pins, you will need an adapter, available at hardware stores, some pharmacies, and airports.

Emergencies

For fire, police, ambulance: call 911. If you have a medical emergency, call 911 or go, preferably by cab, to the emergency room of the nearest hospital. Hospital emergency rooms, open at all times, are often crowded and waits can be long. You will be billed for emergency treatment. If you have health insurance, call your company's emergency number to find which hospitals accept your insurance.

New York Hospital-Presbyterian Hospital/ Weill Cornell Center: 525 East 68th St (York Ave); T: 212 746 5026 (emergencies); T: 212 746 5454 (general).

St. Vincent's Hospital: Seventh Ave (11th/12th Sts); T: 212 604 8000 (emergencies); T: 212 604 7000 (general).

St. Luke's Roosevelt Hospital (Roosevelt division): 10th Ave at 59th St, T: 212 523 4000.

Mount Sinai: Madison Ave (100th/101st Sts); T: 212 241 6693 (emergencies); T: 212 241 6500 (general).

Victims' Services: Call the Safe Horizon hotline, T: 866 689 4357, for counseling and other services if you have been mugged or suffered a crime against your person.

Internet access

There are computer terminals for e-mail at the Times Square Visitors Center, 1560 Broadway (46th and 47th Sts). Many hotels offer Wi-Fi connections as do cafés such as Starbucks, Kinko's copy centers (check the Yellow Pages of the phone book or www.kinkos.com). There is a cybercafé (www.cyber-cafe.com) in Times Square at 250 West 49th St (T: 212 333 4109). Public libraries have computer terminals, but you may have to wait in line and access time may be limited. There are Wi-Fi hotspots in some of the parks; www.nycgovparks.org (go to "Your Park" and check for Wi-Fi info).

Legal holidays

Legal holidays are New Year's Day (Jan 1), Martin Luther King Day (third Mon in Jan),

Presidents' Day (third Mon in Feb), Memorial Day (fourth Mon in May), Independence Day (July 4), Labor Day (first Mon in Sept), Columbus Day (Oct 12, celebrated on second Mon in Oct), Veterans Day (Nov 11), Thanksgiving (fourth Thurs in Nov), and Christmas (Dec 25). Christmas Eve (Dec 24) is an unofficial holiday for many businesses, but not, of course, for stores.

Schools and some businesses in New York are closed on major Jewish holidays: Passover (March or April), Rosh Hashanah (Sept or Oct) and Yom Kippur (Sept or Oct).

Newspapers and magazines

The *New York Times* is the doyenne of daily papers, in print since 1851, and offering, as the front page states, "all the news that's fit to print." Three other major dailies are the *New York Post* and the *Daily News*, both tabloids, and the *Wall Street Journal*, with a focus on the financial markets. The *Post* and *Wall Street Journal*, both owned by Rupert Murdoch, are conservative, while the *Times* is more liberal and is considered the nation's newspaper of record.

Among the weekly magazines is *New York*, which carries news about city life and politics as well as extensive theater, music, and event listings. *The New Yorker* has long been known for fine writing (both fiction and nonfiction), reviews of cultural events, and urbane humor (including cartoons). *Time Out New York*, which arrived here from London in 1995, is the best single source for listings of what's going on in art galleries, restaurants, clubs, concert halls and movie theaters.

Post offices and mail

Most post offices are open weekdays 9am–5pm and Sat until noon or 1pm. The James A. Farley Building, the main post office on Eighth Ave at 33rd St, is open daily 24hrs, though not all services are available outside regular business hours. Branch post offices are located throughout the city; look in the blue section in the Yellow Pages of the telephone book under United States Government, Postal Service, or online at wwwusps.com. Mailboxes are on some street corners; many hotels will perform postal services.

Pharmacies

Pharmacies in the US will not fill foreign prescriptions; many drugs available over the counter elsewhere are not available without a prescription in the US. The Duane Reade at 250 West 57th St and Broadway has a pharmacist on duty 24hrs; T: 212 541 9708; www.duanereade.

Telephones

The US phone system is run by private corporations: rates for long-distance calls vary from carrier to carrier. Hotels add surcharges for both local and long-distance calls, so it is cheaper to use a public pay phone, or a cell phone.

Pay phones can be found on the streets and in building lobbies. Many do not work and some are dirty. Some phones will accept credit cards instead of coins. You can buy

prepaid calling cards in various denominations at chain pharmacies (Duane Reade and Rite Aid), convenience stores, or newsstands.

All telephone numbers in the US consist of a three-digit area code, a three-digit exchange plus a four-digit number. To make a local call, you need only dial the three-digit exchange plus the four-digit number (seven digits).

Information and directory assistance: To reach an operator, dial 0. For information in Manhattan or the Bronx, dial 411 or 555 1212. For Queens, Brooklyn, or Staten Island information, dial 1 718 555 1212. For directory assistance for other parts of the US, dial the area code, then 555 1212. These calls are free at pay telephones.

Making calls: The area codes for Manhattan are 212 and 646; for Brooklyn, Queens, the Bronx, and Staten Island, 718 and 347. The 917 code is used for cell phones and pagers in all five boroughs. To make a **local call** on a public pay telephone, deposit the requisite change (no pennies) for the first 3mins, listen for the dial tone, and dial the seven-digit number. The operator will cut in and tell you to deposit more money when the time has elapsed. To make a direct **long-distance call** to any place in the US or Canada, dial 1 + the area code + the seven-digit number. To make a **direct international call**, dial 011 + the country code, city, code and telephone number. To dial an **operator-assisted long-distance call** (credit card calls, collect calls), dial 0 + the area code + the local number: the operator will come on the line and assist you.

The prefixes 800, 888, and 877 designate toll-free numbers. The code 900 indicates a toll call for some kind of "service" (e.g. horoscopes); these calls are often expensive.

Cell phones: Most US cell phones will work in New York, but you should call your provider to see whether you need to unlock a roaming option. Visitors from outside the US will need a multiband phone and a roaming agreement, but the charges may be very high; check with your service provider. It is also feasible to rent or buy a US phone (or a SIM card), while you are here, depending on how long you intend to stay. ATT, formerly Cingular, offers a relatively inexpensive GoPhone (T: 888 333 6651) for purchase with a pay-as-you-go plan. Alternatively, you can lease or rent a cell phone. InTouch USA rents cellular and wireless equipment, T: 800 872 7626.

Tickets to performing arts events

You can purchase **tickets to Broadway and Off-Broadway shows** at the appropriate box office or over the telephone through Ticketmaster (212 307 4100) or Telecharge (212 239 6200). Both services allow you reserve for Broadway and Off-Broadway shows using a major credit card; both add a surcharge and handling fee to the ticket price. Newspaper ads usually say which service handles tickets for a particular event. Ask about seat locations. The tickets can be mailed to you or held at the box office.

Discounted tickets are available from TKTS discount booths, either in Times Square (day-of-performance tickets only) or at the South Street Seaport (Front and John Sts, near the rear of the Resnick/ Prudential Building at 199 Water St). Pay with cash or travelers' checks only; no phone purchases, no credit cards. For details, check the Theater Development Fund website at www.tdf.org.

The **TKTS Times Square Discount Booth** is temporarily located at the Marriott Marquis Hotel, on West 46th St between Broadway and Eighth Ave. When the renovation of Duffy Square is complete the booth will move back to its former location at the north end of Times Square (West 47th St and Broadway).

You can purchase **tickets to events at Lincoln Center** through Telecharge (212 239 6200), online, or at the box offices of the individual Lincoln Center venues; for additional information, www.lincolncenter.org.

Time

Depending on the season, New York is either on Eastern Standard Time (EST) or Eastern Daylight Saving Time (EDT). Eastern Standard Time is 5hrs behind Greenwich Mean Time (GMT). Daylight saving time begins at 2am on the second Sun in March and continues until 2am the first Sun in Nov. During this period, New York time is 4hrs behind GMT. To find the correct local time, T: 212 976 1616.

Tipping

In restaurants the usual tip is 15–20 percent; many people double the 8.25 percent sales tax. Coat-check attendants will expect at least $1 per coat. Room service waiters and taxi drivers should also receive at least 15 percent (no less than 25¢ for cab drivers); bellhops expect about $1 per suitcase, $2 in luxury hotels. Porters in airports expect at least $1 per bag. Others to tip include doormen who help with packages or summon a taxi ($1–2), hotel chambermaids ($2 per day), and concierges. The size of the concierge's tip depends on the difficulty (and quality) of the service. While $3–5 is adequate for making simple tour arrangements, an unusual or difficult service (getting a seat at a "hot" show or in an exclusive restaurant) should command a larger tip, $10 or more.

Toilets

Public toilets are not easy to find in New York. Restaurants are usually unwilling to let non-customers use their facilities, though you may succeed if you walk boldly and impersonate a customer. Other options are department stores, free museums, libraries, hotel lobbies (ask at the desk if necessary), buildings with public atriums (Trump Tower, CitiGroup Building), mega-stores with cafés, stores that cater to children, and the Times Square Visitors Center (1560 Broadway between 46th and 47th Sts). The Bathroom Diaries (www.thebathroomdiaries.com) is a user-reviewed database of toilets in Manhattan and many other cities worldwide.

SHOPPING

Shopping is a major tourist attraction and, for some New Yorkers, a hobby. Most department stores open at 10am and remain open until 6pm or later; some are open in the evening one day a week; some are open Sun 11–5 or 12–6. Specialty shops and boutiques may open and close later.

Where to shop

In former days, Midtown was the focus of fashionable shopping, with outlying neighborhoods known for special products sold in specialty stores clustered together for the convenience of buyers. Thus there were districts for lighting, kitchen supplies, flowers, sewing and millinery supplies including feathers, and musical instruments. While traces of this older economy remain, shopping areas now reflect the general economic level of the neighborhood rather than a specific trade or product.

Dealers in musical instruments can still be found on 45th St between Sixth and Seventh Aves and also on 48th St in the same crosstown block. There are antique (and junk) shops in the 30s on Second and Third Aves, and on Columbus Ave in the low 80s. Shops with notions, trimmings, millinery supplies, and similar paraphernalia can be found in the Garment District (mid- to high 30s around Seventh Ave). West 47th St, just off Fifth Ave, is "Diamond Street," with upscale jewelers located nearby on Fifth Ave.

Although New York has seen an influx of chain stores whose presence homogenizes the experience of shopping, there are still some neighborhoods with their own special ambience.

Lower East Side and East Village: The Lower East Side, once home to a large Jewish immigrant population from Eastern Europe, has traditionally been the center of bargain shopping. Orchard St is known for discounted clothing and lingerie stores. The Bowery between Grand and Delancey Sts has lighting fixtures. Many stores on the Lower East Side are closed on Sat. In the East Village are shops with books, used records and CDs, vintage clothing, and other paraphernalia.

SoHo: Now too expensive to be home turf for any but the most successful artists, SoHo still has an eye for style—fashions for men and women, home furnishings, cosmetics, even food.

The Meatpacking District: Like SoHo, stylish and expensive. Especially clothing, accessories, and home furnishings.

Chelsea and the Flatiron District: Both have large chain stores including Barnes & Noble, Filene's Basement, as well as stylish clothing stores (to the west of the district near Eleventh Ave). Art galleries have moved to the western fringes of the district near 10th Ave.

Fifth Avenue: From Central Park South down to about 50th St there is a mix of very expensive shops, department stores, and the kind of chain stores familiar from malls across the country. In addition to the toyseller FAO Schwarz and the classic department stores—Bergdorf Goodman, Henri Bendel, and Saks Fifth Avenue—the Japanese department store chain Takashimaya has a branch here, as do the jewelers Cartier, Tiffany, Harry Winston, and Bvlgari. Trump Tower and Rockefeller Center have shops at various price levels.

57th St and environs: A center for luxury shopping, with clothing by internationally known designers. New, and more affordable arrivals west of Fifth Ave include occasional bookshops and a few fabric shops left over from the past, which will probably soon be replaced by fancier establishments. Madison Ave north of 57th St is a center of couture boutiques and art galleries.

New York's grand old department stores

Department stores are known for their wide range of goods and services, and many of the country's most famous have their flagship locations in New York. They offer convenience and ambiance but not bargain prices. The most notable are Bergdorf Goodman (Fifth Ave at 58th St), Bloomingdale's (59th St and Lexington Ave), Henri Bendel (Fifth Ave between 55th and 56th Sts), Lord & Taylor (Fifth Ave at 39th St), Macy's (Herald Square, Sixth Ave at 34th St) and Saks Fifth Avenue (Fifth Ave at 50th St).

EVENTS, FESTIVALS, & PARADES

This is just a sampling of the events that take place in the city. For dates, times, locations, T: 212 484 1222; www.nycvisit.com. Another informative website is www.carnaval.com/cityguides/newyork/parades.htm.

January: *New Year's Day*, public holiday; *Martin Luther King, Jr. Birthday* (Mon closest to Jan 19), public holiday; *Winter Antiques Show*, at 7th Regiment Armory; *National Boat Show*, at Javits Center; *Outsider Art Fair*, Puck Building, Lafayette St at Houston St.

February: *Chinese New Year*, end of Jan/early Feb, Chinatown; *President's Day*, third Mon in Feb, public holiday; *Black History Month*, citywide programs; *Westminster Kennel Club Dog Show*, Madison Sq Garden; *Empire State Building Run-Up*: invitational race up 86 stories.

March: *St. Patrick's Day Parade*, March 17, Fifth Ave, from about 50th–86th Sts; *Ringling Bros and Barnum & Bailey Circus*, Madison Sq Garden, late March/early April; *Greek Independence Day Parade*, March 25 or a Sun close (date shifted during Orthodox Lent), Fifth Ave to about 59th St to 79th St.

April: *Easter floral displays*: Rockefeller Center, Brooklyn Botanic Garden, New York Botanical Garden in the Bronx; *Easter Parade*, Easter Sun 10–4, spring finery and creative hats, Fifth Ave, 49th–57th Sts; *Macy's Flower Show*: thou-sands of plants from around the world; *Cherry Blossom Festival*, late April/early May, Brooklyn Botanic Garden.

May: *Ninth Ave Food Festival*, weekend event, 11am–7pm; Ninth Ave, 37th St–57th Sts; *Fleet Week*, West 46th St at Hudson River, parade of ships; *Memorial Day*, last Mon, public holiday.

June: *Metropolitan Opera in parks*, all five boroughs; *Museum Mile Celebration*, Fifth Ave, 82nd–105th Sts, museums stay open late, special exhibitions, early June; *JVC Jazz Festival*, formerly held at Newport, Rhode Island, performances in various venues, early June; *Mermaid Parade*, Coney Island, Sat in late June; *Shakespeare in the Park*, Delacorte Theater, Central Park at 81st St, through Aug: tickets distributed 6:15 pm day of performance; one per person, line forms early afternoon.

July: *Independence Day*, July 4, public holiday: events at Battery Park, in the rivers around Lower Manhattan, fireworks from river barges; *St. Paulinus Festival*, Williamsburg, Brooklyn. *Italian street festival*, late June–mid-July: procession with towering monument to Our Lady of Mt. Carmel church; *Mostly Mozart Festival* at

Lincoln Center, New York Philharmonic concerts in parks, free, July–early Aug.
August: *New York International Fringe Festival*, two weeks from early Aug, more than 200 companies perform.
September: *Labor Day*, first Mon in Sept, public holiday: Labor Day Parade, Fifth Ave from 44th–72nd Sts; West Indian-American Day Carnevale in Brooklyn. Labor Day weekend, with parade on Mon, along Eastern Pkwy from Utica Ave to the Brooklyn Museum. Extravagant costumes, West Indian music, dancing in the streets. Huge event; *Broadway on Broadway*: free outdoor concert in Times Sq; *Feast of San Gennaro* in Little Italy on Mulberry St, about 10 days in mid-Sept, street fair, procession with saint's image; *New York Film Festival*, Lincoln Center, late Sept–early Oct.
October: *Columbus Day*, second Mon, public holiday: Columbus Day Parade, 5th Ave, 44th–79th Sts, 11am, with Italian-American groups, bands, floats, beauty queens, street festival on Lower Broadway; *BAM Next Wave Festival*, Brooklyn Academy of Music; avant-garde dance, opera, theater, music; *Hallowe'en events*, parade in Greenwich Village.
November: *Election Day*, first Tues, public holiday; *Thanksgiving*, fourth Thur, public holiday: Thanksgiving Parade, Central Park West from 77th–59th Sts, then

down Broadway to Macy's at 34th St. Floats, bands, giant helium-filled balloons pulled by more than 1,000 attendants; *New York City Marathon*, 26.2-mile race through the five boroughs, Sun late in Oct/early Nov, begins at Verrazano Bridge 10:30am and finishes at Tavern-on-the-Green in Central Park; *Veterans Day Parade*, Fifth Ave, 39th–23rd Sts, Nov 11 (morning); *Christmas preparations*: windows along Fifth Ave. Tree and illuminated angels in the Channel Gardens at Rockefeller Center. Radio City Music Hall Christmas spectacular begins, Christmas pageant, Rockettes, mid-Nov–early Jan. Planetarium Christmas show begins, late Nov/early Dec, Hayden Planetarium, American Museum of Natural History.
December: *Christmas*, Dec 25, public holiday: Christmas tree lightings at Rockefeller Center, City Hall, other borough halls. Tuba Christmas, Rockefeller Center, brass choirs. Large Christmas tree with 18th-century Neapolitan carved angels and crèche figures in Medieval Sculpture Hall, Metropolitan Museum; *Hanukkah*: candle lighting at City Hall, Hanukkah Menorah, Grand Army Plaza, 5th Ave at 59th St; *New Year's Eve* in Times Sq, recommended only for those undaunted by celebratory crowds. Midnight ball-drop (*see p. 221*).

HOTELS

New York hotels are the most expensive in the country. The average nightly rate for 2007 was $320.87, 15.4 percent higher than the previous year; rates are expected to rise further. And while that $320.87 will buy a very pleasant room in a four- or-five-star hotel elsewhere in the country, in New York it will get you something small and perhaps not scrupulously clean, with an airshaft or brick-wall view. Since the average occupancy rate in the same period was 83 percent, you should book early.

Probably the most expensive place to stay is the penthouse at the Four Seasons listed at $30,000 a night. (It has a Bösendorfer piano and comes with a chauffeured Rolls Royce and a personal trainer.)

In recent years several hyper-designed boutique hotels with cell-like rooms (you may have to stand on the bed to change your clothes) have joined the scene. Originally their prices were modest, but rates have risen along with the rest of the market.

To the already high tariff, the city and state add a 13.25 percent sales tax (8.375 for the state, and 5 percent for the city) plus an occupancy fee of $3.50 or more. There are, however, a few things you can do to lessen the sticker shock. At certain times of the year, prices double or even triple: in the early autumn after the summer slump; in the pre-Christmas shopping rush; and for special events like the New York marathon. At these peak times even budget chains may charge more than $300. Booking online may ease the pain, even using the hotels' own websites; and there are bargains sometimes at such sites as Orbitz.com, Expedia.com, Hotels.com, and Tablethotels.com. If online rooms are sold out, you can sometimes find space by calling the hotel directly.

Most B&B rooms have minimum stays. City Lights Bed and Breakfast (T: 212 737 7049, www.citylightsbandb.com) and City Sonnet (T: 212 614 3034, www.citysonnet.com) are two agencies that offer listings. In a hosted apartment, you stay in someone's extra room; in an unhosted accommodation, you have the run of the entire apartment. The West Side YMCA near Lincoln Center (T: 212 875 4100, www.ymcanyc.org) and the Vanderbilt YMCA, near the United Nations (T: 212 912 2500, www.ymcanyc.org) both offer basic accommodations.

BLUE GUIDES RECOMMENDED

Hotels, restaurants and cafés that are particularly good choices in their category—in terms of excellence, location, charm, value for money or the quality of the experience they provide—carry the Blue Guides Recommended sign: ■. All these establishments have been visited and selected by our authors, editors or contributors as places they have particularly enjoyed and would be happy to recommend to others. To keep our entries up-to-date, reader feedback is essential: please do not hesitate to email us (editorial@blueguides.com) with any views, corrections or suggestions.

The list below, which reflects prices at the time of writing, includes hotels from all categories and should give a picture of the overall scene.

$$$$ More than $600
$$$ $450–600
$$ $250–450
$ Less than $250

Battery Park–26th Street

$$$$ Ritz-Carlton Battery Park. ■ *2 West St (Battery Place), T: 212 344 0800; ww.ritzcarlton.com. 259 rooms and 39 suites. Map, p. 582, B4.* Wonderful views of New York Harbor (or Downtown skyline) and a high comfort level. Large rooms by New York standards, luxurious appointments, and windows that actually open. Telescopes in the harbor-view rooms let you view the comings and goings in the river; club-level rooms have a separate, private entrance. Rise, the cocktail bar on the 14th floor overlooking the harbor, offers stylish food and drink.

$$$ Gramercy Park Hotel. *2 Lexington Ave (21st St), T: 212 920 3300, www.gramercyparkhotel.com. 184 rooms. Map p. 581, D2.* Celebrity hotelier Ian Schrager's newest venture opened in 2006 amidst a barrage of publicity. The building, a hotel for arty types since the 1920s, was completely done over in a color-drenched eclectic style chosen in collaboration with artist Julian Schnabel. Supersized paintings fill the lobby; giant chandeliers hang from the ceiling; on the roof is a private club, open to hotel guests. Guests have access to Gramercy Park, otherwise open only to neighborhood residents. In addition to the Rose and Jade bars, the hotel has a haute-Chinese restaurant, Wakiya, named for its Japanese-born, Chinese-trained chef.

$$$ Hotel on Rivington. *107 Rivington St (Ludlow and Essex Sts), T: 212 475 2600, www.hotelonrivington.com. 90 rooms and 20 suites. Map, p. 583, D1.* A sleek high-rise, hi-tech newcomer (2005) on the low-rise, still gritty Lower East Side. Many, but not all, rooms offer jaw-dropping views of the city below; Wi-Fi, Frette linens; well-stocked bathrooms (but showers have glass walls facing out, privacy screens available), some with soaking tubs. The neighborhood may not appeal to everyone; service can be uneven; hotel is not close to the main sights. THOR, the in-house restaurant features neo-Austrian cooking; complimentary continental breakfast.

$$$ The Mercer Hotel. ■ *147 Mercer St (Prince St), T: 212 966 6060; www.mercer-hotel.com. 67 rooms and 8 suites. Map, p. 581, D4.* Completed 1997, the Mercer attracted celebrities even before the doors opened. The architectural features of the Romanesque Revival loft building (1892), constructed as an Astor family investment, add to the ambience: large windows, high ceilings, thick walls. Spacious bathrooms. Details are carefully planned, from the cool muted colors and subdued graphics to the clean-lined furniture. In the basement is Jean-Georges Vongerichten's stylish Mercer Kitchen.

$$$ SoHo Grand Hotel. *310 West Broadway (Grand and Canal Sts), T: 212-965-3000, www.sohogrand.com. 369 rooms. Map, p. 582, B1.* The hip SoHo Grand Hotel opened in 1996, the first new luxury hotel in SoHo since the 1870s. Owned by Hartz Mountain Industries, who made their name marketing bird seed and pet products, the SoHo Grand is very pet friendly; pet amenities include chew toys and kitty litter boxes. Among the amenities for humans are complimentary bicycles in warm weather and complimentary in-room goldfish. Rooms decorated in subtle colors with natural materials: wood, clay, canvas and leather. Chic bar with an outdoor patio in warm weather.

$$ Blue Moon. *100 Orchard St (Delancey and Broome Sts), T: 212 533 9080, www.bluemoon-nyc.com. 22 rooms. Map, p. 583, D1.* Occupies a refurbished tenement on the Lower East Side. Updated tenement decor—a mixture of antique and new furnishings, vintage posters, and retro bathroom fixtures. Complimentary breakfast buffet; good-sized rooms. Good neighborhood for restaurants and bars, though distant from the usual tourist sites; lively street life (which can translate as noise). Top-floor rooms have views of the Williamsburg Bridge. Rates vary widely.

$$ The Chelsea Hotel. *222 West 22nd St (Seventh and Eighth Aves), T: 212 243 3700; www.chelseahotel.com. 250 rooms. Map, p. 580, B2.* The legendary Chelsea is famous not for the accommodations but for former clientele—authors, artists, and musicians from O. Henry to Sid Vicious. Depending on your priorities, you may find it quirky and quaint or overpriced and dingy. Walls are famously thick, rooms are large; those facing the street may be noisy. But history remains the Chelsea's chief attraction. The hotel, under new management since June 2007, is more expensive than formerly and will probably be upgraded.

$$ Hotel Giraffe. *365 Park Ave South (26th St), T: 212 685 7700, www.hotelgiraffe.com. 73 rooms and 21 suites. Map p. 581, D1.* A themed boutique hotel; the eponymous giraffe appears in the hotel's graphics and as a statue in the roof garden. The style throughout is comfortably Art Deco, with an attractive lobby (piano music in the early evening) and pleasantly furnished rooms and suites, some with balconies. The neighborhood is not close to any major tourist sites, but is relatively quiet and relaxing. Complimentary continental breakfast, daytime snacks, and wine reception.

$$ Inn on 23rd Street. *131 West 23rd St (Sixth and Seventh Aves), T: 212 463 0330, www.innon23rd.com. 14 rooms. Map p. 580, C2.* Small and family-owned, this bed-and-breakfast offers good value and pleasant surroundings in a restored Chelsea town house. Cozy decor varies from room to room; some rooms lighter than others. Complimentary continental breakfast; double-glazed windows and white noise machines to decrease street noise. Close to public transportation. Reserve well ahead.

$$ Wall Street Inn. ■ *9 South William St (Broad and William Sts), T: 212 747 1500, www.thewallstreetinn.com. 46 rooms. Map p. 582, C4.* Opened in 1999, this landmarked stone-cobbled structure is only seven stories high, which suits its location next to the Stone Street Historic District, a low-profile enclave tucked amidst the area's skyscrapers. Compact rooms are well-appointed with attractive furnishings and marble-tiled bathrooms. Rates here are significantly higher during the week, but on the weekends it can be quite reasonable. The neighborhood can be deserted outside of business hours.

$ The Cosmopolitan. *95 West Broadway (Chambers St), T: 212 566 1900, www.cosmohotel.com. 150 rooms. Map, p. 582, B2.* Popular budget hotel, in business since 1853 (*see p. 96*). Few amenities, but simple, clean rooms. Some rooms are small and some, facing busy Chambers St, are noisy. The location, on the edge of TriBeCa, is close to the World Trade Center site and conveniently near two subway lines. Café in the hotel and a Starbucks in the building.

$ **Washington Square Hotel**. *103 Waverly Place (MacDougal St), T: 212 777 9515; www.washingtonsquarehotel.com. 160 rooms. Map, p. 580, C3.* At the northwest corner of Washington Square, this conglomerate of three buildings has long been favored by writers, musicians, and budget-minded visitors seeking Greenwich Village ambience. Among them (back in its days as the Hotel Earle) were Bob Dylan and Joan Baez. Rooms are small but clean; those in front overlook the square; those in back can be dark. The Art Deco lobby and many of the rooms have been renovated. Free continental breakfast, fitness room, Wi-Fi in the lobby; hotel is smoke free. North Square restaurant serves lunch, tea, and dinner.

41st–59th Streets, Midtown

$$$$ **Four Seasons New York**. ■ *57 East 57th St (Madison and Park Aves), T: 212 758 5700, www.fourseasons.com/newyorkfs. 368 rooms and 63 suites. Map p. 579, D2.* Designed by I.M. Pei, the luxurious Four Seasons New York is executed on a grand scale from the monumental lobby decorated with severe granite columns and a lighted onyx ceiling panel 33ft above the floor to the guestrooms, which are large by New York standards. Rooms above the 25th floor have views either of the skyline or of Central Park. State-of-the-art spa and exercise facilities. The restaurant, L'Atelier de Joël Robuchon, overseen by the celebrity chef, features his signature open kitchen and exquisite minimalist French-Asian cooking, at luxury prices.

$$$$ **The Plaza**. *Fifth Ave at Central Park South, T: 212 759 3000, www.fairmonthotels.com. 282 rooms and suites. Map p. 579, D2.* The Plaza, one of the city's most famous hotels, was upscale when it opened in 1907; a hundred years later it reopened after a $400-million makeover in which the storied public spaces—the Palm Court, the Oak Room and Bar, and the Plaza Grand Ballroom—were returned to their former splendor, but many rooms were converted to private residences. Although pets can check in for $75 a stay, rates for their owners easily reach four figures. Luxury in every detail, from white-glove butlers to gold bathroom fixtures. Prime location, facing Grand Army Plaza at the southeast corner of Central Park.

$$$$ **The St. Regis**. ■ *2 East 55th St (Fifth and Madison Aves), T: 212 753 4500, www.stregis.com. 182 rooms and 74 suites (some former rooms have been reconfigured as private apartments). Map p. 579, D2.* This landmarked hotel was built in 1904 by John Jacob Astor IV and designed by the architects of the J.P. Morgan building on Wall St. Recently updated, it is known for its Gilded Age ambience—high ceilings, silk wall coverings, chandeliers, and, of course, lots of gilding. Impeccable service includes a butler on every floor. Maxfield Parrish's famous mural overlooks the King Cole Bar; Alain Ducasse's restaurant Adour opened in 2008.

$$$ **Jumeirah Essex House**. *160 Central Park South (Sixth and Seventh Aves), T: 212 247 0300, www.jumeirahessexhouse.com. 515 rooms. Map p. 578, C2.* Famous 39-story Art Deco hotel owned by the Dubai-based Jumeirah group and opulently

refurbished to evoke the "golden age of travel" (the 1920s and '30s). Some rooms have views of Central Park, some are smallish. The electronics and other amenities are cutting-edge (high-definition TV, VOIP telephones, self-guided Central Park walks—a combination of audio podcasts, maps, and interactive guides). Chef Kerry Heffernan heads the kitchen at the hotel's South Gate restaurant, featuring contemporary American cuisine.

$$$ W Times Square. *1567 Broadway (West 47th St), T: 212 930 7400, www.whotels.com. 507 rooms and 43 suites. Map p. 578, C3.* W hotels have a reputation for modern minimalist decor balanced by deluxe bedding and bath products. The Times Square location is ideal for visitors determined to be in the thick of the Theater District. This W picks up Times Square's neon vibe and raises the ante with its urban noir lobby and check-in floor-cum-bar. The hotel reaches 52 stories into the sky, so try for a room with a view. Can be noisy. Right downstairs, Steve Hanson's noted Blue Fin offers swanky dining.

$$$ The Waldorf=Astoria. *301 Park Ave (49th and 50th Sts), T: 212 355 3000, www.waldorfastoria.com. 1,235 rooms. Map p. 579, D3–E3.* One of New York's most famous hotels, occupying a niche in the city's social history. On the 50th St side is the Waldorf Towers, a hotel-within-a-hotel, the most expensive and exclusive part of the complex. The Waldorf's Art Deco lobby is famous, built on stilts to absorb the vibrations from the Metro North trains running below. Classic furniture and marble bathrooms; several restaurants including Peacock Alley (American casual). The double hyphen in

the hotel's name is said to express the equality of the original Waldorf and Astoria, and/or to represent Peacock Alley, which separated the two hotels.

$$ The Algonquin. *59 West 44th St (Fifth and Sixth Aves), T: 212 840 6800, www.algonquin hotel.com. 150 rooms and 24 suites. Map, p. 579, D3.* This landmarked hotel has literary associations dating back to the 1920s when the Round Table, a group of well-known editors and writers, met here for lunch (*see p. 214*). The lobby, paneled in dark wood, is comfortably furnished with upholstered chairs. The Oak Room hosts one of the city's best cabarets. The guest rooms are on the small side, but pleasantly decorated, most recently in 2004. Close to Times Square and the Theater District, Fifth Avenue, and Grand Central Station.

$$ City Club Hotel. *55 West 44th St (Fifth and Sixth Aves), T: 212 921 5500; www.cityclub.com. 65 rooms. Map, p. 579, D3.* This block of West 44th St hosts several clubs—the New York Yacht, the Harvard, and since 2001, the City Club Hotel, formerly a gentlemen's political club. The "petite" sized rooms, suitable for a single occupant, were originally for the gentlemen's servants; the duplex suites were carved out of the two-story ballroom. Furnishings combine tradition with innovation, with elaborately plastered ceilings and other original architectural details still intact. The onsite restaurant is DB Bistro Moderne, Daniel Boulud's upscale bistro, where you can lunch on the signature db burger, a sirloin burger stuffed with *foie gras* and truffles.

$$ DoubleTree Metropolitan Hotel. *569 Lexington Ave (51st St), T: 212 752 7000,*

www.metropolitannyc.com. *755 rooms. Map p. 579, E3.* DoubleTree committed to refined 1960s Modernism when it took over the former Summit Hotel, designed by Morris Lapidus, best known for his curvilinear Miami Beach hotels. Building on the Lapidus-designed 1961 exterior (the original 1950s-influenced bubble signage has been nicely adapted), the lobby is colorfully sleek and space-age. The rooms are tastefully subtle; on-site Met Grill and cardio center.

$$ Hotel QT. *145 West 45th St (Sixth and Seventh Aves), T: 212 354 2323, www.hotelqt.com. 140 rooms. Map p. 578, C3.* An updated, cleverly designed take on a European youth hostel, with compact rooms (like cabins on an ultramodern ship), built-in furniture, a small bar, and a very small (22-ft) swimming pool in the lobby. Amenities include a sauna and steam room, wireless internet, DVD players, and a complimentary breakfast. Affordable and frill free, popular with young visitors.

$$ Library Hotel. *299 Madison Avenue (41st St), T: 212 983 4500, www.libraryhotel.com. 60 rooms. Map p. 579, D4.* All the rooms in this European-style boutique hotel are stocked with books; should you run out of reading material it's only a short distance from the New York Public Library and the Morgan Library. The hotel is organized according to the Dewey Decimal System, with each of its ten floors devoted to a Dewey decimal category—religion, history, general knowledge, literature, and so on. Room 800.001, Erotic Literature, is reputedly a favorite. The public spaces include the glass-enclosed wraparound Poetry Terrace, and the Writer's Den with leather seating and a cozy fireplace. Many extras: continental breakfast, complimentary passes to a nearby sports club, a free wine-and-cheese event on weekdays, snacks and bottled water. Close to Times Square (but far enough away to be restful) and a block from Grand Central.

Upper East Side, north of 59th Street

$$$$ The Carlyle. *35 East 76th St (Madison Ave), T: 212 744 1600, www.thecarlyle.com. 187 rooms and suites. Map p. 577, D4.* The luxurious Carlyle, with its familiar Art Deco tower, has long been a favorite of the famous—presidents, foreign dignitaries, and celebrities either seeking the limelight or trying to stay out of it. The rooms are furnished elegantly but conservatively. Pets (under 25lb) can enjoy Fiji water and suitable snacks. The Café Carlyle has a famous cabaret; the Bemelmans Bar retains the noted mural by the illustrator of the Madeline children's books.

$$$ The Lowell. *28 East 63rd St (Park and Madison Aves), T: 212 838 1400, www.lowellhotel.com. 70 rooms and suites. Map p. 579, D1.* A long-standing reputation (since 1926) among people who expect to be treated with the utmost discretion (celebrities know they are secure here) makes this a favored stayover spot. The renowned Post House restaurant is part of the establishment, and the hotel also has its own dining room (afternoon tea, round-the-clock room service). Dogs and cats are welcome. Some rooms have working fireplaces, others have private terraces, all have Wi-Fi.

$$$ The Mark. *25 East 77th St (Madison Ave), www.themarkhotel. com. 118 rooms. Map p. 577, D4.* This already luxurious Upper East Side hotel (opened 1927; scheduled to reopen around press time of this guide) is being refurbished to the highest standards of opulence and comfort. Some of the rooms have been reconfigured as co-op apartments, so the hotel now has fewer rentable rooms. The Mark will also offer amenities ranging from limousine service to in-suite massages and hair styling.

$$ Hotel Wales. *1295 Madison Ave (92nd St), T: 212 876 6000, www.waleshotel.com. 46 rooms and 41 suites. Map p. 577, D2.* Small hotel at the edge of Carnegie Hill, a quiet, upscale residential neighborhood. Rooms are simply decorated but comfortable; the beds have down comforters; the deluxe suites offer views of the Reservoir in Central Park. Sarabeth's Restaurant, a favorite for brunch, desserts, and pastries, is in the building, as is Joanna's, a popular Italian brasserie.

Upper West Side, north of 59th Street

$$$$ The Mandarin Oriental New York. ■ *80 Columbus Circle, (60th St), T: 212 805 8800, www.mandarinoriental.com. 251 rooms. Map p. 578, B2.* Located on the 35th–54th floors of the Time Warner Center's north tower, this is a serious contender for the city's most luxurious hotel, with views of Central Park and/or the Hudson River. The Asian-influenced decor, the high-tech luxuries (surround-sound stereos, face-to-face video conferencing), and impeccable service set this hotel above the crowd. Spa with steam room, soaking tubs, a 75-ft lap pool, and floor-to-ceiling windows so that you can watch the Hudson as you swim. Within the hotel are Asiate, a Japanese-French fusion restaurant; the Lobby Lounge for light fare, desserts, and afternoon tea; and the popular MObar, with Asian-influenced cocktails. The two-bedroom Presidential Suite, with a study and kitchenette, rents for $14,000 nightly.

$$ Excelsior. *45 West 81st St (Central Park West), T: 212 362 9200; www.excelsiorhotelny.com. 200 rooms. Map p. 576, B3.* In a quiet, upscale West Side residential neighborhood, the Excelsior is half a block from Central Park West and across the street from the American Museum of Natural History. A crosstown bus goes right to the Metropolitan Museum. There is nothing trendy about the Excelsior. The public rooms and elevators sport wood paneling; the decor of the guest rooms is old-fashioned, and the rooms are smallish but clean. Some have park views. In the hotel is an upscale restaurant featuring contemporary American cuisine.

$$ On the Ave. *222 West 77th St (Broadway and Amsterdam Ave), T: 212 362 1100; www.ontheave-nyc.com/ main.htm. 260 rooms. Map p. 576, B4.* There are not many hotels close to Lincoln Center, so On the Ave is a good choice for this neighborhood. Some rooms have private balconies; piano in the lobby with nightly music. On the 16th floor a shared balcony space has been outfitted with Adirondack chairs and potted plants for enjoying the view. No restaurant, but convenient eating places nearby.

RESTAURANTS

The New York restaurant scene is as diverse as the city's population. If you want marbled beef or tuna tartare, pizza or a hot dog with kraut, you can find it somewhere in New York. Reservations are absolutely necessary at the most popular restaurants, some of which start booking tables two months in advance. Eating early (before 6pm) or late (10pm) can improve your chances of getting a reservation. If your plans are flexible, you can ask to be put on a waiting list for cancellations. Open Table (opentable.com) is an online service for booking at many restaurants.

Many restaurants will call the day before to ask for confirmation that you still plan to honor your reservation. If the restaurant doesn't call you, call them to reconfirm. If you change your plans, be sure to cancel. A much-told tale recounts André Soltner, owner of the late great Lutèce, calling a no-show at 3am and saying, "My staff and myself are still waiting for you, should we continue?"

A few high-end restaurants are beginning to include service with the price of the meal, and it is often included for groups of more than six people. When service is not included, a tip of 16–20 percent is appropriate. The easiest way to calculate the amount is to double the sales tax of 8.265 percent and add a little more if you're pleased. Tip the bartender at least dollar a drink, and the coat check person at least a dollar a coat.

Almost all restaurants accept major credit cards, though a few small places (for example in Chinatown) do not. Some high-end restaurants require jackets for men. There is no smoking in New York restaurants.

Since there are more than 18,000 places to eat out in New York City, the following list barely scratches the surface. It is intended to give an overview of the possibilities, and to include restaurants close to major tourist attractions. Zagat's *New York City Restaurants*, updated yearly, summarizes and tabulates comments from diners. *New York Magazine* and *The New York Times* also offer reviews, which are available online.

Price ranges for a three-course meal excluding alcohol, tax, and tip:

> $ under $25
> $$ $25–50
> $$$ $50–75
> $$$$ more than $75

Battery Park–14th Street

$$ **Bridge Café**. 279 Water St (Dover St), T: 212 227 3344. *Lunch Mon–Fri, brunch Sun; dinner seven days. Map p. 583, D3.* The old wood-frame building suggests the age of this casual café tucked under the Brooklyn Bridge, possibly New York's oldest continuously operating bar. Good American food, including seafood, steak (beef and buffalo), and home-made desserts. Service is friendly; the room, with its tin ceiling and old oak bar, is cozy and even romantic.

$ Oriental Garden. *14 Elizabeth St (Bayard and Canal Sts), T: 212 619 0085. Open daily, lunch and dinner. Map p. 583, D2.* Good Chinatown Chinese, i.e. brusque service, simple decor, long menu, but good value and many good dishes, especially seafood. Dim sum lunch. No credit cards for bills less than $60.

$$ Peking Duck House. *28 Mott St (Chatham Square and Pell St), T: 212 227 1810, www.pekingduckhousenyc.com. Closed Thanksgiving. Map p. 583, D2.* One of Chinatown's longest-established restaurants, famous for crisp-skinned roast duck. More upscale than most in the neighborhood; uptown branch at 236 East 53rd St (*T: 212 759 8260*).

$ Katz's. *205 East Houston St (Ludlow St), T: 212 254 2246, www.katzdeli.com. Breakfast, lunch, and dinner daily; open late Fri and Sat. Map p. 581, E4.* On the Lower East Side. One of the few remaining authentic New York delis, established in 1888, known for hand-cut pastrami, corned beef, and brisket sandwiches so fully loaded that they could unhinge your jaw. Katz's is not kosher, so the entrées include Reuben sandwiches and bagels with lox and cream cheese, along with the meat dishes. Coffee, tea, seltzer, soft drinks including Dr. Brown's, and also egg creams. Cash only.

$ 'inoteca. *98 Rivington St (Ludlow St), T: 212 614 0473, www.inotecanyc.com. Open seven days, lunch, dinner, and late dining. Map p. 581, E4.* Italian wine bar serving small plates, salads, panini, and sandwiches to a young, stylish Lower East Side crowd. Wine list offers more than 600 wines from all over Italy, more than 30 by the glass. Simple rustic setting; can be crowded; service can be slow.

$$$$ Bouley. *120 West Broadway (Duane St), T: 212 964 2525, www.davidbouley.com. Open seven days, lunch and dinner. Map p. 582, B2.* David Bouley is one of the city's star chefs, and this restaurant in a low vaulted space is the center of a growing TriBeCa empire. Bouley's Gallic creations touched with Asian seasonings leave no doubt as to his talent. Jacket required.

$$$ Danube. *30 Hudson St (Duane and Reade Sts), T: 212 791 3771, www.davidbouley.com. Dinner only, Mon–Sat; closed Sun. Map p. 582, B2.* David Bouley's *fin-de-siècle*-style haute Viennese restaurant in TriBeCa. Golden, Klimt-ish paintings hang on the walls of the dining room, lit with soft amber lighting. The food is good, too, with Austrian favorites modernized and lightened for contemporary tastes, and an eclectic international menu.

$$$$ Chanterelle. *2 Harrison St (Hudson St), T: 212 966 6960. www.chanterellenyc.com. Dinner seven days, lunch Thur–Sat. Map p. 582, B2.* A lovely French restaurant in TriBeCa, with superb food from an award-winning chef, widely spaced tables, and polished service. The menus, written in longhand, have covers with artists' images (Jennifer Bartlett, Merce Cunningham, Cy Twombly), changed twice yearly. In business since 1979 and still admirable.

$$$ Wallsé. *344 West 11th St (Washington St), T: 212 352 2300, www.wallse.com. Dinner daily, brunch Sat and Sun. Map p. 580, B3.* Named for chef Kurt Gutenbrunner's hometown (Wallsee), its logo inspired by Egon Schiele's signature, this friendly West Village restaurant serves sophisticated Austrian-inspired food in a pleasant neighborhood setting. While avocado-and-lobster salad may not be a staple of the Eastern European diet, many other dishes hark back to their country of

origin, including such traditional favorites as *spaetzle* or Wiener schnitzel. Good selection of Austrian wines.

$$$ Fiamma. *206 Spring St (Sixth Ave and Sullivan St), T: 212 653 0100, www. brguestrestaurants.com. Dinner only Mon–Sat, closed Sun. Map p. 582, B1.* Fiamma serves beautifully prepared, imaginative food. While chef Fabio Trabocchi hails from Le Marche (and more recently Washington, D.C.), the cuisine is eclectic, partly Italian regional, partly composed of dishes and ingredients from elsewhere—Maine lobster, tofu, and Wagyu beef. The main dining room on the second floor of a SoHo town house, decorated in warm tones of reds and oranges, is inviting and romantic.

$$$ Babbo. *110 Waverly Place (MacDougal St and Sixth Ave), T: 212 777 0303, www.babbonyc.com. Dinner only, seven days. Map p. 580, C3.* New in 1998, Babbo has become New York's favorite Italian restaurant. Two floors of a Greenwich Village town house are devoted to often adventurous food, including such items as fresh anchovies and head cheese that were unfamiliar to American palates when the restaurant opened. Long and varied wine list. The owners are celebrities of American cooking, Mario Batali and Joseph Bastianich.

$$$ Blue Hill. *75 Washington Place (MacDougal St and Sixth Ave), T: 212 539 1776, www.bluehillnyc.com. Dinner only, seven days. Map p. 580, C4.* Popular cellar restaurant (with garden room in summer) serving seasonal American food. Talented chef Dan Barber gets fresh ingredients from Stone Barns in Westchester County, or from Blue Hill in Massachusetts, where his grandparents were farmers.

$$ Lupa. *170 Thompson St (Bleecker and Houston Sts), T: 212 982 5089, www.luparestaurant.com. Open seven days, noon–midnight. Map p. 581, D4.* Popular restaurant owned by Batali and Bastianich (who also own Babbo). The aim is for traditional Roman trattoria fare, substituting local ingredients where necessary. Many of the Italian cold cuts are made in-house. The wine list includes offerings from all over Italy. The main dining room, with its brick arches and wooden tables, is noisy but convivial; service can be slow.

$$ Pastis. *9 Ninth Ave (Little West 12th St), T: 212 929 4844, www. pastisny.com. Open seven days, breakfast, lunch (or brunch) and dinner. Map p. 580, B3.* Hip and casual, Pastis draws a lively crowd from morning until the wee hours. The menu offers both traditional bistro fare—onion soup, skate au beurre noir, roast chicken—and such decidedly un-French choices as cheeseburgers and a full English breakfast. Bistro decor; seasonal outdoor seating.

$ Café Mogador. *101 St. Mark's Place (First Ave and Ave A), T: 212 677 2226, www.cafemogador.com. Breakfast or brunch, lunch, and dinner seven days; open late. Map p. 581, E3.* Named after a Moroccan port, this East Village neighborhood restaurant serves excellent Moroccan and Mediterranean food at affordable prices. Along with the couscous, *tagines*, and *bastilla* are Middle Eastern dishes and less exotic dinner specials such as roast chicken. Often crowded; service can be slow.

$ Momofuku Noodle Bar. *171 First Ave (10th and 11th Sts, T: 212 475 7899, www.momofuku.com. Open for lunch and dinner seven days. Map p. 581, E3.* Not your usual noodle bar. Korean-American chef David Chang, winner of the James Beard Foundation's Rising Star Chef of the Year award in 2007, has created an

American variation on a Japanese *ramenya*. In addition to ramen dishes—here made with a pork-based broth rather than the traditional dried bonito—Chang serves seasonal specialties, many featuring products from small independent farms. Caveat: tiny restaurant, waiting lines often stretch down the block.

$$ Momofuku SSäm Bar. *207 Second Ave (13th St), T: 212 254 3500. Open seven days, lunch, dinner, and late dining. Map p. 581, E3.* Ssäm is a Korean term for wrapped food, i.e. Asian burritos. This restaurant is larger and somewhat more expensive than the Momofuku Noodle Bar, but offers the same excellent cooking. Also steamed buns, organ meats, plates of cheeses and meats, and small dishes. Beer and sake, water and a few sodas. Livelier later in the evening. Also crowded.

14th–59th Streets

$$$ Gramercy Tavern. *42 East 20th St (Broadway and Park Ave South), T: 212 477 0777, www.gramercytavern.com. Main dining room open for lunch Mon–Fri, dinner seven days; tavern open lunch and dinner daily; closed some holidays; call ahead. Map p. 581, D2.* A well-known restaurant, expensive, sophisticated, yet purposefully rustic (like the initial conception of Gramercy Park itself—a park in a city). The cuisine is new American, the desserts offer new takes on old favorites; thoughtful and energetic service. À la carte menu in the tavern (no reservations) caters to a younger crowd; prix-fixe and tasting menus in the dining room.

$$ Artisanal. *2 Park Ave (entrance on 32nd St, between Madison and Park Aves), T: 212 725 8585, www.artisanalbistro.com. Open seven days, no Sat brunch from July 4–Labor Day. Map p. 581, D1.* Cheerful (and sometimes loud) Murray Hill brasserie offering more than 250 varieties of cheese, complemented by more than 160 wines by the glass. Dishes range from humble mac and cheese to fondues, onion soup garnished with three cheeses, parmesan gnocchi, and a tasting plate for those who prefer their cheese straight. Also classic bistro food: steak frites, fish frites, lamb shanks, and grilled chicken. On-site fromagerie for takeout. Fun with a group.

$$ Oyster Bar. *On the lower level of Grand Central Terminal, T: 212 490 6650, www.oysterbarny. com. Lunch and dinner Mon–Sat, closed Sun and holidays. Map p. 579, D4.* This historic restaurant has been serving seafood since the station opened in 1913. The Guastavino tile ceiling in the "below sea level" dining room makes for noise and odd acoustic effects. Dozens of varieties of oysters, plus traditional pan roasts, chowders, broiled and grilled fish, and a few non-seafood dishes. Eating a pan-roast at the counter is a real New York pleasure. The more elaborate dishes may be less successful.

$$$ Esca. *402 West 43rd St (Ninth Ave), T: 212 564 7272, www.esca-nyc.com. Dinner seven days, no lunch Sun. Map p. 578, B4.* A Batali-Bastianich venture, Esca ("bait") offers Italian seafood in a convenient Theater District location. Menu varies daily according to market offerings. Whole fish, raw fish, fish with pasta, fish stew, and a few other offerings. Good list of Italian regional wines.

$$ Orso. *322 West 46th St (Eighth and Ninth Aves), T: 212 489 7212,*

www.orsorestaurant.com. Open daily for lunch and dinner, closed holidays. Map p. 578, B3. A Theater District standby for Italian food, including individual pizzas. Book early for pre-theater.

$$$$ Le Bernardin. *155 West 51st (Sixth and Seventh Aves), T: 212 554 1515, www.le-bernardin.com. Closed Sun, no lunch Sat. Map p. 578, C3.* One of the city's great restaurants, elegant and civilized, serving impeccable French-influenced seafood. The service is discreet, and rather formal. The dining room is peaceful, with white tablecloths and lots of teak. All seafood, except for a few token items which can be had on request; menu divided into three categories—"almost raw," "barely touched," and "lightly cooked"—plus dessert; menu is prix fixe, more expensive at dinner.

Upper West Side, 59th Street and north

$$$$ Jean Georges. *1 Central Park West (60th and 61st Sts) in the Trump International Hotel, T: 212 299 3900, www.jean-georges.com. Lunch Mon–Fri, dinner Mon–Sat; closed Sun; Nougatine, the casual front room, also serves breakfast and lunch, seven days. Map p. 578, C2.* The most ambitious New York restaurant of chef Jean-Georges Vongerichten's empire, which stretches as far as Paris and Bora Bora. Signature fusion cooking on a foundation of classic French cuisine, inflected with unexpected ingredients and textures. Discreet, attentive service. Jacket required.

$$$ Café Gray. *10 Columbus Circle (Broadway at 60th St), Time Warner Center, third floor T: 212 823 6338, www.cafegray. com. Dinner, seven days, lunch Mon–Sat. Map p. 578, B2.* High-end Asian-influenced French-Italian food overseen by chef Gray Kunz, who earned his stars at the former Lespinasse. Some diners complain of the open kitchen placed between the tables and the view of Central Park, while others enjoy watching the chefs at work. Few complain of the imaginatively conceived, beautifully presented, and carefully seasoned food. Brasserie menu available in the bar area; pre-theater dinner.

$$$$ Per Se. *10 Columbus Circle, Time Warner Center, T: 212 823 9335, www.perseny.com. Dinner seven days, lunch Fri–Sun. Map p. 578, B2.* Chef Thomas Keller had already become a culinary luminary with the French Laundry in Napa Valley before opening Per Se in 2004, and for many, dining at Per Se constitutes a pilgrimage to a gastronomic shrine. American cuisine with classic French influences. The dining room, small and elegant, has lovely views of Central Park. Diners must choose one of two seasonal prix-fixe menus: a nine-course tasting of vegetables and a nine-course chef's tasting menu. Jacket required.

$$ Rosa Mexicano. *61 Columbus Ave (62nd St), T: 212 977 7700, www.rosamexicano.com. Lunch and dinner seven days. Other locations on First Ave at 58th St, and Union Square. Map p. 578, B2.* Right across the street from Lincoln Center and one of the better choices in the neighborhood. Colorful decor, guacamole prepared at your table, and corn tortillas made on-site. Fun and festive. Good margaritas.

$$$ Picholine. *35 West 64th St (Broadway and Central Park West), T: 212 724 8585. www.picholinenyc.com. Dinner seven days.*

Map p. 578, B1. Another Lincoln Center option, this upscale restaurant long known for its cheese selections has recently been redecorated (in lavender and plum tones) and has updated both its menu and spirit. Very busy before the theater, more relaxed other times.

$$ Café Luxembourg. *200 West 70th St (Amsterdam and West End Aves), T: 212 873 7411; www.cafeluxembourg.com Breakfast, lunch and dinner seven days. Map p. 578,*

B1. This Upper West Side restaurant has been around since 1983, serving brasserie food in a (sometimes noisy), casual setting to an urban crowd that includes neighborhood people, musicians, and concertgoers from nearby Lincoln Center. The food is good (though simpler is better here), the service casual and relaxed, and the setting—tiled walls, red banquettes, old mirrors—warm and attractive. Good value.

Upper East Side

$$$$ Daniel. *60 East 65th St (Park and Madison Aves), T: 212 288 0033; www-danielnyc.com. Open Mon–Sat, dinner only; closed Sun. Map p. 579, D1.* Chef Daniel Boulud's first New York restaurant, serving contemporary French cuisine prepared by a classically trained kitchen brigade. Prix-fixe and tasting menus. Wine cellar with 1,500 choices ranging from modest to extravagant.

$$$ Café Boulud. *20 East 76th St (Madison and Fifth Aves), T: 212 772 2600; www.danielnyc.com. Open lunch Tues–Sat; Sun brunch; dinner seven days. Map p. 577, D4.* Daniel Boulud's French-inspired food, reminiscent perhaps of the food served by his ancestors at the family café near Lyon, ranges from traditional, through seasonal, to cosmopolitan. Serene and sedate Upper East Side surroundings, though less formal than Daniel (*see above*).

$ Beyoglu. *1431 Third Ave (81st St), T: 212 650 0850. Open daily, lunch and dinner. Map p. 577, E3.* Named for a district in Istanbul, this modest and inexpensive neighborhood Mediterranean (Greek and Turkish) restaurant serves *meze*—hummus, vine leaves, eggplant—and daily dinner specials. Small, simple, sometimes crowded.

$$ Café Sabarsky. *1048 Fifth Ave (86th St), T: 212 288 0665; www.wallse.com. Open Mon and Wed 9–6, Thur–Sun 9–9; closed Tues; no reservations. Map p. 577, D3.* On the first floor of the Neue Galerie (*see p. 365*), another venture by Kurt Gutenbrunner (*see p. 535*). Very good Austrian food, and irresistible Viennese pastries and desserts. Often crowded, there's a less elegant version on the ground floor.

Brooklyn

$$ Henry's End. *44 Henry St (Cranberry and Middagh Sts), Brooklyn Heights; T: 718 834 1776; www.henrysend.com. Open dinner only, seven days. Map p. 470.* A small neighborhood restaurant in Brooklyn Heights,

serving American food, including (Oct–Feb) exotic game dishes. If peppered ostrich with parsnip purée and barbecued rattlesnake salad do not appeal, you can choose from such regional specialties as

Southern fried chicken and Maryland crab cakes. Good list of mostly American wines. Reservations for groups of three or more.

$$ Noodle Pudding. *38 Henry St (Cranberry and Middagh Sts), Brooklyn Heights; T: 718 625 3737. Open Tues–Sun dinner only; closed Mon. No credit cards. No reservations. Map p. 470.* The name sounds Asian, but this affordable restaurant serves good Italian food in a low-key setting. Crowded and sometimes noisy; lines can stretch out the door.

$$$ Peter Luger Steak House. *178 Broadway (Driggs Ave), Williamsburg, Brooklyn; T: 718 387 7400; www.peterluger.com. Lunch and dinner seven days. Cash only, or Peter Luger credit card (see website).* A carnivore's delight, Peter Luger's has been serving prime, dry-aged beef for 120 years. Straightforward menu with shrimp cocktail and creamed spinach. Rushed service sometimes, but the porterhouse is both marbled and fabled.

BARS

New York offers a wealth of places to imbibe, from historic taverns where famous writers overindulged to chic wine bars in trendy neighborhoods. Some of the establishments in the list below are stand-alone bars, while others are in hotels or restaurants. Bars are permitted to stay open until 4am. The legal drinking age is 21.

Battery Park–14th Street

Rise. *In the Ritz-Carlton Battery Park (14th floor), 2 West St. T: 917 790 2626; www.ritzcarlton.com. Map p. 582, B4.* Fine, expensive drinks with superb views of the Statue of Liberty.

Ulysses. *95 Pearl St (Hanover Sq), T: 212 482 0400; www.ulyssesbarnyc.com. Map p. 582, C4.* Irish-style pub (the eponymous Ulysses is Joyce's) in the Stone Street Historic District; popular after-work hangout for Financial District types; pub food.

Bubble Lounge. *228 West Broadway (Franklin and White Sts), TriBeCa. T: 212 431 3433; www.bubblelounge.com. Map p. 582, B4.* Offers 300 champagnes and sparkling wines by the glass; small plates, salads, charcuterie, sandwiches. Brickwalled and cozy.

Brandy Library. *25 North Moore St (Hudson and Varick Sts), TriBeCa. T: 212 226 5545, www.brandylibrary.com. Map p. 582, B2.* A clubby wood-paneled "library," with bottles on the shelves instead of books; hors d'oeuvres, cocktails, whiskeys, brandies. Expensive.

City Hall. *131 Duane St (Church St and West Broadway), TriBeCa. T: 212 227 7777; www.cityhallnewyork.com. Map p. 582, C2.* Historic photos on the walls at this comfortable, traditional restaurant with bar area; broad selection of American wines.

Megu. *62 Thomas St (Church St and West Broadway), TriBeCa. T: 212 964 7777; www.megunyc.com. Map p. 582, C2.* In a dramatically decorated (and fine) Japanese restaurant, this mezzanine-level bar serves wines, cocktails, and sake.

Ear Inn. *326 Spring St (Greenwich and*

Washington Sts), West Village. T: 212 226 9060. Map p. 582, B1. On the far west side, a contender for oldest surviving New York bar; comfortable with good basic food.

Centovini. 25 West Houston St, (Greene St), SoHo. T: 212 219 2113; www.centovininyc.com. Map p. 581, D4. As the name says, this wine bar offers 100 Italian wines, available by the glass or bottle. Decorated by Murray Moss, whose shop is nearby. Casual Italian food.

Pegu Club. 77 West Houston St (West Broadway and Wooster St), 2nd floor, SoHo, T: 212 473 7348; www.peguclub.com. Map p. 581, D4. Named after a British officers' club in Burma, where the Pegu cocktail (gin, bitters, orange curaçao, and lime juice) was invented, this attractive SoHo bar emphasizes finely crafted cocktails.

One if by Land, Two if by Sea. 17 Barrow St (Seventh Ave and West 4th St), Greenwich Village. T: 212 228 0822; www.oneifbyland.com. Closes 10–11:15. Map p. 580, C4. Set in a town house that once held Aaron Burr's carriages (and now also holds a fine restaurant), this romantic spot is famous as a venue for "popping the question." Bar room with excellent menu, fireplace, and piano music.

Smalls. 183 West 10th St (Seventh Ave South), Greenwich Village. T: 212 675 7369; www.smallsjazz.com. Map p. 580, C3. Jazz club founded in 1993, where many present jazz greats got their starts. Full bar, recently renovated. Music begins at 7.

White Horse Tavern. 567 Hudson St (West 11th St), West Village. T: 212 243 9260. Map p. 580, B3. A poets' bar, once favored by Dylan Thomas (see p. 143) and others, now by literary pilgrims who trek here; run-down but atmospheric. No credit cards.

Joe's Pub. 425 Lafayette St (Astor Place and East 4th St), in the Public Theater, East Village. T: 212 539 8770; www.joespub.com. Map p. 581, D3. Small club with good cabaret; some say "uptown prices with a downtown feel."

McSorley's Old Ale House. 15 East 7th St (Second and Third Aves), East Village. T: 212 473 9148; www.mcsorleysnewyork.com. Map p. 581, E3. Historic pub in East Village, with sawdusty floor, own brews on tap. NYU students have replaced the working-class drinkers of yore. No credit cards.

Pete's Tavern. 129 East 18th St (Irving Pl), Gramercy Park. T: 212 473 7676, www.petestavern.com. Map p. 581, D2. Since 1864 a fixture in the neighborhood; cheerful, historic, and anything but fancy. Nice sidewalk café in season.

Midtown, to 59th Street

Campbell Apartment. In Grand Central Terminal. T: 212 953 0409; www.hospitalityholdings.com. Map p. 579, D4. This bar, popular with commuters, occupies former luxurious office of a railroad magnate. John Campbell, who had it fitted out with lots of dark wood, and installed a pipe organ and a piano on which famous musicians performed for his friends. The bar serves vintage cocktails, with vintage names: Gin-Berry Fizz, Vanderbilt Punch, and the Oxford Swizzle.

Algonquin Hotel. 59 West 44th St (Fifth and Sixth Aves); T: 212 840 6800; www.algonquinhotel.com. Map p. 579, D3. This famous hotel (see p. 214) has two bars: the Lobby Lounge, with upholstered chairs and wood paneling, and the Blue Bar, for

cocktails and bar food. The Oak Room has a historic cabaret.

Royalton Lounge and Bar. *44 West 44th St in the Royalton Hotel (Fifth and Sixth Aves), T: 212 869 4400; www.royaltonhotel. com. Map p. 579, D4.* The Royalton may have lost its cachet with the beautiful people but the bars (expensive) still attract a Theater District crowd.

The Modern Bar. *9 West 53rd St (Fifth and Sixth Aves) in MoMA. T: 212 333 1220; www.themodernnyc.com. Map p. 579, D2.* Bar adjoining the museum restaurant; streamlined, cool; modern Alsatian small plates to accompany your drinks.

Hudson Bar. *356 West 58th St (Eighth and Ninth Aves), T: 212 554 6217, www.hudson-hotel.com. Map p. 578, B2.* On the west side of Midtown in the Hudson Hotel. Draws a stylish crowd, to watch and be watched. The Library Room is smaller and quieter.

Upper East Side

Bemelmans Bar. *35 East 76th St (Madison Ave), T: 212 744 1600, www.thecarlyle.com. Map p. 577, D4.* Upper East Side through and through, elegant, expensive, with good service, older clientele, piano music and Ludwig Bemelmans's *Madeline* murals.

Metropolitan Museum of Art, Balcony Bar and Roof Garden Café. *1000 Fifth Ave at 82nd St, T: 212 535 7710, www.met-museum.org. Map p. 577, D3.* Cocktails and appetizers served with live classical music on the balcony overlooking the Great Hall; April through Oct, weather permitting, the Roof Garden offers drinks and light meals, with a view of Central Park.

Upper West Side

MO Bar. *In the Mandarin Oriental (35th floor), 80 Columbus Circle, T: 212 805 8800, www.mandarinoriental.com. Map p. 578, B2.* Great views in outer lounge, caters to businessmen, out-of-towners; cool and very pricey. An elegant newcomer to the Upper West Side.

Dizzy's Club Coca-Cola. *In the Time Warner Center (5th floor), 10 Columbus Circle, T: 212 258 9595; www.jalc.org. Map p. 578, B2.* Jazz at Lincoln Center's venue for live music in a club setting; great players, great views, but expensive—tickets plus minimums for food and drink.

Café des Artistes. *1 West 67th St (Columbus Ave and Central Park West), T: 212 877 3500; www.cafenyc.com. Map p. 578, B1.* Tucked away in a back corner of a romantic and well- known restaurant. Handy for Lincoln Center.

CAFÉS & DELIS

Financier Patisserie. *62 Stone St (Mill Lane and Hanover Sq), Financial District. T: 212 344 5600, www.financierpastries.com. Map p. 582, C4.* Pastries, sandwiches, quiches, soups at three locations. Closed Sun, but the other two locations are open seven days: *3–4 World Financial Center (Battery Park City), T: 212 786 3220; and*

35 Cedar St (Pearl and William Sts), T: 212 952 3838.

Katz's. The city's most authentic and oldest (*see p. 535 above*).

Zucker's Bagels and Smoked Fish. *146 Chambers St (West Broadway), T: 212 608 5844. Map p. 582, B2.* Opened in 2007, but looks like the old-time "appetizing stores"; hence the T-shirts on the staff noting "A New Tradition" in TriBeCa. The shop is owned by the people who run Murray's Bagels in the Village and Chelsea. Smoked salmon, bagels, sturgeon, etc.

B & H Dairy. *127 Second Ave (7th St and St. Mark's Place), East Village. T: 212 505 8065. Map p. 581, E3.* Small (some call it a hole-in-the-wall) dairy restaurant with a long Lower East Side heritage. Good soup and latkes. Choices for vegetarians.

Bourgeois Pig. *111 East 7th St (First Ave and Ave A), East Village. T: 212 475 2246; www.thepigny.com. Map p. 581, E3.* East Village spot for wine, cheese, chocolate, and coffee.

ChikaLicious. *203 East 10th St (First and Second Aves), East Village. Closed Mon and Tues. T: 212 995 9511; www.chikalicious.com. Map p. 581, E3.* A dessert bar, where a three-course "meal" includes a sweet amuse-bouche, a full-sized dessert, and petits fours.

Joe. *9 East 13th St (Fifth Ave and University Pl), Greenwich Village. T: 212 924 7400; www.joetheartofcoffee.com. Map p. 581, D3.* Some call it the best coffee bar in NY. Now in three locations, including another Village location (*141 Waverly Pl near Gay St, T: 212 924 6750*) and SoHo (*130 Greene St near Prince St in the Alessi store, T: 212 941 7330*).

2nd Avenue Deli. *162 East 33rd St. (Third and Lexington Aves), Murray Hill. T: 212 677 0606. Map p. 581, D1.* Run by the nephew of the murdered Abe Lebewohl, the new restaurant reincarnates its iconic predecessor (*see p. 165*), which went out of business in 2006 after a rent dispute. The day the new place opened (Dec 17, 2007) patrons lined up on the sidewalk in anticipation. The new deli offers the old menu (with a few additions): hand-cut pastrami, roast chicken, chopped liver and matzoh ball soup.

Stage Deli. *834 Seventh Ave (53rd and 54th Sts), Midtown West. T: 212 245 7850; www-stagedeli.com. Map p. 578, C2.* Tourist destination in the Theater District. Sandwiches and other dishes named for stars of stage and screen: the Sid Caesar Salad, the Donald Trump (sliced tenderloin with fries and mashed potatoes). Old-style deli waiters; T-shirts and souvenirs for sale.

Carnegie Deli. *854 Seventh Ave (55th St), Midtown West. T: 212 757 2245; www.carnegiedeli.com. Map p. 578, C2.* Classic (and touristy) deli not far from Carnegie Hall; cheesecake, overstuffed deli sandwiches with comic names (Carnegie Haul). Cash only.

Barney Greengrass. *541 Amsterdam Ave (86th St), Upper West Side. T: 212 724 4707; www.barneygreengrass.com. Map p. 576, B3.* Barney Greengrass, "the sturgeon king." Deli with smoked fish, salads, egg salad and borscht; in business since 1908.

Junior's Restaurant. *386 Flatbush Ave Extension (DeKalb Ave), downtown Brooklyn; T: 718 852 5257.* Family-owned business, famous for cheesecake since 1950. Also burgers, diner food, deli sandwiches. There's a branch in Shubert Alley in the Theater District (*1515 Broadway at 45th St; T: 212 302 2000*).

GLOSSARY

Adirondack chair, sturdy wooden outdoor chair with arms and a slatted back

Ambulatory, typically the section of a church beside and round the high altar

Amphora, antique vase, usually of large dimensions, for oil and other liquids

Annunciation, the appearance of the Angel Gabriel to Mary to tell her that she will bear the Son of God; an image of the "Virgin Annunciate" shows her receiving the news

Anthemion, type of decoration originating in ancient Greece resembling leaf or honeysuckle fronds fanning out from a central stem

Apostles, the name for those sent out by Jesus to spread the Word

Archaic, period in Greek civilization preceding the Classical era: c. 750–480 BC. Art pertaining thereto

Architrave, the horizontal beam placed above supporting columns; the lowest part of an entablature (*qv*); the horizontal frame above a door

Archivolt, molded architrave carried round an arch

Areaway, small yard in front of a row house where the front steps rise, often with a basement underneath

Ashlar, neatly cut square blocks of stone or revetment slabs (*qv*) set smoothly together and used as facing on housefronts (*c.f. fieldstone*)

Back house, a house with no street frontage

Baldachin, canopy supported by columns

Balusters, the upright, vertical elements of a balustrade

Baptistery, separate room or building used for baptisms in a Christian church

Bas-relief, sculpture in low relief

Beaux-Arts, academic, largely eclectic style of architecture taught at the École des Beaux-Arts in Paris, and hugely influential in America in the late 19th century

Belgian block, cube-shaped cobble of hard-wearing stone, used as street paving

Bracket, a supporting strut

Broadway theater, almost all are in the area between West 41st and West 51st Sts around Broadway (the others are Studio 54 and the Beaumont); the present ones seat more than 500 people; shows running in these theaters are eligible for Tony Awards. Off-Broadway theaters seat from 99–500 people, though the Brooklyn Academy of Music has theaters of 870 and 2,100 seats

Broken pediment, a pediment with a gap in the horizontal part, and/or where the cornices do not meet

Brownstone, brown-colored Triassic sandstone, a favored building material in mid-19th-century New York (*see p. 415*)

Bull's eye window, elliptical (not circular) window, often appearing in mansard roofs

Cabochon, an uncut, unfaceted gemstone in a fixed setting

Campanile, bell tower, often detached from the building to which it belongs

Canopic jar (or chest), ancient Egyptian urn used to preserve the internal organs of the deceased, and placed in the tomb beside the mummy

Cantoria, singing gallery in a church

Capital, the top part or "head" of a column

Carolingian, pertaining to Charlemagne and the dynasty he founded in the 9th century

Cartouche, tablet with a scrolled frame, usually round or oval, typically inscribed with initials or a coat of arms

Caryatid, sculpted female figure used as a supporting column

Chamfer, a cut-off corner (in appearance like a triangle with the top removed). Four chamfered corners at a street intersection form an octagon

Chancel, part of a church to the liturgical east of the crossing (*qv*), where the clergy officiate

Choir, part of a church reserved for the singers, usually with stalls; often synonymous with the raised easternmost end of a church where the clergy officiate

Ciborium, casket or tabernacle containing the Communion bread

Classical, in ancient Greece, the period from 480–323 BC; in general, when spelled with a capital C, denotes art etc. from the ancient world as opposed to classical ("classicizing") modern works

Clerestory, upper part of the nave wall of a church, above the side aisles, with windows

Coffered, of a ceiling or vault, having regularly spaced recessed panels, often (but not necessarily) square or rectangular in shape

Colonnette, small column with a decorative, not load-bearing, function

Console bracket, masonry structure, S-shaped with scrolls at top and bottom, placed vertically against a wall to support a projecting horizontal element (c.f. *modillion*)

Corinthian, ancient Greek and Roman order of architecture, a characteristic of which is a capital decorated with acanthus leaves

Cornice, any projecting ornamental molding at the top of a building beneath the roof (exterior) or ceiling (interior)

Crenellations, battlements

Crossing, the part of a church where the nave (central aisle) and transepts (side arms) meet

Cruciform, cross-shaped, from the Latin *crux, crucis*, a cross

Cupola, dome

Curtain wall, a non-load-bearing wall, essentially an infill or a screen between supporting piers or partitions

Dentiled, having a series of small blocks, projecting or hanging down like teeth

Dinette, small alcove or nook, designed, as the name suggests, for (informal) dining

Diptych, painting or tablet in two sections

Doric, ancient Greek order of architecture characterized by fluted columns with no base, and a plain capital

Drip moldings, molding over a hood, arch, or aperture designed to divert rainwater

Egg and dart, molding design consisting of ovoid shapes placed between arrow-like shapes

El, short form for elevated railway

Engaged, of a column, not freestanding, in other words, partly embedded in the wall

Entablature, upper part of a temple above the columns, made up of an architrave, frieze and cornice

Etruscans, influential ancient civilization that dominated central Italy from the 9th–4th centuries BC

Evangelists, the authors of the gospels, Matthew, Mark, Luke, and John. In Christian art they are often represented by their symbols: man or angel (Matthew); lion (Mark); bull (Luke); eagle (John)

Expressionist, art where the forms and/or colors of nature are exaggerated, distorted, or rendered unnatural to produce an emotional response in the viewer

Faïence, glazed decorative earthenware or terra cotta, named for the town of Faenza in Italy, where it originated

Fanlight, semicircular glazed aperture above a door, where the glazing bars are often arranged in a fan-like pattern

Federal style, architectural style which developed in America following the Declaration of Independence (see pp. 9–12)

Fieldstone, type of masonry consisting of irregular blocks of different sizes, held together with mortar

Flatware, cutlery

Flemish bond, style of brickwork where the bricks in each row (course) are placed alternately long (stretcher)-short (header)

Fluted, of a column shaft, having vertical grooves down its length

Foliate, decorated with a leaf pattern

Fresco, painting executed on wet plaster, beneath which the artist had usually made a working sketch

Fretwork, any kind of interlaced, carved or cut out decoration, typically repetitive

Gambrel, a "Dutch barn" roof, pitched in

two stages, the upper stage less steeply inclined than the lower (*c.f. mansard*)

Geometric, in an antique context, refers to a pottery style with complex abstract decoration (900–700 BC)

Gesso, a chalk-based (or, nowadays, acrylic) primer applied to a surface before painting

Gold-ground, medieval Italian devotional painting style where the figures appear against a gold background

Gothic, medieval style of architecture originating in northern Europe, characterized by pointed arches, vaulted interiors and traceried (*qv*) windows

Greek cross, a cross with arms of equal length

Groin vault, type of vaulting where two barrel vaults cross each other at right-angles

Guastavino, a type of majolica tile used as a revetment (*qv*), named after Rafael Guastavino, a Spanish immigrant architect who developed the technique in America

Hellenistic, art and sculpture of the period from 323 BC (death of Alexander the Great) to 30 BC (defeat of Antony and Cleopatra)

Hipped roof, a sloping roof, differing from a simple pitched roof in that it has four sloping sides, meeting not in a ridge at the top, but in "hips" up the sides

I-beam, load-bearing beam with an I-shaped cross-section, used in modern construction

Impost block, block placed above a capital from which an arch rises

Incunabulum (pl. incunabula) any book printed in the same century as the invention of movable type (i.e. between 1450 and 1500)

International Style, 20th-century style of architecture characterized by blocklike shapes, flat roofs, a lack of ornament, and the use of materials such as glass, steel, and reinforced concrete as opposed to old-fashioned masonry

Ionic, an order of Classical architecture identified by its capitals with two volutes (scrolls). Columns are fluted, stand on a base, and have a shaft more slender than in the Doric order

Iron-spot brick, brick flecked with spots of black, from the iron deposits in the clay

Keystone, wedge-shaped strengthening block at the centre point of the curve of an arch

Kouroi, from the Greek word for young man (*kouros*), the standing, nude male statues of the Greek Archaic (*qv*) period

Krater, a large ancient Greek bowl for mixing wine and water

Lady Chapel, chapel devoted to the worship of the Virgin Mary

Lancet window, slender, blade-shaped Gothic window aperture with a pointed arched head

Latin cross, a cross where the vertical arm is longer than the transverse arm

Louvered, with horizontal overlapping slats to admit air but not light

Lunette, semicircular space in a vault or ceiling, or above a door or window, often decorated with a painting or relief

Machicolated, of a parapet: having holes in the floor through which stones, boiling oil etc. could be dropped on attackers

Maenad, female participant in the orgiastic rites of Dionysus, god of wine

Mansard roof, typical roof type of the *hôtels* of Paris: pitched in two stages like a gambrel roof (*qv*), differing from it in that it is hipped, i.e. it has four, not two, sloped sides

Mayor's Lamp, any survivor of the days when it was the custom to erect two lamps outside a mayor's residence

Meneely bell, a bell cast in the Meneely Bell Foundry in Troy, N.Y., which operated between 1826 and 1952

Minton, English firm from Stoke on Trent, the "potteries," known for its blue-printed ware. In the late 19th century its tiles were fashionable, and the company won a tender to produce tiles for the US Capitol

Modillion, supporting bracket or block placed horizontally under a larger, heavier horizontal structure

Mortise and tenon, type of timber joint resembling the interlocking system of a jig-

saw puzzle: a projecting tongue fits into a corresponding notch

Neo-Grec, an eclectic branch of Neoclassicism originating in mid-19th-century France, characterized by a profusion of Greco-Roman classical motifs, Egyptian Revival forms and the austerity of line of the Louis Seize style

Nereid, in Greek mythology, a water nymph

Newel post, upright post or column at the top, bottom, or turning-point of a flight of stairs, usually connected to a banister

Oculus (pl. oculi), round window or aperture

Oriel window, window projecting from an upper story

Palladian window, a window in three parts: a central round-arched aperture is flanked by two flat-topped apertures of lesser height. It derives its name from the Italian architect Andrea Palladio

Paschal, in the Christian church, pertaining to Easter

Pediment, triangular gable above a portico

Pendant, a painting or work which forms a companion or complement to another

Peristyle, court or garden surrounded by a columned portico

Pietà, representation of the Virgin mourning the dead Christ, usually spread on her lap

Pilaster, a shallow pier or rectangular column projecting only slightly from the wall

Pitched roof, a roof made of two sloping sides, meeting in a ridge at the top

Polychrome, from the Greek, meaning many colors

Porphyry, dark blue, purple or red-colored igneous rock

Potlatch, from a Chinook word meaning "gift," a ceremonial present-giving, as practiced by indigenous American peoples

Potter's field, a burial ground

Putto (pl. putti), sculpted or painted figure, usually nude, of a male child

Quadriga, a two-wheeled chariot drawn by four horses abreast

Quatrefoil, four-lobed design

Queen Anne, picturesque, asymmetrical, late 19th-century architectural style characterized by turrets, steeply pitched roofs and gingerbread ornamentation

Quoin, from the French coin (corner), stones placed in courses at the outer corners of buildings, projecting from the wall

Raked, of a cornice, meaning sloping. Thus a cornice that follows the line of a triangular pediment is necessarily raked

Repoussé, relief-work in metal achieved by hammering from the back, thus punching out the design

Reredos, panel or screen behind an altar, which may stand alone or be part of a larger retable (qv)

Retable, screen behind an altar, often a frame or setting for the reredos (qv)

Revetment, cladding, for decorative or protective purposes, applied to floors, ceilings, and interior or exterior walls

Romanesque, architecture of the early Western (i.e. not Byzantine) Christian empire, from the 7th–12th centuries, preceding the Gothic style. A revival of this style, characterized by rounded arches, achieved great popularity in New York in the later 19th century

Rubblestone (see fieldstone)

Rus in urbe, from the Latin meaning "country in the city," referring to the creation of a rural atmosphere in an urban environment

Rusticated, masonry surface where the blocks of stone are not flush with each other as in ashlar (qv), but are separated by deep joints or grooves, making the stone appear more massive

Trefoil, decorated or molded with three leaf- or lobe-shapes

Sanctuary, the part of a church around the high altar. It may be identical to the chancel or choir, depending on the size of the church and the position of the singers' stalls

Scrimshaw, carved or etched ivory or bone, typically whalebone

Second Empire, eclectic, opulent architecture from the reign of Napoleon III in

France (1852–70), historicist in that it borrowed elements from many styles of the past

Segmental arch, arch where the curved part is formed of a simple arc, i.e. a segment of a circle

Setback, the extent to which a building leaves free space around it in its lot, both on the ground and as it rises into the air (*see p. 68*)

Sgraffito, design formed by scratchwork on plaster down to a layer of different-colored plaster beneath

Shawabty (or *shawabti*; also *ushabti*), small figurines from ancient Egyptian tombs intended to perform manual tasks for the deceased in the afterlife

Sidelights, fixed glass panes on either side of a door

Six-over-six, of a sash window, where both panels are divided into six panes

Spandrel, the area between two arches in an arcade or the triangular space on either side of an arch

Splayed, having vertical sides that rise obliquely rather than straight up

Stabile, an abstract sculpture that has no moving parts, a term coined by Alexander Calder to distinguish the artform from a mobile

Stations of the Cross, small paintings, panels, or carvings placed around the walls of a church or chapel depicting scenes from Christ's journey to Calvary

Stele (pl. stelae), upright stone bearing a commemorative inscription

Stoop, narrow porch reached by steps in front of a house, typically a row house. New York's first Dutch settlers elevated the first floors of their houses with high stoops (from the Dutch *stoep*) just as they had in Amsterdam, where flooding was a threat

Stucco, plaster-work, usually molded

Swag, carved or painted design made to resemble bunched drapery

Tempera, a painting medium of powdered pigment bound together, in its simplest form, by a mixture of egg yolk and water

Terra cotta, from the Italian meaning "cooked earth," fired earthenware used in architecture or sculpture

Terrazzo floor, paving made up of small fragments of marble embedded in mortar, smoothed and polished

Tessera (pl. tesserae), small cube of marble, stone or glass used in mosaic work

Tie-rod, transverse truss to prevent walls sagging outward, passed through the wall and fixed with a plate, in the manner of a nut and bolt

Tracery, system of carved and molded ribs within a window aperture dividing it into patterned sections. Particularly associated with Gothic architecture

Transom, horizontal beam across a window; a fixed window above a doorway. When semicircular, this is called a fanlight

Transept, "side arm" of a church, leading to right and/or left off the nave or aisles

Triforium, upper-level arcaded aisle in a Romanesque or Gothic-style church, below the clerestory (*qv*)

Triple-hung window, tall sash window in three sections

Triptych, painting or tablet in three sections

Triton, river god

Trompe l'œil, literally, a deception of the eye; used to describe illusionist decoration and painted architectural perspective

Tuscan, plain order of architecture, with an unfluted column rising from a base to a simple, unornamented capital

Tympanum (pl. tympana), the area between the top of a doorway and the arch above it; also the triangular space enclosed by the moldings of a pediment

Vermiform, "wormlike" decoration; a wriggling pattern

Zoomorphic, from the Greek *zoön* (animal), meaning having an animal form

INDEX

Explanatory or more detailed references (where there are many), or references to places where an artist's work is best represented, are given in bold. Numbers in italics are picture references. Dates are given, where known, for individual artists and architects.

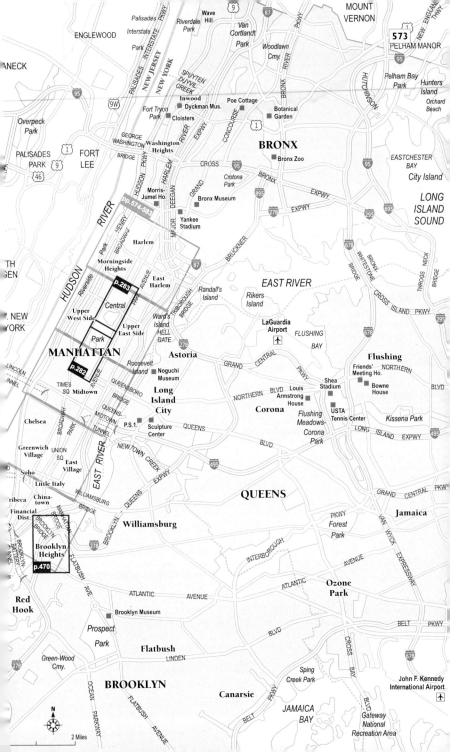

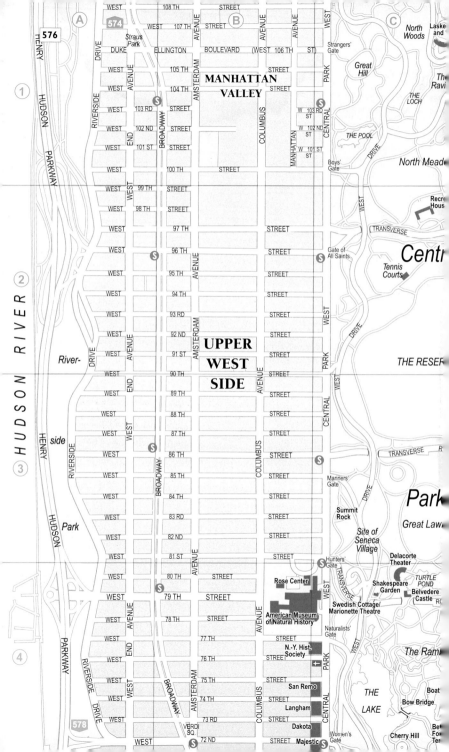

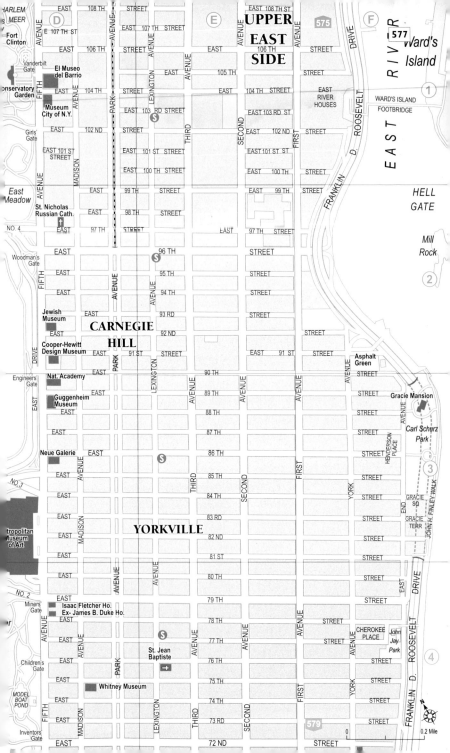

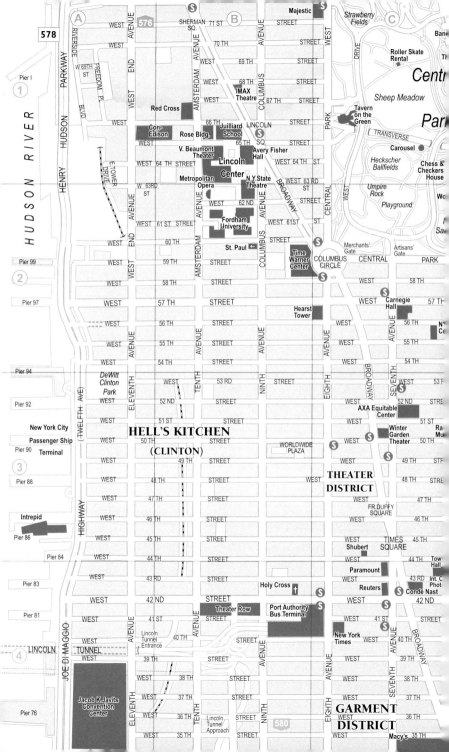

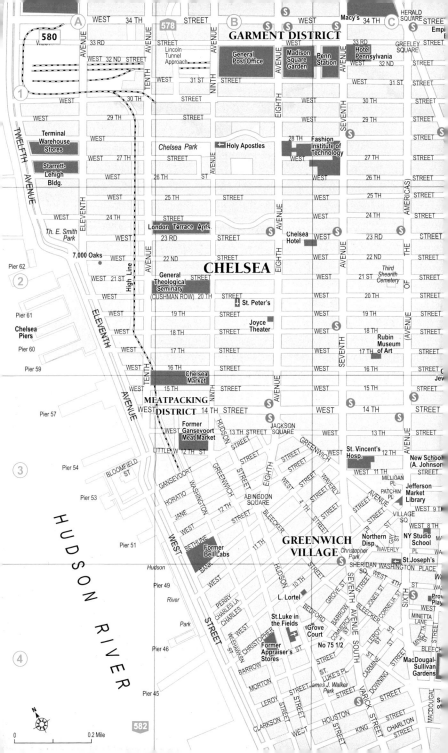

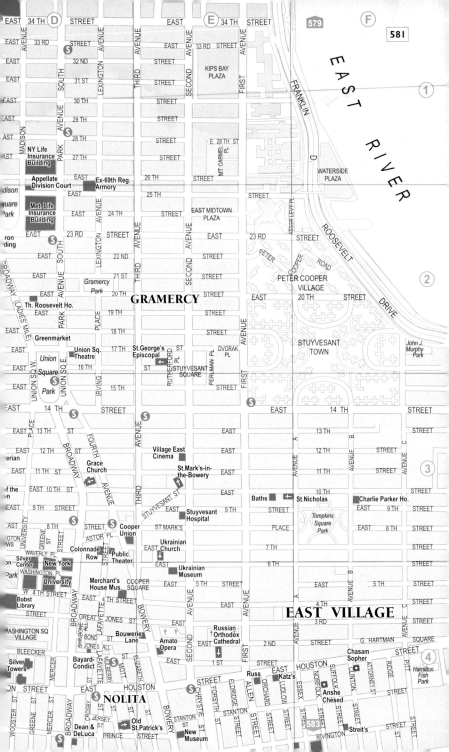

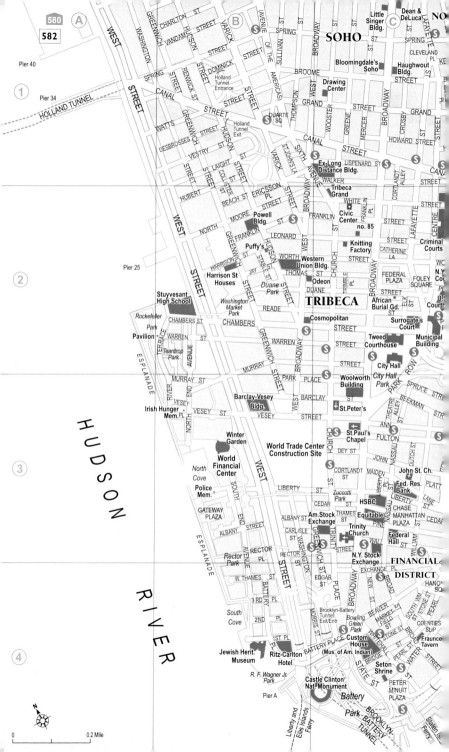

contd. from p. 6

Editor-in-chief: Annabel Barber
Assistant editor: Judy Tither; Editorial assistant: Sophie Livall

Layout and design: Anikó Kuzmich
Maps: Dimap Bt
Floor plans: Imre Bába
Architectural line drawings: Gabriella Juhász & Michael Mansell RIBA

Photo editor: Hadley Kincade
Photographs by Gábor Fényes: pp. 43, 51, 75, 78, 99, 101, 132, 136, 147, 157, 238, 418, 435, 473; Annabel Barber: pp. 47, 66, 245, 253, 291, 295, 297, 415; John Sloan: p. 155; Enrique Sallent: p. 179; P. Neil Ralley: p. 207; Black Star/Alamy: p. 248; Red Dot/Alamy: pp. 71, 111, 233, 255, 372; Red Dot/Corbis: pp. 37, 57, 80, 107, 121, 148, 153, 184, 195, 216, 240, 259; Courtesy of the Battery Conservancy: p. 49; © Peter Mauss/Esto: p. 118; Ed Reed/Office of the Mayor: p. 380; Photography Collection Miriam and Ira D. Wallach Division of Art, Prints and Photographs, The New York Public Library, Astor, Lenox and Tilden Foundations: p. 199; US General Services Administration: p. 90; the Collection of the Bernard Museum of Judaica, Congregation Emanu-El of the City of New York. Photo: Malcolm Varon: p. 312; © D. Finnin/AMNH: p. 396; Collection of the New-York Historical Society: pp. 410, 411; Brooklyn Museum Collection: p. 462; Brooklyn Museum of Art: p. 477. Other images courtesy of the Rubin Museum of Art: p. 191; ©2007 Todd Eberle, the Morgan Library: p. 203; the Morgan Library: p. 204; the Museum of Modern Art: p. 263; the Museum of Modern Art ©1998 Kate Rothko Prizel & Christopher Rothko ARS, NY and DACS, London 2008: p. 267; the Frick Collection, New York: pp. 302, 305, 308; the Metropolitan Museum of Art: pp. 3, 334, 347, 353, 456; the Solomon R. Guggenheim Museum, New York: pp. 369, 370; the Whitney Museum of American Art: p. 318.

Cover photo by Gábor Fényes;
Spine: *Song*, by Hildreth Meière, roundel on Radio City Music Hall, Rockefeller Center; ©Hildreth Meière Dunn 2007.

Author's acknowledgements
The author would like to thank Kate Hill for researching and writing on the Brooklyn Bridge, Brooklyn Museum, Brooklyn Botanic Garden and Prospect Park, and the Rubin Museum; and Julie De Sarbo for her work on the Upper East Side and Brooklyn Heights. Thanks are also due to Jessica Bondi, Lynne Arany, and my agents Mildred Marmur and Lorella Belli.

With grateful thanks also to Eve Kahn, Brad Kulman, and Julie Sloan.

Printed in Singapore by Tien Wah Press, Pte.

ISBN 978–1–905131–23–5